Foreword

The Victorian Society has completed half a century of campaigning, and it is probably fair to say the most of the major monuments that survive are secure for the moment. We lost the Euston Arch, but we still have Paddington. Yet it is an undeniable fact that we know far too little of the details of that vast urban expansion that gave us our Victorian cities. Though the few well known national architects built up and down the country, they did not build the majority of the buildings that were created. Indeed they did not even build the majority of those buildings of quality that we recognise as having heritage value. The making of our Victorian cities was emphatically the work of local people establishing an urban fabric where local self-government (as the Victorian preferred to call it) could make the city in which they lived and worked. And that is why our great Victorian cities all have their own individual character. Birmingham, often seen as the cradle of local self-government, is no exception; and fostered a strong local body of architects. They cannot easily be described as the 'Birmingham school' because of the variety that is found in their works, which is why this volume is so important.

The Birmingham group of the Victorian Society is celebrating its 40th anniversary by publishing this volume on Birmingham Architects. A series of essays detail the individual careers of no less than twenty six different architects who made their careers in Birmingham and the West Midlands. Often they were, or became, men of substance, always they were creative in their response to local problems, and it was they, above all, who created the built environment we know as Birmingham. This book, which celebrates the major impact people such as Thomas Rickman, John Henry Chamberlain or Frederick Martin had on the development of Birmingham, will surely take its place among the leaders of this generation of architectural studies. The volunteers of the Birmingham Group of The Victorian Society have opened up a new and important area in the history of the West Midlands, and they are very much to be congratulated for the result. This book is the result of wide collaboration. The twenty six essays represent the scholarship of no less that twenty two men and women members of The Society. The essays have been carefully assembled to lead the reader from the slow growth of the small early Victorian town through the expansion that accompanied the development of a Civic Gospel, the modernity of terracotta, to the fascinating explosion of artistic talent that occurred in Birmingham under the influence of the Arts & Crafts. It is, for instance, interesting (and important) to learn how far the local architects mastered the potential of terracotta, a new material in the mid-century when the most celebrated master of that material, Alfred Waterhouse, built virtually nothing in the city.

This is a book not only for Birmingham but for the wider public with an interest in the Victorian heritage that still, just, survives to give character and individuality to our cities. The more that is learned about the work of local architects the more we shall understand what makes each of out towns and cities special, and the more we shall appreciate the varied heritage of urban Britain. That is something vital in an age when planners are giving our cities up to anonymous glass and concrete towers that make Birmingham look like Bolton or Leeds like Manchester. The Birmingham Group of The Victorian Society are to be congratulated for dreaming up this project, and for carrying it through in so thorough a way.

COLIN J. K. CUNNINGHAM
Chairman, The Victorian Society

Editor's Acknowledgements

This book owes much to the initiative and perseverance of Barbara Shackley, chairman of the Birmingham and West Midlands Group of the Victorian Society (2001–2009), in turning a pipe dream into a reality. She was indefatigable in securing authors for specific architects, especially when due to work commitments individuals had to withdraw and a replacement had to be found, and inspiring in her belief that 'the book' would at last emerge.

Special thanks are also due to several of the contributors to this book, especially Toni Demidowicz, Andy Foster, Niky Rathbone and above all, Donald Abbott, for answering my queries and supplying additional information, and to Robin Fryer, David Shackley, Sutton Webster and David Low for their timely help. I would also like to thank Derek Brown and Jackie Maidment of Oblong and Neil Wells who provided the index.

The first port of call for any research on Birmingham is always the Central Library, and the staffs of the City Archives and the Department of Local Studies, now Archives and Heritage Services, have provided invaluable assistance.

The financial support provided by the Victorian Society Mary Heath Fund is gratefully acknowledged.

Lastly, my husband, Ted Collins, has been a great support. Although not, as I was, brought up in Birmingham, he shares my enthusiasm for the City and my nostalgia for the historic built environment as it was in the 1950s prior to its redevelopment.

ILLUSTRATION ACKNOWLEDGMENTS

The majority of the photographs for this book have been taken by Robin Fryer, with additional photography by Jonathan Farmer. The following have also contributed photographs: Andy Foster (AF); Margaret Herbert (MH); Peter Leather (PL); David Low (DL); Barbara Shackley (BS); David Shackley (DS); Adam Wood (AW) and Mary Worsfold (MW).

Introduction

PHILLADA BALLARD

In 1826 a popular Music Hall song entitled 'I can't find Brummagem' indicated the level of development and rebuilding that had prevailed in the town since the singer had been there twenty years previously. Had he returned again half a century later his perplexity would have been greater for now he would have found the town almost wholly rebuilt as a splendid Victorian City with a wide range of buildings in a multiplicity of styles and materials. J. T. Bunce wrote in 1885 'In Birmingham the physical conditions of the place have undergone changes which the most powerful memory, based on the most prolonged term of residence, can scarcely enable one to realize.'[1]

Birmingham less than a century later presented yet another picture again. Wartime bombing, comprehensive postwar redevelopment and the lack of sentimentality about replacing buildings – as encapsulated in the words of Herbert Manzoni, Birmingham's City Engineer from 1935–1963 – 'future generations should be applying their thoughts and energies to forging ahead, rather than looking backward,'[2] had destroyed what had remained of the 18th century town and made serious inroads into the Victorian City.

Nicholas Cooper and Nicholas Taylor in their preface to the Victorian Society's 1965 exhibition on 'The Nineteenth Century Architecture of Birmingham' had pointed to the fact that little was known about Birmingham's Victorian architecture:

The principal reason for the 'obscurity' of Birmingham's architecture is local pride. Buildings were only rarely designed by the big names from London. They were local buildings for local people by local people – local businessmen bursting with confidence, local architects fearlessly independent of influences from outside.

More recently in 2005, Andy Foster in his *Pevsner Architectural Guides: Birmingham* again highlighted 'Birmingham's practice whereby almost all available commissions went to local men.' He also emphasized the paucity of published sources on Birmingham's architecture in general.[3]

There clearly exists a need for more research, and, in particular, detailed appraisals of the local architects who were responsible for so much of the built environment of the nineteenth and early twentieth century city. This book, sponsored by the Birmingham and West Midlands Group of the Victorian Society, focuses wholly on these local architects. Clearly it cannot be wholly comprehensive, the tripling of the population between 1841 and 1911 and the economic boom which fuelled the great expansion in building in the second half of the nineteenth century, is reflected by the numbers of architects practicing in Birmingham which rose from 55 in 1858 to 160 in 1908. It is, however, concerned with the work of twenty six architects or architectural practices which by virtue of the scale and importance of their output might be termed the 'leading' architects of the period and whose work dates from the 1820s to the First World War. For most of them, the sphere of activity was Birmingham and its immediate surroundings, though many did some work further afield quite frequently because of a Birmingham connection or because they came to specialise in a particular type of building. Examples of the latter include Thomas Rickman (1776–1841) who, although he spent twenty one years of his twenty three years as an architect based in Birmingham, the greater part of his large ecclesiastical output was not in the town. Likewise one of his pupils, Daniel Rowlinson Hill (1810–57) the architect of the Birmingham Borough Gaol was one of the most active designers of prisons for other local authorities. John George Bland (1820–1898) who specialized in designing factories was responsible for a large number of carpet factories in Kidderminster. Exceptionally some practices, such as that of Oliver Essex subsequently Essex Nicol and Goodman, had a London office from 1886.

In Birmingham, as with all the major British industrial cities, the transformation of its centre took place in the second half of the nineteenth century. Prior to this the town had few buildings of much architectural significance in spite of being one of the most economically advanced and highly specialized industrial centres in England. The concentration on the small metal trades requiring small amounts of raw materials and high degrees of skill was characterized by small masters operating in workshops, though some larger enterprises had emerged by the third quarter of the 18th century and there were significant numbers of wealthy individuals. Until 1838 the government of the town was based largely on the antiquated manorial village system, except for the addition of the Street Commissioners formed in 1769. In the early 1820s the major buildings of note were the medieval parish church of St Martin's, three 18th century churches and one from the early 19th century, several large Dissenter's chapels, two theatres, the General Hospital, the General Dispensary and the Public Office. This latter building was designed, unlike most of the other significant buildings, by a local architect, William Hollins, and provided the offices for the Street Commissioners and the magistrates. In the town there was a number of elegant town houses for the wealthier members of society together with detached villas in the surrounding countryside. There was no public assembly building or covered market.

The first impetus in building in the 1820s was the provision of a number of Anglican churches to meet the needs of the growing population, several of them designed by Thomas Rickman who was also responsible for the Society of Arts building in New Street. In the 1830s two public buildings of note were erected on the initiative of the Street Commissioners. In both cases buildings in other industrial centres provided a precedent. Prior to commissioning the Town Hall enquiries were made concerning public assembly buildings in Liverpool, Manchester, Leeds, Sheffield, Hull and Bristol.[4] An outside architect, Joseph Hansom was chosen, but he went bankrupt in 1834 and the building was finally completed and extended by a local architect Charles Edge, in the 1840s. Edge had earlier been the architect of the Market Hall of 1831–5, a building inspired by a similar one at Sheffield.[5] Prior to this a competition had been held for the design of the Smithfield livestock Market in the Moat, which had been won by a London architect. However this design was not used and a much less expensive building was erected, designed by one of the Street Commissioners.

Future architectural competitions in Birmingham frequently led to controversy and the trend certainly developed to favour local candidates. Equally, if contracts were awarded without competition and architects were suspected of a monopoly this could lead to professional jealousy.

The new system of local government after Birmingham achieved borough status in 1838 resulted in the commissioning of a wide range of buildings for which there were no existing precedents in the town. The local architect, D. R. Hill having been appointed as architect for the first of the Council's buildings, the borough gaol at Winson Green in 1842, was then appointed, partly for reasons of economy, for all the succeeding buildings as a matter of course, although he was never officially the borough architect. The prison was followed by the Pauper Lunatic Asylum on an adjoining site, the first public baths and washhouses and police stations. These buildings were based on London models. The proposal to make Hill the Inspector of Buildings led to suggestions in the local press that he was being unfairly advanced and that he was not the only competent architect operating in the town.

Although Birmingham architects were growing in numbers in the 1830s and 40s they did not at this stage monopolize all the important commissions. The three railway stations were by London architects, the rebuilt King Edward's Grammar School of 1837 and the new Roman Catholic Cathedral of 1839 were by Augustus Pugin, while E. M. Barry was commissioned to design the Birmingham and Midland Institute in 1855. Gilbert Scott and S. S. Teulon were each responsible for a church in Ladywood, and Teulon carried out other work in Edgbaston for Lord Calthorpe, the ground landlord.

However an architectural competition which took place in 1849 for the new Birmingham Workhouse demonstrates a clear preference on the part of civic dignitaries for local architects. The competition attracted fifty four entries, and of the short list of six, five were Birmingham architects. Due to protests at the result, the competition was held again, and the winner was again the Birmingham firm of Drury and Bateman.

The twin factors of economy and a preference for a local architect is nowhere better demonstrated than over the competition to appoint an architect for the Municipal Buildings, later known as the Council House, which was held in 1871. The decision of the adjudicator, the London architect, Alfred Waterhouse, was ignored in favour of Yeoville Thomason, a local architect. He was manager of the architects' department in the Borough Surveyors' Office, and as a Council employee would not be paid the winner's premium. Intervention by a Council committee meant that the elevations as built differed considerably from those originally submitted. When the Municipal Art Gallery was commissioned ten years later as a major extension of the Council House, no competition was held and Thomason was again the architect.

In the municipal provision of Free Libraries under the Act of 1850, Birmingham was slower than Liverpool and Manchester, but when funds were finally allocated local architects had been to the fore. For the Central Library initially the Council had decided to employ E. M. Barry for a building that would have continued the façade of the uncompleted Midland Institute but he was dismissed after underestimating the costs, and an architectural competition was held in 1862 which was won by the local architect, William Martin. The Central Lending Library was opened in 1865 and the Reference Library in 1866. The three branch libraries built in the 1860s were all the work of another local architect, J. J. Bateman. Martin's partner, John Henry Chamberlain, was responsible for the extension to the Midland Institute in 1881 and the rebuilding of the Central Library, after a fire, in 1882. These buildings occupied the west side of what became known as Chamberlain Square, with the Memorial fountain to Joseph Chamberlain in the centre, the south side was formed by the north face of the Town Hall, the north side by Mason's College of 1880, and the East side by Thomason's Art Gallery of 1885, became arguably the most impressive group of 19th century buildings in Birmingham. Mason's College of Science, built and endowed entirely by Josiah Mason, a Birmingham pen manufacturer, had been designed by a then little known local architect, Jethro Cossins, selected by Mason. Not far away in Margaret Street was the Ruskinian Gothic Municipal School of Art of 1883 by John Henry Chamberlain.

Educational provision at the elementary level expanded hugely after the 1871 Education Act and many Board schools were built in the highly populated districts of poor housing close to the town centre where their quality made them stand out from their surroundings. The firm of Martin and Chamberlain, and its successor, Martin and Martin, had an almost total monopoly as architects for these schools, being responsible for twenty nine schools between 1871 and 1884, up to the death of John Henry Chamberlain, and another eighteen from 1884 until 1902. This invited protests from other of Birmingham's architects, as had been the case with D. R. Hill, and in 1896 the School Board were forced to hold a competition, which was won by Martin and Chamberlain. Martin and Martin ceased designing schools in 1902 when their request for a higher percentage fee was turned down and a salaried architect, Herbert Buckland of Buckland and Farmer was appointed architect to the Council's Education Department. The firm of Crouch and Butler designed several elementary schools in the adjoining parishes that were later absorbed into Birmingham.

The period from the 1850s onwards saw a rising number of commercial and public buildings in the centre of Birmingham. The work of Birmingham architects dominated the scene in the design of the main offices of the large joint stock banks, mainly in Italianate style. Rickman and Edge had designed banks in the 1830s but such buildings became more numerous and were the work of architects such as J. A. Chatwin, Edward Holmes, Osborn and Reading and Yeoville Thomason. Thomason was responsible for several banks in Colmore Row, together with new types of buildings such as manufacturers' showrooms and a gentlemen's club. Other clubs were designed by Osborn and Reading and Jethro Cossins. Chatwin designed hotels in the urban centre as did Thomas Plevins. Also appearing for the first time were large top lit galleried shops such as the one for Hyam and Co designed by J. J. Bateman in New Street in 1857, and shopping arcades such as the Great Western Arcade of 1876 and the Central Arcade of 1881 both by W. H. Ward. Other arcades were the work of Jethro Cossins, Newton and Cheatle, and Nicol and Nicol. Another innovation was the the making of an entirely new street, Corporation Street, as an improvement scheme to demolish slum housing implemented under the terms of the Artisan's Dwelling Act of 1875, Birmingham being the first local authority to do so.[6] This provided the opportunity for impressive three storey developments of shops, office chambers, insurance buildings and restaurants with many buildings designed by W. H. Ward, Martin and Chamberlain, and Essex, Nicol and Goodman. The improvement scheme marked the new dynamism in local government and public life in Birmingham as a result of the 'Civic Gospel' preached by prominent non-conformist ministers to increase the commitment of the wealthy to public service and private munificence and to extend the range of public services to the poor as well as the better off.

The greater number of public buildings included much work in the provision of hospitals either as extensions to existing hospitals or in the construction of large new buildings. No non-Birmingham architects appear to have been employed, the contracts all going to local firms. Drury and Bateman designed Queen's Hospital in 1840, Martin and Chamberlain were responsible for extensions to the General Hospital in 1857 and to the Accident Hospital in 1870, Yeoville Thomason designed the Homeopathic Hospital in 1873 and the Jaffray Suburban Hospital in 1884, Cossins and Peacock designed the Ear, Nose and Throat Hospital in 1891, and the Lying in Hospital in 1906. The new General Hospital was designed by William Henman in 1894. Frederick Martin designed extensions to it in 1914 having also been responsible for the Women's Hospital of 1907 and the Children's Hospital of 1913.

Unusually, in the 1880s outside architects were responsible for two important public buildings. The General Post Office was designed by Sir Henry Tanner in 1889 and he also designed the one at Leeds. In 1884 Birmingham was granted the right to have an Assize, and the Council wanted to appoint Alfred Waterhouse who had designed the Manchester Assize Courts of 1859–64. Protests from local architects led to the holding of an open competition assessed by Waterhouse, with only one Birmingham firm, Bateman and Hunt, coming in the top five.[7] The winners were Aston Webb and Ingress Bell and the Victoria Law Courts were notable for the extensive use of terracotta, which although it had been used by local architects for some time as a decorative element, now became immensely popular. It was used more in Birmingham than anywhere else in the country.[8] Several further buildings in Corporation Street were built using terracotta as a facing material, notably W. H. Ward's Salvation Army Citadel of 1891, Ewen and J. Alfred Harper's Ruskin Buildings and Methodist Central Hall both of 1900 and their King Edward Building of 1900–1. James and Lister Lea were responsible for many public houses in the city centre in Jacobean style with much terracotta internally or externally. Essex, Nicol and Goodman were also notable for their use of terracotta, including premises in Old Square for Lunt and Co. of 1894 and a large department store, The Louvre, in High Street of 1895. Frederick Martin's National Telephone Exchange in Newhall Street of 1896 is considered 'the finest commercial building of Birmingham's brick and terracotta period.'[9]

By the late 19th century Birmingham was generally acknowledged as the 'capital' of the Midlands, serving a region, although its central shopping area was smaller than that of any large city.[10]

The great number of places of worship built in the second half of the nineteenth century in Birmingham and its expanding suburbs, again demonstrate the dominance of Birmingham's architects. Bryan Little in *Birmingham Buildings* notes that Birmingham now possesses 'no work by such national figures as Sir George Scott, Street or Butterfield.'[11] Apart from two churches in Bordesley by J. L. Pearson, there is little that did not emanate from a Birmingham drawing board. However, demonstrating their versatility with building types, most of the leading architects included churches and chapels in their output. Yeoville Thomason was responsible for a number of non-conformist chapels as well as what is now the oldest surviving 'cathedral synagogue' in Britain, Singers Hill in Blucher Street, together with churches. J. J. Bateman designed the Unitarian's Church of the Messiah in Broad Street, and F. B. Osborn, Martin and Chamberlain, Mansell and Mansell all produced ecclesiastical work. Of all the denominations, only the Catholic Church employed non Birmingham architects, though from the 1890s increasingly new commissions went to Barry Peacock, himself a Catholic, of the Birmingham firm of Cossins, Peacock and Bewlay. Nevertheless from the 1860s one architect, J. A. Chatwin, dominated the scene,[12] his most notable work being the rebuilding of Birmingham's medieval parish church of

St Martin's and the addition of the chancel to St Philip's. Of the Arts and Crafts architects, St Agatha's, Sparkbrook by W. H. Bidlake of 1899–1901 is the best known, whilst Arthur Stansfield Dixon designed several churches on a basilica plan.

By the 1860s the changing face of Birmingham was also apparent in the increasing number of purpose built industrial premises as larger concerns developed. As an industrial centre Birmingham had lacked the impressive industrial architecture of places such as Leeds with its huge textile mills, the mills and warehouses of Manchester and the dock complexes of Liverpool. In Birmingham from the 1830s a number of enterprises were operating in factories particularly in the electro-plating, brass and pen trades, with some factories being designed by Charles Edge and Bateman and Drury. In the 1860s J. G. Bland was responsible for a number of large factories in a flamboyant Venetian Gothic style including Wiley's Pen Works of 1862–3, now the Argent Centre. Yeoville Thomason designed factories in the same style. By the late 19th century other trades, originally operating at the workshop level such as jewellery and engineering had a number of large firms operating at the factory level. Among the architects designing such factories were Mansell and Mansell, Crouch and Butler, and Newton and Cheatle and these practices were notable for also executing domestic commissions for the same clients. J. L. Ball, noted for his Arts and Crafts houses, was responsible for some manufactories for the new products of bicycles and cars.

The domination by local architects of major building projects at the turn of the century had a notable setback in the selection of a London firm to design the new University buildings at Edgbaston in 1901. Aston Webb and Ingress Bell were selected by the Chancellor, Joseph Chamberlain, not on the strength of their highly successful Birmingham Law Courts, but as leading designers of national educational institutions. Oliver Lodge, the Principal would have preferred a local firm. The request by local architects for a competition was ignored.[13] The only work for the University by a Birmingham firm was the women's hall of residence, University House by Buckland and Haywood-Farmer of 1908.

The versatility of Birmingham's architects is also evidenced by the fact that those practices that undertook the major civic, commercial and industrial buildings also had considerable output of domestic architecture. In the period from the 1820s to the mid century those of means had largely ceased to occupy town houses in favour of villas in the suburban areas in proximity to the town. Rickman, Hill, Edge and J. J. Bateman were all responsible for villas for such clients, although this aspect of their work is not well documented and it is probable that much villa work was undertaken by jobbing builders. However when wanting a country house on a more substantial scale, wealthy Birmingham clients generally chose an outside architect who specialized in such work.[14]

The majority of the leading Birmingham architectural practices in Birmingham in the third quarter of the 19th century undertook a substantial number of domestic commissions, a consequence of the considerable increase in the number of prosperous manufacturers, and commercial and professional men in the flourishing Birmingham economy. J. H. Chamberlain of Martin and Chamberlain designed several residences set in substantial grounds for the civic elite in the suburbs of Harborne, Edgbaston and King's Heath in a characteristic Ruskinian Gothic style. His first gothic incursion in polychromatic brickwork in Edgbaston in the 1850s was regarded as startlingly novel by a public comfortable with stuccoed classicism. There was also considerable demand for large detached houses in relatively modest plots of half an acre in suburban areas, two to three miles from the city centre. These were built in the western area of Edgbaston where the new roads of Norfolk and Augustus Roads were created and where F. B. Osborn was particularly active, as well as in Yateley Road and Farquhar Road where Buckland and Haywood-Farmer designed some notable houses. In Moseley there were several residential developments including the Russell's estate and the Moseley Hall Estate of the Taylors where Owen Parsons and the practices of Cossins, Peacock and Bewlay, and Essex, Nicol and Goodman predominated.

In contrast the only exception to the suburbanisation of the business and professional classes occurred in the medical profession, many of whom continued to occupy town house in the City centre as residences and consulting rooms. The redevelopment of the Colmores' Newhall Estate in the 1890s was notable for the building of several such town houses by F. B. Osborn, Newton and Cheatle, Essex, Nicol and Goodman, Mansell and Mansell, and C. E. Bateman.

From 1890s with the improvement of suburban railway services, wealthy clients were able to live much further from the urban centre, the most notable developments being the Earl of Plymouth's Barnt Green Estate and the Four Oaks Estate at Sutton Coldfield, as well as many substantial houses in Northfield, Yardley, Olton and Solihull. The Four Oaks Estate was notable for its large houses in the Arts and Crafts style, the majority being by Birmingham architects, with the exception of a house each by the London architects W. R. Lethaby, Ernest Newton and Balfour and Turner. W. H. Bidlake, one of the few Birmingham architects with a national reputation, designed several houses there, as did Newton and Cheatle, C. E. Bateman, Owen Parsons, and Crouch and Butler. Although J. L. Ball, a leading Birmingham architect, did no work at Four Oaks he did design several large Arts and Crafts houses in Edgbaston, notably Winterbourne for J. S. Nettlefold. Ball's relatively low output is accounted for by his commitment to architectural education in the city.

As well as the acceleration in the volume of house building for wealthy clients from the 1880s onwards, many architects were involved in designing substantial additions to existing houses in response to changing taste. Billiard rooms and smoking rooms were frequently added, and occasionally picture galleries, as well as lodge cottages to give more formality to entrances. From about 1910 motor houses began to be built.

Increasingly the phenomenon developed among a number of upper middle class of possessing a suburban house and a country retreat. Some of the latter were newly built, such as several houses in Lickey Hills designed by Ernest Bewlay of Cossins, Peacock and Bewlay for members of the Cadbury family, who were mostly resident in Northfield in houses designed by W. A. Harvey or Ernest Bewlay, whilst Arthur McEwan designed Wast Hills for W. A. Cadbury. There was also the fashion to restore timber framed farmhouses or small manor houses. De Lacy Aherne restored Eastcote Hall near Meriden for Samuel Jevons and Yeoville Thomason upgraded Tyseley Grange for J. C. Onions. Some of the country retreats could be of exceptional size such as Berry Hall, near Solihull designed by J. A. Chatwin for Joseph Gillot the younger, or Moor Hall near Sutton Coldfield by Henman and Cooper for Edward Ansell.

Others commissioned additions to existing substantial properties such as the Muntz family's 17th century Umberslade Hall near Tanworth which were designed by W. H. Bidlake, after an earlier remodelling by the London architect Phéne Spiers.

The domestic output of several of Birmingham's leading architects in the late 19th and early 20th centuries was not confined to detached upper middle class housing. Newton and Cheatle, and Owen Parsons designed alterations and improvements to back to back housing in the inner city area, whilst Frederick Martin designed some of the regrettably few artisans' dwellings built to replace slum housing under the 1875 Improvement Scheme, as originally envisaged. Crouch and Butler undertook a large number of working class terraced housing schemes for developers in Winson Green, Small Heath and Saltley. Other architects such as De Lacy Ahearne and C. E. Bateman designed speculative middle class housing. Buckland and Haywood-Farmer were responsible for the village for the dam maintenance workers of Birmingham's Elan Valley scheme in Wales whilst two housing developments were notable for their contribution to model housing and town planning. These were the work of W. A. Harvey designing the model village at Bournville for George Cadbury, and the Harborne Tenants' Estate by Frederick Martin at Moor Pool, Harborne, initiated by J. S. Nettlefold, chairman of the Council's Planning Committee. These were influential in the layout and high quality of Birmingham's local authority housing finally undertaken after the First World War.

The quality of Birmingham's suburbs, and in particular its Arts and Crafts architecture of the late 19th and early 20th century attracted considerable praise in the contemporary architectural press. This was in contrast to the reaction to much of what was built from the mid 19th century onwards: a writer in *The Builder* in 1890 stated that the paper in recent years had hardly ever been able to accept as illustrations any drawings sent in from Birmingham, and that he considered the Midland capital 'one of the most architecturally depressing of all our large towns'.[15] A local observer in the *Birmingham Gazette* in 1884 commented 'taken in detail the Birmingham buildings are as magnificent as are her institutions, but en masse the effect is an architectural jungle'.[16] However not everything was condemned in the London press, a writer in the *Pall Mall Gazette* in 1894 said 'in Birmingham you may generally recognize a Board School by its being the best building in the neighbourhood'.

It is difficult to be objective about architecture, and as noted earlier Birmingham has had a particular fondness for reinventing its built environment. In the late 1950s and early 1960s much of central Birmingham was reconfigured to accommodate the car, leading to the loss of many of the important buildings by architects featured in this book. However as Jonathan Meades writing in *The Times*[17] has observed, 'central Birmingham today has abandoned its love affair with the car, the love whose name this city alone dares speak.' He regretted the lack of protection for Birmingham's modernist buildings of the 1960s – 'whose sum constituted the most complete plastic expressionism of postwar optimism' but 'for the casual visitor the greatest attraction is the sheer extent of its prodigious later Victorian streets and buildings'.

NOTES

[1] Quoted in Asa Briggs, *History of Birmingham* vol 11 'Borough and City 1868–1938' (1952), p. 10.
[2] Quoted in Andy Foster, *Pevsner Architectural Guides: Birmingham* (New Haven and London) p. 197.
[3] *Ibid* p. 27; p. x.
[4] Conrad Gill, *History of Birmingham* vol 1 'Manor and Borough to 1865' (1952) p. 199.
[5] *Ibid* p. 172.
[6] Foster, *Birmingham*, p. 16.
[7] *Ibid*, p. 74.
[8] *The Builder*, 73, 27 Nov 1897, p. 435; Briggs, *History of Birmingham* p. 24.
[9] Foster, *Birmingham* p. 130.
[10] Briggs, *History of Birmingham*, p. 16.
[11] Bryan Little, *Birmingham Buildings: The Architectural Story of a Midland City* (Newton Abbot, 1971) p. 27.
[12] *Ibid*, p.27; Foster, *Birmingham*, p. 19.
[13] Eric Ives, Diane Drummond and Leonard Schwarz, *The First Civic University: Birmingham 1880–1980* (Birmingham, 2000) p. 116; Little, *Birmingham Buildings*, p. 37.
[14] Phillada Ballard, 'A Commercial and Industrial Elite, Birmingham's Upper Middle Class 1780–1914,' (unpublished Ph.D thesis, University of Reading, 1983) p. 776. For example Hubert Galton's Warley Abbey was designed by Robert Lugar, John Howard Galton's remodelling of Hadzor House, near Droitwich, was by Matthew Habershon and John Moilliet employed Samuel Dawkes for Abberley Hall.
[15] Little, *Birmingham Buildings*, p. 32.
[16] Quoted in Briggs, *History of Birmingham*, p. 23.
[17] *The Times* 5 March 2005.

Part One • The Early Victorian Town

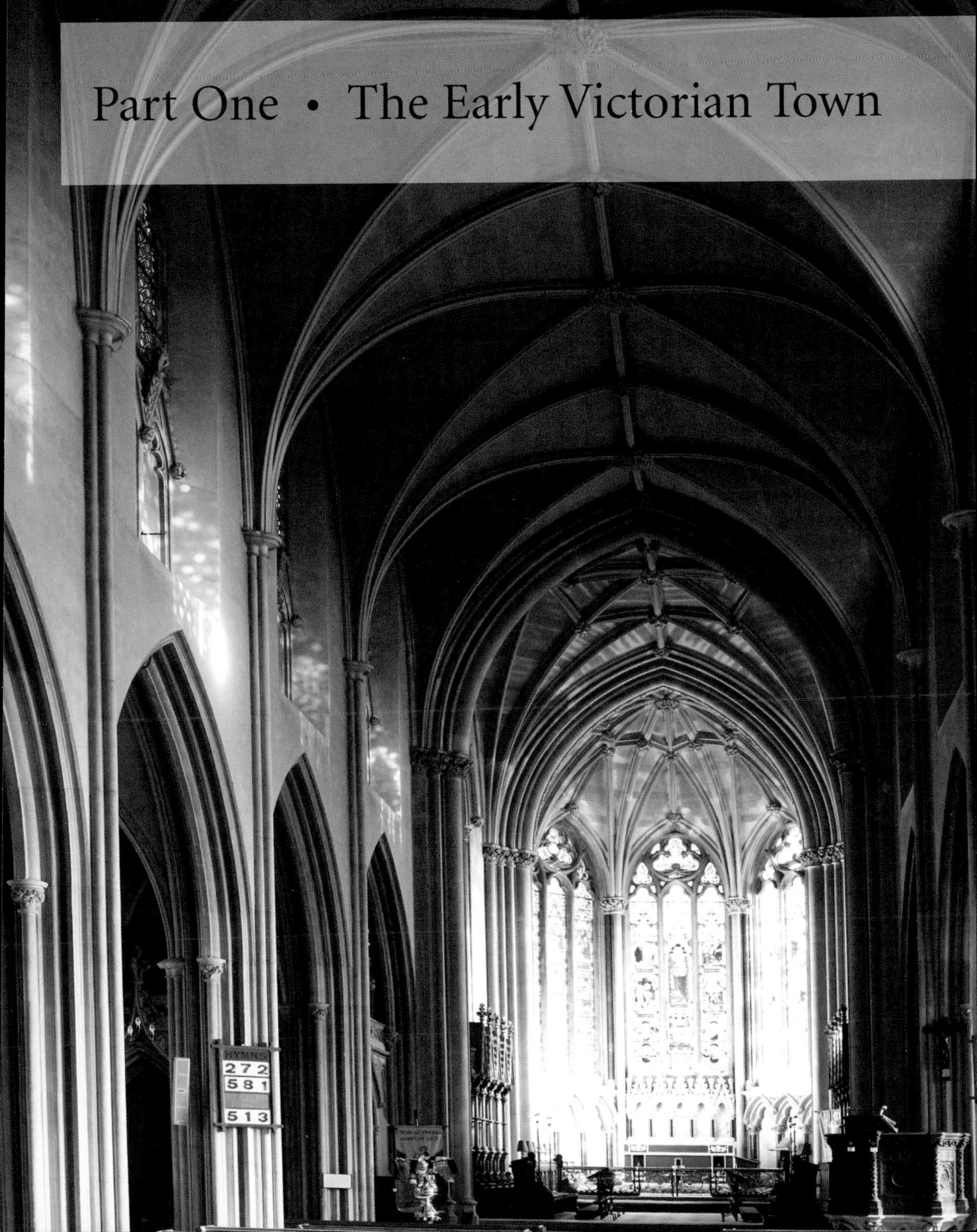

1 Thomas Rickman

REMO GRANELLI

In person Thos. Rickman was rather below the middle height, inclining to corpulency, with a rather large head, and a very short neck. His features were not refined, but the expression of his countenance was pleasant, especially when animated by lively conversation, which he always heartily enjoyed. His temperament was quick, but without acerbity, and although he was sometimes under sudden provocation roused to anger, the irritation generally immediately subsided and left no taint of bitterness. His vision was affected with colour blindness.[1]

Thus Thomas Rickman (1776–1841) was described shortly after his death by R. C. Hussey who had become his partner in 1835 and thereafter carried on the firm's practice at 45 Anne Street (later Colmore Row)[2] in the following years.

This accurate description of Rickman in his later years can be seen from the portrait by W. S. Cruickshank of 1826 when Rickman was fifty years of age, and a close study of the architect's diaries from 1807 to 1834[3] will fully vindicate Hussey's assessment, for in them there are the thoughts of a man who exuded determination and activity, and the studious intention of not staying down for long. His importance to British architecture, however, must be seen as an historian rather than an architect, for as a practitioner he cannot be compared with Soane, Nash and several others of his time even though his practice became large and extended throughout the country. His importance lies in his understanding of Gothic architecture and his dissemination of the succeeding stages of this style. He was the first person to investigate the style's change of detail and to date the introduction of those changes. His book,

Thomas Rickman from a portrait by
W. S. Cruickshank in T. M. Rickman's *Notes on the Life of Thomas Rickman*

An Attempt to Discriminate the Styles of Architecture in England, based upon his first-hand studies, was published in seven revised editions throughout the nineteenth century,[4] and from its first publication in 1817 the book became a standard work of reference for all architects and students until the end of the century when other standard works were published. But Rickman did not begin his career as an architect and historian in earnest until he had reached middle age and after he had been engaged in many occupations.

Thomas Rickman was born in Maidenhead, Berkshire on 8 July 1776,[5] the eldest of nine children born of Joseph and Sarah, Quakers of that town. Joseph had been was born in 1749 in Lewes then the home of a large contingent of Rickmans. There is little information on Thomas during his formative years apart from his work as a trainee chemist in his father's business after he had left school, but we do know from what his son has written about him that he was a methodical young man with a serious cast of mind, who during the early period of his life was interested in sketching parish churches – an interest that would rekindle in later years.[6]

Rickman was not the first to manifest an interest in Gothic architecture. Wyatt had been involved in the re-introduction of the style in the eighteenth century, but before him there was James Essex (1722–84) who was perhaps the first practising architect to take an antiquarian interest in the style, and there had been early, tentative essays in a plagiarised 'Gothick' by both designers and clients who did not fully understand the organic constructive elements in the style but were entertained only by its element of fantasy. There was someone, however, able to show a more serious interest in Gothic at this early period. The Hon. Roger North (1653–1734), the sixth son of Dudley, the fourth Lord North, perceived that there were '3 periods of ye Gothic building' – obviously referring to Early English, Decorated and Perpendicular, but not naming them; a responsibility left for Rickman a century later. Although a barrister, North carried out new designs, and alterations to existing buildings while he worked at the bar. The best of his known buildings being the Middle Temple Gateway in Fleet Street of 1683–84.[7]

In 1813 Thomas married Christiana Horner, a governess who died shortly afterwards in childbirth, the baby girl dying eighteen months later. In the same year the last part of his initial work on medieval architecture in England was published in James Smith's *Panorama of Arts and Sciences*, a periodic publication to which Rickman had begun contributing the previous year and in which he delineated and described the three main styles noting the characteristics of each period and tracing their evolution. This had not been attempted previously and the article made a deep impression on members of the Society of Archaeologists of which Rickman was later voted a member, and upon architects throughout the country. He was now becoming known in both architectural and archaeological circles, and in his spare time – for he was still employed as an accountant – he continued his first-hand study of Gothic architecture and he attracted a large number of small architectural commissions which became larger in scope as the years passed.

He was becoming known in the Liverpool area by his work, writing and lecturing, and in 1817 he published the work born of years of first-hand study *An Attempt to Discriminate the Styles of English Architecture from the Conquest to the Reformation*. The publication of this important work and its distribution throughout the country to architects, historians and interested gentlemen brought him considerable publicity and the architectural practice he had begun some years previously began to grow quickly and extensively.

In 1818 at the age of forty-two years he left his position as an accountant with the firm of Messrs Case to practice full-time as an architect.[8] On opening his office in Liverpool Rickman appointed an assistant to deal with the many junior tasks that are to be found in an architect's office, but very soon he needed someone able to give technical assistance. He made possibly the best decision of all his years in practice when he appointed Henry Hutchinson (1800–31) as his assistant in June 1818. Henry was born in 1800 in, or near, to Birmingham, and he is first recorded when he and his elder brother Thomas, an architect practising at 57 New Street, became members of the Society of Birmingham Artists (forerunner of the RBSA) when the Society opened new premises in Union Street in 1814. It was probably in his brother's office that Henry received his initial instruction before joining Rickman in Liverpool. Henry was then a young man of eighteen years with ability and promise. There is a coloured lithograph in the Liverpool Athenaeum showing a caricature of Rickman and Hutchinson embarking upon a survey expedition. Rickman is shown to be a rotund and powerful man of average height and almost bald, whereas Hutchinson is fair-haired, long and thin with stooping shoulders. He was already, when first joining Rickman, a first-class draughtsman with a keen intellect and an ability to handle classical design in an assured manner. He proved to be a godsend to Rickman who had little experience of classical buildings so early in his practice, and, as time passed, Hutchinson proved to be a great asset to the practice.

In Birmingham Rickman's first important commission was St George's Church in Tower Street awarded by the Church Commissioners. This was the first church to be built under the 1818 Act which had been allocated £1,000,000 for the erection of churches in newly developed areas. This was not however a straight forward appointment and Rickman, with little practical experience 'was called before Architects Nash, Soane and Smirke and underwent a long minute (& I fear reversing) Examination of near 4 hours'.[9] This gruelling interview took place on 27 August 1818 and a little later Thomas realised that his fears were groundless when he heard that he had been appointed for the new church building.

With his appointment as the architect for St George's Church Rickman began a long and successful association with Birmingham by opening a small office at 5 Canon Street and installing Hutchinson to take charge. But what determined him to establish his practice in this burgeoning town, for he had no personal or family connections here? A number of considerations led to his decision. Firstly, there was Henry's knowledge of the town together with his connections there. Secondly, Thomas had made the acquaintance in 1816 of Charles Barber (1784–1854) who was then living in Liverpool but was a member of the large Birmingham family of painters descended from Joseph Barber (1757–1811) who had been drawing master at King Edward's Grammar School in New Street and teacher of David Cox, among others. Neither should the fact be ignored that Thomas was a strong Quaker, and Birmingham was a centre for nonconformists, who were able to give strong support to Thomas in his effort to establish a thriving practice. In addition he was able to obtain financial help from a bank in the town, when he was refused in Liverpool.

After many years of uncertainty and misfortune Thomas at last settled to a mode of work and a life style which suited him entirely. By 1820 his Birmingham office was so busy and its future in the bustling town so promising, that he left Liverpool for good and took residence in Birmingham where he oversaw the running and rapid growth of his practice which in its first year produced a thousand drawings – quite an achievement for a practice of any size in any age, but for one so small and in its infancy the feat was remarkable.

Competition from architects practising in the town was sparse, and when Thomas set up practice there in 1818 apart from Joseph Bateman, a surveyor and father of John Jones Bateman, there was only William Hollins (1763–1843) the architect and sculptor who had been responsible for the Old Library in Union Street (1798), the Public Offices and Prison in Moor Street (1805), and the Dispensary in Union Street (1806–08). He was an adequate architect as engravings of his work shows, but today perhaps better remembered as the father of the sculptor Peter Hollins whose work can be seen throughout the country. St George's Church is the building that readily comes to mind when historians speak of Rickman's importance in furthering the early progress of the Gothic Revival. How unfortunate that this important pioneer building should be demolished in 1960 without opposition by the Church of England when it was deemed to be of no further use to the Church. In the late 1950s Rickman's tomb, designed by his last partner R. C. Hussey, and standing in the surrounding churchyard, was left to decay.

The church of St George was the most important project that the office worked upon during its first two years in practice and set a standard for other practitioners in the Gothic style. In common with Revival churches of the early nineteenth century the plan form was reminiscent of the eighteenth-century Georgian church in its symmetry and simplicity, until it is remembered that many churches of the twelfth and early thirteenth centuries began quite simply with a nave and chancel, sometimes an aisle, crossing and tower. Transepts and chapels which give to the building their amorphous character were added as time passed and enlargement was considered necessary. Consequently St George's was simple, its form dictated by the needs of the congregation and the materials used were chosen by the dictate of economy, so there should be little surprise at the difference between

ABOVE Church of St George, Tower St, 1819–20 (demolished 1960). *Courtesy of Birmingham Archives and Heritage Services (WK/N4/282)*

LEFT Church of St George, interior. *Courtesy of Birmingham Archives and Heritage Services (WK/N4/285)*

the Gothic Revival church built under the financial restrictions of the 1818 Act and the genuine Gothic church of the medieval period.

Between 1820 when Rickman settled in Birmingham and 1825 when he again married, his practice made progress with a great amount of gothic and classical work throughout the country. In Birmingham and the surrounding countryside the practice was engaged upon new churches at Erdington, Dale End, Hampton Lucy, Ombersley and Holloway Head, and the extension of churches at Moseley, Handsworth and Hagley; and during this period secular works were carried out at Down House and Ettingham Park.

To give a fair assessment of the ability of the practice attention should be paid to works which were undertaken beyond the confines of Birmingham, when it will be seen that given the opportunity Rickman and his practice were able to show abilities which were not always apparent, particularly in their ecclesiological work. Three such projects which belong to this period may be briefly mentioned here.

Down House at Redmarley in Gloucestershire, was designed for the Hon. George Dowdeswell through an introduction by Thomas Fulljames of nearby Hasfield Court, who was uncle to one of Rickman's pupils. Work began on site in 1822 and was completed in 1824 when the practice created a classical styled house on the high point of the site having excellent vistas. Much material was reused from the existing house situated further down the site which was later entirely demolished. The house has an attractive interior which has been little altered over the years, and the nearby E-shaped stable block of the same date and style, has a well balanced façade with a central entrance arch and a pierced rotunda above.

While the building of Down House was in progress work began on the erection of St Peter's Church at Hampton Lucy in Warwickshire, (1822–26), for the Lucy family of Charlecote Park, to replace an earlier church which Rickman advised against retaining. A member of the family, the Revd John Lucy, was vicar of the church, and it was he who paid for the rebuilding with monies left to him by his mother some years previously. The new church of St Peter, due largely to the design skills of Hutchinson, is one of the finest of religious buildings, by the partnership, and of this period throughout the country. The decorated style of the thirteenth century was used, in common with most new churches at this time, and was built with warm golden-brown ashlar with opulent detailing of that period, all afforded by private monies. Henry Hutchinson died at Leamington where he was convalescing, on 22 November 1831, and was buried at Hampton Lucy where his gravestone may be seen.

The New Court of St John's College at Cambridge is a further example which readily substantiates the above assessment. The practice was appointed to this contract in 1826 and work on site commenced the following year. Here, the architect took full advantage of the fairy-tale site overlooking treed parkland and bounded by the River Cam, to design a romantic cluster of Gothic buildings set about two enclosed courtyards with central ambulatory, and having a cloistered

Church of St Peter, Hampton Lucy, 1822–26

approach from the 'Bridge of Sighs', detailed and scaled so aptly by Hutchinson, to span the adjacent river. This is one of the finest achievements by the partners to whom, at the completion of the contract in 1831, the Governors presented inscribed silver writing stands, only a short time before Hutchinson's death.[10]

When design work was in progress in 1822 on the Hampton Lucy church, St Barnabas at Erdington was also in the drawing stage and was being designed in the Gothic style, but the result is quite different. This was a Commissioners' church with the usual building fund economy. The church was planned as a single-cell building, with only a nave and no aisles, but Rickman gave handsome proportions to the broad nave and the space is pleasing even though the long and slender cast iron windows in Geometric and Flamboyant styles give insufficient light to enliven the interior. At the west end there is a substantial timber gallery sitting upon Rickman's slender and elegant cast-iron screen with four equally elegant columns and end wall fixings. The church was designed in the Decorated style, at this time most favoured by ecclesiastical architects. The natural lighting at the east end was improved by J. A. Chatwin in 1883 when he extended the chancel and provided new windows, at the same time he added the transepts, and later came back, in 1893, to add an imposing open timbered roof.

In August 1824 Rickman toured the north of England supervising projects at Wigan, Chorley and Preston, and went on through the Lake District pausing at

Kendal, and then on to a contract at Carlisle. From there he crossed the border into Scotland to gather material for the revised edition of his book which was now widely read throughout the country. At Edinburgh he met the printer George Miller and visited his home at Hope Park. There he met the printer's daughter, Elizabeth, a lady much younger than himself who quite captivated him. The initial friendship quickly developed into much more for Rickman as his diary shows, 'This morning I walked to Fairlie with EM & during the day had some other opportunities with her & tho every interview only shows me how much deserving she is of love & admiration I am almost in despair ... but it is yet early days & I hope and trust a further acquaintance will give me more hope.'[11] When he returned to Birmingham a correspondence developed between them, and their wedding subsequently took place in Edinburgh on 20 January 1825.[12] After their marriage they moved into the house in Islington Row that Rickman had taken and furnished late in 1824.

The marriage brought Rickman a happiness which was new to him. Elizabeth showed herself to be a good wife, as can be judged from the diaries which frequently refer to her, and her visits with Rickman to his building sites around Birmingham and further afield. She visited his friends and business acquaintances, and was able to help Rickman in the preparation of the revised editions of his book.

The second Commissioners' church by Rickman and Hutchinson was begun on site in July 1825 with St Peter's Church at Dale End.[13] This was the subject of a competition for which the partners submitted both Gothic and Classic designs. The accepted scheme was Classic and based upon the ancient Temple of Minerva at Athens and provided accommodation for 1,900 parishioners as required by the Commissioners. The west front of the building which was presented to the street was dominated by a massive Doric portico of four columns which encompassed the full height of the building, and stood upon stylobates raised above the ground by four steps. Within the portico was the central entrance to the church, with at both north and south sides separate entrances to the galleries within the church. The traditional bell tower, which also provided the 'rising to the heavens' motif, was represented by a short tower above the roof at the west end and was encircled with attached columns on a stylobate. The church was completed, and opened for divine service on 10 August 1827.

Being one of the few architects in the town and the only one with a national reputation Rickman continued to receive commissions from its dignitaries. James Watt junior, Mathew Robinson Boulton's partner at the Soho Works employed him to supervise the construction of a chapel at St Mary's Church, Handsworth[14]

OPPOSITE Interior of Church of St Peter, Hampton Lucy, 1822–26

to house a statue sculpted by Francis Chantrey (1781–1841) to commemorate his father who had died in 1819.

There were three architects at work on the James Watt Memorial Chapel when it was erected in 1826. This appears to be excessive when the competent William Hollins had only recently carried out major works at the church, and Birmingham had the services of Rickman, a reputed ecclesiastical architect. Given that, it is surprising to find that Richard H. Bridgen, a small-time architect who had probably met Rickman in 1818 when both men were in Liverpool, now appears to have been the designer of the Watt Chapel, leaving Rickman as supervising architect and Hollins as main contractor. The diaries show that Rickman spent a great deal of time not only on site supervision when he often met both Hollins the builder, and Watt the client, but also in producing architectural details for the builder. Hollins produced samples of 'flags for the Chapel which are to be Bidford with a black border'[15] for Rickman to approve which suggests the duty of a contractor. We hear little of Bridgen when the work is under construction in 1826 except for an entry in the diary for the 19 May which refers to a drawing for a mullion sent to him. Whoever was responsible for its concept the memorial chapel is a success. Sited on the south-east corner it is a chaste Gothic design in natural stone with a groined roof supported by attached columns from which spring the elegant supporting arches. The entrance to the chapel from the body of the church is enclosed by a four-point arch of fourteenth-century design with ogee decorations. Chantrey's fine statue of Watt is in white marble depicting him seated at ease and considering a scaled manuscript. It is a fitting tribute to one the great men of this revolutionary period. In the church are sculptured commemorations to his colleagues, Boulton, Murdock and Eginton.

St Thomas's at Holloway Head was the third and last new church to be erected in Birmingham by the Commissioners under the supervision of the Rickman office. The contract was won in competition with other

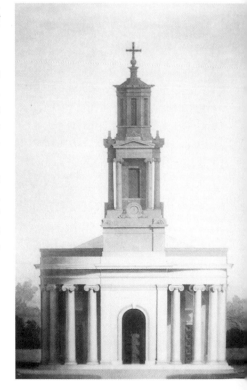

West end of Church of St Thomas, Granville St. Elevation drawing, 1826.
Courtesy of RIBA Architects Drawings Collection, V&A Museum

OPPOSITE Surviving portion of Church of St Thomas, 1826–29 damaged in 1940

architects and was handled in the main by Hutchinson who shortly after he had produced design drawings suffered a periodic illness and left for Leamington in April in order to recover. He appears to have suffered from illness often throughout his partnership with Rickman and because of it would work from his home in St Paul's Square where he had settled after his marriage in 1822.

On 23 May 1826 news came that the Commissioners had approved the design drawings and wished Rickman to proceed with the working drawings and obtain tenders.[16] The winning tender was approved on 26 August and the first stone laid by the Bishop on 2 October at a ceremony attended by five hundred people.

It was an elegant design in the classic manner completed in 1829, of which only the west end with entrance porch and tower remain after an enemy air attack during the 1939–45 war. What remains however gives an impression of Hutchinson's facility in classical design. The building has bold yet sensitive lines with little ornamentation on its external face but relies upon a strong handling of the elliptical portico, with the western tower breaking through the composition above the doorway, and with a sweeping weathering course running through the entrance elevation and continuing along the sides of the nave.

The classical buildings produced by the partnership were usually small in scale, precisely and invariably successful. Two excellent examples showing these characteristics are The Birmingham Society of Arts in New Street which was completed in 1829, and the Birmingham Banking Company in Waterloo Street of 1832.

The Society of Birmingham Artists was first formed in 1809 with its membership including the brothers Charles and Joseph Barber, and Samuel Lines, meeting at a building in Peck Lane immediately south of New Street.[17] Five years later, in 1814, the Society moved to a new building in Union Street and now included in its membership the brothers Thomas and Henry Hutchinson. Thomas was then practising as an architect at 57 New Street and Henry was probably working with him. In 1826 the original Society broke up and a new one was formed under the title of 'The Birmingham Society of Artists' which met at a circular exhibition building in New Street where the first exhibition of the Society was held in 1827. The catalogue issued to commemorate this first exhibition contained an illustration of the new exhibition building proposed by Rickman and Hutchinson who had become members of the Society in 1826. Their published design won general approval and work soon began on the new building. The small classical building which Hutchinson designed to sit upon the New Street site was, possibly, the most elegant of those in the town at this time, and is now a great loss to the city.

The architect based his design upon the Roman Temple of Jupiter Stator in Rome, and the end product was a delicate expression of classical design in Bath stone. The four fluted Corinthian columns supported a rich entablature which oversailed the pavement and stood upon moulded bases at its edge. Blind recesses were placed on the slightly projecting wall on either side of an attractive entablatured doorway. Inside the building a flight of stairs led to a landing from which

Society of Arts Building, New
Street, 1828 (demolished in 1911).
*Courtesy of Birmingham Archives
and Heritage Services (Whybrow
Collection)*

on either side opened rooms used as a library/committee room, and a sculpture
exhibition room. Immediately facing the staircase was the opening to the circular
main exhibition room which was given a coffered-dome ceiling with a central roof
light. Adjoining this space were two smaller rooms, one being circular for the
exhibition of watercolours, and an octagonal room for prints.

In 1911 the building was demolished to make way for a larger building which
provided a home for what had become the Royal Birmingham Society of Artists
and one of the most important art societies in the country. The Society again
moved its premises to Brook Street, St Paul's Square in 1999.

The building contract for the Birmingham Banking Company[18] was awarded to
the partners after they had competed against another firm of architects in the
latter months of 1830, and work commenced on the corner of Waterloo Street and
Bennett's Hill with the entrance of the building being placed at the end of the
façade facing Bennett's Hill. The Banking Company had begun in New Street a
few years before under the management of Joseph Gibbons, and had then moved

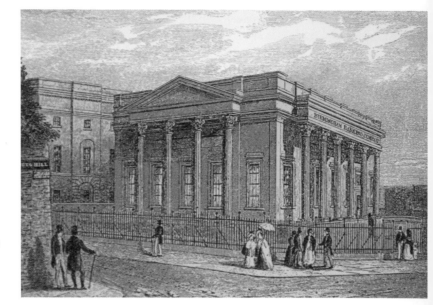

Engraving of Bank for the Birmingham Banking Co., Temple Row, 1830, from R. K. Dent *The Making of Birmingham* 1894

Bank for Birmingham Banking Co., with alterations by Yeoville Thomason of 1869

Drawing for Wood House, Tettenhall, 1831–36. *Courtesy of RIBA Architects Drawings Collection, V&A Museum*

on after a period of consolidation to premises in Union Street. It was the first purpose built bank to be erected in Birmingham, and for this scheme Hutchinson used the Corinthion order – at the same time he was using the Ionic order in a classical design for the Town Hall competition for which the practice was awarded third prize – with a plain tympanum within the pediment on the Waterloo Street frontage. Its simplicity is more reminiscent of the early Greek temple than the later Roman derivation which its order follows and which became popular in English architecture some years later. In 1869 the original entrance to the bank was sealed and a new entrance with a pedimented head was introduced to the corner of the building giving access from Waterloo Street. The doorway and curved upper storey are typically Roman in character and out of place on a Greek façade. This uncomplimentary alteration was made by Yeoville Thomason (1826–1901), an Edinburgh born architect who practised in Birmingham after his apprenticeship with Charles Edge.

Henry Hutchinson died on 22 November 1831[19] before the completion of the bank contract, one of his last works. Indeed, he was only a little connected with site supervision due to his persistent illness which plagued him throughout the year and which convalescent visits to the Isle of Wight for several months, and later in the year to Leamington where presumably he had family ties, did nothing to abate. His subsequent death threw a heavy burden upon Rickman who had always undertaken most of the travelling throughout the country to supervise site work and meet clients, whilst at the same time visiting churches and compiling notes for his book. Now he also had to supervise the work in his office, for his younger brother, Edwin, who had been made a partner in the firm, began to manifest the mental instability that had affected his father in his latter years, and had to be put under restraint and treated at Rickman's home, finally leaving the practice in 1834.[20] It is unclear what happened to Edwin after this time except that he lived a long life, dying in 1873 in his eighty-third year.

The extra work and responsibility began to take its toll on Rickman's robust constitution and matters came to a head when he was building Wood House at Tettenhall near Wolverhampton for Miss Hinckes for whom he began designs in 1832.[21] By 1834 he began to show signs of persistent illness, having several seizures and falls during his travels about the country, and it was during this period that Wood House, the large and attractive Gothic house, finally cost far more than the contract figure, a situation never before experienced by the careful accountant/ architect who had always completed his buildings at or below the contract figure. In this instance the spinster client held her architect responsible for the ensuing extras – as he probably was in legal terms – when the contract was completed in 1836, and on finding that he did not have monies to meet the financial extras, Miss Hinckes took a legal option on his home in Islington Row, which he was forced to sell a few years later in order to meet financial obligations when he retired through illness.[22]

The growth of the town called for a new thoroughfare for housing in the Gosta Green district, and Great Lister Street came into being. The district also needed a new church to serve the inhabitants of the area. The Bishop of Lichfield, Dr Ryder, with the financial support of prominent people, appointed Rickman to design a new church in 1836. The church, demolished during Birmingham's rebuilding era of the 1960s, was a Gothic design in red brick with stone dressings, the brick tower with chequered stone corner piers bearing a similarity in design to the church of St Botolph at Barton in Lincolnshire, though the tower there is entirely in stone. The church was consecrated in December 1838 when Rickman attended the ceremony. An adjoining street was named after Dr Ryder and a life-sized medallion of the Bishop designed by Peter Hollins later formed part of a monument erected in the parish church of Lutterworth where, earlier, Dr Ryder was the incumbent.

The Bishop Ryder Church was the last building with which Rickman was personally connected.[23] With increasing illness he retired leaving the practice to Richard Hussey who carried on the work of the practice competently but on a smaller scale. The financial problems of two later troublesome contracts left Rickman with considerable expenses which he met by selling his property in Islington Row in the spring of 1838 – the house was demolished a little before the 1939 war – and moving to 17 Albion Street in the Jewellery Quarter, also now demolished. There he died of his illness on 4 January 1841 aged sixty-three years.[24] In his retirement his work was not forgotten and he was made one of the first Honorary Members of the Oxford Society, and the Cambridge Camden Society, both of which becoming influential in the forthcoming Ecclesiastical Movement.[25]

His last partner, Richard Hussey, designed a monument which was placed above Rickman's grave in the churchyard of St George's church in Tower Street

Bishop Ryder Church, Gem St, Aston, 1838 (demolished c. 1960). *Courtesy of Birmingham Archives and Heritage Services*

bearing the inscription, 'Thomas Rickman F.S.A. who first correctly named the several styles and clearly elucidated the principles of our ecclesiastical architecture. This monument was dedicated by a few of his friends in the cemetery of one of his many churches which he erected. He died January 11 MDCCXXXI aged LXIV years'.[26]

Richard Hussey continued as sole principal of the practice and trained Rickman's son, Thomas Miller. Shortly after Rickman's death Elizabeth sold his book rights to J. H. Parker[27] who edited and published the next three editions culminating with the seventh edition in 1881 after the content of Rickman's writing had been brought up to date in line with improving scholarship. The book remains an excellent primer in its subject.

Elizabeth, with her son and daughter, went to live at Houghton Place, Somer's Town, Middlesex, where she died in 1877. Her son, Thomas, became an FSA and President of the Architectural Association; he married Mary Lynam and lived at Seacombe Lodge, King's Road, Clapham, Surrey, where he practised successfully as a surveyor employing fourteen assistants.[28] He had one son who died in infancy. Thomas lived until 1912. His sister, Mary Ann, remained a spinster living at St Pancras, London, where she died in 1900.

List of Architectural Works of Thomas Rickman (1776–1841)

Thomas Rickman practised as an architect from 1812 to 1838. He opened his practice in Birmingham in 1820. From 1818 until 1831 he was assisted by Henry Hutchinson (1800–31). His brother, Edwin Rickman, was a partner from 1831 to 1834, and in 1835 R. C. Hussey became a partner and continued the firm after Rickman's death.

This list is based upon H. M. Colvin's *A Biographical Dictionary of English Architects 1660–1840* (1954). Alteration and additions have been made by the author of this essay.

WORK IN BIRMINGHAM AND ITS ENVIRONS

PUBLIC

1819–22 Church of St George, Tower St [D]. Rickman's tomb is in the graveyard

1822 Church of St Barnabas, High Street, Erdington (enlarged by J. A. Chatwin 1883; re-roofed 1893)

1823–24 Rebuilding of Church of St Mary, St Mary's Row, Moseley (rebuilt by J. A. Chatwin 1884–1910)

1825–27 Church of St Peter, Dale End, repaired after fire (rebuilt by Charles Edge 1835) [D]

1826 The Watt Chapel in the Church of St Mary, Hamstead Road, Handsworth, (orig. design R. H. Bridgens)

1826 Addition of aisle and arcade to Church of St John Baptist, Hagley, Worcs.; internal works 1839 (rebuilt by G. E. Street 1858–60)

1826–29 Church of St Thomas, Bath Row, Holloway Head (war damaged 1940)

1827–29 Church of St Mary, Harborne; enlarged by Rickman (later considerable alterations by Yeoville Thomason)

1828 Additions to Public News Room, Temple Row [D]

1828 Exhibition Rooms for Society of Arts, New Street [D]

1829 Master's House at Deaf and Dumb Asylum, Edgbaston [D]

1831 Bordesley School, Camp Hill, Birmingham [D]

1832 Lodge entrance to Birmingham Botanical Gardens, Edgbaston.

1833 Church of All Saints, All Saints Street (chancel added in 1881)

1834 Rebuilding of Church of St Margaret, Ward End (attrib. to Rickman by VCH *Birmingham*, attrib. to J. Frith by Goodhart-Rendal. Frith however was Rickman's clerk of works and only supervised the firm's contracts)

1838 Bishop Ryder Church, Great Lister Street [D]

COMMERCIAL

1826 New Offices for Rickman practice at 45 Anne Street (later 19 Colmore Row)

1830 Bank for Birmingham Banking Company (now Midland Bank), Temple Row (altered by Yeoville Thomason c. 1870)

DOMESTIC

1823 Alterations to drawing room of Thornhill House, Handsworth for Anne Boulton

1830 Two houses in Islington Row, Edgbaston for Thomas Rickman, one of which he occupied [D]

WORK OUTSIDE BIRMINGHAM

PUBLIC

1812–14 Church of St George, Everton, nr Liverpool

1814–15 Church of St Michael in the Hamlet, Liverpool; cast iron was used extensively in this church and that of St George

1816 Church of St Philip, Liverpool [D 1882]

1819 Church at Runcorn, Cheshire (rebuilt by A. Salvin 1849)

1819–21 Church of St Mary, Birkenhead, Cheshire (enlarged) [D]

1820 The Town Hall, Clithero, Lancs.

1820–21 Rebuilding of Church of St Mary, Barnsley, Yorks.

1820–24 Church of St George, Chorley, Lancs. (Chancel added 1891)

1821–22 Church of St George, Barnsley, Yorks.

1822 News Room, Preston, Lancs.

1822–23 Christ Church, Brunswick Square, Gloucester (rebuilt in a Romanesque style 1899–1910)

1822–26 Church of St Peter, Hampton Lucy, Warks (enlarged by Scott 1856)

1823–25 Church of St Peter, Preston (spire added 1852)

1823–25 Church of St Paul, Preston (chancel added 1882)

1824–25 Church of St David, Glasgow

1825 The Court House, Preston, Lancs.

1825–27 Church of St Mary, Mellor, nr Blackburn, Lancs. (restored by Austin and Paley 1899)

1825–29 Church of St Andrew, Ombersley, Worcs.

1825–29 Lower Darwen Church nr Blackburn, Lancs. (Colvin says it is a Commissioners' church but the author has been unable to locate it)

1826–27 Repairs and additions to Church of St Michael, Great Tew, Oxon.

1826–29 Christ Church, Coventry; nave added to C14 steeple [bombed 1940]

1827–29 Church of Holy Trinity, Over Darwen, nr Blackburn, Lancs.

1827–29 Church of St John, Oulton, Yorks.

1827–30 Church at Pemberton, nr Wigan, Lancs. (Colvin says it is a Commissioners' church but the author has been unable to locate it)

1827–31 The New Court, St John's College, Cambridge, and 'Bridge of Sighs' over River Cam

1828–29 Rebuilding of Church of St Mary Magdalen, Clithero, Lancs.

1828 Church of All Saints, Canterbury [closed 1902]

1828–30 Christ Church, Carlisle

1828–30 Church of Holy Trinity, Carlisle

1828–30 Church of St John, Whittle-le-Woods, nr Leyland, Leics. (rebuilt 1880–82 by Myers, Veevers and Myers)

1829 Drapers' Hall, Bayley Lane, Coventry

1829–31 Church of Holy Trinity, Bristol

1830 Addition of south aisle to Church of St Andrew, Rugby, Warks. (rebuilt by Butterfield 1877–79)

1830 The News Room and Library (now Barclays Bank), Carlisle

1830 Rebuilding of Church of St Helen, Albury, Oxon for the Earl of Abingdon

1830–32 Christ Church, Greyfriars, Warwick Lane, Coventry [bombed 1940]

1831 Church of St Jude, Liverpool (altered 1882 by James Brook)

1831–32 Addition of belfry and tower to Church at Saffron Walden, Essex

1831–33 Church of St David, Haigh, nr Wigan, Lancs.; chancel added 1886–87

1831–33 Church of St Stephen, Tockholes, nr Blackham, Lancs. (only the south porch has been preserved leading into church of 1965–66 by Houston and Forbes)

1831–33 Church of Our Lady of Mount Carmel, Redditch, Worcs.

1832 Church at Lower Hardress, Kent

1832–34 Extensions and repairs to Bablake School and Bonds Hospital, Coventry

1833–35 Church of St Mathew, Kingsdown, Bristol

1834–37 Asylum For The Blind (with chapel), Bristol [D]

1835–37 Church of All Saints, Stretton-on-Dunsmore, Warks.

1835–37 Emmanuel Church, Loughborough, Leics.

1836 Restoration and alterations to Church of St Mary, Henbury nr Bristol

1836–37 Rebuilding of nave of Church of St James, Hartlebury, Worcs.

1837–38 Church of Holy Ascension, Settle, Yorks.

1838 Christ Church, Clevedon, Somerset

1838–39 Church of St Stephen, Sneiton, Notts. (tower only remains, rest rebuilt by C. G. Hare)

1838–39 Rebuilding of Church of St Martin, Horsley, Gloucs. (medieval tower retained)

1838–39 Internal works to Church of St John the Baptist, Halesowen, Worcs.

DOMESTIC

1823 The Down House, Stourton, Gloucs for the Hon. George Dowderswell

1824 Alterations to Ettington Park, Warks. for E. W. Shirley (reconstructed by John Pritchard in 1862)

1825 The Grove, Kirkpatrick-Irongray, nr Dumfries for Wellwood Maxwell

1827 Badgeworth Court, Badgeworth, nr Gloucester (rebuilt 1895 by Paul Crompton)

1827 Lough Fea, Ireland for E. P. Shirley

1827–28 Brunstock, near Carlisle for George Soul

1827–28 Burfield Lodge, near Bristol for E. P. Fripp

1828–29 Additions to Rose Castle, Cumberland for the Bishop of Carlisle

1828–32 Matfen Hall, Matfen, Northumberland for Sir Edward Blackett

1830 Additions to Baynards Park, Surrey for Rev. Thurlow

1830–31 Alterations to Weston Park, Staffs. for Lord Bradfield

1830–31 Alterations to Stanwick Park, Yorks. for Lord Prudhoe

1831–36 Wood House, Tettenhall, Staffs. for Miss Hinckes [D]

1833 House at Rugby, Warks. for H. S. Gipps

1833 House at Liverpool for Colin Campbell [D]

1833 House at Liverpool for George Smith [D]

NOTES

[1] Quoted from notes by Richard C. Hussey, FSA, which he left to Thomas Miller Rickman who subsequently published them in his book *Notes on the Life of Thomas Rickman*, (1901), p. 57.

[2] *Ibid* p. 50.

[3] Victoria and Albert Museum, RIBA Library Drawings and Archives Collection, (hereafter V&A RIBA) RIT/1–3, Personal Journals of Thomas Rickman, October 1807–1834.

[4] Rickman contributed several articles on architecture to James Smith's *Panorama of Science and Art* in 1812, and on 1 July 1817 Rickman distributed the first edition of his book, *An Attempt to Discriminate the Styles of English Architecture from the Conquest to the Reformation* which was based on his essay in *Panorama of Science and Art*. The second edition was enlarged and republished in 1819, as was the third edition of 1825. The fourth edition published in 1835 included an etching by J. Le Keux from a drawing by Rickman's late partner, Henry Hutchinson, of the Ruined Perpendicular Chapel at Evesham in Worcestershire. The fifth edition was enlarged and published by J. H. Parker in 1848 after he had purchased the copyright from Elizabeth Rickman in 1842, she retaining the remaining copies of the fourth edition. The sixth edition was published in 1862, and the seventh and last edition in 1881. In addition to the *Attempt* Rickman published several articles on architecture including, 'A Tour in Normandy and Picardy in 1832' and 'Four Letters on the Ecclesiastical Architecture of France and England' published in *Archaeologia* of 1833 and 1834 respectively; 'Architectural Observations' in *Specimen of Architectural Remains in various Counties of England* by Dawson Turner (1838).

[5] V&A RIBA holds a Rickman family tree which traces the Rickman family from Richard of Wardleham, born c. 1512, to Thomas Miller Rickman who died in 1912.

[6] Rickman, *Life* pp. 5–7.

[7] See Howard Colvin 'Roger North' *Architectural Review* October 1951, 257–59.

[8] Sources for Rickman's architectural work include a Collection of Architectural Drawings in the RIBA Library at the V&A and Rickman's Time Books in 10 volumes in the British Library (Add. MS 37793–802). Recent studies of Rickman include B. A. James 'The Architectural Work of Thomas Rickman' (unpublished finals thesis c. 1955) and Remo Granelli 'Thomas Rickman 1776–1841' (unpublished finals thesis, 1957).

[9] V&A RIBA, RIT/1–3 Rickman's Personal Journal, 27 August 1818.

[10] For recent studies of Rickman's work in Cambridge see Marcus Whiffen, 'Rickman and Cambridge' *Architectural Review*, 98, December 1945, 160–65: B. A. James, 'Rickman and the Fitzwilliam Competion', *Architectural Review*, 110, April 1957, 270–71

[11] *Ibid*, 12 August 1824.

[12] Rickman, *Life*, p. 33.

[13] [Dr Yates] *An Historical and Descriptive Sketch of Birmingham with some account of its environs and forty four views of the Principal Public Buildings* (Birmingham, 1830).

[14] V&A RIBA, Rickman's Personal Journal, entries for January to October 1826; Douglas Hickman, *Birmingham* (1970) p. 23.

[15] Rickman Journal, entries for January to October, 1826.

[16] *Ibid.*

[17] R. K. Dent, *The Making of Birmingham* (Birmingham, 1894) pp. 324–27; J. Hill and W. Midgley, *The History of the Royal Birmingham Society of Artists* (Birmingham, 1928) pp. 12–16.

[18] Rickman, *Life*, p. 42.

[19] *Ibid* p. 45.

[20] *Ibid* p. 45, p. 50.

[21] *Ibid* p. 46, p. 53.

[22] *Ibid* p. 54.

[23] *Ibid* p 53; Dent, *Making of Birmingham*, p. 406.

[24] Rickman, *Life*, p 54.

[25] *Ibid*, p. 54. The Oxford Society, originally called The Oxford Society for Promoting the Study of Gothic Architecture, purchased over 2000 of Rickman's sketches of medieval buildings, mostly churches, in 1842. These are now held in the Society's archives in the Ashmolean Museum, Oxford.

[26] The author first saw this inscription in 1956 when he made an accurate copy. On seeing it for the second time in 1975 the church of St George had been demolished and its graveyard neglected. The incised lettering on Rickman's tomb had been so obliterated by weather and vandals that it was not longer readable; Richard Hussey, as well as designing the monument, wrote an obituary of Rickman which was published in *The Gentleman's Magazine*, March 1841, p. 322. For the first recognition in the twentieth century of Rickman's work in Birmingham see R. Stanley Morgan 'Thomas Rickman – an Architect of Birmingham' *Birmingham Post*, 13 May 1953.

[27] Rickman, *Life*, p 78.

[28] 1851 Census.

2 Charles Edge

PETER BAIRD

One of the most fascinating treasures kept in the Birmingham Central Library is a magnificent collection of architectural drawings by Charles Edge (1801–67) and his son, Charles Allerton Edge (1845–1900).[1] They date from 1829 to 1880. It seems that when the firm was taken over following Charles Allerton's death, the quality of their old drawings was recognised, and fortunately they were kept. They were given to the library in 1932 by the successor firm, rather than simply being thrown away. Unfortunately, however, they are not a reliable guide to the work of the Edges. Many of the buildings shown in the drawings have been demolished, and probably many of the designs were never in fact built. Edge must also have designed and built a large number of other buildings whose drawings do not survive. The existing drawings, therefore, however unique and valuable a survival, are not a complete or accurate record of Edge's work.

Many of these drawings are of astonishing beauty and elegance in themselves, but their historical importance is that they show the development of taste from the pure Greek classicism of the 1820s through the Italianate style into polychrome brick gothic of the 1880s with all the trimmings. Edge's work illustrates how a Georgian town became a Victorian city.

The earliest drawings show a strict adherence to the classical style. In the unlikely event that Vitruvius had been asked to design a bank or a Wesleyan chapel, the result would have been very much like Edge's earlier drawings.[2] As time goes on almost imperceptibly scrolled plaster brackets begin to appear under window sills, neo-baroque details are added, proportions become less strict, and then unplastered brick makes its appearance, as in the house for Mr Barlow.[3] Finally the later drawings of Edge and those of his son, Charles Allerton Edge, as for example Mr Powell's Gun Shop, provide examples of high Victorian taste.[4]

Charles Edge was born in 1801 in Edgbaston, then a country village in Warwickshire. No portrait or details about his background or education have come to light, but there are indications in his drawings that he did not go to a very good school. For example, although his drawings are so meticulous, he labels a room anti-room (instead of the correct ante room) and he spells accommodation with one 'm', and cemetery without the last 'e.' Nobody with Latin and Greek could make such errors. His contemporary and patron, Thomas Unett was educated at Rugby School, where he would surely have had such errors beaten out of him by Dr Arnold. Perhaps Edge, like many of the men who made Birmingham a great

Elevation of New Wesylan Chapel, Constitution Hill, 1827. *Courtesy of Birmingham Archives and Heritage Services (MS 1703/17)*

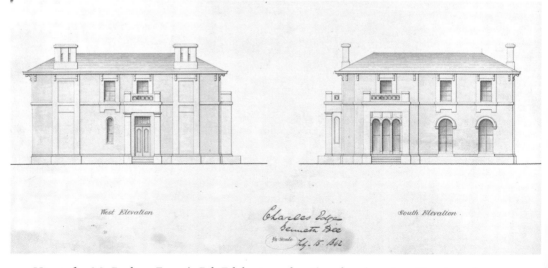

House for Mr Barlow, Francis Rd, Edgbaston, elevation drawing 1842. *Courtesy of Birmingham Archives and Heritage Services (MS 1703/30)*

city, depended at first on innate talent. Hollins, the earlier architect of the Public Office was self-taught, as was Rickman himself.[5] The Royal Institute of British Architects, which might have provided such details, was only founded in 1841, by which time Edge was already very well established.

Although Edge's early work is strictly classical, it is doubtful whether he travelled abroad. The rules and conventions of classical style could be learned from the books of design by people who had been to Italy, available from the end of the eighteenth century.[6] Edge's work is not only beautifully drawn and not at all provincial, but correct, ingenious and elegant. He was highly talented, but must also have been well trained.

It might have been that the young Edge showed exceptional talent at drawing and somehow came to the notice of the celebrated Thomas Rickman (see Chapter One). Rickman had a house in Islington Row, which was large enough to take several pupils. In the biography of Rickman by his son,[7] it is stated that 'with his pupils he had some troubles. Sometimes he was depressed for the want of suitable and reliable assistance'. It is not likely that Edge can have been one of these unsatisfactory pupils. When Hansom and Welch went bankrupt in 1833 whilst building the Town Hall Rickman, who had himself entered the competition for its design, was consulted. Then Edge was appointed as the new architect to finish the work, presumably on Rickman's recommendation. There is another example of Rickman's regard. In 1825 Rickman built the Commissioners' church of St Peter's at Dale End. Only five years later it was badly damaged by fire, and the drawings for the repairs are signed by Edge, (and also by Hansom) and are dated 1835.[8] Edge seems to have started on his own account in about 1830, and it is probable that Rickman put these pieces of work in Edge's way.

Another work in which Edge probably worked at first jointly with Rickman was on one of the enlargements of the Public Office in Moor Street. This had been finished in 1807 and was the only public building of its time. Due to Birmingham's lack of municipal status, it had to serve as a court, prison, police station, an office for the Birmingham Street Commissioners and as a hall for public meetings. It kept proving too small, and for example in 1827 an enlargement was approved at a cost of £7,700. In the Birmingham Collection there are drawings by Edge for further enlargements, dated 1829 and 1832, more than doubling the size of the building. Edge's design provides such things as separate yards for male and female prisoners and rooms for overseers, magistrates, witnesses and so on. Edge's design cleverly keeps a strictly classical appearance, with Ionic columns at the front and Doric at the side, topped with a splendid statue of Justice.[9] The drawings are particularly fine showing such details as the green baize on the tables, and the fittings of the cupboards. The building was perhaps not popular with the masses, and was besieged in the Chartist riots of 1837. It was enlarged again in 1844 and finally demolished in 1911.

As well as his skills as an architect, Edge must have been a capable artist. There are a few of his sketches included among the architectural drawings, including an attractive pen and ink sketch of the interior of the market hall, with elegant gentlemen in top hats looking at the piles of fruit and vegetables displayed for sale.[10] There is also a pencil sketch showing the exterior of one of his villas set among mature shrubs.

It is rather hard for us to imagine Birmingham in the early nineteenth century. The medieval town remained in the Digbeth area, but as the eighteenth century advanced, the area around the new churches of St Philip and then St Paul were cut from agricultural land. As the town grew like a balloon, in addition to houses and factories, new public buildings were needed, such as a Town Hall, Post Office, Market Hall, schools, churches, chapels, shops, offices, banks, workhouses, even cemeteries. From drawings in the Birmingham Central Library we can see that Edge essayed all these genres. In particular, many prosperous citizens were moving out into the semi-rural Edgbaston, where they employed Edge to build them classical villas.

Edge's practice was almost all conducted in Birmingham. He was not only prolific but also adaptable. For example when the railway came to Birmingham in 1838, the terminus, designed by Hardwick, was at Curzon Street, and a road was needed to connect it to the centre of town. Edge drew up plans for the road, signing himself for this purpose not 'architect' as usual, but as C. Edge, Surveyor. This elegant boulevard from Curzon Street to High Street, named Albert Street was started but never finished because New Street Station was opened in 1856 making the road unnecessary.[11]

Edge, like Rickman, did a lot of work in the Bennett's Hill area, to the North of New Street, which was laid out from about 1827, and was at first a fashionable residential area. Edge himself lived at 18 Bennett's Hill until about 1840 and always had his office there. After his death, Charles Allerton also continued the practice from here. (No. 23, an Edwardian building, now stands on the site). Edge's drawings for offices of the New Hall Coal Company in Bennett's Hill are in the Birmingham Collection. The proprietor and his family and servants lived above the offices which were on the ground floor. There are also drawings for the Norwich Union Life and Fire Office in Temple Street. This building survives much altered as the Trocadero public house. Here again the manager and family lived above the offices. There is another house dated 1837 for a Mr Flavell in Bennett's Hill with attractive pilasters. It may be that Burne-Jones may have grown up here. Designs are found in the collection for a bank in Bennett's Hill.[12] The houses at the top of the hill, numbers 1 to 6, are said by Hickman[13] to be Edge's work, but in any case they have been facaded.

It is rather surprising how many people seem to have lived 'over the shop' in early Victorian times. Edge's offices for the Inland Revenue, for example, had living quarters, and all his schools have accommodation for the schoolmaster. The chapel at Key Hill Cemetery had a flat for a porter, and an attendant lived in the Town Hall. Each of these dwellings has its own cess pit and private well for water supply, which must have contributed to the cholera and fearful infant mortality of the period.

In 1830 the Liverpool architects Joseph Hansom and Edward Welch won a competition to build a Town Hall in Birmingham, by which was meant a grand assembly room rather than a municipal headquarters. Construction was begun but the architects went bankrupt and were unable to finish the splendid design, for which they had taken personal financial responsibility with a very low tender.[14] The Town Hall is not made of stone but is of brick construction faced with Anglesey marble, which had to be brought at great expense to Birmingham by sea and canal. It may be that Edge's acceptance of the job may have regarded by Hansom with some bitterness. It is to be hoped that the patenting of the hansom cab in the next year, 1834, restored Hansom's fortunes.

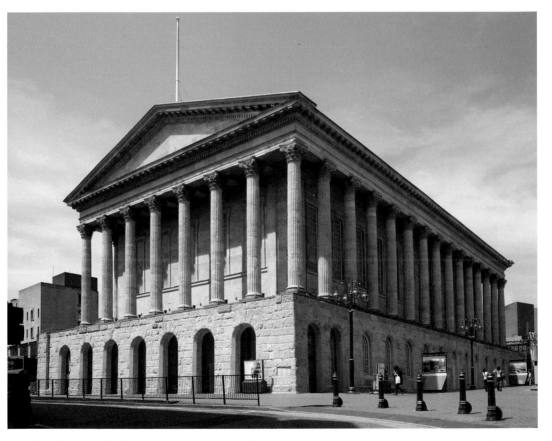

The Town Hall designed by Hansom and Welch, 1832–34 and completed and extended by Charles Edge, 1837, 1849–51

In completing the building, Edge was still hampered by a lack of money, and the Town Hall was not finished until 1850. But a drawing of the music festival of 1834[15] shows the interior already apparently complete, with a small organ and two windows in the Northern end. It seems as if the 'cella' of the temple-like structure was roofed and usable long before the peristyle was complete. Further delays were caused when the largest organ in the world at that time was presented to the town, by the General Hospital. Edge had to add a rectangular 'alcove' at the North end of the building. But it is cleverly disguised so few people realise that the inner building is not rectangular. In order to accommodate the alcove, Edge added two further columns, so that there are fifteen on the sides, and not thirteen as before.[16] Edge originally intended to go along with Hansom's economical plan that the North end should be a flat wall, decorated by pilasters with moulded capitals. But in the end he succeeded in finding funds to complete the entire peristyle of Corinthian columns. Mendelssohn gave the first performance of the Oratorio 'Elijah' here and played on the great organ, and the musical life of the city largely depended on the Town Hall for almost 150 years. Elgar's 'Dream of Gerontius' was first performed here.   The recent multi-million pound refurbishment of the

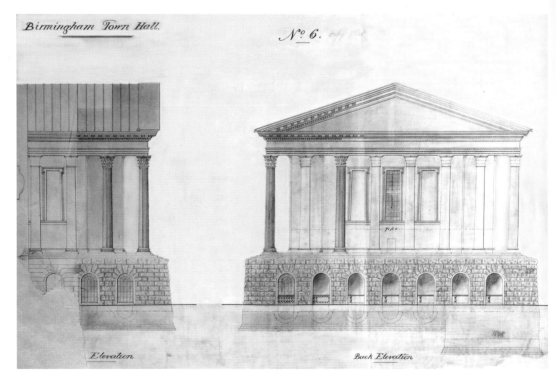

The Town Hall, elevation drawings of Edge's extension to the northern end 1848.
Courtesy of Birmingham Archives and Heritage Services (MS 1703/15/14)

building has restored the interior to something much more like Hansom's original scheme, which had been spoiled in the twentieth century by a second balcony.

Whilst very splendid and grand from the outside, the Town Hall has never been quite satisfactory in its interior, owing perhaps to the lack of an obvious portal, and the fact that the horizontal contrast between the base and the peristyle is not reproduced inside the building. Temples in the ancient world (and in Birmingham) are best from the outside. But if anyone is at fault, it is Hansom, not Edge, who triumphantly completed this splendid project.[17]

Perhaps Edge's greatest single achievement was the retail Market Hall, also built for the Street Commissioners, and opened in 1833 at a cost of £73,266.[18] This enormous building was over 120 yards long and 60 feet high. Inside there was space for 600 stalls and four thousand shoppers. It was possible to buy here not only fruit, vegetables, fish and meat, but also pets and prams.[19] The whole hall was lit by gas, which made evening shopping possible. From 1851, in the middle of the hall stood a decorative fountain 'of bronze adorned with well-designed figures representing the various manufactures, with groups of fish, flowers, etc'. This fountain was moved to Highgate Park, but it is now no longer there, and has probably irretrievably vanished. Beneath the hall were large vaults on iron girders for storing produce. At each end there were magnificent Doric porticos, and on either side there were three and four storey buildings consisting of shops on the ground floor and living space above. The difficult slope of the ground was ingeniously disguised by Edge's design.[20]

This much loved building was badly damaged by enemy bombing in August 1940. But much of it still looks fairly intact in an aerial photograph of 1962 when the roofless interior was still in use as an open air market. Nevertheless in that year the City Council decided to demolish the whole thing as part of their Bull Ring

Main elevation of The Market Hall, 1833. 19th century lithograph

Interior of Market Hall of 1833 showing dedication of fountain, 1851

scheme. An unworthy Sixties market hall took its place, and this market hall has now been replaced in its turn after only forty years of use. It seems inexplicable that the old market hall should not have been repaired and restored, but such was the enthusiasm of the council for modernity that they swept away a building which nowadays would be considered as one of the finest in the city. At least all Edge's splendidly detailed drawings for it survive.[21]

On 18 October 1832 a group of businessmen including Edge met in the New Royal Hotel in New Street and decided to float a new company to be called the Birmingham General Cemetery Company. There were 1000 shares at £10 each. Edge took twenty six shares. Space to bury the dead was urgently needed as almost the only places of burial were the churchyards of the established church, which were overflowing with graves, such was the rapid growth of the town. And anyway it may have been rather distasteful to dissenters to have to await the general resurrection in the company of Anglicans. The new cemetery was to be non-denominational.[22]

Edge was appointed a director of the company and its surveyor, and he remained so for the rest of his life.[23] The directors authorised him to take borings in various places, and to report back to the board. Land at Monument Lane and

Key Hill Cemetery, engraving *c.* 1860s

Holloway Head was found unsuitable, but a sandy site at Key Hill was thought ideal. Eight and a half acres were purchased from the Poor Law Guardians for £5,750. Edge saw that 'a considerable number of poor (i.e. paupers) might at once be engaged by the cemetery company in forming and levelling the site.' And this was done. In their annual report of 1834 the directors concluded as follows, 'Your committee beg to congratulate the proprietors on the establishment of a company which will be an honour to its promoters, a source of sacred pleasure to the inhabitants of this densely populated town, and they doubt not of ample remuneration to the proprietors.'

This somewhat smug conclusion was proved correct. Not only were the paupers useful, and doubtless cheap, in digging the graves, but the sand was found to be very suitable for casting. The minutes of the monthly meetings of the directors for the whole of the rest of the century are in Birmingham Central Library.[24] Edge seems very rarely to miss a meeting, and often took the chair. Every month there is a record of how many dozens of tons of sand were dug out by the paupers and carted to Soho Wharf to be taken by canal to the foundries which needed it. The last sand was excavated as late as 1930. Furthermore the Great Western Railway was forced to pay dearly for a slice of the cemetery for their new line to Wolver-hampton which opened in 1854. More or less expensive conventional plots for burial were successfully sold to prosperous non-conformists throughout the next century, and even Joseph Chamberlain himself rests here. The official guide of 1915 describes Key Hill as the Westminster Abbey of the Midlands.[25] It is almost gratifying to note that so long ago the Company had a lot of trouble from drunks and hooligans, and had to employ several attendants to keep order. Today inter-ments no longer take place at the cemetery, and the place appears abandoned to anyone who enjoys overturning a gravestone for a dare.

The established church soon imitated the scheme by building another cemetery next door in Warstone Lane, but there were easily enough customers for both, and for the municipal cemetery at Witton (1859) as well.

Edge seems to have been fascinated by the technology for disposal of bodies. Along the back of the site he devised a series of what he called catacombs dug into the sandy cliff. Each catacomb could take about 20 bodies. The coffins are not buried but rest in sealed vaults. As each batch of new catacombs was sold, Edge constructed a further series, so that now they run all around the northern side of the site. And Edge invented a compact way of dealing with the paupers' bodies as

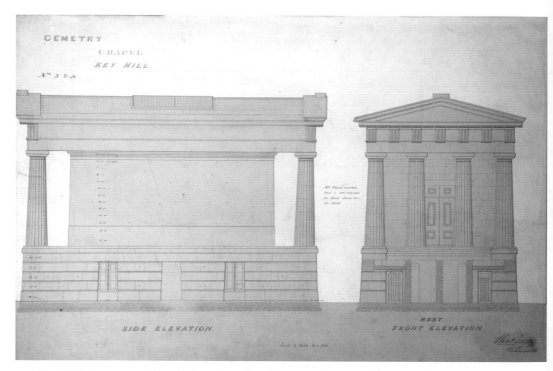

Key Hill Cemetery Chapel, elevation drawing 1834. *Courtesy of Birmingham Archives and Heritage Services*

well. A slit trench a few inches wider and longer than a coffin and about 25 feet deep was dug. As each pauper's coffin was interred, concrete was poured over it. When the trench was full, another trench could be dug a short distance away with no fear of collapse from the first trench, there being in effect a concrete wall between the two trenches. The morbid visitor to Key Hill can still see large tomb-stones with the names and ages of the forty or so paupers buried beneath each one. In addition Edge designed the splendid and surviving listed piers and railings to the cemetery, and a modest but attractive chapel with four Doric columns at each end. It was lit from above, which caused a certain amount of trouble from leaks in the roof. But the directors were so pleased with the chapel that they put a picture of it on the company seal. This delightful little chapel was demolished when the city council municipalised the cemetery in 1966. This was a regrettable act, although it must be admitted that Edge had himself robbed the stone for the chapel from the ruins of Weoley Castle.

A very remarkable survival of the Edges' work is the shop of Messrs Powell in Carr's lane. This firm is still carrying on their business as gun makers and retailers in the same premises. The drawings for this building, dated 1860, are in the Library.[26] Most of the drawings are in the hand of his father, but it may be the

Entrance to Key Hill Cemetry, 1835

Shop for Mr Powell, Carr's Lane, 1860

rather clumsy captions are by the hand of the fifteen year old Charles Allerton Edge. An earlier factory that still survives is the Victoria Works in Graham Street built in 1839–40 for Joseph Gillott the penmaker, which has been attributed to Charles Edge.

In the Library Collection there are many drawings for large, attractive villas on the Calthorpe estate at Edgbaston. It is hard to discover how many of them were in fact built, and subsequently demolished, or if some were simply plans for houses which were never built in the first place. For example the drawings include two different, but similar, houses for a Mr Meredith in Chad Road.[27] The house that stands here today, No. 15, is different in the number of bays, but at the same time has characteristics that suggest that it must be by Edge. Apart from a porch added to a house at 39 Wellington Road, there is nothing else standing on the Calthorpe Estate which can be unequivocally attributed to Edge. It is possible to go round Edgbaston tentatively attributing houses to Edge because their style and details seem so similar to things found in his drawings. But perhaps these villas are in fact by rival architects, and Edge was simply working in the latest fashion. Unfortunately the Lease Books of the Calthorpe Estate[28] do not record more than the name of the tenant, the definition of the plot and the ground rent to be paid.

Victoria Works, Graham Street of 1839–40. The second floor is a later extension

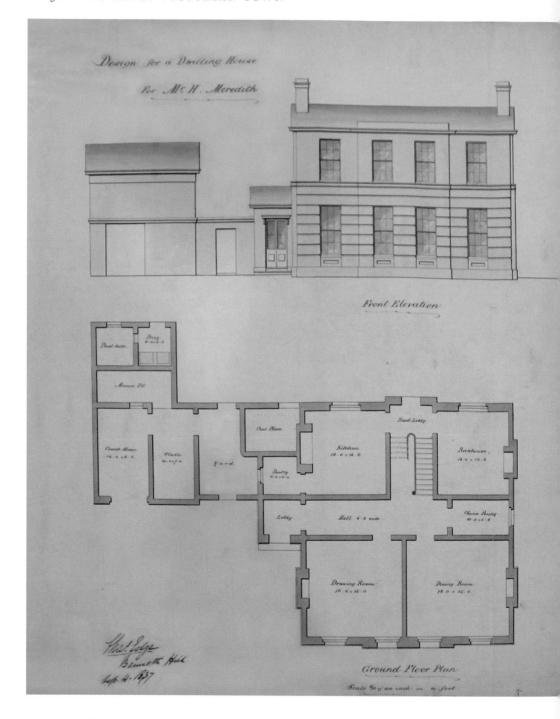

House for Mr Meredith, Chad Road, Edgbaston, main elevation drawing and plan.
Courtesy of Birmingham Archives and Heritage Services (MS 1703)

15 Chad Road, Edgbaston, probably designed by Charles Edge

The Lily House (now called the Tropical House) in the Birmingham Botanical Gardens, with its pleasant and restrained cast iron columns and Corinthian pilasters, is by Edge (1852), but there are no drawings for it. Edge also designed (without charging a fee) the fountain on the lower walk, which remains in place today. He was on the committee of the Gardens, which are very close to his own house in Harborne Road, and was elected Chairman of the committee for 1848.[29]

There are drawings for alterations in 1844 to Rigby Hall near Bromsgrove in the Collection, and Rigby Hall is still standing.[30] But the present buildings, dating from the 1860s, are not those to which the drawings refer. But they are so similar to a demolished lodge, for which there are drawings, that the building, much altered by its use as a County Council maternity and a children's home, and now in use as professional offices, is very likely to be by Edge.

Edge could also design satisfying gothic buildings. The Early English enlarge- ment of St George's church in Westbourne Road was carried out in 1856.[31] A lot of Edge's work here was swallowed up in J. A. Chatwin's subsequent enlargement of 1881 (see chapter 5). There are designs for a Scottish Presbyterian chapel in Broad Street,[32] and also for Holy Trinity church in Smethwick,[33] a gothic school and chapel in Bordesley,[34] and a gothic pumping station at Witton (1851).[35] Holy

Trinity, Smethwick remains, but much enlarged by another architect in 1889. Of Edge's work, only the Western spire and his crypt remain. He has used his cemetery experience to construct family vaults in the crypt, for sale to parishioners. Many still remain vacant. Edge also turned his hand to schools,[36] extensions, farm houses, even a cow shed in a vernacular manner. One of the most attractive of his drawings is for a cast iron pillar box, dated 1841. This is literally a pillar, being in the shape of a Doric column, with a vertical slit for posting letters.[37]

Edge worked almost exclusively in Birmingham and nearby places like Smethwick, Dudley and Hagley. The only exception to this was a speculative development in Filey in the East Riding of Yorkshire for the rather aristocratic Birmingham solicitor John Wilkes Unett, who was the father of Edge's contemporary Thomas Unett, who also gave him work, and was killed at Sebastopol. In 1830 Filey was an obscure fishing village between Scarborough and Bridlington, with a really attractive sandy beach. Unett saw its potential as a seaside resort and employed Edge to design a rather grand shallow crescent with its curved side facing the sea, and a private garden at the front. His beautifully drawn plans for this development are in the Collection, signed 'C. Edge, Surveyor'.[38] Construction of the crescent began in the classical style in the 1830s, but houses cannot have sold

The Crescent, Filey. 19th century photograph

very well at first, perhaps because the railway only came to Filey in 1846. So by the time the crescent was finished in about 1860, with a large hotel by Edge at its apex, the houses were not uniform and many show Italianate features. The whole crescent is stuccoed, and does look quite attractive today. Pevsner calls it the 'Brighton spot of Filey'.[39] Charlotte Bronte visited the town twice. In Edwardian times Filey did become a successful resort attracting the aristocracy and even minor royalty, not to mention the family of the composer Frederick Delius when he was a child.[40] Today in the era of the foreign package holiday, it is a little sad, with the big hotel split into holiday flats and the owners of the terrace houses asserting their individuality by all painting their stucco in different shades of cream.

Although Edge never practised outside Birmingham, apart from the Filey crescent, he became very prosperous. He moved from Bennett's Hill to a house, now demolished, in Harborne Road. The 1841 census records that he had a wife, Ellen, some twelve years his junior, a daughter and two female servants. By the 1851 census he had a wife, several servants, a governess and six children, Charles Allerton being the third. Altogether there were eight children, five died in childhood. His daughter Frances married Mr Barrow, who was a grocer, and for whom Edge designed a large villa in Francis Road and a warehouse in Snow Hill.[41]

As a successful local architect, Edge was asked to help resolve a dispute in 1849 about the new Birmingham Workhouse. The journal *The Builder* for that year is full of this scandal. The Guardians had advertised a competition for a huge workhouse, and received fifty four entries from all over the country, including six from Birmingham firms. Without the benefit of any architectural advice they selected a short list of six, five of whom, including the winner, were from Birmingham. The editor of *The Builder* was appalled. As laymen the Guardians were said to be as suitable to judge between the complex designs as they were to write verses in Greek. The Guardians were compelled by a public outcry to resign, hold fresh elections, and then to hold a further competition. Edge and an architect from London and another from Derby were appointed as assessors. This time there were forty three entries, and the firm of Bateman and Drury (see chapter 4) were announced as the winners. But this was not the end of the matter, as a sardonic correspondent, who signed himself 'A Lover of Fair Play' complained in a letter to *The Builder* that Edge had canvassed the Guardians in favour of Bateman and Drury, and that furthermore their name was partially legible on one set of plans. In the end, the 'Lover of Fair Play' was compelled to take out an advertisement in *The Builder* with a grovelling apology to Edge.[42] The workhouse was eventually begun in 1850 by Bateman on the site of the present Summerhill Hospital, part of City Hospital, Dudley Road.

As he got older Edge left more of the work of the firm to his son, Charles Allerton Edge. He was born in 1845, so that he was only twenty two at the time of his father's death. But he had been apprenticed to his father, and it is sometimes hard to decide which of them is responsible for plans of the 1860s. After his father's death in 1867, Charles Allerton kept the business going at Bennett's Hill, commuting to the office from his home in Blackwell. His works seems to have consisted mainly of more or less conventional large neo-gothic residences in places like Richmond Hill Road in Edgbaston, where five of his houses survive,[43] and at Barnt Green. These houses, whilst doubtless well built and pleasant to live in, lack, at least to some eyes, very much aesthetic merit as architecture, especially when compared to the achievements of his father. Many have been demolished, presumably for their large gardens. Carefully drawn designs for these houses and other buildings are to be found preserved in the Collection.

C. A. Edge

Charles Allerton died in 1900, aged 55. In Pike's 'Contemporary Biographies,' in *Birmingham at the Opening of the Twentieth Century,* presumably written by Edge, he boasts not of his buildings but of his promotion and construction of tramways, and in particular to the adoption of a sort of fender in front of the locomotive, which saved the lives of many children.[44] Perhaps it is due to his filial piety that his father's drawings have survived. Another of Edge's pupils was Yeoville Thomason (see chapter 6).

Edge himself died in July 1867, leaving an estate worth almost £25,000 to his wife. This is an indicator of the solid success that Edge had earned in his professional career. His wife died four years later in 1871, and they are both buried in one of Edge's own catacombs, with a dozen or so of his descendants (but not Charles Allerton). The last interment in this catacomb was in 1962.

The twentieth century has not been kind to the built work of Charles Edge. Perhaps if he had done more work outside Birmingham, more of his buildings would have survived redevelopment. (Consider how few are the surviving works of Rickman in Birmingham). But there does remain one splendid memorial to Edge – apart from the hideous 1970s teaching block named after him at the University of Central England in Perry Barr – and that is the magnificent collection of his drawings which demonstrate the changing architectural tastes of the early Victorian period in Birmingham.

30 Richmond Hill Road, Edgbaston

Selected List of Architectural Works of Charles Edge

Charles Edge(1801–1867) was a pupil of Thomas Rickman. He practised in Birming-ham from the late 1820s to 1867. From c. 1860 his son, Charles Allerton Edge, assisted him and continued the firm until his own death in 1900.

WORK IN BIRMINGHAM AND ITS ENVIRONS

PUBLIC

1827 Wesleyan Chapel, Constitution Hill, Birmingham [D]

1828–1835 Market Hall, High Street, Birmingham; 1851 fountain [D].

1829–1838 enlargement of Public Office, Moor Street, Birmingham [D]

1834–62 Key Hill Cemetery, Key Hill, Birmingham [chapel only D]

1835–1851 completion of Town Hall, New Street and Paradise Street, Birmingham

1835 rebuilding of St Peter's Church, Dale End after fire of 1831 [D]

1838 Road, Albert Street, Birmingham [not completed]

1838 Chapel, King Street, Dudley [D]

1838 Holy Trinty Church, Smethwick 1838 [mostly D]

1838 enlargement of St George's Church, Westbourne Road, Edgbaston; 1856 further enlargement

1852 Lily House at Birmingham Botanical Gardens, Westbourne Road, Edgbaston

1853 Infant School and mistress' house for parish school, Ampton Road, Edgbaston

COMMERCIAL

1832 Office for New Hall Coal Co., Bennett's Hill, Birmingham [D]

1833 Bank of Birmingham, Bennett's Hill, Birmingham [D]

1846 Norwich Union Fire engine house, 17 Temple Street, Birmingham

INDUSTRIAL

1838 Regent Works, Regent Street, Birmingham (attrib. by A. Foster)

1839 Victoria Works, Graham Street, Birmingham (attrib. by A. Foster)

1860 Proof Hole, Proof House, Banbury Street, Birmingham

1860–1 Shop and works for Mr Powell, gunmaker, 35–37 Carr's Lane, Birmingham

DOMESTIC

c. 1827 1–6 Bennett's Hill, Birmingham (attrib. by Young and Taylor) [facaded]

c. 1828 102 Colmore Row (attrib. by D. Hickman)

1831 Wassell Grove, Hagley [D]

1837 15 Chad Road, Edgbaston

1850 portico to Apsley House, 39 Wellington Road, Edgbaston; probably also main house c. 1830.

1855 Charlmont Hall, West Bromwich, 1855[D].

WORK OUTSIDE BIRMINGHAM

DOMESTIC

1844 and later, Rigby Hall, Bromsgrove [some D]

1835–38 The Crescent, Crescent Road, Filey, Yorks

NOTES

[1] Birmingham Central Library, Archives and Heritage Services (hereafter BCL AHS) have three collections relating to the Edges. The major collection is MS 1703 'Architectural Drawings of Charles and C. E. Edge' which has 108 sets of plans. Further drawings are to be found in MS 1446 'Birmingham School Building Plans' and MS 1460 'H. R. Yeoville Thomason'.

[2] BCL AHS, MS 1703/1 Elevation of New Wesleyan Chapel, Constitution Hill, 1827.

[3] BCL AHS, MS 1703/30 House for Mr Wm. Barlow, Francis Road, 1842.

[4] BCL AHS, MS1460/7 Shop for Mr Powell, Carr's Lane, 1860.

[5] Bryan Little, *Birmingham Buildings: The Architectural Story of a Midland City* (Newton Abbot, 1971) p. 122, and Andy Foster, *Pevsner Architectural Guides: Birmingham* (New Haven and London, 2005) p. 8.

[6] See for example, Sir John Soane, *Designs for Public and Private Buildings* (1828).

7 T.H. Rickman, *Notes on the Life of Thomas Rickman* (privately printed, London, 1901) p. 67.

8 BCA AHS, MS 1703/8/1–4.

9 BCA AHS, MS 1703/2 Public Office, Elevation, 1829.

10 BCA AHS, MS 1703/6.

11 Victor Skipp, *The Making of Victorian Birmingham* (Studley, 1983) p. 31.

12 BCL AHS, MS 1703/4. Subsequent alterations to the bank for Birmingham Banking Co. are MS 1460/50.

13 Douglas Hickman, *Birmingham* (1970) p. 23.

14 *Ibid*, p. 31.

15 R. K. Dent, *The Making of Birmingham* (1894) p. 396.

16 Jo Holyoak, *All About Victoria Square* (Birmingham, 1989). Edge's drawings for the Town Hall are MS 1703/15/1–36.

17 K. Turner, *Central Birmingham 1870–1920: Old Photograph Series* (Bath, 1994) p. 116.

18 J. T. Bunce, *History of the Corporation of Birmingham* (Birmingham, 1885) p. 172.

19 Peter Baird, *The Bull Ring* (Stroud, 2004) p. 86.

20 see fig. 7 in *Ibid*, p. 80–81.

21 BCL AHS, MS 1703/6/1–13.

22 F. H. Manning, *Official Guide to Birmingham General Cemetery* (Birmingham, 1915) p. 7.

23 Edge's drawings for Key Hill cemetery are MS 1703/12/1–13. His work included the Chapel of 1834–5, alterations to the Registrar's House of 1835 and designs for the catacombs in 1837, 1840, 1854 and 1862.

24 BCL AHS, Other Cemetery Records, Birmingham General Cemetery Box 1 Minutes and Reports October 1832–December 1877, Box 2 January 1878–December 1909.

25 Manning, *General Cemetery*, p. 11.

26 BCL AHS, MS 1460/7/1–7

27 BCL AHS, MS 1703/18/1–4.

28 BCL AHS, MS 2126/3/5/d/3.

29 Phillada Ballard, *An Oasis of Delight* (1983) p. 39; p. 41; p. 119.

30 BCL AHS, MS 1703/34/1–2.

31 BCA AHS, MS 1703/54/1–4.

32 BCA AHS, MS 1703/9.

33 BCA AHS, MS 1703/19/1–4.

34 BCA AHS, MS 1703/33/1–3.

35 BCA AHS, MS 1703/49/1–3.

36 His designs for schools include BCA AHS, MS 1446/17 St George's Church of England Primary School, Edgbaston, c. 1853; MS 1446/36 St Paul's Church of England Primary School c. 1846; MS1446/47 Little Bromwich National School, Ward End *c.* 1859.

37 BCA AHS, MS 1703/29/10.

38 BCA AHS, MS 1703/13/9 Crescent Road Filey, Yorkshire layout of building estate 1835–38 and erection of hotel 1836.

39 Nikolaus Pevsner, *Buildings of England: Yorkshire and East Riding* (1st pub 1966, 1972 ed.) p. 229.

40 Filey Borough Council *Official Town Guide* (Filey, 1980).

41 BCA AHS, MS 1703/25 and 1703/30

42 *The Builder*, 7 (1849) p. 68; p. 3; p. 94; p. 196; p. 327; p. 406; p. 411; p. 425; p. 434; p. 459; p. 482; *The Builder*, 8 (1850) p. 82.

43 The Richmond Hill Road houses are nos.30, 33, 35, 36 and 37. He also designed no. 69 Westfield Road. House in Richmond Hill Road. MS 1703/71 (elevations)

44 *Birmingham at the Opening of the Twentieth Century*, ed. by W. T. Pike (Brighton, n.d.) pp. 155–6.

3 Daniel Rowlinson Hill

PHILLADA BALLARD

In July 1844 at the age of 34, D. R. Hill (1810–57) was appointed as architect of the Borough Gaol at Winson Green, his first commission for the Borough of Birmingham. A succession of borough commissions followed in the next thirteen years until his early death in 1857 – in 1846 the Lunatic Asylum, in 1848 the Kent Street Baths and additions to the Moor Street Public Offices, additions to the Borough Surveyor's Office in 1852, and further commissions such as Corporation stables, police stations and the lighting system for the Town Hall. Many of his major projects required extensions as soon as they were completed, notably the Borough Gaol, which he was still working on at the time of his death. He also undertook work outside Birmingham, particularly four further prisons at Lewes, Wandsworth, Warwick, and Cardiff. In Birmingham the bulk of his energies were taken up with Borough work. By the late 1840s he was engaged not only on all the Borough's new buildings but also in inspecting all buildings in their ownership and assessing potential land purchases, and in 1852 was proposed as Superintendent of Public Buildings but not appointed due to the jealousy of other local architects. However, in effect he was the 'Borough architect' in all but name.

D. R. Hill was responsible for a wide range of buildings many of which were without precedent in the town but which were the result of the Council's responsibilities after 1838 when Birmingham became a borough, together with the increase in public provision as a result of national law-making. His preferred style was Tudor though he was competent classical architect.

The biographical details of Hill's life are sketchy. His father Daniel Hill, was a plater, who married Elizabeth Rowlinson daughter of Daniel Rowlinson at Edgbaston Church[1] in June 1806 and Daniel Rowlinson Hill was born in Birmingham in 1810.[2] Details of his education prior to becoming an architect are not known. In 1829 he was articled to the Birmingham architect Thomas Rickman.[3] Some evidence survives of Hill's interest in architecture and his early training. In a diary of 1827 he made notes on beauty in architecture and recorded a visit to St Paul's Cathedral, whilst in June 1829 he made a tour to Gloucestershire where he saw Thomas Fulljames, also a pupil of Rickman, and made notes and sketches on Tewkesbury Abbey, Toddington Manor and Cheltenham and Bristol.[4] The diary of the Gloucestershire visits had notes on obtaining visas and it is clear that a continental tour was planned, and indeed this took place in 1831. His parental means were obviously adequate to provide for this journey, an experience that relatively

Self Portrait of D. R. Hill, 1834. *Courtesy of Birmingham Archives and Heritage Services (MS 1421/5)*

few Birmingham architects were able to enjoy. The 'Grand Tour' mainly to Rome and Naples took place in 1831 and subsequently some of the sketches were worked up and printed as lithographs such as the Temple of Neptune in 1835.[5]

In 1834 Hill set up his architectural practice in an office in Union Passage, New Street and an early, if not his first, commission was for St James's Church, Mere Green Road Sutton Coldfield,[6] possibly a commission passed to him by Rickman. The small church, completed in 1835 was in the Early English style with lancet windows and a west tower.[7] This church served as the parish church for the Four Oaks development and, in 1906–08, had large additions by C. E. Bateman. Also in the early years of his practice he prepared some drawings for Key Hill Cemetery at the request of one of the members of the Board when Edge's early drawings were considered too expensive to execute. However other members of the Board rejected this approach and Edge resubmitted successful drawings.[8]

Apart for this commission there appear to be no other recorded buildings for a considerable period. However, in the early 1840s his practice expanded and he had his office in Waterloo Street. In 1843–44 he obtained commissions to design three schools.

The first was a National school, St Luke's school, in St Luke's Road which adjoined the newly built church of that name in Bristol Street, consecrated in 1842 and designed by Henry Eginton in the Norman style.[9] A simple two storey building provided accommodation for boys on the ground floor and girl's above. The elevation had round headed windows echoing the style of the church and was opened in 1843.[10] The following year he designed St Luke's Infants School, a single storey building with an attached two storey house for the teacher in matching style to the first building. Both schools were demolished after being bombed in 1941.[11] This was followed by another National school, All Saints' School in Lodge Road, Hockley, built to adjoin the church of that name which had been designed by Rickman and Hutchinson in 1833.[12] The long two storey building provided accommodation for 616 children in three rooms, boys on the ground floor, girls and infants above, together with an apartment for the master.[13] It was in a restrained gothic style with a large tri-partite window on its south front and a band of raised stone gothic lettering reading 'All Saints Schools A.D. MDCCCXLIII'.[14] It still survives although with alterations and additions, apart from the south front.

In July 1844 Hill obtained his first major commission when he was appointed architect of the Borough Gaol.[15] The background to his appointment is unclear as the known corpus of his buildings discussed above would hardly indicate that he had the experience to tackle such a major project. For the Council this was the first building undertaken since Birmingham became a borough in 1838 and the gaol would mean that the Council would be free of the expense of housing prisoners in the County Gaol at Warwick.

The plans were prepared following the principles laid down by the Home Office. By the 1840s new prisons in Britain were being designed to be managed on the separate system. Each inmate was completely separated for sleeping, eating, working, worship and exercise in order to prevent communication between prisoners and the contamination of first and minor offenders by habitual criminals.[16] To assist in the promotion of the separate method the government erected Pentonville in 1840–42 that would serve as a model. It was designed by Major Joshua Jebb, who became Surveyor General of Prisons in 1844. Hill was appointed in July 1844 and by November, having visited Pentonville and other prisons currently being erected, had prepared his plans.

In May 1846 Hill gave the second of two lectures on 'Prisons and Prison Discipline' at the Philosophical Institute in Cannon Street and referred to the

All Saints National School, Hockley, 1843

misapprehension that existed in Birmingham with regard to the separate system, a feeling which he had initially shared, but 'as facilities have been given me of seeing this system in operation and contrasting it with the other systems adopted in many of our prisons my objections have been removed'. His talk was illustrated by drawings of the plans for the forthcoming gaol which according to the report in the *Midlands Counties Herald* 'excited much attention and greatly contributed to the elucidation of the subject'.[17]

Birmingham Borough Gaol was designed to accommodate 400 prisoners, with provision for extension to 500 and to cost over £50,000. For managing the prison, in addition to the separate system, distinct accommodation for different categories of prisoners was required. Hill's layout combined a radial and linear plan, with sections for women, men, juveniles and debtors along one axis, each section radiating from a central hall from where staff could observe the whole area.[18] Each wing had four storeys with galleries for the upper floors. The cells were 13 feet long, 7 feet wide and 9 feet high and provided with 'soil pan or water closet, washing basin with sufficient supply of water'. They were lit by a high, non-opening single window, Jebb having altered Hill's original plan for a double window. A separate heating and ventilation system by Hadens of Trowbridge was supplied to each cell. The chapel, which was also used as a school room accommodated two hundred and thirty eight prisoners with tiered banks of high sided pews, the 'stalls or seats constructed that the Prisoners can see and be seen by the Clergyman, and yet neither see or communicate with each other'. The exercise yards were wedge shaped and arranged in circular blocks.

The prison was built of brick with Derbyshire stone dressings and had Romanesque and Jacobethan overtones and was designed to look like a miniature castle. It was entered by a castellated gateway topped by crenellations with diaper patterned walls connecting the houses for the governor to the right and the chaplain on the left. The tops of these were also crenellated.

The gaol was built to the north west of the town adjoining the Birmingham Canal on a thirteen acre site acquired from Piddock's Charity for £3,250. The prison occupied five acres and was surrounded by a high brick wall with turrets and topped by chevaux de fries, a system of spikes.

When the estimates were received it was decided to reduce the number of cells to 300 and to exclude the juvenile wing. The original builder, John Malthew proved unsatisfactory and was replaced after his death in 1846 by Pashby and Plevins. Hill had to select the specialist contractors who supplied the heating systems, water apparatus and gas supply. In the spring of 1849 the building of the Gaol was nearly complete with Hill preparing plans and elevations of the fittings and furniture he preferred for the various offices at the prison including for the magistrates room, medical officer's sitting room, solicitor's room, chaplain's room, the parlour for the matron, and the Governor's office. After putting out tenders for the prisoners' bedding – mattresses and pillows of coconut fibre

Birmingham Borough Gaol, Winson Green, elevation 1846. *Courtesy of Birmingham Archives and Heritage Services (MS 1421/9)*

Gatehouse, Birmingham Borough Gaol, Winson Green. *Courtesy of Birmingham Archives and Heritage Services (WK 16/177)*

covered with ticking – to go on wooden beds which Hill designed, his final job was to obtain machines for hand labour in the cells, either steel hand mills for grinding wheat or handlooms for weaving stockings together with gardening, shoemakers' and tailors' tools. The prison was completed in September 1849. Two years after it opened Hill was instructed to design a series of additions which were not complete by the time of his death. These were additions to the female wing in 1851 and from 1854 a debtors' wing and additions to the male wing, new kitchens and offices. Alterations to the prison chapel were also carried out as the accommodation for female prisoners had not allowed for their separation and 'scenes of great impropriety had occurred'.[19]

In 1849 Hill designed the first of four prisons for other local authorities. The prison for the county of Surrey at Wandsworth was a much larger undertaking than Birmingham, being designed on the radial plan with 700 cells and with provision for extensions to 1000 and was completed in 1851.[20] Both the men and women's prisons were extended by one wing in accordance with Hill's original plan, in 1857–60.[21] By 1850 he was at work on his third prison that at Lewes, designed on a cruciform plan with 256 cells. It was built of flint with brick quoins. Warwick was started in 1853 for c. 350 cells on a radial and linear plan completed in 1860. In partnership with William Martin he designed Cardiff in 1854–57. Hill is considered on stylistic grounds to also be the architect of Swansea prison.[22]

In 1846 two years after the commission for the prison, Hill was appointed to another Borough project that of designing the Pauper Lunatic Asylum[23] so that from July 1846 he was managing two major Birmingham projects concurrently, and a third, the Kent Street Baths, started the following year. The 22 acre site to build the Asylum was acquired next to the Gaol for £6,650,[24] the Lunatic Asylum Committee at its meeting of 10 June 1846 noted

The situation was elevated and healthy with good drainage and sufficient land for outdoor recreation and proximity to the borough for visits of friends of patients and visitations of the Committee

At their meeting of 20 July they recorded their reasons for appointing Hill

The Committee being decidedly of the opinion that economy will be materially promoted by employing the same architect for erecting the Asylum as is employed for superintending the erection of the Gaol and being satisfied with the ability and conduct of Mr Hill

Another factor that favoured Hill's appointment was that he lived not far from both projects, having moved at the Corporation's request from Edgbaston to the vicinity of Winson Green in order to be close at hand to supervise the building of the prison, and from 1846 lived at Camden Villa, Warstone Lane.[25]

As with the prison, the plans for the Asylum had to be approved by outside bodies in addition to the Town Council, in this case the Commissioners in Lunacy

Entrance front of former Borough Lunatic Asylum, Lodge Road, 1847

and the Home Office, and it was not until January 1847 that Hill's plans were presented after considerable consultations with both bodies 'without an existing asylum as a model.' The asylum was estimated to cost nearly £39,000 and was for three hundred pauper lunatics. The report prepared by the Lunatic Asylum Committee on 6 January 1847 testified to Hill's skill in designing institutions:

The building is also arranged that at a future period its extent might be increased with much facility, and at comparatively moderate cost. In various arrangements of the building your committee cannot but express their admiration of the intelligence and talent displayed by the Architect in combining with simplicity and uniformity, every provision considered essential for the superintendence, classification and sanitary amendment of the Patients.

The asylum was built of brick with stone dressings in Tudor style. The principal front had a central five bay block of three storeys with large stone mullioned windows, open work stone parapets and diaper brickwork either side of the entrance. Two pavilions in a similar style but of three bays were linked to the centre by recessed two storey blocks. In the words of a recent commentator it looked 'almost as grand as a great country house'.[26] To the rear there were a series of interlinked two storey blocks with simpler detailing.

By January 1848 the building was well advanced and Hill was instructed to find a landscape gardener for laying out the grounds and he engaged Edward Williams who subsequently did the landscaping at the prison. The asylum was notable for the provision of open space as pleasure grounds, vegetable gardens and a 22 acre farm in which the inmates were encouraged to work as well as walk. In December of that year Hill was organising the painting of the interior and submitting to the Committee samples of furniture and clothing for the staff and inmates as well as drawing up plans for the farm buildings. The asylum was opened in June 1850.

After becoming All Saints' Hospital much of the former Lunatic Asylum has been demolished but the principal front remains and is now used by the prison service. The area of the former two storey blocks is now within the curtilage of the prison and the farmland is now a public park.

In the early years of his borough commissions Hill also undertook work for private clients. Evidence survives for three of these commissions. These comprised a church, a private house and a private almshouse.

St John the Evangelist Church at Walmley, Sutton Coldfield was the second of Hill's churches though here he completed the work of H. J. Whitling.[27] The church was founded in 1843 when Walmley was designated a separate parish from Sutton Coldfield.[28] It was designed in neo-Norman style which was fashionable in the 1840s. The material used dark blue vitrified bricks with stone used sparingly on the shafts and arches in the short chancel. The church had a hammer beam roof and a rose window and bell cote at the west end.[29] It was consecrated in 1846. A watercolour by Hill of the elevation and section of the chancel survives in the collection of Hill's papers in the Birmingham City Archive.[30] Memorial windows in the chancel to the ironmaster Joseph Webster of Penns, who was largely instrumental in founding the church, were added in 1856.[31]

Hill's only known commission for a private house was for 12 Carpenter Road Edgbaston, for Mr Goodman carried out in 1849. The stuccoed classical style house has an Ionic porch and segment-headed windows.[32] Hill may well have carried out other domestic commissions, and particularly on the Calthorpe estate which was still a favoured location for upper middle class housing, but the evidence to identify the architects in this period is very scanty.

The Licensed Victuallers' Asylum in Bristol Street was designed by Hill in 1847 and completed in 1849. It adjoined another building in Bristol Street designed by Hill, St Luke's Infants School of 1844. The Licensed Victuallers' Society had been founded in 1845 by the Mayor, Thomas Phillips, who was familiar with Hill's work for the Borough, and may well have recommended him as the architect. It was modelled on a much larger institution in the Old Kent Road in London, and provided almshouse accommodation for aged and needy members of the trade.[33] The linear building was of two storeys with a raised central block containing a hall with a Board Room above, and lower wings on either side, and was built of brick with stone dressings in the Tudor style.[34] The building was in use until the Second

Licensed Victuallers' Asylum, Bristol Street, lithograph, 1848. *Courtesy of Birmingham Archives and Heritage Services (MS 1421/6)*

World War when its inmates were evacuated. In 1947 the front of the building was removed and it was converted to a car showroom, and was finally demolished in 1964.[35]

From the late 1840's Hill's work in Birmingham seems to have been exclusively for the Borough and he designed two public baths, a police station and additions to the Public Office and the Borough Surveyor's Office.

The movement for a public baths in Birmingham was as a result of the Public Baths and Wash-Houses Act of 1846[36] and the formation of Public Baths Association. In November 1846 a site was bought from Sir Thomas Gooch in Kent Street, formerly let as Guinea Gardens, and Gooch stipulated 'a handsome elevation should be erected'.[37] Hill was asked by the Gaol and Buildings Committee to report on the site, and by April 1848 he was asked to prepare plans for a building to include a swimming bath 84 ft by 36 ft, a plunging bath 15 ft by 17 ft for men and another 13 ft by 18 ft for women, 51 private baths 5 ft 9 in. square 36 of which were for men and 15 for women with vapour and shower baths, 25 stalls for washing, a room for a centrifugal drying machine, laundry with mangles and residential accommodation for the governor, matron and servants. Provision was made for future extensions. As with the prison, no building of this nature had been erected in Birmingham previously and Hill had accompanied the members of the Baths sub-committee on a visit to four public baths in London in order to refine his plans.

The Baths were built of brick with stone dressings and had a sumptuous elevation to the road with a prominent two storey central block in Jacobean style with large mullioned windows. This provided accommodation for the bath's staff and a committee room. Single storey blind aracaded walls on either side concealed the baths and terminated in two end-on pavilions with Dutch gables. The boiler house had a massive brick chimney in complementary style.

Front of Kent Street Baths, 1848. This elevation was masked by a new frontage in 1933.
Courtesy of Birmingham Archives and Heritage Services

Building started in 1849 and the builder John Cresswell submitted an estimate for £7,888. In July 1850 Hill prepared plans for the water supply to the Baths and was negotiating terms for the Water Works Company. The Kent Street Baths opened on 2 April 1851 and in Easter week 70,000 people visited them. By June Hill was asked to provide plans for showers for the bathers, additional plunge baths and extensions to the boiler house, and these were completed in the following year. So successful were these baths that Hill was soon instructed to inspect land for a second baths, and a site at Woodcock Street was bought from Lench's Charity. Hill designed baths for this site in 1854 but they were not executed and the Woodcock Street Baths were erected to a design by Edward Holmes in 1859.

However Sir Thomas Gooch who visited the Kent Street Baths in 1853 had 'expressed himself so pleased with the usefulness of the institution and the manner in which he building had been erected' that he presented half an acre of land on Birmingham Heath for 'new baths of a similar character'.[38]

Hill's Kent Street Baths are still standing but extensions, including a Turkish Bath suite and a new art deco frontage, designed by Hurley Robinson in 1931–33, obscures Hill's work.[39]

Kent Street Baths 1848, lithograph of the interior. *Courtesy of Birmingham Archives and Heritage Services*

In the 1850's Hill work for the Borough expanded when he took over the role of Surveyor of Public Buildings in January 1852, although not the title. The Council's powers had been increased by a local Act of 1851 when they acquired the responsibilities hitherto executed by the Street Commissioners.[40] This meant they could appoint a Borough Surveyor and a Surveyor of Public Buildings. The Surveyor of Public Buildings would be responsible for inspecting and reporting on new and existing buildings and designing alterations not to exceed a cost of £500, for a salary of £250 per annum, but would not be excluded from competing for the erection of public works. Hill's appointment was recommended by the General Purposes Committee 'after considering the intimate acquaintance which he has with all the complicated details of the important public buildings which the Corporation has completed as well as his acknowledged character, ability and talents'. This aroused a storm of protest from a number of Birmingham's architects as to what they perceived as Hill's monopoly and in a letter in *Aris's Gazette* they argued that the Council

by allowing the architects to compete for any appointment deemed necessary (would) rescue their character from the imputation cast upon it by the General Purposes Committee that there was only one man in the town capable of doing the business of the Corporation.

The General Purposes Committee then received a memorial signed by eighteen architects protesting against Hill's appointment, and it was not ratified.[41] However the evidence would suggest that Hill carried out the work, even if he had no official title.

The public buildings owned by the Corporation in 1852 were the gaol, the lunatic asylum, the Kent Street Baths, the Town Hall, the Market Hall, the Public Office, six Police Stations, and the Meat and Smithfield Markets. In the period up to his death in May 1857 Hill was responsible for major additions to the prison and to the public baths, as already described.[42] His new buildings for the Corporation were the police station in Duke Street completed in 1853, Corporation Stables in Park Street of the same date and a weighing machine house on Bordesley Wharf, the layout of which was designed by the Borough Surveyor, Pigott Smith. He also did unexecuted designs for the Woodcock Street Baths. In 1852 he designed minor alterations to the Public Offices in Moor Street, which William Hollins had designed in 1805–07. This was raised by two storeys and a gallery built from the entrance to the Council Chamber and a new entrance to the offices.[43] In 1853–54 Hill designed alterations to the Council Chamber which was to have improved ventilation and a new system of gas lighting and a new heating system in the whole building. He was also responsible for a new lighting system in the Town Hall where he installed a large gas chandelier in 1852. In the Town Clerk's Office he designed and oversaw the fitting up of a new filing system for the borough records.

Much of his time was also spent on inspecting buildings owned by the Corporation or ones they considered acquiring, and in some cases ordering demolitions, disposing of the materials and making the site safe. This was mainly in the area of Ann Street, Congreve Street, Edmund Street and Paradise Street near the Town Hall where the Council was considering building new corporation buildings and a county court.

In April 1857 Hill's reports to Committee are recorded as from Hill and Martin. He had taken William Martin (1828–1900) into partnership, Martin having been previously his managing clerk. Martin was born in Shepton Mallet and had been articled to Thomas Plevins of Birmingham. Martin continued the business as Hill and Martin for a number of years doing work for the Corporation and for the prison service, and went into partnership with John Henry Chamberlain in 1864.[44]

Daniel Hill died suddenly on 1 May 1857 aged 47. The meeting of the Estates and Buildings Committee on 4 May noted

The committee having heard of the sudden death of Mr D. R. Hill desires to offer Mrs Hill and her bereaved family their sincere sympathy on the loss they have sustained irreparable to them and serious to the Borough which has been deprived of a respected inhabitant and an architect of distinguished professional attainment.

The same minute was reported in *The Birmingham Journal* for 9 May under the heading 'the late Borough Architect,' an indication that he had occupied this office in effect if not in name.

He left a wife, Eleanor, and three surviving children, the youngest two having died in infancy in 1852 and 1854 respectively.[45] Hill's oldest son, Daniel Shenton Hill born in 1844 also became an architect and was articled to J. R. Botham in 1861 and made a classical tour in 1873. He died at Knowle in 1930.[46]

The work of Daniel Rowlinson Hill has been underrated, possibly because he died relatively young and little has been written about him.[47] However, in Birmingham in a period of only thirteen years he produced a number of highly important corporation buildings which had no precedents in the town, whilst elsewhere, as a prison architect he was one of the most prolific designers of the period.

Selected List of Architectural Works of D. R. Hill

D. R. Hill (1810–57) was born in Birmingham and was articled to Thomas Rickman. He set up in practice in Birmingham in 1834 and took William Martin (1828–1900) into partnership in the 1850s. After Hill's death the firm of Hill and Martin continued until 1864.

WORK IN BIRMINGHAM AND ITS ENVIRONS

PUBLIC

1834–35 St James' Church Mere Green, Sutton Coldfield

c. 1834 Drawings for Key Hill Cemetery (unexecuted)

1843 St Luke's National School for boys and girls, St Luke's Road, Edgbaston [D 1941]

1844 St Luke's Infants School, St Luke's Road, Edgbaston [D 1941]

1844 All Saints' National School, All Saints Street, Lodge Road, Hockley

1845–49 Birmingham Borough Goal, Winson Green; additions to Female Wing 1851–53; extension to Debtor's Wing, new kitchen and offices, alterations to chapel 1853–57; additional Male Wing 1855–59

1845 St John the Evangelist Church, Walmley, Sutton Coldfield

1846–50 Birmingham Borough Asylum for Pauper Lunatics, Winson Green

1848 Licensed Victuallers' Asylum, Bristol Road [D]

1848 Alterations to prison department of the Public Office, Moor Street

1848 Public Baths, Kent Street; extensions 1851–52; new boiler house 1853

1852 Additions to Borough Surveyor's Office, Moor Street

1853 Police Station, Duke Street

1853 Corporation Stables, Park Street

1853 Machine House, Bordesley Wharf

1854 Woodcock Street Baths, nr Aston Road (not executed)

DOMESTIC

1846 12 Carpenter Road, Edgbaston for Mr Goodman

WORK OUTSIDE BIRMINGHAM

PUBLIC

1849–51 Surrey County Gaol, Wandsworth; 1857–60 additional wings to male and female prisons

1850–53 East Sussex County Gaol, Lewes

1853–60 Warwick County Goal, Warwick

1854–57 (with William Martin) Cardiff County Gaol, Cardiff

? date Swansea County Goal (attributed)

NOTES

[1] Dugdale Society, *The Registers of Edgbaston Parish* Church vol. 2 *Marriages 1636–1812* (Oxford, 1936).

[2] 1851 Census Enumerators' Records.

[3] Thomas Mill Rickman, *Notes on the Life of Thomas Rickman* (privately printed, London, 1901), p. 35.

[4] Birmingham Central Library, Archives and Heritage Services (henceforth BCL AHS), MS 1421/1 Diary of D. R. Hill 1827, 1829.

[5] BCL AHS, MS 1421/2 Diaries of a Tour in Italy May–October 1831; MS 1421/3 Pencil sketches and watercolours made in Italy; MS1421/4 engraving of Temple of Neptune.

[6] Nikolaus Pevsner and Alexandra Wedgwood, *The Buildings of England: Warwickshire* (Harmondsworth, 1966, 1974 edition), p. 426.

[7] BCL AHS MS 1446/11 Lithograph of St James's Church 'printed from the drawing by H Harris, 1835, dedicated to the Bishop of Lichfield by D. R. Hill, architect.'

[8] BCL AHS, Other Cemetery Records, Birmingham General Cemetery Minutes and Reports Oct 1832–Dec 1877. The author is grateful to Toni Demidowicz for this information.

[9] *Victoria County History of Warwickshire* vol. 7. *The City of Birmingham*, ed. by W. B. Stephens (1964), p. 390.

[10] BCA MS 1446/26 Signed and dated elevations of St Luke's National Schools for Boys and Girls, and for Infants.

[11] VCH *Birmingham*, p. 532.

[12] *Ibid*, p. 379.

[13] BCL AHS, MS 1446/1.

[14] The building is still extant but it has had additions and the fenestration has been considerably altered. It is currently used as offices for the Birmingham Youth Offenders Team Unit.

[15] The section on the Borough Gaol is predominantly based on BCL AHS, Birmingham Borough Committee Minutes: Gaol and Buildings Committee 1844–51; Estates and Buildings Committee 1851–56; Gaol Committee 1856–57; Birmingham Corporation Plans BCC /90 and /157 Borough Gaol; and C. Gill and A. Briggs, *History of Birmingham,* vol 1 (Oxford, 1952), pp. 276–77.

[16] Allan Brodie, Jane Croom and James O. Davies, *English Prisons, an Architectural History* (Swindon, 2002), p. 84.

[17] BCL AHS, MS 1421 ms of lecture and newscutting, 14 May 1846.

[18] *English Prisons*, p. 101.

[19] BCL AHS, Birmingham Borough Committee Minutes, Estates and Buildings Committee 16 May 1853

[20] BCL AHS, 1421/10 Plans and sections of East Surrey County Gaol.

[21] *English Prisons*, p. 99.

[22] *Ibid*, p. 100, p. 107, p. 110. Martin and Chamberlain did work on a number of other prisons including additions to Kirkdale, Mold, Camarthan, Swansea and Cardiff in the late 1860s.

[23] The section on the Birmingham Borough Pauper Lunatic Asylum is based on BCL AHS, Birmingham Borough Committee Minutes: Gaol and Buildings Committee 1844–51 and Lunatic Asylum Committee 1845–50; Birmingham Corporation Plans BCC/131 and /132 All Saints' Asylum, Lodge Road.

[24] The majority of the land was bought from Capt. Inge and the remainder from the Guardians of the Poor.

[25] BCL AHS, Gaol and Buildings Committee 8 Sept 1845, letter from D R Hill stating he had not yet found a suitable residence for himself at Winson Green but 'as soon as I can do so I shall remove to that neighbourhood'; 1851 Census Enumerators' Record HO 107 2051.

[26] Victor Skipp, *The Making of Birmingham* (Birmingham, 1983), p. 99.

[27] Andy Foster, *Pevsner Architectural Guides: Birmingham* (New Haven and London, 2005), p. 153.

[28] VCH *Warwickshire*, vol. 4 (London and Oxford, 1947), p. 245.

[29] The church was designated by Pevsner 'a fascinating horror' – Pevsner, *Warwickshire*, p. 44; p. 426.

[30] BCL AHS, MS 1421/12.

[31] John Horsfall, *The Iron Masters of Penns* (Kineton, 1971), p. 73.

[32] Foster, *Birmingham*, p. 227.

[33] BCL AHS, Section 140083 Annual Report of the Licensed Victuallers' Asylum, Birmingham, 1879; R. K. Dent, *Old And New Birmingham* (orig pub 1878–80, reprinted East Ardesley, 1973), pp. 552–53.

[34] BCL AHS, MS 1421/6 Two lithographs of the Birmingham Licensed Victuallers' Asylum.

[35] Information on mount of lithograph of the Asylum in BCL AHS WK/E1/442; *Kelly's Directories of Birmingham*, 1964, 1965.

[36] Rachel Wilkins, *Turrets, Towels and Taps* (Birmingham, 1984), p. 7.

[37] The money for the purchase of the site came from the £6000 subscription raised from the public for the provision of a public park, but later devoted to the Baths – *Public Parks Gardens and Recreation Grounds* (Birmingham, 1892), p. 7. The section of the Baths is based on BCL AHS, Borough Committee Minutes: Gaol and Buildings Committee 1844–51; Baths and Washhouses Committee 1851–57 and Birmingham Corporation Plans BCC/150 14 drawings by D. R. Hill for the Kent Street Baths, 1849.

[38] These were the Monument Road Baths opened in 1863.

[39] Wilkins, *Turrets, Towels and Taps*, p. 7; Foster, *Birmingham*, p. 202.

[40] Gill and Briggs, *Birmingham*, p. 356.

[41] James MacMowan, *Municipal Public Works and Planning in Birmingham, 1852–1972* (Birmingham, 1973), p. 47.

[42] The section on Hill's work in the surveying of public buildings is based on Birmingham Borough Committee Minutes, Estates and Buildings Committee 1851–57.

[43] BCL AHS, Birmingham Corporation Plans BCC/19. Hill had carried out minor alterations to the prison department of the Public Offices in 1848 improving the foundations and the ventilation, see drawing BCC/185.

[44] Obituary of William Martin, *The Builder*, 79, 28 July 1900, p. 84.

[45] Notices in *Aris's Gazette* 2 Feb 1852; 13 Feb 1854.

[46] Will of Daniel Shenton Hill 18 March 1930.

[47] Hill is not included in RIBA's *Directory of British Architects 1834–1914*, (London and New York, 2001).

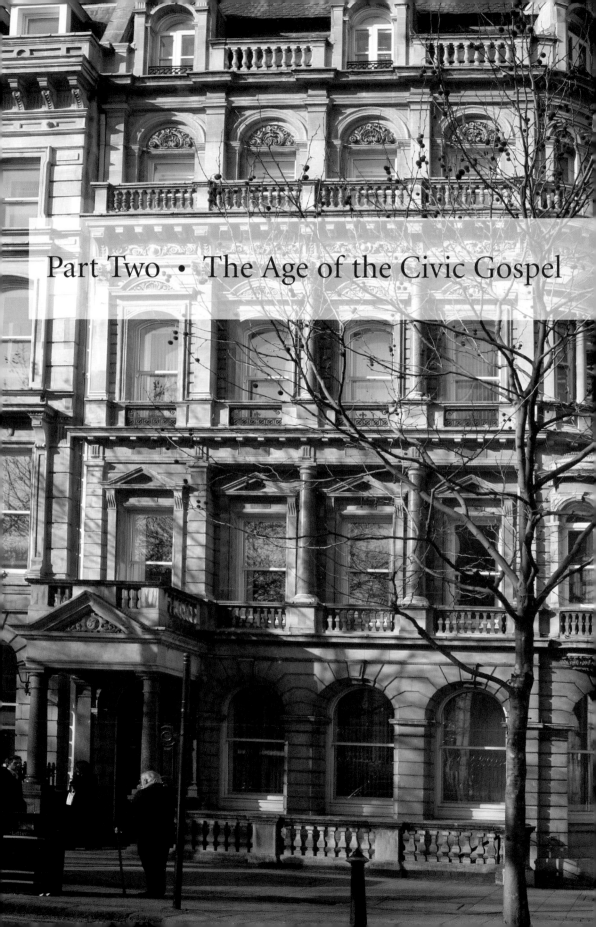

Part Two • The Age of the Civic Gospel

4 John Jones Bateman

TONI DEMIDOWICZ

In his long and prolific career as an architect John Jones (J. J.) Bateman (1817–1903) demonstrated an easy versatility, producing designs for a wide variety of building types. With George Drury (see below) he was one of the earliest proponents of the Tudor Revival in Birmingham but was equally proficient in Classical, Italianate and Gothic Revival styles. Of all his works in the city he was probably best known for the Birmingham Workhouse on Dudley Road, Queen's College on Paradise Row, the Church of the Messiah on Broad Street and the Fish Market on Spiceal Street. J. J. Bateman was a member of the Birmingham Architectural Society and then a founder member of the Birmingham Architectural Association. He served as its first president in 1882 and was elected an honorary member in 1884, remaining active in its affairs throughout the remainder of his life. Bateman was greatly interested in the education of young architects, believing that competition entry was the best means of developing their skills.[1] His various practices won a number of important commissions through architectural competition.

John Jones Bateman was born in Birmingham in 1817, the oldest child of the architect Joseph Bateman (1778–1857) and his wife Mary Ann. He was named after his maternal grandfather, John Jones, probably the Birmingham joiner and builder active around the time of his parents' marriage in 1810. At the time of his son's birth Joseph Bateman was in business with his older brother Thomas, a building surveyor and auctioneer and Bridgemaster for Worcestershire.[2] The firm had been founded by their father, also

J. J. Bateman

Joseph Bateman, a carpenter and joiner and 'builder of much repute' in the 1790s.[3] The younger Joseph joined the business after his father's death in 1811.

Joseph Bateman shared a busy practice with Thomas as auctioneer, surveyor and architect, working in Birmingham and throughout Warwickshire and Worcestershire. He 'built in the Greek style'[4] and the most notable surviving example of his work in Birmingham is Hagley Terrace (1819–20), 97–109 Hagley Road.

Bateman and his brother worked together until Thomas' death in 1829. Joseph then lived and worked in Leamington Spa where he designed the Warneford Hospital (1832–34) and Victoria Place (1834). He established a second office there in 1835 when he took the architect George Drury into partnership. He seems to have retired about 1848, closing the Leamington office and returning to live in Birmingham where he died in 1857. Drury (1806–1851) was born in Evesham, Worcestershire, the son of John Drury, a friend or relative of the Bateman family. He remained with the practice in Birmingham from 1835 to his death in 1851. His principal works in Birmingham were the Queen's Hospital (1840), Queen's College (1843) and the New Workhouse (1850–1851).

J. J. Bateman was educated in Birmingham and articled to his father, working in the practice, based at 9 Duddeston Row (now Albert Street), from the mid 1830s. He became a full partner in 1848.[5] Following the older Bateman's retirement, the practice moved to offices at 42 Cherry Street and John Jones Bateman worked with Drury, as Drury and Bateman, until the latter's death. Bateman then practised alone until 1862 when he took the young architect Benjamin Corser into partnership.

Corser (1840–1918) had been articled to J. J. Bateman and had then worked for a time in London with the architect, John Gibson, a friend of Bateman and sometime president of RIBA. Gibson had trained in Birmingham as the pupil of Joseph Hansom, the architect of Birmingham Town Hall. He acted as clerk of works to King Edward VI School (1834–1842), designed by Charles Barry, whose work Bateman greatly admired. Gibson later became architect to the National Provincial Bank (now NatWest). In 1869 he designed the Birmingham branch on Bennett's Hill in typical Renaissance style. Corser remained in partnership with Bateman until 1882, when he established his own practice in the offices at 59 Colmore Row which he and Bateman had occupied since 1880.

J. J. Bateman moved to premises at 13 Waterloo Street and, in 1883, was joined by the older of his two sons John Joseph (1855–1885), who worked as a surveyor and auctioneer. John Joseph died in an accident in 1885. The younger son Charles Edward (C. E.) Bateman (1863–1947) was articled to his father in 1880 and in 1885 moved to London to work in the practice of Verity and Hunt. He returned from London to become his father's partner in 1887, the firm moving to new premises at 81 Edmund Street in 1892. In 1898 they were joined by Alfred Hale, the son of the architect William Hale. J. J. Bateman remained an active partner in the practice until shortly before his death in 1903.

Bateman first worked as a surveyor. In 1834, at the age of seventeen he surveyed property in High Street for the gunmaker Westley Richards[6] and in 1835 he helped his father assess the damage caused by the Chartist riots which took place in Birmingham that year.[7] His first independent architectural design seems to have been a warehouse entrance porch for the gunmaker Westley Richards' High Street property which he completed in 1838 at the age of twenty-one.[8] He continued to work for Westley Richards, producing designs for rebuilding the firm's manufactory on High Street in 1852 and for a shooting shed at Camp Hill in 1860.[9]

Bateman worked with George Drury on a range of commissions in Birmingham including dwelling houses in Edgbaston and other expanding suburbs, commercial properties and manufactories. He was involved in work for the Queen's Hospital on Bath Row for which Drury had designed a building 'in the Italian character ... [its] depth of shadow and simplicity of detail ... [producing

Design for the new Chapel, Queen's Hospital, 1859. *Courtesy of Birmingham Archives and Heritage Services (MS 1542, Box 23)*

an] imposing effect'.[10] After Drury's death Bateman continued to be employed as hospital architect, working on additions and alterations to the buildings, including, in 1859, a new Italianate chapel.[11] He also continued to work on Queen's College on Paradise Street, Birmingham's medical school, founded in 1828, replacing the original anatomical museum with 'a public museum of arts and manufactures' and adding a new public lecture room (all 1860–1865) in a Tudor Perpendicular style which matched Drury's earlier designs.[12] Only the façade of the building, refaced in 1904, now remains.

In 1850 the Guardians of the Poor of the Parish of Birmingham awarded the commission for the new workhouse in Winson Green (1850–1852) (now the site of City Hospital, Dudley Road) to Drury and Bateman. This was one of the largest of the institutions erected in the 1850s under the Poor Law Amendment Act of 1834. Built to accommodate just over 1,600 staff and inmates the 'principal features of the design [were] the isolation of each from the other, of the workhouse, the infirmary, the tramp department, and the asylum for children, and of the perfect separation of classes in each department'.[13] The separate infirmary especially was unusual at this date.[14] The red brick workhouse was designed in a Tudor Revival style with, at Bateman's suggestion and at a greater cost, the exterior of the chapel having a 'more distinctively ecclesiastical character given to it by the addition of

Queen's College, photographed in 1901

New Birmingham Workhouse, from *The Builder*, 1 January 1852. *Courtesy of Birmingham Central Library*

ornamental stonework to the windows'.[15] After Drury's death in May 1851 Bateman directed the building work alone, *The Builder* crediting him in January 1852 as the sole architect.[16]

Bateman and Drury were responsible for the design of a number of dwelling houses, ranging in type from small cottages and modest terraces to large detached villas. These were mostly plain classically proportioned buildings and included, for example, the house built for John Lowe in Small Heath about 1850.[17] In 1849 the practice designed a house in the Tudor Revival style for James Boyce in Balsall Heath.[18] Bateman later produced designs in a similar style for Robert Gillam's house, 11 Ampton Road (1855)[19] and for Edward Barnsley's house, 51 Carpenter Road (1855–60)[20] both in Edgbaston, although Barnsley's house displays more straightforwardly Gothic elements in the porch and front entrance. In the early 1850s, he also employed the Italian villa style, popularised in the early nineteenth century by the architect John Nash. 13 and 14 Charlotte Road and 105 and 107 Gough Road, built for Edward and George Baker, were designed in 1851 with projecting end bays containing an extra or third storey,[21] now altered in the case of 107 Gough Road. Interestingly none of the houses is stuccoed, as was usual with this style, but rather of brick with plain stucco details.

A notable commission for Bateman in the years from 1851 to 1862 during which he practised alone was the extension of the Deaf and Dumb Institution on Church

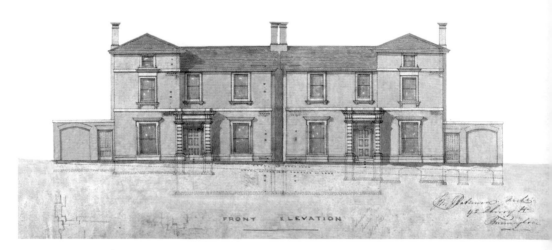

Two houses for Edward Baker in Charlotte Road, Edgbaston 1851. *Courtesy of Bimingham Archives and Heritage Services (MS 1542, Box 227, Bundle 9)*

Deaf and Dumb Institute, Church Road, Edgbaston, extended by J. J. Bateman, 1859. The Master's House designed by Thomas Rickman is on the left. *Courtesy of Birmingham Archives and Heritage Services (WK/E1/495)*

Road in Edgbaston founded in 1812 and opened in 1815. The Committee proposed to enlarge the schoolroom to accommodate 120 children, to extend the dormitory space for both boys and girls and to provide an infirmary and accommodation for the assistant masters, all this to be 'in harmony with the present building'.[22] Bateman joined with the Birmingham architect Frederick Fiddian to submit plans which were accepted by the Committee in 1857. As required, the regular design with shouldered gables, hoodmoulds, casements and pier buttresses carefully complemented both the Gothick original and the Master's House of 1829 by Thomas Rickman.[23]

Following this success, J. J. Bateman was one of four architects asked to submit designs for St Barnabas' National School Rooms, Ryland Street in February 1861.[24] The two schoolrooms were to accommodate 300 children, 150 boys and 150 girls. Both rooms were to be 'on the ground floor ... with two classrooms, two cloakrooms, a reading room, water closets and a coal cellar and soup kitchen in the Basement storey'.[25] The Committee also thought it 'might be advisable if the reading room could open into the schoolroom by folding doors so as to make one large room for tea drinking etc'.[26] The proposed layout was typical of a large parish school of the period, comprising two schoolrooms, one for boys, one for girls, each with a smaller attached classroom, a cloakroom and lavatories. Bateman's first plan, the one chosen by the Committee, had two ground floor schoolrooms side by side, each with a separate entrance and its own playground and lavatory accommodation at the rear. This probably proved too expensive however, for the school was built as a two storey structure, the girls' schoolroom and classroom above the boys' although still with a separate entrance door. The schoolrooms and classrooms were separated by folding doors, but there was no reading room, again probably because of limited funds. The building was in the Gothic style, popularised for school design from the 1840s, of brick and blue brick dressings with a circular opening in the principal gable and large arched windows grouped to admit the maximum amount of light. The upper schoolroom was open to the roof, supported on a timber roof structure. The two schoolrooms, each 60 by 30 feet, were capable of accommodating 500 children. The school, built at a cost of £1250, was opened on 24 October 1861, the Committee commending 'the skill and ability displayed by John Jones Bateman Esquire, the architect, in the construction of the National School Rooms of St Barnabas now satisfactorily completed'.[27] In 1869 Bateman and Corser added a third classroom to the school and designed a new schoolmaster's house in the Gothic style.[28]

Bateman and Drury began work for the drapers Hyam and Company on a series of additions to their town centre premises in 1839,[29] shortly after the firm moved into 'the queer old building known as the Pantechnetheca'[30] on New Street. Hyam and Co. were one of the earliest and most successful retailers of ready-made clothing on a major scale and by the early 1850s had established a chain of large stores in major cities.[31] In 1857 J. J. Bateman was commissioned to design a new

Messrs. Hyam's, New Street, from *The Builder*, 25 June 1859. *Courtesy of Birmingham Central Library*

building for the Birmingham branch,[32] the central and most impressive part of which was to be occupied by Hyam's as a retail shop and workrooms and the remainder let to other businesses as retail shops and offices. Designed in Renaissance style with lavish use of Italianate detail, the principal frontage on New Street and a secondary elevation on Union Passage, Hyam's premises comprised three storeys and a basement. The shop was divided into three departments; workmen's clothing was sold in the basement, ready-made clothes on the ground floor and 'bespoke' on the first floor. The workroom for two hundred tailors and seamstresses was on the second floor overlooking New Street where there was more natural light. The ground and upper floors were arranged as galleries supported on cast iron columns, so that the 'visitor, standing in the basement, looks right up through the shop and the upper floor to the great central lantern 70 feet above him which gives light to the interior of the whole building'.[33] This type of galleried top-lit retail space was a relatively new form which had found favour with the ready to wear specialists from the time the large scale trade began to develop in the 1840s. Hyam's entire building, 110 feet in length along New Street, 150 feet along Union Passage, 100 feet in height, containing offices, showrooms and seven shops, centrally heated and expensively finished and fitted out, cost nearly £25,000.[34] *The Builder*, imagining a Londoner's astonishment 'at the size and costliness of many of the new buildings for commercial purposes' constructed in provincial towns, particularly Manchester and Liverpool (where, incidentally, Hyam's had already opened large stores), judged Bateman's design as 'calculated to produce a similar effect in Birmingham'.[35]

In 1858 Bateman was appointed architect to the Aston Hall and Park Company, established to save the Jacobean mansion by subscription and to open it as a museum of arts and industries and place of public recreation. The Company bought the property in March 1858 and Queen Victoria was persuaded to come and open it to the public in June, leaving the managers only three months to prepare the house and grounds and assemble the exhibition. Bateman won a limited competition for the design of a glass pavilion at a cost not exceeding £1, 200.[36] This was set against the west front of the Hall on the terrace, allowing access to the series of rooms under the Long Gallery. The structure housed the Art Treasures Exhibition and was intended to save heavy objects of marble, bronze and iron being dragged through the old building as well as to show them to best advantage.[37] The pavilion, a 'Crystal Palace in miniature,'[38] was designed in the Elizabethan style 'to harmonise' with the Hall and was constructed of cast iron and glass, the structure supplied by the Coalbrookdale Company of Ironbridge.[39] Bateman also produced designs for the conversion of the stables into refreshment rooms[40] and a bandstand or orchestra in the Gothic style.[41] He presumably also advised on other works carried out, including the restoration of the long gallery, the great dining room and King Charles Room (the best bedchamber) 'to their original and pristine state'[42] for the use of Queen Victoria during her visit.

Perhaps Bateman's most important commission during the years in which he worked alone was the design of the Unitarian Church of the Messiah. The Unitarian Society wished to leave their Meeting House on Moor Street (now St Michael's Roman Catholic Church) and build a new and more imposing church in Broad Street on the north west edge of the town, closer to the elite suburb of Edgbaston where many of the most important members of the congregation lived. Sites on Broad Street proved expensive however, and, after a long search, it was finally resolved to erect the building on an arch alongside the road bridge over the Birmingham Canal. The Committee issued instructions for an architectural competition in January 1859.[43] Designs for a new chapel and Sunday schools to hold 600 subscribers, 250 schoolchildren and a choir were to be submitted to the Congregation by the end of April.[44] Bateman's designs were selected and he over-saw the work.[45] The arch over the canal was finished in August 1860,[46] the foundation stone laid in the same month and the church opened for worship on New Year's Day 1862.[47] *The Builder* was impressed:

when the high parapet wall of the old bridge was removed, and the façade of the church was found running parallel with the existing footway, no-one would ever have guessed that the new edifice was built over the canal, especially as the wall on the other side of the roadway is so high as to keep the water quite out of sight. This is probably the only example of a highly decorative church capable of holding something like a thousand people being artificially supported at a considerable height above a line of busy water traffic that passes beneath its whole length. ... The Unitarian Church extends, supported on its own archway parallel with the whole northern side of the old bridge, at some little distance from the footway, and is, beyond comparison the most remarkable structure in the entire line of Broad Street ...[48]

The large church and the school building to its rear were designed in the Decorated Gothic style popular among Non-Conformist congregations at that time. During the 1840s the cheap and simple Dissenter's chapel with a classically treated principal façade gave way to more elaborate compositions, frequently in the Gothic styles now associated with church architecture. In the 1850s Gothic, and particularly Decorated Gothic, became firmly established as the preferred Non-Conformist style. Built of Hampstead stone with Bath and Hollington stone dressings, Bateman's church was richly ornamented. The principal entrance on Broad Street was composed of a highly decorated recessed porch with granite columns supporting three gables and a parapet covered in quatrefoil diaper work. The slender splayfooted spire on the corner of Broad Street with St Peter's Place rose to 150 feet, providing a considerable local landmark. Internally there was a 'fine open timbered roof'[49] another currently fashionable Gothic Revival feature. The building was much admired in the town, although *The Builder* objected to the 'coarse rustication' of the walls and to the 'parasitic buttresses' beneath the windows,[50] opining that any necessary strengthening here should have been carried out in 'a less objectionable manner'.[51]

Church of the Messiah, Broad Street. Etching of 1862. *Courtesy of Birmingham Archives and Heritage Services*

Despite all their efforts the Aston Hall and Park Company were unable to raise sufficient funds to maintain the Hall and park and the property was bought by Birmingham Corporation. Before the purchase in September 1864 the Baths and Parks Committee instructed J. J. Bateman to report on the construction and state of repair of the buildings and to estimate the annual maintenance costs.[52] In the report he submitted to the Committee Bateman recommended the removal of the glass pavilion and the refreshment rooms he had designed for the Aston Hall and Park Company in 1858. His recommendations caused a public furore and both he and the Company were condemned for their profligacy,[53] although the glass pavilion at least was never meant to be a permanent arrangement.[54] Following its acquisition by the Corporation Bateman was commissioned to take on the repairs to the hall and the removals were carried out. These had the effect, as Bateman intended, of both giving more ground to the park and improving views of the house.[55]

Bateman's specifications for the repair of Aston Hall show a concern for the retention of ancient fabric wholly in tune with the times. Architectural opinion was turning towards the careful conservation of ancient buildings rather than damaging wholesale restoration. Listing the repairs to the main building and to the two small cottages known as the Falcon Houses in minute detail, he nonetheless adds ...

The architects beg to state generally that the preservation of the antiquity and present character of this building is to be retained as far as possible and those parts only are to be new which impair the substantiality of the structure. It being difficult to describe in detail every reparation required and in order to define as far as possible the extent of the restorations (more particularly) to the exterior stonework and to arrive at an uniform basis of tender, the architects require the parties tendering to submit lists of questions to which written replies will be given to doubtful new work.[56]

Birmingham finally adopted the 1850 Free Libraries Act in 1860 and later that year the Council approved a scheme which included the establishment of four district lending libraries with attached news rooms to serve the north, south, east and central and western parts of the town.[57] The first library to be opened, in 1861, was that serving the northern district. The Libraries Committee rented a building on Constitution Hill from the brassfounder John Cartland,[58] in fact part of a manufactory in the Gothic style designed for Cartland by Bateman in 1859.[59] There was some difficulty in obtaining suitable sites for the remaining district libraries. It was not until 1865 that four local architects' practices were asked to submit designs for the free library in Deritend to serve the southern district. The plans had to include a library and librarian's room, both to be lit from the roof, a vestibule and entrance, with a cellar beneath to contain the heating apparatus, and a lavatory and water closet, the total cost to be no more than £1,000.[60] The Committee resolved to accept the design 'in the Tudor style of Gothic architecture' submitted by Bateman and Corser.[61]

The site on Heath Mill Lane was irregularly shaped and caused Bateman and Corser some difficulty:

The Land being of irregular shape and the various buildings only one storey in height it became difficult to design an imposing Front to the Street. The Entrance is at the end towards Digbeth. The Library being at the other end of the site and approached by a corridor. The Library is 42 feet long and 38 feet wide it has an open timbered roof and is lighted by a lantern light running the whole length of the building and also by a small window in the gable end toward the street.[62]

What are presumably earlier drawings show a Classical front but this was obviously abandoned.[63] A few days after accepting the 'Tudor Gothic' design the Library Committee asked for a window in the principal gable to 'improve the building'[64] and for larger gable doors and side windows, requests to which the architects acceded.[65]

Deritend Free Library was opened in October 1866, on the same day as the foundation stone for Gosta Green library, serving the eastern district, was laid. Bateman and Corser's design for the corner site on Aston Road and Legge Street

Former Deritend Free Library, Heath Mill Lane, 1866

had been successful in a limited local competition in which the architects were again required to plan for an awkwardly shaped site.[66] Bateman and Corser submitted two designs, the first with one entrance on the corner, the second with an entrance on each street.[67] The second design was accepted.[68] The library, 'of red brick with stone dressings, [was] in the Tudor style',[69] and very similar to that in Deritend[70] except for the 'clock turret about 45' high' which marked the 'acute angle' between the two streets.[71] Internally, as at Deritend 'the walls [were] internally recessed with Gothic headed recesses for the reception of book-cases'.[72] Gosta Green Free Library was opened in 1868.

Besides their many plans for the workshops and warehouses which comprised the typical Birmingham manufactory, Bateman and his various partners worked on a number of more specialised industrial buildings. These included malthouses and hopkilns,[73] glasshouses[74] and specialist works associated with the gun trade. The Birmingham Gun Barrel Proof House, founded by Act of Parliament in 1813 to test guns and gun barrels, stands on Banbury Street by the Birmingham and Fazeley Canal. Thomas and Joseph Bateman had acted as surveyors to the Proof House[75] and in 1866 Joseph's successors, Bateman and Corser, began an extensive programme of additions, alterations and repairs to the buildings.[76] These included in 1868 the reroofing of the 'large proof house and pistol proof house' and repairs to the coal house and powder magazine and to the canal and wharf walls.[77] Between 1868 and 1870 the west side of John Horton's original building was sensitively converted from dwelling houses to workshops.[78] A new magazine was built in 1876[79] of 'specially fired bricks closely jointed for safety'.[80]

The warehouse and manufactory on Great Hampton Street in the Jewellery Quarter designed by Bateman and Corser for the silversmith John Stokes in 1871[81] provides an excellent example of a typical Birmingham works of the time. The principal building on Great Hampton Street is in the Italian Gothic style with a façade of polychromatic brick. It appears on the left of the photograph of the Great Hampton Street Works by Yeoville Thomason, in chapter six, p. 141. Two parallel ranges of workshops (twentieth century replacements of the originals) run at right angles to the rear and are separated by an open yard. The ground floor of the principal building, with a cellar beneath, was originally occupied by a kitchen, scullery and living room and the first floor by a warehouse and workshops.[82] A private stair led to domestic accommodation on the second floor.[83] The passage to the right leads into the principal building, that on the left to the workshops.[84] The domestic accommodation has since been converted to business use.

In 1869 Birmingham Corporation bought land on the corner of Spiceal Street and Bell Street for the erection of a new Wholesale Fish Market.[85] Plans were invited through competition and four architects' practices submitted designs[86] for the irregularly shaped site, which was much narrower on Spiceal Street than at the 'opposite or west end'.[87] The Market and Fairs Committee voted to adopt the

Birmingham Fish Market, Spiceal Street, 1869–71. Late 19th century photograph. *Courtesy of Birmingham Archives and Heritage Services*

plans prepared by Bateman and Corser, costed at £1,350, stipulating that the actual cost of construction should not exceed £1, 400[88] and the foundation stone was laid on 4th July 1870. The iron and glass construction of the Crystal Palace in 1851 had inspired a brief and limited fashion for market halls with glass walls and roofs, but these were soon realised to be entirely unsuitable for the sale of perishable goods, and the architects' winning design was typical of a conventional late Victorian market hall. A single nave, aligned east-west, was covered with a timber roof structure supported on masonry piers or columns. The roof covering was of slate; the skylights glazed in patent roll plate glass and the louvred wooden ventilators were covered in corrugated zinc. The walls were brick, the 'arcade opening to the streets [closed by] wrought iron gates and palisading',[89] the heads of the arches filled with fixed sash windows. The building was designed in a restrained Classical style, with an 'ornamental brick façade'[90] on Bell Street and a Bath stone front containing two cast iron columns, a pediment, cornice and rusticated quoins on Spiceal Street.[91] In the mid-1880s, with the purchase of more land on Spiceal and

Bell Streets, the Fish Market was considerably extended.[92] Plans for the extensions were drawn up by the borough surveyor William Till.[93]

Bateman's practice continued to receive commissions for house designs from Birmingham's commercial and industrial elite. The pen manufacturer Joseph Gillott had bought what remained of the Rotton Park estate on the north side of Hagley Road in 1851 and had immediately begun to lay the land out for building. In 1864 he gave the site for a new church and a sum of money towards its erection. St Augustine's, designed in the Gothic style, was consecrated in 1868. It provided the focus for three new streets, St Augustine's, Melville and Lyttleton Roads. The businessman Edwin Antrobus acquired the whole of the area on the west side of St Augustine's Road '3668 yards of freehold land ... on which it [was] proposed to build 10 houses'[94] as a speculative venture. Bateman and Corser appear already to have been involved in designing a new detached house on the corner of Hagley Road and St Augustine's Road for Antrobus and, in 1873, produced plans for this and for ten semi-detached villas.[95] The architects chose a Gothic design in which to build, perhaps to reflect the style of the church. Based on the ideas of Ruskin and other proponents, the Gothic style had become steadily more popular in domestic architecture and by the 1870s was commonly used in designs for speculative schemes. The three pairs of villas actually constructed, with their arched sash windows, blue brick detailing, finials, fretted bargeboards and prominent decorated porches, display an adept and confident use of the style. Building costs for the ten villas were estimated at £7,000 and the completed houses were valued at £9,000.[96]

Commercial offices began to emerge as a building type in the early Victorian period and the concept of office 'chambers', a series of separately tenanted office suites within a single building, was firmly established by the 1860s. Classical styles, particularly the Renaissance *palazzo*, were adopted for early and mid-Victorian office buildings but from the late 1850s onwards designs gradually became more varied. St Philip's Buildings, 59 Colmore Row, is the best example in Birmingham of a grand commercial building by Bateman and Corser. The Midland Land and Investment Company had outgrown their 'old premises' in the city.[97] Bateman had recently completed the Inns of Court Hotel in London for them[98] and in 1878 his practice was commissioned to design their new offices in Birmingham.[99] Although the site, on the corner of Colmore Row and Church Street, is beside the country's 'best ensemble of mid-Victorian palazzo splendour,'[100] built between 1869 and 1874,[101] Bateman and Corser moved away from the *palazzo* form, choosing to build in the ornate classical style derived from the French Renaissance and known as Second Empire. The building, despite later alterations, is 'the best piece of Second Empire French in the city'.[102] It has a richly detailed yet carefully

OPPOSITE   St Philip's Buildings, Colmore Row, 1878

ordered principal frontage onto Colmore Row with a restrained classically styled long secondary frontage on Church Street. The two essential requirements demanded in office buildings of the period are met. The closely set windows, larger on the ground floor, allow plenty of precious natural light through to the interior and the height of the building (in the days before lifts were commonly installed) ensured a good rental income from the site. The Midland Land and Investment Company occupied the

ground and first floor fronting Colmore Row ... the corner on the ground floor being the banking room, over which is the Board–room, the requisite offices for the manager, secretary, surveyor and clerks fronting Church-Street. The other portions are let off in suites of offices. Beneath a well-lighted basement is a sub-basement let off as vaults.[103]

The building is constructed in Bath stone with free-standing granite columns articulating the principal frontage. The original internal finishings and fittings were mahogany.[104] Total building costs were about £20,000, Bateman and Corser themselves supervised the building work.[105]

J. J. Bateman had a long professional involvement with the Cartland family, designing and altering both industrial and residential properties for various of its members.[106] In 1845 the brassfounder James Cartland bought a house and land in King's Heath to the south of Birmingham. Following his death in 1855 his son and heir, John Cartland, employed Bateman to alter and extend the house in 'Tudor Gothic' style.[107] Formerly known as Bleak House it was renamed The Priory. Cartland continued to acquire land around the property and, in 1887, as King's Heath grew, seized the opportunity to profit from housing development, instructing Bateman to plan an estate layout off Vicarage Road.[108] After his death in 1889 his son and successor, John Howard Cartland, continued with the development.

Bateman designed the first houses on the Priory estate for John Cartland, four semi-detached 'cottages', 255 Vicarage Road and 2 Melstock Road, 1 Melstock Road and 257 Vicarage Road, in 1887.[109] The houses have conventional late Victorian domestic details – tile-hung or half-timbered gables and casement windows. Each pair is asymmetrical and could be interpreted as a single house. In the same year however, Bateman was joined in partnership by his son Charles, newly returned from working and studying in London, and, under his influence, the Arts and Crafts style became gradually more apparent in the designs produced by the practice. 241–243 Vicarage Road, a pair of semi-detached houses built for Cartland in 1889[110] provide a good example of the style and are almost certainly largely the work of the junior Bateman, who was to become one of its most accomplished proponents. The buildings have elements in common with his father's work, but show the beginnings of a distinctive vocabulary that is clearly different. 'The long ridge line, sweeping roofs with projecting eaves, sturdy chimneys and casement

241–243 Vicarage Road, King's Heath, 1889

windows are all part of an architectural language which [C. E. Bateman] would later develop'.[111] The bay window is a later addition.

In 1894 Bateman and Bateman designed 'professional offices and printing offices for John Feeney, the proprietor of the Birmingham Post and Daily Mail'[112] on Cannon Street in the city centre. The design is interesting for its early use of reinforced concrete to strengthen the walls,[113] the *Building News* observing that a 'large amount of steelwork enclosed with concrete is employed in the construction in order to keep the basement, which is one large room, as free as possible from obstructions to the printing machines'.[114] The first known patent for reinforced concrete was taken out by the British firm of W. B. Wilkinson and Co. in the 1850s and by the turn of the century a number of systems or means of disposing the steel reinforcement within the concrete had been devised and patented. In Britain however the use of the material was largely confined to floors and roofs and the construction of whole concrete frame buildings was developed in France and the USA. From 1892 the inventor and entrepreneur Francois Hennebique took out British patents for his building system which he had developed in France and Belgium and in 1897 his company erected Weaver's Mill in Swansea, the first complete concrete frame building in Britain. The use of reinforced concrete beams in 1894 therefore, to allow the maximum space for Feeney's printing presses in his office basement, and no doubt to withstand their vibration, demonstrates a willingness and capacity to employ new construction techniques on the part of the Batemans' practice.

J. J. Bateman was by now in his late seventies and, although still involved in the practice, appeared to be leaving most of the work to his son. The design of the 'quiet and pleasing house front in Cannon-street'[115] in the Queen Anne style, was almost certainly the work of the younger Bateman. The building was of brick with simple detailing, Hollington stone used for the ground storey and dressings, including banding along the fourth storey, side gables and chimney stacks, and Welsh green slates on the roof.[116] A refined and successful attempt to move away from late nineteenth century architectural excess, it was an 'unpretentious building' with a 'taste for unpretentiousness and sobriety in architecture which especially requir[ed] fostering in Birmingham'.[117]

John Jones Bateman had married Mary Ann Culbard in Lambeth, London in 1847. They lived at first in Moseley, moving to Hawkesford House, Castle Bromwich in 1853. Of their seven children the two sons, John Joseph and Charles Edward, joined their father's practice. In 1902 Bateman moved from Castle Bromwich to Hawkesford, the house his son had designed for him in Four Oaks, Sutton Coldfield. He was taken ill at Easter 1903, when he gave up his involvement in the practice, and died in June aged 85.[118]

Selected List of Architectural Works of J. J. Bateman

John Jones Bateman(1817–1903) was articled to his father, Joseph Bateman, and in 1848 became a partner with George Drury (1806–51) as Drury and Bateman. Between 1851 and 1862 he practised alone, and then entered into partnership with Benjamin Corser (1840–1912). In 1887 his son, C. E. Bateman (1863–1947) became a partner, and in 1898 they were joined by Alfred Hale. J. J. Bateman was active in the firm until shortly before his death in 1903.

WORK IN BIRMINGHAM AND ITS ENVIRONS

PUBLIC

1850–52 New Workhouse, Dudley Road (with George Drury) [D]

1853 Deritend and Bordesley Sunday Schools, Bull Ring/Smithfield [D]

1857 Extension, Deaf and Dumb Institution, Church Road, Edgbaston, (with Frederick Fiddian) [D]

1858 Alterations, restoration and new buildings, Aston Hall, Aston Park, for Aston Hall and Park Co [D]

1859 New Chapel, Queen's Hospital, Bath Row [D]

1859–60 Infirmary for Birmingham Free Industrial School, Gem Street [D]

1859–62 Church of the Messiah, Broad Street for the Unitarian Society [D]

1860–65 Museum and Public Lecture Room, Queen's College, Paradise Street [D]

1861 St Barnabas' National School, Ryland Street, 1861; 1869 addition of classroom and schoolmaster's house [D]

1862–63 Alterations and additions to Birmingham Lying-In Hospital, Broad Street [part D]

1864–66 Repairs to Aston Hall, Aston Park for Birmingham Corporation

1865–66 Deritend Free Library, Heath Mill Lane (with Benjamin Corser)

1866–68 Gosta Green Free Library, Aston Road/Legge St (with Benjamin Corser) [D]

1872–73 Alterations to St Mary's Church, Whittall Street (with Benjamin Corser) [D]

COMMERCIAL

1857–1859 Shops, workrooms and offices for Hyam and Co, drapers, New Street/Union St [D]

1871–73 Alterations to Bingley Hall, Broad Street (with Benjamin Corser) [D]

1872–73 Warehouses, Newhall Hill [D]

1878 St Philip's Buildings, Colmore Row/Church St for Midland Land and Investment Company

1869–71 Corporation Fish Market, Spiceal Street/Bell St (with Benjamin Corser) [D]

1894–97 Newspaper Offices and Print Rooms for Birmingham Post and Daily Mail, Cannon Street (with C. E. Bateman) [D]

INDUSTRIAL

1859 Manufactory for John Cartland, brassfounder, Constitution Hill [D]

1859 Workshops and Warehouse, Whittall Street [D]

1866–76 Repairs, additions and alterations to the Gun Barrel Proof House, Banbury Street

1871 Manufactory and warehouse for John Stokes, silversmith, 83–84 Great Hampton Street, Hockley (with Benjamin Corser)

DOMESTIC

1851 13–14 Charlotte Road, Edgbaston for Edward Baker

1851 105–107 Gough Road, Edgbaston for Edward and George Baker

1854–55 House, Soho Hill, Handsworth

1855 11 Ampton Road, Edgbaston for Robert Gillam

1855–56 Alterations and extensions, The Priory, King's Heath for John Cartland [D]

1856 Six terraced houses, Ledsam Street, 1856

1860–67 Oakfield House, Wellington Road, Edgbaston

1873 Three pairs of villas, St Augustine's Road, Edgbaston for Edwin Antrobus

1887 Four semi-detached houses, 255 Vicarage Road and 2 Melstock Road, and 257 Vicarage Road and 1 Melstock Road, King's Heath for John Cartland

NOTES

1 *The Builder*, 16, 15 June 1858, p. 873.

2 'Three Generations of Birmingham Architects', *The Architects' Journal*, 50, 9 July 1919, p. 57.

3 *Aris's Gazette*, 1 July 1811.

4 *The Architects' Journal*, 50, 9 July 1919, p. 57.

5 Birmingham Central Library, Archives and Heritage Services (henceforth BCL AHS), MS 1542 Papers of Messrs Bateman and Bateman, Architects and Surveyors, Partnership Accounts.

6 BCL AHS, MS 1542, Box 16, bdl. 8.

7 *Birmingham at the Opening of the Twentieth Century: Contemporary Biographies,* ed. by W. T. Pike (Brighton, n. d.), p. 150.

8 BCL AHS, MS 1542, Box 16, bdl. 8.

9 *Ibid.*

10 BCL AHS, MS 1542, Box 23, bdl. 22.

11 BCL AHS, MS 1542, Box 23, bdl. 23.

12 BCL AHS, MS 1542, Box 34, bdl. 10.

13 *The Builder*, 9, 31 January 1852, p. 71.

14 Roger Dixon and Stefan Muthesius, *Victorian Architecture* (1978), p. 110.

15 BCL AHS, MS 1542, Box 7, bdl. 1.

16 *The Builder*, 10, 31 January 1852, p. 12.

17 BCL AHS, MS 1542, Box 14, bdl. 10.

18 BCL AHS, MS 1542, Box 2, bdl. 7.

19 BCL AHS, MS 1542, Box 15, bdl. 5.

20 BCL AHS, MS 1542, Box 46, bdl. 4.

21 BCL AHS, MS 1542, Box 27, bdl. 9; MS 1542, Box 47, bdl. 8.

22 BCL AHS, MS 1542, Box 15, bdl. 3.

23 Andy Foster, *Pevsner Architectural Guides: Birmingham* (New Haven and London, 2005), p. 227.

24 BCL AHS, MS 1542, Box 3, bdl. 2.

25 *Ibid.*

26 BCL AHS, MS 1542, Box 3, bdl. 3.

27 *Ibid.*

28 BCL AHS, MS 1542, Box 3, bdl. 2.

29 BCL AHS, MS 1542, Box 21, bdl. 4.

30 'The Late Mr Eliezer Edwards', *Birmingham Faces and Places*, III, 2 March 1891, p. 183.

31 Kathryn A. Morrison, *English Shops and Shopping: An Architectural History* (2003), p. 128; p. 195.

32 BCL AHS, MS 1542, Box 21, bdl. 4.

33 *The Builder*, 17, 25 June 1859, pp. 423–25.

34 *The Builder*, 17, p. 423.

35 *Ibid.*

36 BCL AHS, MS 1542, Box 24, bdl. 7.

37 D. J. O'Neill, *How Aston Hall and Park were 'Saved'* (Birmingham, 1910), p. 48.

38 W. C. Aitken, *Official Guide to Aston Hall and Park and to the Exhibition of Fine Arts and Art Manufactures inaugurated by Her Most Gracious Majesty the Queen on Tuesday June 15 1858* (Birmingham, 1858), p. 11.

39 O'Neill, *Aston Hall*, p. 48.

40 BCL AHS, MS 1542, Box 24, bdl. 7.

41 BCL AHS, MS 1542, Box 28, bdl. 20.

42 Aitken, *Guide to Aston Hall*, p. 11.

43 BCL AHS, MS 1542, Box 1, bdl. 7.

44 *Ibid.*

45 BCL AHS, MS 1542, Box 1, bdl. 7.

46 BCL AHS, MS 1542 Box 12, bdl. 1.

47 Robert K. Dent, *Old and New Birmingham* (orig. pub. Birmingham 1880, reprinted Menston, 3 vols, 1973), p. 580.

48 *The Builder*, 21, 28 February 1863, p. 150.

49 Dent, *Old and New*, p. 580.

50 *The Builder*, 21, 28 February 1863, p. 150.

51 *Ibid.*

52 BCL AHS, MS 1542, Box 24, bdl. 7.

53 *Ibid.*

54 O'Neill, *Aston Hall*, p. 48.

55 *Ibid.*
56 BCL AHS, MS 1542, Box 12, bdl. 18.
57 J. T. Bunce, *History of the Corporation of Birmingham*, 2 vols (Birmingham, 1878–80), vol 2, pp. 206–209.
58 *Ibid.*
59 BCL AHS, BCL MS 1542, Box 11, bdl. 4.
60 BCL AHS, MS 1542, Box 26, bdl. 10.
61 *Ibid.*
62 BCL AHS, MS 1542, Box 26, bdl. 10.
63 *Ibid.*
64 BCL AHS, MS 1542, Box 26, bdl. 10.
65 *Ibid.*
66 BCL AHS, MS 1542, Box 41, bdl. 5.
67 *Ibid.*
68 BCL AHS, MS 1542, Box 41, bdl. 5.
69 *The Builder*, 24, 3 November 1866, p. 813.
70 *Ibid.*
71 *Ibid.*
72 *Ibid.*
73 BCL AHS, MS 1542, Box 18, bdl. 15.
74 *Birmingham at Opening of Twentieth Century*, p. 150; BCL AHS, MS 1542, Box 20, bdl. 8.
75 BCL AHS, MS 1542, Box 47, bdl. 10.
76 BCL AHS, MS 1542, Box 18, bdl. 2, Box 27, bdl. 13.
77 BCL AHS, MS 1542, Box 27, bdl 13.
78 Foster, *Birmingham*, p. 188.
79 BCL AHS, MS 1542, Box 27, bdl. 13, *Foster*, p. 189.
80 Foster, *Birmingham*, p. 189.
81 BCL AHS, MS 1542, Box 4, bdl. 6.
82 *Ibid.*
83 BCL AHS, MS 1542 Box 4, bdl. 6.
84 *Ibid.*
85 BCL AHS, MS 1542, Box 12, bdl. 7.
86 *Ibid.*
87 BCL AHS, MS 1542, Box 12, bdl. 7.
88 *Ibid.*
89 BCL AHS, MS 1542, Box 12, bdl. 7.
90 *Ibid.*
91 *Ibid.*
92 C. E. Goad, *Birmingham Fire Insurance Maps* (1889–1959), sheet 215.
93 Bunce, *History of the Corporation*, p. 174.
94 BCL AHS, MS 1542, Box 33, bdl. 1.
95 *Ibid.*
96 BCL AHS, MS 1542 Box 33, bdl. 1.
97 *The Builder*, 36, 29 June 1878, p. 692.
98 *The Builder*, 36, 5 January 1878, p. 10; *Birmingham at Opening of Twentieth Century*, p. 150.
99 *The Builder*, 36, 29 June 1878, p. 692.
100 Dixon and Muthesius, *Victorian Architecture*, p. 131.
101 Foster, *Birmingham*, pp. 96–98.
102 *Ibid*, p. 98.
103 *The Builder*, 36, 29 June 1878, p. 692.
104 *Ibid.*
105 *The Builder*, 36, 29 June 1878, p. 692.
106 BCL AHS, MS 1542, Box 15, bdl. 12; MS 1542, Box 11, bdl. 4; MS 1542, Box 52, bdl. 7; MS 1542, Box 37, bdl. 2; BCL AHS, King's Norton and Northfield Building Register, app. no. 800, January 1886.
107 BCL AHS, MS 1542, Box 52, bdl. 7.
108 David Davidson, 'The Work of C. E. Bateman' (unpublished M.A. Thesis, De Montfort University, 1995), p. 21.
109 *Ibid*, p. 22; BCL AHS, King's Norton and Northfield Building Register, app. no. 890, 13 May 1887.
110 Davidson, 'Bateman', p. 26; BCL AHS, King's Norton and Northfield Building Register, app. no. 1071, 12 April 1889.
111 Davidson, 'Bateman', p. 26.

[112] *Building News*, 68, 23 November 1894, p. 713.

[113] BCL AHS, Birmingham Building Register, app. no. 9765, 5 October 1893. For a discussion of the use of ferro-concrete see Patricia Cusack, 'Agents of Change: Hennebique, Mouchel and ferro-concrete in Britain, 1897–1908', *Construction History*, 3 (1978), 61–74.

[114] *Building News*, 68, 23 November 1894, p. 713.

[115] *The Builder*, 73, 27 November 1897, p. 440.

[116] *Building News*, 68, 23 November, 1894 p. 713.

[117] *The Builder*, 73, 27 November 1897, p. 440.

[118] *Building News*, 82, 19 June 1903 p. 855.

5 J. A. Chatwin

TIM BRIDGES

St Philip's Cathedral, erected at the heart of Birmingham between 1709 and 1725 is rightly celebrated for its fine baroque design by Thomas Archer. However, in the 1880s the building was extended almost seamlessly to the east with a substantial chancel by J. A. Chatwin. In 1905 his son, Philip, refurbished the chancel at the time that the church was given cathedral status, and in 1947 it fell to Philip along with his nephew, Anthony, to restore bomb damage to the roof and later restore the tower.[1] Thus three generations of the Chatwin family have worked on this fine building, taking their lead from J. A. Chatwin, who became renowned for his church designs in the Birmingham area during the second half of the nineteenth century. However, the number of church buildings associated with his name in Birmingham, and the lack of examples outside the Midlands, has perhaps led in the past to somewhat dismissive critiques of his work and indeed several of his churches and other buildings have been demolished. Yet the achievements of J. A. Chatwin were wide ranging and his versatility as an architect is increasingly gaining appreciation. His designs for houses, schools, public and commercial buildings, as well as churches, show competence in a variety of styles from Gothic and Tudor to Italianate and Baroque.

Chatwin was christened Julius Alfred and although he used Alfred, these were forenames he disliked, and he was known to his friends as Timmy. He spent much of his life in the vicinity of St Philip.[2] The family has strong Midland roots. The name is derived from Chetwynd, a village near Newport Shropshire, and J. A. Chatwin had ancestors in Halesowen from the late

J. A. Chatwin

seventeenth century.[3] He was born on 27 April 1830, the sixth child and fourth son of John and Harriet Chatwin, and was baptised in St Philip. The family was living at 92–93 Great Charles Street, and John Chatwin's button works were in premises to the rear of the house. John Chatwin had invented the method of covering metal buttons with fabric, which was patented in 1843.[4] Later, the family moved to Soho Hill, Handsworth, living in a house known as Soho Villa, since demolished, at the corner of Villa Road. After attending school in Heathfield Road, Handsworth, J. A. Chatwin went to King Edward's School in New Street at the age of eleven.[5]

The drawing master at King Edward's, R. Hamilton, exhibited several designs for buildings at the Birmingham Royal Society of Artists, and it is probable that his influence helped to develop Chatwin's interest in architecture. However, Chatwin also attended Samuel Lines's Academy of Arts in Temple Row, where he studied architecture and watercolour. There he became a friend of Lines's son, Henry Harris Lines, who was himself to become noted for his drawings and paintings of archaeological sites and historic buildings under threat of destruction. Chatwin also attended the academy with Henry Gillott, and through him became a lifelong friend of his brother, Joseph. They were sons of the celebrated pen maker Joseph Gillott, who had moved to Birmingham in 1821 to seek work in the light steel toy trade. Gillott had adapted the pressing process to invent the modern steel pen nib. His nibs were sold throughout the world, and he used his considerable wealth to become an important patron of the arts. Gillott was amongst the first to recognise the importance of Turner and, at his death succeeded him as President of the Royal Birmingham Society of Artists. The young Chatwin became a frequent guest at Gillott's house for artistic gatherings.[6]

Chatwin left school when he was sixteen and went to work as a draughtsman for Branson and Gwyther. The company was one of the largest contractors in the country, and deeply involved in both the civil engineering and building aspects of the rapidly developing railways. Edwin Gwyther was a friend of Chatwin's father, and advised that to become an architect, the young Chatwin would need first to learn draughtsmanship and acquire a basic knowledge of both building construction and the management of contracts. Chatwin developed his draughting skills by copying engineers' drawings for bridges and tunnels on the Birmingham and Oxford Railway.[7] During the five years that he worked for the firm he was given increasing responsibility, and in 1848 aged only seventeen was presented with an award by the firm for his successful settlement of a dispute between contractors on the railway near Banbury on behalf of an indisposed Gwyther.[8] Chatwin worked on the construction of the tunnel on the Great Western Railway between Bordesley and Snow Hill. He also produced the drawings for a footbridge at Bartholomew Street on the extension of the London and North Western Railway from Curzon Street to New Street.[9]

However, perhaps his most significant achievement whilst at Branson and Gwyther was the design and construction of Bingley Exhibition Hall. This

Bingley Hall, Broad St, 1850. Illustration by Thomas Underwood

successfully combined his newly acquired railway engineering knowledge with architectural and artistic skills. The story of the hall is described by his great grandson, John Chatwin:

When I was six, I was taken to the Circus inside Bingley Hall. My father told me to look up into the roof and asked what I could see. Through the guy wires for the trapeze, I could just see long timber trusses; they seemed to be floating but my father said they were held up on round iron columns. Then I saw a thin column coming down within the audience — but the circus ring itself was column free. 'This building was designed by your great grandfather' my father said, 'Those columns are hollow so that the rainwater from the roof runs through them and into the canal.

Nearly fifty years later, I came across several rotting timber trusses, a few cast iron brackets and three of the columns when walking round the Brindley Place site before redevelopment started. They had been stored on site after the mysterious fire which destroyed Bingley Hall in the 1980s. However, it was sadly not practical to incorporate these remnants into the design of Brindley Place.

Chatwin had thoroughly managed the construction of Bingley Hall. It covered one and a quarter acres at a cost of £5,000, and was completed within eight weeks, in time for the Birmingham Cattle Show in 1850. The building had been commissioned as a temporary structure: cast iron columns intended for new railway stations and bricks for cuttings and embankments were re-directed; the unusually large timber trusses were purpose designed and 11,700 square feet of glass sheets was procured. The building remained Birmingham's principal large assembly building for the next one hundred years.[10]

First Cattle Show in Bingley Hall, December 1850

New buildings had been designed for King Edward's School New Street by Sir Charles Barry in 1835, a few years prior to the young Chatwin's attendance as a schoolboy. In 1851 Chatwin left Branson and Gwyther to become articled to Barry. In London, Parliament had been destroyed by fire in 1834 and Barry worked on the designs for the new Parliament buildings from 1837 and building work started in 1840. Although the opening of the House of Lords was in 1847, the House of Commons was not opened until 1852. There is a family tradition, which may be apocryphal, that Chatwin concealed himself in a ventilation duct directly over the throne to see Queen Victoria open the House of Commons. However, it is known that Chatwin worked on the stone detail of St Stephen's Tower and part of his instruction was to study buildings and mouldings previously designed by Barry.[11] Apparently he was so successful that on one occasion when asked directions in the London fog, Chatwin was able to locate himself precisely by feeling the mouldings of a nearby facade and identify the building as a particular club.[12] Barry was a great exponent of neo-classicism as is shown in the design of 1824 for the City Art Gallery in Manchester, whilst the Italianate Reform Club of 1837 and his Bridgewater House in 1846 'helped establish the unshakeable centrality of the palazzo style in nineteenth century architecture'.[13] However, from 1835 A. W. N. Pugin was assisting Barry in producing impressive Perpendicular gothic designs. Pugin believed in the Middle Ages as the ideal of Christian civilisation.[14] This is reflected in his interior decorations for King Edward's School, including the stained glass and gothic style woodwork, such as the current Chief Master's chair

'Sapientia'.[15] Pugin's work thus gave the school buildings by Barry a strong medieval character, and led to Barry involving Pugin in the competition for rebuilding Parliament. The successful aesthetics of Pugin's gothic veneer to Barry's classical proportions of Parliament appear to be reflected in Chatwin's understanding of the balance of buildings, and may have contributed to his later versatility as an architect.[16]

During his time in London with Barry, Chatwin attended evening classes of the first Schools of Design at the old Royal Academy Rooms, Somerset House under the direction of R. Redgrave and J. R. Herbert.[17] In 1853 his articles were completed and Chatwin continued to be employed as an assistant to Barry for a further two years. This association and influence proved enduring, and it seems probable that Chatwin's previous work for Barry was instrumental in securing his appointment as consultant architect to the King Edward's Foundation in 1866.[18]

In the summer of 1855, Chatwin left Barry's office and returned to Birmingham to establish his own practice in a small office in Bennett's Hill. He designed many small extensions and alterations to houses in Edgbaston; most early commissions seem to have been either from friends such as Joseph Gillott junior or recommendations through Branson and Gwyther. Commissions for larger houses followed as his reputation grew. A house possibly for a site at Lutley, Halesowen, was designed in 1858 for Charles Birch of Metchley Abbey in Harborne; the fee was a watercolour by the increasingly celebrated local artist David Cox, which marked the beginning of Chatwin's life long passion for collecting art.[19]

Chatwin's father died in 1855, and in 1857 he took an extended holiday studying architecture on the continent, which would have a lasting influence on his work. He went to Ghent and Cologne to look at Northern Gothic and then made an extensive tour in Italy to widen his understanding of classical buildings first gained during his apprenticeship to Barry. For most of this trip, his travelling companions were the sons of his former employers, George Branson and Edwin Gwyther junior.[20]

Within three years of becoming established in Birmingham, Chatwin's practice had secured commissions for several schools and at least one new church. As a result, on Christmas Eve 1858, Chatwin moved to larger premises at 20 Temple Row where the office remained until the building was demolished in 1900. During these early years Chatwin continued to live with his family at Soho Hill. Then the family moved in 1864 to 8 Frederick Road, though by the time of his marriage in 1869 Chatwin was living at 14 Calthorpe Road.[21]

During the 1860s Chatwin often met Joseph Gillott junior at the Hen and Chickens Hotel in New Street. Gillott discussed with Chatwin his proposal to develop a new residential area at the Noel estate of Rotton Park to the north of Hagley Road, which was to be modelled on the Calthorpe developments to the south, and would provide housing away from the city centre for the lower middle and skilled working classes.[22] Chatwin agreed to make a plan for the road layout, and as a result of a competition, Gillot later commissioned Chatwin to design a church as the centrepiece, namely St Augustine built in 1868. The church had probably been in Chatwin's mind from the outset, to be surrounded by houses also to his design. However, in the event the houses in Lyttleton Road around the church seem largely to have been built after 1896 to designs by John Statham Davies. Other earlier houses in St Augustine's Road may be to Chatwin's design. Several other commissions were to come from organisations where Gillott was either a participator, such as Solihull Public Hall in 1899, or a benefactor, including the church and school at Catherine de Barnes in 1880. One of Chatwin's first independent projects in domestic architecture was his work at Berry Hall Solihull, which Gillott senior had purchased in 1855 for his own house.[23]

Branson and Gwyther publicly acknowledged the young Chatwin as the architect of his first houses, which he designed whilst still working for the practice in 1850. The client was J. D. Goodman, proprietor of the Birmingham Small Arms Company.[24] These houses, Needwood and Beechwood, still stand at 38–39 Frederick Road Edgbaston. They comprise a richly detailed, almost symmetrical pair of Italianate villas in stucco, with Venetian and round headed windows arranged around central doorways. The doorways display distinctive rusticated

Needwood and Beechwood, Frederick Road, Edgbaston, 1850

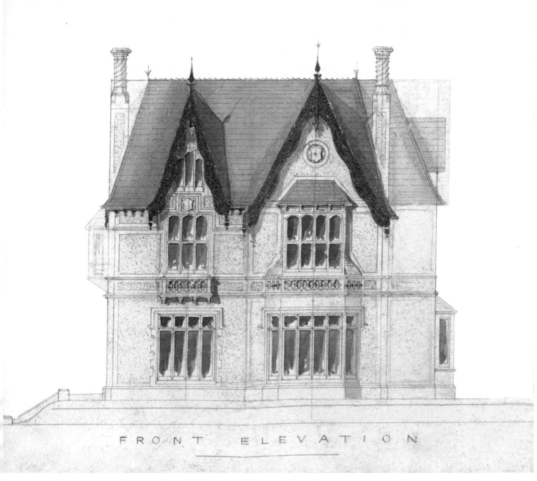

2–3 Augustus Road, Edgbaston. Elevation drawing, 1859. *Courtesy of Birmingham Archives and Heritage Services (MS 891/83)*

surrounds with decorative shell and feather fanned motifs to the lunettes.[25] Whilst working for Barry, Chatwin designed a terrace of houses in a similar style at Gloddaeth Crescent on the seafront at Llandudno for Branson and Gwyther. These early pieces of domestic architecture reflect the regency villas in both Edgbaston and the seaside resort. However, in 1859 he was commissioned to design another pair of houses in Edgbaston at 2–3 Augustus Road. By contrast, this building, in a domestic high gothic, with prominent steep gables and decorated bargeboards, was much admired and gave rise to a number of further commissions for large houses.[26] They have since been demolished.

Another of Chatwin's key domestic works to have been lost is Berry Hall, Solihull with Tudor style chimney stacks, Jacobean style windows and Italianate entrance portal designed for the Gillott family in 1870. However, Berry Hall Lodge of 1884 does survive nearby. In a more defined Elizabethan style, it too has cut brickwork chimney stacks, but the timber-framed gable and coved eaves are echoes of Cheshire, which together with the turned wooden supports to the porch show an attention to detail similar to that used by Edward Ould after 1887 at Wightwick.[27] Knutsford Lodge, 25 Somerset Road Edgbaston, shows the excellence of Chatwin's design for a gentleman's residence. Of 1861 it is in a Jacobean style with its splendid two storey porch with oriel window and gabled bays and mullioned and transomed windows to the frontages.[28] The vicarage at Catshill built in 1870 echoes these more substantial domestic designs with its gables and Tudor style chimneys, whilst Upper Skilts near Studley built in the 1880s in the Tudor style for Sir John Jaffray, founder of the *Birmingham Post*, incorporated panelling from the nearby Tudor house.[29]

Chatwin's domestic architecture was not confined to the homes of the more well-to-do. Next to Pearson's church of St Alban stand his Lench's Trust Alms-houses of 1878–80, in the midst of what was the terraced workers' housing of Highgate. The cottages surround three sides of a rectangular green with the warden's house at the centre, and seem to represent the first use of the 'Queen Anne' style in Birmingham. The fine late seventeenth century style detailing is in moulded and cut brickwork on the pilasters, string courses and eaves of the facades nearest to the road, but sadly the tall star-shaped chimneys have since been removed.[30]

The destruction of the Great Western Hotel, by Snow Hill Station in Colmore Row was a great loss to Birmingham. Designed by Chatwin in 1875 it has been described as the finest nineteenth century hotel in the city.[31] Though his role is unclear, Chatwin may also have been involved with work on the Grand Hotel which was designed by Thomas Plevins in 1876–78, with its classical front and French chateau roofscape.[32] The Hen and Chickens Hotel in New Street, now demolished, was designed by Chatwin in 1898 to replace the building where he used to meet his friends Gillott and Lines. 'He was as skilful in his drawings for terracotta work as for stone, as witness the Hen and Chickens Hotel, New Street'.[33] The White Horse Cellars, Constitution Hill, erected in 1890 in the 'Queen Anne' style is Chatwin's only known public house design, whilst the facade of 20–26 Albert Street of 1898 survives as a rare example of his later designs for commercial premises.[34]

Chatwin's first school, St Silas's National, was designed in 1851 to go in a newly created square with small terraced houses next to J. W. Fiddian's church in Lozells. St Clement's School followed in 1858, built next to the church in Nechells he designed at the same time.[35] He produced several other school designs during the 1860s prior to the creation of the Education Board in 1870. Thereafter Chatwin worked on private and public schools, including that at Catherine de Barnes as a private commission for the Gillott family, and he appears to have undertaken

St Silas's National School, Church St, Lozells, 1851

work at Uppingham School in Rutland in 1870.[36] In 1883–86 major extensions were made by Chatwin to 31 Calthorpe Road, a villa of 1830, for Edgbaston College for Girls.[37] However, the Solihull Grammar School building on Warwick Road is an excellent example of Chatwin's larger school buildings, with its Perpendicular style hall and battlemented tower porch contrasting with the domestic Jacobean style of the frontage of the main range. The display of moulded brick and terracotta is similar to that to be found at Berry Hall Lodge, perhaps reflecting the interest of Gillott in the project.[38]

As Surveyor of the Fabric to the Governors of King Edward's School, Chatwin was responsible for repairs and redecorations across the school sites. The extension of the New Street buildings in 1883 included a Gymnasium and the 'splendidly designed and equipped' Girls' High School of 1895–96 next to the school he had attended as a boy.[39] All have since been demolished. King Edward's Schools Aston were established in 1881 in buildings to Chatwin's design. The schools for boys and girls formed a pair, but subsequently were amalgamated into one boys' school.[40] Also in 1881 King Edward's School took over Edgbaston Proprietary School at Five Ways for which Chatwin designed a large extension.[41]

Meanwhile in 1878, plans for an Aquarium designed by Chatwin for the public display of marine life near the Hen and Chickens in Birmingham came to nothing. Not long afterwards Chatwin's commission for a glass palace in India, which is believed to have been secured by Benjamin Stone for an unidentified

Solihull School, Warwick Road, 1879–82, 1900

maharaja, foundered in 1880. The patron received an ill omen, as his horse stumbled on the day that final arrangements for the scheme were to be completed, and plans for what would have been Chatwin's only work outside the country were abandoned.[42]

However, Wolverhampton Art Gallery was completed in 1885 to Chatwin's designs, using ashlar and polished granite in the Italianate style to house the borough's growing public collection of works of art. Access to the galleries on the upper floor is by a fine staircase with a wrought iron balustrade. These galleries are lit from above and have no windows to the front and side elevations, allowing maximum use of the walls for hanging pictures and the amount of natural light in the rooms to be more readily controlled. The blind exterior walls are decorated at first floor level with fine sculptures by Boulton of Cheltenham, similar to those on Chatwin's nearby Lloyd's Bank. These show male and female figures in classical dress enjoying the arts to the front and in period costume demonstrating science and industry to the side. This building is an excellent example of a provincial Victorian art gallery, and together with the adjacent art school, comprises one of Chatwin's finest public buildings.[43]

Solihull Public Hall, later the Council House, was built by private enterprise in 1876 and forms a pair with his contemporary Lloyd's Bank on Poplar Road. Both

Lloyd's Bank and Solihull Public Hall, Poplar Rd, Solihull, 1876–77

are of brick with stone dressings. The fine run of pointed Gothic windows of the hall with central balcony over the gothic entrance arch recalls the civic buildings of the Low Countries and contrasts with the Tudor style of the bank. Chatwin's competence to work in differing styles yet achieve harmony is demonstrated on this new street, the focus of nineteenth century Solihull's civic pride.[44]

The Joint Stock Bank, Temple Row West of 1864 was Chatwin's first important bank building; it was much admired, leading to commissions of other banks.[45] The facade facing St Philip set a new trend in this Regency square. Little describes 'a rich little palazzo with its Doric and Corinthian façade'[46] and the ingenious design of the ground floor window arrangement which creates an unusual relationship between the exterior and interior has been admired.[47] Chatwin's commercial work was frequently Italianate and shows further strength in his versatility as an architect. This and the success of his subsequent Baroque chancel on the neighbouring St Philip appear to be connected with his training by Barry. Although heightened by a storey in the late nineteenth century, his Lloyd's Bank at Wolverhampton of 1878 displays more of this detailed understanding of Italianate architecture. The pilasters, plinth and cornice are moulded, Doric

columns enhance the large porch, and sculptures above the ground floor windows depict coal mining, agriculture and engineering, interpreting the Renaissance for a great industrial and commercial age.[48]

Indeed it was for Lloyd's, whose founder came from Birmingham, that Chatwin undertook his principal bank building works. In 1870 he won the competition to design the new office in Colmore Row, on the corner of Eden Place opposite the Council House. Since demolished, this building was considered to have a less than satisfying exterior as it was constructed of brick faced with cement, contrary to the Colmore Estate policy for stone buildings on the north side of the street. The elevations also had to be heightened by the use of a tall parapet and coat of arms as it was dwarfed during construction by the unexpected completion of a taller neighbouring building. Further internal alterations to the design to suit the needs of the bank at the request of its director, Joseph Chamberlain, led to the cost of the building being higher than planned, though Chamberlain and Chatwin were able to resolve the situation amicably. Several other commissions for bank buildings followed in the West Midlands area, not least as a result of company policy to open a large number of branches in the region.[49]

In 1885 Chatwin designed Lloyd's head office in Lombard Street, London. This was an impressive classical building of which he was justly proud, and he took his sons, including Philip, to visit when it was nearing completion. It was the first building in the City to have electric light. However, by 1931 it had been demolished to make way for a new headquarters building.[50] Still surviving is the facade of the Palladian Lloyd's Bank in High Street, Cardiff of 1892, which with giant pilasters is well suited to the prominent site with other significant commercial premises in the city centre close to the castle.[51]

Many of Chatwin's banks were stone faced and Italianate, like the six bay frontage of 1892 to Lloyd's Bank, Malvern, or the classical proportions and details of Lloyd's Bank, Stratford-upon-Avon, of 1899, where Italianate windows blend with Doric columns and Corinthian capitals and a canted oriel supports a short spire to the corner.[52] This concept continued into the early twentieth century with the fine Lloyd's Bank in High Street Leicester of 1903–06 with its tall round-arched windows, separated by Ionic columns to the ground floor, reflecting some of Chatwin's earlier designs for houses and banks. The style was perpetuated by Philip Chatwin's classical Lloyd's Bank at Five Ways, Edgbaston of 1908.[53]

By contrast, Lloyd's Bank in Deritend shows the development of Chatwin's domestic gothic with a stepped cornice and lancets in the gable.[54] Lloyd's Bank in Poplar Road Solihull of 1877 is more like his later Elizabethan style Berry Hall Lodge. It is of brick, and domestic, almost Arts and Crafts architecture.[55] Indeed his smaller banks for Lloyd's further demonstrate Chatwin's versatility as an architect. These include purpose built premises such as the since demolished building

OPPOSITE   Former Joint Stock Bank, Temple Row West, 1864

of Georgian proportions in Netherton, the more French gothic style ediface in Hagley Street, Halesowen and the conversion to banks of several eighteenth and early nineteenth century buildings, mainly town houses, with the introduction of Italianate ground floor frontages, as at Lloyd's Bank at Ironbridge.[56] Chatwin's work for banks also extended to the Compton Evans Bank in Derby, as well as the Bucks and Oxon Bank further south. The bank of 1884 at the foot of High Street, Hemel Hempstead, has Tudor type details reflecting Chatwin's domestic architecture in the Midlands, with mullion windows and corner turret complete with oriel and short spire.[57]

J. A. Chatwin is perhaps best known for his church architecture, though his considerable achievements in this field have perhaps been less than enthusiastically commented on in the past. As Brian Little pointed out 'Chatwin's church building dominance well illustrates Victorian Birmingham practice whereby almost all available commissions went to local men'.[58] Indeed the city has few examples of Victorian church building by nationally noted architects; St James Edgbaston by Teulon and St Alban Highgate by Pearson being amongst the exceptions. Whilst Nikolaus Pevsner and Alexandra Wedgwood in *The Buildings of England: Warwickshire* seem generally dismissive of most churches in the county from the period between 1875 and 1900, and refer to Chatwin as 'ubiquitous', they do stress his competence and versatility as an architect, and contrast the 'noble early fourteenth century rebuilding' of St Martin with the 'brilliant Archerish chancel' to St Philip, recording that he 'never entirely failed'.[59]

Chatwin's first church commission was for the now demolished St Clement, Nechells in 1858. Described as a 'thorough though uninspiring Gothic design', the church made good use of available funds in a poor area. It cost £3,200 and had a nave, chancel, and transepts. Its rose window, doorways and octagonal turret with gabled spirelet were all in the early Decorated style.[60] In 1864, but built to designs made four years earlier, Holy Trinity, Birchfield Road, Handsworth gave Chatwin a 'reputation for solid gothic work at a reasonable price'.[61] Indeed this Early English to Decorated style building is most striking with an aisled nave, chancel with polygonal apse, short transepts and south porch tower with spire. Such features can also be found in the design of many of his subsequent church buildings. The same is true of his geometric tracery windows to the aisles, the cusped lights to the groups of three clerestorey windows and the tall two light windows with Geometric tracery in the apse. Inside, the five bay arcades with double chamfered arches resting on cylindrical columns, the deeply carved capitals and the scissor braced roof, with principal rafters rising from angel corbels positioned lower down the clerestorey walls would all have parallel derivatives in later churches.[62] In 1862, he is also described as using 'rogue gothic' at St Lawrence, Dartmouth Street, which along with the plain gothic St Gabriel, Barn Street of 1869 are lost churches in north-east Birmingham from this early building phase.[63]

St Augustine, Edgbaston, amongst the finest of Chatwin's surviving church buildings, was designed as the centrepiece for Joseph Gillot's Rotton Park Estate, and is approached from the south along an avenue from Hagley Road. The chancel and nave were started in 1868, and were funded through public sub-scription which raised £9000, and the tower and tall spire added in 1876 at a further cost of £4000. Several tall two light windows and the three-sided apse to the chancel are typical features of Chatwin's work, as is the fine deep carving to the arcade capitals. The spire rises to 185 feet and makes a dramatic landmark in this area of two and three storey buildings. Unusually for Chatwin, the spire is attached to the tower using a perpendicular style corona in the manner of St Patrick Patrington in Yorkshire and is reminiscent of St Michael Coventry. Chatwin was dissatisfied by modifications to the original design for the church by the estate committee, and the opportunity to add the tower and spire somewhat mitigated the situation.[64]

'In most of the church restorations...it appears...that the architect had one all-pervading idea, and that has been to produce, by ample breadth of treatment and harmony of form, what is artistically called "a feeling of repose"'.[65] The rebuilding and extension of existing churches by Chatwin shows considerable understanding for what was already there; there is a degree of archaeological correctness to his work and his successful treatment of both medieval gothic at St Peter and St Paul, Aston and classical at St Philip, is remarkable. Whilst following the example of other Gothic Revival architects in these works, he was not imposing the ubiquitous fourteenth century gothic on churches of other styles as is demonstrated by his work at the significant medieval Birmingham churches of St Martin, St Bartholomew Edgbaston, and St Mary Handsworth.[66] Chatwin's earliest restoration work seems to have been in 1862 on the nave at the medieval church at Waddesdon in Buckinghamshire, and subsequent restorations of the medieval All Saints Preston Bagot in Warwickshire, St Michael Penkridge in Staffordshire and St Mary Kidderminster in Worcestershire were generally sensitive to the existing buildings. Indeed Chatwin's nave roof in the Perpendicu-lar style and his raising of the Early English style chancel arch at Penkridge in 1881 along with the refacing of the tower and rebuilding of the clerestorey at Kidder-minster in 1893 can be said to have replenished the medieval character.[67] However, the erection of dominant new naves parallel to the earlier nineteenth century churches at St George Edgbaston, St James Handsworth, and St John Kidder-minster, whilst preserving much of the earlier buildings as side aisles, represents a new departure. The external additions at St George[68] appear more harmonious than the other more incongruous examples, especially at St James, where the short tower of Robert Ebbles's church of 1839 is invisible from the south behind Chat-win's nave and chancel erected at a cost of £7000 in 1895 to house seven hundred people. Similarly much of Gordon Alexander's St John Kidderminster was rebuilt to create a church which could seat over a thousand people, leaving just the brick

Church of St Augustine, Edgbaston, 1868

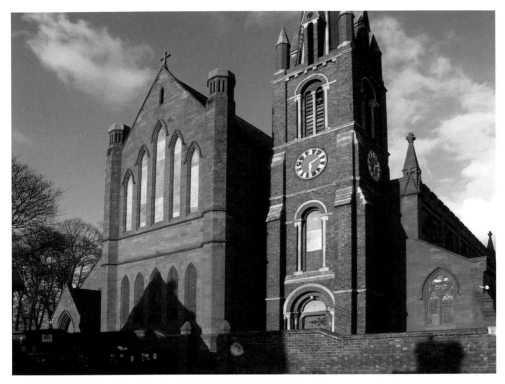

Rebuilding of Church of St John, Kidderminster, 1892 and 1902

tower and spire at the west end of the earlier nave, which was then reconstructed by Chatwin in red sandstone in 1902, but in any case overshadowed by his larger new nave and chancel to the north.[69]

One of Chatwin's more significant ecclesiastical commissions was the rebuilding of the medieval and Georgian parish church of St Martin in the Bull Ring. One parishioner commented 'we saw with no regrets, the destruction of that ugly brick building which successive generations of meddlers and muddlers had tacked on to a fine spire'.[70] Whilst the significance of the loss of earlier fabric might be debatable, Chatwin proposed a bold rebuilding from the foundations upwards of everything but the medieval tower and spire, which itself had been refaced and embellished by Philip Hardwicke in 1853–55. The earlier work was carefully demolished and rebuilt by Chatwin who slightly enlarged the medieval plan.[71] Medieval wall paintings were uncovered and recorded, but regrettably not saved. Chatwin did, however, believe in reclaiming parts of the existing building for re-use: the choir stalls were made from the roof timbers, whilst the pulpit and other panelling were incorporated within the re-modelling of his own house.[72] A strength of St Martin is his typical sympathetic approach to the surviving work,

West Elevation of Church of St
Martin in the Bull Ring

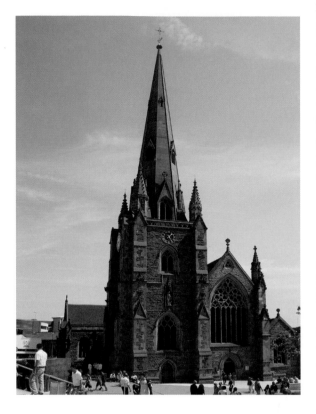

as in the nave arcades being designed to echo the style of the medieval arch to the tower.[73] There is a fine hammerbeam roof which is believed, like that at St Peter and St Paul Aston, to be derived from the roof of Westminster Hall, which would have been a familiar sight to Chatwin whilst he was working for Barry on the Parliament buildings.[74] The Decorated style windows with their reticulation provide a wonderful setting for the fine south transept window of 1876–77 by Sir Edward Burne-Jones, which anticipates Chatwin's work with Burne-Jones and William Morris at St Philip in the 1890s.

'An even finer achievement than St Martin's was Mr Chatwin's restoration and enlargement of Aston church. The first part of the work was carried out in so admirable a manner that the late Mr John Feeney gave Mr Chatwin practically *carte blanche* in the manner of completing it by the erection of a costly chancel, which was undertaken as a costly memorial'.[75] The reconstruction of the entire body of St Peter and St Paul Aston, leaving just the tower and spire, was commenced in 1879, of which the chancel and the Erdington Chapel were endowed anonymously during his lifetime by John Feeney, owner of the *Birmingham Post*. Work was conducted in phases, concluding with the erection of the south porch in 1908 after Chatwin's death. The style of Chatwin's work is Decorated to Perpendicular combining Perpendicular transoms with Decorated heads to several of the windows.[76] The absence of a chancel arch, but inclusion of a large polygonal apse is again reminiscent of St Michael Coventry. Indeed, the interior becomes richer towards the east end. Deep and elaborate carving embellishes the arcades to the sides of the chancel. The fine hammerbeam roofs are low pitched, with a distinguishing treatment for the shape of the apse. In the nave the trusses are supported by shafts rising from mouldings above the arcades, with their lowest points below the clerestorey and proud from the wall, similar to Holy Trinity Birchfield Road. This particular detail was characteristic of several of Chatwin's other churches, but with so many wonderful features and fittings St Peter and St Paul Aston has been described as the 'mature work of Birmingham's most prolific architect'.[77]

Whilst the arcades with their octagonal piers and clerestorey at St Martin are distinctly Decorated in style, round Transitional or Early English piers are to be found in the arcades of a number of Chatwin's churches, though they alternate between round and octagonal at St Peter and St Paul Aston reflecting a transition between Decorated and Perpendicular.[78] The side aisles at the Catholic Apostolic Church comprise 'passage aisles through the buttresses' of the early Decorated style under Chatwin's usual steep pitched roofs.[79] These are similar in type to those at St Augustine Edgbaston and St James Handsworth. A higher clerestorey at St George Edgbaston and lancet windows is more thirteenth century Early English and parallels have been drawn to Gilbert Scott's All Souls Haley Hill, Halifax.[80] Polygonal eastern apses were favoured as at St Augustine Edgbaston, St Paul Lozells, Christ Church Summerfield[81] and the demolished St Saviour Hockley. This distinguishing feature can also be seen further afield at his St Martin Bedford of 1888.[82] However Chatwin also used three sided apses as west baptistries. Such baptistries became something of a tradition in Birmingham churches, though not all were apsidal.[83] Good examples of Chatwin's apsidal baptistry designs can be seen at St Ambrose Edgbaston and the Catholic Apostolic Church, where Hickman particularly liked the west elevation with the baptistry beneath a window.[84] The west end at St Andrew Bournemouth of 1891 is thus instantly recognisable as Chatwin's work.[85] Although the baptistry at St James Handsworth was not built until 1921, nor that at All Saints Stechford until 1937, both complete Chatwin's earlier designs for these churches.[86] He was indeed capable of achieving great unity in his churches, as is demonstrated in Holy Ascension Mappleborough Green, a large Early English style Warwickshire church, erected in 1888 for Sir John Jaffray. It remains unaltered, still with its original fittings.[87]

The lost St Saviour Hockley of 1874 followed the design of Holy Trinity Birchfield with gables to the side aisles.[88] Double gables to transepts were used in the extensions to Teulon's St John Ladywood in 1881 and can also be seen at St Martin Bedford.[89] Large, sometimes crocketed, pinnacles were often placed to emphasise externally the division between nave and chancel as at St Peter and St Paul Aston

Catholic Apostolic Church, Summer Hill, 1873

Interior of Catholic Apostolic Church

and St Martin. At St Mary Old Swinford the large pinnacles are actually retained from the east end of the Commissioners' type church by Ebbles of 1843.[90] Chatwin added sympathetic gothic eastern extensions to Harvey Eginton's Christ Church Catshill in 1887, and Thomas Rickman's St Barnabas Erdington in 1883, though this latter was seriously damaged by fire in 2007.[91] His north aisle is a seamless addition of 1883 to Frederick Preedy's All Saints King's Heath.[92] He also achieved a masterly unifying effect with his own and previous work at St Bartholomew Edgbaston. The medieval and seventeenth century fabric of this church had undergone several part rebuildings in the earlier nineteenth century, but in 1885–86 Chatwin added a new chancel, chapel, north arcade and clerestorey, followed by an extra south aisle in 1889.[93] It is all in the Perpendicular style, and both this and the similar work at St Mary Moseley, which was continued after his death by his son Philip, overshadow the earlier short towers adding perhaps to a sense of antiquity in these churches.

At St Bartholomew Edgbaston Chatwin's nave columns complement the early nineteenth century work to create a Perpendicular style interior which could easily be mistaken for a prosperous North Midlands medieval church. This contrasts with St Mary Handsworth, where the 1820 work by William Hollins in the nave and aisles was virtually replaced by Chatwin in the Decorated style in the manner of St Martin. The Perpendicular style was also used successfully by Chatwin in the largely brick St Paul Lozells with its striking north west tower and

Church of St Mary, Handsworth. Elevation of proposed alteration, 1875. *Courtesy of Birmingham Archives and Heritage Services (MS 891/83)*

higher stair turret. Perpendicular details are also very convincing at Christ Church Summerfield, where there were ample funds to build a church as a memorial to Reverend George Lea and so stone was used.[94] The unfinished St Peter Handsworth of 1905, is regarded as Chatwin's last church design, but may in fact be by his son, Philip. It is Arts and Crafts Perpendicular and has a massive, if squat, battlemented rectangular tower, which stands over the east end of the nave dwarfing the short chancel with characteristic three sided apse.[95]

Chatwin's interiors vary in their finish. The stone facing at St Peter and St Paul Aston and St Martin is more in keeping with their medieval origins. Red brick is used at St Ambrose Edgbaston and St Paul Lozells, whilst yellow brick is dominant at St John Kidderminster and St Martin Bedford.[96] Hickman considered the Catholic Apostolic Church to show Chatwin 'at his most powerful and his best' having an 'interior of cathedral proportions with heavy brick arches to the aisles on circular Norman columns and clerestorey windows between clustered wall shafts supporting a high arched roof. The west end is particularly successful with a tall archway set in a diapered brick wall leading to a well lit baptistry'.[97] It thus forms a fitting setting for the Greek Orthodox Cathedral today.

The range of fittings and furnishings ascribed to Chatwin is large, and their survival often has a further unifying effect on his interiors. Of particular significance are Chatwin's pews, pulpit, reredos, sedilia and other chancel fittings at St Martin, or his choir stalls with carved biblical figures, pulpit, low chancel screen, floors, sedilia and reredos grouped beneath Hardman's five windows at the magnificent east end of St Peter and St Paul Aston.[98] All these represent Chatwin's work with companies manufacturing stained glass and fittings, of which Hardman is probably the most notable, but others include Boulton of Cheltenham or Bridgeman of Lichfield. Further interiors with noted collections of Chatwin's furnishings can be seen at St Philip Dorridge, Holy Trinity Birchfield and Holy Ascension Mappleborough Green.[99]

Chatwin added a new vestry and organ chamber in 1891, followed by a chancel in 1894, to J. G. Bland's church, St Mary Acock's Green. Work on Bland's design for this church had been undertaken in phases from 1864, but following completion of the nave Chatwin was employed to continue the scheme, although it remains incomplete with the tower, spire and transepts still unbuilt.[100] Indeed a number of Chatwin's schemes remain unfinished. St George Edgbaston, where completed extensions had cost £12,000, never received its planned south tower;[101] St Philip Dorridge has Chatwin's grand stone chancel and vestries of 1896 still attached to the earlier simple lower brick nave of 1878 by E. J. Payne;[102] and the west end of St Peter Handsworth has remained incomplete since 1907, the year of Chatwin's death. Whilst the new chancel at St Mary Old Swinford added almost forty feet to the east end of that church in 1898, it was built with springers for future arcades to be added in the wide box-pewed nave to the west of the chancel arch.[103]

However, the nave was never replaced, although Philip Chatwin was asked to prepare plans in 1910. He did however continue until 1910 with his father's rebuilding of Rickman's work at St Mary Moseley.[104]

Although Chatwin established a considerable reputation for the design of new churches in the gothic style, perhaps his most significant church commission was a comparatively modest extension in a classical style, uncharacteristic in the context of his ecclesiatical work. St Philip's church completed in 1725 had been Thomas Archer's first significant commission. In 1865 Chatwin had been responsible for re-facing the fine baroque tower which, together with its pair of side porches and strong stone detailing, is the focus of this magnificent building. However, the interior of Archer's building was uncompromisingly rectangular with raised galleries on either side, and with only a small apse at the east end to provide space for a simple communion table. Such short chancels were typical of most eighteenth century churches. The spread of the Oxford Movement in the second half of the nineteenth century meant there was a desire to enlarge the chancel with the altar as a focus for worship and to house a large robed choir. It is also probable that improvements at St Philip were driven by an aspiration to support Birmingham's ambition to become a diocese in its own right. Consequently, in 1883 Chatwin was commissioned to prepare plans to re-order the building and extend the chancel, which had been under consideration for some time, but funds to support the work had been lacking.[105] The opportunity to move forward came when Miss Emma Chadwick Villiers Wilkes proposed a tablet and stained glass window in memory of her brother, Arthur Salt Wilkes. Chatwin suggested that a new chancel might provide a fitting setting for this memorial. As the likely cost might have jeopardised the project, the full proposal was eventually established over a series of meetings. Miss Wilkes paid for the construction of a new chancel as well as the extension of the side aisles to form choir and clergy vestries. She further made an anonymous donation for the new east window which was to be the first of the spectacular set of four stained glass windows designed by Sir Edward Burne-Jones and installed between 1885 and 1897.

A stylistically sensitive extension was relatively easy to deal with externally, however it posed difficult design problems for the interior. A classical chancel arch would have been awkward in form and scale; but without one it was not clear how the liturgical importance of the chancel could be properly expressed. Chatwin's elegant solution simply extends the form and height of the flat nave ceiling into the chancel, where it is enriched with elaborate coffer plasterwork. The simple pilasters of Archer's nave arcade contrasted with two columns of a giant Corinthian order at the east end either side of the reredos. Chatwin multiplied the number of these freestanding columns to define and enclose the chancel, using their capitals and entablature to articulate and intensify its spatial qualities. This set piece terminates in a pair of attached columns framing the east window, with the splendid Burne-Jones Ascension.[106]

St Philip's Cathedral, exterior of East End

Chatwin had already established a close working relationship with Burne-Jones and William Morris at St Martin, but he had to proceed cautiously to achieve the full design. One window only had been envisaged in the east end, but its artistic success paved the way for the two surrounding windows to be filled with stained glass. Miss Wilkes agreed to donate funds and was keen that they illustrate her choice of subjects, the Good Shepherd and Christ at the Well. However, Burne-Jones and Morris proposed the Crucifixion, which Morris wished to see treated 'as an event and not mystically: that is with figures of soldiers and the like' and the Nativity. Initially this latter suggestion did not meet with Miss Wilkes's approval, who declared 'I particularly dislike the introduction of cattle in the Nativity ... I wish the Nativity of our Lord and not a cattle show'.[107] An extensive correspondence followed during which Morris asked Chatwin to convey to Miss Wilkes that Burne-Jones was considering his withdrawal from the commission as a result of what he clearly saw as small-minded meddling. However, the cattle were omitted and when the two additional windows were installed in 1888, the triptych was

OPPOSITE   East End of St Philip's Cathedral, with the central window, the Ascension by Edward Burne-Jones, 1885 (inset)

agreed to be a triumph not just for Burne-Jones and Morris, but also the realisation of Chatwin's important architectural set piece. The final window of the set, the imposing Doom at the west end, was not installed until 1897 following public subscription for a memorial to Bishop Bowlby, a former rector. Viewed from the nave through Chatwin's tower arch it is an unforgettable sight. Chatwin's work at St Philip possibly comprises his most memorable ecclesiastical architecture.[108]

In 1869 Chatwin had married Edith Isabel, the second daughter of Edmund Boughton, J. P.[109] After their marriage the Chatwins settled in Court Oak Road Harborne, but shortly after the birth of their eldest son Leslie in 1871, they were persuaded to move to Erdington by his father-in-law, who had just purchased a house there, and wanted his daughter and her young family as neighbours. Chatwin and Edith never really settled in this house, Mount Pleasant, although he improved the property, using for instance the gallery balusters from St Martin on the staircase. After his wife's parents moved to Coventry in 1879, Chatwin wished to move his growing family back to Edgbaston.[110] Their second son Philip had been born in 1873, followed by four daughters, and finally two younger sons, the last born to be in 1887.[111] In November 1880 Chatwin bought Wellington House, 57 Wellington Road, as a large family home. The house has since been demolished. Before the family moved in June 1881 he undertook a number of improvements, not least installing in the dining room some oak cornices said to have been made of Elizabethan woodwork from Kenilworth Castle.[112] Chatwin was to remain at this address until his death, and evidently life there with his wife and children was extremely happy. Philip describes family evenings gathered together with Edith reading stories to the younger children whilst Chatwin worked at his drawing board, occasionally asking for a pause in the reading whilst he concentrated on resolving a difficult architectural problem.[113]

Throughout his adult life Chatwin was expanding his art collection. Inspired by his acquaintance with David Cox, he acquired several of his works along with paintings by H. P. Briggs and Richard Wilson. A noted exception to his reputation never to spend more than £5 on a painting at a sale came in 1887, when he secured a particularly desirable *Still Life* by William Etty.[114] He was highly regarded as one of two customary architect members of Royal Birmingham Society of Artists, and, following the death of J. H. Chamberlain in 1883, became Vice-President until ill health prompted his resignation in 1902.[115] During this period he and Edith entertained many noted artists and visitors to the galleries. He also had a great interest in history and archaeology, which was inherited by his son Philip. Chatwin was a Fellow of the Antiquarian Society of Scotland and a member of several local archaeological societies.[116]

In his professional life, Chatwin was elected a fellow and life member of the Royal Institute of British Architects in 1863.[117] The practice, now J. A. Chatwin and Son, moved to Great Charles Street three years after Chatwin had been joined by Philip in 1897. In his later years Chatwin only occasionally worked in the office, though he continued to prepare designs from home until just before his death.[118] Pevsner describes him as noteworthy 'as a local Birmingham man and founder of a dynasty of Birmingham architects'.[119] Indeed Philip Chatwin continued to practice at Great Charles Street, where the repair of churches remained a specialism. Philip was joined in 1936 as partner by his nephew, Anthony Chatwin, the son of his elder brother Leslie. In the mid 1970s the practice finally moved to George Road, Edgbaston.[120] Amongst many descendants, his great-grandson, Bruce Chatwin, achieved fame in the late twentieth century as a traveller and author.

J. A. Chatwin died aged 77 on Thursday 6 June 1907. The well attended funeral was the following Monday, 10 June, at St Bartholomew Edgbaston.[121] His grave memorial, a stone tomb chest decorated with a foliate cross, is now grade II listed in the churchyard and stands close to one of the many churches he successfully restored and extended.[122]

List of Architectural Works of J. A. Chatwin

J. A. Chatwin (1830–1907) was born in Birmingham and educated at King Edward's School and Samuel Lines's Academy of Arts. After gaining experience as a draftsman for the Birmingham building firm of Branson and Gwyther he was articled to Sir Charles Barry in London. In 1855 he set up in independent practice in Birmingham. In 1897 he took into partnership his son, Philip and the practice became J. A. Chatwin and Son.

WORK IN BIRMINGHAM AND ITS ENVIRONS

PUBLIC

1850 Exhibition hall at Bingley Hall, King Alfred's Place, for Branson and Gwyther [D]

1851 St Silas's National School, Church St, Lozells

1858 St Clement's Church, Nechells Park Rd, Nechells [D]

1858 St Clement's National School, High Park St, Nechells [D]

1859 St Matthew's National School, Lupin St, Duddeston [D]

1860–64 Holy Trinity Church, Birchfield Rd, Handsworth

1861 St John's Infants' Church School, Coplow St, Ladywood [D]

1861 St Anne's National School, Devon St, Duddeston [D]

1861 St Laurence's National School, Dartmouth St, Duddeston [D]

1867 St Mary's Church, Whitehouse Avenue, Aston Brook [D]

1867–68 St Laurence's Church, Dartmouth St, Duddeston [D]

1867–69 St Gabriel's Church, Barn St, Deritend [D]

1868 St Anne's Church, Devon St, Duddeston (unexecuted)

1868–76 St Augustine's Church, Lyttleton Rd, Edgbaston

1868 Bishop Ryder School, Staniforth St [D]

1868 Fire Brigade Headquarters, Little Cannon St [D]

1869 St Paul's School, Legge Lane

1871–74 St Saviour's Church, Bridge St West, Hockley [D]

1872–75 Additions and restoration to St Martin's Church, Bull Ring

1873 St Andrew's Catholic Apostolic Church (now Greek Orthodox Cathedral), Summer Hill Terrace

1875 Organ case for St Nicolas's Church, King's Norton

1876–80 Additions and restoration to St Mary's Church, Hamstead Rd, Handsworth

1878–81 Work to St Silas's Church, Church St, Lozells

1879–1907 Additions and restoration to St Peter and St Paul's Church, Witton Rd, Aston (with Philip Chatwin from 1897)

1880 St Paul's Church, Lozells Rd

1881 Addition to Edgbaston Proprietory School, Five Ways, Edgbaston for King Edward VI School [D]

1881 Addition to St John's Church, Monument Rd, Ladywood

1881–83 King Edward's Grammar School for Boys, Aston

1883 Addition to St Barnabas' Church, High St, Erdington [Damaged in fire, 2007]

1883 Addition to All Saints' Church, King's Heath

1883 Gymnasium for King Edward VI School, New St [D]

1883–84 Additions and Alterations to St Philip's Church (now Cathedral)

1883–85 Christ Church, Summerfield Crescent, Edgbaston

1883–86 Additions to Edgbaston College for Girls, 31 Calthorpe Rd, Edgbaston

1884–85 Addition to St George's Church, Edgbaston

1885–89 Additions and restoration to St Bartholomew's Church, Edgbaston

1886–97 Additions and restoration to St Mary's Church, Moseley, (with Philip Chatwin from 1897)

1887 Additions to St John's Church, Perry Barr

1887–88 St Mary's Church, Bearwood, Sandwell

1890 St Mark's Church, Washwood Heath

1890 St James' Church, Frederick Rd, Aston [D]

1890 White Swan Cellars, Constitution Hill.

1891–94 Additions to St Mary's Church, Acock's Green

1894 Tower added to Bishop Ryder Memorial Church, Gosta Green

1894–95 Additions to St James' Church, Crocketts Rd, Handsworth

1895 Additions to St Michael's Church, Boldmere, Sutton Coldfield

1895–96 King Edward VI School for Girls, New St [D]

1897–98 St Mary and St Ambrose's Church, Pershore Rd, Edgbaston

1897–98 All Saints' Church, Stechford

1899 Public Hall, Poplar Rd, Solihull

1905 St Peter's Church, Grove Lane, Handsworth

COMMERCIAL

1862–64 Joint Stock Bank, 4 Temple Row West

1865 Great Western Hotel, Colmore Row [D]

c1865 Engine House for appliances, Alliance Fire Insurance Co., Temple Row [D]

1870 Lloyd's Bank Offices, Colmore Row [D]

1874 Lloyd's Bank, High Street Deritend

1875 Works to Grand Hotel, Colmore Row

1875 Lloyd's Bank, Aston Brook [D]

1877 Works to Exchange Building, Stephenson Place

1877–78 Commercial premises at 135 Edmund St for J. D. Goodman [D]

1878 Designs for an Aquarium, New St (unexecuted)

1898 Rebuilding of Hen and Chickens Hotel, New St [D]

1898 Commercial premises at 20–26 Albert St

1899 Additions to Lloyd's Bank, Great Hampton St

Undated

Lloyd's Bank, Bristol St [D]

Lloyd's Bank, Dudley Rd [D]

Lloyd's Bank, Handsworth

Lloyd's Bank, Harborne

Lloyd's Bank, Jamaica Row [D]

Lloyd's Bank, Moseley Rd, Highgate [D]

Lloyd's Bank, New St [D]

Lloyd's Bank, Stirchley

DOMESTIC

1848/50 Two houses for J. D. Goodman, 38–9 Frederick St, Edgbaston [now Frederick Rd]
    for Branson and Gwyther

1851 House for George Branson at 89 Harborne Rd

1856 House for John Leonard, Hagley Rd

1857–58 Estate layout and various houses in Rotton Park, Edgbaston for Joseph Gillott
    (largely unexecuted)

1858 House for Dr W. Fletcher, Acock's Green

1859 Pair of houses, 2–3 Augustus Rd, Edgbaston [D]

1861 Knutsford Lodge, 25 Somerset Road, Edgbaston

1870 Berry Hall, Solihull for Joseph Gillot; 1884 Lodge, Marsh Lane [Hall D]

1878–79 Lench's Trust Almshouses, Conybere St

1880 Alterations and extensions to Wellington House, 57 Wellington Rd, Edgbaston [D]

WORK OUTSIDE BIRMINGHAM

PUBLIC

1851–52 Work on Palace of Westminster for Sir Charles Barry

1862 and 1877 Restoration of St Michael's Church, Waddesdon, Buckinghamshire

1870 Work at Uppingham School, Rutland

1879 Restoration to All Saints' Church, Preston Bagot, Warwickshire

1879–82 and 1900 Solihull Grammar School, Warwick Road, Solihull

1880 Church and School, Catherine-de-Barnes, Solihull for the Gillott family

1880 Design for a Glass Palace, India (unexecuted)

1881 Restoration to St Michael's Church, Penkridge, Staffordshire

1883–85 Art Gallery, Lichfield St, Wolverhampton

1885 Restoration to St Michael's Church, Salwarpe, Worcestershire

1887–88 Restoration to All Saints' Church, Church Lench, Worcestershire

1888 Holy Ascension Church, Mappleborough Green, Warwickshire for Sir John Jaffray

1888–89 St Martin's Church, Clapham Rd, Bedford

1888–89 St Michael's Church and lychgate, Underwood, Nottinghamshire for Earl Powys
   of Beauvale

1891 St Andrew's Church, Bennett Rd, Charminster, Bournemouth

1891–96 Restoration of St Mary's Church, Warwick

1892–95 Restoration of St Mary's Church, Kidderminster

1893–94 and 1902 Additions to St John's Church, Bewdley Rd, Kidderminster,

1896–97 Additions to St Philip's Church, Dorridge

1898 Additions to St Mary's Church, Old Swinford, Stourbridge, Dudley

1899 Additions to St John, St Lawrence and St Anne's Church, Knowle

1901 Additions to St Thomas' Church, High St, Dudley (unexecuted)

COMMERCIAL

1876 Lloyd's Bank, Hagley Street, Halesowen, Dudley

1877 Lloyd's Bank, Poplar Rd, Solihull

1878 Lloyd's Bank, Dudley St, Wolverhampton

1880 Compton and Evans' Bank, Irongate, Derby

1884–85 Bucks and Oxon Union Bank, High St, Hemel Hempstead

1885 Lloyd's Bank Head Office, Lombard St, London [D]

1892 Lloyd's Bank, Belle Vue Terrace, Malvern, Worcestershire

1892 Lloyd's Bank, Victoria Square, Droitwich, Worcestershire

1892 Alterations to Lloyd's Bank, King St, Carmarthen, Dyfed

1897 Lloyd's Bank, High St, Cardiff

1899 Lloyd's Bank, Bridge St, Stratford-upon-Avon, Warwickshire

1903 Lloyd's Bank, High St, Leicester

1904 Lloyd's Bank, The Bridge, Walsall

Undated

Lloyd's Bank, Chatham, Kent

Facade for Lloyd's Bank, Ironbridge, Shropshire

Lloyd's Bank, Netherton, Dudley [D]

Lloyd's Bank, Redditch, Worcestershire [D]

Lloyd's Bank, Rye, East Sussex

Lloyd's Bank Shrewsbury

Lloyd's Bank, Smethwick, Sandwell

Lloyd's Bank, West Bromwich

DOMESTIC

1854–55 Houses for Branson and Gwyther at Gloddaeth Crescent, Llandudno, Clwyd

1857 House for W. Taylor, Llandudno, Clwyd

1870 Catshill Vicarage, Bromsgrove, Worcestershire

1880–90 House at Upper Skilts, Mappleborough Green for Sir John Jaffray

1890–95 Additions to The Firs, College Grove, Malvern, Worcestershire

---

NOTES

[1] A. Foster, *Pevsner Architectural Guides: Birmingham* (New Haven and London, 2005), p. 41.

[2] P. B. Chatwin, *Life story of J. A. Chatwin 1830–1907* (Oxford, 1952), p. 5. In addition much vital research on J. A. Chatwin has been undertaken by his great grandson, John Chatwin, himself a qualified architect in the family tradition. The author is most grateful to him for making his working notes freely available in order to write this chapter. Those sections which rely heavily on his research are acknowledged below. The archival material relating to J. A. Chatwin in public collections is limited. Birmingham Central Library, Archives and Heritage Services hold some of Chatwin's plans for schools in MS 1446 'Birmingham School Building Plans' and a few works by him are to be found in MS 891 'Plans of P. B. Chatwin, Architect'. The Building Registers for Birmingham and parishes later incorporated into Birmingham, which date from the late 1870s onwards are valuable for dating much of J. A. Chatwin's work.

[3] John Chatwin, Notes and family tree; N. Shakespeare, *Bruce Chatwin* (1999), p. 14

[4] *Chatwin*, p. 5.

[5] *Ibid*, pp. 5–6.

[6] John Chatwin, Notes.

[7] *Chatwin*, p. 7.

[8] *Ibid*, p. 8.

[9] 'Mr J. A. Chatwin F.S.A. (Scot), F.R.I.B.A.' *Edgbastonia*, 9, no. 9 (1889), p. 34.

[10] John Chatwin, Notes; see also B. Ainsworth, 'Chatwin's Exhibition Hall', *Birmingham Historian* No 27, Winter 2005, pp. 20–26.

[11] *Chatwin*, p. 16.

[12] *Ibid*, p. 15.

[13] Andy Foster personal communication; D. J. Watkin, 'Holford, Vulliamy and the Sources for Dorchester House' in *Influences in Victorian Art and Architecture*, ed. by S. MacReady and F. H. Thompson, Society of Antiquaries of London Occasional Paper (New Series) VII, (1985), pp. 81–82.

[14] Nikolaus Pevsner, *An Outline of European Architecture* (Harmondsworth, 1963), p. 381.

[15] Alexandra Wedgwood, 'The Early Years' in *Pugin: A Gothic Passion* ed. by P. Atterbury and C. Wainwright (New Haven and London, 1994) p. 32.

[16] Pevsner, *European Architecture*, p. 382. It is interesting to note in this context that in 1823 Barry did not consider his church of St Peter, Brighton to be a complete Gothic building as it lacked a spire.

[17] *Edgbastonia*, 1889, p. 34.

[18] *Chatwin*, p. 44.

[19] *Ibid*, p. 25.

[20] *Ibid*, p. 21–24.

[21] *Ibid*, p. 47.

[22] J. Mckenna, *Birmingham: The Building of a City* (Birmingham, 2005), p. 54.

[23] John Chatwin, Notes

[24] Goodman was the great uncle of Cecily Couchman who married Philip Chatwin in 1906.

[25] A. Foster, *Pevsner Architectural Guides: Birmingham* (New Haven and London, 2005), p. 238; *Chatwin*, p. 9; List Description.

[26] *Chatwin*, p. 20; Birmingham Central Library, Archives and Heritage Services (hereafter BCA AHS) MS 891/51

[27] Nikolaus Pevsner, *The Buildings of England: Staffordshire* (Harmondsworth, 1974) p. 310: List Description.

[28] Foster, *Birmingham*, p. 252; List Description.

[29] BCL AHS, Cotton Collection, vol 58; G. Tyack, *Warwickshire Country Houses* (Chichester, 1994), p. 264.

[30] BCL AHS, Birmingham Building Register, app. no. 1308 12 August 1878; BCL AHS, ZZ329 Lench's Trust Minutes; Foster, *Birmingham*, p. 195; List Description.

[31] *Ibid*, p. 100.

[32] *Ibid*, p. 98.

[33] Obituary, *Birmingham Daily Post*, June 7, 1907; see also obituaries *Building News*, 92, No 2736, 14 June 1907, p. 818, *Birmingham Biography*, Vol 6, 1906–09, containing Obituary, *Evening Despatch*, 7 June 1907, p. 93, Obituary, *Birmingham Weekly Mercury*, 15 June 1907, p. 98, and Obituary, *Gazette and Express*, 8 June 1907, p. 94.

[34] BCL AHS, Birmingham Building Register app. no. 7263 5 March 1890; Foster, Birmingham, p. 84, p. 174; Obituary in *The Builder*, 92, 15 June 1907.

[35] John Chatwin notes: BCL, AHS MS 1446/14 and 1446/39.

[36] *Chatwin*, p. 40.

[37] BCL AHS, Birmingham Building Register app. no. 5390 5 March 1887.

[38] Nikolaus Pevsner and Alexandra Wedgwood, *The Buildings of England: Warwickshire* (Harmondsworth, 1966) p. 40; List Description.

[39] R. Cary Gilson, 'The Schools of King Edward VI' in *Birmingham Institutions*, ed. by J. H. Muirhead (Birmingham, 1911), p. 550; see also Rachel Waterhouse, *King Edward's High School for Girls Birmingham 1883–1983* (1983).

[40] BCL AHS, Aston Building Register, app. no. 1024, 8 November 1881.

[41] *Chatwin*, p. 45; BCA AHS MS 891/23.

[42] *Chatwin*, p. 42.

[43] Pevsner, *Staffordshire*, p. 317; List Description.

[44] S. Bates, *Solihull: A Pictorial History* (Chichester, 1991), fig 35; see also S. Bates, *Solihull Past* (Chichester, 2001), and S.Bates *Greater Solihull* (Stroud, 1999).

[45] D. Hickman, *Birmingham* (1970), p. 33.

[46] B. Little, *Birmingham Buildings: The Architectural Story of a Midland City* (Newton Abbot, 1971), p. 27.

[47] Foster, *Birmingham*, p. 120.

[48] List Description.

[49] *Chatwin*, p. 43; BCA AHS MS 891/130; 891/146; 891/157.

[50] *Chatwin*, p. 44.

[51] J. Newman, *Buildings of Wales: Glamorgan* (1995), p. 126.

[52] Alan Brooks and Nikolaus Pevsner, *Pevsner Buildings of England: Worcestershire* (New Haven and London, 2007).

p. 469; List Description.

[53] Nikolaus Pevsner, *The Buildings of England: Leicestershire and Rutland* (Harmondsworth, 1960), p. 156; Foster, *Birmingham*, p. 215.

[54] Foster, *Birmingham*, p. 174, p. 183; BCA AHS, Birmingham Building Register app. no. 14824 4 May 1899.

[55] Bates, *Solihull: Pictorial History*, fig 35.

[56] BCL AHS, MS891/109; J. Hunt, *A History of Halesowen* (Chichester, 2004); List Description

[57] List Description

[58] Little, *Birmingham Buildings*, p. 27

[59] Pevsner and Wedgwood, *Warwickshire*, p. 57, p. 106, p. 109, p. 179.

[60] *Ibid*, p. 130; *Chatwin*, p. 26; BCL AHS, NS 891/108.

[61] Foster, *Birmingham*, p. 19.

[62] Pevsner and Wedgwood, *Warwickshire*, p. 182; List Description.

[63] Foster, *Birmingham*, p. 19.

[64] *Ibid*, p. 239; *Chatwin*, p. 26; List Description; BCL AHS, MS 891/60–66.

[65] *Edgbastonia*, 1889, p. 34.

[66] Foster, *Birmingham*, p. 19.

[67] List Description; *Worcestershire*, pp. 365–67.

[68] BCL AHS, Birmingham Building Register, app. no. 15 May 1884.

[69] Digital Handsworth; Obituary, *The Builder*, 92, 1907; *Worcestershire*, p. 401; K. Simpson, 'Anglican Church Extension in and around Nineteenth Century Kidderminster' in *Transactions of the Worcestershire Archaeological Society* (Third series), vol 17 (2000), pp. 253–78.

[70] John Chatwin, Notes.

[71] Foster, *Birmingham*, p. 53.

[72] *Chatwin*, p. 45.

[73] Foster, *Birmingham*, p. 54

[74] P. Howell and I. Sutton, *The Faber Guide to Victorian Churches* (1989), p. 12.

[75] Obituary, *Birmingham Daily Post*, 1907; see also W. Eliot, *The Parish Church of Aston-juxta-Birmingham: its Ancient History and Modern Restoration* (Birmingham, 1889).

[76] Foster, *Birmingham*, p. 259; BCL AHS, MS 891/5–6.

[77] Howell and Sutton, *Victorian Churches*, p. 12.

[78] *Ibid*, p. 12.

[79] Hickman, *Birmingham*, p. 36.

[80] Foster, *Birmingham*, p. 224.

[81] BCL AHS, Birmingham Building Register, app. no. 3898, 15 November 1883.

[82] List Descriptions; Church Plans Online; Nikolaus Pevsner, *The Buildings of England: Bedfordshire, Huntingdon and Peterborough* (Harmondsworth, 1968), p. 49.

[83] Foster, *Birmingham*, p. 289.

[84] BCL AHS MS 1047/1–13 Architectural Drawings of the Catholic Apostolic Church, Summer Hill, Birmingham; MS 891/56–59; Hickman, *Birmingham*, p. 36.

[85] Nikolaus Pevsner, *The Buildings of England: Hampshire and the Isle of Wight* (Harmondsworth, 1967), p. 121.

[86] Pevsner and Wedgwood, *Warwickshire*, p. 181, p. 212.

[87] *Ibid*, pp. 347–48; List Description.

[88] Pevsner and Wedgwood, *Warwickshire*, p. 138.

[89] List Description; Pevsner, *Bedfordshire*, p. 49.

[90] R. Peacock, *St Mary's Old Swinford: A Victorian Church* (Stourbridge, 2003), p. 40; Worcs Record Office, Parochial box BA3090/1 ref 728 Old Swinford faculty 14 August 1896; *Dudley Herald*, 28 May 1898.

[91] Brooks and Pevsner, *Worcestershire*, pp. 216–17; Pevsner and Wedgwood, *Warwickshire*, p. 176.

[92] Pevsner and Wedgwood, *Warwickshire*, p. 187.

[93] BCL AHS, Birmingham Building Register, app. no.4700, 31 August 1885; Foster, *Birmingham*, p. 231.

[94] List Description; obituary, *The Builder*, 1907.

[95] BCL AHS, Handsworth Building Register app. no. 4040, 4 July 1905; Pevsner and Wedgwood, *Warwickshire*, pp. 181–82; List Description.

[96] List Description; Pevsner, *Bedfordshire*, p. 49.

[97] Hickman, *Birmingham*, p. 36; BCL AHS, MS 1047/1–13.

[98] Foster, *Birmingham*, pp. 279–81.

[99] List Descriptions.

[100] Pevsner and Wedgwood, *Birmingham*, p. 145.

[101] Obituary, *The Builder*, 1907.

[102] Pevsner and Wedgwood, *Warwickshire*, p. 145.

[103] Peacock, *St Mary's Old Swinford*, p. 40.

[104] Pevsner and Wedgwood, *Warwickshire*, p. 192; BCL AHS, MS 891/107.

[105] BCL AHS, Birmingham Building Register, app. no. 3279 27 June 1883.
[106] John Chatwin, Notes; *Chatwin*; pp. 34–39; BCL AHS MS 891/30–32.
[107] *Ibid*; J. Hunt, 'Miss Wilkes's Windows', *Birmingham Historian*, 9, 1993, p. 15.
[108] *Ibid*.
[109] *Edgbastonia*, 1889, p. 35.
[110] *Chatwin*, p. 45.
[111] John Chatwin, Notes.
[112] *Chatwin*, p. 46.
[113] *Ibid*, pp. 46–47.
[114] *Ibid*, pp. 47–50.
[115] *Ibid*, p. 50; *Edgbastonia*, 1889, p. 35.
[116] *Edgbastonia*, 1889, p. 35.
[117] *Ibid*.
[118] *Chatwin*, p. 52.
[119] Pevsner and Wedgwood, *Warwickshire*, p. 47.
[120] Chatwin, Notes.
[121] Obituary, *Birmingham Dispatch*.
[122] List Description.

6 H. R. Yeoville Thomason

BARBARA SHACKLEY

In the latter half of the nineteenth century, Henry Richard Yeoville Thomason (1826–1901) was one of the most important architects in Birmingham. Although, at first, Thomason's family connections provided him with regular work in the form of house commissions, this was soon augmented, and superseded, by his own efforts. His position as manager of the Council's Architect's department gave him a unique insight into the needs and demands of the time. As a hard working and conscientious officer, he won the competition to build the prestigious new Civic Centre, even though his original plans for the Council House were drastically altered.

He was trained by Charles Edge, and used classical styles, showing a preference for the Renaissance and Italianate, especially when designing for civic, commercial and domestic buildings and, wherever possible, with stone and carved decoration. He used gothic styles and brick for industrial, religious and educational buildings.

In 1848 when Henry Richard Yeoville Thomason began his career at the age of twenty two, Birmingham would have been unrecognisable, from the city that we know today. The Town Hall, built to house the Triennial Music festival, was hardly completed; the Council House, the Art Gallery and Museum, the Birmingham Public Library and all civic open spaces with statuary and fountains were nonexistent. There were few school buildings and most of the inner city was dominated by squalid, congested and unhealthy dwellings. Although by 1838, Birmingham had become a Municipal Corporation, the old institutions still continued, the Street Commissioners were not abolished until 1851 and a High Bailiff was elected as late as 1854. Non-conformist preachers such as George Dawson, began to

Yeoville Thomason, from *Edgbastonia* June 1884.
Courtesy of Birmingham Archives and Heritage Services

teach what became known as the 'Civic Gospel'. They preached that Christ would bless those who supported a municipal policy which helped the poor and stimulated the love of art and learning in the town; and that Birmingham should have wide, beautiful, tree-lined roads and open spaces similar to those in Paris. It was not until Joseph Chamberlain became a councillor in 1869 and Mayor in 1873–76, that any ameliorating action was taken. Chamberlain municipalized gas and water, and then developed council buildings, schools, and libraries. In 1878, Birmingham's first municipal Improvement Scheme in Corporation Street was followed by a second in John Bright Street.

Thomason, finding himself in the centre of all this activity, took advantage of these opportunities and developed a successful practice. A contemporary description of Thomason noted that he was 'unobtrusive and retiring in his manner, unassuming, modest, friendly and sincere. He talks about plans in a practicable way, discussing them rather than enforcing his own views and consequently he is popular amongst his profession'.[1]

Thomason's father and grandfather were from an old established Birmingham family and although Thomason was born in Edinburgh, it was in Birmingham that he was educated, trained and practised as an architect. His grandfather, Sir Edward Thomason, (1769–1849) was a wealthy industrialist with a manufactory in Church Street. He had been apprenticed to Matthew Boulton, and had inherited his father's gilt and plated button business at the age of twenty one and eventually became a famous medal maker.[2] Sir Edward had married Phillis Bown Glover, daughter of Samuel Glover, a successful merchant and iron worker of Great Charles Street and Abercarn, Monmouthshire and their only child was Thomason's father, Henry Botfield Thomason (1802–43). Henry eventually lived at Mathon Lodge, Worcestershire, and remained unmarried until 1838, when he married Jane Price Pinhorn who was less than 20 years old.[3] However, prior to marriage he had a long liaison with Elizabeth Yardley with whom he had five children. Henry Botfield died at the age of forty one in 1843,[4] six years before his father. This event could have accounted for the closure of the manufactory around 1845.

Henry's mother, Elizabeth Yardley, was born in 1798 to Richard and Mary Yardley, and remained a single women all of her life. She had five children, (probably all by Henry Botfield Thomason,) three daughters and two sons born between 1824 and 1835. They were all baptised in 1836 at St Martin's, Birmingham, under the name of Yeoville Yardley.[5] In the 1841 census, Elizabeth Yeoville was described as independent, living with five children at 262, Watery Lane, Bordesley, where Henry, although only 15, is described as having an office. Although never marrying, in the 1851 census, Elizabeth Thomason was described as a widow with four children, living at 16, Spring Hill Terrace, where Henry and his younger brother George were both described as 'architects with offices at home'.[6] This somewhat irregular background never seemed a hindrance to Thomason's career as an architect in Birmingham.

After a private education, in 1841 at the age of fifteen, Thomason was articled to the leading Birmingham architect, Charles Edge. Edge was responsible for designing the first Market Hall and the extension to the Town Hall in the 1840s. Thomason helped to plan street improvements in the vicinity of the Town Hall and in 1844 he worked on the Carr's Lane Schools. Sometime during this period he travelled in Europe making a study of architecture in Italy. His career began in 1848, when at the age of twenty two, he began to lease several plots on the Calthorpe Estate. In 1854, he worked on 15–16, Broad Street designing alterations to the brass and iron bedstead manufacturers of Messenger and Sons, and also at R. C. Hussey's Office in London It was in this year, at the age of twenty eight, that Thomason became manager of the architect's department in the Borough Surveyor's Office, under Mr Pigott Smith, and also set up practice on his own at Wellington Chambers, 40 Bennett's Hill, near to Edge's Office.[7] At first he practised as H. R. Yeoville, but by 1860, he was using his full name Yeoville Thomason, and in 1862, he became a Fellow of the Royal Institute of British Architects.[8] George Yeoville, his brother, although never described as a partner, also worked as an architect at Wellington Chambers in 1864. Cooper Whitwell became Thomason's partner from 1867 until his retirement.

In 1863, Thomason married Harriet, the twenty five year old, youngest child of the large family of Abel and Rachael Rollason of Shepherd's Green House, Erdington. This house still survives.[9] Abel, a Congregationist, was a well established metal roller and owned a mill on the River Tame at Bromford. Harriet and Henry made their family home in Avondale, 4 Ampton Road in 1864 and by 1881 there were three children; Florence, fifteen years, Edith thirteen years, and Philip eleven years.[10]

For the first years of his career, Thomason worked mainly on domestic commissions, building and extending houses and working as a speculative architect on the Calthorpe Estate.[11] From around 1853, it was Thomason who introduced the Lombardic Romanesque style in brick to Edgbaston. He leased sites on Pakenham, Ampton and Arthur Roads. The large, red brick dwelling with steep gables, barge boards and a strong geometric brick design, at No. 4, Arthur Road, now the Calthorpe Clinic, is almost certainly by Thomason. By 1860, he had designed No. 10, Ampton Road, a robust red brick palazzo with round-arched windows, and had bought leases in Gough Road and Hagley Road. In Wheeleys Road, family members commissioned houses, numbers 57–64, classical and stuccoed contrasted with numbers 65–66, built in Lombardic red and blue patterned brick. Thomason was probably also responsible for a similar surviving pair in Charlotte Road.[12]

Altogether, thirteen plans for domestic dwellings in Birmingham survive. Three are outside Birmingham for wealthy established Birmingham clients. For

4 Arthur Road, Edgbaston, *c.* 1853

example, a large double fronted villa with two gables and decorative barge-boards, now the Vicarage in Sherbourne, (1860–63) was built for Miss Ryland, the Birmingham heiress.[13]

For Mr Harwood at Victoria Road, Aston Park, in 1862, Thomason designed a house of two bays, two floors and an attic. It was long and narrow with a parlour, sitting room, (no dining room), kitchen and service area, four bedrooms on the first floor and two bedrooms in the attic. There was only one w.c. for the whole household and no bathroom.[14] The alteration of Fox Hollies Hall, Hall Green (now demolished), situated on an ancient site and purchased by Zaccheus Walker was another important project. In 1869 Thomason was employed to modernise the old building and make considerable additions, including that of a large gallery to contain a valuable collection of paintings. An illustration of the rear view of the hall survives as does a plan of the rear elevation. A three storied, brick house of four bays had tall decorative chimneys, a two storey double bay window and an Italianate tower of five floors. The Art Gallery extension had five bays with five long windows.[15] The grounds surrounding the Hall, although not extensive, contained fine old timber and shrubs. This building is now demolished and the whole estate developed for council housing.

Thomason designed a house for Thomas Padmore, the billiard table maker, at Church Road, Moseley in 1870. This was a double fronted house of three bays with two storeys and attic, had two Jacobean type gables with a decorative balustrade at cornice level. It had an imposing front door with steps and a double storied bay window on the right side of the house. There were three reception rooms, a large service area with a privy, a yard but no coach house, four bedrooms, two dressing rooms, a w.c. and a bath room. Also, there were two bedrooms in the attic.[16] A house for John Feeney, on Hagley Road, was of three bays with two Jacobean gables and a front door of style. This design was used by a Mr. Wilson for four houses in Wheeleys Road.[17] No. 79, Hallfield House, formerly Convent of the Holy Child, now Priory School, was built for Samuel Messenger, a Broad Street lamp manufacturer, in the 1830s and was probably re-modelled by Thomason in the 1860s.

His first big public commission was the Hebrew Synagogue, Singer's Hill, on Blucher and Ellis Streets, built between 1854 and 1858 in a restrained Italianate

Front elevation, Singer's Hill Synagogue, 1854

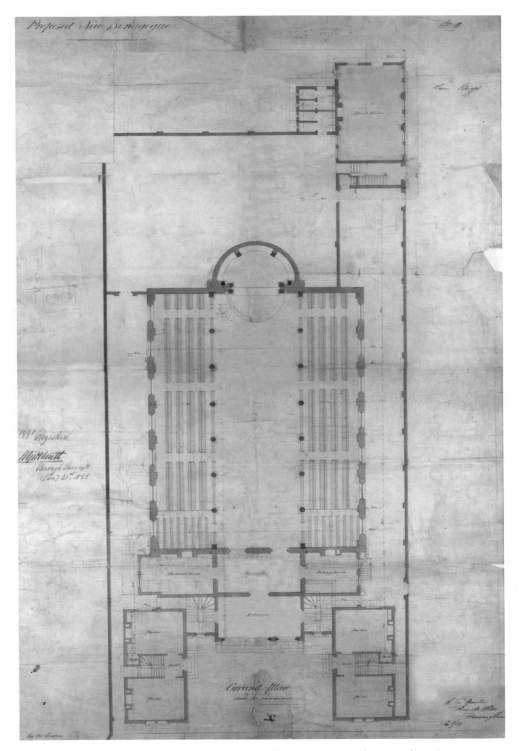

Singer's Hill Synagogue. Plan 1854. *Courtesy of Birmingham Archives and Heritage Services, (MS 1460/5/11)*

style with Renaissance and Romanesque references. This was situated near to the British School, the first Birmingham non-conformist school in Severn Street part of which was also constructed by Thomason in 1867. The Synagogue, costing £9,363 accommodated a congregation of one thousand people and was built by Samuel Briggs in red brick with dark stone dressings. It had paired round headed windows, a big bracket cornice and an elegant portico; three slender arches and a rose window dominated the central triangular pediment recessed behind two projecting wings which formed a courtyard in front. In 1937, the whole of this gable wall was rebuilt and moved forwards one bay by Harry Weedon, to increase the seating capacity. Oscar Deutsch, for whom Weedon designed Odeon Cinemas, was President of the Synagogue at this time. The side elevations had two tiers of big round headed windows. The round headed doorways with leaded hoods which serve these wings were added by Cotton, Ballard and Blow in 1957–59.

The interior of the synagogue, of six bay arcades with Corinthian columns above the galleries had square piers with Byzantine leaf capitals below. The barrel roof had ornamented ribs and a vaulted, apsed east end containing the modern Ark. The galleries were reconstructed and the ground floor seating re-done by Weedon in 1937. The thirty six decorative gasoliers converted to electricity in 1904, were the original cast and gilded lights. The original windows of pale blue, red and yellow stained glass were replaced in the 1950s–70s by pictorial styled stained glass windows, by Hardman's Studios. At the east end, Thomason's school hall of 1862 was reconstructed as a Social Centre in 1934 by John Goodman, who also re-fitted Thomason's 1884 Council Room in a 30s style. This building is now listed Grade II* and is considered by the Jewish community as the oldest functioning 'cathedral synagogue' in the country.[18] The falling congregation has given rise to anxiety about the future of the building.

Thomason's career as an architect of public buildings now accelerated. In 1859, Thomason began the design of the Temperance Society's Hall in Temple Street inspired by Joseph Sturge, the Quaker philanthropist. In a classical style, it cost £2,300, had a square plan and held eight hundred people and had an elliptical shaped platform with excellent acoustics, for orchestral use. It was built of white Rugby brick with Bath stone dressings, round windows, bold key stones and had a heavy string course with a pronounced cornice surmounted by an ornate balustrade and decorative urns. Two storey windows were set in shallow relieving arches. In 1900, the front elevation was altered by Ewen Harper and again in 1931 by Charles Bateman.[19] This is now the headquarters of the Birmingham Law Society.

An obituary of Thomason states that the Aston Union Buildings were among his more important work and indeed he was involved with these designs for the rest of his career, his partners C. Whitwell & Son taking over designs after his retirement.[20]

Temperance Society's Hall, Temple Street, from *The Builder* 24 March 1860. *Courtesy of Birmingham Central Library*

In the 1860s, Aston Union decided that the existing workhouse in Erdington was too small and a ten acre site was purchased at Gravelly Hill for the new workhouse to be built in several phases. The second phase, completed in 1871 was the most important, costing £35,000. Thomason used a Gothic style with classical details, the design of the buildings being typical of workhouses of the era. Built of red brick with stone dressings, blue brick plinths and bands, it had polychromatic arches. The ensemble was made up of the Gate House, 300 feet in length, the Main

Former Aston Union Workhouse, Gravelly Hill, main block, 1871. *Photo: BS*

Building of three storeys with a central spired tower and an Infirmary. On the main gable was the inscription, 'Aston Union, This Memorial Stone was laid by Thomas Colmore Esquire, Chairman of the Board of Guardians AD 1869, Yeoville Thomason Architect, Jeffrey Pritchard, Builders'.[21] In 1909, Aston Board of Guardians amalgamated with Birmingham to form the Greater Birmingham Union.[22] This building became the Highcroft Hospital, Erdington. The Gatehouse range and the Main Building were listed Grade II in 1999 and were restored and converted into apartments by George Wimpey West Midlands Ltd. The other buildings have been demolished and the land developed for housing.

At the same time a much more luxurious building was being designed by Thomason. The Union Club, the first clubhouse in Birmingham, was selected by an open architectural competition, and built on the corner of Colmore Row and Newhall Hill, between 1868 and 1869. It was to form part of the first instalment of the proposed improvements in Colmore Row. Costing £16,000 and this time built in his favourite Italianate style, the stone front elevation, on two streets, was

Former Union Club, 1868–69

designed in two storeys. Massive balustrades, rusticated stonework, square headed windows, boldly carved keystones, columns with rich Corinthian capitals, balconies, friezes of carved foliage with shields, and armorial bearings including that of Mr Colmore the landlord, were all features of the design.[23] He altered it and rebuilt the facades in 1885 to match the new street line. This Grade II listed building is considered by many critics to be Thomason's most successful design. Two additional storeys were added in 1988 and the building is now in commercial use.

In the High Street Smethwick, the library of 1866–67, built as the Public Hall, was designed by Thomason; it has lost its central porch and, according to Pevsner, was in very poor Gothic.[24] However, in 1871, Thomason was fortunate to have the opportunity to produce his 'chef d'oeuvre', designing the Municipal Buildings now known as the Council House. Between 1874 and 1884 he was almost continuously engaged in the construction of a series of major important civic buildings of the Council House, the Art Gallery and the Gas Department offices. The site had been acquired in 1853, but the 'economists', one section of the Liberal Party, had dominated decisions until 1869, when with the election to the Council, Joseph Chamberlain became the leader of the 'progressives' and introduced social reform.

The competition for the Birmingham Assize Courts, and Corporation Build-ings was announced in February 1871. The seven architects entering from Birmingham included Yeoville Thomason, W. H. Ward, Edward Holmes, Bateman and Carver, Thomas Naden, F. B. Osborne, and C. A. Edge. Of other plans sub-mitted, nine were from London and two were each from Liverpool, Flint, Man-chester, Leicester, Plymouth and Nottingham, with one from Belfast. There were therefore a total of twenty nine entrants.[25] The *Building News* queried why there were only twenty nine sets of drawings submitted whereas forty sets were sub-mitted to the Town Hall competition in West Bromwich.[26]

The building, to be erected at a cost of £120,000 close to the Town Hall, was in two parts, firstly, the Law Courts and Judge's Lodgings and secondly the Munici-pal Buildings.[27] Alfred Waterhouse, having recently completed the designs for the much acclaimed gothic Manchester Town Hall, accepted the invitation to judge the competition. By 18 March, twenty nine designs had been submitted, seventeen in a gothic style, eleven in a classical style and one in a renaissance style. Water-house examined the plans on the 20 to 22 March 1871, each identified by a motto or sign. If the architect who won was employed by the Council, the premium (that is the prize), was to be part of his commission. The plans were first exhibited for the members of the Council, Justices of the Peace and the Press and the following week for the public. Before the results had been published the *Birmingham Daily Post* wrote, 'none of the designs are of a sufficiently meritorious character to justify their creation'. Both *The Architect* and the *Building News* were critical of these newspaper reports — 'we object to "penny a liners" criticising architectural competitions'.[28] Thomas Charles Sorby of Brunswick Square complained in an article in the *Birmingham Morning News* that one architect had unfairly sent all the members of the Corporation lithographed copies of his design. In April 1871, the *Building News* stated that authorship of the designs had been known since the beginning of the competition. It was believed that the mottoes *Perseverentes* and *Forum* were those of local architects and this indeed proved to be correct. One plan not having a motto, referred to as No. 9, was disqualified as it had no motto and did not use the designated site.[29] However, Waterhouse who thought the plans of No. 9 which were classical, 'most masterly and eminently suited to require-ments and not a copy of an existing building' recommended that the committee should attempt to acquire the drawings.

On the 8 May, Waterhouse announced the results of the competition to the Estates and Building Sub-Committee. *Maltese Cross*, a gothic design was first and was to win a £200 premium, *Perseverentes*, a renaissance design was second with a £100 premium and *Forum* another gothic design was third with a £50 premium. On the 12 June, the committee received a request from *Perseverentes* to be allowed to submit a model of his proposal 'in further explanation of the elevation'. The Town Clerk said that this was an unorthodox idea.[30]

However, in July, the Town Council decided to ignore Waterhouses's decision. Mr Cornforth moved an amendment that the best plans were *Perseverentes* and that *Maltese Cross* although very beautiful 'could not be built in two separate times'. Alderman Osborne declared that *Maltese Cross* 'was the worst in the series and the Council was as capable of forming an opinion as Mr. Waterhouse'. Mr Ellaway suggested that 'Mr. Waterhouse had not had time to consider the plans fully and thought that the opinions of other scientific gentlemen should be taken'. However Alderman Brindley thought the Council should know that Mr Water-house had been induced to change his mind.[31]

With heavy sarcasm, *The Architect* in July made the following observations — 'in Birmingham we have a complete breakdown of Mr. Waterhouse as professional adjudicator before the local partiality. Mr. Waterhouse examined twenty nine designs which would have cost each of the authors £2000 for labour and expense but, when the sealed envelopes were opened, to the utter amazement of everyone *Perseverentes* and *Forum*, the winners, were the work of Birmingham men'. *Perseverentes* was in fact Yeoville Thomason, manager of the Surveyors' Department. He had offered to show his model to the committee in June, and he received the first prize of £200. *Forum*, designed by Ward, was second and received £100 and *In Uno*, a classical design by Mr L de Ville of Duke Street, Adelphi, London, was third with £50. No. 9 by W. Henry Lynn of Belfast was acquired for use by the Council, as strongly advised by Waterhouse.[32]

In conclusion, it is hard to believe that the competition had been fair. Obviously, it had become common knowledge at an early stage of the competition that *Perseverentes* and *Forum* were both local men. If an employee of the council won the competition, his prize became part of the commission which would have been financially more acceptable to the Council.

It is worth pointing out that the competition for the Town Hall in Manchester, won by Waterhouse in 1867 had had none of these problems. The competition attracted one hundred and thirty seven entries and from those, the judging committee composed of city councillors assisted by professional assessors elected a short list of nine schemes. The second stage of the competition was judged by the classicist, and first President of the RIBA, Professor T. Donaldson, and the gothicist architect G. E. Street and all nine competitors received £300 for the provision of more detailed drawings. Waterhouse gained the contract on grounds of 'architectural merit, construction, excellence of plan and arrangement, light, cost and provision of spare room. It was superior in respect of ventilation ease of access and general excellence of the plan'.[33]

On 17 June 1873, the Mayor Joseph Chamberlain 'laid the first stone at whose invitation the principal inhabitants met and celebrated the event at the Great Western Hotel with a display of fireworks in the evening in Aston Hall'.[34] Thomason was paid £1500 commission, one third to be paid at the signing of the

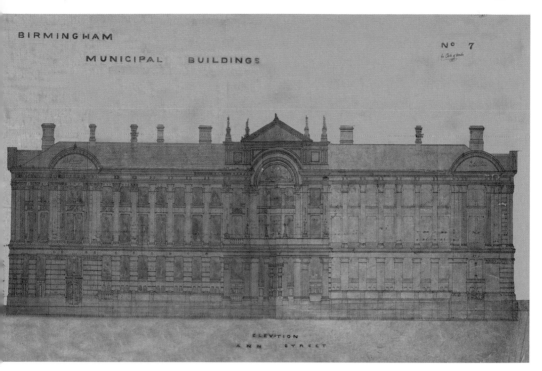

Council House, elevation to Ann Street, 1873, before the dome was added to the design.
Courtesy of Birmingham Archives and Heritage Services (MS 1460/45/7)

contract, one third to be paid as work proceeded and one third to be paid at completion. The tender of J. Barnsley & Sons of £83,220 was accepted.[35]

In July 1873, a Corporation Buildings Sub-Committee was appointed 'to confer with Thomason on the alterations to the elevations and plans of the Corporate Buildings thought desirable'. The elevations were a larger version of his Italianate commercial designs, round headed windows separated by paired Corinthian columns, similar to the *Daily Post* building, with a huge tower in the centre.[36] Alternative elevations, totally different from those originally adopted were submitted, the cost remaining the same.[37] A giant order was introduced, a much praised feature of the plan known as No. 9, by W. Henry Lynn and more in keeping with the Town Hall. It was suggested by Robert Dent that 'as the new elevations were so different from those adopted, it was re-modelled in accordance with a committee'.[38] It was decided to build only the Municipal Buildings at this time and not to erect the Assize Courts until Birmingham became an Assize District.

The old line of Ann Street and Colmore Row was altered and straightened giving a better view of the Town Hall. The new buildings were to harmonise with the Town Hall, with a rusticated base of a similar height and rows of columns dividing the windows as in the Town Hall. Thomason was able to build in his

The Council House, 1874–79, with a small section of the Town Hall on the left

favourite Italo-French/Renaissance style. The principal front had a length of 296 feet, the pediment over the central entrance rose to a height of 90 feet the stone cornice of the dome to 114 feet and the top of the finial is 114 feet high. The dome above the top of the main staircase was covered entirely with lead and the terminal was of gilded copper. In the centre was a portico projecting 16 feet carrying a balcony, behind which a central arch with a mosaic by Salviati was flanked by Corinthian piers carrying a pediment with carved relief. The sculpture by Lockwood, Boulton & Sons portrayed Britannia rewarding the manufacturers of Birmingham. At Congreve Street and Eden Place the angle of the building was curved and surmounted by a bold semi-circular pediment, enriched with a sculpture of high relief.

Four floors were divided into eighty rooms of varying sizes. The principal entrance had a grand staircase supported by polished marble columns with a balustrade of various coloured marbles. The marble came as gift from the City of Milan.[39] The facilities for the Council Chamber were upgraded and equipped with a public gallery and cloakrooms at additional costs of £2,750. The members' seats were arranged in a semi-circular plan with the spectators' gallery on the west side.

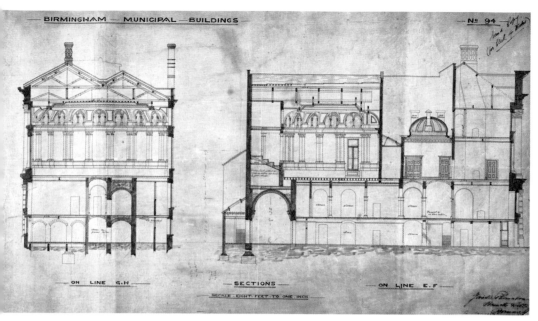

Council House. Section, 1875. *Courtesy of Birmingham Archives and Heritage Services (MS 1460/145/4)*

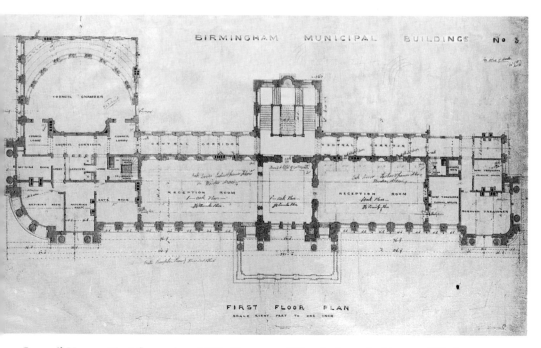

Council House. First floor plan, 1875. *Courtesy of Birmingham Archives and Heritage Services (MS 1460/145/1)*

The mayor's chair at the east end of the chamber was on a dais and behind this was a screen of Riga oak with panels of Italian walnut, richly carved with the arms of the borough.[40] All the chairs and tables were designed by Thomason. A suite of reception rooms 160 feet in length by 30 feet wide and 30 feet high was approached from the central entrance.[41] In 1879, it was decided to name the building, the Council House, and not the Municipal Hall.[42]

Thomason claimed that his arrangement of the seating in the Council Chamber provided a model for the arrangement of several subsequently erected Council rooms.[43] His excellent planning is not quite matched by his Italo-French architecture and there have been many architectural criticisms of this building such as this comment by Bryan Little in his *Birmingham Buildings* of 1971:-

Ceremonially, and in its administrative capacity, the new building served a good purpose, yet when one compares it with a classical masterpiece as Broderick's Town Hall at Leeds it fails to strike the right note. It is too long for its other proportions. Its central element is awkwardly composed, the dome is too small, and much of the renaissance detail is heavy and coarse while its curved council chamber and its grand staircase are imposing. It is hard to reckon Thomason as a designer of more than average capacity.[44]

One feels that he was solid, reliable, conscientious and hardworking, but not inspirational or innovative. He never upset the establishment, followed fashionable trends and produced few original ideas. Nationally, he could not be called one of the first rate architects of his time. However, the Council House has been statutory listed Grade II* and is regarded affectionately by Birmingham people and demonstrates the civic pride felt by citizens in its time.

Thomason was responsible for another major civic building, the Art Gallery and Museum. The passing of a Museums Act in 1845 and 1850 created an interest in the establishment of a Corporation Museum. J. T. Bunce, editor of the *Daily Post*, and W. C. Aitkin, a brass and glass manufacturer, argued that an Industrial Museum would provide better designs for Birmingham products. In 1880, the Tangye Brothers offered the sum of £5,000 for the purchase of objects of art if the Council were to provide a permanent Art Gallery. If this amount was equalled by other donations, they would offer a further £5,000. Land to the rear of the Council House which had been retained for the new law courts was suggested as a site. The Gas and Water Departments needed accommodation in the Council House and the area allotted to the Assize Courts was now considered too small. It was therefore decided that the Art Gallery should be built on this site and the Council House extended. The basement and ground floor of the new building were to be offices and the first floor was to be used as the Art Gallery. There was no architectural competition this time and Thomason was asked by the Corporation in 1881 to sketch plans for three galleries. The Gas Department agreed to pay for the erection of their own offices and, at their expense, to provide the first and upper floors for the Art Gallery. One gallery was to be 80 by 48 feet with a height of 16

Museum and Art Gallery,
1881–85

feet and another 98 by 48 feet was set aside as an Industrial Museum. Richard Chamberlain laid the foundation stone, and urged the need for money or works of art for the art gallery.[45] The designs of the elevation of the Council House continued to Congreve Street (now Victoria Square) with an entrance portico of two storeys, and the junction with Edmund Street was terminated by a clock tower. Thomason had provided an excellent solution to the problem of a grand entrance in limited space. Also excellent was his portico and tower combination. The Art Gallery was opened on the 28 November, 1885, by the Prince of Wales, later King Edward VII. The memorial stone in the entrance hall bears the words, 'By the Gains of Industry we promote Art'.

However, in 1897, *The Builder* conducting a survey of the city's architecture had said that 'we fear it is impossible the building is one of which the City can be proud, the coarse character of the detail is only too much emphasised by the classic refinement of the Town Hall; and the clock tower is one of the poorest erections of the kind we have ever seen, without dignity, proportion or character'. However, by 1914, Birmingham had built up two collections of national importance, a water-colour collection, based on the works of the local painter, David Cox and a collection of the school of Pre-Raphaelites. Sir Edward Burne-Jones, born in Birmingham, gave many paintings as did many Birmingham families. From this beginning the major collections were formed.

Detail of Pediment, Museum and Art Gallery

Thomason's role in designing religious buildings, apart from the Synagogue, included several churches. He designed the Congregational Church in Acock's Green, in 1860, now demolished,[46] the church of St John the Baptist, Harborne in 1857, the church of St Asaph's in Great Colmore Street in a spiky decorated style with cross gabled aisles and apses in 1868, now demolished[47] and in 1867–68, a new south aisle to St. Peter's Church, Harborne.[48] In 1871, he repaired the west front and redecorated internally the east end of St. Philip's Cathedral.[49] The East end was rebuilt in 1883–84 by J. A. Chatwin. In 1873 he altered and built additions to Holy Trinity Church in Sutton Coldfield. This included the gabled north aisle, built of stone with large pointed windows with varied tracery designs. Inside, he designed the north gallery to match those on the west and south walls. It is of fine oak panelling, decorated with carved pilasters set between carved panels. The wooden vaulting over the aisle and gallery is well constructed.[50] In 1875, he erected a west front and gallery and the re-arrangement of the east end at Carr's Lane Chapel, re-fronting it in a 'Renaissance style' and provided new seating for the chapel in 1883.[51] He also designed the reredos for St Catherine's Church, Scholefield Street in 1878, now demolished.[52] Thomason worked on St Paul's church in 1861 and 1884, and probably designed the font, in pink granite and white marble.[53]

Other public buildings included hospitals such as the Homeopathic Hospital, Easy Row, designed in 1873, now demolished.[54] The nursing home and mortuary for the General Hospital designed in 1879 have also been demolished[55] as has the Jaffray Suburban Hospital in Erdington designed by Thomason in 1884. Built in terracotta and moulded brick, it was a symmetrical building with two wings and a terracotta centre gable with baroque details. It was of four bays with six beds in the centre and two wings of dormitories.[56]

Thomason developed new skills in industrial design and he used a striking gothic style in great contrast to that of his usual Renaissance or Italianate style in 1872. Great Hampton Street Works, Nos 80–82 Great Hampton Street was a

Great Hampton Street Works, 1872. John Stokes's Manufactory by Bateman and Corser is on the left

Atlas Electro-plating Works, Paradise Street from *The Builder* 6 July 1878. *Courtesy of Birmingham Central Library*

purpose built button manufactory, designed by Thomason for Joel Cadbury, of the button makers Messrs. Green, Cadbury and Richards. An imposing facade designed in the Venetian Gothic style had a three storied showroom, warehouse and office range, with basement and attic. Indeed, some of the foliate details resembled those found in the buildings of J. H. Chamberlain. The street range, built of brick with stone dressings had two centred arches for the windows and a bold moulded, corbelled stone cornice. On the left hand side a cart entrance led to a long courtyard around which stood the workshop ranges. In its early years the works was engaged in the manufacture of the 'Very Button', a linen-covered button manufactured in vast quantities. The company continued in production until 1936.[57] This building, including its workshop ranges, still survives although slightly altered and is listed Grade II. It was restored in 1995–96 for the Birmingham Conservation Trust by Frank Brophy Associates.

The Atlas Electro-Plating Works in Paradise Street was commissioned in 1874. This was a very decorative building erected by Messrs. Horace Woodward & Co. at a cost of £25,000 with machinery. The buildings, extending from Paradise Street to Edmund Street were constructed of stone and red brick. Over the keystone of the principal entrance was a figure of Atlas. Shops, offices, workshops and rooms for casting, plating, gilding, stamping, modelling and burnishing were accommodated. The entrance gateway was in Edmund Street at the back with the engine and boilers and the engine stack of 110 feet high. This was considered to be at the forefront of the newer type of Birmingham manufactory. The builder was Messrs William Parker & Sons.[58] This building no longer survives.

Thomason almost certainly designed what is now called Newhall Place in Newhall Hill, in 1860–70, now listed Grade II.[59] This is a muscular, symmetrical blue brick manufactory with grey and red dressings and some stone. The cornices of the capitals form a string course with the transoms and door frames and the two floors are pierced with round headed windows with some medallions in the spandrels.

In the commercial world, Thomason led in his designs for the Town and District Bank. The first block for the Town and District Banking Company was built from 1869 to 1870 and formed the second instalment of the proposed improvements in Colmore Row. This was added to on each side by two more blocks. All were originally faced in Bath stone and ornamented with a rich cornice (still surviving) by the builder, Hardwick & Son and again the general style was 'free style Italian'. Beneath the hall was a series of strong rooms for bullion and securities, served by a hydraulic lift. The cost was between £11,000 and £12,000.[60] Next door, a continuation of the four storeyed range by Thomason was numbers 69–71 of 1873–74, more restrained, probably part of the original shop front for Rogers & Priestly, piano makers. Nos 75–77, built in 1872–73 were for Sanders & Co., metal brokers, a richly decorated building with a central feature.[61] These buildings have now been facaded, only the front elevations remaining. However, the grand,

Factory, Newhall Hill, 1860–70

classical, banking hall interior with round headed arches and Corinthian pilasters, listed Grade II, has been retained.

Towards the end of his career Thomason became architect to the Birmingham, Dudley & District Banking Co. and in partnership with Whitwell, he was responsible for over a dozen banks in the West Midlands.

In 1862, Thomason designed the offices and works for *Aris's Birmingham Gazette* in High Street, now demolished, with many shops and offices. From 1867 to 1887, he was responsible for designing the building and the alterations on New Street, Cannon Street and Corporation Street to the premises for the *Birmingham Journal*, with shops and offices in a gabled Flemish style. In 1879, the buildings on Corporation Street were extended for Messrs Jaffray & Feeney for the *Birmingham Mail* and eventually became the headquarters of the *Birmingham Post and Mail*, until 1965. They were made up of three, stone-faced, commercial palazzos with rich arched windows in the Italianate style. During the 1990's the facades were refurbished but the buildings behind were re-built and new shop fronts constructed.[62] In 1877, Thomason added the corner to what was Rickman & Hutchinson's Birmingham Banking Co. 23–3, Bennett's Hill and which became the Midland Bank. (See illustration on p. 16) He continued Rickman's façade and

Birmingham Post Building, New Street

cornice down the hill, designed a doorway with Aberdeen granite pilasters, and modelled the paired arched chimneys over the pediment.[63] He also remodelled the interior with paired Corinthian columns. In 1880 Nock's Hotel which became the Cathedral Tavern was built for a Mr Mason in Church Street. This is now part of a new development on Edmund Street and Church Street.

In 1880, his last important project before retirement, were the plans for Lewis's, a department store, on the corner of Bull Street and Corporation Street. This was the first iron and concrete building in Birmingham and unfortunately, many of the plans have been destroyed. Built of brick it had large windows, the corner feature embellished by a turret standing on stone columns. Each floor had a circular corner decorated with columns and highly decorated capitals. The spectacular roof line was broken with decorative pinnacles.[64] This shop, now closed, was replaced in 1924–25 by a new building.

The practice of Thomason and Whitwell moved to 1 Cannon Street in 1887, Thomason going into retirement. Henceforth Cooper Whitwell appears to have undertaken most of the firm's work and he changed the name of the partnership in 1894 when it became C. Whitwell & Son. It was dissolved in 1953.

Henry Richard Yeoville Thomason died at 9, Observatory Gardens, Campden Hill in London in 1901, described in his will as 'Gentleman'. Probate in London on the 16 December was given to Philip Rollason Thomason, barrister-at-law and Florence Mary Thomason spinster. Edith is not mentioned and must have died before her father. He left £1,820.[65] Thomason took no part in public life, his work absorbed his interest, and after retirement took an interest only in matters connected with architecture. He never contributed to life outside his profession and as far as is known he did not lecture or teach others from his own experience.

The historian, G. M. Young, says that as Manchester had done in earlier times, Birmingham epitomized late Victorian England which to some extent coincides with 1854 to 1887, the thirty four years that Thomason was in practice. Strong local government and a rapid growth in the size, population and industrial capacity of the Birmingham area created huge opportunities. Thomason took advantage of these and became one of the most important architects in late Victorian Birmingham. Many of his buildings survive and make a huge contribution to the character of the city centre. He was responsible for the distinguished set of buildings on Colmore Row creating a suitable setting for St Philip's Cathedral. He designed the grand commercial buildings on lower New Street and of course, the Council House and Art Gallery buildings. It would be hard to think of Birmingham without the input by Thomason. His career can only be described as successful and fulfilling. He is commemorated by a monument on the west wall of St Philip's Cathedral.

List of Architectural Works of H. R. Yeoville Thomason

H. R. Yeoville Thomason(1826–1901) was articled to Charles Edge of Birmingham. He set up in independent practice in Birmingham in 1854 and entered into partnership with Cooper Whitwell in 1867. Thomason retired in 1887 and the firm's name was changed to C. Whitwell & Son in 1894. It continued to operate until 1954.

BIRMINGHAM AND ITS ENVIRONS

PUBLIC

1854–58 Hebrew Synagogue, Blucher and Ellis Streets, for President and Council of the Hebrew Congregation; 1878–84 alterations and additions including Council Room

1855–56 Congregational Chapel, Francis Rd, Edgbaston

1857 Church of St John the Baptist, High St, Harborne [D]

1860 Congregational Chapel, Acock's Green [D]

1862 School Room for Hebrew School, Ellis St

1865 Masonic Hall, New St [D]

1867–68 St Asaph's Church, Gt Colmore St [D]

1865–73 New south aisle to St Peter's Church, Church Rd, Harborne

1869 Aston Union Workhouse, Gravelly Hill, Erdington; subsequent additions by Thomason up to 1887 and continued by Whitwell

1871 Repairs to west front and internal redecoration of east end, St Philip's Cathedral. (Some of front may survive)

1873 Homeopathic Hospital for Trustees of the Hospital, Easy Row [D]

1873–79 Additions and alterations to Holy Trinity Church, Sutton Coldfield

1874–79 Council House for Mayor and Corporation of the Borough of Birmingham.

1875 Addition of new west front and gallery and rearrangement of east end, Carr's Lane Congregational Chapel; 1883–84 Addition of cast iron arcading and re-seating [D]

1878 Design of reredos for St Catherine's Church, Scholefield St [D]

1879 Addition of Nurses' home and mortuary for Trustees of the General Hospital, Steelhouse Lane [D]

1879–87 Extension of Council House for Museum and Art Gallery and offices for Gas Dept., for Mayor and Corporation

1880 Municipal Buildings for Smethwick Urban Sanitary Authority, Smethwick

1884 Council House, proposed erection of block across courtyard [unexecuted]

1884 Jaffray Surburban Hospital for Trustees of the Hospital, Erdington [D]

COMMERCIAL

1860 Shops and warehouses for George Heaven, High St and Carr's Lane [D]

1862 Offices and works for *Aris' Birmingham Gazette*, High St, James Wilson, builder [D]

1863–64 Offices and printing works for *Birmingham Journal*, (later *Birmingham Daily Post*), New St; 1871 extensions Cannon St; 1879 extensions 9–13 Corporation St; 1882 extensions Cannon St; 1887 extensive additions behind facades, for Jaffray and Feeney [High St and Cannon St elevations facaded 1996–97]

1865–77 Alterations to bank, for Birmingham Banking Co. Bennett's Hill

1866 Union Club, 67–69 Colmore Row; 1885 new facade following road widening

1867 Shop and offices for Mr Richard Cooper, New Town Row [D]

1867–70 Head Office premises for Birmingham, Dudley and District Bank, 63–67 Colmore Row; 1872–75 extensions; 1891–95 furnishing and screens, 1898 'Roman' mosaic floor [facaded]

1868 Offices for Messrs Padmore, New Edmund St [D]

1870 Offices for Messrs Hirsch & Stern, New Edmund St [D]

1872 Shops and offices for Mr Wilson and design of shop fittings for Mr Allport, Colmore Row and Livery St

1872–73 Offices for Sanders & Co. metal brokers, 75–77 Colmore Row [facaded]

1873–74, Offices probably for Rogers & Priestly, piano makers, 69–71 Colmore Row [facaded]

1873–74 Bank for Birmingham, Dudley & District Banking Co, Cradley Heath.

1876 Bank adjoining St Paul's Churchyard for Birmingham Dudley & District Bank, Tipton.

1880–01 Addition of new banking hall for Birmingham Dudley & District Bank, Bilston.

1880 The Nock's Hotel (renamed Cathedral Tavern) for Mr Mason, Church St [part survives]

1880, Business premises, 25 Paradise St [D]

1880 Department Store for Messrs Lewis's, Bull St [D]; 1884 Extension [not executed]

1888 Alterations to bank for Birmingham, Dudley & District Bank, Oldbury.

1891 New bank for Birmingham District and Counties Bank at Hockley Hill/Well St (T&W)

1891 Banking premises for Birmingham District & Counties Bank, Aston Cross (T&W)

INDUSTRIAL

1854 Alterations to Manufactory of Messenger & Sons, brass and iron bedsteads manufacturers, Broad St (in the hand of Thomason but from the office of R. C. Hussey of London) [D]

c. 1860–70 Newhall Works, Newhall Hill (probably by Thomason)

1864 bridge over Hockley Brook, for Robert Cooper at New Town Row [D]

1867 Mill for P. H. Muntz, Great Bridge, Tipton, Staffs

1868 Warehouse for George Heaven, Moor St [D]

1871 Extension to Phoenix Bolt & Nut Works, Smethwick

1872 Factory for Messrs. Wynn, edge tool manufacturers, Commercial St

1872 Manufactory, 'The Great Hampton Street Works' for Joel Cadbury, button manufacturer, Gt Hampton St, Hockley

1874–75 Manufactory, 'Atlas Electro-Plate Works' for Woodward & Co, Paradise St [D]

1875 Exchange works for John Yates & Co, Aston

1882 Addition of oriel window to warehouse for Mr Charles, Smallbrook St [D]

1889 Extension of rolling mill, Pitney St

DOMESTIC

1848–77 houses on the Calthorpe Estate, Edgbaston including:- c. 1853 houses in Pakenham Rd, Ampton Rd and Arthur Rd; 1853–54 17–18 Charlotte Rd and ? Speedwell House, 51 Calthorpe Rd; 1858–60 57–64 and 65–66 Wheeley's Rd; 1860 10 Ampton Rd and houses in Gough Rd and Hagley Rd; 1877 Houses in Carpenter Rd and 5 Augustus Rd

1860s? Alterations to Hallfield House, (now Priory School) for Samuel Messenger, Sir Harry's Rd, Edgbaston

1862 House for Mr Harward, Victoria Park, Aston Park [D]

1866 House for Dr A. Fleming, Hagley Rd [unexecuted]

1869 Alterations and additions to Fox Hollies Hall for Z. Walker, Hall Green, Yardley [D]

1869–70 Alterations and additions to New Hall, for J. Chadwick, Sutton Coldfield

1870 House for T. Padmore, Church Rd, Moseley. [D]

1870 Four villas to same design for Mr Wilson, Augustus Rd, Edgbaston [D]

1871 Four houses for Mr Wilson, Wheeley's Rd, Edgbaston [D]

1871 House for Mr Feeney, Hagley Rd, Edgbaston from a plan used in Wheeleys Rd.

1871 House, 'Mountfield' for Mr J. Sherwood, King's Norton

1872 Survey plans of Perry Hall and a gardener's cottage, for the Hon. A. C. G. Calthorpe, Perry Barr [Cottage demolished for road widening]

1875 House, 'The Lindens', for T. Padmore, Alcester Rd, Moseley

1879 House for J. W. Yates, Birches Green, Erdington [D]

1881 House for E. V. Whitby, Dudley Rd

1884 Additions to Tyseley Grange, Tyseley for J. C. Onions

WORK OUTSIDE BIRMINGHAM

PUBLIC

1890 Baptist chapel for unknown client, Salop Rd, Oswestry (T&W)

COMMERCIAL

1888 Bank for Birmingham, Dudley & District Bank, Ludlow (T & W)

1889 Bank for Birmingham, District & Counties Bank, Wem, Salop. (T & W)

1889 Bank for Birmingham, District & Counties Bank, Longton, Staffs.
(T & W)

1889 Bank for Birmingham, District & Counties Bank, Derby (T & W)

1890 Bank for Birmingham, District & Counties Bank, Kington, Herefordshire (T & W)

1890 Bank for Birmingham, District & Counties Bank, Bishop's Castle, Salop. (T & W)

1891 Alterations to bank for Birmingham, District & Counties Bank, Leominster, Hereford (T & W)

DOMESTIC

1861 Rebuilding of Bridgetown Farm, for Miss Ryland, Stratford-on-Avon, John Hardwick & Sons, builders.

1863 House for Miss Ryland at Sherbourne

1863 Pair of cottages for Rev. C. Girdlestone, Stanford in the Vale, Berkshire

NOTES

1 *Edgbastonia*, 4, No. 38, June 1884, pp. 81–83.
2 George Learmonth, *Thomason's Warwick Vase* (Birmingham, 1981), pp. 1–2.
3 Malvern Census, 1841; Will, Ludlow, September Quarter, 1836, vol. 18, p. 86.
4 *Worcester Directory*, 1843.
5 Yeoville appears to be an invented name as no other can be found in the 1881 census.

[6] Much of the family information is from the *International Genealogy Index* with additional information from the *Rate Books of All Saints*, Birmingham 1850–53. The author wishes also to acknowledge the assistance of John Bassindale. Elizabeth's eldest daughter was married in 1848 at St Peter and St Paul, Aston. At the wedding Elizabeth gave the father's name as Henry Yardley, Gentleman. This was untrue. Henry Richard Yeoville Yardley was a witness. In 1858 they were living in Arthur Rd and in 1861, Elizabeth Thomason, widow was living at 56, Calthorpe Rd with her two sons. In 1871, Elizabeth Thomason was living with George at 88, Hagley Rd.

[7] Birmingham Central Library, Archives and Heritage Services (hereafter BCL AHS) MS 1460, papers of the architects Whitwell & Sons, 3 Newhall Street (hereafter *Whitwell Collection*), introduction by W. A. Whitwell, 1951. Cooper Whitwell was Thomason's partner from 1867 to 1885. Thomason's name was dropped in 1894 and the business became known as C. Whitwell & Son.

[8] RIBA, *The Directory of British Architects*, vol. 2, (2001), p. 185.

[9] *Aris's Gazette* 14 March 1863.

[10] 1881 Census.

[11] *Whitwell Collection*, Introduction.

[12] BCL AHS, MS 500, Calthorpe Estate Register of leases 1848–60, item 7.

[13] *Whitwell Collection*, item 13, 5 drawings, Sherbourne 1863.

[14] *Whitwell Collection*, item 11, 2 drawings, Victoria Rd 1862.

[15] *Whitwell Collection*, item 26, 1 drawing, Hall Green Fox Hollies, 1869; *Birmingham at the Opening of the 20th Century, Contemporary Biographies*, ed. by W. T. Pike, (Brighton, n.d.) p. 46.

[16] *Whitwell Collection*, item 28, 3 drawings of new house, 1870.

[17] *Whitwell Collection*, item 32, 3 drawings of house elevations. One of the drawings was apparently used later as a design for a house for Mr Feeney in Hagley Rd, in 1871.

[18] *Whitwell Collection*, item 5, 18 drawings, erection and alterations to Synagogue, 1878–84; Andy Foster, *Pevsner Architectural Guides: Birmingham*, (New Haven and London, 2005), p. 209; Zoe Josephs, *Birmingham Jewery, More Aspects, 1740–1930* (Birmingham, 1956), pp. 22–80; Joseph Cohen, *Stained Glass Windows of Singers Hill Synagogue 1956–63* (Birmingham, 1963).

[19] *The Builder*, 18, 24 March 1860, p. 185.

[20] *Whitwell Collection*, Introduction.

[21] *The Builder*, 27, 10 July 1869, p. 545, p. 547, p. 549.

[22] Birmingham University Field Archaeology Unit, *Historic Building Re-ordering at Highcroft Hospital* (Birmingham Planning Dept. EB File).

[23] Foster, *Birmingham*, pp. 96–97.

[24] Nikolaus Pevsner, *The Buildings of England: Worcestershire* (Harmondsworth, 1968), p. 91.

[25] *Building News*, 21, 8 July 1871, p. 48.

[26] *Building News*, 20, 14 April 1871, p. 283.

[27] *The Architect*, 5, 15 March 1871, p. 146.

[28] *Building News*, 20, 14 April 1871, p. 48.

[29] *The Architect*, 5, 15 March 1871, p. 146.

[30] BCL AHS, Estates and Building Sub Committee Minutes July 1871; *Building News*, 21, 22 July 1871, p. 37.

[31] *Building News*, 21, 15 July 1871, p. 27.

[32] Estates and Building Committee, Minutes, July 1871; *Building News*, 21, 22 July 1871, p. 37; *Whitwell Collection*, item 45, 180 drawings, surveys, elevations, designs for furniture for Birmingham Municipal Building.

[33] John J. Parkinson-Bailey, *Manchester: An Architectural History*, (Manchester, 2000), pp. 106–08.

[34] *Building News*, 21, 22 July 1871, p. 37.

[35] Estates and Building Sub-Committee, Minutes, January 1875.

[36] Foster, *Birmingham*, p. 61.

[37] *Building News*, 24, 7 March 1873, p. 290.

[38] R. K. Dent, *Old and New Birmingham* (Birmingham 1880), p. 525.

[39] Colin Cunningham, *Victorian and Edwardian Town Halls* (London, Boston and Henley, 1981), p. 80.

[40] R. K. Dent, *The Making of Birmingham* (Birmingham, 1894), p. 466; *The Architect*, 9, 15 February 1873, p. 83.

[41] BCL AHS Birmingham Corporation Minutes, Main Council, 4 March 1879, minute no. 11,357.

[42] Obituary, *Journal of the Royal Institute of British Architects*, August 1901.

[43] Stuart Davies, *By the Gains of Industry: Birmingham Museums and Art Gallery 1885–1985* (Birmingham, 1985), p. 12, p. 20; *Building News*, 38, 10 July 1880, p. 545.

[44] Bryan Little, *Birmingham Buildings: The Architectural Story of a Midland City* (Newton Abbot, 1971), p. 30.

[45] *Building News*, 41, 23 July 1881, p. 39; *Whitwell Collection*, item 56, 160 drawings of elevations, heating and ventilation systems and structural designs, 1879–87 for Art Gallery.

[46] *Whitwell Collection*, item 8a, 1 drawing, copy of plan to let the seats, 1860.

[47] *Whitwell Collection*, item 21, 8 drawings of elevations, 1867–68.

[48] *Whitwell Collection*, item 39, 5 drawings of plans of church and new south aisle, 1865–73.

[49] *Whitwell Collection*, item 31, 4 drawings, repairs to west front and internal decoration of east end, 1871.

[50] *Whitwell Collection*, item 42, 22 drawings additions and alterations 1873–79.

[51] *Whitwell Collection*, item 47, 8 drawings erection of new front and gallery, rearrangement of east end, 1875.

[52] *Whitwell Collection*, item 52, 1 drawing for reredos, 1878.

[53] Foster, *Birmingham*, p. 162.

[54] *Whitwell Collection*, item 40, 3 drawings of survey of area and elevation of hospital, 1873.

[55] *Whitwell Collection*, item 53, 4 drawings of nursing home and mortuary, 1879.

[56] *Whitwell Collection*, item 67, 18 drawings of internal and external designs for Jaffray Hospital.

[57] John Cattell, Sheila Ely and Barry Jones, *The Birmingham Jewellery Quarter*, (Swindon, 2002), p. 238; Little, *Birmingham Buildings*, pictures 55–56.

[58] *The Builder*, 36, 6 July 1878, p. 698.

[59] *Birmingham Post*, 19 October 1974.

[60] *The Builder*, 27, 19 July 1869, p. 545; *The Architect*, 1, 16 January 1869, p. 39.

[61] Foster, *Birmingham*, p. 98.

[62] *Whitwell Collection*, item 12, 3 drawings; erection of office and works, High St for *Aris's Birmingham Gazette*; item 15, 16 drawings of re-building and alteration of premises for *Birmingham Journal*, Cannon St and High St construction of shop and offices for Mr Feeney; item 54, 2 drawings for erection of extension of offices for the *Birmingham Mail* for Messrs Jaffray & Feeney.

[63] Foster, *Birmingham*, p. 127.

[64] *Whitwell Collection*, item 68, 6 drawings of departmental store for Messrs Lewis's 1884–87 (Proposed extension not carried out).

[65] Obituary, *JRIBA*, 31 August 1901.

7 John Henry Chamberlain

JOE HOLYOAK

On 16 July 1877, John Ruskin wrote Letter LXXX of *Fors Clavigera*, his Letters to the Workmen and Labourers of Great Britain, from Bellefield, the house in Winson Green of Birmingham's Mayor, George Baker.[1] In it he complained that a new Gothic school was fast blocking out the once pretty country view from his window. That was the new Dudley Road School of the Birmingham School Board, across the road from Bellefield, and its architect, John Henry Chamberlain (1831–83) was surely one of the 'representative group of the best men of Birmingham' whom Ruskin reports that Baker invited to Bellefield to meet the visitor during his two day stay.

Ruskin was frequently dismissive of the efforts of contemporary architects to translate faithfully into brick and stone his inspirational precepts of what a modern Gothic architecture should be. But we have another view of Ruskin's visit from the Mayor's son W. Moseley Baker. He recorded how memorable for him the visit was, and adds that 'close by a Board School was being erected – and J. R. was up and down ladders like a schoolboy'![2]

George Baker had two hard acts to follow. He had become Mayor of Birmingham the previous year in succession to Joseph Chamberlain (no relation to the architect), and was to become Master of the Guild of St George in succession to its founder, John Ruskin. For John Henry Chamberlain, that high tea at Bellefield to which he and others were invited must have been a significant event. It brought together the two greatest influences in his life; the author of 'The Nature of Gothic' in *The Stones of Venice*, whose advice on architecture he was inspired to follow since he read it soon after its publication in 1853,[3]

J. H. Chamberlain, drawing. *Courtesy of Birmingham Archives and Heritage Services*

William Martin. *Courtesy of Martin,
Ward and Keeling*

and the Birmingham Liberal Association, to whose political aspirations so many
of his buildings endeavoured to give form.

The successful career of J. H. Chamberlain, and his partner from 1864 onwards,
William Martin, was a striking example of talented men being in the right place
at the right time. Birmingham in the late 19th century was reshaped by the phenomenon of what came to be called 'The Civic Gospel'. This was the growth of civic
and municipal ambition, fuelled by religious non-conformism and Liberal politics, one of whose results was the huge expansion of urban institutions. These
institutions delivered to the citizens of Birmingham such facilities as education,
health, water, gas, recreation, policing, fire fighting, and library services. All of
these required buildings, and the firm of Martin and Chamberlain enjoyed almost
a monopoly in their design. They designed schools, hospitals, pumping stations,
police stations, fire stations, and libraries, as well as houses, churches and commercial buildings.

The representation of political ideology through architectural form is a tricky
matter. It is tempting to look for, but usually difficult to find, a direct illustrative
relationship between one and the other. The Nazi leadership certainly believed
that the neo-classical language was expressive of the doctrines of National Socialism, and neo-classical architecture has consequently and unfairly been politically

tainted since. But this same architectural language elsewhere is capable of com-
municating the virtues of democracy and justice, as many US state capitols testify.
In Birmingham in the 1870s and 1880s, due to the near-monopoly in municipal
and quasi-municipal commissions which they enjoyed, Martin and Chamberlain's
lively Ruskinian Gothic style of architecture came *de facto* to express the Liberal
revolution in municipal management. Looking back from a distance of one hundred and thirty years or so, Ruskinian Gothic in red brick and terracotta is certainly the epitome (is the *brand*, we might now say) of the Civic Gospel.

But it is hard to construct a convincing argument in support of the inevitability
of this. Martin and Chamberlain were fine architects, certainly, albeit slightly old-
fashioned in terms of the development of the Gothic Revival by national standards, and clearly very responsive, able and reliable in business terms. However,
one may conclude that their success in representing in architectural terms the
great municipal advances in Birmingham was less due to the appropriateness of
their architectural style, than to the fact that they were both active and committed
in the Liberal cause, and extremely well connected to the city's political and social
elite. But, as will be described later, when it came, in 1871, to the choice of an architect for the most important representation of municipal ambition, the new Council House, the Gothic Revival style was rejected in favour of a rather pompous
neo-classicism.

That said, two arguments at least can be advanced for the appropriateness of
Martin and Chamberlain's polychromatic and naturalistic kind of Gothic architecture for Birmingham's Civic Gospel. The first lies in the exoticness of the architecture, placed in the mundane streets of 19th century Birmingham. The town,
when Chamberlain arrived there in 1856, though prosperous, was utilitarian,
undistinguished and dull, with few buildings of note. One intention of the Liberal
caucus, when it achieved political dominance in the 1860s, was to raise the cultural
aspirations of the town above the utilitarian. Robert Dale, one of the influential
non-conformist ministers behind the Civic Gospel, recorded how speakers in the
late 1860s would suggest that 19th century Birmingham might become the equivalent of Renaissance Florence, 'the home of a noble literature and art'.[4]

Martin and Chamberlain's architecture fitted this aspiration. It spoke of culture
and fine art, and of craftsmanship, it had literary resonances, and it was capable
of turning functional necessities such as pumping stations, maternity wards and
ventilation towers into things of beauty. The Board Schools designed by Martin
and Chamberlain, in particular their ventilation towers, prominent landmarks in
mean working-class streets of terraced houses and back-to-back courts, were perceived as exceptional symbols of learning (Sherlock Holmes's description of
London Board Schools as 'beacons of enlightenment' is even more apt for those of
Birmingham).[5]

The second argument lies in the flexibility of the Gothic style, in both plan and
section, in adapting itself to a variety of functional programmes in buildings, for

the design of some of which, such as fire stations and swimming baths, pre-19th century historical precedent offered little help. Martin and Chamberlain had thoroughly absorbed Ruskin's observation that the Gothic language employed a series of forms 'of which the merit was, not merely that they were new, but that they were capable of perpetual novelty'.[6] They were able to deploy the language of gable, buttress, lancet window, tower and apse to achieve endless variety; not as an end in itself, though it frequently produced delight, but to meet the needs of widely differing programmes. This mediaeval, organic sensibility which saw no division between function and form was one of their great assets. It reflected Ruskin's belief that '... Gothic is not only the best, but the *only rational* architecture, as being that which can fit itself most easily to all services, vulgar or noble'.[7] The exception to this was a situation such as the planning of Corporation Street where, as we shall see, their lack of an alternative, more formal manner, let them down.

Martin and Chamberlain designed two monuments to the person who most embodied the Civic Gospel in Birmingham, its Mayor from 1873 to 1876, Joseph Chamberlain – one explicit, one implicit. The explicit monument, unusual in that it was built during the lifetime of its subject, is the Chamberlain Memorial, which stands in what is now Chamberlain Square. This was erected by public subscription to mark Joseph Chamberlain's election as MP for Birmingham in 1880, in what was then a scruffy piece of neglected land behind the Town Hall. The Memorial, although Gothic, is uncharacteristic of the architects' work, being rather French in flavour, and composed all of limestone. It has a portrait medallion of Joseph Chamberlain by the sculptor Thomas Woolner. The inscription makes explicit reference to the Mayor's municipalisation of the gas and water industries, and the fountain and pool at its base may perhaps be read as symbolic of the latter of the two.

At the same time the architects were designing a large house for the ex-Mayor in Moor Green, which was then countryside to the south of the town, and which is now part of King's Heath.[8] Highbury, named after the part of London from which Joseph Chamberlain originated, is the best of Martin and Chamberlain's houses. A number of rooms on ground and first floor are planned around a large, central two-storey high hall. The hall, which has the staircase rising from it at one end, is elaborately decorated with naturalistic motifs in marquetry, encaustic tile, and carved wood and stone. There is a considerable amount of dissonance between the various patterns and materials, which was presumably quite intended, as Ruskin recommended. The wide south front, facing the large garden, most of which is now Highbury Park, demonstrates one of Chamberlain's favourite compositional strategies, of three dissimilar gables, left, right and centre, punctuating the elevation, which recurred later in the School of Art.

It also appeared in The Grove, Harborne, a house which Martin and Chamberlain remodelled in 1875–67 for William Kenrick, the brother-in-law of Joseph

Highbury, Yew Tree Road, 1878, the garden front. The second floor of the right hand bay was added in 1888

Highbury, the hall

Highbury, detail of hall

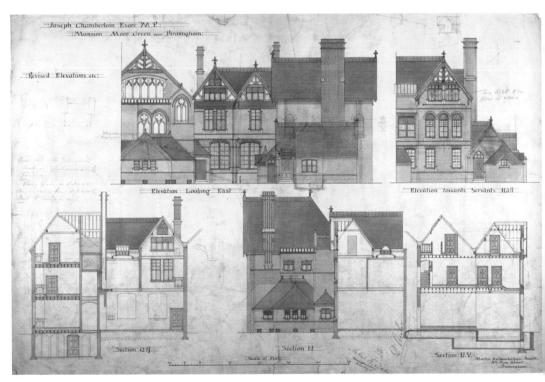

Highbury, drawing of elevations, 1878. *Courtesy of Birmingham Archives and Heritage Services (MS 1338/3)*

Chamberlain. This was one of a number of houses which the architects designed in the 1870s for members of the town's civic elite. It was a freely-planned essay in Italian Gothic, very similar to the later Highbury, with much ornate and natural-istic interior decoration. It was demolished in 1963, but the ante-room, or boud-oir, and its furnishings, was removed to the Victorian and Albert Museum.[9]

Of a similar nature were Berrow Court in Edgbaston for J. A. Kenrick of 1878,[10] and Harborne Hall of 1884 for Walter Chamberlain,[11] also extensive remodellings, resulting in rather raw, muscular, gabled red-brick houses, that teeter on the edge between beauty and ugliness. These two still stand, together with the lodge added to Oakmount in Edgbaston, for Richard Chamberlain of 1879, but J. H. Chamber-lain's own house in Edgbaston, Whetstone, of 1875 has been demolished.

John Henry Chamberlain's association with Birmingham was an accidental one. He was born in Leicester, on 26 June 1831, his father, Joseph, being a Calvin-istic Baptist minister of Salem Chapel in the town.[12] He was educated at Mr Franklin's Academy in Leicester and showing an early interest in art, he was articled to the Leicester architect, Henry Goddard (1792–1868). During the five years he spent in Goddard's office, he encountered Ruskin's writings on architec-ture.

Fired by Ruskin's passion for Italian Gothic architecture in *The Stones of Venice*, and after a brief period working in London, Chamberlain visited Italy to see the sites of Ruskin's inspiration for himself. On his return to Leicester, he concluded that his career would not prosper there, and decided to try his luck in Birming-ham, where his cousin (confusingly, another Joseph Chamberlain) was a partner in the carpet and furnishing business of Eld & Chamberlain.

This family association brought Chamberlain his first two commissions in Birmingham; a house for the father of his cousin's partner, John Eld in Edgbaston, Shenstone House, 12 Ampton Road in 1856, and a shop for Eld and Chamberlain in Union Street in the city centre in 1857. The house survives but the shop does not. Both buildings show Chamberlain's interest in the polychromatic treatment of flat surfaces, using coloured and patterned brickwork and encaustic tile.

After these two buildings, Chamberlain's practice did not go well in Birming-ham, although he continued to have a few commissions in Leicester, and it seems that the startlingly exotic nature of the Ampton Road house may have been part of the reason. Edgbaston was a prestigious, low-density suburb where many of the town's commercial, political and cultural elite had their homes. In the 1850s its architectural character was almost uniformly Italianate; symmetrical, white painted stucco boxes, with low-pitched roofs behind parapets. Introduced into this cool, uniform environment, Mr Eld's house had the shock effect of an offensive gesture. But upon the occasion of Chamberlain's death in 1883, the magazine *Edgbastonia* could declare 'The reign of sham in architecture has ceased. We see no stucco now'.[13]

12 Ampton Road, Edgbaston, 1856

He was married in 1859, to Anna Abrahams, the daughter of another Baptist minister, and in his first few years in Birmingham, Chamberlain began to establish the political and social connections that were to be the basis of his future success. An important element was a business partnership, albeit brief, with the engineer William Harris. Harris was to become a key member of the Liberal caucus that came to power in the town in the 1860s. He is described by Asa Briggs as '. . . a most active and intelligent political wire-puller behind the scenes'.[14] He became Secretary of the Birmingham Liberal Association in 1868, and is credited for the organisation of the successful outcome of the general election of that year, when the Liberals won all three Birmingham seats. Harris's friendship must have been critical to Chamberlain.

But despite Chamberlain's increasing integration into the power structures of the town, the development of his architectural practice did not match his talent, and in 1864 he almost emigrated to New Zealand. He had an offer from Lord

Lyttelton of Hagley Hall, the first President of the Birmingham and Midland Institute, for whom he had done some minor jobs, to design a new cathedral in Christchurch. It seems that a number of friends were alarmed by his intended departure from the town, and instead of emigration, a partnership was arranged between Chamberlain and the architect William Martin, which was formed in April 1864.

William Martin was born in 1828 in Shepton Mallet, and moved with his parents, first to Worcester and then to Birmingham. He was apprenticed to the architect Thomas Plevins, and having completed his articles became the managing clerk in the practice of D. R. Hill, later to become Hill and Martin. Hill was, neither then nor now, a celebrated architect, but he had a national reputation as a designer of prisons and asylums, in which he specialised, in all parts of the country. Martin continued the practice after Hill's death in 1857, until his partnership with Chamberlain was formed in 1864. His established reputation must have been useful to Chamberlain.

The relationship between the skills of William Martin and J. H. Chamberlain is usually characterised as Chamberlain being the partner driven by design theory, and possessing the creative design skills, and Martin having the complementary practical abilities, in planning, structural design and costing. One suspects that this polarisation is too neat, and questions are raised by the continuation of the Ruskinian Gothic style in the firm's buildings between Chamberlain's death in 1883 and Martin's death in 1900. But there does seem to be substantial truth in the characterisation. Martin certainly was a skilled engineer in steel and cast iron, seen most dramatically in the Free Library of 1879, and the storey-high supporting structure of the Grosvenor Room in the Grand Hotel of 1891. In addition to his design skills, he was a valuer, arbitrator, and expert witness. He negotiated the purchase of the whole of the property acquired for the Corporation Street Improvement Scheme of 1878.

In any case, one should certainly not undervalue the contribution of the more practical and utilitarian design skills to the Civic Gospel. Discussion of the Birmingham Board Schools, for example, has emphasised the aesthetic nature of the Gothic forms, the elegance of towers, lancet windows and gables, and the naturalistic ornamentation. But the provision by a public body of spacious, well-planned accommodation, well-lit, heated and ventilated, for poor working-class children who had no other experience of these conditions, was a radical expression of the Liberal Association's civic ambitions. It was equally an expression of the nonconformists' idea of practical Christianity; their leaders frequently emphasised the duty of the municipality to meet its citizens' needs for utility and convenience.

Chamberlain was certainly the more high profile partner in the practice, playing a number of roles in the public life of the town. From 1858 he was Professor of Architecture at Queen's College, a college with faculties of theology, medicine and arts, in Paradise Street, opposite the Town Hall. From 1865 he was Honorary

Secretary of the Birmingham and Midland Institute, and from 1874 Chairman of the Society of Arts and School of Ornamental Art which was housed within the BMI. Chamberlain negotiated the transfer of the School of Art from the BMI to the Town Council, and designed its new building in Margaret Street. He was a member of the congregation of the Church of the Saviour, and a close friend of its founder, George Dawson, a central figure in the Civic Gospel. He founded the local branch of Ruskin's Guild of St George.

Chamberlain's introductory lecture as Professor at Queen's College, 'The Offices and Duties of an Architect', gives a good indication of his architectural philosophy. He cites Ruskin, but challenges Ruskin's definition, in 'The Lamp of Sacrifice',[15] of the difference between building and architecture (or rather, Architecture), as the adding of 'an unnecessary feature'. Instead, he paraphrases Pugin's earlier principle[16] (also originally delivered to a theological college, just a few miles to the north), saying that building becomes architecture 'by making those very necessities of construction otherwise than ugly'. That is, ornament is in the construction, not added to it.

He emphasises the social, and even medical, benefits of good architectural design; the benefits that well-considered housing may bring to the health of the urban poor. In stressing the continuity of architecture from the humblest cottage to the cathedral, he paraphrases Ruskin in *The Seven Lamps*, 'Whatever style is best for the domestic ... that style is the only right style for the chapel or the church ... '[17]

The principle of *Naturalism* in 'The Nature of Gothic', of a reverence for nature from which it follows that ornament can only properly consist of natural forms, is developed, and in connection with this Chamberlain introduces a more original idea, which he calls Compensation. Every building necessarily destroys part of the loveliness of the natural world, and architecture has a responsibility to replace it with a beauty of its own. 'Compensation is the first duty required of Architecture in its character of a fine art. So much of the beautiful has been taken away, and its restoration must be effected'. It is a distant parallel with today's concerns for an eco-architecture, though expressed more in spiritual than in resource terms. It is not clear whether or not Chamberlain meant the compensation for lost birds, leaves and berries to be made specifically through their inanimate equivalent in terracotta, stone, oak or coloured glass, or more generally. One hopes that it was the latter, as otherwise the rule of Compensation would be rather a naive one.

Chamberlain's association with the Birmingham and Midland Institute was central to his life in Birmingham, and ultimately led to his last, and possibly his best building, the School of Art. The history of the Institute's building is entangled with that of the Free Library, and Martin and Chamberlain designed parts of both. The BMI occupied the building designed for it in 1855 by Edward Barry in Ratcliffe Place, opposite Hansom's Town Hall. Barry designed a building behind a huge continuous classical facade which was to stretch from Paradise Street to

Birmingham and Midland Institute and Free Library from Paradise Street, 1881.
Photograph *c.* 1900. *Courtesy of Birmingham Archives and Heritage Services*

Edmund Street. But by 1860 only half had been built, as the Institute's money ran out, and the Town Council negotiated the purchase of the vacant land as the site for the new Free Library, following its adoption of the Free Libraries and Museums Act, to be built behind the completion of Barry's facade. Barry was appointed, but made the same mistake as Joseph Hansom across the road thirty years earlier; the lowest tender exceeded his estimate by a long way, and he was dismissed. William Martin won a competition in 1862 to be appointed as architect, to Barry's public dismay.[18] The Lending Library was opened in 1865, and the Reference Library the following year.

The popularity of the Free Library was such that the Town Council decided to build an extension, acquiring land in Edmund Street for the purpose. Martin and Chamberlain, by now in partnership, were appointed architects.[19] Work had just started on site in 1879, when a careless workman started a fire. Barry's facade, built by Martin, survived, but the major part of the building, and the stock of books, were destroyed.

Birmingham and Midland Institute and Free Library. Elevation drawing for extension in Paradise St, 1879. *Courtesy of Birmingham Archives and Heritage Services (MS 1338/8)*

Meanwhile, following Chamberlain's appointment as Honorary Secretary in 1865, the fortunes of the BMI had prospered over the following years. Expansion of the building was required, particularly the lecture theatre, which was proving too small to accommodate the popular public lectures. In 1877 the Institute appointed Martin and Chamberlain as architects to build an extension in Paradise Street.[20] Progress on site was slow, quite apart from the delay caused by the fire, and the new building opened in 1881.

Naturally, the frontage paid scant regard to Barry's adjacent classical facade. Horizontal mouldings roughly corresponded to the heights of Barry's rusticated

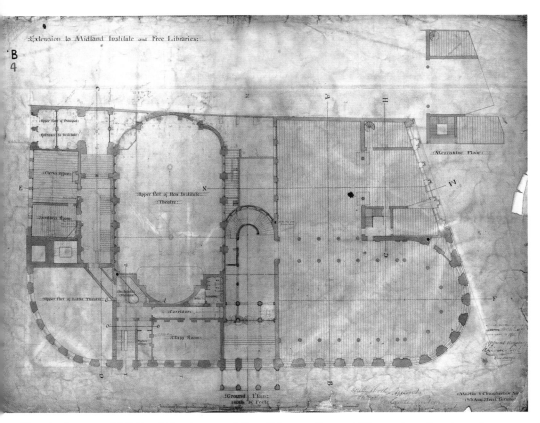

Birmingham and Midland Institute and Free Library. Ground Floor plan, *Courtesy of Birmingham Archives and Heritage Services (MS 1338/8)*

base and the entablature above the Corinthian pilasters, but that was all. Four elaborate Venetian Gothic bays, each topped with a crocketed gable, fronted the street. The major elements were four large lancet openings on the first floor, each with mosaic panels in the arch by Salviati, divided by niches intended for statuary. The interior was an exercise in revealed construction; fair-faced brick and stone walls, Minton tiles, and ornamental wrought-iron girders in the Lecture Theatre.

At the other end of the block, Martin and Chamberlain were re-commissioned after the 1879 fire to rebuild the library.[21] Martin's original library had stayed fairly close to Barry's intended plans, and it is unlikely that the interiors had any outstanding qualities. But the fire gave the architects the opportunity to replan both the original area and the unbuilt extension as one, and the result was Martin and Chamberlain's most memorable spatial composition, opened in 1882.

Through Barry's central portico, one entered into a tall staircase hall about 18m long, and about half that in width, fair-faced in red brick inset with floral blue and white Minton tiles, lit by tall red and green stained glass windows in the semicircular apse at the far end. A wide, extremely comfortable staircase curved

First floor of the Reference Library, restored after the fire of 1879

up inside the apse; the flights divided by twin handrails on coupled iron columns, and the treads surfaced by grids of tiny wood blocks. Proceeding around nearly the entire perimeter of the hall, it delivered the reader to the entrance to the Reference Library, accessed by a turn through 90 degrees. At this point, the staircase was cantilevered into space at the very top of the hall, and the effect was dizzying.

The interior of the Reference Library saw Chamberlain showing considerable deference towards Barry's classical language. It was vaulted like a Romanesque cathedral; an apsed nave surrounded by aisles, the two separated by round arches supported on pink Shap granite columns with neo-grec capitals. A rectangular wing of similar height branched off this nave, and the entrance from the staircase was placed at the junction of the two spaces. Within the aisles, iron galleries and iron spiral staircases gave access to walls of books lining the rooms.

At the far end of the rectangular wing, an unostentatious door led to an outstanding display of design and craftsmanship in timber, the Shakespeare Memorial Library. This housed the library's considerable Shakespeare collection, which was given to the town in 1864 by the Our Shakespeare Club. This was a dining club composed of Birmingham's Liberal intellectual leadership, including J. H. Chamberlain himself, formed in 1862 with the aim of raising the level of scholarship in the town. Chamberlain had designed a room for the collection in 1868, which was destroyed in the fire.

The Shakespeare Memorial Library is the only substantial part of the 1882 library which survived the demolition of 1974, and is incorporated into the present Central Library. It is a rectangular room, not large, lined by glass-fronted oak bookcases, with moulded and coloured plaster covings and ceiling. The general impression is an eclectic kind of Tudor style, with naturalistic ornament in marquetry, glass and plaster. Here, as elsewhere in the 1882 library, we are told that Chamberlain designed every piece of ornament himself. The autonomy of the craftsman, free to contribute independently to the total architectural work of art, was one of Ruskin's precepts which Chamberlain disregarded. Martin and Chamberlain laid great importance on quality of craftsmanship, and employed highly skilled and artistic craftsmen. But they always worked on the interpretation of designs by Chamberlain himself. Consistency of style was more important than individual creativity.

However, as always in Chamberlain's work, the naturalistic ornament follows Ruskin's principle of changefulness; that there should be constant invention, with no one piece repeating another. This was equally visible in the new elevation to Edmund Street which adjoined Barry's facade, which was Martin and Chamberlain's most extravagant piece of external design. It was hardly an example of organic design, having little or no relationship to the Shakespeare Memorial Library and other spaces that lay behind it. Its five bays were in a round-arched Lombardic style, elaborately ornamented in encaustic tile, carved stone, and moulded terra cotta. Above the central three bays was a large concave mosaic cornice by Salviati, with acanthus leaves in gold leaf and scarlet on an azure ground. Before it became neglected and grimy, the facade must have been amazingly colourful.

Up until the middle of the following century, the clustering of the Free Library, the BMI, the Chamberlain Memorial, and J. H. Chamberlain's gabled canopy to the adjacent statue of George Dawson, with the School of Art just around the corner, continued to contribute to one of the most eloquent statements about 19th century civic ambition of any city in the country.

In 1882, as the new library triumphantly opened, Martin and Chamberlain were commissioned by the Town Council to design the building to house the new Municipal School of Art.[22] This was to follow the transfer to the council from the BMI of the Society of Arts and School of Ornamental Art. Chamberlain had been its Chairman since 1874, and negotiated its transfer. Ironically, the first municipal school of art in the country was enabled by private gifts of land and money. In a letter to the Mayor, Richard Chamberlain, one of the donors, the industrialist

Shakespeare Memorial Library, 1882

Richard Tangye, expressed 'a very strong feeling as to the architect who should be employed to carry out the work. Mr J. H. Chamberlain possesses in an eminent degree all the requisite qualifications'.[23]

The School of Art is the finest expression of Chamberlain's Ruskinian Gothic manner, and of the municipalisation ethos of the Civic Gospel. It does not possess the drama and scale of the Free Library, but it is a purer, less compromised work of art. Sadly, Chamberlain did not live to see it, as he died on the day that he opened the tenders for its construction, 22 October 1883.

The land given by Cregoe Colmore for the school necessitated the cutting of a new street, Margaret Street, between Edmund Street and Great Charles Street. The main front of the school lies upon Margaret Street, with secondary frontages on Edmund Street and Cornwall Street. The organisation is roughly symmetrical about the central entrance on Margaret Street, but the composition of this elevation, and the relationship of the three elevations exemplify the principles of changefulness and organic planning. Each of the three gabled bays to Margaret Street is different, with the least emphasis being given to the central one. Instead, emphasis is given to the two end gables which contain, on their top floor, the north lit drawing and painting studios. They are unequal, the right-hand bay being of three storeys compared with two on the left. It is likely that this composition of this elevation derives from the earlier precedent of Highbury, designed for the MP, previously Mayor, Joseph Chamberlain. At Highbury, the tall right-hand bay was caused by a late addition of second floor rooms to the plan, but the irregular result must have pleased the architect.

The left-hand bay, on the corner of Cornwall Street, contains the most striking feature of the exterior. In the unfenestrated gable is placed a 3.6 m diameter roundel in buff terracotta, designed by Chamberlain and executed by one of his regular collaborators, Samuel Barfield of Leicester. Lilies trail wildly across a rectilinear trellis; faithfully naturalistic, but prefiguring Art Nouveau in their fluidity and dynamism.

In the toplit, arcaded entrance hall, originally called the Museum, the naturalistic ornament continues, with the carved stone capitals to the Shap granite columns illustrating berries, acorns, crocuses and pansies. The walls are bare red brick, with a simple pitch pine boarded dado. The floor is patterned in mosaic, and there is a relief portrait of Chamberlain in one wall. The Museum has the intense character of a small chapel.

School of Art, 1883–85. Margaret Street front

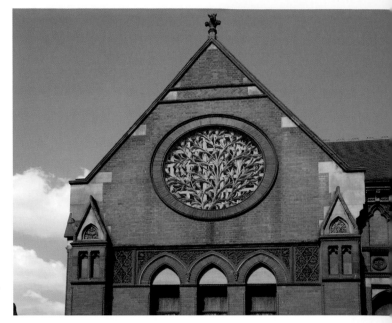

School of Art, detail
of left-hand bay

OPPOSITE School of
Art, entrance hall

Elsewhere, the interior has a plainer and more utilitarian manner, but every-where designed and executed with refinement. The staircases on either side of the Museum are lit by large lancet windows with stylised flower patterns in geometric leaded glass. The treads of the stairs have the same grid of end-grain wood blocks that was used in the Free Library, delightfully comfortable to the foot. In its early years, the School of Art gained a national reputation for its progressive teaching methods. The processes of painting, drawing and designing, in a city which earned its living by manufacturing, were reconsidered, and related to modern cir-cumstances. The building, which made a refined art from largely industrialised modern materials, was itself an exemplar of this.

In 1893, William Martin extended the School considerably, adding another nine bays to Chamberlain's five on Cornwall Street, entirely satisfactorily and sympa-thetically. In the 1990s, the building was immaculately cleaned and renovated by its present owners, Birmingham City University, with new accommodation cleverly inserted without being visible from any of the streets.

Martin and Chamberlain's Board Schools were not, strictly speaking, municipal buildings, although they were certainly conceived and perceived as being part of the town's Civic Gospel. Indeed, the Education Act of 1870, which sought to create for the first time secular education available to all, through local School Boards, was itself largely a product of the Civic Gospel. The 1870 Education Bill promoted by William Forster MP grew out of the work of the National Education League, based in Birmingham, chaired by George Dixon and containing all the other prominent Birmingham Liberals of the time.

However, despite this, the Liberals were defeated in the first election for the Birmingham School Board, in November 1870, which was won by the Tories. The Liberals took control in the next election of 1873, and continued to run the School Board until its dissolution in 1903.

The first commission of the first Board was for five schools; Bloomsbury Street, Jenkins Street, Farm Street, Steward Street and Garrison Lane. Martin and Chamberlain were the chosen architects, despite their Liberal associations, and they (and as Martin and Martin) continued to design the Birmingham Board Schools in a virtually unbroken succession until 1902. Forty seven schools in all were designed by the practice, twenty nine of them being designed before Chamberlain's death in 1883.

Collectively, these schools represent an extraordinary display of architectural consistency and invention, of endless variety upon a theme. Comparing the last school, Marchmont Road in Bordesley Green, with the first, Bloomsbury Street in Nechells, it is clear that they are members of the same family, although nearly thirty years separate them. No two schools of the forty seven have the same plan; each assembles the familiar elements of gable, lancet window, wall, ridge, ventilation tower, into a unique pattern which responds to the programme and the site. It is a compelling demonstration of the Ruskinian principle of change-fulness, put to work in the service of practicality, and producing visual delight.

The first five schools, which were completed in 1873, were comparatively simple in their planning. Junior boys and junior girls were each accommodated on an identical floor of a two-storey building, each with about six classrooms grouped in a rather pedestrian way around a main schoolroom. The infants were in a separate single-storey block. Although a system of ducted air extract was already present, the prominent ventilation towers which are such a characteristic feature of later schools were not yet present, the ducts terminating in louvred belfries on the ridge of the roof.

The effectiveness of the heating and ventilation systems of the Birmingham Board schools was remarked upon by several contemporary commentators. We may assume that these were primarily the contribution of the practically-minded William Martin. But for the poor children living in insanitary and overcrowded back-to-back houses in Nechells, Ladywood and Deritend, whose parents were paying 3d per week for their schooling, the environmental conditions in the schools were as much an illustration of the principle of Compensation, if not greater, than the naturalistic terracotta mouldings and ornamental cast iron arches of the architecture.

The environmental conditioning depended upon natural air movement, gener-ated by temperature difference and the passive stack effect of the tower, until the Floodgate Street School in 1891, when mechanical fan-assisted air movement was introduced. But despite the effectiveness of the systems of air ducts, with later exceptions in the 1890s they do not appear to have been a generator of the

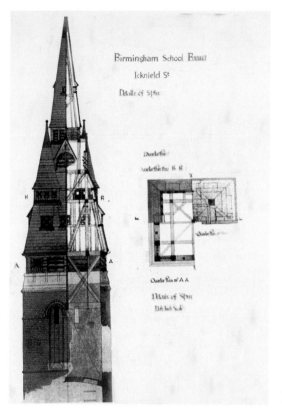

Birmingham School Board
Icknield St
Details of Spire

Icknield St School Tower, 1883

architectural pattern of the schools. The planning and three-dimensional form of the schools is derived primarily from spatial utility and educational needs, and the devices for the tempering of the air are pragmatically fitted in, not always in the most efficient manner possible.[24]

By the completion of Bristol Street School in 1876, the design of the Birmingham Board Schools had reached maturity. The planning was moving towards the so-called Prussian system, with all children in separate classrooms, each with their own teacher. This was not in fact fully achieved until Dudley Road School in 1878, due to a shortage of qualified staff.[25] But the central hall plan is here evident in both the infants' and juniors' parts, with classrooms arranged almost symmetrically on either side of a central schoolroom, which in the infants' case terminates in a semicircular apse.

The infants' and juniors' parts are connected by a third cluster which contains the girls' and infants' entrance hall, the caretaker's accommodation, rooms for the two heads, lavatories, and the magnificent gabled and spired ventilation tower. The main elevation facing Bristol Street displays the full and varied complexity of the three parts, in a freely-formed assembly of ten gables, containing diverse groupings of single, double and triple lancet windows of various sizes. It evokes

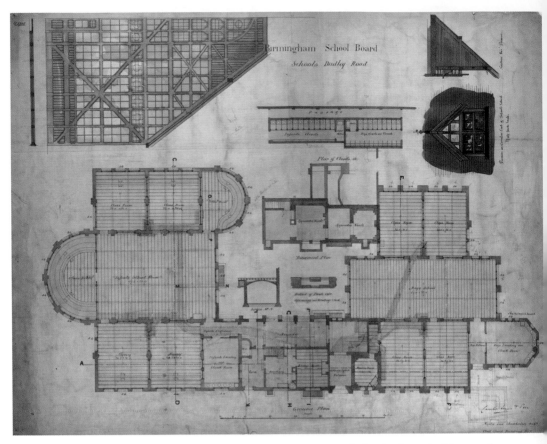

Dudley Road School, 1879. Ground floor plan. *Courtesy of Birmingham Archives and Heritage Services*

Ruskin's characterisation of the virtues of the Gothic builders; ' ... they never suffered ideas of outside symmetries and consistencies to interfere with the real use and value of what they did. If they wanted a window, they opened one; a room, they added one; a buttress, they built one; utterly regardless of any established conventionalities of external appearance'.[26]

The picturesque compositions such as this that resulted from the freely-planned Gothic Revival mode are indeed strikingly reminiscent of mediaeval ecclesiastical precedent as translated by doctrinaire 19th century propagandists such as A. W. Pugin. It is an irony apparently not remarked on at the time that a political movement dedicated to the wresting of education out of the hands of the church, and to the creation of an explicitly secular educational system, should result in Birmingham in school buildings which contained so many familiar signs of what was widely recognised as a Christian architecture. This was certainly not the case in, for example, London, where E. R. Robson's Board Schools in Queen

Anne Revival style were equally as successful as Martin and Chamberlain's in establishing the visual evidence of a coherent local and democratic educational system.

The pattern of two-storey junior block and single-storey infant block became the standard formula for the Board Schools, with a few exceptions such as Oozells Street of 1878, now converted to the Ikon Gallery, Icknield Street of 1883,[27] and Floodgate Street of 1891, where land values obliged the Board to build three-storey schools on restricted sites. As Birmingham's urban development spread and became more suburban in the 1880s and 1890s, the more expansive single-storey form became more typical, such as in Somerville Road of 1894.

Clearly Martin and Chamberlain's monopoly of the School Board's output (they also designed the Board's offices in Edmund Street in 1875)[28] reflected the Board's confidence both in the architects' design ability and in their ability to build within budget. However, it is clear that there was some opposition. An intriguingly defensive paragraph in the 1877 School Board report explains; 'In order to improve the ventilation of the schools, and to render the use of artificial means unnecessary, that part of the building containing the staircase has been carried up ... and forms a tower on the upper part of which the vitiated air from the boys' and girls' schools is carried. In no instance have these towers been provided for other than directly useful purposes.'[29]

The former Oozells Street School, 1878

Presumably drafted by the architects, it continues, referring to Pugin's second True Principle, 'With regard to the ornamental appearance of the buildings ... the attractiveness of the schools has not been caused by adding to their expense by any appreciable extent. The ornament is in nearly all instances part of the construction and could not be removed without loss to the stability of the schools; and it is the result of the care and thought that has been given to the design of these buildings, and has not been gained by unnecessary expenditure'.[30]

Commissions continued without a break after Chamberlain's death in 1883. Rumblings of complaint about the monopoly continued, however, and in 1896 the Board was obliged to hold a competition for the design of the Marlborough Road School. Martin and Martin won it. But in 1901, after the death of William Martin, and only a year before the 1902 Education Act abolished the School Boards and transferred their duties to the municipalities, Martin and Martin demanded a higher percentage fee, and their services to the School Board were terminated. The Board decided to employ its own salaried architect, and appointed Herbert Buckland, who later succeeded to the post of architect to the Council's Education Department in 1903.

Martin and Chamberlain, as has been shown, dominated municipal and public building in Birmingham in the 1870s and 1880s, and their architecture came to be the physical expression of the Civic Gospel. The major exception to this is right at the very top, in what could have been the greatest expression of the Civic Gospel – the Council House itself. The architect for the Council House was selected by a competition in 1871. The conduct of the competition was a shambles, and appears to have been significantly interfered with by local political interests.

The twenty nine entries to the competition were anonymous, identified only by mottoes. But it appears that Martin and Chamberlain were not among them. This may be explained by the shortness of time given to entrants, but is surprising, given the importance of the commission. Their non-appearance is an unexplained puzzle.

Martin and Chamberlain may have had a good reason for not entering the Council House competition, but they have to bear considerable responsibility for what was a major civic disappointment, that of the building of Corporation Street. This was a personal vision of the Mayor, Joseph Chamberlain, and was enabled by the Artisans' Dwellings Act of 1875. The Act provided for the compulsory purchase of slum areas, and their redevelopment including new working class housing. In Birmingham this took the form of the redevelopment of ninety three acres in the town centre, named the Improvement Scheme by the Mayor. The area was to be unified by a grand new street, to be named Corporation Street, nearly a mile long, running north from New Street. Martin and Chamberlain were appointed as surveyors.

It is clear that the urban surgery of the great Parisian boulevards planned by Baron Georges Haussmann, at that time being constructed, was an important source of the vision of Corporation Street. The Mayor and Councillor William White, the Chairman of the Improvement Committee, talked of the example of Paris, and described the future street as 'a great street, as broad as a Parisian boulevard from New Street to the Aston Road'.[31]

But Haussmann's rational engineering linked to classical axiality, supported by building codes which ensured regular, disciplined architecture, was entirely foreign to Martin and Chamberlain's gothic, organic sensibility. Started in 1878, the line of the new street curved pragmatically and picturesquely, uphill and downhill, and new buildings, including some by Martin and Chamberlain themselves, reflected a *laissez-faire* policy in which random variety was certainly allowed, if not encouraged.

A Parisian boulevard it was not, but neither did Corporation Street particularly illustrate the Civic Gospel. Critics pointed out that it was more a product of civic pride, and the term was not used complimentarily. Despite the terms of the enabling Act, no new housing was built within the Improvement Scheme. It effectively extended the commercial centre of the town, and benefited business, but as a piece of social engineering it failed.

John Henry Chamberlain died before Corporation Street was completed, but we might imagine that as a disciple of John Ruskin and a Trustee of the Guild of St George, he was disappointed by what he saw. More than any other late 19th century architect, he managed in his work to translate into form not only Ruskin's architectural precepts, but, through Birmingham's Civic Gospel, its social and ethical precepts too. He and William Martin would surely have welcomed, whether as architects or as master planners, the opportunity to represent in the town centre the importance which Ruskin placed on the proper housing of the working class. But, even in Liberal Birmingham, they were no more able than anyone else to put into practice Ruskin's radical economic precepts.

List of Architectural Works of John Henry Chamberlain (1831–1883)

John Henry Chamberlain was born in Leicester, and was articled to the Leicester architect, Henry Goddard (1792–1868). After a tour of Italy he set up in practice in Birmingham in c. 1855 and in 1864 entered into partnership with William Martin (1828–1900) as Martin and Chamberlain. Martin was born in Shepton Mallet and was articled to the Birmingham architect Thomas Plevins and then worked for D. R. Hill. William Martin continued the firm after Chamberlain's death, taking into partnership his two sons, Frederick and Herbert.

The list below covers J. H. Chamberlain's work as a sole practitioner from 1857 to 1864, and his work in partnership with William Martin from 1864 until 1885. The work of Martin and Chamberlain after 1885 is listed in the chapter on Edward Martin.

BIRMINGHAM AND ITS ENVIRONS

PUBLIC

c. 1860 Wesleyan Chapel, Essington St [D]

1863 Islington Wesleyan Methodist Chapel, St Martin's St [D]

1865 Free Library, Ratcliffe Place [destroyed by fire 1879]

c. 1867 Alterations to, and redecoration of, Town Hall, Paradise St

1870 Church of St Stephen, Serpentine Rd, Selly Park

1870 Infant School, Severn St

1870 Additions to Birmingham Accident Hospital, Steelhouse Lane [D]

? date Police Station, Dudley Rd

1873 Bloomsbury Board School, Lingard St for Birmingham School Board; 1875 additions; 1878 additions [D]

1873 Jenkins Street Board School, Small Heath for BSB; 1874 additions [D 1940]

1873 Farm St Board School, Summer Lane for BSB [D]

1873 Steward St Board School, Spring Hill for BSB

1873 Garrison Lane Board School, Bordesley for BSB

1874 Elkington Street Board School for BSB [D]

1874 Lower Windsor Street Board School, Duddeston for BSB [D]

1875 Allcock Street Board School, Bordesley for BSB[D]

1875 Rea Street South Board School, Deitend for BSB [D]

1875 Osler Street Board School, Ladywood for BSB [D]

1876 Dartmouth Street Board School for BSB [D]

1876 Baptist Chapel, Pershore Rd

1876 Smith Street Board School, Hockley for BSB [D]

1876 Bristol Street Board School for BSB [D]

1876 Nelson Street Board School for BSB [D]

1876 Norton Street Board School for BSB [D]

1877 Police Station, Moseley St

1877 Moseley Road Board School for BSB [D]

1877 Fox Street Board School for BSB [D]

1877 Summer Lane Board School for BSB [D]

1877 Brookfields Board School, Pitsford St for BSB [D 1940]

1877 Canopy to George Dawson statue, Chamberlain Place [D]

1878 Oozells Street Board School for BSB

1878 Dudley Road Board School for BSB

1878 Little Green Lane Board School, Small Heath for BSB [D]

1878 Lunatic asylum & cottages, Rubery for Birmingham Corporation

1879 Hutton Street Board School, Nechells for BSB [D]

1879 Montgomery Street Board School, Sparkbrook for BSB

1879 Dixon Road Board School, Small Heath for BSB

1879 Extension to Free Library, Edmund St [destroyed by fire 1879]

1879 Hope Street Board School for BSB [D]

1880 Memorial to Joseph Chamberlain, Chamberlain Place

1881 Extension to Birmingham and Midland Institute, Paradise St [D 1965]

1882 Free Library, Ratcliffe Place [D 1974 except Shakespeare Library dismantled and relocated in present Central Library]

1883 Public Baths, Monument Rd, Ladywood [D 1939]

1883 Central Fire Station, Upper Priory [D]

1883 King Edward VI Grammar School for Boys, Stratford Road, Camp Hill for BSB

1883 Branch Library, Constitution Hill [D]

1883 Icknield Street Board School, Hockley for BSB

1883 Foundry Road Board School, Winson Green for BSB

1883 Loxton Street Board School, Bloomsbury [D]

1883 Rubery Board School, Bristol Road South, Rednal for King's Norton School Board

1885 Municipal School of Art, Margaret St

COMMERCIAL

1857 Shop, 28–29 Union St, for Eld and Chamberlain [D]

187? Alterations to Birmingham Waterworks Company Offices, Broad St

1873 Offices for the Birmingham School Board, Edmund St

1880 New Premises for Averys, Corporation St/Bull St

1881 Premises for Birmingham Household Supply Association Ltd, Corporation St [D]

1883 Premises for Ray and Prosser, Corporation St [D]

1883 Shop front and warehouses, 17 Bull St

1883 Warehouse, Lower Priory

INDUSTRIAL

1862 Edgbaston Waterworks, Waterworks Rd [partly D]

1867 Aston Pumping Station [D]

1874 Selly Oak Pumping Station

DOMESTIC

1856 Shenstone House for Mr Eld, 12 Ampton Rd, Edgbaston

1863 Ferndale for W. A. Winkler, 50 Carpenter Rd, Edgbaston

1875 Whetstone, Somerset Rd, Edgbaston for J. H. Chamberlain [D]

1875 Four houses, Edgbaston Lane for Messrs Gibbs and Harrison

1875 Additions to The Grove, Harborne for William Kenrick [D, anti-room at V&A]

1876 Penryn, Somerset Rd, Edgbaston for James Deykin [D]

1878 Additions to Berrow Court, Edgbaston for J. A. Kenrick; 1895 additions

1878 Additions to Park Grove, Edgbaston for John Jaffray

1878 Highbury, Moor Green, King's Heath for Joseph Chamberlain

1879 Lodge to Oakmount, Westbourne Rd, Edgbaston for Richard Chamberlain

1884 Additions to Harborne Hall, Church Rd, Harborne for Walter Chamberlain

1884 Additions to Kelton, Church Rd, Edgbaston

WORK OUTSIDE BIRMINGHAM

PUBLIC

1859 Stoneygate School, 254 London Rd, Leicester for George Franklin

1859 Brooklands House, Uppingham School, Rutland

1870 Church of St Barnabas, Franche, Worcestershire

INDUSTRIAL

1880 Pumping station at Whitacre, Warwickshire

c. 1880 Offices for Archibald Kenrick and Sons Ltd, hollow-ware manufacturers, Spon Lane, West Bromwich

---

NOTES

[1] John Ruskin, *Fors Clavigera: Letters to the Workmen and Labourers of Great Britain*, ed. by Dinah Birch (Keele, 2000).

[2] E. H. Scott, *Ruskin's Guild of St George* (1931), pp. 27–8.

[3] John Ruskin, *The Stones of Venice* (1st vol. 1851, 2nd and 3rd vols 1853).

[4] R. W. Dale, quoted in R. A. Armstrong, *Henry William Crosskey: his Life and Work* (1895), p. 245 *passim*.

[5] Sir Arthur Conan Doyle, *The Memoirs of Sherlock Holmes: The Naval Treaty* (1893).

[6] John Ruskin, *Stones of Venice*, ed. by Jan Morris (1981), p. 122.

[7] *Ibid*, p. 123.

[8] Birmingham Central Library, Archives and Heritage Services (henceforth BCL AHS) King's Norton Building Register, app. no. 279, June 4 1878 mansion for Joseph Chamberlain; BCL AHS, MS 1338/3 Kenrick Architectural Drawings, plans of Highbury and BDS 1999/33 Drawings for Highbury.

[9] BCL AHS, Harborne Building Register, app. A, 2 Jan 1875, house 'The Grove' for William Kenrick.

[10] BCL AHS, Birmingham Building Register, app. no. 1535, 11 January 1878.

[11] BCL AHS, Harborne Building Register, app. no. 4 29 February, 1884, additions to Harborne Hall.

[12] The author is indebted to Brenda Piper, a great, great niece of John Henry Chamberlain for some biographical details.

[13] *Edgbastonia*, 3, 3 November 1883.

[14] Asa Briggs, *Victorian Cities* (1963, 1968 ed.) p. 190.

[15] John Ruskin, 'The Lamp of Sacrifice', Chapter 1 in *The Seven Lamps of Architecture* (first pub. 1849, 1907 edition), p. 15.

[16] A. W. Pugin, *The True Principles of Pointed or Christian Architecture* (1841).

[17] J. H. Chamberlain, *An Introductory Lecture on the Offices and Duties of Architecture* (Birmingham, 1858), pp. 6–7.

[18] E. M. Barry in letter to *The Builder*, 10, 26 April 1862.

[19] BCL AHS, MS 1338/9–10 Martin and Chamberlain's drawings for Birmingham Central Library and Reference Library 1878–79; Birmingham Building Register, app. no. 1049, 3 April 1878.

[20] BCL AHS, MS 1338/8 J. H. Chamberlain's drawings for extension to Birmingham and Midland Institute, 1879.

[21] BCL AHS, Birmingham Building Register, app. no. 1956, 21 October 1879.

[22] BCL AHS, Birmingham Building Register, app. no. 3971, 1 February 1884.

[23] J. T. Bunce, *History of the Corporation of Birmingham*, vol. 11 1852–1884 (Birmingham, 1885), p. 249.

[24] P. Buchan, 'Piped Air', unpublished Diploma dissertation, Birmingham School of Architecture, University of Central England, 1975.

[25] BCL AHS, Birmingham Building Register, app. no. 78, 5 October 1876.

[26] Ruskin, *The Stones of Venice*, ed. Morris, p. 123.

[27] Birmingham Building Register, app. no. 3023, 24 November 1881.

[28] BCL AHS, MS 1338/1 Martin and Chamberlain's drawings for Birmingham School Board Offices, *c.* 1875.

[29] BCL AHS, Birmingham School Board, Annual Report, 1877.

[30] *Ibid.*

[31] Conrad Gill and Asa Briggs, *History of Birmingham* vol 2 (1952), p. 19.

8 John George Bland

PETER LEATHER

Research into the life and career of John George Bland (1820–98) was initially hampered by the lack of a detailed obituary. Neither the local papers nor the Birmingham Architectural Association saw fit to mark his passing. This is surprising and not a little mysterious (as is the fact that he was not a member of the BAA) when it is considered that he had been an architect for over fifty years and had spent more than forty of them in Birmingham. The one obituary he did get, in *The Builder* for May 1898, reads simply, 'Mr. John Bland, who for many years practiced as an architect in Temple-street, Birmingham, died suddenly in his office on the 16th inst. Mr Bland was about seventy years of age.'[1]

Subsequent discoveries about Bland's career set out in this chapter may explain in part his relative anonymity in Birmingham; but questions remain, upon which one can only speculate at present.

The statement in *The Builder* obituary that he was 'about seventy years of age' at the time of his death is presumably the source of the statement in the *Directory of British Architects 1834–1914* that he was born in 1828 or 1829. This is incorrect. He was in fact born in 1820, in East Farndon, Northamptonshire to George Bland, freeholder and his wife, Maria.[2] He was baptised in August, so his age at death would therefore be seventy-seven. By 1832 the family was living in Dingley, still in Northamptonshire, but only three miles from Market Harborough in Leicestershire – both of these places were to play an important part in Bland's early career.[3] No details have yet emerged of his general education (although a good starting point might be the registers of Market Harborough and Clipston grammar schools) but he received his architectural training from a noted church builder, William Adams Nicholson of Lincoln.[4]

Bland's career started in the 1840s when he was still based in Dingley; but by 1849 his address was St Mary's Road, Market Harborough.[5] The principal source for this phase of his career is the two editions of J. D. Bennett's *Leicestershire Architects*.[6] His first known building may be the School at Wilbarston (1846), just three miles from Dingley.[7] He also worked locally (within ten miles of Dingley) on the Church of St Michael, Cranoe, Leicestershire, rebuilding all but the 13th-century tower in the Perpendicular style (1847–49),[8] and on the various outbuildings and structures at Lamport Hall (*c.* 1849).[9] He is also recorded as working at an unspecified date on the Church of St Mary at Brampton Ash, two miles from Dingley.[10] Contacts at the church have no idea what he might have done as

St Mary's is an unspoilt and 'un-victorianised' 13th-century building — perhaps he was consulted as the local architect on minor repairs?

A little farther afield, he built the School at Irchester, twenty three miles from Dingley, in 1848,[11] but his most distant project was at Papworth St Agnes over forty miles away in Cambridgeshire, where 'the former Rectory, W of the Church, of brick, in a free Georgian style, was built in 1847–8 by John Bland'.[12] The Rector of Papworth St Agnes at that time was J. H. Sperling, a noted Ecclesiologist, who was engaged in rebuilding the medieval parish church of St John the Baptist with a new tower in 1848 and nave and chancel in 1854.[13] In 1851 Bland was appointed surveyor to the Market Harborough Vestry.[14]

Bland's work in the East Midlands – at least in terms of known buildings – ceases at this point and he seems to have left Dingley by 1854 at the latest.[15] But he is not recorded in Birmingham until 1856 (see below) and no evidence has emerged for where else he may have been based in the interim. One thing however is sure: a series of major and possibly life-changing commissions at this time brought him almost eighty miles away from Dingley to Kidderminster in Worcestershire.[16]

The Gothic Longmeadow Mills (1853–54) and Classical Stour Vale Mills (1855–56) are among the first of Kidderminster's big new Victorian carpet factories.[17] Indeed the latter has been hailed as the standard for all the others.[18] He also built the Crane & Barton Carpet Factory of 1856.[19] The question of how a revivalist church architect came to be the principal builder of Kidderminster carpet factories will be discussed at the end of this chapter but for the moment suffice to say that this would seem to prove the reason and motivation for Bland's move to Birmingham.

The date of his arrival can be deduced from the local Directories, where he first appears in 1856, living at 5 Wellesley Place, Wheeley's Road, Edgbaston[20] and with an office in the almost brand new Unity Buildings (1853–54) on Temple Street (then Upper Temple Street).[21] He was to stay in the same office throughout his time in Birmingham and, as seen from his obituary above, actually died there.

His residential arrangements, however, were more varied. By 1860 he had moved to Acock's Green where, as shall be seen later, he had one of his major commissions. No actual address is known until 1864 when he is in Sherbourne Road. This house may or may not be the 'Riversdale' listed in 1875 or perhaps this was the one in Station Road listed in 1878? By 1880 he had returned to Edgbaston and 14 Speedwell Road. This is where he was living at the time of the 1881 Census, where he is listed as the head of a household comprising his wife, Caroline, who at 28-years-old was thirty years younger than him and only a few years older than his three elder children, and who must therefore have been the products of a previous marriage or marriages, his daughter, Maria (24), sons, George and James (22 and 21), daughter, Grace (10), a cook and a housemaid. His final house-move was to Church Road, Moseley by 1884 – always presuming that this is the same

Transepts and Chancel of
Church of Ascension, Hall
Green, 1860s. *Photo: PL*

house as the one given as 'Queenswood Villas, Church Road' in 1890 and '35
Church Road' in 1898.

His first recorded commission while in Birmingham was another departure in
the form of a house 'in a kind of Rundbogenstil with central porch tower' near
Stroud built in 1858.[22] That this was probably built for the owner of a nearby mill
begs a question as does the fact, perhaps coincidental, that his young wife in the
1881 Census came from Stroud.

Bland's first recorded work in Birmingham is the addition of transepts and
chancel in the same style to the Queen Anne Church of the Ascension of 1703, then
known as the Marston Chapel, in Hall Green. The date for this is given as 1860 by
both Pevsner and Foster but the latest edition of the church guidebook is more
cautious, saying only '1860s' but adding: 'According to notes found in a diary kept
by a member of the King family the builder was Mr. Samuel Briggs and the architect was Mr. Bland. At present no formal record has been found to confirm this'.[23]

While churches, chapels and schools continued to remain part of Bland's portfolio, it is no surprise, given what we now know about his activities in Kidderminster, that his best Birmingham building is a factory. This was the Albert Works
(now The Argent Centre) of 1862–63, on the corner of Legge Lane and Frederick
Street in the Jewellery Quarter.[24] The polychrome brickwork of this 'Lombardic
castle' is a far cry from the Revivalist styles of his early buildings.[25] It is among the
first of the new breed of Italianate architecture which was to transform Birmingham 'from a largely drab and dreary Georgian town ... to a vibrant Victorian
city'.[26] The building is not only significant for its architecture but also for its
fireproof construction: 'The details of construction are of considerable interest,
and stand out from the general trends of manufactory construction at the time'.[27]
In addition, 'J. G. Bland probably also designed a fireproof manufactory at
Nos 84–86 Vittoria Street, now part of the School of Jewellery, built in about 1865

Argent Centre, formerly Albert Works, 1862–63

Vittoria Street Manufactory, *c.* 1865

for William Randel, goldsmith'.[28] Two further Kidderminster carpet factories date from the same time as these: the Waterside Mill of 1862 and the Imperial Mill of 1864.[29]

Bland also had several major church commissions at this time. St Mary the Virgin in Acock's Green (1864–66) was in a simple, lofty Early English style, never to be crowned with the steeple he intended, but later 'Chatwinised' with Decorated chancel, vestry and organ chamber.[30] The New Wesleyan Chapel in Summer Hill of 1866 was also Early English[31] but the Aston Villa Methodist Chapel of 1865 combines Early English with a more High Victorian Gothic.[32] Outside Birmingham he added the reredos to St Mary, Wythall in Worcestershire in 1866[33] and undertook repairs to All Saints, Emberton in Buckinghamshire in 1868–69.[34]

This is, furthermore, the period of Bland's only known buildings in the London area: a classical Baptist Chapel in Camberwell in 1863,[35] and two Venetian Gothic schools for the Russell Hill Schools of the Warehousemen, Clerks and Drapers, the first in Russell Hill (Purley) itself in 1863–64,[36] and the second in Croydon in 1864.[37] The Russell Hill School is the only one of his buildings to be featured in *The Builder*.[38]

Bland's longstanding links with Kidderminster re-emerge at the end of the decade with another carpet factory, Morton's Works (1869–70)[39] and his most prestigious project in the town, the 'High Victorian Gothic' Kidderminster Infirmary/General Hospital (1870–71), which he won in competition with eighteen other architects, perhaps an indication of how well he was regarded there.[40]

A plan of 1871 in Birmingham Central Library shows an 'educational Gothic' extension to St Saviour's Junior and Infant School in Alum Rock Road, which later maps and photographs show that this was indeed built, although demolished in the 1970s.[41] It is incredible and so far inexplicable, given all he had achieved in the

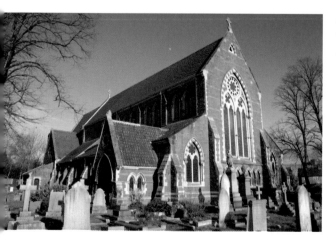

St Mary the Virgin, Acock's Green, Aisle and Nave.
Photo: PL

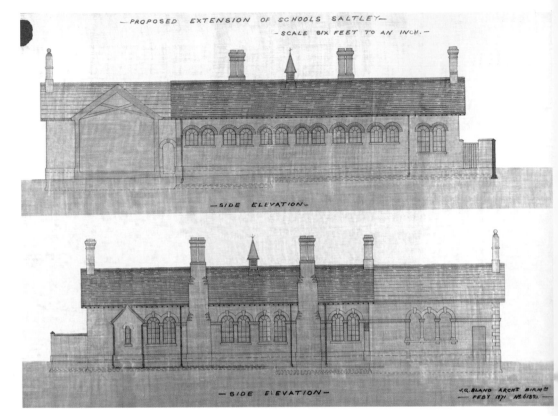

St Saviour's School, Alum Rock Road, plan drawing of extension, 1871. *Courtesy of Birmingham Archives and Heritage Services (MS 1446/38 2)*

1860s, and the fact that he had twenty-seven more years ahead of him, that this is the last Birmingham building project that can definitely be assigned to Bland.

Sometime between 1872 and 1875 Bland went into partnership with Jethro Anstice Cossins.[42] This almost certainly lasted until 1882/83.[43] The majority of buildings known from this time are assigned to Cossins and are dealt with in the appropriate chapter. It is possible that the Warwick House commission of 1880 was Bland's work and his expertise in factory building might suggest that the 1882 Manufactory in New Bartholomew Street was his too.[44]

Whatever the case in Birmingham, Bland was still much sought-after in Kidderminster. He built the polychromatic Barton's Carpet Factory Offices, Showroom and Warehouse in 1872 fronting his Crane and Barton Factory of 1856, and the Queen Anne-style Worcester Cross offices of Willis & Co in 1878–79.[45] Willis went on to be Mayor of Kidderminster in 1880–81 and in 1882 commissioned Bland to build him a 'fairy-tale mansion' in Scottish Baronial style at Brockencote Hall, Chaddesley in Worcestershire.[46]

ABOVE Offices of Stour Vale
Mills Carpet Factory. Green St,
Kidderminster, 1855–56

LEFT Offices of Barton's Carpet
Factory, Vicar Street,
Kidderminster, 1872

This is currently the last known building by Bland. Perhaps other later ones await discovery or perhaps, now in his sixties, he decided to take things easier and kept up his office for occasional consultancies. Why he did not devote some of his time to membership of the Birmingham Architectural Association, to which almost all Birmingham's architects belonged, remains a mystery.

Whatever the reason, the next record of Bland is the stark notice of his death in the Probate records, 'Bland John George of Church-road Moseley Worcestershire architect died 16 May 1898 at Temple-street Birmingham Administration Worcester 17 June to Caroline Teresa Bland widow Effects £45'.[47] The need for Administration means that there was no will; but neither the absence of a will nor the relatively small amount, by professional standards, left to his widow is necessarily a sign of reduced work and circumstances in has final years. It could equally be a case, common enough in the Victorian period, of a wealthy man passing on his wealth to his benefactors before death – and taxes!

What then are we to make of Bland? His training with Nicholson set him on the road to be a revivalist church architect. It is possible that his work at Papworth St Agnes, so far from home by comparison with his other early commissions, brought him into contact with the ecclesiological ideas of Rev. Sperling and his time there may even have been expressly for that purpose. Unsurprising, then, that almost all his work while based in Dingley and Market Harborough was church-related, if we count church schools in that category.

So what happened to him in the 1850s to make him a factory builder? One of the obstacles to answering this question is that factories, unlike churches, have only recently become an object of architectural interest. It is especially noteworthy in Bland's case that Pevsner's *Worcestershire* makes no mention of him and it is only Alan Brook's reworking of the volume that has acknowledged his importance as a builder of carpet factories in Kidderminster. In the town itself, Bland has long been considered one of its most significant architects. As more work is done on the historic factories of the Midlands, information may come to light enabling Bland's evolution as a factory builder to be traced, perhaps all the way back to his home county.

Stylistically, Bland borrowed widely from his own revivalist background, earlier architecture both Classical and Gothic and from the changing trends of the 1860s, 70s and 80s. He is in fact a model of Victorian eclecticism, drawing inspiration from all architectural styles but never concentrating sufficiently on one to make it his own. As such it cannot be claimed that he contributed significantly to any particular trend in Victorian architecture, although the Italianate style of his Albert Works/Argent Centre is among the first of its kind in Birmingham.

However, looking not so much at the artistic as the engineering merits of his buildings, Bland's reputation is worthy of re-evaluation. Now that it is known that the Argent Centre is not the one-off exercise it once seemed and instead formed part of a whole series of fireproof factories, it may well be the case that Bland has to be considered for possible inclusion among the foremost practitioners in this field.

The final question to be addressed is why Bland died in comparative anonymity in the city where he had been working for over fifty years. Does his non-membership of the Birmingham Architectural Association hint at some rift between him and his fellow architects or was it simply that he was already too long in the tooth by the time it was formed to bother to join? And what of his much younger wife – was there any social impropriety there or was he simply one of those unfortunate Victorian men whose previous wife or wives had died young, perhaps in childbirth?

This is all of course pure – some might say baseless – speculation. In terms of both his professional and personal life, only time – and more research – will tell.

Selected List of Architectural Works of John George Bland

J. G. Bland (1820–98) was articled to W. A. Nicholson of Lincoln. His early career was in Leicestershire, and by 1856 he had set up in practice in Birmingham. From c. 1875–82 he was in partnership with Jethro Cossins, and then continued as a sole practioner until his death in 1898.

WORK IN BIRMINGHAM AND ITS ENVIRONS

PUBLIC

1860? Extension to Church of the Ascension, Hall Green (then known as Marston Chapel)

1864–66? Church of St Mary the Virgin, Warwick Rd, Acock's Green

1865 Aston Villa Methodist Chapel (now New Testament Church of God), George St/ Lozells Rd, Lozells

1866? New Wesleyan Chapel, Summer Hill [D]

1871 Extension to School, St Saviour's Junior and Infants, Alum Rock Rd [D 1972]

INDUSTRIAL

1862–63 Albert Works pen factory (now Argent Centre), Legge Lane

1865? Goldsmith's Factory and offices, 82–86 Vittoria St (later incorporated into school of Jewellery)

Also Perryan Pencil Manufactory? Ironmongers' Hall? (listed in Bland's entry in the *Building Trades' Directory*, 1868 as Birmingham buildings but not otherwise recorded – perhaps the Perryan Pencil Manufactory is in fact the Albert Works, which is not otherwise included, and the Ironmonger's Hall, an unlikely prospect in Birmingham in any case, was never built?)

1882– Manufactory, New Bartholomew St (Bland and Cossins) [D]

COMMERCIAL

1880 Shops and Offices, Corporation St (Bland and Cossins) [D 1950s?]

1880 Vaults to Warwick House, New St (Bland and Cossins)[D 1930s?]

1882 Four Shops, [189–195] Hagley Rd (Bland and Cossins)

DOMESTIC

1876 House, Augustus [actually Augusta] Rd, Moseley (Bland and Cossins) [D]

1882 Villa, Oxford Rd, Moseley (Bland and Cossins)[D]

WORK OUTSIDE BIRMINGHAM

PUBLIC

1846 School, Wilbarston, Northants.

1847–49 Church of St Michael, Cranoe, Leics. (rebuilding of all but W tower)

1848 School, Irchester, Northants.

1863 Baptist Chapel, Rye Lane, Camberwell, London

1864 Russell Hill Schools of the Warehousemen, Clerks and Drapers, Croydon, Surrey

1866 Reredos, Church of St Mary, Wythall, Worcs.

1868–69 Reseating/Repairs, Church of All Saints, Emberton, Bucks.

1870–71 Kidderminster General Hospital (originally Kidderminster Infirmary), Mill St, Kidderminster, Worcs. (converted into flats)

INDUSTRIAL

1853–54 Carpet Factory, Longmeadow Mills, Dixon St, Kidderminster, Worcs. [D 1980s?]

1855–56 Carpet Factory, Stour Vale Mills, Green St, Kidderminster, Worcs.

1856 Carpet Factory for Crane & Barton, Kidderminster, Worcs. [D]

1862? Carpet Factory, Waterside Mill, Kidderminster, Worcs. [D]

1864? Carpet Factory, Imperial Mill, Kidderminster, Worcs. [D 1976]

1869–70 Carpet Factory for Morton's, New Rd, Kidderminster, Worcs.

1872 Carpet Factory, Offices, Showroom & Warehouse for Barton's, Vicar St (fronting Crane & Barton factory of 1856), Kidderminster, Worcs.

1878–79 Carpet Factory Offices, Worcester Cross, Oxford St, Kidderminster, Worcs.

Also the *Building Trades' Directory*, 1868, after a list of the five Kidderminster carpet factories above built between 1853 and 1864 by Bland, states '… and others. Also, Flour and Cotton Mills, at Kidderminster; and numerous other works.'

DOMESTIC

1847–48 Rectory, Papworth St Agnes, Cambridgeshire

1848–50 Lodges to Lamport Hall, Northamptonshire – also Lamport Manor Home Farm

1858 House, 174 Slad Rd, Stroud, Gloucestershire

1882 Brockencote Hall, Chaddesley, Worcestershire [almost entirely rebuilt after fire
    damage in 1920s]

NOTES

¹ *The Builder*, 74, 1898, p. 497.

² A. Brodie *et al*, *Directory of British Architects 1834–1914* (2001); The route to discovering the details of Bland's birth was a roundabout one. The 1881 Census gives his place of birth as 'Faindon' which does not exist, and it was at first assumed that this was Finedon, By sheer coincidence, a John Bland had been born there in 1822 (information kindly supplied by Diane Hodge of Finedon Library). However J. D. Bennett, in researching the second edition of *Leicestershire Architects*, had correctly identified Bland's place of birth from the 1851 Census but falsely assumed that, since he was then thirty, he must have been born in 1821. The final detail of Bland's genealogy came from Andrea Pettingale of Kettering Library to whom many thanks.

³ Based on the 1832 Poll Book – information supplied by Andrea Pettingale.

⁴ Brodie, *Directory*.

⁵ He is referred to as 'Bland of Dingley' in association with his works at Slawston in 1848 (J. D. Bennett personal communication) and Cranoe in 1847–49 (Nikolaus Pevsner, *The Buildings of England: Leicestershire and Rutland* 2nd ed. revised by E. Williamson and G. K. Brandwood (Harmondsworth, 1984) pp. 142–43) but appears under Market Harborough in 1849 and 1851 directories and 1851 Census (J. D. Bennett personal communication).

⁶ J. D. Bennett, *Leicestershire Architects* (1st ed. Leicester, 1968) no pagination; (2nd ed. Leicester, 2001) p. 17.

⁷ *Ibid*, in 1st ed. only.

⁸ *Ibid*. In Bennett the date is given as 1849 but more information and a date of 1849–50 is given in Pevsner, *Leicestershire* pp. 142–43.

⁹ Bennett lists the Steward's House and Porter's Lodge and dates them to 1848. Nikolaus Pevsner in his *The Buildings of England: Northamptonshire* 2nd. edn. rev. by B. Cherry (Harmondsworth, 1973) p. 289, says 'Lodges 1849–50, probably by J. G. Bland, who designed Lamport Manor Home Farm in a similar Tudor style'; Northamptonshire SMR gives Swan Lodge *c*. 1849 (SMR No. 4292/2/9–MNN 109016) and Gates, gatepiers and wall, *c*. 1849 also by Bland (SMR No. 4392/2/10–MNN 109017); contacts at Lamport Hall think that the lodges in Pevsner are Swan Lodge and Porter's Lodge and that the Steward's House in Bennett may be the building which is now Swan Inn.

¹⁰ Bennett, *Leicestershire Architects*.

¹¹ *Ibid*.

¹² Nikolaus Pevsner, *The Buildings of England: Cambridgeshire* (2nd. ed. Harmondsworth, 1970), pp. 448–49.

¹³ *Ibid*; www.friendsoffriendlesschurches.org.uk/papworth/papworth.htm (accessed 01/03/2007).

¹⁴ Bennett, *Leicestershire Churches*.

¹⁵ *Ibid*.

¹⁶ Bland's work in Kidderminster was first brought to the author's attention by Alan Brooks, who generously supplied information in advance of publication of A. Brooks, and N. Pevsner, *Pevsner Architectural Guides: Worcestershire* (2007); this was subsequently confirmed and expanded by the *Building Trades' Directory 1868*; K. Tomkinson, and G. Hall, *Kidderminster since 1800* (2nd ed. Kidderminster, 1985), p. 106: M. Thompson, *Woven in Kidderminster* (Kidderminster, 2002), p. 41, p. 45, and D. Gilbert, *Town and Borough: A Civic History of Kidderminster* (Kidderminster, 2004), pp. 14–15, p. 81, p. 88.

¹⁷ Bland's first five Kidderminster carpet factories are listed by name of company in the *Building Trades' Directory* 1868 and can be identified by cross-referencing with Thompson, *Woven*, Chapter 6, 'Company Review' pp. 136–91.

¹⁸ Thompson, *Woven*, p. 45.

¹⁹ See note 17.

²⁰ This and all subsequent information about where Bland lived and worked in Birmingham is taken from the street directories in Birmingham Central Library.

²¹ Andy Foster, *Pevsner Architectural Guides: Birmingham* (New Haven and London, 2005), p. 120.

²² D. Verey and A. Brooks, *Pevsner Architectural Guides: Gloucestershire 1: The Cotswolds* (Harmondsworth, 1999), p. 667.

²³ Nikolaus Pevsner and Alexandra Wedgwood, *Buildings of England: Warwickshire* (Harmondsworth, 1966), p. 178; Foster, *Birmingham*, p. 269; A. M. Brown, *The Church of the Ascension, Hall Green* (2003), no pagination.

²⁴ Foster, *Birmingham*, p. 166.

²⁵ Douglas Hickman, *Birmingham* (1970), p. 43. He wrongly dates it to *c*. 1885.

²⁶ Peter Leather, *The Buildings of Birmingham* (Stroud, 2002), p. 91.

[27] J. Cattell, S. Ely and B. Jones, *The Birmingham Jewellery Quarter: an Architectural Survey of the Manufactories* (Swindon, 2002), pp. 117–18, p. 186, p. 244.

[28] *Ibid*, p. 118, p. 145.

[29] See note 17.

[30] *Building News*, 14, 28 October 1866; Pevsner *Warwickshire*, pp. 143–44.

[31] *Building Trades' Directory 1868; Building News*, 14, 12 October 1866; *A History of the County of Warwick*, vol. 7: *Birmingham*, ed. by W. B. Stephens (1964), p. 423 implies that the chapel was erected in 1855 but the 1866 date seems far more likely.

[32] *Building Trades' Directory*, 1868; 'Aston Villa Methodist Church, Handsworth', *Digital Handsworth*, www.digitalhandsworth.org.uk (accessed 01/03/2007). It may be of interest to know that this is the church from which Aston Villa Football Club was founded!

[33] *Ex inform* Alan Brooks, see note 16.

[34] www.churchplansonline.org (accessed 01/03/2007).

[35] B. Cherry and Nikolaus Pevsner, *The Buildings of England, London 2: South* (Harmondsworth, 1983), p. 617, p. 227.

[36] *Ibid*, p. 227.

[37] I. Nairn and Nikolaus Pevsner, *The Buildings of England: Surrey* (Harmondsworth, 1962), p. 162.

[38] *The Builder*, 24, 1866, p. 11 (illustration), p. 13.

[39] *Ex inform* Alan Brooks (see note 17); Thompson, Woven, p. 151.

[40] Gilbert, *Kidderminster*, p. 81; *ex inform* Alan Brooks; www.institutions.org.uk/hospitals/england/worcs/kidderminster_infirmary.htm (accessed 01/03/2007).

[41] Birmingham Central Library, Archives and Heritage Services (hereafter BCL, AHS), MS 1446/38 Birmingham School Building Plans; J. M. Jones, *Saltley and Little Bromwich* (Birmingham, 1974), p. 15.

[42] The last of the local directories in Birmingham Central Library to show Bland on his own is 1872 and the first to show him with Cossins is 1875.

[43] According to his obituary in the *Birmingham Post* of 6 December 1917, Cossins established his own practice in 1879. However building plans in the name of Bland & Cossins exist for 1880 and 1882, and the Directories list them together until 1882, Cossins first appearing on his own in 1883.

[44] BCL AHS, Birmingham Building Register, app. no. 2513, vaults to Warwick House, New Street, 13 November 1880; *Ibid*, app. no. 3114, manufactory, New Bartholomew Street, 6 March 1882.

[45] *Ex inform* Alan Brooks (see note 17).

[46] Gilbert, *Kidderminster*, p. 15.

[47] *Calendar of the Grants of Probate and Letters of Administration*, 1898.

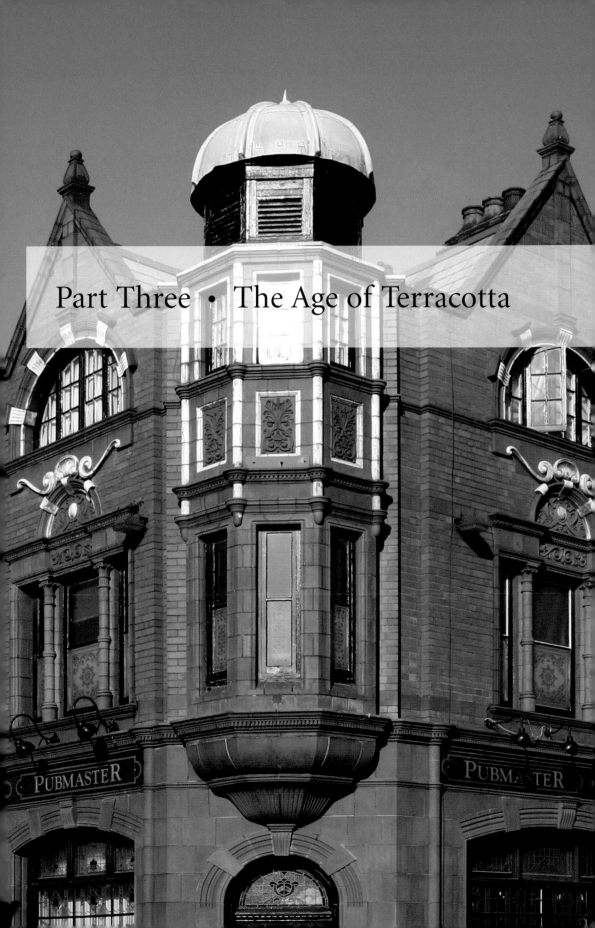

Part Three • The Age of Terracotta

9 Essex, Nicol & Goodman

DONALD ABBOTT

The architectural practice which was to become known to late-Victorian Birmingham as Essex, Nicol & Goodman originated in 1883, when the newly qualified Oliver Essex (1855–1939) first set up practice on his own account at 35, Paradise Street. Three years later, in 1886, he moved to 8, Newhall Street, where, in the following year, 1887, he was joined by John Coulson Nicol (1848–1933) and the name of the firm became Essex & Nicol. In 1892, as a consequence of the additional amount of work being generated by the practice, John Goodman (1864–1951) was also admitted into partnership, and so the firm of Essex, Nicol & Goodman finally came into being.[1] The three partners continued in practice together under this name for the next thirteen years, until 1905, when Coulson Nicol left, together with his recently qualified son, George Salway Nicol, in order to set up their own firm of Nicol & Nicol. Oliver Essex and John Goodman however, continued in partnership, the name of the firm changing once more, this time to Essex & Goodman, which was to remain its name until the death of Oliver Essex in 1939.

Essex, Nicol & Goodman, together with its preceding and succeeding partnerships, was one of Victorian and Edwardian Birmingham's most prominent architectural practices, being responsible for many outstanding buildings in and around the City centre. These included offices, shops, stores and factories in the private sector, together with public works for the Corporation. Noted as being one of the first firms in the City to make an extensive use of terracotta, they incorporated this into buildings mainly of late Gothic or varying types of Renaissance design. They were also responsible for two of the City's earliest and best known cinemas. However, their work was far from being confined to Birmingham. Their practice extended far beyond the Midlands, and from their earliest days they had an office in London, where they gained many commissions.

Oliver Essex, the younger son of Benjamin and Hannah Essex, was born in a terraced house in Great King Street, Hockley, Birmingham, in 1855. His father, who was from London, was by trade a journeyman silver engraver, who later set up shop as a book and music seller in Constitution Hill. It is not known where Oliver received his education, but it would almost certainly have been at one of the many Church schools available at that time. In 1870, when Oliver was only fourteen years of age, both of his parents died of tuberculosis, within a few months of each other, and he was temporarily forced to abandon his ambition to become an architect.[2] Three years later, however, he became a pupil in the offices

Oliver Essex and John Goodman. John Goodman's photograph *courtesy of Mary Goodman*

of W. H. Ward, where he financed the cost of his training to be an architect during the day, by means of his working for the Post Office by night.[3] He stayed with Ward for ten years, becoming first an assistant, and then manager. In 1883, he was admitted as an Associate of the Royal Institute of British Architects, becoming a Fellow in 1892. During his time with Ward, around 1881, Essex took up lodgings in the house of Edward Short, an accountant's clerk, in Sandford Road, Moseley, where he met the Shorts' eldest daughter, Effie. They were to be married eleven years later; there were no children of the marriage. Amongst his other interests, Essex included painting, being an exhibitor of water colours at the Birmingham Society of Artists and the Midland Arts Club. He was also a member of the committee of the Archaeological section of the Birmingham and Midland Institute.[4] He never retired, working right up until his death in 1939, at the age of eighty-three. He was buried in Harborne Parish Churchyard, following a service at St George's Church, Edgbaston. By the time he died, he had amassed an estate which was valued at £177,174, (equivalent to an astonishing £4,580,000 today).

John Coulson Nicol, who joined Oliver Essex in partnership in 1887, was born in Aberdeen in 1848, the son of George Nicol, a brewer, and his wife Catherine. He was apprenticed to Alexander Ellis in Aberdeen, later joining W. Hamilton Beattie in the offices of George Beattie and Son, in Edinburgh, where he gained experience in the erection of Craiglockhart Workhouses, the North Berwick Hotel and other buildings. He then worked in New Zealand, San Francisco, Chicago and New York, before returning to the UK, where he became district surveyor in the parish of Marylebone. Around 1880 he came to Birmingham, where he worked as a managing assistant, first to Thomas Plevins, and then to Osborn and Reading, before joining Oliver Essex in partnership in 1887.[5] In the same year he was admitted as an Associate of the Royal Institute of British Architects, becoming a Fellow in 1918. In 1877 Nicol married Sarah Salway, the daughter of a builder, and it was their eldest son, George Salway Nicol, with whom in 1905 he set up the firm of Nicol & Nicol. Coulson Nicol was a Freemason, being a Past Master of the Athol

Lodge No. 74.[6] He died in 1933, at the age of eighty-five, his funeral being held at St Mary's, Acock's Green. His estate was valued at £35,549 (equivalent to £1,118,000 today).

John Goodman, the third member of the firm of Essex, Nicol & Goodman, was born in 1864 in the village of Gumley in Leicestershire, the son of John Goodman, a farmer, and his wife Mary. He was educated at Kibworth Grammar School. It is thought that the restoration of St Helen's, the parish church of Gumley, by G. F. Bodley in 1875–76, inspired the young Goodman to become an architect.[7] Following the death of his father in 1881, he and his mother moved to Birmingham, where John became a pupil in the offices of Messrs Bland & Cossins. In around 1887 he joined Essex & Nicol as assistant and surveyor, becoming a partner in 1892. He was admitted as a Member of the Society of Architects in 1906, becoming a Fellow of the Royal Institute of British Architects in 1925, when the two professional bodies merged. From the time of their coming to Birmingham, Goodman and his mother were regular worshippers at St Alban's Church, Conybere Street, and it was here that Goodman met, and married in 1917, Dorothy Hill. Although they had two sons and a daughter, none followed him into the practice. During the course of his seventy years' service to St Alban's Goodman was at various times churchwarden and school manager. Like Nicol, he was a Freemason, being a Past Master of the Grosvenor Lodge. He was also a member of the Union Club, Warwickshire County Cricket Club and Moseley Golf Club. During the First World War he served as a volunteer in the 1st Volunteer Regiment of the Royal Warwickshire Regiment.[8] Like Essex, Goodman never retired, dying peacefully at home after a very short illness at the age of eighty-seven. He was buried in his home village of Gumley, following a Requiem Mass and funeral service at St Alban's. He left an estate valued at £90,983 (worth £1,371,000 at today's prices).

At the time that Oliver Essex first started up in business on his own account in Paradise Street in 1883, the development of the village of Moseley into a suburb of Birmingham was beginning to take place, and the consequent explosion in demand in that area for domestic architecture played a large part in ensuring the success of the new practice. During the course of its first seven years the firm was responsible for the design of no less than fifty-seven houses in and around Moseley, including in 1886 a block of twenty-one three-storied semi-detached houses on the Highfield estate.[9] Further commissions for domestic architectural work in Moseley continued to be received in the years immediately following 1890, including thirteen detached and eight pairs of semi-detached houses in Chantry Road alone. In the main this was largely speculative building, carried out by various developers, including Oliver Essex himself.

All three partners were responsible for the design of their own homes. First, in 1892, Coulson Nicol built a house in Elmdon Road, Acock's Green which he called 'Elmdon Lodge'. In 1903, however, he built another house, on the corner of Elmdon Road and Yardley Road, into which his family moved, taking with them

the name of 'Elmdon Lodge'.[10] Six years later, however, in 1909, this house wit-
nessed the tragic early death of his youngest daughter, Etta, aged only twenty-four,
as a result of which the family left the house and moved back across the road into
their earlier home, which once more became 'Elmdon Lodge'. Nicol remained
there until his death in 1933. In 1894 Oliver Essex submitted his plans for 'The
Chains', in Church Road, Edgbaston.[11] It is believed that this was the first private
house in Birmingham to have a lift installed.[12] Two years later, in 1896, John
Goodman designed and built a house, 'Beverley', for himself and his mother in
Salisbury Road.[13] A photograph taken in 1900 just after this had been built, shows
a large double-fronted house, with twin gables at the front and side, together with
an extensive conservatory. On the ground floor were breakfast, dining and drawing rooms, kitchen, pantry and hall. The first floor comprised five bedrooms,
bathroom, and laundry, while the second floor held two further bedrooms.
'Beverley' was the first house to be built in Salisbury Road, which was a new road,
cut in 1896 through the grounds of Moseley Hall.[14] Although four more houses
were built soon afterwards in Salisbury Road, together with three in Edgbaston,
the large scale domestic commissions of the practice's early years had by the turn
of the century largely fallen away, and work on this front soon formed only a
relatively minor part of the firm's output.

Commissions for commercial building work, however, continued unabated.
Work of this nature, in addition to the housing development in Moseley, had
played an important role in the expansion of the new practice. As early as 1886
Essex had opened an office in London, in Chancery Lane, in order to deal with
several important commercial commissions, including the £250,000 development
of the Salisbury Estate in the Strand. In the same year he designed and built the
Grand Theatre, Derby. In Birmingham, commercial work in the early years was
steady, if not so prestigious, comprising in the main small shops, or additions and
alterations to existing buildings.

In 1894, however, Essex, Nicol & Goodman designed impressive new terracotta-
faced commercial premises in Old Square for R. Lunt & Co., haberdashers and
hosiers.[15] Terracotta had been introduced into Birmingham in 1891, in the form of
the prestigious Victoria Law Courts, designed by the London architects, Aston
Webb and Ingress Bell. In an extended feature on the architecture of Birmingham
in its issue dated November 27 1897, *The Builder* commented that 'half a century
ago Birmingham was, so far as the most important buildings were concerned, a
city of stone architecture; it seems to be now tending to become a city of terracotta architecture, and it is pretty evident that this is due to the example set in the
Law Courts, and the great admiration with which that building was, very justly,
regarded'.[16] Terracotta was particularly suited to Birmingham's needs, since it not
only made up for the lack of local stone, but was also resistant to smoke and soot.

The building for Lunt & Co. was amongst the first of a number of noted terracotta buildings in Birmingham designed around this time by Essex, Nicol &

John Goodman's House, 'Beverley', Salisbury Rd, Moseley, 1896.
Courtesy of Mary Goodman

Goodman, the style of which was to become the hallmark of the firm, helping to make their work immediately identifiable. Building on Oliver Essex's experience of Renaissance architecture, acquired during his time with W. H. Ward, they incorporated into this the use of colourful terracotta, which, combined with a profusion of intricately detailed ornamental design and tracery, topped by eye-catching features such as finials, pinnacles, turrets, cupolas, lanterns and Dutch gables, made their work quite distinctive.

The terracotta building designed for Lunt & Co. in 1894 displayed many of these characteristics. Standing six stories high, it was crowned with Dutch gables, cupolas and finials. The six large ground floor shop windows were all surmounted by detailed tracery. Praised in *The Builder*'s 1897 feature, the building was described as showing 'a good deal of richness and breadth of treatment; the continuation of the row of small arched windows in the third story, in an unbroken line across the front is very valuable in the design and a very good point'.[17] In the next

'The Louvre', High Street, from *The Builder* 27 December 1897. *Courtesy of Birmingham Central Library*

year, 1895, came a further outstanding terracotta building, for 'The Louvre', a drapery store in High Street.[18] Also featured in *The Builder*, this was another tall six-storied building, with arched windows and corner pinnacles, topped by a tower with cupolas at each corner, the whole being crowned with a lantern surmounted by a weathercock. The tracery above the ground floor windows was described by *The Builder* as 'dropping like lace curtains from the soffits'.[19] In 1896, as part of the redevelopment of Newhall Street, the partnership was responsible for a doctor's consulting rooms and residential premises on the corner of Cornwall Street, designed for Dr Edward Malins.[20] This building, which still survives, is now grade II listed, and is described in the booklet *Birmingham Terracotta* as being 'a relatively plain redbrick building with elegant and restrained detailing provided by buff terracotta'.[21] Two further fine examples of city centre terracotta were produced in 1897, and these also survive, both again being grade II listed buildings. The first of these, 'Cornwall buildings,' originally housing a workman's hall, club, savings bank and offices, and commissioned by W. T. Smedley and others, is also in Newhall Street, again on the corner of Cornwall Street, but on the opposite side of the road.[22] An impressive Rennaissance styled four-storied building, with

Cornwall Buildings, 43–51 Newhall Street, 1897

terracotta decoration including 'ornate porticoes, horizontal banding, fenestration decoration, scroll work, flower motifs, moulded cornices, a pierced parapet and decorated gables', it has, on the corner with Cornwall Street, an octagonal tower capped by a cupola.[23] This building now houses an All-Bar-One wine bar. The third of these three surviving grade II listed terracotta buildings is Newton Chambers, in New Street, which occupies the whole of the space between Needless Alley and Cannon Street.[24] As described by *Birmingham Terracotta*, 'the entire block is entirely faced with buff terracotta and red terracotta banding. Built in an Italian Renaissance style it also incorporates French arches and Belgian gables. It is an ornate building, richly decorated with cartouches above the original corner entrances capped with cupolas, medallions, scrolled string courses and an elaborate central gable.'[25] For many years, up until the 1970's, Newton Chambers was probably best known to the public at large as being the home of the Kardomah café.

While these new terracotta buildings were in the process of going up, one of the City's older buildings was about to come down. Christ Church, on the junction of New Street and Colmore Row, which had been consecrated in 1813, was demolished, despite protests, in 1899. This valuable site, covering an area of 2,460 square yards bounded by New Street, Colmore Row, Waterloo Street and Christ Church Passage, was to be developed commercially, mainly as offices, showrooms and shops, and the commission for this prestigious development was awarded to Essex, Nicol & Goodman. The new five-storied building, in French Renaissance style, which opened in 1901, was illustrated in *The Builder*, where it was described as being of 'Horsley Castle stone with green slate roofs ... [with] a dome over the circular corner at the junction' of Colmore Row with New Street.'[26] Although the official name of this development was Christ Church Buildings, it was to become far better known to generations of Birmingham families as 'Galloway's Corner', after the photographic equipment shop which occupied the extended corner frontage looking out over Victoria Square. Sadly, the entire building was demolished in 1970, as part of an ill-conceived plan to transform Colmore Row into an additional part of the Inner Ring Road.[27] However, this scheme was fortunately stopped, and the site now forms part of the extended and improved Victoria Square.

The turn of the century saw Essex, Nicol & Goodman designing yet more commercial buildings in the city centre. These included new premises in the Minories in 1899 for Newbury's (drapers), in Station Street in the same year for Lockerbie and Wilkinson (hardware merchants), and in Bull Street in 1903 for Barrows (grocers). They were also responsible for alterations to existing buildings, such as the Stock Exchange in Newhall Street in 1901, and Grey's (drapers) in Bull Street in 1903. After the departure of Coulson Nicol in 1905, Essex & Goodman

OPPOSITE   Newton Chambers, New Street, 1897

Christchurch Buildings (Galloway's Corner) 1901. *Courtesy of Birmingham Archives and Heritage Services (FA- GRE)*

continued to prosper in the commercial field, receiving many commissions, including in 1910 the design of new premises in Bull Street, Harborne for the London, City & Midland Bank, in 1911 a warehouse in Great Hampton Street for Newbury's,[28] and in 1913 new premises including a post office, in Acock's Green.

The 20th-century brought with it a new form of entertainment, in the shape of the cinema, and in 1911 Essex & Goodman prepared plans for the proposed conversion of the City [Roller Skating] Rink in John Bright Street into a 1,200 seater 'electric theatre', but this development appears never to have materialized.[29] In 1913, however, they designed what was to become one of Birmingham's best known cinemas, the Scala, in Smallbrook Street.[30] Billed as 'The last word in kinemas', this cost £10,000 and was claimed to be 'the finest of its kind in the Midlands'.[31] This was soon to be followed by another popular cinema, the Futurist, planned originally in 1915, (as 'The Majestic'), but not opened until 1919,

The Scala Picture House, 1913. *Courtesy of Birmingham Archives and Heritage Services* (*WK/B11/4261*)

completion having been delayed by the war.[32] Nicol & Nicol however, were already ahead of Essex & Goodman in this new field. They were responsible for the Picture House, New Street, which opened in 1910, and which modestly claimed to be 'the most luxurious cinematograph theatre [with] the best programme in Europe'.[33] The imposing New Street elevation may still be seen today as the entrance to the Piccadilly Arcade.

In designing the buildings necessary to house this new form of entertainment, Essex & Goodman leant heavily on Oliver Essex's early experience of designing conventional theatres. Architecturally, they were very similar, but built on a smaller scale. These cinemas unlike the theatres, had only two floors, the pit and the gallery, while provision had, of course, to be made for the 'operating' and 'winding' rooms. A small stage was retained, together with changing rooms, as variety acts were employed to entertain the audience while the reels were being changed. The Scala and the Futurist both also had an orchestra pit, the orchestra being used to accompany the films.[34]

In contrast to Oliver Essex's early heavy involvement in domestic and commercial work, commissions for industrial buildings were conspicuous by their relative absence during the practice's opening years. In 1887, however, Essex & Nicol were commissioned to design a manufactory in Upper Trinity Street for Mary Hoskins (ships' berth manufacturers). More industrial work soon followed, including in 1888 a factory in Earl Street for S. Mason (beer machinery manufacturers), in 1890 an engine room in High Street, Bordesley, for Hoskins & Sewell (bedstead manufacturers), in 1891 factories in Northwood Street for C. B. Partridge & Son (platers), and in Vesey Street for Thomas Cross (gun action makers), and in 1892 more manufacturing premises in Northwood Street, this time for P. G. Allday (brass founders).

In the following year, 1893, a purpose-built factory was designed by Essex, Nicol & Goodman for A. H. Woodward (pen, pen holder and pencil case manufacturers), and this may still be seen today.[35] Situated in Legge Lane, in the Jewellery Quarter, this three storey building is another fine example of the partnership's expertise in terracotta, and is now grade II listed. Featured in English Heritage's *The Birmingham Jewellery Quarter*, it is described as being 'particularly notable for its Dutch-gabled terracotta facade'.[36] Eleven years, (and several factories) later, in 1904, the firm was responsible for yet another surviving red-brick and terracotta building, again in the Jewellery Quarter, and again listed grade II. This three-storied building was designed for Charles Arnold, a solicitor, and was originally intended for multiple-occupation as offices and showrooms. Situated on the corner of Vittoria Street and Regent Street, it has seven window bays in Vittoria Street, three on the corner section and two in Regent Street. The fenestration is described in *The Birmingham Jewellery Quarter* – 'the windows are treated differently at each level; there are elliptical-arched openings on the ground floor, keyed segmental-arched heads to the first floor, and flat-headed openings on the second floor'.[37]

During the years up to 1918 Essex & Goodman continued to design factories and workshops for a variety of clients. These included manufacturers of such diverse products as spurs (W. Bach, Coleshill Street 1908), saddlery and leather goods (Martins B'ham Ltd., Granville Street 1911), electric light fittings (Armorduct Manufacturing Co., Farm Street, Witton 1911), pinafores (Crown Lockstitch Mfg., Co., Hinckley Street 1915), and buttons (E. Armfield & Co., St Paul's Square 1918). They also designed industrial premises for motor engineers (F. E. Baker Ltd., Eckershall Road 1912), fire-proof construction engineers (Stuart Granolithic Co., Bartholomew Street 1918) and wire workers (Lander & Sons, Barford Street 1918).

The practice's early involvement in domestic and commercial work and its subsequent continuing expansion in both the commercial and industrial fields

Pen Factory, Legge Lane, 1893

Drawing of Technical School, Suffolk Street, 1895

would appear to have been gained at the expense of their participation in the creation of Birmingham's Victorian public architecture. Up until 1893, the practice's only work recorded in the public field was a plan for alterations and additions to the Masonic Hall in Severn Street, prepared by Essex & Nicol in 1891. In 1893 and 1894 however, commissions were received from the Corporation of Birmingham for the design of the two public buildings in Victorian Birmingham for which Essex Nicol & Goodman were to become noted. As with their best known commercial work, these were to display an extensive use of terracotta. The first of these commissions was for the City's new Technical School, the late Gothic facade of which was to dominate Suffolk Street, and which opened in 1895.[38] Comprising six stories, it was referred to in *The Builder* as 'the great pile of the Technical School', the journal going on to comment that 'it is a remarkable looking building ... the great segmental arch embracing the four doors under its shadow, and the bay windows running through two or three stories between the solid buttresses, and built boldly out on the extrados of the arches of the basement windows, are bold features which cannot but impress one'.[39] The second of these two buildings was the new meat market and slaughter house in Bradford Street, which was in Flemish-Jacobean Renaissance style, and which opened in 1897.[40] This was later described as being 'conspicuous for its tall tower and corner turrets, for its plaques of rams' heads and skulls and of bullocks' heads, and for the attractively rounded feature at its north-eastern corner'.[41] Regrettably neither of these two outstanding public buildings survived the frenzied Corporation rebuilding programme of the nineteen seventies.

Amongst the other public works later carried out by the practice were commissions relating to St Alban's Church Schools. In 1902 they were responsible for extensions to the existing buildings and in 1915 for the rebuilding of the schools.[42] The opening of the new schools in 1915, which coincided with St Alban's 50th Jubilee Festival, was reported in the *Church Times*, which commented that 'the new schools, admirably designed by Mr. John Goodman, an old Churchwarden of many years' service, are of two stories, remarkably well lighted and airy and unique in Birmingham in having a roof playground which will be used for out-door school in good weather'.[43]

Like their contemporaries Martin & Chamberlain, Essex, Nicol & Goodman did not build many churches. The one and only church building attributable to the practice was the mission church of St Benedict, Hob Moor Road, Small Heath, opened in 1905, shortly before the two Nicols left to start up business on their own.[44] Described as being 'an unpretentious but substantial building of red brick',[45] this was superseded in 1910 by the present Parish Church.[46] Designed by George Salway Nicol, (who would almost certainly therefore have been responsible for its humble predecessor), this is a Romanesque red brick structure, of which a contemporary account reported that 'its simple and direct construction produces an effect of repose and dignity'.[47] The church and its vicarage, also by Nicol & Nicol and built shortly afterwards, are now both grade II listed buildings. The original mission church is now used as the church room.

In the years following 1918 the firm of Essex & Goodman continued to design commercial buildings for the City centre. Well known amongst these were Grey's Department Store in Bull Street (now demolished), Waterloo House in Waterloo Street, Lancaster House on the corner of Newhall Street and Great Charles Street, Somerset House in Temple Street and King Edward House in New Street. In the field of domestic architecture they were responsible for blocks of flats in Edgbaston, such as Kenilworth Court, Norfolk Court and Moorland Court. Following the death of Oliver Essex in 1939, the name of the firm changed once more, this time to Essex, Goodman & Suggitt, and although the firm regrettably no longer has a presence in Birmingham itself, there is still a practice of that name active in London, with a Midlands' office close by Birmingham, in Lapworth.

In 1983, a hundred years after Oliver Essex first set up in practice on his own account, Essex, Goodman & Suggitt hosted a commemorative banquet in the banqueting suite of the Council House in Birmingham, in the presence of the Lord Mayor and many other dignitaries. The ambitious young man from Great King Street, whose parents had both died when he was only fourteen years of age, could surely never have imagined the extent to which he would eventually succeed, and the legacy which he would leave, when he first joined W. H. Ward in 1873 to learn his profession, at the same time working by night for the Post Office, to enable him to pay his way.

List of Architectural Works of Essex, Nicol & Goodman

Oliver Essex (1855–1939) was articled to W. H. Ward of Birmingham. In 1883 he set up in independent practice. He went into partnership with John Coulson Nicol (1884–1933) in 1887. Nicol had been articled to Alexander Ellis in Aberdeen. In 1892 Essex and Nicol took into partnership John Goodman (1864–1951) who had been articled to Bland and Cossins of Birmingham. John Nicol left the firm in 1905 to set up in partnership with his son, as Nicol and Nicol. Essex and Goodman continued in practice until Oliver Essex's death in 1939.

Buildings are by Essex, Nicol and Goodman unless otherwise stated.

WORK IN BIRMINGHAM AND ITS ENVIRONS

PUBLIC

1891 Alterations and additions, Severn St Masonic Hall, (E & N)

1893 Technical School, Suffolk St, for Corporation of Birmingham [D]

1894 Meat Market, Bradford St, Sherlock St, for Corporation of Birmingham [D]

1895 Additions to Midland Conservative Club, Waterloo St

1896 Extension of fire station, Upper Priory, for Corporation of Birmingham [D]

1898 Additions to premises, Whitall St, for the Sisters of Charity of St Paul

1901 Additions to Friends' Hall, Farm St, for Committee of Friends

1902 Extensions to St Alban's schools, Dymoke St, for the Trustees; 1904 alterations, w. c.s etc

1904 Mission church, Hobmoor Rd, for Rev. H. Jacob

1914 Alterations to St Alban's church schools, Dymoke St, Leopold St, for the Trustees; (E & G); 1915 amended drainage plan (E&G)

COMMERCIAL

1884 Public house and 5 shops, Dale End and James Watt St, (Oliver Essex) [D]

1884 Shops and show rooms, Bull St/Dalton St, (Oliver Essex)

1884 Seven shops etc., Parade and Edward St, (Oliver Essex)

1885 Alterations and additions, New Street, for Birmingham Colonnade, (Oliver Essex) [D]

1886 Shopping, stabling and coach house, rear of 20, Great Charles St, (Oliver Essex)

1886 Additions to theatre, Snow Hill, for Mr Melville, (Oliver Essex) [D]

1887 Alterations and additions to Angel Hotel, Ladypool Rd/Stratford Rd, (Oliver Essex)

1888 Shop front and internal alterations, 24, Ledsam St, for Chas. Holden, (E & N)

1888 Rebuilding and restoring public house after fire, Corporation St/Cannon St, (E & N) [D]

1888 Alterations and additions to public house, Bolton Rd, Oakley Rd, (E & N)

1889 Shopping, Bradford St, for Mr Mohr, (E & N)

1890 Seven residential shops, Alcester Rd, for John Collins, butcher, (E & N)

1890 Bakehouse, High St, King's Heath, for John Collins, (E & N)

1891 Alterations and additions to public house Bordesley Rd for Atkinsons Breweries, (E & N)

1891 Shopping, 2 rows, St Mary's Row, for Ward & Sons, gun manufacturers, (E & N)

1891 Maltings, Dartmouth St, for J. & C. H. Evans, Maltsters (E & N)

1892 Alterations to premises, 'The Louvre', High St, for Edwin Fletcher, draper, (E & N) [D]

1892 Furnishing warehouse, Bristol St, for J. W. Lill, draper, (E & N)

1893 Five shop fronts and slaughter house, Ladypool Rd, for John White

1893 Builders' premises, Welches Hill, for E. J. Charles

1894 Business premises, warehouse and shops, Old Square, for R. Lunt & Co. haberdashers and hosiers; 1897 additions; 1904 additions [D]

1895 Premises, 'The Louvre', High St, (above) [D]

1895 Shops, cottages at rear, Alcester Rd, for John Bowen, builder

1896 Premises, Newhall St/Cornwall St, for Ed. Malins, MD, MRCP

1896 Business premises, Old Square, for Newbury's Ltd., drapers [D]

1896 Business premises, Upper Priory, for Essex & Nicol

1897 Business premises, Cannon St/Needless Alley/New St, for Clarence Property Co. [D]

1897 Workmen's hall, club, etc., Newhall St/Bread St, for W. T. Smedley & Others

1897 Business premises, Bull St/Minories, for George Berrill & Son, grocers

1897 Four shops, Bristol St/Bell Barn Rd, for Essex & Nicol

1897 Three shops and offices, Broad St, for Oliver Essex

1898 Business premises, Edgbaston St, for J. Collins [D]

1898 Business premises, Steelhouse Lane, for J. C. Nicol [D]

1898 Warehouse, Moseley Rd/Edgbaston Rd, for Mr Grew

1899 Shops, offices & business premises, Colmore Row, New St, Waterloo St, ('Christchurch Buildings'), for Birmingham Central Estates Co. [D]

1899 Shop fronts, 18, 19, 20, 21 Great Barr St, for F. Pickering

1899 Business premises, Minories, for Newbury's Ltd., drapers; 1901 w.c.s [D]

1899 Business premises, Station St, for Lockerbie & Wilkinson, hardware merchants

1900 Two shops with offices above, Paradise St, for Oliver Essex [D]

1900 Business premises, Church St, for Oliver Essex

1900 Three shops and dwellings, Bell Lane/Bristol Rd, for E. H. Morrison, grocer

1901 Shops, offices and consulting rooms, Easy Row/Edmund St, for Buildings Ltd

1901 Alterations and additions, 7, Newhall St, for the Stock Exchange

1901 New premises, The Crescent, Handsworth, for Hill & Egginton, shop fitters

1901 Business premises, Upper Priory, for J. C. Nicol [D]

1902 New premises, Moat Lane, for A. Shorthouse, meat salesman

1903 New premises, High St, for High Street Ltd

1903 New premises, John Bright St/Suffolk St, for E. B. S. Musgrave

1903 New premises, Bull St, for Barrows Ltd, grocers, tea and coffee merchants [D]

1905 Shop front, 13, Jamaica Row, for A. Shorthouse, meat salesman (E & G)

1905 Four shops, Horse Fair, for Clarence Property Co. (E & G)

1906 Shops and commercial premises, Broad St/Bishopsgate St, for P. C. Isacke (E & G)

1907 Alterations, Digbeth, for Warriner & Mason, tea merchants, grocers (E & G)

1909 Four shops, Sandon Rd, for Dr E. C. Rogers (E & G)

1909 Business premises, High St, Harborne, for Essex & Goodman (E & G)

1910 New business premises, Bull St, Harborne, for London, City & Midland Bank (E & G)

1911 Electric Theatre, John Bright St, for Electric Playhouse Ltd (E & G)

1911 Warehouse, Great Hampton Street, for Newbury's Ltd, drapers, (E & G)

1912 Showroom etc., Moseley Road, for B. C. Jackson (E & G)

1913 Alterations to Billesley Hall Farm, Brook Lane, for Moseley Golf Club (E & G)

1913 New premises, post office, etc., Warwick Rd, Acocks Green, for Essex & Goodman (E & G)

1913 New picture house, ('The Scala'), Smallbrook St, for George Murray (E & G)

1913 Warehouse, Great Hampton St, for Newbury's Ltd, drapers (E & G)

1913 Shelter over footpath, verandah, Smallbrook St, for Picture House Co. (E & G)

1914 Shopping, Cherrywood Rd, for Calthorpe Motor Co. (E & G)

1914 Business premises, Lower Temple St, for Ebenezer Parkes; 1914 alterations (E & G)

1915 Strongroom etc. Bull St, Harborne for London Counties and Midland Bank (E & G)

1915 Picture house, ('The Futurist'), John Bright St, for Majestic Ltd; 1916 verandah and generating room (E & G)

1915 Extension of works, Cherrywood Rd, for Calthorpe Motor Co; 1916 offices and petrol and oil store (E & G)

1916 Block plan, 214, Bradford St, for A. J. Grant (E & G)

1916 Workshop, Smallbrook St, for Scala Theatre (E & G)

1918 Commercial building, Easy Row/Edmund St, for Clarence Property Co. Ltd. (E & G)

INDUSTRIAL

1887 Manufactory, Upper Trinity St/Bowyer St, for Mary Hoskins, ships' berth makers (E & N)

1888 Shopping and business premises, Earl St and Chapel St for S. Mason, beer machinery manufacturer; 1888 Factory buildings; 1890 additions (E & N)

1889 Shopping, High St, Bordesley, for Hoskins & Sewell, bedstead manufacturers; 1890 engine room and warehouse; 1892 warehouse (E & N) 1893 office extension [D]

1889 Shopping and alterations, 181, 2, 3, Moseley St, for Crane & Son, file manufacturers (E &N); 1894 machine shop additions; 1895 shopping

1890 Manufacturing premises, Granville St, for Martin & Martin

1891 Manufactory, shopping, Northwood St, for C. B. Partridge & Son, nickel platers (E & N); 1895 shopping and factory extension

1891 Manufacturing premises, Vesey St/Price St, for Thos. Cross, gun action maker (E & N)

1892 Steel warehouse, Weaman St, for Edwin Bayliss (E & N)

1892 Manufacturing premises, Northwood St, for P. G. Allday, brass founders (E & N); 1908 alteration (E & G); 1911 shopping (E & G)

1892 Alterations and additions, 89, Vyse St, for George Payton, manufacturing jeweller

1893 Manufactory, Legge Lane, for Cornelius Davenport

1894 Manufactory, Bromsgrove St, Hindes Ltd, brush manufacturers; 1907 additions (E & G)

1896 Manufactory, Livery St/Northwood St, for J. Setton

1896 Shopping, High St, for Westley Richards & Co., gun makers

1896 Business premises, Steelhouse Lane/Upper Priory, for Chapman Felix, wire manufacturers

1897 Shed, Conybere St, for Parkers Ltd, joinery manufacturers

1897 Additions, Newtown Row, for Ingram & Kemp, chandelier manufacturers

1897 Shopping, Newtown Row, for R. Baker

1898 Shopping, Northwood St, for Bent & Parker, buckle manufacturers

1899 Alterations, Legge Lane, for Mrs Davenport; 1903 rebuilding of shopping

1899 Shopping, Stafford St, for Harris & Sheldon, shop fitters and brass founders

1906 Business premises, Coleshill St, for W. Bach, spur manufacturer (E & G)

1907 Factory, Lionel St, for A. Clarke (E & G)

1911 Shopping, Granville St, for Martins B'ham Ltd, saddlers and leather goods manufacturers (E & G)

1911 Shopping, Farm St Witton, for Armorduct Manufacturing Co., electric light fittings manufacturers (E & G)

1912 New factory, Eckershall Rd, for F. E. Baker Ltd, motor engineers (E & G); 1913 lavatories (E&G); 1916 factory extensions (E&G)

1913 New premises, Bishopsgate St, for Alfred Roberts, rubber manufacturers (E & G)

1913 New premises, The Crescent, for Eccles Walker & Co. (E & G) [D]

1915 New works, Burbidge Rd, for H. Joyce (E & G)

1915 Metal warehouse, New Canal St, for P. Collins: 1915 temporary warehouse (E & G)

1918 Alterations and additions to 67–68, St Paul's Square, for E. Armfield & Co. button makers (E & G)

1918 Office and lavatory, Bartholomew St, for Stuart Granolithic Co., fire proof construction engineers (E & G)

1918 Proposed factory, Barford St, for Lander & Sons, wire workers (E & G)

DOMESTIC

1884 Four villas, [51, 53, 55, 57] Mayfield Rd, Moseley, for Sam Mason (Oliver Essex)

1885 Seven villas, School Rd, Moseley, for Thos. Gough (Oliver Essex)

1886 Two villas, [11 & 13] Park Hill, Moseley, for Oliver Essex (Oliver Essex)

1886 Two semi-detached villas, King's Norton, for W. B. Weatherstone (Oliver Essex)

1887 Four houses, Park Hill, Moseley for John Munro (E & N)

1887 Four villas, [2, 4, 6, 8] Church Rd, Moseley, for H. R. Hall (E & N)

1887 Two houses, [128, 130] Anderton Park Rd, Moseley for Oliver Essex (E & N)

1888 Two villas, Prospect Rd, Moseley for John Pickering (E & N)

1888 Dwelling house, Earl St/Chapel St for S. Mason (E & N)

1888 Two houses, [125, 127] Anderton Park Rd, Moseley, for Chas. Collins (E & N)

1889 Residence, 'Shepley Grange', Barnt Green, for Thomas Walker (E & N)

1889 Two villas, [10, 12] Wake Green Rd, Moseley for W. Percy Harrison (E & N)

1889 Six dwelling houses and shops, 19–24, Digbeth, for Jos. Horton (E & N)

1889 Alterations, Woodbridge House Moseley, for W. H. Sabin (E & N)

1889 House, 'Hill Crest', Church Rd, Moseley for Edward Hurley (E & N)

1889 Two houses, [32, 34] Wake Green Rd, Moseley for Oliver Essex (E & N)

1889 Dwelling house, Tindal St, for Mr Parkes (E & N)

1889 House, 'Revesby', [36] Wake Green Rd, Moseley for Edwin Fletcher (E & N)

1889 House, Edgbaston Rd/Park Hill, Moseley for John Pickering (E & N)

1890 Villa, 3, Park View, Alcester Rd., Moseley, for Thos. Wilkinson (E & N)

1890 Two houses, [41, 43] St Agnes Rd, Moseley for Geo. Collins (E & N)

1891 House, Wake Green Rd, Moseley for F. Bromhall (E & N)

1891 House, [17] Wake Green Rd, Moseley for H. R. Hall (E & N)

1891 Two houses, Highfield Rd, for John Parker (E & N)

1892 Stable etc., 15, Carpenter Rd, for Harry Berrell (E & N)

1892 Dwelling house, Edgbaston Rd/Oakfield Rd, for Walter Flewitt (E & N)

1892 House, 'Athol Lodge', [6] Elmdon Rd, Acock's Green, for J. C. Nicol

1892 House, 'Elie Lodge', [8] Elmdon Rd, for J. C. Nicol

1892 House, 'Elmdon Lodge', [10] Elmdon Rd, for J. C. Nicol

1892 Four houses, Chantry Rd, Moseley for Oliver Essex

1892 Three residences, Yardley Rd, Acock's Green, for C. Harvey

1892 House, 'Newstead', [44] Yardley Rd, Acock's Green for Henry Allsop

1892 House, Elmdon Rd, Acock's Green, for F. Cook

1893 Residence, 'Greylands', Lichfield Rd, [85, Gravelly Hill North], Erdington, for
 Dr Aspinall

1893 Residence, 'Glandore',]45] Sutton Rd, Erdington, for Dr Donovan

1893 Three pairs of semi-detached houses, Chantry Rd, for Oliver Essex and J. Parker

1893 Two pairs of houses, Chantry Rd, for Oliver Essex and J. Parker

1893 Dwelling house, 'La Fontaine', 40, Heathfield Rd, King's Heath for G. Hynd

1893 Coach house, stable and conservatory, 54, Chantry Rd, for G. W. Dawes

1893 Dwelling house, Westfield Rd, Moseley for Patrick A. Martin

1893 Three pairs of semi-detached houses, Chantry Rd, for Essex, Nicol and Parker

1894 Six houses, Ashfield Av, for R. Morton Hughes

1894 Dwelling house, 'The Chains', [1] Church Rd, Edgbaston, for Oliver Essex

1894 Pair of semi-detached houses, Prospect Rd, for John Lewis

1894 House, 'Wych Elms', coach house and stable, [15] Forest Rd, for Edward Hurley

1894 Six houses, Chantry Rd, for E. J. Charles, builder

1894 Residence, Chantry Rd, for James Percival

1895 Dwelling house, stabling, 35, Westfield Rd, Moseley, for Walter Jones

1896 House, 'Beverley', [52] Salisbury Rd, for John Goodman

1896 Two greenhouses and conservatory, Wake Green Rd, for Mr Harrison

1896 Dwelling house, 'Hill Crest', Lyttleton Rd, for E. Smallwood

1897 Stable, coach house, etc., Westfield Rd, for H. Wright

1897 House and business premises, [19] Drayton Rd, for R. Webb

1897 Residence, 37, Chantry Rd, for F. Pickering

1897 Additions to 'Monaco', Chantry Rd

1897 Two houses, [48 & 50] Salisbury Rd, for John Goodman

1897 Annesley House (formerly 'Lisshicawn'), Birmingham Rd, Solihull for
   C. J. Newbury

1897 Additions, Farquhar Rd, for W. H. Cox

1898 House, 323, Hagley Rd, for J. F. Craig

1898 House, stabling, coach house, [93] Alcester Rd, for J. F. Taylor

1898 Two houses, St Bernard's Rd, Olton, for J. P. Achurch

1899 Detached residence, Chantry Rd, for Parker and Adie

1899 Two residences, Salisbury Rd, for John Goodman

1899 House, Chantry Rd, for John Parker

1899 Extension of Moseley Park Mews, Alcester Rd, for J. F. Taylor

1900 Detached villa, Chantry Rd, for John Parker

1903 House, 'Stukeley', [27] Farquar Rd, Edgbaston, for J. P. Achurch

1903 House, 'Elmdon Lodge', [50] Yardley Road, Acock's Green, for J. C. Nicol

1904 Alterations and additions to 'Penlee', Chantry Rd, for J. D. Prior

1911 Motor house, Norfolk Rd, for Mr Horsey (E & G)

1911 Additions, Harborne Park Rd, for A. D. Brooks (E & G)

1913 Additions, Cromer Rd, for J. Parkin (E & G)

1914 Additions, South Rd, Northfield, for F. Sherwood (E & G)

1914 Additions and bay windows, Park Rd, Moseley, for H. Joyce (E & G)

1915 Alterations, Westfield Rd, for P. R. Martin (E & G)

WORK OUTSIDE BIRMINGHAM:

COMMERCIAL

1886 Development of Salisbury Estate, Strand, London (Oliver Essex)

1886 Grand Theatre, Derby, for Andrew Melville (Oliver Essex)

1886 Abbey Hotel, Kenilworth (Oliver Essex)

1888 Coventry Theatre, Coventry (E & N)

1893 New Offices, 17, Pall Mall East, for The Imperial Live Stock Ins. Corp.

1895 Arcade and Shopping, Preston

1900 Offices, Lichfield St, Wolverhampton, for Royal London Mutual Insurance

DOMESTIC

1890 House, Alum Chine, Bournemouth, for W. C. Ginder (E & N)

NOTES

[1] The circular letter sent out by Essex & Nicol to the firm's clients advising them of the admission of John Goodman into partnership, explained that 'we have adopted this course owing to our increasing practice'.

[2] Oliver Essex's Obituary, *Birmingham Post* 2 February 1939, p. 16.

[3] *Ex inform* Rev. John Goodman, August 2004. The author is grateful to Mr Goodman for providing him with notes based on the Goodman family archives and for his personal recollections of his father and Oliver Essex.

[4] *Birmingham Post* 2 February 1939.

[5] Obituary of Coulson Nicol *Birmingham Post* 15 March 1933, p. 12.

[6] *Ibid.*

[7] *Ex inform* Miss Mary Goodman, August 2004. The author is grateful to Miss Goodman for giving him a summary of her father's life, including his long association with St Alban's Church.

[8] *Ibid.*

[9] Also included in these fifty seven houses were nos 10 and 12 Wake Green Road, see King's Norton Building Register, app. no. 1105, 20 July 1899 for W. Percy Harrison, in Birmingham Central Library, Archives and Heritage Services (hereafter BCL AHS). These houses are now listed Grade II. The block of twenty one houses planned for the Highfield Estate, (King's Norton Building Register, app. no. 866, 11 February 1886) comprised six houses in Wake Green Road, seven in Church Road and eight in a new road to be cut across the Estate. However this commission was not proceeded with.

[10] BCL AHS Yardley Building Register app. no. 1047, 22 April 1902, for house, 50, Yardley Road, for Coulson Nicol.

[11] BCL AHS Birmingham Building Register, app. no. 1099, 29 March 1894, for house, 1, Church Road, for Oliver Essex.

[12] *Ex inform* John Goodman.

[13] BCL AHS King's Norton Building Register, app. no. 2492, 19 August 1896, for house, 52, Salisbury Road, for John Goodman.

[14] *Ex inform* Mary Goodman.

[15] BCL AHS Birmingham Building Register, app. no. 10144, 19 April 1894, for Retail business premises, Old Square.

[16] *The Builder*, 73, 27 November 1897, p. 435.

[17] *Ibid*, p. 489.

[18] BCL AHS Birmingham Building Register, app. no. 11380 7 November 1895, for Retail business premises, High Street. Previously, in 1889, Essex, Nicol & Goodman had designed a house, Reversby, [36] Wake Green Road for Edwin Fletcher, proprietor of The Louvre.

[19] *The Builder*, 27 November 1897, p. 438, p. 446.

[20] BCL AHS Birmingham Building Register, app. no. 11528 28 January 1896, for Doctor's consulting rooms and residential premises, Newhall Street.

[21] Birmingham City Council Planning Department, *Birmingham Terracotta* (Birmingham, 2001) p. 9.

[22] BCL AHS Birmingham Building Register, app. no. 13049 17 June 1897, for Workman's hall etc, Newhall Street.

[23] *Birmingham Terracotta*, p. 11.

[24] BCL AHS Birmingham Building Register, app. no. 12982, 26 May 1897, for shops, offices and business premises, New Street.

[25] *Birmingham Terracotta*, p. 21.

[26] BCL AHS Birmingham Building Register, app. no. 14675, 15 March 1899 for shops, offices and business premises, Colmore Row/New Street; *The Builder*, 80, 29 September 1900, p. 272.

[27] Joe Holyoak, *All About Victoria Square* (Birmingham, 1989) p. 25.

[28] Prior to the building of the premises in the Minories and the warehouse in Great Hampton Street for Newburys, Essex, Nicol & Goodman had designed a house, Lisshichawn, in Solihull for Mr C. J. Newbury in 1897.

[29] BCL AHS Birmingham Building Register, app. no.22225, 6 June 1911, for an Electric Theatre, John Bright Street.

[30] BCL AHS Birmingham Building Register, app. no. 24538, 17 July 1913, for a Picture House, The Scala, Smallbrook Street.

[31] *Birmingham Daily Post*, 2 March 1914 p. 1, and 4 March 1914 p. 12.

[32] BCL AHS Birmingham Building Register, app. no. 27233, 29 November 1915, for a Picture House, John Bright Street. The Futurist subsequently became the first cinema in the City to show a 'talkie' film, 'The Singing Fool' starring Al Jolson, on Monday 18 March 1929.

[33] BCL AHS Birmingham Building Register, app. no. 21301, 18 February 1910 for a Picture House, New Street; *Birmingham Daily Post*, 21 October 1910, p. 1.

[34] It has been suggested by C. and R. Clegg in *The Dream Palaces of Birmingham* (Birmingham, 1983) p. 13, that 'at cinemas like the Scala and the Futurist, patrons went along just as much to hear a first class orchestra play as to see what was on the silver screen'.

[35] BCL AHS Birmingham Building Register, app. no. 9201, 23 January 1893, for Pen manufactory for A. H. Woodward, Legge Lane.

[36] J. Cattell, S. Ely and B. Jones, *The Birmingham Jewellery Quarter* (Swindon, 2002), p. 246.

[37] *Ibid*, p. 274.

[38] BCL AHS Birmingham Building Register, app. no. 9776, 9 October 1893 for Technical School, School, Suffolk Street.

[39] *The Builder*, 27 November 1897, 74, p. 439.

[40] BCL AHS Birmingham Building Register, app. no. 10592, 6 November 1894, for Meat Market, Bradford Street.

[41] Bryan Little, *Birmingham Buildings* (Newton Abbot, 1971) pp. 33–34.

[42] BCL AHS Birmingham Building Register, app. no. 16785, 25 March 1902 and app. no. 26097, 6 October 1914, for extensions and alterations to St Alban's Schools, Dymoke Street/Leopold Street.

[43] *Church Times*, 2 July 1915, p. 7.

[44] BCL AHS Birmingham Building Register, app. no. 18164, 22 August 1904, for Mission Church, Hobmoor Road.

[45] *Birmingham Daily Post*, 29 March 1905, p. 5.

[46] BCL AHS Birmingham Building Register, app. no. 20071, 8 January 1908, for Church, Hobmoor Road.

[47] *Birmingham Daily Post*, 2 May 1910, p. 453.

10 Cossins, Peacock and Bewlay

ANNE BAKER, JOANNE BUTLER AND PAT SOUTHWORTH

The long-lived partnership comprised three individuals, of different generations, with distinctive styles. It spanned the transition from Gothic through to Arts and Crafts styles and its prolific output was credited with having contributed much to the architectural improvement of Birmingham. Civic and public buildings, industrial and commercial premises as well as domestic architecture were all well represented in the output. A measure of the firm's success is that it won contracts to build schools, when Birmingham had used mainly the prestigious firm of Martin and Chamberlain, for those flagship buildings redolent of civic pride. The various styles in which the partners worked reflected their times and their personal philosophies. Jethro Cossins (1830–1917) the senior partner, was a forward thinking liberal, an active supporter of William Morris's Society for the Protection of Ancient Buildings. He produced not only Gothic buildings, but those forerunners of the Arts and Crafts buildings variously described as Free Classic, Cadogan Square, or Queen Anne.[1] None of his buildings can be identified earlier than the 1870s when he was already in his forties. However, in 1875 he won the major contract from Josiah Mason to build a Science College in the civic heart of Birmingham, so he must have gained something of a reputation. Around 1890 he took as his partner Frank Barry Peacock (1859–1937), then in his thirties, who had trained in Manchester, articled to Alfred Darbyshire, a lover of amateur theatricals who had built a number of theatres.[2] Peacock also espoused the Free Classic style. At the turn of the nineteenth century the firm became 'Cossins, Peacock and Bewlay', with Ernest Chawner Bewlay (1872–1942), not yet thirty, joining it after working for some years on his own account. Ernest Bewlay worked in the Arts and Crafts styles then coming into vogue, and produced well regarded buildings while pursuing his interest in art and sketching.

Jethro Anstice Cossins

The initial identification of the work of Cossins, Peacock and Bewlay was through the Registers of Building Applications which provide a relatively comprehensive overview of their work and usually give the name of the client, and indicate a chronology of building work.[3] Although many of the accompanying plans are now in a very fragile condition, they may not only aid identification of the building itself, but also provide the only record of a now demolished building, and show the intention of the architect.[4] When it is included, additional correspondence between the various parties may help to illuminate discrepancies between the plan and the finished building.

The biographies in the RIBA *Directory of British Architects*, obituaries in newspapers, and in the Birmingham Architectural Association reports, and wills, census records and register office records, along with snippets here and there in various publications (such as architectural journals) provided the biographical details of the architects, including their involvement in various interests, especially those of leisure. Inevitably, the more renowned the architect, the more likely will be the record of their activities. It is unsurprising therefore that there is more biographical information for Jethro Cossins than for the lesser-known Barry Peacock. Unfortunately, Cossins, Peacock and Bewlay were a relatively small firm of architects and only the briefest of information about their business arrangements exists and is usually limited to the entries in the various Trades Directories.[5]

Perhaps the best source of evidence is that of the building works themselves which record what the architects wanted to be known about themselves. Where identification was possible, the buildings demonstrate changes in style over time, and the various influences impacting on the style.[6] However, it was not always possible to be certain that the correct building had been identified.

Before discussing the buildings and architectural styles, an outline of the practice will be given, along with a summary of what is known about the individuals it comprised. As 'Cossins, Peacock and Bewlay' the firm was in business from the late 1890s until 1917.[7] However, before their involvement with that firm, all the individuals had worked with other architects or on their own. Jethro Cossins, the senior architect of the firm, came to Birmingham in the early 1850s with the architect to whom he had been apprenticed, Frederick William Fiddian.[8] Jethro Cossins was in partnership with John George Bland, in offices at 14 Temple Street, as evidenced by extant plans for work by Bland and Cossins dating from 1876 to 1882.[9] For eight years from 1882, Cossins appears to have practised on his own account, first with offices in Warwick Chambers, Corporation Street, and then at 83 Colmore Row, which was to remain the firm's location for a considerable period. From around 1890, after Cossins had taken F. Barry Peacock into partnership, plans were submitted in the name of 'Cossins and Peacock,' with the additional name 'Bewlay' first appearing in 1896.[10] This initially was Jethro Cossins's nephew by marriage, Hubert Rawson Bewlay, the son of a Moseley Civil Engineer.

Perhaps owing to Hubert's illness, after 1900 Ernest Chawner Bewlay, Hubert's younger brother, replaced him in the partnership.[11]

The firm continued with the name of Cossins, Peacock and Bewlay until shortly before Jethro Cossins died in 1917, when the name changed to Peacock, Bewlay and Cooke.[12] The firm then took the name of Peacock and Bewlay. Barry Peacock remained in active partnership until his retirement at the age of 75 in 1934.[13] The firm retained the same name for some time after the deaths of Peacock in 1937, and Ernest Bewlay in 1942, and was using it into the late 1950s.[14]

Jethro Anstice Cossins, who founded the partnership, was a 'historically minded architect,'[15] and the only one without an early background in the Midlands. He was born in Kingsdon, Somerset, in 1830, the son of John Cossins and Elizabeth, née Anstice, and was educated at Taunton and Castle Cary.[16] His interest in architecture manifested itself from an early age and was said to have been inspired by a visit to Wells Cathedral. He was articled in 1847 to an architect and surveyor, Frederick William Fiddian, who was practising in London.[17] Jethro Cossins moved to Birmingham with Frederick Fiddian in 1850, and directories record Fiddian working from Bennett's Hill from 1852. Cossins worked in various Birmingham offices before becoming the partner of John George Bland (see chapter 8).[18] Between 1876 and 1882 plans appear in their joint names, specifically for a house in Moseley,[19] shops in Corporation Street,[20] a shop front and vaults in New Street, Birmingham,[21] a factory in New Bartholomew Street,[22] and shops in Hagley Road.[23] In 1882 Jethro Cossins began his own practice. As a result of one major commission, that of Mason's Science College, he travelled extensively on the Continent, visiting many European schools and colleges to gain ideas for design and layout. He was also drawn overseas when he directed the building of premises in the West Indies for an Assurance Company.

His obituary described him as 'architect and archaeologist', and he wrote several archaeological papers and was President of the Birmingham Archaeological Society.[24] He was interested in church antiquities, particularly old Warwickshire churches.[25] He was a member of the Committee of the Society for the Protection of Ancient Buildings, established by William Morris in 1877, and became its Midlands' Area Reporter. The Society's aim was to conserve buildings by traditional techniques, avoiding drastic interventions such as removing wall plaster. In putting these aims into practice he appears to have been notably successful.[26] Much of his leisure time was spent exploring Warwickshire, and on his death, he left a large collection of manuscripts, notes and sketches.[27] He was President of the Birmingham Architectural Association from 1881–82, and Vice-President of the Royal Society of Artists from 1902–05. He was also a Member of the Council of the Midland Institute, of the Committee of the Municipal School of Art, and the Management Committee of Birmingham Museums.

He died aged eighty-seven, on 5 December 1917, at the Midland Institute where he had been attending a meeting of the Birmingham Archaeological Society, when he became ill. He retired to the Principal's office, but died before a doctor could reach him. At the time of his death he was living at 'Kingsdon', in Forest Road, Moseley. He had applied to build a villa in Forest Road in 1884, and a house in Forest Road in 1890.[28] His wife, Fanny Seddon Cossins, outlived him, and his will shows that he left effects valued at about £11,500.[29]

The second partner, Barry Peacock, was Jethro Cossins's junior by almost thirty years.[30] He was born in Cheetham, Manchester on 12 December 1859, the son of a master tailor,[31] but attended Bishop Vesey Grammar School in Sutton Coldfield.[32] In his obituary in *The Builder* in 1937 he was described as 'one of the best-known architects in Birmingham', although the Report of the Birmingham and Five Counties Architectural Association speaks of his 'very retiring nature'. On leaving school, he joined a firm of Manchester architects, being articled to Alfred Darbyshire FSA, FRIBA, 1875–80.[33] Darbyshire was described as 'architect and antiquary' and appears to have been particularly well-known as a theatre architect. Barry Peacock returned to the Birmingham area where from 1880 he was an assistant to Jethro Cossins, with whom he went into partnership in *c.* 1890. He was elected a Fellow of the Royal Institute of British Architects some twenty years later in 1907.

He was described as taking little part in public affairs outside of his profession,[34] but was a keen supporter of Warwickshire County Cricket Club. Although not a player himself, he was a member of the Committee for about thirty years, and acted as honorary architect for repairs and renovations to the Edgbaston ground. He was also Vice-President of the Birmingham Architectural Association from 1890–92. His work extended outside Birmingham and he was the architect for St Augustine's Priory, Ealing; the Oratory School at Caversham, Reading; the Church of the Sacred Heart and St Catherine, Droitwich in 1919; and Nuneaton's Municipal Buildings in 1934. His adherence to Roman Catholicism perhaps helped him in getting the church contracts.[35] He was favoured by the philanthropists, Barrow and Geraldine Cadbury[36] who were involved in building Bilberry Hill Tea Rooms (1904),[37] a Children's Court (1905),[38] a Remand Home specifically for juveniles (1910)[39] and two open-air schools in the Birmingham area: Uffculme in Moseley, around 1911[40] and, in 1922–25, adapting Cropwood, in the Lickey Hills. Geraldine Cadbury, daughter of Barrow and Geraldine, recalled that her mother designed the schools 'with the help of the architect Mr Peacock' suggesting that he by no means had a free hand in the work![41]

He is known to have travelled to Italy, where he studied the famous Byzantine church of Sant' Appollinare in Classe, Ravenna, which acted as a model for his church of the Sacred Heart and St Catherine in Droitwich.

Barry Peacock died on 17 February 1937, at the age of 77, at his home 'Silverwood', Four Oaks Road, Sutton Coldfield, a house that he had designed and built around 1899.[42] He had married Jessie Caroline, the eldest daughter of Mr Charles Winn of Selly Park.[43] The firm had worked on Charles Winn's house on Upland Road in 1901.[44] Although ten years his junior, Jessie Peacock died less than

Ernest Chawner Bewlay

three weeks before him. They left a daughter, Joan Barry, whose married name was Brooke-Pike.

The youngest member of the partnership, Ernest Chawner Bewlay, born in 1872, was the son of Alderman Hubert Bewlay of Moseley. The 1881 census records his father's occupation as 'Manufacturer Engine Driver', but by 1901, he was described as 'Civil Engineer'. Ernest had two older brothers, Hubert Rawson, born in 1870, and Harry, who became a Land Agent and Auctioneer, born 1871. Ernest's mother, Sarah, died around the time of his birth in 1872. She had been born in 1844 at Stourbridge, Worcestershire. She appears to have been the younger sister of Jethro Cossins's wife, Fanny, also born at Stourbridge, in 1839. The three orphaned boys may have been brought up by their maiden aunt on their mother's side, Mary Ryland, born 1836, who was living in the house of Hubert senior in 1901.[45] Ernest Bewlay was educated at Greenhill School, Moseley, at Architectural Association Schools, and was articled to Jethro Cossins 1888–92, becoming a partner in the firm from around 1900. He stepped into the vacancy left by his brother, Hubert, who served for only four years in the practice.[46] From 1892 to 1894 he was assistant to George Kenwrick, quantity surveyor, and then began independent practice. In 1895 he acted as executive architect when Moorcroft, Moseley, was being built by one of the first generation of Birmingham Arts and Crafts architects, Herbert T. Buckland.[47] Bewlay's new Coroner's Court won the accolade of being judged the best new building in the Birmingham and Five Counties area during the three years ending in 1937, leading to the firm being awarded the RIBA bronze medal. He became architect to Birmingham City Council, and the restoration of Blakesley Hall as a late Elizabethan Manor house, was another architectural achievement.

Ernest Bewlay was a Fellow of the Royal Institute of British Architects from 1911 and the Vice-President from 1931 to 1933. On the Institute's recommendation he advised Whitby Council on the preservation of old Whitby. It was a town he knew well, as he had earlier done many water-colour sketches of the old part of the town. He was a noted artist, and a member of the Royal Birmingham Society of Artists and of the Civic Society, and a Vice-President of the Association of the Friends of Birmingham Art Gallery.[48] He travelled in Belgium and Holland. He was a President of the Birmingham and Five Counties Architectural Association, 1927–28 and a member of its art advisory committee. His obituary in the Association's Annual *Report* of 1942–43 describes him as 'respected by clients, his professional brethren and builders alike, he was in great request as an arbitrator and adviser'. It also mentions his devotion to sport, and describes him as 'one of the best golfers and billiard players in the Midlands,' and as an accomplished speaker. His love of the countryside is demonstrated by his involvement in the Society for the Preservation of Rural England.

He died aged 70, on 18 November 1942, leaving a widow.[49] At the time of his death, he was residing at 68 Wellington Road, Edgbaston; a house he had applied to build, as owner, in January 1913.[50] He had formerly lived in Park Hill, Moseley.

The background against which the firm worked was favourable to architecture. From 1873 when Joseph Chamberlain became Mayor, Birmingham sought to establish a pro-active local government which would provide numerous public services. This phenomenon also occurred in other large industrial towns and cities, but Birmingham's provision was especially comprehensive and high quality, and was reflected in buildings like schools and libraries. The spirit of growing civic pride and private philanthropy arising from the industrial wealth created in Birmingham, led to a mushroom growth in public buildings in the late nineteenth century. It was also a time when the middle class of Birmingham and its environs was expanding, and new suburbs were growing to meet their need for out of town housing in airy spacious surroundings which emulated the country house living of the gentry. The expanding professional classes needed churches and shops in their suburbs, and in town they needed new business premises. All this led to an expansion in building of all kinds. There was a reaction among the professional classes against the showy architectural styles favoured by the industrialists, and a more restrained, gentle, less muscular style, inspired by Norman Shaw's Free Classic styles, came into favour, along with the vernacular Arts and Crafts styles. The latter styles represented reaction against increasing mass production in building, and followers of the new styles sought to re-introduce craftsmanship.

Jethro Cossins employed Gothic, Free Classic and Flemish styles during his career in Birmingham. Mason College of 1875–80, and the Liberal Club of 1883 are symmetrical Italianate Gothic buildings, which show the influence of the Gothicist Alfred Waterhouse who was credited with having extended the Gothic beyond its allotted span. He again employed Gothic motifs, using trefoil headed windows, in Cromwell Street Board Schools of 1888.[51] However, from as early as 1880 he had used Free Classic style pioneered by Norman Shaw, which drew on seventeenth century motifs. In that year he built The Dell, No. 15 Westbourne Road, Edgbaston, now listed Grade II.[52] His shops at 189–195 Hagley Road of 1882 and 8a–10 Bordesley Street/Allison Street of 1882 as well as the Proof House's Curator's House and Workshop of 1883 and the Ear and Throat Hospital, Edmund Street of

Cromwell Street Board School, Nechells, 1888

1891 show him working in the Free Classic style.[53] When he built the Free Libraries at Saltley in 1890 and Balsall Heath in 1895 in red brick and terracotta he used Flemish Renaissance and sixteenth century French models.[54] He introduced some Arts and Crafts features into the Balsall Heath Library, which is described below.

Barry Peacock worked largely in Shaw's Free Classic style, for example in the Tea Rooms, Bilberry Hill, Rednal of 1904, and his Gas Department buildings in Cotteridge of 1911.[55] His Jacobean Renaissance work at the Birmingham and Midland Institute, formerly the Birmingham Library, of 1898–99,[56] did not impress Wedgwood who described it as 'a right old mix up of styles: red brick with gables, mullions, and banded Ionic columns and pilasters'.[57] However, in the latest Pevsner on Birmingham, Andy Foster calls it 'loose but friendly Jacobean'.[58]

Ernest Bewlay used Gothic styles for his Arts and Crafts churches at Cotteridge of 1902[59] and Maney of 1904.[60] For domestic architecture he used both Norman Shaw's Old English Arts and Crafts style, as in Priorsfield, Edgbaston Park Road of 1899,[61] and a more austere Arts and Crafts style, pioneered by W. R. Lethaby and Philip Webb, as in the houses in Park Hill, Moseley built in the 1890s, before he joined Cossins and Peacock in 1900. His domestic work was undertaken in such middle class suburbs as Moseley, Edgbaston, and Four Oaks in Sutton Coldfield.

The Ear and Throat Hospital, Edmund Street, of 1890 photographed in 1897

The former Ear and Throat Hospital, 1890

Priorsfield, Edgbaston Park Road, 1899

15 Wentworth Road of 1907, an example of one of the firm's houses in Four Oaks

Bewlay became known for his designs for banks, and his plain, symmetrical fronted banks, Bordesley High Street of 1902, Bennett's Hill of 1904, and Warstone Lane 1905 tend towards Norman Shaw's neo Georgian style.[62]

The various major commissions which the firm obtained over time reflect the public and private need for buildings demonstrating the status of the city, the industrial company, commercial firm, or individuals. Clients would want the buildings to reflect their good taste, and to show their appreciation of current styles, and architectural firms responded to that desire.

Jethro Cossins gained prominence when chosen by Sir Josiah Mason to build the Science College (1875–80), which cost £60,000.[63] Other public buildings followed: the Liberal Club of 1883, in a similar style but rated architecturally superior to the College;[64] the Old Meeting Church which opened in 1885 and had cost £26,000;[65] and Cromwell Street Board Schools of 1888, which were to accommodate 1080 pupils.[66] A 23-shop arcade, called Hen & Chickens Arcade, after the hotel forming its entrance, was built by the firm in 1885.[67]

In the 1890s the firm built the Ear & Throat Hospital in 1890, two Libraries for the City Council, the first, Bloomsbury Library, Saltley Road in 1890, and Balsall Heath Library in 1895, and the New Library in 1899, now the Birmingham and Midland Institute. For the Corporation, the firm also built the Pig Market, Montague Street in 1899.[68] Perhaps the fact that Jethro Cossins shared the Liberal politics of those controlling the City helped in gaining contracts for public works.[69]

The former New Library, Margaret Street, 1899

St Peter's Church, Maney Hill Road, Sutton Coldfield, 1904

Jethro Cossins was an antiquarian and a member of the Society for the Protection of Ancient Buildings. This background qualified him for reparation work which he undertook both locally and further afield. His best known repair was to Burton Dassett's All Saints Church, Warwickshire, in 1890. It had been semi-derelict and in a dangerous state before he undertook the difficult task of restoring it without destroying original features. Indeed, in the process of repair, he uncovered much of the church's earlier history because of the careful way in which he worked.[70]

Ernest Bewlay, like Barry Peacock, was favoured by the Cadbury family, and built for them in a modest Arts and Crafts style which suited their Quaker antipathy to excessive ornamentation. The Cadbury commissions were three small country houses in the Lickeys near Birmingham: Heanor for Edward C. Cadbury in 1904, Beaconwood for George C. Cadbury junior, in 1905, and Cropwood for Barrow Cadbury in 1906.[71]

Among the firm's later major works are Fentham Street School for Aston School Board of 1904;[72] Loveday Street Lying-In Hospital of 1906;[73] and the two Gothic churches mentioned previously, St Agnes at Cotteridge of 1902 and St Peter at Maney, Sutton Coldfield of 1904. Bewlay became a noted bank builder, and by 1917 he had built for Birmingham District Counties a bank in Bordesley High Street of 1902, together with the bank in Warstone Lane of 1905, and for Parr's Bank in

Waterloo Street/Bennett's Hill of 1904 as well as all over the Midlands.[74] Barry Peacock also undertook some bank work.[75]

The firm was responsible for a number of industrial buildings, for example, in 1899 it built a factory for Williams Brothers/Piggotts in Arthur Street,[76] and one for Linde British Refrigeration Company in Digbeth.[77] In 1909, the firm built a warehouse in Kenyon Street for Cannings, a firm which also used them for other designs.[78]

The Catholic Church employed the firm, specifically Barry Peacock, for the apsidal chancel of 1893 and presbytery of 1896 for St Catherine's, Horsefair, as well as to build its tower/steeple of 1908, and school.[79] The Parish Hall for the Oratory, Hagley Road, of 1909,[80] is the firm's work as is Coventry Road School of 1902,[81] and the new presbytery for the Church of the Holy Family, Coventry Road of 1910.[82]

Numerous domestic commissions, large and small, came the firm's way throughout the period, including such additions as billiard rooms and motor houses. The List of Works has had to reflect just a small part of that output. Some commissions from the Cadbury family to F. Barry Peacock and Ernest Bewlay

The former Parr's Bank, Bennett's Hill, 1904. The upper storeys are a later alteration.

The former Linde
Refrigeration Cold
Store, Digbeth, 1899

have been mentioned. The firm also altered Southfield, Wheeleys Road in 1901–04 for Barrow Cadbury.[83] Domestic commissions were frequently in the suburbs where Birmingham's leading families lived and examples include additions for Charles Gabriel Beale in 1895 at Maple Bank, Church Road, Edgbaston;[84] for Edward Nettlefold of a lodge to Westbourne, Westbourne Road, Edgbaston in 1894,[85] and additions for Arthur Chamberlain in 1889 at Moor Green Hall, Moseley.[86]

The concluding part of this chapter will examine in more detail some of the firm's significant commissions, in order to give a picture of its legacy to Birmingham's architecture.

Mason's Science College was the first major commission for Jethro Cossins. It was situated on Edmund Street and the site, which extended back to Great Charles Street, was chosen for its proximity to other important civic buildings, such as Birmingham's Free Library, the Midland Institute, the Town Hall and the new Council House.[87] Sir Josiah Mason wished his college to compete with the famous German science schools, and so Cossins was sent to study several Continental schools and colleges before completing the design.[88]

The foundation stone was laid on 23 February 1875,[89] and opened by Sir Josiah Mason on 1 October 1880.[90] The building, which was mainly four storeys high, cost about £60,000 including all the laboratory fittings.[91] The exterior of the building was described as '13th-century Gothic with details of a somewhat French character'. The frontage was symmetrical and constructed of a deep red brick from Kingswinford, with windows and various details in Portland, Bath and other stone.[92] It had several gables and turrets, and on top of the central gable was a statue of a Mermaid, the crest of the founder.[93] Below this was a large oriel

ABOVE Mason College

RIGHT Inside Mason College: central corridor and main staircase. *Courtesy of Birmingham Archives and Heritage Services (WK/B11/4261)*

The Liberal Club, 1883

window, two storeys high. The central entrance to the college was through a moulded and deeply recessed arch, which led into a vestibule whose groined arches, carved capitals and geometrical tracery were reported to be in 'admirable harmony with the exterior of the building.'[94]

The interior of the College was arranged around two open courtyards, which were divided by a central stack of corridors that ran from the front to the back of the building. These were connected by the main staircase which opened off the ground floor corridor with an arcade of four moulded arches on granite columns. Lecture theatres, reading rooms, administrative offices, a library, assembly room, a museum, laboratories and common rooms were incorporated into the design, which was described as 'complete and perfect for the purposes required as any building in this Country or on the Continent'.[95] There were a number of subsequent additions, including new laboratories, and a club house, all carried out by the firm, between 1892 and 1905.[96]

The Liberal Club, also designed by Cossins in the Gothic style, was built almost adjoining Mason's College in 1883.[97] These buildings formed one side of Chamberlain Place, opposite to the rear of the Town Hall. The entrance to the new Museum and Art Gallery, and the Central Free Library were on the other two sides, with the Chamberlain Memorial in the middle of the square. The College, which became the foundation for the University of Birmingham, was demolished in 1964, and the present Central Library was built on the site.[98]

This history of the next case study, Balsall Heath Library, goes back to the take over by the Birmingham Board of Health of the Balsall Heath Board in 1891. One of the conditions was that the City provided a library. The architectural firm of Martin and Chamberlain was used very extensively for municipal contracts, which in Birmingham were always built to a notably high standard. Cossins and Peacock managed to secure the library contract, perhaps helped by their already having built the Cromwell Street Schools of 1888[99] and the Bloomsbury Library of 1890.[100]

Sir Aston Webb's and Ingress Bell's building of the Victoria Law Courts in 1891, in which terracotta was used lavishly, heralded a major change in Birmingham's architecture. The use of terracotta as a subsidiary decoration had been common-place and Jethro Cossins had used it in the Liberal Club in 1883 and also in Bloomsbury Library in 1890. However, Aston Webb took use of that material to new heights. Not only did Birmingham architecture now change in the material used, but it also moved away from Italianate styles in favour of Jacobean/Renaissance ones. In his Bloomsbury Library of 1890 Jethro Cossins had already adopted the new styles, and they were developed further in his Balsall Heath design.

The exterior of the trend-setting Victoria Law Courts is built of red bricks and red terracotta, making it somewhat 'loud'. Cossins and Peacock's Bloomsbury Library is also striking in its redness, but uses a little buff terracotta for decorative window heads. At Balsall Heath, the architects used buff terracotta extensively making a strong design against red brick. The Library sits on a deep plinth of buff terracotta, and then there are thin horizontal bands of it which continue through the double transoms of the wide, elliptical arched, mullioned windows which light the Library Hall. Above each window there rises a shaped gable in terracotta containing an aedicule niche. The Library Hall is aisled inside, with square columns supporting arches resembling those of the exterior hall windows, and which similarly have spaced voussoirs rising periodically. There was a plaster frieze beneath the Library Hall ceiling.

The tower to the north of the Library Hall forms the main entrance and has a Flemish Renaissance doorway flanked by banded columns, topped by a terracotta gable pediment, which sweeps up towards a relief plaque of the City arms. The tower has curved chamfer corners with terracotta banding, and its clock stage and dome are in terracotta. The shape of the swept spire on top of the tower echoes that of the doorway's gable pediment below. Capping the tower is a small cupola. North of the tower there is a small extension to the building. Overall, the design is well balanced and harmonious.

Balsall Heath Library, 1985

The tower design may have been influential. Douglas Hickman wrote in *City Building Series — Birmingham* of 1970, 'it is interesting to compare the tower with that of the Horniman Museum, Lewisham, built in 1902, the masterpeice of C. Harrison Townsend. Townsend's tower is similar in composition, but dispenses with the spire and surface decoration and carries the curved corners up to circular pinnacles.'

The last case study looks at a group of domestic buildings. A fine group of five houses, (nos 35, 37, 39, 43 and 45) all designed by Ernest Bewlay, on Park Hill, Moseley were built between 1898 and 1899. All the houses are built to a different design and in various ways exemplify the Arts and Crafts style of architecture. Three of the five houses were built by the same firm of builders, R. Fenwick of William Edward Street. Unfortunately, although the building plans for all the properties are extant, they are all in too fragile a condition to be examined.

'Clydesdale,' No. 35, was built for a brassfounder, George F. Piggott, in 1898. Built of brick with pebble dash decoration and Bath stone edgings, it has a complex front elevation with varied window types, including a long window on the stairwell, and a sunken porch. A motor house was added in 1911.[101] 'The Red House,' No. 37, was built in 1899 for Mr J. R. French, of Allesley near Coventry.[102] It is of red brick construction and has two wings protruding from a central sec-

'Clydesdale' 35 Park Hill, Moseley, 1898

tion. The bay windows on ground and first floor level are separated by an area of hanging tiles. There is an arch above the first floor windows constructed in a contrasting brick. The front door within the recessed porch has ornate curvilinear hinges.

'The Cottage,' No. 39, was designed by Ernest Bewlay for himself. It is of pebble-dash and brick construction, set back from the road with a recessed porch. Several of the windows to the rear are bay windows, in contrast to those on the front elevation. To the right of the front door is inscribed on a terracotta plaque 'EBD 1898' – referring to Ernest Bewlay and his wife Dorothy. There are some fine examples of original Arts and Crafts brass door furniture on internal doors. A dressing room extension was added in 1905.[103] Ernest Bewlay lived here from 1898 to around 1913, when he moved to Bewlay House, 68 Wellington Road, Edgbaston.[104] The new house was more symmetrical and exemplified the neo-classic style.

Nos 43 and 45 Park Hill comprise a pair of large semi-detached properties, of red brick construction , built in 1899 for Mr W. E. Adland using the building firm of W. H. Gibbs.[105] They are three storeyed, rising to twin gables in the central section of the slightly projecting front elevation. The gables contain semi-circular windows, and below, on the first floor, there are bay windows. The houses are more symmetrical than the other Bewlay houses in Park Hill.

The houses exemplify Bewlay's views which he expressed in a report to the Birmingham Architectural Association in 1896–97, following a visit to the church of the Cowley Fathers, Oxford. He said of that building it 'shows how dignity and grace may be obtained by studied proportions and mass of wall surface without the aid of costly and elaborate details: here a plain building of stone and plaster bears upon its surface at every point the hand of a master, and possesses the subtle charm which only the work of artists really has.'

The firm of Cossins, Peacock and Bewlay adapted well to the changes in style which occurred during the period, and survived to flourish well beyond the Victorian period. In this it was no doubt helped by each of the partners coming from a different generation. Jethro Cossins, who made the reputation of the firm, worked in Free Classic, Gothic, and Flemish Renaissance idioms. He had been among the earliest to introduce Free Classic styles to Birmingham, and also earned commendation for his careful repairs of ancient buildings. Barry Peacock favoured the Free Classic style, and undertook significant works beyond Birmingham. Ernest Bewlay espoused the vernacular Arts and Crafts styles as well as the Free Classic style, and lived in houses exemplifying both. It would appear that the three partners were versatile and able to take on commissions for all sorts of buildings. Each made a unique contribution to the partnership's long life and prolific output. Even after many of its works have suffered demolition, sufficient survive to leave the stamp of the firm on twenty-first century Birmingham.

Selected List of Architectural Works of Cossins, Peacock and Bewlay

Jethro Cossins (1830–1917) was apprenticed to Frederick Fiddian of London and came to Birmingham with Fiddian in 1850. By 1876 he was working in partnership with John George Bland. From 1882 he was in practice on his own until c. 1890 when he went into partnership with Barry Peacock (1859–1937). Peacock had been articled to Alfred Darbyshire of Manchester. In 1896 they took into partnership, Hubert Rawson Bewlay, who had been articled to Cossins. He was replaced by Ernest Chawner Bewlay (1872–1942) in 1900. The firm continued as Cossins, Peacock and Bewlay until shortly before Cossins's death in 1917.

Work is by the three partners unless individuals are indicated.

Buildings below with a date range of 1897–1912 have been ascertained from BCA AHS MS 2004/2/1 C. S. Underhill's Records of an Architect's Practice

WORK IN BIRMINGHAM AND ENVIRONS

PUBLIC

1875 Mason Science College, Edmund St, Birmingham, University of Birmingham from 1904, J. A. Cossins; alterations and additions 1892; 1895; 1897; 1899 (new laboratories);

1900; 1902; 1903; 1904 (Club House); 1905: (Laboratory and additions to Bacteriological Laboratories); 1910 (w.c.s); 1914 (new refectory) [D, 1964]

1883 Liberal Club, Edmund St, Birmingham, J. A. Cossins [D]

1885 Old Meeting Church, Bristol St, J. A. Cossins; 1900 Caretaker's house [destroyed by bomb, 1940]

1888 Cromwell Street Board School and dwelling house, Cromwell St and Rupert St, Nechells for Birmingham School Board, J. A. Cossins

1890 Ear and Throat Hospital, [Nos 103–07] Edmund St and Barwick St, Cossins and Peacock; 1902 alterations and additions, Barwick St [frontage only survives]

1890 Bloomsbury Free Library, Lingard St and Saltley Rd, Cossins and Peacock

1891 Birmingham Town Hall, alterations and improvements, Cossins and Peacock

1892 Additions and alterations to St Catherine of Siena's Roman Catholic Church, Horse Fair, Cossins and Peacock; 1908 Steeple; 1896 Dwelling House, for the Rev. G. Fenn [D, c. 1964]

1893 Alterations and closets for Roman Catholic Schools, Windmill St, Cossins and Peacock [D]

1895 Balsall Heath Branch of Free Library, Moseley Rd, Cossins and Peacock

1896 Alterations to Free Library, Aston Rd and Gosta Green [D]

1897–1912 Bell gable for St Barnabas Church, High St, Erdington

1897–1912 alterations to Liberal Union Club, Six Ways, Aston

1897 Alterations and additions to Deritend Library, Heath Mill Lane

1898 New Library (now the Birmingham and Midland Institute), Margaret St/Cornwall St

1898 Additions to Convent of Saint Paul, Selly Park Rd, Selly Park

1898 Alterations to Gate Fronts, Adderley Park, Saltley

1899 Pig Market, Montague St [D]

1900 Bishop Vesey's Grammar School, Lichfield Rd, Sutton Coldfield

1901 Additions to Club House for King's Norton Golf Club, Wychall Lane, King's Norton; 1906 additional Club Rooms [D]

1902 Roman Catholic Schools, Coventry Rd [D]

1903 St Agnes's Church, Pershore Rd, Cotteridge [D]

1904 Fentham Road School, Fentham Rd, Erdington (now King's Centre, and Ashbourne Centre)

1904 St Peter's Church, Maney Hill Rd, Sutton Coldfield

1904 Recreation Room for Gas Department, Devon St, Vauxhall & Duddeston

1904 Tea Rooms, between Rednal & Bilberry Hill, Rednal, for Barrow Cadbury

1904–5 Women's Hospital, Showell Green Lane, Sparkhill [D]

1905 Additions to Board School on Bristol St [D]

1905 New Night Shelter for Girls, Tennant St [D]

1906 Memorial School, Windsor St [D]

1906 Loveday Street Lying In Hospital, Loveday St [D]

1906 Addition to School of Art, Vittoria St; 1909 and 1911 alterations and additions

1908 Additions to Friends Meeting House, Upper Priory [D]

1908 Two blocks of lavatories at Uffculme, Queensbridge Rd, Moseley; 1911 Open Air School, in grounds of Uffculme, Moseley

1909 New Parish Hall for The Oratory, Plough & Harrow Rd, Edgbaston; 1913 Rifle Range; 1914

1910 Remand Home, Moseley Rd [D]

1910 Alterations and additions to Woodbrooke Settlement, Griffin's Hill, Selly Oak; 1914 Dining Hall, and additions

1910 New Presbytery for Church of The Holy Family, Coventry Rd

1911 Home for Feeble Minded Women (Agatha Stacey Homes) off Leach Lane, Rednal [D]

1911 Premises for City of Birmingham Gas Department, Pershore Rd, Cotteridge; 1914 additions

1912 Women's Baths, Kent Street [D]

1914 Additions to Friends' Institute, Berkeley Rd

1914 Almshouses, Church Road, Yardley

COMMERCIAL

1876 New shop front, New St, Bland and Cossins [?D]

1880 Four shops and offices, Corporation St, Bland and Cossins

1880 Vaults to Warwick House, New St, for Holliday and Son, Drapers and Ironmongers, Bland and Cossins; 1899 additions to Warwick House, New St; 1901 new w.c.s; 1896 Shop and workshops, Union Passage & Warwick Passage [D]

1882 Four shops, [189–195] Hagley Rd, Bland & Cossins

1882 Three shops, stabling [8A–10] Bordesley St/Allison St, J. A. Cossins; 1899 stabling, Allison St

1885 Arcade of twenty three shops (back of Hen & Chickens), New St, J. A. Cossins [D]

1889 Alterations and additions to Premises, Temple St, J. A. Cossins

1891 Alteration to front of Tangyes, 114, New St, corner of Lower Temple St, Cossins & Peacock

1892 Alterations, closets etc, for Northern Assurance Co., [81] Colmore Row, Cossins & Peacock

1897–1912 Metropolitan Bank, Hockley

1897–1912 Shops for Goodmans, Builders' Materials Merchants, Gravelly Hill

1897–1912 New shopping for S. Holiday, The Crescent, Birmingham

1897–1912 Birmingham and District County Bank, Bearwood

1897–1912 Birmingham and District County Bank, Dudley Market Place

1897–1912 Birmingham and District County Bank, High Street, Dudley

1897–1912 United Counties Bank, Walsall

1897–1912 United Counties Bank, Sedgley

1897 Business Premises for W. C. Heap, 36 Ludgate Hill

1898 Alterations to *Daily Mail*, Building, Cannon St; 1899 new Composition Room

1901 Additions for Evans and RDLAS, Paternoster Row

1902 Birmingham & District Counties Bank, 122, Bordesley High St, Bordesley

1902 New Offices for J. J. Taunton & Co, Spring Mattress Manufacturers, Sherborne Road, [D]

1903 Alterations for John Feeney, Newspaper Publisher[38] New St

1904 New Premises for Parr's Bank, Waterloo St and Bennett's Hill corner

1904 Alterations to Birmingham & District Counties Bank, High St [?Dudley or Bordesley]

1905 Garage for Barnetts Motors, [128] Bristol St [D]

1905 New Bank & Workshop for Birmingham & District Counties Bank, Warstone Lane

1905 Alterations for Loan & Deposit Co, Easy Row [D]

1908 Alterations to Metropolitan Bank, Great Hampton St

1909 Shop etc. for Barrows Stores Ltd, 94 Bull St; 1913 additions [D]

1909 New Front for Caledonian Insurance Co., 77 Colmore Row

1909 Addition of new office for Metropolitan Bank, [33] Bennett's Hill

1910 Additions to D. and M. Davis, Silversmiths, [13] Colmore Row

1910 United Counties Bank, Gooch St [D]

1913 Alterations to Scottish Widows Society, [12] Bennett's Hill

1914 Additions for Messrs R. Streather & Sons, Builders, Lichfield Rd , Four Oaks

1914 Alterations to United Counties Bank, Coventry Rd

1914 Alterations to United Counties Bank, Bristol Rd

1914 Alterations to United Counties Bank, Hagley Rd

INDUSTRIAL

1880 Manufactory, New Bartholomew St, Bland & Cossins [D]

1883 Curator's House & Workshop, Proof House Yard, Banbury St, J. A. Cossins

1887 Alterations and additions to Shopping, for Cadbury & Co, Princip St, J. A. Cossins [D]

1890, Additional Store/Warehouse for Alfred Field & Co, Hardware Merchants, Edmund Street, Cossins and Peacock

1892 Additional Shopping and Offices for J. & E. Wright, Rope and Twine Manufacturers, Universe Works, Garrison Street, Cossins & Peacock; 1896 w.c.s [D]

1896 Alterations to premises for Peyton and Peyton, Bedstead Manufacturers, High Street, Bordesley; 1898 additional Shopping

1897–1912 Alterations to Factory for Hoskins & Sons, Bedstead Manufacturers, Neptune Works, Bordesley

1897–1912 Alterations to premises for Howes & Burley, Moseley Street (manufacturers of carriage lamps) — see below under 1908, Bishop St premises; 1912, Barford St premises; 1913 Holloway Head premises.

1897 Alterations & additions for Crofts, Assinder & Co, Bedstead Manufacturers, Heath Mill Lane [D]

1898 Store and roof over yard for Sanderson & Co, Mineral Water Manufacturers,149 Camden St, E. C. Bewlay

1898 Manufactory for Williams Bros. & Piggott, Brassfounders, Arthur St, Small Heath, E. C. Bewlay; 1900 additional shopping [D] See 1911 below for Herbert Rd premises.

1898 Additional shopping for C. Winn & Co, Brassfounders [140] Granville St; 1907 additions [D]

1898 Chimney Stack for H. Jutson, Manufacturing Chemist, Liverpool St

1899 Laundry for J. R. French, Alfred St, Sparkbrook, E. C. Bewlay [D]

1899 Shopping for J. & J. Taunton, Spring mattress Manufacturers, River St & Sherborne Rd [D]

1899 Manufactory, Cold Stores and Offices for Linde British Refrigeration Co., Digbeth, E. C. Bewlay; 1904 new Machine shops

1899 Shopping for A. B. Reeves & Co, Brassfounders, Crescent, Cambridge St, E. C. Bewlay; 1904: additions to Factory; 1905 additional Shopping

1900 Alterations and additions to factory premises for Amster Ltd [D]

1900 Shopping for Thomas Piggott, Tube Manufacturers, Western Rd , Spring Hill; 1913 alterations [D]

1904 Additions for Marks & Cohen, Manufacturing Jewllers, [94 & 96] Camden St; 1908 additions; 1909 alterations, Cossins, Peacock and Co.

1904 Additions for Messrs J. Smith, Bedstead Manufacturers, Athole St

1905 New Shopping for Reeves, plumbers, [7 & 8] Tennant St

1906 Additional business premises for J. Archdale & Co., machinery manufacturers, Ledsam St

1907 Alterations for H. L. V. Pryse, Aston St

1907 Additions for Wilmot Ltd, Gold Chain Manufacturers, [62, 63, 64] Albion St

1908 Alterations for Webly & Scott, Revolver and Arms Manufacturers, Bagot St

1908 Additional shopping for Chamberlain, King & Co., (cabinet makers, carpet factors, decorators, removal contractors) Suffolk St

1908 Alterations for Howes & Burley, carriage lamp manufacturers, Bishop St; 1909 additions

1909 Warehouse for W. Canning and Co., Chemical Company, Kenyon St; 1911 addition of shopping

1910 Additions to Warehouse for W. Canning & Co., Great Hampton St; 1912 New Premises for W. Canning & Co, Great Hampton St

1911 Alterations for Morris & Co, Brassfounders, Freeth St

1911 Roofing for Williams Bros. & Piggott, Brassfounders, Herbert Rd

1912 Shopping for Burman & Co, Sheet Metal Workers and Spinners, Windmill St [D]

1911 New Premises for P. Southall, Harford St [Possibly not erected]

1912 Shopping for Howes & Burley, Carriage Lamp Manufacturers, Barford St

1913 Shopping for Weberley & Son, Canal St

1913 Alterations for Howes & Burley, Carriage Lamp Manufacturers, Holloway Head; 1913 Dipping Shed

1913 Alterations for Ansells, Brewers, Western Rd

1914 Outbuildings for H. L. Y. Pryse, Ashted Row; 1914 new drainage [D]

1914 Alterations to Premises of Glover & Main, Manufacturers of gas stoves and meters, King Edward's Rd [D]

DOMESTIC

1876 House for J. E. Hollis, [? West View Cottage], Augusta Rd, Moseley, Bland & Cossins; 1898; alterations [D]

1880 House, The Dell, 15 Westbourne Rd, Edgbaston

1882 Villa for Albert Good, Oxford Rd, Moseley, Bland & Cossins

1883 Two villas for A. H. Assinder, [45 & 47] Mayfield Rd, Moseley, J. A. Cossins

1884 Villa for J. A. Cossins, Forest Rd, Moseley, J. A. Cossins [D]

1885 House for A. Heath, Armadale, 8 Wake Green Rd, Moseley (Moseley Society thought that J. A. Cossins might be architect as it is Free Classic style)

1886 Dwelling House, [13] Westbourne Rd, J. A. Cossins [D]

1887 Alterations and Billiard Room, for Henry Hollis, Beechcroft, Westbourne Rd, Edgbaston, J. A. Cossins

1889 Additions for C. G. Beale to Dwelling House, Maple Bank, Church Rd, Edgbaston, Cossins & Peacock; 1890 additions to Lodge, Cossins & Peacock; 1895 additions to Billiard Room [D]

1889 Alterations and additions for W. A. Wiggins to The Park, Park Rd, Moseley, Cossins & Peacock [D]

1889 Additions to Moor Green Hall, Moseley, for Arthur Chamberlain, Cossins & Peacock [D]

1889 Alterations and additions to Westbourne, [12] Westbourne Rd, for Edward Nettlefold, J. A. Cossins; 1894 additions to Lodge, Cossins & Peacock [D]

1889 Stabling, etc., for Samuel Taylor, Brockenhurst, Anderton Park Rd, Moseley, Cossins & Peacock [D]

1890 Billiard Room and alterations to Dwelling for R. Peyton Esq., Westfield, Augusta Rd, Moseley, J. A. Cossins [D]

1890 House, for J. A. Cossins, Forest Rd, Moseley, J. A. Cossins [If this is Kingsdon, [18] Forest Road the site of which is near the south west corner of Forest Road's intersection by Anderton Park Road, it has been demolished]

1891 Bay Window for J. A. Marigold, 50 Frederick Rd, Edgbaston, Cossins & Peacock [D]

1893 Two houses for R. Plant, [71 & 73] Springfield Rd, Moseley/Kings Heath, Cossins & Peacock

1894 House, for J. A. Cossins, Anderton Park Rd, J. A. Cossins [A contemporary map with 'Ownership' indicated shows Cossins owning the corner plot, on SW junction with Forest Road, so the extant house [The Gables] on the site may be the one built]

1894 Billiard room at Milton Grange for James Whitfield, Forest Rd, Moseley, Cossins & Peacock [D]

1895 Vicarage, The Brooklands [34] Selly Wick Rd, Selly Park, Cossins & Peacock

1895 New Stables, for A. W. Auster, [23] Park Hill, Moseley, Ernest Bewlay [D]

1895 Additions for S. H. Padmore, Carlton Lodge, School Rd, Moseley, E. C. Bewlay

1896 Alterations and additions for John G. Smith, Robinshurst, [22] Westfield Rd, Edgbaston

1896 House for J. A. Cossins, [?32] Mayfield Rd, Moseley

1897 Additions for Isaac Myers, 24 Westfield Rd, Edgbaston

1897 Additions for A. Elkington, 5 Westfield Rd, Edgaston

1897 Alterations for Gerald Phillips, 117 Hagley Rd

1897 Additions to Red House for W. H. Dawes, School Rd, Moseley, E. C. Bewlay

1897 House for H. F. Sabin, Priory Dene, Priory Rd, Edgbaston [D]

1897–1912 Alterations and additions for W. Holcroft, Barnt Green

1897–1912 House for J. Morgan, Barnt Green

1897–1912 House for Stanley Evans, Solihull

1898 Billiard Room for Lionel Spiers, Lynthorpe, 13 Augustus Rd, Edgbaston

1898 House for G. F. Piggott, [35] Park Hill, Moseley; 1911 Motor House

1898 Additions for W. Shakespeare, The Limes, Albert Rd, Harborne

1898 House for E. C. Bewlay, The Cottage, [39] Park Hill, Moseley, E. C. Bewlay; 1905 alterations

1898 Billiard Room for W. W. Wiggin, The Forehill House, The Forehill, Cotteridge

1899 House for F. B. Peacock, Hermitage Rd (?Edgbaston)

1899 House, out offices and stabling for J. R. French, The Red House, [37] Park Hill, Moseley, E. C. Bewlay

1899 Billiard Room for George Myer, 166 Hagley Rd, Edgbaston

1899 House for S. W. Smith, Priorsfield, Edgbaston Park Rd, Edgbaston; 1912 alterations and additions

1899 Two houses for W. E. Adland, [43 & 45] Park Hill, Moseley, E. C. Bewlay

1899 One house near Chantry Rd for Walter B. Incledon, Alcester Rd, Moseley, E. C. Bewlay [1904 Kelly's has W. B. Incledon at 56 Chantry Rd]

1899 House for Mr F. Barry Peacock, [Silverwood] Walsall Rd/Four Oaks Rd

1899 House for E. Pearson, Homestead, Bracebridge Rd, Sutton Coldfield

1899 Additions to Bath Room for Eric Meakay Carter, Greenland Rd

1900 Additions for Frank S. Pearson, Avon Lodge, [28] Upland Rd, Selly Park [D]

1900 Smoking Room and bedrooms over for Sir Hallewell Rogers, Greville Lodge, Wellington Rd/Sir Harry's Rd , Edgbaston; 1911 additions; 1912 additions

1900 Alterations and additions for H. R. Padmore, [11] Wharfdale, Church Rd, Edgbaston [D]

1900 Additions for Henry Rabone, [Ambleside] Somerset Rd , Edgbaston [D]

1901 House for W. Charlton, Gate House, [32] Barker Rd, Four Oaks

1901 Alterations and additions for Barrow Cadbury, Southfield, [64] Wheeleys Rd [later Edencroft, when it became YWCA]; 1904 additions

1901 House for Wallis Whitworth, Mead End, [7], Meadow Rd, King's Norton

1901 Extension to Drawing Room, Charles Winn, The Uplands, [65], Upland Rd, Selly Park; 1902 extension to Dining Room

1902 House for Mr Wilcox, Streetly Lane, Sutton Coldfield [Probably Ingleneuk (sic)]

1902 Alterations for J. H. Lloyd, Edgbaston Grove, Church Rd, Edgbaston; 1904: Stabling etc. [D]

1903 Alterations for A. Wigley, Westfield Rd, Edgbaston

1904 House for Edward C. Cadbury, Heanor, Beacon Hill, Lickeys

1904 House, for G. F. Goodman, Fountain Rd (unidentified)

1904 Bay window, H. Monckton, [40] Calthorpe Rd, Cossins, Peacock & Bewlay

1904 New House, for E. B. Winn, Rosemary, Woodbourne Rd, Edgbaston; 1909 garage; 1912 additions, (both for James Dixon)

1905 House, Moorcroft, 93 Moorcroft Rd, Moor Green, Herbert T. Buckland and E. Bewlay as executive architects

1905 House for George C. Cadbury, Beaconwood, Beacon Hill, Lickeys

1905 Alterations for O. Kauffman, Rosemary, Hermitage Rd, Edgbaston

1905 House for G. Prince, Clovelly, [30], Barlow's Rd, Harborne

1905 House for H. T. Nock, Highcliffe, Victoria Rd

1905 Alterations and additions for M. Carter, 3 Westbourne Rd, Edgbaston

1905 House for F. Holliday, [9] Pritchatt's Rd, Edgbaston; 1906 Stabling

1905 Alterations for C. A. Carter, Spring Cottage, Wellington Rd, Edgbaston

1906 House for Barrow Cadbury, Cropwood, Spirehouse Lane, Blackwell, Lickeys

1906 House for C. H. Barnsley, Somerset Rd, Edgbaston

1906 Alterations for Dr E. J. Beards, 430 Moseley Rd; 1913 alterations

1906 motor house for William Wiley, Briarwood, Hartopp Rd, Four Oaks

1907 House for W. Y. Sapcote, Cromford [42] Farquhar Rd, Edgbaston

1907 Additions for W. L. Powell, [44] Wellington Rd, Edgbaston

1907 House for Mr Lloyd Owen, Vrondeg, [15] Wentworth Rd, Four Oaks

1907 House for Walter Goodrick Clarke, [probably 48 & 50] Meadow Hill Rd, King's Norton

1908 House for Philip Winn, The Grey House, Four Oaks Rd, Four Oaks

1908 Additions for A. P. Cary Field, Woodbourne, [63] Wheeley's Rd, Edgbaston

1908 Additions for George Cadbury, The Dell, Oak Tree Lane [D] (had been 'Fircroft', a Selly Oak College prior to Primrose Hill becoming 'Fircroft' — see 1913 below)

1909 Alterations and additions for J. A, Marigold, [7] Augustus Rd, Edgbaston

1911 Additions for J. Cadman, Fieldgate, [61] Wellington Rd, Edgbaston

1911 Additions for R. C. Gibbins, Fayrestowe [62] Wellington Rd, Edgbaston

1911 Addition for Mrs Parsons, Mountlands, Norfolk Rd, Edgbaston

1912 House for R. Pinsent, Selly Wick Rd, Selly Park [Pinsent lived in Selly Wick House. Grade II, probably late 18th-century house, and perhaps the plans were for extending that old house?]

1913 Alterations for Smith, [? Oakdale], Wychall Lane, King's Norton

1913 House for E. C. Bewlay, Bewlay House, [68] Wellington Rd, Edgbaston

1913 Additions for George Cadbury, Primrose Hill, Bristol Rd. [now Fircroft College, part of Selly Oak Colleges]

1913 House for Miss M Sheldon, [29] Selwyn Rd, Edgbaston

1913 House for E. Canning, Hamstead Hall Rd

1913 Additions to Clive House, 27 Plymouth Rd, Barnt Green

1913 Additions for C. F. Lloyd, Berkely Rd

1914 Alterations for E. M. Carter, Sunybreak, Wellington Rd, Edgbaston

1914 Alterations for D. Davis, [15] Augustus Rd (Redeposited 22/7/19)

1914 Additions for J. D. Smith, Wellington Rd, Edgbaston

1916 Additions for, Dr Thomas Wilson, Marchmont, Birmingham Rd, Wylde Green [D]

WORK OUTSIDE BIRMINGHAM

PUBLIC

(all the buildings below are extant)

1879 Rebuilding of Little Packington Church, Warwickshire, J. A. Cossins

1886 Darlaston Town Hall, J. A. Cossins (cost £5,500)

1887 Drinking Fountain and Clock Tower, Stratford-upon-Avon (top of Rother Street), J. A. Cossins

1897–1912 new roof and lead work for Holy Trinity Church, Stratford-upon-Avon

1897–1912 alterations and seating for St Peter's Church, Portishead, Avon

1897–1912 new gallery for Darlastan Town Hall, J. A. Cossins (built 1886)

1889 Repairs to St Michael's Church, Alkerton, Oxfordshire, J. A. Cossins

1890 Repairs to Burton Dassett Church, Warwickshire, J. A. Cossins

1896 Repairs to St Michael, Cropthorne, J. A. Cossins

1899–1900 Repairs to St Peter and St Paul, Long Compton, Warwickshire, repairs, J. A. Cossins

1919 Church of the Sacred Heart and St Catherine of Alexandria, Droitwich, F. B. Peacock

COMMERCIAL

(Whether extant or demolished is unknown)

1897 Birmingham and District County Bank, Newport, Salop.

1897–1912 Shops for C. H. Everton, Droitwich, Witton

1897–1912 Alterations to United Counties bank in Cornmarket, Derby

1897–1912 Bank alterations for United Counties Bank, Castle St, Shrewsbury

1897–1912 United Counties Bank, Church Stretton, Shropshire

1897–1912 United Counties Bank, High St, Cheltenham

INDUSTRIAL

(Whether extant or demolished is unknown)

1897–1912 Alterations to Factory for W. Hall & Co. Studley

DOMESTIC

(Whether extant or demolished is unknown)

1897–1912 House alterations, Fladbury, Cropthorne Mill

1897–1912 Boarding House for Mrs Reilly, Corbett Avenue, Droitwich (perhaps related to a private boarding establishment run by Mrs and Miss Reilly)

1897–1912 Cottage for Mrs Yardley, West Malvern

1897–1912: Alterations to Woodrow Farm for W. R. Nash, Lydiate Ash

1897–1912: House and alterations for A. Slater, Bescot

1897–1912: Cottage for Reeves & Co., Malvern

NOTES

[1] An early example of a building by Jethro Cossins in that style was 15, The Dell, Westbourne Road, Edgbaston built in 1880 (Listed Grade II), in Norman Shaw style. Probably the earliest example of the Cadogan Square style in Birmingham is Chatwin's Lench's Trust Almshouses in Conybeare Street of 1878–80.

[2] The Palace Theatre, Oxford Street, Manchester, was designed by Alfred Darbyshire and F. Bennett Smith in 1889; the 2nd Theatre Royal, Plymouth, was built in 1889 by Alfred Darbyshire (Plymouth Library Theatre Archive).

[3] Most Building Plan Registers for the Greater Birmingham area are available in Birmingham Central Library, Archives and Heritage Services (henceforth BCL AHS). Those for Birmingham pre expansion are in volumes 1876–1883, 1883–1888; 1888–1890, and for subsequent years there is one volume for each year. AHS also holds the following Building Plan Registers: Handsworth; King's Norton and Northfield; Harborne (incorporated into Birmingham in 1891); Aston; Yardley; and Perry Barr. For the latter four districts the registers may not provide the name of the architect. Sutton Coldfield building plan registers are in the Sutton Coldfield Library and cover the following years: 1887–1894 Vol 1 (no provision to name architect); 1894–1898 Vol II; 1898–1905 Vol III; 1905 Vol IV.

[4] Available for Birmingham from 1876 onwards and later for parishes subsequently incorporated into Birmingham.

[5] Edward Berks Norris (1880–1961) joined Cossins, Peacock and Bewlay in 1901. His obituary in the Green Book, 1962–63, p. 5, mentions that he worked on the tower of St Catherine, Horsefair and also St Catherine, Droitwich.

[6] The identification of the buildings on the ground was often problematic and very time consuming. Even if building plans were available, they did not often give the building's location. In the period before houses were numbered and house names changed over time, identification was often impossible.

[7] *Kelly's Directories of Birmingham*, 1899–1917.

[8] Fiddian was a Birmingham-born architect, appearing in the 1841 and 1851 Birmingham censuses. A Frederick William Fiddian, son of Charles and Sarah Fiddian, was baptised on 30 July 1810 at the New Meeting House (Unitarian), Moor Street, Birmingham. Fiddian built a number of houses in Edgbaston, as well as working further afield.

[9] *Hulley's Directory of Birmingham* 1876–77; *Kelly's Directory of Birmingham*, 1875, 1879, 1881; *Post Office Directory* 1882; King's Norton and Northfield Building Register, app. no. 55, 5 June 1876; Birmingham Building Register app. no. 2469, 13 October 1880; app. no. 2513, 13 November 1880; app. no. 3114, 6 March 1882; app. no. 3121 8 March 1882.

[10] Peacock appears to have used Barry rather than his first name, Frank.

[11] In the 1901 census records, Hubert Rawson Bewlay is recorded as 'retired architect', although aged only thirty-one (and erroneously shown as Herbert R. Bewlay – but identifiable as living with his wife, Adela Maud (née Slater) whom he married in Dolgelly in the July quarter 1897. The Green Book or Birmingham Architectural Association *Annual Report 1899–00* gave Hubert Bewlay's address as Moseley whereas before it had listed him with the other practice members at 83 Colmore Row. Hubert Rawson Bewlay's death was registered in 1904, in King's Norton.

[12] Cossins's obituary, *Birmingham Post*, 8–9 December 1917. The style 'Peacock, Bewlay and Cooke' appears to have been short-lived.

[13] Barry Peacock's Obituary, *Birmingham Mail*, 18 February 1937.

[14] For example the Mechanical Engineering Building of the University of Birmingham was completed by that firm in 1957.

[15] Frances O'Shaughnessy, *The Story of Burton Dassett Church*, (n.d.), p. 12.

[16] Biographical details are based on the following sources: Cossins's obituary; RIBA *Directory of British Architects, 1834–1914* (1993); Census Enumerators' Records 1901; *Slater's Directory of Birmingham* 1852–53; Bryan Little, *Birmingham Buildings: the Architectural Story of a Midland City* (Newton Abbot, 1971) p. 124; BCL AHS, will of Jethro A. Cossins, 15 May 1918.

[17] Information is sparse about this architect, who flourished between 1841 and 1871. St Thomas Church, Stourbridge, contains a reredos donated 1916 in memory of Mary Ann Fiddian. Both Jethro Cossins's wife, Fanny, and Hubert Bewlay snr's wife, Sarah, were Rylands and born in Stourbridge, christened in nearby Old Swinford. This coincidence may hint at some connection between the wives of the two partners and the family of the architect, Frederick Fiddian, to whom Jethro Cossins was apprenticed.

[18] Perhaps that architect's best known Birmingham building is the former Albert Works (later Argent Centre) of the 1860s, described by Peter Leather in *A Guide to the Buildings of Birmingham* (Stroud, 2000) p. 91, as 'magnificent Butterfield-style, polychrome brick'.

[19] King's Norton and Northfield Building Register, app. no. 55, 5 June 1876, for a house, etc. for I. E. Hollis in Augustus Road, Moseley (which must be Augusta Road).

[20] Birmingham Building Register, app. no. 2469, 13 October 1880.

[21] Birmingham Building Register, app. no. 1257, 12 August 1879, New Street Shop Front; app. no. 2513, 13 November 1880 for vaults to Warwick House (which stood on New Street).

[22] Birmingham Building Register, app. no. 3114, 6 March 1880.

[23] Birmingham Building Register, app. no. 3121, 8 March 1882, for four shops.

24 He correctly identified tunnels at Lifford Hall, King's Norton, as mill culverts. See BCL AHS, MS 285811, Notes by J. A. Cossins on 'Old houses, cottages, churches and other buildings, chiefly in Warwickshire, including memoranda on subterranean passages in Birmingham,1885–1899'. This was cited by George Demidowicz in his 'Lifford Hall: Preliminary Report, (unpublished Report, 1985). For Lifford Hall see also Steve Litherland *An Archaeological Evaluation near Lifford Hall, King's Norton* (Birmingham University Field Archaeology Field Unit, 1990).

25 He is recorded as having undertaken repairs on a number of Midland churches, including Edgbaston Old Church, Edgbaston. See P. B. Chatwin 'Edgbaston', *TBAS*, 39, 19 March 1913, 5–35 (p. 21); other Midlands churches included St Michael, Alkerton, Oxfordshire (1889–90); All Saints, Burton Dassett, Warwickshire (1888–89); St Peter & St Paul, Long Compton, Warwickshire (1899–1900); St Michael, Cropthorne, Worcestershire (1896) www.churchplansonline.org/retrieve, searching on Cossins, J. A.

26 The quality of Cossins' conservation work at All Saints, Burton Dassett was commended by Nikolaus Pevsner in *The Buildings of England: Warwickshire* (Harmondsworth, 1966) p. 221.

27 BCL AHS, MS 285811.

28 On 20 February 1884 he had applied to build a villa for himself in Forest Road (King's Norton and Northfield Building Register, app. no. 655). On 3 September 1890 he applied to build a house for himself on Forest Road (Kings Norton and Northfield Building Register, app. no. 1263). 'Kingsdon' Forest Road was given as Jethro Cossins's address in the 1888 *Kelly's Directory*, implying that the earlier building plan may have referred to 'Kingsdon'. It is not possible to identify any existing house in Forest Road which may be Cossins's work.

29 Fanny Seddon Cossins was born Fanny Seddon Ryland and christened at Old Swinford in 1839. Ernest Bewlay's mother, Sarah, who appears to have died shortly after his birth in 1872 (In Memoriam card of 1872 in BCL AHS for Sarah Bewlay, wife of Hubert of Springhill), was Sarah Ryland, born 23 April 1844, at Old Swinford, Worcestershire. Fanny and Sarah's parents were William and Sarah Ryland (née Thomas); BCL AHS, will of Jethro A. Cossins, 15 May 1918.

30 The biographical details are based on the following sources: Obituary in *Birmingham Mail*, 18 February 1937; Obituary in *The Builder*, 152, 5 March 1937, p. 534; RIBA *Directory of British Architects, 1834–1914*.

31 Although his obituary in the *Birmingham Mail* states that he was born in Birmingham, his 1901 Census entry correctly shows his place of birth as Manchester, Lancashire. His birth certificate confirms he was born in Cheetham, Manchester, on 12 December 1859, to Henry Barry Peacock, 'Tailor Master', and Ellen Whitfield Peacock, formerly Armstrong.

32 Peacock obituary. 1871 and 1881 census records (RG10/3188/23 and RG11 3084/7) show that his widowed mother, Ellen W. Peacock, had married William Gibson (Auctioneer 1871, Land Agent 1881) who lived in Yardley and Moseley.

33 Born 20 June 1839 in Salford; died 15 July 1908 in Manchester.

34 Birmingham and Five Counties Architectural Association, *Annual Report*, 1937–38, pp. 82–83.

35 Personal communication from Andy Foster, based on information from Douglas Hickman.

36 Frances Wilmot and Pauline Saul, *A Breath of Fresh Air: Birmingham's Open-Air Schools 1911–1970*, (Chichester, 1998), p. 14, p. 21.

37 King's Norton and Northfield Building Register, app. no. 1659, 15 February 1904.

38 The building does not appear in the Birmingham Building Register but it is attributed to Barry Peacock in his obituary.

39 Birmingham Building Register, app no. 21392, 9 April 1910.

40 King's Norton and Northfield Building Register, app. no. 3320, 17 March 1911.

41 Wilmot and Saul, *A Breath of Fresh Air*, p. 14, p. 21.

42 Sutton Coldfield Building Register, application of 3 August 1899, for 'one house, Walsall Road'. *Kelly's Directories* list Barry Peacock's house as 'Silverwood, Walsall Road' in 1904, but by 1916 it had become 'Silverwood, Four Oaks Road'.

43 His marriage is recorded for the quarter ending September 1891 in King's Norton.

44 King's Norton and Northfield Building Register, app. no. 1155, 11 December 1901, also app. no. 1330, 28 August 1902.

45 Census Enumerator's Record, Public Record Office RG13/2807, p. 61 (King's Norton)

46 Hubert Rawson Bewlay's death at the age of thirty-four was registered in the quarter ending March 1904, in King's Norton.

47 In Nikolaus Pevsner and Alexandra Wedgwood, *The Buildings of England: Warwickshire*, p. 187, it is described as 'one of the best Arts and Crafts houses in Birmingham'; The Victorian Society, *Nineteenth Century Architecture of Birmingham*, (1965), referring to building no. 93.

48 Ernest Bewlay's obituary in the Birmingham and Five Counties Architectural Association, *Annual Report*, 1942–43, p. 8, refers to his work being of sufficient merit to be represented in the permanent collection of the Birmingham Art Gallery. Some of his sketches of buildings in Gloucestershire and Worcestershire were published in *The Builder*, 67, 8 September 1894, p. 171.

[49] He married on 6 April 1899, at Redditch Parish Church, Ethel Ann Morgan, then aged twenty-six, the daughter of the late John Morgan, Needle Manufacturer. It appears that his wife adopted the name 'Dorothy', and there is a record of a birth of a Dorothy Bewlay in King's Norton in the quarter ending June 1907, perhaps the couple's daughter.

[50] Birmingham Building Register, app. no. 23899, 27 January 1913.

[51] Birmingham Building Register, app. no. 5957, 7 April 1888.

[52] Andy Foster, *Pevsner Architectural Guides: Birmingham*, (New Haven and London, 2005), p. 227.

[53] Birmingham Building Register, shops, Hagley Road, app. no. 3121, 8 March 1882; shops, Bordesley Street app. no. 3462, 22 November 1882; House at Proof House, app. no. 5503, 4 January 1883; Ear and Throat Hospital app. no. 7465, 26 June 1890.

[54] Birmingham Building Register, app. no. 7706, 30 October 1890; app. no. 10769, 19 February 1895.

[55] King's Norton Building Register, app. no. 3350, 1 June 1906.

[56] Birmingham Building Register, app. no. 13902, 30 April 1898. Now Listed Grade II*.

[57] Pevsner and Wedgwood, *Warwickshire* (1990 edition) p. 125.

[58] Foster, *Birmingham*, p. 140.

[59] Pevsner and Wedgwood, *Warwickshire* (1990 edition) p. 189.

[60] Edwin F. Reynolds, architect of the church of St Germain (1915–16), City Road, Edgbaston, worked in the firm during his early career (details from Green Books of Birmingham Architectural Association *Annual Reports*).

[61] Birmingham Building Register, app. no. 14901, 7 June 1899.

[62] Birmingham Building Register, app. no 7043, 10 September 1902; app. no. 18108, 4 June 1904; app. no. 18441, 6 March 1905.

[63] Eric Ives, Diane Drummond and Leonard Schwarz, *The First Civic University: Birmingham 1880–1980* (Birmingham, 2000) p. 22.

[64] Birmingham Building Register, app. no. 3711, 18 June 1883; Birmingham Victorian Society, *Nineteenth Century Architecture of Birmingham.*

[65] *Victoria County History: Warwickshire*, vol. VII, 'The City of Birmingham' ed. by W. B. Stevens (1964) p. 474.

[66] Birmingham Building Register app. no. 5957, 7 April 1888.

[67] Birmingham Building Register, app. no. 4396, 22 January 1885.

[68] Birmingham Building Register, Ear Nose and Throat Hospital, app. no. 7465, 26 June 1890, (now listed Grade II); Bloomsbury Library, Saltley Road, app. no. 7706, 30 October 1890 (now listed Grade IIb), Balsall Heath Library, app. no. 10769, 19 February 1895 (now listed Grade IIb); New Library, app. no. 13902, 30 April 1898 (now listed Grade II*); Pig Market, app. no. 14892, 2 June 1899.

[69] Obituary of Jethro Cossins, *Birmingham Post*, 8–9 December 1917.

[70] Frances O'Shaughnessy, *The Story of Burton Dassett Church*, (no date), p. 12.

[71] Alan Crawford, 'The Birmingham Setting' in *By Hammer and Hand: The Arts and Crafts Movement in Birmingham*, ed. by Alan Crawford, (Birmingham, 1984) p. 36 and listings in the List of Works.

[72] Roy Thornton 'The Board Schools of Birmingham', *Birmingham Historian*, No. 21, 2002, p. 36.

[73] Birmingham Building Register, app. no. 19189, 18 May 1906.

[74] Birmingham Building Register, Bank, Bordesley High Street, app. no. 17043, 19 September 1902; Bank, Warstone Lane, app. no. 18441, 6 March 1905; Bank, Waterloo Street, app. no. 18108, 4 June 1904; further Banks which the firm built are listed in BCL AHS MS 2094/2/1 Baron C. S. Underhill, Architect, Records of Architect's Practice, 1897–1996. This lists architectural drawings provided by the firm 1897–1912. These include banks at Dudley; Hagley Road (Birmingham); Bearwood; Newport, Salop; Walsall; Church Stretton, Salop; Castle Street, Shrewsbury; Derby; Sedgley and Cheltenham.

[75] Barry Peacock's obituary in the Birmingham and Five Counties Architectural Association *Report*, 1937–38, p. 82, refers to Wolverhampton, Hereford and Cradley Heath banks as his work.

[76] Birmingham Building Register, app. no. 15003, 17 July 1899.

[77] Birmingham Building Register, app. no. 15105, 13 September 1899.

[78] Birmingham Building Register, app. no. 21020, 21 August 1909; app. no. 22166, 11 May 1911; app. no. 22884, 21 March 1912.

[79] Birmingham Building Register, Church of St Catherine, Horsefair, app. no. 86941, 9 May 1892; app. no. 12081, 29 July 1896; app. no. 20260, 18 May 1908; app. no. 9385, 17 April 1893.

[80] Birmingham Building Register, app. no. 21004, 11 August 1909.

[81] Birmingham Building Register, app. no. 17188, 15 December 1902.

[82] Birmingham Building Register, app. no. 22291, 18 July 1910.

[83] Birmingham Building Register, app. no. 16478, 19 September 1901, and also app. no. 17947, 23 March 1904.

[84] Birmingham Building Register, app. no. 11285, 1 October 1895.

[85] Birmingham Building Register, app. no. 10412, 8 August 1894.

[86] King's Norton Building Register, app. no. 1104, 20 July 1889.

[87] Ives, Drummond and Schwarz, *The First Civic University*, p. 16.

[88] Little, *Birmingham Buildings*, p. 124.

[89] Maurice Cheesewright, *Mirror to a Mermaid*, (Birmingham, 1975) p. 9.

[90] Brian Jones, *Josiah Mason 1795–1881, Birmingham's Benevolent Benefactor*, (Studley, 1995), p. 91.

[91] Ives, Drummond and Schwarz, *The First Civic University*, p. 22.

[92] Cheesewright, *Mirror to a Mermaid*, p. 9.

[93] Preserved within the Union of Students' building of the University of Birmingham, Edgbaston.

[94] Robert K. Dent, *Old and New Birmingham* vol. 3, (1st pub. Birmingham 1878–80, reprinted Wakefield, 1973), pp. 592–93, quoting an extract from the *Daily Mail*.

[95] Ives, Drummond and Schwarz, *The First Civic University*, p. 17; 22.

[96] Birmingham Building Register, app. no. 8499, 2 February 1892; app. no. 11453, 12 December 1895; app. no. 12918, 5 May 1897; app. no. 14868, 26 May 1899; app. no. 15816, 11 October 1900; app. no. 16914, 18 June 1902; app. no. 17044, 11 September 1902; app. no. 17385, 3 April 1903; app. no. 18106, 1 July 1904; app. no. 18151, 8 August 1904; app. no. 18484, 30 March 1905; app. no. 22041, 8 March 1910.

[97] Birmingham Building Register, app. no. 3711, 18 June 1883.

[98] Keith Turner, *Old Photographs Series: Central Birmingham 1870–1920*, (Stroud, 1994), p. 119 (from caption of photo).

[99] Birmingham Building Register, app. no. 5957, 7 April 1888.

[100] Birmingham Building Register, app. no. 7465, 26 June 1890.

[101] King's Norton Building Register, app. no. 3170, 11 March 1898; King's Norton and Northfield Building Register, app. no. 3343, 30 April 1911.

[102] King's Norton and Northfield Building Register, app. no. 271, 5 April 1899.

[103] King's Norton Building Register, app. no. 3360, 30 June 1898; King's Norton and Northfield Building Register, app. no. 1981, 1 September 1905.

[104] Birmingham Building Register, app. no. 23899, 27 January 1913.

[105] King's Norton and Northfield Building Register, app. no. 395, 20 June 1899.

11 William Henry Ward

STEPHEN HARTLAND

In an interview for the magazine *Handsworth* in January 1897, the eminent local architect William Henry Ward (1844–1917) confessed to being a great admirer of Joseph Chamberlain, whose visionary reforms had made such a difference to his adopted city and had so greatly improved the lot of Birmingham's citizens.[1] While it is not recorded if Chamberlain had equal regard for W. H. Ward, there is no doubt that the celebrated architect was also prominent in changing the face of Birmingham, his French Renaissance or Second Empire style being wholly consistent with the civic aspirations of 'the best governed city in the world.' While in practice in Birmingham, Ward was responsible for designing no fewer than thirty-six business premises in Corporation Street, four theatres in the district, two hotels, and a considerable number of other important buildings elsewhere in the city.

The boldness and confidence of the development of the city centre owed much to Joseph Chamberlain's stroke of commercial adeptness in letting out corporation-owned land on seventy-five year leases, which he foresaw would provide a useful income for the city in future years. Chamberlain had appointed an Improvement Committee in July 1875 to examine ways of improving the city by whatever means were possible under the terms of the Artisans' Dwelling Act of 1875. This committee held an inquiry and one of the results was a proposal to demolish a large number of slum dwellings and lay a new road from New Street to Aston Street, sixty-six feet in width and cutting through the Georgian Old Square. So it was that the opportunity arose for so many of Birmingham's architects to contribute to creating the grand civic boulevard that Chamberlain envisaged, an opportunity that led to the creation of Corporation Street and in which William H. Ward would be fully involved. Unfortunately, not even the far-sighted Chamberlain could

W. H. Ward

predict that, when these seventy-five year leases expired, the stately grandeur of Victorian architecture would be out of fashion and the bulldozers would move in to demolish many of the buildings so lavishly created to symbolise Birmingham's status as the second city of the greatest Empire in the world.

William Henry Ward was born in Allanton, Lanarkshire, on 31 December 1844, the eldest son of Henry Ward, a Chartered Engineer.[2] The Ward family, however, were not Scots and originated from Hampshire. Ward was educated at Glasgow and then at Hereford and was subsequently articled to James Cranston, of Oxford and later of Birmingham.[3] Cranston's practice excelled in the field of church architecture. Much of his work was in Herefordshire and its environs and included the Pump Rooms, Round Market, Corn Exchange and National School in Tenbury Wells. Cranston's designs were influenced by early English or gothic architecture and, indeed, the Pump Rooms at Tenbury were described as being in a 'Chinese Gothic' style. For those who know W. H. Ward's designs, and as this essay will demonstrate, Ward's affections were much more for the French Renaissance or Second Empire style, certainly in his civic or public buildings, and it may have been for this reason that he declined Cranston's offer of a partnership in the firm.

Before becoming articled to Cranston, Ward had been a keen all-round sportsman. As a youth he had often stayed with friends at Draycott Hall in Derbyshire, which was the family seat of the baronets of the Denys family. Ward had on many occasions spent time duck and goose hunting on the River Derwent, notably with the 4th Marquess of Hastings, who was also a regular visitor. At school and afterwards he was noted for his ability in running and jumping and particularly boxing, becoming the best heavyweight boxer in the Midlands. In addition to this, he was able to give good service to his local cricket teams and on many occasions succeeded in getting into the All England XXIIs. In latter years, however, when maintaining his practice as an architect in Birmingham he settled for games requiring less physical prowess and more skill or patience. He took up fishing and shooting as pastimes and was particularly noted for the latter, maintaining at his home in Handsworth a fine gun-cabinet containing an impressive array of rifles and guns.[4]

Ward commenced independent practice in Birmingham in 1864 and established his offices at 27 Paradise Street.[5] Soon, however, he moved to 29½ Paradise Street, towards the junction with Suffolk Street and overlooking Alfred Hughes' Garden Restaurant and the Birmingham Coffee House Co. Ltd. There he remained until his retirement fifty years later in 1914, at the age of seventy.[6] One of Ward's first noteworthy commissions in his adopted city was the Corporation Depôt in Sheepcote Street, which still stands today. This, however, is a fairly perfunctory building, giving few indications of the bold and ornate style that would become his signature in the next few years. It is built of brick and has two small gatehouses standing sentry to the courtyard area.[7]

Much more typical of Ward's hallmark style is one of his best-known works, his Great Western Arcade of 1874, linking Temple Row with Colmore Row (then called Monmouth Street). The first and certainly the most beautiful arcade in Birmingham, it owes its 'line' to a newly-built railway tunnel which had formerly been a cutting for the Great Western Railway from Snow Hill Station. The land over the new tunnel was bought by the Great Western Arcade Company, which had been formed with the sole purpose of building an arcade on the site, and the foundation stone was laid in April 1875, the 400-foot-long arcade being opened to the public on 19th August 1876. The façade of each entrance arch was wrought in stone and crowned with sculpted allegorical figures. The Temple Row façade represented Science and Art; a male figure represented science and held dividers and compasses, while a female figure held a painter's palette and had an easel by her side. The Monmouth Street façade represented Music and Literature, with literature represented by a man holding a book and music symbolised by a woman holding a classical harp. These allegorical figures would become an oft-used

Great Western Arcade, interior

Engraving of Great
Western Arcade,
Colmore Row, 1874

device by Ward in much of his future work. The arches at each end of the arcade were decorated with low-relief foliation and flowers, as were the bases of the columns that rose from ground level to the second storey.

Ward was a great traveller, especially in Continental Europe, and his inspiration for the interior of the arcade probably came from the many such galleries to be found in Paris. The arcade itself, containing 94 shops, was covered with a glazed roof set in cast-iron semi-circular ribs that carried on where the numerous pilasters finished. While each end of the arcade was four storeys high, the rest of it had just two storeys and on the top floor there was a series of galleries. The centre of the arcade widened out into a large circle, above which there was originally a large octagonal dome from which was suspended an impressive chandelier by the Birmingham firm of Oslers. Unfortunately, the original roof and dome, along with the Colmore Row façade and the two upper storeys of the Temple Row façade, were destroyed by enemy action during World War II. In 1986, however, the arcade was

OPPOSITE   Great Western Arcade, Temple Row, 1874

refurbished and a new façade was installed at the Colmore Row entrance by Douglas Hickman of John Madin Design Group.[8]

On 7 February 1877, at the age of thirty-two, Ward married Fanny Harriet Taylor, the twenty-two-year-old daughter of Christopher Taylor, a Handsworth wine merchant.[9] The marriage took place at St Michael's Church, Handsworth, and they set up home together at Stafford House, 52 Holyhead Road, Handsworth, in the parish of St James.[10] The house, a villa typical of those belonging to the Victorian professional classes and one in which Ward would happily spend his leisure moments, was described as being one of the handsomest and best appointed of such suburban residences. It was set back from the main road and was notable for its trimmed lawns, gravelled paths and unobstructed views across to Barr Beacon. It was at this time also that Ward became Master of the St James Lodge of Freemasons, subsequently becoming a Provincial Grand Officer.[11]

In 1878 his first daughter, Binnie, was born. In the same year he restored part of St Mary's Church in Handsworth and presented to the church a stained glass window, which was installed in the tower.[12] The following year saw the realisation of a commission from Alfred Humpage, a local Contractor, or speculative developer as we would call him these days. The commission was for the site on the corner of Corporation Street and New Street, which was to be called Queen's Corner. Ward here had to complete the end of Yeoville Thomason's palazzo on New Street, built for the *Birmingham Post and Mail*, and provide an entrance to Corporation Street.[13] This was followed in 1880 with a commission for another building on Corporation Street, just north of Queen's Corner.[14] Known as Victoria Buildings, this had a stone fronted façade and had five storeys and an attic. It was described as 'a striking early example of Free Style architecture'[15] with some Spanish and Elizabethan detailing, and Ward included in its design pilasters of pink sandstone, carved pediments and an abundance of carved fruit.

By 1881 Ward was a father of three. In addition to his eldest daughter, Binnie, there were also a son, William, aged one, and the newest arrival, Constance. Ward kept two servants at Stafford House, twenty-one-year-old Emily Copestake from Birmingham and a twenty-three-year-old cook from Dudley by the name of Charlotte Broughtfield.[16]

It was in that year that he completed his commission for the Central Arcade at 15–17 Corporation Street, again for Alfred Humpage. Built originally as the Central Restaurant, 15–17 Corporation Street also contained the Central Arcade, which ran through the building to Cannon Street and was the second arcade to be built in the City after the Great Western Arcade.[17] The building survives today and is largely of Bath stone, although the ground floor is of Darley Dale stone. Ward was now starting to develop the style that would become his hallmark, namely, that of highly decorated French Renaissance, and in this instance his design included a large decorative oriel window. The floor of the arcade was made up of glass fixed in a cast iron frame, so that the restaurant at basement level would be

Queen's Corner, New Street and Corporation Street, 1879

bathed in natural light. After a fire in 1888 it was partly rebuilt to the designs of the Birmingham firm of Essex & Nicol. Oliver Essex was a former pupil of Ward's, having commenced working for him in 1873 and qualified as an architect in 1883.[18]

Ward was now doing very well and commissions were flowing, as his popularity spread and his impressive French Renaissance buildings attracted increasing public notice in Birmingham. Also in 1881 a design for a country house for the notable Birmingham industrialist and subsequent MP for Tamworth, P. A. (later Sir Albert) Muntz was completed at Clifton-upon-Dunsmore, near Rugby, Warwickshire. Muntz had bought the estate belonging to Clifton Lodge in 1880 and engaged Ward to create a handsome residence and extensive stabling for him

The Central Arcade, 1880. Elevation drawings of the Corporation Street and Cannon Street entrances, 1880 and modern photograph of former Corporation Street entrance, *courtesy of Birmingham Archives and Heritage Services*

(he would go on to breed prize Shire Horses from the stud here). The new Muntz family home was christened Dunsmore House and demonstrated Ward's versatility in that it is in the Tudor-Gothic Revival style and differed considerably from his more characteristic Second Empire style, although Ward's bold treatment of the roofline, with impressive finial-topped gables and large chimneys, betrays its creator. The house was built by a local Rugby firm of builders, J. Parnell & Son Ltd.[19]

Perhaps one of Ward's best years in terms of prominent commissions was 1883, as in addition to his spectacular Grand Theatre it saw him complete two other very fine buildings, the Stork Hotel and the Colonnade.

The Colonnade, which Alfred Humpage had invited him to design on the corner of New Street and Ethel Street, was built in 1882 at a cost of just £70,000 and was opened on 10th January 1883.[20] It was a free-standing edifice in the French Renaissance style and of an interesting design, having a colonnade running around the whole of the building. The mansard roof had metal railings running along its length but was punctuated by a central convex mansard dome topped with a large flagpole. It was at this time that Oliver Essex was about to finish his articles with Ward and set up his own practice, and it may be surmised that Essex

Dunsmore House, Clifton-upon-Dunsmore, 1881

had a hand in the design of this building, since the upper floors lack the usual boldness of Ward himself. The building also exhibited a number of the elaborate gables that would become Essex's signature, although he would later adapt it into a more Flemish form. An example of this were the premises designed by Essex on the corner of Dale Street and James Watt Street in 1884, the gables on which show a demonstrable similarity to the gables on the Colonnade.[21]

At ground level the building contained shops, but above these was housed the Midland Conservative Club while the remainder of the building functioned as a Temperance hotel and the Colonnade Restaurant. The building was later converted into an arcade whilst the hotel traded for thirty-three years until it closed in 1916 – perhaps as an unsung casualty of the Great War, which was still raging.[22] After the hotel had closed, the Birmingham Chamber of Commerce, which had been seeking permanent premises, bought the lease and subsequently the freehold too. The Chamber of Commerce remained in the building until 1960, when it moved to new premises designed by John Madin on the Calthorpe Estate in Edgbaston. The Colonnade provided the money for the move to the new site, as it was sold off for redevelopment and demolished in 1961 to make way for the Woolworth building, which remains on the site to this day.[23]

The Colonnade, New Street and Ethel Street, 1882. Photograph c. 1900. *Courtesy of Birmingham Archives and Heritage Services (WK/B11/1063)*

The other high point for Ward in 1883 was the completion of the Stork Hotel in Corporation Street, on a site near Old Square. Ward had been invited to become involved in a project to replace the old Stork Hotel, which originally stood a few hundred yards away, with a new hotel. The original building was bought at auction on 26th September 1881 and was quickly razed to the ground. Ward completed the design in 1882 and the new hotel opened for business in 1883.[24] It was in his usual French Renaissance style with Second Empire detailing and faced with stone. On the top of the central pediment stood a large carved stork looking down into Old Square.

The hotel was particularly ornate, displaying a riot of rich carvings above its many window-bay pediments. Its site was on the corner of the Minories and Lower Priory and it was said at the time to stand boldly forth as one of the magnificences of Corporation Street.[25] The Stork Hotel managed to maintain its magnificence for another seventy-seven years, before the onslaught of progress and the requirements of the Inner Ring Road decreed that it too should fall victim to redevelopment. It was demolished in 1960 to make way for the Priory Ringway.

Ward's plans for the magnificent Grand Theatre also came to fruition in 1883. Situated just across the road from the Stork Hotel and, like it, also looking on to Old Square, Corporation Street, it had been commissioned by a well-known citizen of Birmingham in the 1880s and 1890s, Andrew Melville. A Welshman from Cardiff and the son of George Melville, a notable Shakespearean actor of the time, Melville was steeped in the tradition of the Victorian theatre and was at once an actor and theatre proprietor as well as a theatre manager, director, producer and writer of plays. In the early 1880s he had been undecided whether to buy a theatre in Manchester or to build one in Birmingham, but eventually he decided that Birmingham was the better option.[26]

A previous plan for part of the site had been put forward by Messrs McDermott & Bennett, who had sought to build a 'Coffee Tavern Theatre of Varieties.' However, their plan failed and so Melville seized his opportunity by arranging with the Birmingham Corporation Improvement Committee to take a bigger piece of land, which would be suitable to build a larger theatre than that which was originally planned by McDermott & Bennett.[27]

Unusually for an actor and theatre proprietor, Melville was generally held to be a modest man. He was still, however, a man of his time and so the pediment of the eventual building would display his initials, 'AM', quite prominently carved into a cartouche at the top of the façade. The new theatre was renowned for being especially commodious and for having very good ventilation and good views from most seats. It had a capacity of 2,200, its two circles, a gallery, stalls and eight boxes making it the largest theatre in the town. The original intention had been to open the theatre as the New Theatre (the name carved in the gable over the main entrance), but perhaps because of Ward's customary architectural ostentation it became known as the Grand Theatre and was hailed as one of the handsomest

The Stork Hotel, Corporation Street, 1883. Photograph c. 1883. *Courtesy of Birmingham Archives and Heritage Services (WK/B11/0270)*

edifices of the city.[28] An anecdote reported in *Birmingham Faces & Places* of 1892 tells that Melville received the first proof of the theatre billing with the heading New Theatre. While watching the last remnants of the scaffolding being removed, however, he remarked "Well, it's a Grand Theatre, and I think it will be better to call it so." He accordingly sent back the proof with the new heading. In true theatrical style, Melville always maintained that he would change the name on the front of the theatre from 'New Theatre' to 'Grand Theatre' – when he could borrow a ladder that was long enough.[29]

At this point it seems appropriate to touch upon another of Ward's stylistic predilections, which was his penchant for carving the name of the building into its façade. It was all too clear in the case of the 'New' Theatre, but the Stork Hotel also had its name writ large below the pediment, as did the Colonnade on its New Street façade. As will be discussed subsequently, the device was again employed on the tower of the Parish Offices.

Like so many of Ward's buildings, the Grand Theatre was designed in the French Second Empire style. Its façade was highly decorated, the enriched gable being topped with a bold roof adorned by a central convex mansard dome crowned by a large allegorical figure of Aurora, goddess of the dawn, in a horse-drawn chariot and holding up a trumpet to herald the new day. The façade was indeed a very attractive one and vividly showed the influence of the church of Saint-Étienne-du-Mont in Paris (that celebrated sixteenth-century combination of Gothic, Renaissance and Baroque), repeating as it does the design of a central

The Grand Theatre, Corporation Street, 1883. Photograph c. 1900. *Courtesy of Birmingham Archives and Heritage Services (WK/B11/0887)*

pediment beneath a central gable that almost gives the impression of one building rising from another. The tympanum of the pediment was as rich in ornament as was the gable above it, which contained two reclining figures in low relief (similar to those found on the Great Western Arcade façades, and which were to become a consistent feature in Ward's designs) and this was held aloft by four caryatids. The main entrance to the building was crowned with a large convex mansard dome. The interior was equally lavishly decorated in crimson and gold and featured a beautiful marble staircase leading to an ornamental foyer floor. The plasterwork in the auditorium repeated the harp motifs that were carved into the pediments above each of the theatre's flank entrances.

The building work began in March 1883 and was undertaken by the local firm of Bradney & Co. They took just eight months to complete the work, enabling the theatre to open for business on 14th November 1883 with a special programme consisting of two items – 'Ici on parle Français,' and 'Good as Gold' – and a musical entitled, 'At the Seaside.' Joseph Chamberlain was expected as a guest on the opening night, but he telegraphed an apology at the last minute to say he had been detained in London. While it is not recorded whether Ward was present at the opening, it seems highly likely given what we know to have been his great love of the theatre. He counted among his friends many actors whose names would mean nothing to us now but who regularly visited him at his home on the Holyhead Road, where many of their portraits in the form of drawings or photographs were displayed on his walls.[30]

In 1907 Moss Empires bought the theatre and engaged Frank Matcham to redesign the interior at a cost of £20,000 for it to be re-opened as a Music Hall. The Grand Theatre continued to run successfully in this form until the late 1920s, when competition from the new cinemas together with the Depression and its location 'out of town' at the end of Corporation Street conspired to make it a less attractive venue and caused it to close its doors in May 1933. It was subsequently re-opened as the Grand Casino Dance Hall, but even this failed, and eventually it became part of a market before succumbing to the ubiquitous bulldozer in 1960.[31]

It is hard to comprehend how such a great building, so perfectly embodying the Victorian era in its social tastes, was ever allowed to be lost to us with such ease. In this context one can understand all too clearly why the Victorian Society came to be founded in 1958. However, an equally majestic building of Ward's that survives today (or, at least, its façade does) is the Board of Guardians Parish Offices built between 1882 and 1884 and bounded on three sides by Edmund Street, Newhall Street and Cornwall Street (or Bread Street as it was then called) while maintaining a central square courtyard at its core.

The Birmingham Parish Board of Guardians were elected by the ratepayers under the provisions of the Poor Law to administer relief to the poor and destitute, which would often result in those assessed becoming inmates of a local workhouse or infirmary. Ward was to do well from the need to construct workhouses

Board of Guardians Parish Offices, 1882–84. Photograph c. 1900. *Courtesy of Birmingham Archives and Heritage Services*

and infirmaries, acting as expert adviser to Boards of Guardians such as those of Solihull, Wolverhampton, Doncaster, Alcester, Bradford, Sheffield, Nottingham, Brentford, London and, of course, Birmingham.[32] He was also to design the Dudley Road Infirmary in Birmingham in 1888 which was of a considerable size, west of the workhouse. The City Sanatorium in Yardley Road was built in 1893 and the sanatorium at Salterley Grange, Cheltenham in the early years of the twentieth century.[33]

Work began on the Birmingham Parish Offices in June 1882 by Messrs Webb & Son, the contract price for the building being £25,490 together with a further £5,000 for fixtures, fittings and interior decorations. The memorial stone was laid in the following year on 15th February by E. J. Jerrett, then Chairman of the Board of Guardians, and the building was formally opened in March 1885 by Mr Price, the Chairman of the Board in that year.[34] Above the main entrance in Edmund Street was a large clock tower and cupola which reached a height of 105 feet. The Edmund Street entrance was also the entrance to the office of the Registrar of

Births, Marriages & Deaths, where citizens could use an imposing and attractive waiting room as well as a rather unusually-designed staircase with scrolly balustrading.

The rusticated stonework is banded on the first and second storey in Coxbench sandstone from Derbyshire, while above the larger arched windows to each of the pavilions at the corners of the building are to be found Ward's usual sculptural devices of low relief allegorical figures, although these are much smaller, and in greater number, than at the Grand Theatre and Great Western Arcade. At the third storey the windows are embellished with segmental (or rounded) pediments, although at the corners the windows again change to triangular pediments which are themselves framed by columns set within larger square engaged columns, both sets of columns having Corinthian capitals. These are topped by pediments containing decoration varying from roundels surrounded by foliage to griffins (which were symbolic of watchfulness and courage, and were later used to symbolise the Dual Nature of Christ). In addition, there were balusters at parapet level upon which sat a number of urns.

The Newhall Street side has a banded colonnade of red granite along the central pavilion of the building, which is treated differently from the other parts of this façade in that it originally culminated in a small-segmented ornamental pedestal bearing a sculpture (now sadly gone). The windows between each of the columns extend almost to the full height of the columns, the purpose of the windows' height being to create enough light for the Boardroom, which was two storeys high. The Boardroom itself was an imposing space, measuring sixty feet long, thiry-six feet wide and twenty-four feet high and approached by a broad flight of stairs. Such generous dimensions were necessary. The Boardroom (which was in some respects similar to the Council Chamber at the Council House) had to accommodate 120 Board members, who were seated in a long double oval. At one end stood a raised dais for the Chairman, Vice Chairman, Clerk and Assistant to sit, and the furniture was of massive oak, the chairs alone costing £5 each in 1884. Beneath the Boardroom, at first floor level, was a hall decorated by pilasters and a coved ceiling, and having a balcony at one end and a reredos flanked by two doors with segmental pediments at the other.

In the basement of the building was the Muniment Room, where all the records of the parish were kept (including thousands of rate books and documents about the town dating back to the early eighteenth century). This room was of the same proportions as the Board Room, but had a much lower ceiling constructed of arched concrete resting on rows of iron pillars. The boast was that if the building were to fall down or be burnt to the ground, then the Muniment Room would remain unscathed.

The Parish Offices were somewhat more restrained – or perhaps refined – than some of Ward's earlier works, although still very much in his characteristic style and incorporating his customary mansard roof and central mansard dome. An essay in Ward's favourite Second Empire style that was thought to equal the grandeur of the Council House, the Parish Offices were termed a 'Municipal Palace.' It was a building that was designed to impress, although an architectural magazine of the time referred to it as being in a 'severe form' of the style of the French Renaissance. Unfortunately, the clock tower and cupola were lost to enemy action in Word War II and yet worse was to come in the 1980s when the city council decided to gut the whole building and retain just the façade. At that time the beautiful château-style mansard roofs were lost, along with the urns, metal railings and all the finials and other embellishments at roof level. What remains is very much impoverished as a result, but at least Ward's façade remains for us to appreciate as an example of his boldness and his architectural abilities.[35]

In 1885 Ward was responsible for designing a further set of buildings in Corporation Street, known as Lincoln's Inn (subsequently to be renamed the Gazette Buildings).[36] This remains pretty much intact, although its roof was damaged in Word War II and the central mansard dome was destroyed, to be replaced by a rather poor square flat roof. Although similar in some respects to the Colonnade he designed a couple of years before, Lincoln's Inn (or the Gazette Buildings) is not nearly so successful and is more Mannerist in its approach than the lavish Second Empire of Ward's earlier work. Central to the façade is a substantial arched entrance surmounted at a height of two storeys by a large broken segmental arch with some moderate decoration (including his customary reclining allegorical figures). However, overall the façade contains much less detailing and lacks any of Ward's richness of embellishment noted in his earlier works. Nonetheless, Alfred Humpage obviously thought them worthy offices and he took a lease at 4 Lincoln's Inn.[37]

An altogether more successful later work is Ward's Salvation Army buildings building on Corporation Street, which was commissioned by J. Booth for the Salvation Army Headquarters in Corporation Street and built in 1892.[38] This was Ward's last major 'civic' building, so many of which had contributed to the realisation of Chamberlain's dream as the grand boulevard of a great city of the foremost commercial power in the world. It is in a classic form, far more freely treated and containing none of reminiscences of Ward's earlier French Renaissance style that had weakened the impression of the Lincoln's Inn building. The most notable features of the design were the two flanking towers wrought from Bath stone which topped in height the four sedate lower storeys, the ground floor being in York stone and granite. Both the domes had smaller finials at each corner of the tower from which they rose. Most of the façade contains some rusticated banding, which lessens with each storey, the third storey having an enriched pediment along with a sparse smattering of garlands below and to the tower flanks. The following year in 1893 saw his last big commission in wider Birmingham, namely that of the Infectious Diseases Hospital for Birmingham Corporation at Yardley Road.[39]

The Salvation Army Citadel, 1892, with Ewen and J. A. Harper's Methodist Hall on the left

Further afield Ward had been commissioned to re-build the Brentford Work-house at Isleworth, near London to include an Infirmary. The new buildings were based on a pavilion block layout and were officially opened by the Duchess of Teck in 1897.[40] In 1906 he designed Salterley Grange Sanatorium in Cheltenham for the Birmingham Corporation to send tuberculosis sufferers to.[41] This was the first Municipal sanatorium in the country.[42] In Birmingham he was responsible for rebuilding the Castle & Falcon Public House on the corner of Digbeth and Meriden Street, the design of which included a chamfered corner with bands of blue and yellow brick.[43] However, apart from these last few buildings mentioned, Ward's golden years were over in Birmingham and much of his work in the twentieth century would be the more mundane work occasioned by alterations and additions, with just one house built in Monument Road, Edgbaston in 1906.[44]

Ward moved from Handsworth in 1912, where he had lived for nearly fifty years, and bought a house nearer to the city at 65 Sandon Road, Edgbaston, just off the Hagley Road. He continued in his practice until early in 1914, when he retired in

favour of his son, also William Henry Ward, who had been educated at Rugby
School and had then become a partner in his father's firm.[45] However, Ward's
retirement was short lived, as Henry (who was a reservist in the Territorial Army)
was soon called up to serve in the Great War. Ward Senior carried on the practice,
still in Paradise Street although now renumbered No. 30, until 1917, when he died
on 15 March in his 73rd year. His obituary in the next day's *Birmingham Post*
lauded the breadth and quality of his contribution to the architecture of Birmingham, listing not only a good number of the works examined here but also
including some of the work he had done for social luminaries of the countryside
surrounding his adopted city. These commissions included work for Sir Charles
Featherstone Dilke in restoring Maxstoke Castle at Coleshill in Warwickshire,
extensive alteration at Netherseal Hall in Derbyshire for Colonel Robertson and
the restoration of parts of Warwick Castle for the Earl of Warwick.

The work of Ward in Birmingham had made him a well-known character and
his fine buildings had certainly contributed to making Birmingham into a great
and indeed beautiful Victorian city. Many of his buildings still stand for us to
enjoy them first hand, though unfortunately some of the striking features, such as
bold rooves and clock towers have been lost during the twentieth century. His
major works can undoubtedly be defined as grand edifices and it is to be regretted
that many of his buildings were demolished in the 1960s, when all that was
Victorian was considered unfashionable and unworthy of retention.

Selected List of Architectural Works of William Henry Ward

*W. H. Ward (1844–1917) was articled to James Cranston of Oxford, and later of
Birmingham. Ward started in independent practice in Birmingham in 1865. He
retired in 1914 in favour of his son, also William Henry Ward, who had been in
partnership with his father. He soon re-entered the firm on his son being called up,
and continued working until his death in 1917.*

WORK IN BIRMINGHAM AND ITS ENVIRONS

PUBLIC

1873 Corporation Depot, Sheepcote St

1887 Infirmary, Dudley Rd for Birmingham Board of Guardians

1882–84 Parish Offices for Board of Guardians, Edmund St/Newhall St/Cornwall St
[facaded 1984–86]

1891 Salvation Army Building, Corporation St

1893 Infectious Diseases Hospital, Yardley Rd for Birmingham Corporation; 1903
addition of pavilions and nurses' home

1906 Additions to Moseley Rd Working Boys Home for Rev. G. Hudson

COMMERCIAL

1871 84–86 New St [City Chambers] for E. C. Osborne, stationer (attrib. by A. Foster)

1874–76 Great Western Arcade, Temple Row/Colmore Row for Great Western Arcade Company [damaged 1941]

1879 Two shops with offices [Queen's Corner], Corporation St for Alfred Humpage

1879 Shops and offices [Victoria Buildings], Corporation St

1880 Central Arcade with nine shops and offices, 15–17 Corporation St for Alfred Humpage

1881 The Colonnade Building including Temperance Hotel and restaurant, shops and offices, New St/Ethel St for Alfred Humpage; 1901 alterations to hotel and restaurant [D]

1881 Temporary Bazaar, New St for Alfred Humpage

1882 New Stork Hotel, Corporation St [D]

1882 Lincoln's Inn Building including shops and lawyers' offices [Gazette Building], [8] Corporation St

1883 New Theatre [Grand Theatre], Corporation St for Andrew Melville [D]

1884 Stabling and alterations to Warehouse, Clement St, Sand Pits

1885 Rebuilding of Woolpack Hotel, Moor St [D]

1885 Two shops and warehouse, Moor St

1886 Red Stone Cross Public House, Dale End for J. C. Bourne

1886 Central Club and shops, Corporation St

1887 Alterations and reconstruction of Club, High St for Edwin Fletcher

1890 Shops and Offices, Lower Temple St for J. and H. Creamer

1890 Newspaper Offices for *Birmingham Argus*, Corporation St

1891 Cannon St Chambers, business premises and warehouses, Cannon St for S. C. Larkins; 1895 roof and staircase; 1906 alterations

1895 Alterations to shop front, Hockley Hill for Harry Smith

1896 Alterations and additions to Clarendon Chambers, Temple St/Temple Row for C. F. Price; 1896 additions

1897 Additions to offices, Temple St for Bikkow and Co.

1899 Alterations to shop, Broad St

1901 New frontage to Offices at 29, 29½ , and 30 Paradise St

1914 Offices, 189, Hagley Rd, Edgbaston for J. B. Webster

INDUSTRIAL

1887 Workshops and warehouse, Vyse St for C. Peyton and Sons, brassfounders

1894 Shopping and shop, Bromsgrove St/Pershore St for W. Price; 1900 shop front

1899 Addition of shopping to Griffin Foundry, Vyse St for Frank Moore

1899 Additions to premises, Livery St for Webb and Co.

1900 Addition of shopping and warehouse, 187–188 Broad St for T. Oram

1901 Alterations, Livery St for S. G. Larkins and Sons; 1909 additions; 1911 additional storey; 1916 additional escape and staircases

1905 Alterations, Icknield Square for Gough and Co.

1906 Alterations to Castle and Falcon Public House, Digbeth St/Meriden St, for J. J. Affleck

DOMESTIC

1890 Twenty-three terraced houses, Green Lane, Small Heath

1890 Twelve terraced houses, Green Lane, Small Heath

1892 Addition of billiard Room, Somerset Rd, Edgbaston for Henry Barber

1894 Two houses, Tudor St for Emery Davies (not approved)

1906 House and Stabling, Monument Rd for Dr Trout

1913 Motor house, St Mary's Rd, Harborne for R. J. Curtis

1914 Additions, Church Hill Rd, Handsworth for J. F. Burton

WORK OUTSIDE BIRMINGHAM

PUBLIC

1897 Brentford Workhouse, Isleworth

1906 Salterley Grange Sanatorium, nr Cheltenham for Birmingham Corporation

DOMESTIC

c. 1865 Work at Maxstoke Castle, Coleshill for Sir Charles Featherstone Dilke

1891 Dunsmore House, Clifton on Dunsmore nr Rugby for P. A. Muntz

Dates unknown: Alterations at Netherseal Hall, Derbyshire

Alterations at Warwick Castle

NOTES

[1] *Handsworth*, 3, no. 31, January 1897, p. 3.

[2] *Birmingham at the Opening of the Twentieth Century: Contemporary Biographies* ed. by W. T. Pike (Brighton, n. d.) p. 164.

[3] *Handsworth*, 3, no. 31, January 1897, p. 1; Obituary of W. H. Ward, *Birmingham Post* 16 March 1917.

[4] *Handsworth*, 3, no. 31, January 1897, p. 3.

[5] RIBA, *Directory of British Architects 1834–1914*, 2 vols, (2001) p. 914.

[6] Kelly's *Directory of Birmingham*, various dates 1867–1917.

[7] Andy Foster, *Pevsner Architectural Guides: Birmingham* (New Haven and London, 2005) p. 150.

[8] *The Architect*, 11, 14 March 1874, p. 157; Public Monuments & Sculpture Association, *National Recording Project* Work ID 793; Department of the Environment *List of Buildings of Special Architectural or Historic Interest: Birmingham*, (1982), 0787 SW 30/7; Foster, *Birmingham*, p. 118.

[9] Marriage certificate no. 331, Parish of Handsworth, County of Staffordshire, West Bromwich District 6B 785 1st Quarter 1877.

[10] Kelly's *Directory of Birmingham*, various dates, 1867–1917; Census Enumerators' Records 1881 and 1891.

[11] *Handsworth*, 3, no. 31, January 1897, p. 3.

[12] Obituary, *Birmingham Post*, 16 March 1917.

[13] Birmingham Central Library, Archives and Heritage Services (hereafter BCL AHS) Birmingham Building Register, app. no. 1696, 30 April 1879, one shop, Corporation Street/New Street.

[14] *Ibid*, app. no. 1749, 6 June 1879, two shops with offices, Corporation Street; app. no. 1874, 28 August 1879, shops and office, Corporation Street.

[15] The Victorian Society, Birmingham Group, *Three City Trails* (Birmingham, 1998) p. 6.

[16] 1881 Census Enumerators' Records.

[17] BCL AHS, Birmingham Building Register, app. no. 2237, 8 May 1880, Central Arcade plus 9 shops and offices, Corporation Street; *The Architect*, 25, 12 February 1881, p. 115.

[18] *How Does Your Birmingham Grow?* ed. by John Wybrow, (Birmingham, 1972) p. 70.

[19] Obituary of Sir P. A. Muntz, MP, *Birmingham Daily Post*, 22 December 1908; Warwickshire Record Office, MS 14 GB 0152 Records of J. Parnell & Son Ltd (builders).

[20] BCL AHS, Birmingham Building Register, app. no. 2747, 16 May 1881, Colonnade, Shops and offices New Street; *Showell's Dictionary of Birmingham*, 1885, p. 43; illustrated in *How Does Your Birmingham Grow?* p. 70.

[21] *The Architect*, 32, 19 July 1884, p. 39.

[22] *Birmingham Post*, 2 December 1960.

[23] *Birmingham Post*, 20 July 1988.

[24] BCL AHS, Birmingham Building Register, app. no. 3225, New Stork Hotel, Corporation Street, 16 May 1882; *Showell's Dictionary of Birmingham*, 1885, p. 107; illustrated in *How Does Your Birmingham Grow?* p. 38.

[25] *Showell's Dictionary of Birmingham*, 1885, p. 107.

[26] *Birmingham Faces and Places*, 4, 1892, pp. 38–39.

[27] *Ibid* p. 38.

[28] BCL AHS, Birmingham Building Register, app. no. 3573, 1 March 1883, New Grand Theatre for Andrew Melville, Corporation Street; Derek Salberg, *Ring Down the Curtain* (Luton, 1980) pp. 68–71; *Showell's Dictionary of Birmingham*, 1885, p. 300; *Birmingham Faces and Places*, 4, 1892, pp. 38–39; illustrated in *How Does Your Birmingham Grow?* p. 40; Victor Price, *Birmingham Theatres, Concert and Music Halls 1740–1988* (Studley, 1988) pp. 32–33.

[29] *Birmingham Faces and Places*, 4, 1892, pp. 38–39.

[30] *Ibid*.

[31] *Handsworth*, 3, no. 31, January 1897, p. 2.

[32] *Birmingham at the Opening of the Twentieth Century* p. 164.

[33] Obituary, *Birmingham Post*, 16 March 1917.

[34] BCL AHS, Birmingham Building Register, app. no. 3254, 10 June 1882, New Parish Offices; *Birmingham Faces and Places*, 5, 1893, pp. 155–57; *Showell's Dictionary of Birmingham*, 1885, pp. 259–60; Obituary of W. H. Ward, *Birmingham Post*, 16 March 1917.

[35] Foster, *Birmingham*, p. 130.

[36] BCL AHS, Birmingham Building Register, app. no. 3305, 20 July 1882, Lincoln's Inn, offices plus 10 shops, Corporation Street.

[37] Kelly's *Directory of Birmingham* 1886

[38] BCL AHS, Birmingham Building Register, app. no. 8162, 29 July 1891, Salvation Army Building, Corporation Street.

[39] *Ibid*, app. no. 9567, 16 March 1893, Infectious Hospital for Birmingham Corporation, Yardley Road.

[40] *Birmingham at the Opening of the Twentieth century*, p. 164; *Handsworth*, 3, no. 31, January 1897, p. 1.

[41] Obituary, *Birmingham Post*, 16 March 1917.

[42] *Victoria History of the County of Warwick: Vol 7 The City of Birmingham* ed. by W. B. Stevens (1st pub 1964, reprinted 1965) p. 345.

[43] Foster, *Birmingham*, p. 180.

[44] BCL AHS, Birmingham Building Register, app. no. 19258, 25 June 1906, House & stabling at 260 Monument Road, Edgbaston for Dr Trout.

[45] Obituary, *Birmingham Post*, 16 March 1917.

12 Frank Barlow Osborn

DONALD ABBOTT

Frank Barlow Osborn (1840–1907) was born, educated, and, apart from a short period of training in London, spent the whole of his professional career in Birmingham. His father, Thomas Osborn, a silversmith, originally came from Sheffield, but for most of his life he was in business in Birmingham, for some time representing Edgbaston on the Town Council. Frank's mother, Ann, was the sister of William Barlow, a well known and respected local solicitor, who for twenty eight years held the appointment of Clerk to the Justices of Birmingham.

Frank Osborn was born in Hagley Road, Edgbaston, in June 1840, and received his initial education at the preparatory school in Harborne Road run by the Misses Ryland. From there he moved on to the Proprietory School at Five Ways, an establishment founded by influential members of the Edgbaston community. As might be expected, the sons of many of the leading Edgbaston families of the time attended the school. Some years later the school was closed, but the building was taken over by the King Edward Foundation, to become Five Ways Grammar School.[1]

On leaving school, having settled on a career in architecture, the young Frank was articled to Charles Edge, the Birmingham architect who designed the Market Hall (1828–35) and supervised the completion of the Town Hall (1835–61). In order to widen his experience, Osborn later transferred to the offices of Samuel Sanders Teulon, a London architect specialising in the design of ecclesiastical buildings. Examples of Teulon's churches in Birmingham include St James, Edgbaston (1852), and St John the Evangelist, Ladywood (1852–54). In 1864, having been elected an Associate of the Royal Institute of British Architects, Osborn returned to Birmingham to set up business on his own account, practising under his full name of Frank Barlow Osborn. His first business address was 1, Cherry Street, but in 1866 he moved to 11, Temple Row. In 1872 he was

Frank Barlow Osborn

elected a Fellow of the Royal Institute of British Architects, and in 1874 he moved office once more, this time to 13, Bennett's Hill, where he was to remain for the rest of his career. Two years later, in 1876, Osborn took into partnership Alfred Reading, a former pupil, thus creating the firm of Osborn & Reading. Amongst Osborn's other pupils were Charles Lea and Thomas Newton. The firm of Osborn and Reading continued until the end of the year 1890, when Reading left the practice, leaving Osborn once more to carry on business in the name of Frank Barlow Osborn, which he did successfully until his death in 1907.

This success was reflected in his accumulated wealth at the time of his death, his total effects being valued at £22,444, which in today's terms would be worth over £930,000. Unfortunately, there was no one left in his family to carry on his practice. In 1867 he had married Mary Anne Whitehead, the daughter of a local merchant, by whom he had a son and two daughters. Their son Philip did not however take after his father and become an architect, but made a career for himself in the Army; the elder daughter Lucy married a clergyman, while the younger daughter Marion remained unmarried. In 1874 their mother Mary had died, following the birth of Marion, but in 1880 Osborn married for the second time, his new wife being Marion Georgina Taynton, the daughter of a London solicitor. She also predeceased him.

During the course of his forty-three years in business Osborn produced a wide ranging variety of architecture. As might be expected from his training under Teulon, a number of his commissions were for churches and other ecclesiastical buildings, but he was also responsible for many other different kinds of buildings, including a large number of private residences, notably in Edgbaston, where he continued to live throughout his life.

A contemporary account of Osborn's career confirms that soon after starting up in practice in 1864 he was 'receiving and executing a fair share of commissions',[2] but unfortunately there are very few records of, or references to, any of his work during this early period. It is known that in 1868 he entered the competition for the design of the new workhouse to be built for the King's Norton Union,[3] but he failed to win the contract. Also around this time it would appear that Osborn's father, Thomas, had five large houses built on the Hagley Road, near to the junction with Westfield Road, one of which, no. 205 (later no. 222), was occupied by Osborn, who continued to live there until his death in 1907.[4] Although there is no documentary evidence available to show that Osborn in fact designed these houses for his father, it is surely inconceivable that Osborn senior would have employed the architectural services of anyone other than those of his own son, newly set up in practice. Shortly afterwards, around 1869–71, it would seem that Osborn carried out further work for his father, in the form of alterations to his father's property, 13, Bennett's Hill, prior to his own move there in 1874.[5]

Osborn's earliest known fully authenticated building, dating from 1873, is also arguably his finest, and certainly his most interesting. Described by Pevsner as 'nicely eccentric',[6] the church of St Cyprian, Hay Mill was commissioned not by the Church of England to meet the spiritual needs of an expanding urban population, but by James Horsfall, the proprietor of the wire-making firm of Webster and Horsfall, for the benefit of his own workforce. An already existing chapel, originally built in 1861 as a schoolroom for the children of the workforce, was seamlessly incorporated by Osborn into his overall design, becoming the chancel of the new, extended church, which was, (and indeed still is), situated literally outside the gates of the factory. The original source of power of Hay Mill, the mill race, which somewhat inconveniently ran straight through the centre of the proposed site of the new church, was channelled by Osborn underneath the building by way of a tunnel. The original chapel with its lancet windows was described as being 'of brick, in the Thirteenth Century style of architecture',[7] and the extensive additional work was therefore executed in the same style. The new church comprised chancel, nave, north and south aisles, vestries, children's gallery, porch, tower and spire. The pattern of lancets established by the chapel was continued into the new side aisles, with plate tracery in the clerestory windows. The interior of the church is of red brick with stone dressings, with the exterior being of red and blue brick. The tower and slated broach spire are positioned in the south-west corner of the church, above the porch. The Horsfall Mortuary Chapel, also designed by Osborn, was added to the south side of the nave in 1877. The church was consecrated as the parish church of Hay Mill on 23 April 1878 and is now a grade II listed building. For many years, for some as yet unexplained reason, the design of St Cyprian's was erroneously attributed by all of the leading authorities to Martin and Chamberlain, but it has now been conclusively shown that the architect was in fact Frank Barlow Osborn.[8]

In the years immediately following the completion of St Cyprian's, commissions were received first by Frank Barlow Osborn, and then by the new firm of Osborn & Reading, for the building of two more new churches. St Margaret's, Ledsam Street, a daughter church of St John's, Ladywood, (one of Teulon's churches), was opened on 2 October 1875, while St Catherine's, Scholefield Street, in the parish of St Clement's, Nechells, was consecrated on 8 November 1878.[9] Both churches were built in a style similar to that of St Cyprian's, in red brick with tile roofs, both having north and south side aisles containing lancet windows, with larger clerestory windows above. Neither church, however, was provided with a tower or spire, since, unlike St Cyprian's, there was no wealthy patron.

Although Osborn was not to build another church in Birmingham until the turn of the century, his expertise in ecclesiastical architecture continued to find expression in the form of designs for the original Methodist Central Hall, the Boatmen's Mission Hall, and three mission rooms for Birmingham churches. All of these were multi-purpose buildings, combining a place of worship with classrooms and other amenities.

St Cyprian's Church, Hay Mill, 1873

The first of these commissions was for the Boatmen's Mission Hall, in Bridge Street, erected by the Seamen and Boatmen's Friend Society for the benefit of the families of those working on the canals.[10] Opened in March 1885, it was 'of the style of the latter half of the sixteenth century',[11] and had a large Perpendicular traceried window over the entrance to emphasize the religious nature of the hall. There was a large coffee and reading room at ground level, with a chapel and vestry (or schoolroom), on the first floor, and a further room in the basement, which took advantage of the drop in ground level along Bridge Street to provide natural light.

In the following year, 1886, Osborn & Reading won a competition for the design of a new Wesleyan Chapel, to replace the influential Cherry Street Chapel which had been demolished under the Improvement Scheme. The site was on the junction of Corporation Street and Upper Priory, and the design included not only a chapel but also a large hall, classrooms, a house for the caretaker, and three shops for letting.[12] The building, which was to become known as the Central Hall, and which opened on 8 September 1887, was 'in the English Gothic style of the thirteenth-century, the materials used being Darley Dale stone for the greater part of the ground floor story, and red brick with stone dressings for the remainder of the elevations'.[13] In 1903, when the new Methodist Central Hall was opened further along Corporation Street, this building was renamed King's Hall, and as such became much better known in later years as the home of the King's Hall Market.

The first of the three mission rooms was built in Dollman Street for St James's, Ashted, in 1889.[14] 'An absolutely plain structure, with brick masonry, and roof and floor of wood',[15] the room was intended eventually to form one transept of a larger church. By contrast, the mission room in Ellis Street, built for St Thomas's, Bath Row, in 1892 by Osborn, now once more a sole practitioner, was referred to in the Vicar's annual report for that year as 'the large and beautiful mission hall, recently opened'.[16] Osborn's third mission room, opened in 1896, and later to become known as St Peter's, Belmont Row, was another commission for St James's Ashted. Unlike its 'absolutely plain' sister mission in Dollman Street, this was a large two storied building, 'designed in the Perpendicular style ... constructed of red brick and stone, with stone mullioned and traceried windows'.[17] Similar in style to the Boatmen's Mission Hall, it also had a large Perpendicular traceried window over the entrance.

Osborn's last church, St Peter's Spring Hill, consecrated on 19 July 1902, was built under the provisions of the Birmingham Churches Act, to replace the old church of St Peter, Dale End, and the attendant costs were met out of the fund created by that Act. Whether or not this was Osborn's finest church is open to debate, but it was undeniably his largest, and certainly his most expensive. The building costs alone amounted to between £13–14,000, more than twice those of St Cyprian's. At the time of its opening St Peter's was described as being 'one of the largest and most important of the new churches of Birmingham', the internal measurements being 145 ft. by 68 ft., and with accommodation being provided for up to 800 people. The style employed was Early Perpendicular, quite unlike that of Osborn's earlier churches. In addition to the chancel, nave and gabled baptistery, the church has north and south aisles, transepts with separate entrances, and a chancel aisle on the south side. A tower is at the west end of the south aisle. There are a large number of traceried windows, including two very large ones at the east and west ends. The materials used were red brick internally and externally, with stone arcades, windows and dressings, and a tiled roof. It was remarked at the time of its opening that 'the church depends for its effect chiefly upon its proportions, stability, and spacious interior, without much expensive ornament'.[18] In 2002, its centenary year, St Peter's, having been made redundant by the Church of England, was given a new lease of spiritual life when it was taken over by the New Testament Church of God.

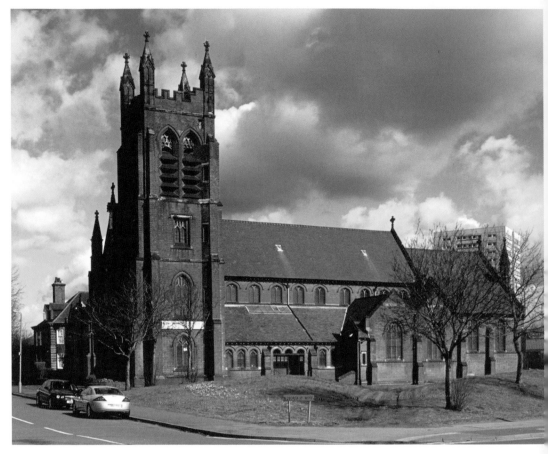

St Peter's Church, Spring Hill, 1902

Out of all of Osborn's ecclesiastical buildings in Birmingham, sadly only two survive: St Cyprian's, his first, and St Peter's, his last. However, Osborn's role in public architecture in Birmingham was far from being confined solely to ecclesiastical work. One of his earliest public buildings, opened on 17 December 1880 by the Mayor, Alderman Richard Chamberlain, was the Birmingham Medical Institute in Edmund Street.[19] Originally a library and reading room for the medical profession, in later years, after it had become the headquarters of the Conservative and Unionist Party, it became much better known as Empire House. A classical building of red brick and terracotta, with a portico of red sandstone, it unfortunately suffers by direct comparison with its next door neighbour, John Chamberlain's Grade I listed School of Art. The facade alone survives and is listed Grade II.

In the following year, 1881, Osborn & Reading received a commission for another public building of a much different kind. One of Osborn's principal interests outside architecture was his involvement with the 1st Volunteer Brigade of the Royal Warwickshire Regiment. He first enlisted as a private when the Brigade was initially formed in 1859, eventually rising to the rank of Hon. Lieut-Colonel, and receiving the Volunteer Decoration. It was hardly surprising, therefore, that in 1881, when choosing an architect to design a new drill hall, the Brigade should look no further than Osborn & Reading.[20] Opened on 5 November 1881, again by the Mayor, the new buildings in Thorp Street included orderly rooms, offices, armouries, mess rooms, kitchens, and store rooms. The drill hall itself, 250 ft. x 80 ft., and 45 ft. high, was covered in one span by a glazed roof, supported on iron girders, and was claimed to be 'the largest hall used for Volunteer Head-quarters in the kingdom'.[21]

Another public building designed by Osborn & Reading was opened three years later in October 1884. The Edgbaston Assembly Rooms, on the corner of Francis Road and Hagley Road, provided suites of function rooms of various sizes, each with its own entrance and own set of facilities.[22] The main assembly room was capable of accommodating 600–700 visitors, and included a musicians' gallery, stage, and dressing rooms. The local magazine, *Edgbastonia*, noted how 'the eleva-tion is in the style of the Elizabethan Renaissance, and is of elegant design and pleasing outline'.[23]

In the following year, 1885, Osborn & Reading were commissioned to design the Conservative Club to be built in Temple Row. As with the Wesleyan Central Hall a year later, this came about as the result of winning a competition. A tall four-storied building, facing St Philip's Churchyard, with an imposing portico on the right hand side, the style of architecture was 'Roman of the Early Italian Renaissance'.[24] A later article in *Edgbastonia* later described it as being 'without doubt the most convenient and handsome Club in Birmingham'.[25]

1886 must have been a busy year for Osborn & Reading, for it also saw comple-tion of their large scale improvement scheme for the Corporation Market Build-ings, Smithfield, the commission for which had originally been won, (again in a competition), some five years earlier, in 1881. The new buildings stretched from Moat Lane, through St Martin's Lane, to Jamaica Row, and comprised a new main entrance, a new hotel (St Martin's), shops, and offices. Constructed of red brick, with terracotta and stone dressings, the style was 'of the English Renaissance of the Stuart period'.[26]

Further prestigious public building work came Osborn & Reading's way in 1889, in the form of the out-patients' department of the Birmingham Royal Orthopaedic Hospital in Great Charles Street. This work, part of a scheme for the rebuilding of the old hospital, comprised 'dispensary and waiting hall, and on the upper floors two isolation wards, nurses' rooms, etc., after the Elizabethan style'.[27]

Although many of Osborn's larger buildings, such as the Market Buildings and the Hospital, were produced for the public sector, this did not preclude him from also being active in the commercial and industrial fields. Indeed, one of Osborn's

The Conservative Club, 1885 (From *Birmingham Faces and Places*, vol. v, 1893)

earliest known buildings was the Birmingham Joint Stock Bank, New Street, opened in 1876. This was of three stories, in Portland stone, and was 'Early Italian Renaissance in design'.[28] The front of the bank, on the ground floor, was divided into three bays by four stone columns, which supported a central pediment over the entrance. This bank was followed by another in 1880, the Worcester City and County Bank, in what was then Ann Street, but is now Colmore Row, on the corner of Newhall Street. This was 'in the French Renaissance style … the columns and architraves … of red stone, the body of the work Bath stone'.[29]

Some years later, when the leases of many of the Georgian buildings on the Colmore Estate began to expire, Osborn was commissioned to design further buildings in that area. The first, built in 1895, and still surviving, is on the junction of Newhall Street and Edmund Street, and was originally used as medical consulting rooms.[30] Positioned on a prominent corner site, built of red brick with terracotta and stone dressings, it has a circular turret, capped by an octagonal cupola, which runs vertically down all four storeys. There are gabled windows and

Former Medical Consulting Rooms, 29 Newhall Street, 1895

balconies in both Newhall Street and Edmund Street. This building, better known as 'The Hogshead', and now 'The Corner House', is listed Grade II.

Further buildings in Newhall Street were commissioned in the following year. No. 41, on the corner of Bread Street (now Cornwall Street), was a General Dispensary for Dr D. C. Lloyd Owen.[31] Another, No. 10, towards Colmore Row, comprised offices and premises for Edwin Docker, a solicitor.[32]

So far as industrial buildings were concerned, Osborn & Reading designed a number of workshops in the Jewellery and Gun Quarters of Birmingham, and also, in 1887, a manufactory in Weaman Street, for P. Webley & Sons, the well known gun manufacturers.[33] In 1890 they were responsible for additional offices and premises in Sheepcote Street for James Booth & Co., tube manufacturers.[34] In the following year, Osborn, once more in practice on his own, was commissioned to design a warehouse in Slaney Street, for Pilkington Brothers, the St Helen's glass manufacturers, whose presence in Birmingham up until that time had been limited to an agent. This proved to be a huge building, with five floors connected by a lift, and although described as a warehouse, the building also included workshops.[35] Six years later, in 1897, Pilkington's expanded their Birmingham base further by building a manufactory, also in Slaney Street, which was again designed by Osborn.[36]

The vast majority of Osborn's public, commercial and industrial work was almost inevitably sited either in the city centre or in what is now the inner city area. Just as inevitably, therefore, due to the City Fathers' passion for periodically reinventing the city's environs, little of his legacy in this field remains. Apart from his two churches, the facade of the Medical Institute, and 29 Newhall Street, out of all the commissions detailed above there are known to survive only the impressive entrance to the Thorp Street Barracks (now a car park), and Booth & Co.'s offices in Sheepcote Street, (now residential accommodation).

Despite the demand on his services for public, commercial and industrial work, Osborn still managed to produce a substantial amount of domestic architecture. The Birmingham Building Plans Register, from 1877 to 1907, records fifty-three plans submitted during that period either by Osborn, or by Osborn & Reading, in respect of new houses, or work on existing houses. It appears reasonable to assume, therefore, that a fair amount of domestic work had previously come Osborn's way in the thirteen years prior to 1877 during which he was in practice. The vast majority of the houses which Osborn either built or worked on were in Edgbaston, and were therefore mostly substantial properties. In his introduction to the first omnibus edition of *Edgbastonia*, published in 1882, the editor explains that 'Edgbaston is unquestionably the fashionable suburb of Birmingham. The fact that the land is the property of one man, who will permit none but first-class houses to be erected, renders it the favourite site for the residences of independent persons and the wealthier classes of professional men, merchants and traders'.[37] Westfield Road and Augustus Road, which were developed during the 1880s and

Former Offices for James Booth and Co., 2 Sheepcote Street, 1890

1890s, with their large detached houses and tree lined fronts, and where much of Osborn's domestic architecture is to be found, reflected this philosophy. Typical of the houses built at that time is 32, Westfield Road, which Osborn and Reading designed for H. S. Thompson in 1882. This was a substantial three storied house with a gabled front, and bay windows at both front and rear. On the ground floor were to be found dining room, drawing room, study, kitchen, scullery, and two pantries. The two upper floors included a total of eight bedrooms, plus bathroom, billiard room, box room and laundry. There was also a basement with a cellar and a wine cellar.[38]

Amongst the other private residences built by Osborn were three parsonages, the first of which was not however in Edgbaston. This was the new St Philip's Rectory, in St Philip's Place, the building plan for which was submitted for approval in August 1885,[39] within days of that for the Conservative Club, to be situated in the neighbouring Temple Row, also facing St Philip's. Given these twin circumstances, therefore, it is not surprising to learn that the Rectory was of an identical Early Italian Renaissance style to that of the Conservative Club. The other two parsonages were however in Edgbaston. The new vicarage for St George's, built in 1897 in Calthorpe Road, of red brick and terra cotta was 'in the Renaissance style of architecture, with large bay windows at the front and west sides'.[40] Osborn's third and final vicarage, in Raglan Road, was built in 1905 for the adjoining new church of St Mary and St Ambrose.[41] This was a large Edwardian style house, which can still be seen today, close by Edgbaston Cricket Ground, although it no longer serves as a vicarage.

Unlike Birmingham city centre, the leafy suburb of Edgbaston has remained largely undisturbed since the Victorian era, and Osborn's domestic architecture has therefore been in a better position to survive than his other work. Although many of the houses in Edgbaston which he designed unfortunately cannot now be identified, based on those which can, it seems safe to assume that most survive and continue to be lived in today. Regrettably, however, his own home at 222 Hagley Road no longer stands.

It will be appreciated from the wide range of buildings and architectural styles described above, that Osborn was nothing if not versatile. In addition to churches in differing styles of Gothic, he produced many other buildings, both public and commercial, of Classical and various Renaissance designs. His works included ecclesiastical buildings, hotels, hospitals, drill halls, banks, offices, shops, warehouses, factories, and numerous private residences. He also moved with the times. In the twilight of his long career Osborn found himself successfully designing buildings for which he could not possibly have had any training, since these were buildings of a type that would have been literally unthought of in his early days. Amongst them were three tram depots, those at Moseley Road (1906), Rosebery Street (1906) and Kyott's Lake Road (1907), an electricity sub-station in Upper Trinity Street (1905),[42] (now locally listed), and the still operational, privately owned Birmingham Crematorium (the City's first), at Sheldon Coppice, Perry Barr (1903).

On 6 April 1907, less than four years after the Crematorium had opened, Osborn collapsed at the Union Club, Colmore Row, and died shortly afterwards.

St George's Vicarage, Calthorpe Road, 1897 (From *Edgbastonia*, Vol. XVIII, February 1897)

He was not however cremated. His funeral, conducted by two archdeacons, and attended by a large number of mourners, including many local architects, was held in Harborne Parish Church, following which he was interred, in the conventional manner, in the family vault in the churchyard.[43]

Selected List of Architectural Works of Frank Barlow Osborn

F. B. Osborn (1840–1907) was articled to Charles Edge and later worked in the London office of S. S. Teulon. In 1864 he set up in independent practice in Birmingham. Between 1876 and 1890 he was in partnership with Alfred Reading as Osborn and Reading, and then worked independently until his death in 1907.

WORK IN BIRMINGHAM AND ITS ENVIRONS

PUBLIC

1874 St Cyprian's Church, The Fordrough, Hay Mill; 1877 mortuary Chapel

1875 St Margaret's Church, Ledsam St, Ladywood [D]

1878 St Catherine's Church, Scholefield St, Nechells [D]

1880 Medical Institute, Edmund St, Birmingham

1881 Volunteer Headquarters, Royal Warwickshire Regiment, Thorp St; 1892 enlargements

1881 Volunteer Headquarters, 1st South Staffs Regiment, Belgrave Terrace, Handsworth

1884 Edgbaston Assembly Rooms, Francis Rd, Edgbaston [D]

1885 Boatmen's Mission Hall, Bridge St, Birmingham [D]

1885 Conservative Club, 53, Temple Row [D]

1886 St Martin's Hotel and Market Entrance, St Martin's Lane, for Corporation of Birmingham [D]

1886 Edgbaston Vestry Hall, Islington Row, Edgbaston [D]

1887 Methodist Central Hall, Corporation St [D]

1889 Mission Room, Dollman Street, for St James's Ashted [D]

1889 Out-Patients Department, B'ham Royal Orthopaedic Hospital, Gt Charles St [D]

1890 Girls' Friendly Society Diocesan Lodge, Barwick St [D]

1890 Rebuilding Christ Church, Hagley Rd West, Quinton

1892 Mission Room, Ellis St, for St Thomas's Church, Bath Row

1894 Mission Room, Belmont Row, for St James's Church, Ashted

1894 Renovation and redecoration, Holy Trinity, Bordesley

1897 Extension to Deaf & Dumb Institute, Church Rd, Edgbaston

1899 Private Hospital, 70, Newhall St

1899 Additions to Nurses' House, The Crescent, for the Institute for Nursing

1901 Extension of Vegetable Market and Cattle Market, Jamaica Row/Moat Row, for Corporation of Birmingham [D]

1902 St Peter's Church, George St West, Spring Hill

1903 Birmingham Crematorium, Sheldon Coppice, Walsall Rd, Perry Barr

COMMERCIAL

1876 Joint Stock Bank, New St, Birmingham [D]

1880 Worcester City & County Bank, Colmore Row, Birmingham [D]

1880 4 Retail shops, 206, 209, Deritend [D]

1881 Stables, 205, 209, Deritend [D]

1883 2 Shops, 221, 223, Lower Priory

1887 Assurance building, Colmore Row, Birmingham [D]

1888 New shop front, 71, High St, for Messrs Hall & English [D]

1888 Business premises, 19–21, Corporation St, for Messrs Norton & Co.

1890 Extension to warehouse, Bridge St/Broad St, for Wm. Pearce

1893 Warehouse and retail shops, Edmund St/Livery St, for G. Jackson

1895 Medical consulting rooms, 106–110, Edmund St/29, Newhall St, for W. H. Smythe

1896 Offices and premises, 10, Newhall St, for Edwin Docker [D]

1897 Business premises, Newhall St, for C. G. Beale [D]

1898 Business premises, Great Charles St, for W. H. Smythe

1900 New business premises, Barwick St/Edmund St, for Messrs Willcocks, Wheeler & Co

1902 Alterations and additions to shops, 23, 27 Summer Row, for E. H. Wynne

1902 Alterations, 10 Ludgate Hill, for Crawley, Parsons and Co.

1906 Tramcar depot, Moseley Rd, for Tramways Committee

1906 Tramcar depot, Rosebery St, for Tramways Committee [D]

1907 Tramcar depot, Kyott's Lake Rd, for Tramways Committee [D]

INDUSTRIAL

1880 Additions and alterations to workshops, Warstone Lane

1881 Additions to manufactory, Weaman St

1882 Workshop, Park Mills

1883 Shopping, back of 63, Northampton St

1887 Manufactory, 88, 89, Weaman St, for P. Webley & Sons [D]

1888 Shopping, 88, 89, Weaman St, (see above) [D]

1889 Shopping, rear of 53, 54, Whitmore St, for Jas. Morrison

1890 Workshops, 77, Bath St, for Geo. Jones

1890 Shopping, 80, Bath St

1890 Additional offices and premises, Sheepcote St, for James Booth & Co.

1891 Glass Warehouse, Slaney St, for Pilkington Bros.

1892 Office and Manufactory, Great Charles St [D]

1892 Warehouse and w.c., 20, 21, Loveday St, for Ed. Rawlings

1892 Shopping and offices, Thorp St, for W. Hopkins

1893 Rebuilding, Atlas Works, Charles Henry St

1897 Manufactory, Slaney St, for Pilkington Bros. [D]

1900 Shopping, Bridge Row, Deritend, for W. Jennens

1905 Electricity sub-station, Upper Trinity St

DOMESTIC

1877 Stable and Coach House, Augustus Rd, Edgbaston

1877 House, Augustus Rd, Edgbaston

1877 House and Out Offices, Hagley Rd, Edgbaston

1878 House, Woodbourne Rd, Edgbaston

1879 House, Hagley Rd, Edgbaston

1882 House, Westfield Rd, Edgbaston

1882 House, Augustus Rd, Edgbaston

1882 House for H. S. Thompson, [32] Westfield Rd, Edgbaston

1883 Additions and lodge to Westfield, [44] Augustus Rd, Edgbaston;

1884 House, Westfield Rd, Edgbaston

1886 St Philip's Rectory, St Philip's Churchyard, Birmingham [D]

1887 House, Clovelly, [4] Manor Rd

1888 House, Endcliffe, [2] Manor Rd

1889 House, Woodbourne Rd, Edgbaston

1889 7 Houses for Thos. Harris, Kenyon St, back of the Wheel Tavern

1889 House for Ben Tilley, Cromartie, [17] Westfield Rd, Edgbaston

1889 Billiard Room for Arthur Warden, The Vale, [25] Edgbaston Park Rd; 1891 stables, alterations and additions

1892 Conservatory and alterations for A. E. Wilson, Wyddrington, Church Rd, Edgbaston

1895 House for F. M. Mole, 33, Westfield Rd, Edgbaston

1896 Residential chambers, Newhall St/Bread St, for Dr D. C. Lloyd Owen

1896 New Billiard Room for A. C. Osler, Fallowfield, [29] Norfolk Rd, Edgbaston

1897 St George's Rectory, 52, Calthorpe Rd, Edgbaston [D]

1898 House for E. M. Sage, Clare Gate, [19] Farquhar Rd, Edgbaston

1905 St Mary & St Ambrose Vicarage, Raglan Rd, Edgbaston

1906 Motor house for Dr Martin, St James' Rd, Edgbaston

WORK OUTSIDE BIRMINGHAM

PUBLIC

1888 Rebuilding St James's Parish Church, Norton Canes, Cannock

1894 Enlargement, Berwick Church, Shrewsbury

1894 Church Schools, Langley

COMMERCIAL

1896 London & Midland Bank, Coventry

DOMESTIC

Stretton Croft, Barnt Green, Worcs.

Alterations, Berwick Hall, Shrewsbury

Alterations, Eccleshall Castle, Staffs.

Alterations, Stratton Grange, Northants.

NOTES

[1] 'Edgbastonians Past and Present — Lt. Col. Osborn, V. D.', *Edgbastonia*, 14, no. 155, April 1894, p.50.

[2] *Ibid.*

[3] Birmingham Central Library Archives and Heritage Services (hereafter BCL AHS) MS 690/72 King's Norton Union New Workhouse Competition 'Explanation and Particulars of Design', 15 December 1871.

4 BCL AHS, Edgbaston Rate Book, 25 March 1871.

5 Birmingham City Council Conservation Group file.

6 Nikolaus Pevsner and Alexandra Wedgwood, *The Buildings of England: Warwickshire* (1966), p. 145.

7 *The British Architect*, 1, 6 March 1874, p. 151.

8 D. Abbott, 'The Church of St Cyprian, Hay Mill', *The Birmingham Historian*, 22, May 2002, pp. 19–23. See also 'The Re-opening of St Cyprian's Hay Mill', *Aris's Birmingham Gazette*, 3 January 1874.

9 BCL AHS, Birmingham Building Register, app. no. 476, 19 May 1877, for Church of St Catherine.

10 *Ibid*, app. no. 4179, 28 January 1884, for Boatmen's Mission Hall

11 *Birmingham Daily Gazette*, 18 March 1885, p. 6.

12 BCL AHS, Birmingham Building Register app. no. 4901 9 March 1886 for Central Hall, Corporation Street.

13 *Birmingham Daily Post*, 9 September 1887, p. 8.

14 BCL AHS, Birmingham Building Register, app. no. 6137 6 July 1888 for Mission Room, Dolman Street.

15 *Birmingham Daily Post*, 25 March 1889, p. 5.

16 *Birmingham Daily Gazette*, 8 February 1892, p. 8; BCL AHS, Birmingham Building Register, app. no. 8075, 4 June 1891, for Mission Room, Ellis Street.

17 BCL AHS, Birmingham Building Register, app. no. 11783, 27 April 1896, for Church of St Peter's, Belmont Row; *Birmingham Daily Post*, 7 December 1896, p. 9.

18 BCL AHS, Birmingham Building Register, app. no. 15625, 5 June 1900, for Church of St Peter's, Spring Hill; *Birmingham Daily Gazette*, 18 July 1902, p. 8.

19 BCL AHS, Birmingham Building Register, app. no. 1048, 5 April 1878, for Birmingham Medical Institute, Edmund Street.

20 BCL AHS, Birmingham Building Register, app. no.2273, 20 May 1880, for Drill Hall, Thorp Street.

21 *Edgbastonia*, 14, no. 155, April 1894, p. 53.

22 BCL AHS, Birmingham Building Register, app. no. 3436, 8 November 1882, for Edgbaston Assembly Rooms, Hagley Road.

23 'The Edgbaston New Assembly Rooms,' *Edgbastonia*, 4, no. 42, October 1884, pp. 151–53.

24 BCL AHS, Birmingham Building Register, app. no. 4671, 6 August 1885, for Conservative Club, Temple Row; 'The Conservative Club', *Birmingham Faces and Places*, vol. 5, 1893, p. 187.

25 *Edgbastonia*, 14, no. 155, April 1894, p. 51.

26 *The Builder*, 44, 17 April 1886, p. 574.

27 BCL AHS, Birmingham Building Register, app. no. 6178, 25 July 1888, for Outpatients' Dept., Orthopaedic Hospital; *The Builder*, 97, 13 April 1907, p. 453.

28 *The Builder*, 34, 26 May 1876, p. 497.

29 BCL AHS, Birmingham Building Register, app. no.1340, 27 August 1878, for Worcester City and County Bank, Ann Street; *The Builder*, 38, 3 April 1880, p. 425.

30 BCL AHS, Birmingham Building Register, app. no. 10541, 15 October 1894, for Medical Consulting Rooms, Newhall Street.

31 BCL AHS, Birmingham Building Register, app. no. 11747, 13 April 1896, for Offices, 41, Newhall Street.

32 BCL AHS, Birmingham Building Register, app. no. 11771, 22 April 1896, for Offices 10, Newhall Street.

33 BCL AHS Birmingham Building Register app. no. 5653, 12 September 1897, for Manufactory, Weaman Street for Webley and Sons.

34 BCL AHS, Birmingham Building Register, app. no. 7690, 24 October 1890, for Premises, Sheepcote Street, for J. Booth and Co.

35 BCL AHS, Birmingham Building Register, app. no. 7962, 15 April 1891, for Warehouse, Slaney Street for Pilkington's.

36 BCL AHS, Birmingham Building Register, app. no. 13114, 15 July 1897, for Manufactory, Slaney Street for Pilkington's.

37 *Edgbastonia*, 1 , no. 1, 1882.

38 BCL AHS, Birmingham Building Register app. no. 3383, 21 September 1882, for House, 32 Westfield Road for H. S. Thompson.

39 BCL AHS, Birmingham Building Register, app. no. 4698, 29 August 1885, for St Philip's Rectory, St Philip's Place.

40 BCL AHS, Birmingham Building Register, app. no. 12565, 27 January 1897, for St George's Vicarage, Calthorpe Road; 'The Proposed New Vicarage for St George's, Edgbaston', *Edgbastonia*, 17, no. 189, February 1897, p. 41.

41 BCL AHS, Birmingham Building Register, app. no. 18455, 17 March 1905, for Vicarage for St Mary and St Ambrose, Raglan Road.

42 BCL AHS, Birmingham Building Register, app no. 18836; for Tram Depot, Moseley Road, 26 October 1905, app. no. 18721, 10 July 1905, for Tram Depot, Rosemary Street; app. no 18721, 31 August 1906, for Tram Depot, Kyott's Lake Road; app. no. 18853, 26 October 1905, for Electricity Sub-station, Upper Trinity Street.

43 *Harborne and West Bromwich News*, 13 April 1907, p. 7.

13 James and Lister Lea

CHRIS UPTON

For 150 years the English public house has been a battleground. Nor is this a state that afflicts it solely on Saturday nights. From the mid-19th century onwards arguments have raged over opening hours and staff working hours, the impact of drinking (and smoking) upon the health and budgets of the poor, and the influence of the pub upon social mores. The pub is contested ground, no more so than in times of strong local or national government, when officialdom has felt itself empowered to intervene in individual behaviour, and in the sale and distribution of alcohol.[1]

This has been the case in all corners of the British Isles, but no more so than in Birmingham. The presence of Unitarians and Quakers in the Victorian Council House encouraged strong interventionist (and patriarchal) tendencies in the way it managed the city. No local authority involved itself more thoroughly in the ways of the working classes – where they lived, how they lived, how long they lived – than Birmingham. It was a battle, not only for hearts and minds, but for lungs and livers too. When Joseph Chamberlain attempted (and failed) to take the brewing industry under municipal control in January 1877 under the so-called 'Gothenburg system', it was symptomatic of a desire to reform the public house, and alter what it meant to the Midland town.[2] If drinking was to continue – and there were plenty in the Temperance Movement who would have preferred it not to – it would have to change its image.

This engagement is not simply a matter of social history. It affected the very architecture and design of the public house, its position in the high street and its place in the local economy.[3]

No one featured more prominently in the campaign to lift the Birmingham pub from drinking den to drinking palace than the firm of James & Lister Lea. Under their hand the Birmingham pub was transformed in the 1890s. Using architectural details borrowed principally from the Gothic, Tudor and Jacobean styles, and features as likely to be seen in churches as in pubs, the Leas and their architects made drinking palatable and attractive to a new class of Birmingham people. That they could do so reflects the fact that new money and new commercialism was at work in the brewery industry.

What is now the archetypal image of the high Victorian public house – a place of tiles and terracotta, pilasters and stained glass – was pioneered in Birmingham by James and Lister Lea, though they were by no means the only firm involved in the transformation. C. J. Hodgson, Matthew J. Butcher, Wood and Kendrick, and William Jenkins – to name but four – were also notable contributors to the trend. Yet the dominance of James and Lister Lea is still remarkable. Andy Foster draws attention to eleven pubs designed by the firm still standing in the central area of Birmingham – the largest group by a single architectural practice – and many more have since been demolished.[4] Roy Thornton calls the firm 'the most prolific of all pub architects',[5] whilst Andrew Maxam, using the archives of Michells & Butlers, Atkinson's and William Butler's, records twenty three pubs designed by the company.[6]

No firm of Victorian architects could afford to concentrate on one kind of building exclusively, but the unique elements of the public house demanded some degree of specialization. Not only was a close partnership with the interior designer essential, as well as with the suppliers of exterior decoration such as terracotta and glass, but the pub's traditional location at the intersection of two streets likewise required a particular kind of spatial awareness. In addition, the design, architectural quality and symbolism of the pub had a message to convey to potential customers about what kind of establishment it was (and was not), what sort of clientele lurked within its walls, and what kind of retreat it provided from the outside world. The ideal, evident in most of the best designs, was a building that blended in with its neighbourhood at first-floor level, but demonstrated its uniqueness and difference on the ground floor. The result was advertising in stone and glass, and James and Lister Lea were past masters of the technique.

There were two key developments in this change of emphasis from beerhouse to public house. The 1869 Wine & Beerhouse Act gave the licensing magistrates increased powers to refuse or withdraw licences in an early attempt to squeeze out what were seen as 'undesirable' establishments. On a local level the so-called 'Birmingham Scheme' between the City Council and the major brewers, or, as Andrew Maxam calls it, 'fewer and better', encouraged the latter to surrender the licences of smaller pubs in the central area on the understanding that they would be allowed to open larger, 'reformed' houses in the suburbs or on the approaches to the city. As a result, in the decade between 1904 and 1914, as Maxam notes, no fewer than one thousand pubs closed in Birmingham. Many of those which remained fell into the clutches of the brewery companies, who spent much money upgrading them.[7]

It is possible to get some sense of the issues involved from an examination of one of the firm's best examples, which is arguably also (since the demolition of the Woodman in Easy Row) Birmingham's most famous drinking establishment.

The Bartons Arms now stands in magnificent semi-isolation on Newtown Row.[8] The place where it lies was designated as one of the city's five Central Redevelopment Areas in 1947 and comprehensively rebuilt during the late 1950s and early 1960s. As a popular local landmark the pub survived the onslaught, though many of its former patrons did not. In 1982 it was accorded listed building

The Bartons Arms, High Street, Aston, re-built 1899–1901

status at Grade II*, the first public house in the city to be awarded such an accolade.

Even stripped of its original surroundings, it is clear that The Bartons Arms was designed as a flagship pub in a notable entertainment quarter. (The Aston Hippodrome, also designed by James & Lister Lea, stood nearby.) Mitchells & Butlers purchased the lease of its predecessor for £12,000 and appointed James and Lister Lea to transform it (at a cost of £10,000). Mr Brassington of the firm produced the design, and rebuilding and refitting took place between 1899 and 1901. Alan Crawford argues that Brassington's design took its cue from nearby Aston Hall, though the firm's architects had already shown an affection for Jacobean styling elsewhere. 17th-century gabling was on the palette of most Victorian architects, and the closest parallel is perhaps with The Fighting Cocks in Moseley, also dating from 1899 and by Newton & Cheatle. Both buildings have prominent clock towers and present a three-storey facade, with bay windows and gables, to the main road. The addition of tall Elizabethan or Jacobean chimneys on The Bartons Arms underlined its antiquarian credentials.

Prominent though it was on Aston High Street, it was (and is) the interior of The Bartons Arms that set it apart. Not all those original features survived a series of refits from 1969 onwards, but much remains to show the opulence of this late Victorian gem. Mintons provided two tile-paintings of which the hunting scene survives in the staircase hall. The lobby, from which the staircase ascends, is one of the most striking features of The Bartons Arms. Here the central serving space curves back behind an arch, and the original snob-screens permit the kind of private conversations impossible in the public bar. There were once three smoke rooms leading off the lobby, separated by wooden partitions, but brewery preferences in the 1970s were for more open-plan drinking, and the partitions were taken down. Ironically, it is easier to see today how Brassington's spacial design flows from room to room than it would have been before these recent 'readjustments'.

Nevertheless, enough of the glass (much of it monogrammed with M&B), ceiling and wall tiles, wrought-iron balustrades, bronze light-fittings and elaborate chimney-pieces survive at The Bartons Arms to show just how lush this interior was. Of course, we cannot attribute all the features of the interior design to James and Lister Lea, but undoubtedly they provide the stage upon which the actors strut. Using information supplied by Kelly and Surman, who took over the Leas' architectural practice in the 1930s, Crawford and Thorne describe the considerable delegation in place at James and Lister Lea, particularly evident in their dealings with the Hathern Station Brick and Terracotta Co. of Loughborough, who supplied the terracotta for subsequent approval at the Cannon Street office.[9]

As noted earlier, the firm was also responsible for the Aston Hippodrome, which fronted onto Potter's Lane, immediately behind The Bartons Arms. It was the only theatre designed by the firm and opened on 7 December 1908, a relatively late date for a variety theatre. The building was demolished in September 1980, and The Drum now occupies the site.[10] Surprisingly few images of the Aston Hippodrome survive; those that do show a terracotta and stone facade, with a wrought iron verandah at ground floor level and two cupolas adding to the overall symmetry of the frontage. Derek Salberg mentions the unusually ample headroom between the three levels of seating, and 'the scientific method used to air the theatre'. The Hippodrome was constructed by a local firm of builders – Messrs Parkinson of Aston – seated 1,800 people and cost £10,000 to build. It ceased to be a variety theatre in June 1960 (then being converted into a bingo hall), but in its day attracted such stars as Laurel & Hardy, George Formby, Sid Fields, and Morecambe and Wise.[11]

The closest equivalent to The Bartons Arms, for sheer sumptuous display, is probably The Red Lion on the Soho Road in Handsworth.[12] Built in 1901–02 for

The Red Lion, Soho Road,
Handsworth, re-built 1901–02

the Holt Brewery Company The Red Lion also replaced an earlier original building, dating back at least to 1829. Here too the prevailing style is Jacobean, but
employed far more eclectically, mixing classical and Flemish influences. Much of
this we must attribute to the designers at Hathern Station Brick and Terracotta
Co., who filled the facade with all the Jacobean strapwork, capitals and heraldic
lions in their catalogue. The ground storey, in red terracotta, is less elaborate than
the buff-coloured terracotta on the floors above. But the polygonal tower at the
corner of the facade, topped by a curious little cupola, shows that James and Lister
Lea are at work too.

There is one indication on the plan for this building that hints at the battles
being waged before the licensing justices and in the council chamber. One of the
smoke rooms at The Red Lion is labelled 'Coffee Room', a sure sign that Holt's
were prepared to embrace Temperance, rather than simply to defy it. That was
true of James and Lister Lea as well. Indeed, one of the earliest commissions (3327
in the Birmingham Building Plans Register) was for a coffee house in Spring
Hill.[13]

These two examples – The Bartons Arms and The Red Lion – show that James
and Lister Lea were not exclusively employed by a single brewery. Indeed, they

produced designs for all four of the major brewery companies in late Victorian Birmingham: Holts, Mitchells (afterwards Mitchells and Butlers), Davenports and Ansells. Many of these commissions were, in fact, the rebuilding of earlier premises, as were the two already described. As such they date from the period, roughly 1890–1910, when the larger breweries were buying out smaller, independent publican-brewers and re-fashioning their pubs as tied houses. The kind of refurbishment seen at The Bartons Arms would have been well beyond the budget of an individual owner.

If Jacobean was the default option for the Leas, the office was ready and willing to reproduce other styles too. In 1890 the architects tackled a late 18th-century house on the corner of Bristol Street and Bromsgrove Street, which from at least 1818 had been known as the Wellington Hotel.[14] Enough has survived of that hotel to see that the firm was perfectly capable of extending that regency style into the new extension to the tune of bow windows and Corinthian pilasters. Perhaps it is only the acute angle at which the extension connects to the original which alerts the careful observer that all is not all of a piece. Sadly there is little of the interior that preserves the work of the firm other than the 1890 billiard room.

Many of the firm's best public houses were to be found in and around the Gooch estate to the south and east of the city centre. Indeed, a more than testing pub crawl can still be made between half a dozen examples only a few streets apart. The Woodman at the corner of Albert Street and New Canal Street (built in 1897 for Ansells) shows the company at its creative height, radically adapting the Jacobean model to a corner site. Crawford and Foster single out this building for being the first to abandon the traditional format of pilasters on the ground floor (which had a tendency to isolate the ground from the upper storeys) and effectively to unify the architecture.[15] In addition, the alternation of narrow and broader bays helps the building to flow effortlessly from the one street into the next. The same technique can be seen at The Anchor (1902), on the corner of Rea Street and Bradford Street.[16] The interior bar has lost its original partitions, but retained its bar front and back, as well as much of its Minton tiling. The Market Tavern in Moseley Street is a standard corner site design with crisp terracotta detail and makes an attractive addition to the street scene in this industrial area.

Minton tiles can be seen to even greater effect at The White Swan in Bradford Street, dating from 1899–1900, which preserves most of its interior fittings, apart from the partitions.[17] At this point the firm was working on two pubs for two breweries at almost the same time and the results are very similar. The White Swan was designed for Ansells; The Dog and Partridge (later renamed The Market Tavern) for the Holt Brewery Co. In both cases the brewery committed to rebuild at a cost of no less than £1,000, allowing much use of tiling in passageways, bars and (in the case of The White Swan) on the ceiling.

The differences in design between these public houses are often slight, evident if we compare The Swanpool Tavern (1898) on Lichfield Road and The Dog and

The Wellington Hotel, Bristol Street, 1890

The Woodman, Albert Street, 1887

The Anchor, Rea Street, 1902

The Market Tavern, 1899–1900

The White Swan, Bradford Street, 1899–1900

Partridge (1900) on Moseley Street.[18] Both are seen to occupy corner sites, at which a round-arched entrance is surmounted by an oriel, topped by a cupola. Both have large, round-arched windows at ground floor, and square windows on the first floor with pediments above. Each relies on terracotta for external decoration, with painted glass and tiling within. Nevertheless, there are striking differences between the two buildings too. The Swanpool has terracotta roundels above the doors; The Dog and Partridge has its terracotta in the pediments above the first-floor windows and in the oriel. At The Dog and Partridge the oriel extends into a third storey with windows and pilasters, and the gables culminate in finials. At The Swanpool Tavern the gables curve at the top.

It needs to be stressed, however, that James and Lister Lea did not devote themselves entirely to public houses, even if these are what they are best remembered for. Indeed, the Birmingham Building Register shows them submitting designs for everything from domestic housing and water closets to factories and workshops. The earliest recorded plan is for a manufactory in Ledsam Street in Ladywood, submitted on 26 January 1881.[19] Such variety of work kept the firm more than usefully employed: ten plans were submitted in 1881, rising to fifteen in 1886. From this point onwards the firm's name appears on average every month in the plans register. The earliest public house with which James & Lister Lea are associated was The New Inns (later The New Inn Hotel) in Bromsgrove Street in August 1884, closely followed by The Smithfield Arms in Jamaica Row.[20] The former was in a traditional, half-timbered style, predating the Leas' adoption of Jacobean or Dutch gables, while the latter equated more to a 'Queen Anne' style.[21]

The earliest indication of the firm's presence in Birmingham is in the Corporation Directory for 1863, where they are listed as 'auctioneers and land agents' at 19 Cannon Street.[22] At no point in the trade directories is the company listed or advertised as architects. As the appended gazeteer indicates, the firm's most important work dates from the last decade of the 19th-century and the early years of the 20th. This coincided, argue Crawford and Thorne, with the arrival of Robert Roberts to take charge of pub design at the Cannon Street office.[23]

Of the significant public buildings, other than public houses, designed by the firm, mention should be made of the Birmingham and Midland Hospital for Skin and Urinary Diseases on John Bright Street. The first Skin and Lock Hospital opened in pre-existing premises on the corner of Newhall Street and Lionel Street in January 1881, but plans for a purpose-built hospital were announced in 1885,

The former Skin Hospital, John Bright Street, 1888

Portrait of Lister Lea 1833–1908, watercolour, private collection

and James and Lister Lea were enlisted as architects.[24] The plans were submitted in July 1887.[25] The total cost, including furniture and equipment, was £5,702 15s 2d and the opening ceremony took place on 7 June 1888. The building still survives, but is no longer used as a hospital.

Of significance too was the brick Bristol Hall in Bristol Street, built in 1899 as a Primitive Methodist chapel to replace an earlier church in Gooch Street. The chapel cost £7,000 and comprised a lecture hall, mission hall, five classrooms and

Three shops in Bristol Street, 1898–99

other rooms. The chapel closed in 1928 'owing to the removal of the usual congregations and the large increase of the Jewish population in the immediate neighbourhood'. It was subsequently used as a synagogue.[26] Significant commercial development was undertaken by the firm in Bristol Street. Notable survivors are three shops from the original block of four. Further south on the corner of Thorp Street, the former White Lion of 1896 is the Elizabethan-styled stone and brick,

OPPOSITE   Former White Lion public house, 1896

three-storied building. Numbers 76–94 Bristol Street are an excellent group of brick and terracotta shops. Above the shop line these survive intact.

James and Lister Lea was a genuine family firm. According to his obituary in the *Birmingham Daily Post*, the first Lister Lea died, at the age of 75, on 10 May 1908 at Greenhill House in Moseley. Struggling to fill a paragraph, the obituarist noted that the dead man 'was of a very retiring disposition and took no part in public life'.[27] Of his five sons, three continued the practice, of which Lister Lea jnr and Charles Lea were the most prominent. As the eldest son, Lister Lea jnr inherited Greenhill House, and was the senior partner in the practice, though by his death on 21 May 1919, at the age of 64, his role was as an estate agent.[28] They continued to use the offices at 19 Cannon Street. This second Lister Lea was buried at Brandwood End cemetery.[29]

Charles Herbert Lea, born 9 March 1861, was more centrally involved in architectural design. Articled to Messrs Osborn & Reading, he commenced practice at

Cannon Street in the 1880s. Charles Lea was responsible for the overall design of the Skin and Lock Hospital in John Bright Street, the Bristol Street Primitive Methodist chapel, the Drill Hall for the Smethwick Volunteer Corps and a large number of residential properties, hotels and public houses. His entry in *Contemporary Biographies* in 1900 records him as 'specialist in brewery architecture'.[30]

James and Lister Lea continued to design public houses well into the 1930s. The George V, built in what became known as 'Birmingham Tudor' style on the Bristol Road in Longbridge, was one of their final designs in 1937. After this time the firm operated only as estate agents, and the architectural practice was taken over by John B. Surman of Kelly and Surman.

BELOW   Shops, 76–94 Bristol Street, 1896–97

Selected List of Architectural Works of James and Lister Lea

The Birmingham firm of James and Lister Lea, auctioneers and land agents were practising as architects from the 1880s, specialising in pub architecture. The firm was continued by two of Lister Lea's sons, Lister and Charles. Charles had been articled to Osborn and Reading.

BIRMINGHAM AND ITS ENVIRONS

PUBLIC

1897 Skin and Lock Hospital, John Bright St

1899 Primitive Methodist chapel (Bristol Hall), Bristol St

COMMERCIAL

1882 Coffee House and houses, Spring Hill

1884 New Inns, Bromsgrove St

1885 Black Swan, Bromsgrove St

1885 Smithfield Arms, Jamaica Row

1886 Bell Hotel, Bristol Rd

1886 Birmingham Arms Hotel, Bradford St

1886 Engineer's Arms, New Canal St

1887 Gate Inn, Icknield St

1887 Plough Inn, Jamaica Row

1888 7 shops, Bromsgrove St

1889 Queen's Head, Steelhouse Lane

1890 Unicorn Inn, Digbeth

1890–91 Extension to Wellington Hotel, Bristol Street

1891 Black Horse, Bristol Rd

1892 Golden Lion, Lionel St

1892 Old Fox, Hurst St

1894 White Swan, Summer Row

1894 Queen's Tavern, Essex St

1894 5 shops, Bristol Rd, 1894

1895 Warwick Arms, Bradford St

1896 Coach & Horses, Norwood Rd, Bordesley Green

1896–97 Shops, Bristol St

1896 White Lion, Thorp St

1897 Woodman, 106 Albert St for Ansells

1897 Australian Bar, Hurst St

1897 Offices, Temple Row

1898 4 shops, Horse Fair for A. Rodway

1899–1900 Shops, Bristol St

1898–99 Swan & Mitre, Lichfield Rd, Aston, for Holt Brewery Co.

1899 Market Tavern (formerly Dog and Partridge), 210 Moseley St, for Holt Brewery Co.

1899 Summer Hill Tavern, Summer Hill for Isaiah Food

1899 White Swan, 276 Bradford St for Ansells

1899–1901 Bartons Arms, 152 High St, Aston, for Mitchells and Butlers

1900 Salutation Inn, Snow Hill, for Holt Brewery Co.

1900 Eagle & Tun, New Canal St, for Ansells

1901 Roebuck Inn, William St, for Holt Brewery Co.

1901 Bull's Head, 75–77 The Green, Kings Norton

1901 Bull's Head, Bishopgate St, for Ansells

1901 City Tavern, Bishopgate St

1901 King's Arms, Bishopgate St, for Mitchells and Butlers

1901–02 Red Lion, Soho Rd, Handsworth, for Holt Brewery Co.

1902 Anchor, Rea St, for Ansells

1905 Country Girl, Raddlebarn Rd,

1906 Navigation Inn, Wharf Rd, 1906

1906 White Lion, High St, Bordesley

1906 Birmingham Horse, Moseley St, for Davenports

1907 Black Horse, 22 Jennens Rd, for Mitchells and Butlers

1907 White Hart, Nechells Park Rd

1907 Lloyd's Bank, Bristol St

1908 Aston Hippodrome

1908 Forge Tavern, Fazeley St for Ansells

1908 Dolphin, Irving St, for Mitchells and Butlers

1908 Hen & Chickens, Lower Dartmouth St, for Davenports

1913 Cross Guns, Washwood Heath Rd, for Atkinsons

1913 Crown Inn, Lower Tower St, for Mitchells and Butlers

1913 New Inn, Alum Rock Rd, for Michells and Butlers

1913 Old House at Home, Lordswood Rd, Harborne, for Rushtons

1923–24 British Oak, 157 Pershore Rd, Stirchley, for Mitchells and Butlers

? Grapes, Winson Green

White Horse Cellars, 106 Constitution Hill

INDUSTRIAL

1881 Factory, Ledsam St

1882 Factory, New Spring St

1884 Mill and workshop, Clifford & Sons, Fazeley St

1891 Hide & Skin market, 32 Bradford St

1891 Offices and workshops, Imperial Enamel Co., Watery Lane

1896 Factory, Little Bow St

1897 Factory and house, Essex St

1899 Stables and shopping, Gibb St for Alfred Bird

1911 Ice Cream factory, Banbury St, for Sir Thomas Gooch

1919–20 Factory, Fazeley St

DOMESTIC

1881–82 6 houses, New Spring St

1883 5 houses, Back of Abbey St

1886 7 houses, Meriden St

1886 3 houses and shopping, New Canal St

1889 House, Ascot Rd

1892 13 houses, Oakfield Rd

1892 7 houses, Willows Rd

1897 House, Salisbury Rd, Moseley

1898 12 houses, Beaconsfield Rd and Oakfield Rd, 1898

1900 House, Wake Green Rd, Moseley

NOTES

[1] The national (though principally London) picture is outlined in Mark Girouard, *Victorian Pubs* (1975) pp. 54–73.

[2] John Thackray Bunce, *History of the Corporation of Birmingham*, Vol. II. (Birmingham, 1885), p. 568. The measure was proposed and approved in the council chamber by 46 votes to 10. Alan Crawford and Robert Thorne examine the impact of the Chamberlain regime (both Joseph and Arthur) upon pub design in Alan Crawford *et al*, *Birmingham Pubs*, (Gloucester, 1986), pp. 40–41.

[3] Crawford and Thorne chart the growth (and eventual triumph) of the larger breweries in Crawford, pp. 7–15.

[4] Andy Foster, *Pevsner Architectural Guides: Birmingham*, (New Haven and London, 2005).

[5] Roy Thornton, *Victorian Buildings of Birmingham*, (Stroud, 2006), p. 125.

[6] Andrew Maxam, *Time Please! A Look Back at Birmingham's Pubs* (Smethwick, 2002).

[7] Joseph McKenna, *Birmingham Breweries*, (Studley, 2005), pp. 35–35, outlines the success of the brewery giants.

[8] The Bartons Arms is discussed by Thornton in *Victorian Buildings* p. 126, and Crawford in *Birmingham Pubs*, pp. 82–83.

[9] Crawford, *Birmingham Pubs*, p. 28.

[10] Derek Salberg, *Ring Down the Curtain* (Luton, 1980), pp. 114–16.

[11] Victor J. Price, *Birmingham Theatres, Concert and Music Halls* (Studley, 1988), p. 39.

[12] The Red Lion is discussed by Crawford in *Birmingham Pubs*, pp. 118–19.

[13] Birmingham Central Library, Archives and Heritage Services (hereafter BCL AHS) Birmingham Building Register, app. no. 3327, coffee house, Spring Hill, 1882.

[14] BCL AHS, Birmingham Building Register, app. no. 7449, alterations to Wellington Hotel, 1890. The Wellington Hotel is discussed by Foster in *Birmingham*, p. 202.

[15] Crawford, *Birmingham Pubs*, p. 137; Foster, *Birmingham*, pp. 189–90.

[16] The Anchor is discussed by Foster in *Birmingham*, pp. 190–91.

[17] The White Swan is discussed by Crawford in *Birmingham Pubs*, pp. 134–35 and by Foster in *Birmingham*, p. 191.

[18] The Dog and Partridge is discussed by Thornton in *Victorian Buildings*, p. 125 and by Crawford in *Birmingham Pubs* p. 134.

[19] BCL AHS, Birmingham Building Register, app. no. 2578, 26 January 1881, manufactory, Ledsam Street.

[20] BCL AHS, Birmingham Building Register, app. no. 4241, August 1884, New Inns, Bromsgrove Street; *Ibid*, app. no. 4412, 1884, Smithfield Arms, Jamaica Row.

[21] Crawford, *Birmingham Pubs*, pp. 21–24.

[22] *Corporation Directory for Birmingham*, (Birmingham, 1863), p. 234.

[23] Crawford, *Birmingham Pubs*, p. 24.

[24] J. Ernest Jones, A *History of the Hospitals and Other Charities in Birmingham*, Birmingham, n.d., pp. 92–94.

[25] BCL AHS, Birmingham Building Register, app. no. 5543, July 1887, for Skin and Lock Hospital, John Bright Street.

[26] *Victoria County History of Warwickshire: Birmingham*, vol. 7 (1964), p. 464.

[27] *Birmingham Post*, 11 May 1908.

[28] *Birmingham Mail*, 22 May 1919.

[29] *Birmingham Post*, 27 May 1919.

[30] *Birmingham at the Opening of the 20th Century*, ed. by W. T. Pike, (Brighton, n.d.), p. 160.

14 Mansell and Mansell

ALLAN EVANS

Without any doubt the contribution of the father and sons architectural partnership of Thomas Henry Mansell (1834–1911), Edward Mansell (1861–1941) and Thomas Gildart Mansell (1866–1929) was one of important significance in the development of Victorian Birmingham. A few of the buildings they designed still remain, with some having become familiar landmarks, both in the city centre and further afield. While this can be said, a full assessment of their works does prove difficult. Very little remains in the form of archive material and a number of the buildings that were built to their designs have disappeared with the passing of time. Also it must be taken into account that the number of buildings that were commissioned for this company was not as great as those of other Birmingham architects of the time.[1] From an examination of their surviving works, it is quite clear that there is a strong influence of Tudor, Elizabethan and Jacobean styles mixed in with a form of Gothic. They also built some significant buildings faced with terracotta. Furthermore, there are striking similarities in the works of these men.

The earliest known reference to the existence of their business is in 1868, when a Thomas Henry Mansell had his business premises at the Argyle Chambers in Colmore Row. On the evidence of local directories by 1879 his offices moved to new premises in Bennett's Hill off Colmore Row. In 1883, Thomas Mansell moved his premises once more, this time to 2 Newhall Street. Edward and Thomas Gildart Mansell were to follow in their father's footsteps. Edward was a pupil of the Birmingham contractors, Messrs Barnsley and Sons from 1878 to 1881 and then served his articles with his father. Thomas Gildart was articled to Osborn and Reading of Birmingham from 1882 to 1887, and then worked in London. By 1892 both sons appear to have been in practice with their father as Mansell and Mansell although Thomas Mansell had probably retired by the mid 1890s. In 1905 the firm was operating from Midland Chambers in Temple Row. Edward Mansell became a Fellow of the Royal Institute of British Architects in 1908 and Thomas Gildart Mansell became an Associate of RIBA in 1892.[2]

Mansell and Mansell carried out a wide range of different types of buildings. Of their domestic work Tudor Grange, Solihull was their most significant commission. The client was Alfred Lovekin, a jeweller and silversmith and co-partner in the jewellery manufacturing company of Adie and Lovekin based in the city's Jewellery Quarter, by the mid 1880s planning to move away from the city suburbs

Tudor Grange, Solihull, entrance front. *Photo: B. S.*

to the rural tranquillity of Warwickshire. Land formerly used for agricultural purposes was made available for building along Blossomfield Road in Solihull. Within close proximity to a railway station, this could provide easy access to the city centre for many of the businessmen who had decided to take up residence in this locality. He appointed Thomas Henry Mansell to design a large dwelling to be described as a 'gentleman's residence' along this stretch of road in 1887.

Tudor Grange was built in the Elizabethan/Jacobean style with no expense spared in its construction. The exterior was of brick with bath stone dressings. The interior was very elaborate and was panelled in oak and mahogany by Plunketts of Warwick, who were also responsible for the many fireplaces on the ground floor of the house. These incidentally, were inlaid with tiles by William de Morgan and Ruskins of Smethwick. After the death of his wife in 1900, Alfred Lovekin decided to put Tudor Grange on the market. Alfred Bird, a leading Birmingham industrialist and manufacturer of Bird's custard powder, purchased the property, perhaps persuaded by Mr Lovekin's business partner James Adie who was a contemporary of Bird's. Both had been educated at King Edward's School, New Street. Alfred Bird was soon to realise the potential Tudor Grange had to offer. Already a large dwelling, his intention was to enlarge it considerably. By now Thomas Mansell would have been 66 years of age and in semi-retirement, so it was to the sons that he was to turn to, for this work to be carried out. Once the extensions to the house were completed, Bird decided to embellish it further by placing near life size statues on the roof top parapets. He commissioned Robert Bridgeman the sculptor, who had already achieved fame for his work on the façade of Lichfield Cathedral, to carry out this assignment.[3]

Another significant domestic commission, but of a completely different character was the town house and consulting rooms designed by Thomas Mansell for Dr Thomas Savage at No. 133 Edmund Street in 1895–96. The consulting rooms would have been on the ground floor, with the upper storeys providing living accommodation for the doctor's family. The building has been reconstructed into office premises and the original façade retained. It has been described by Andy Foster as being strongly influenced by the work of Norman Shaw and he continues thus:

The brick front has stone bands linking the cross windows. Cornice with Savage's initials and the date, swept-up parapet, and tall hipped roof with finials. The doorcase is a combination of two demolished Shaw designs in the City of London, New Zealand Chambers and Barings Bank. A large segmental pediment supported on long consoles and short pilasters, the pediment broken by a tiny two light window, itself pedimented and with a big keystone.[4]

Industrial Birmingham was rapidly expanding by the end of the Victorian Era and there was a great need for purpose built factories and warehouses. Mansell and Mansell were responsible for a number of industrial buildings, on one occasion for clients for whom they had carried out other work. Alfred Lovekin must have been more than satisfied with the work by Thomas Mansell at Tudor Grange, and

Tudor Grange, garden front. *Photo: B. S.*

LEFT Former town house and consulting rooms, 133 Edmund Street, 1895–96

BELOW Former Jewellery Manufactory of Adie and Lovekin, Frederick Street and Regent Street, 1894

his partner, James Adie had also employed him to design additions and generally alter the appearance of his own home on the Hagley Road in 1891. No assessment can be made of this work, as the house has been demolished. In 1894 Adie and Lovekin appointed Thomas Mansell to design a new building for their jewellery manufactory on the corner of Frederick Street and Regent Street in the Jewellery Quarter. Foster describes it as being 'in fine restrained Jacobean, with curly broken pediment to the N doorway.'[5] The company of Adie and Lovekin was to cease trading by the mid 1930s but the building still survives and is occupied by the firm of Thomas Fattorini who moved to the Jewellery Quarter in 1928. The present owners have, alas, painted the exterior brickwork a ghastly mixture of mauve and pink, which completely destroys the appearance and is totally out of keeping with other surrounding buildings.

Mansell and Mansell were responsible for two important buildings in the City Centre and both were probably the work of the Mansell brothers, rather than their father. In 1900 the Ocean Accident Insurance Company asked Edward Mansell to design their new business premises at the junction of Temple Row West with Waterloo Street. This five storey building of brick and terracotta is still standing and is a mixture of Gothic and Tudor styles and has a conical corner turret which makes it an attractive feature to the surrounding area. The second building was commissioned in 1903 when the Mansells reconstructed the façade to Queen's College on Paradise Street which had been built as a training college for Anglican priests in 1843. The new façade featured brick and terracotta again. The Mansells may have been influenced by Charles Barry's design for King Edward's School in New Street. Noticeable too are the strong similarities with windows and gables to that of his work on the building at the Waterloo Street/Temple Row junction. Recently this building has been converted into apartments and has sensitively retained all the features to the frontage.[6]

Whereas Thomas Mansell resided at various addresses in Edgbaston, culminating with 38 Harborne Road,[7] Edward Mansell after his marriage, was to set up his home in Clarendon Square in Leamington Spa. The Birmingham to Oxford Railway Line would have provided easy access to him for Snow Hill Station. In 1905 the Diocese of Birmingham was created and he was appointed as its Surveyor. The only church to his credit is St Luke's along Bristol Street, which is of brick with stone dressings and is of plain Gothic style and which replaced an earlier church by Henry Eginton which was pulled down because it was unsafe. The roof of this church has within the last few years been replaced with concrete tiles, which on the whole is totally out of keeping with the building.[8]

Mansell and Mansell were to continue in business until 1934.[9] Thomas Gildart Mansell died in 1929, and Edward Mansell died at the Warwickshire and Coventry Mental Hospital on 11 March 1941 and his estate was only valued at £2,174.11.3d, which seems considerably less than what would have been expected from an architect of such standing of the day. An architect's journal of the day, while giving

Former Offices of the Ocean Accident Insurance Company, Temple Row West and
Waterloo Street, 1900

Façade of the former Queen's College, Paradise Street, 1903

biographic type obituaries to others it only gave his passing a very brief mention.[10] This was a very sad end indeed to this father and son partnership. Tudor Grange now forms part of Solihull College and extensive restoration work has been carried out on the house in recent years. If ever there should be a monument to the talents of this artistic partnership, then this surely would be the house.

List of Architectural Works of Mansell and Mansell

Thomas Mansell (1834–1911) was born in Stourbridge and was working in Birmingham as an architect and surveyor by 1868. In c. 1892 his sons, Edward Mansell (1861–1941) and Thomas Gildart Mansell (1866–1929) became a partners. Edward had served his articles with his father and Thomas had been articled to Osborn and Reading. The firm of Mansell and Mansell continued until 1934.

BIRMINGHAM AND ITS ENVIRONS

PUBLIC

1898 Alterations to School, Beaufort Rd, Edgbaston for the Trustees to the Schools

1901 New classrooms and gymnasium to School, New John St West for the Birmingham School Board

1903 Alteration's to Queens College, Paradise St for the Trustees; 1909 addition of w.c.s

1903 Church of St Luke, Bristol St

1904 St Giles Institute, Storr's Place, Green Lane for Rev. J. Richards; 1914 extensions

1910 Club, Lower Trinity St for Rev. J. L. Ropes

1912 Alterations, High St, Bordesley for Rev. J. L. Ropes

1913 Chapel, High St, Bordesley for Rev. J. L. Ropes

COMMERCIAL

1895 Doctor's premises for Dr Thomas Savage, 133, Edmund St [now offices Chamberlain House]

1900 New premises for Ocean Accident Insurance Company, Waterloo St/Temple Row West [now café Nero]

1910 New shop front 173/175 High St, Deritend for Rev. J. L. Ropes

INDUSTRIAL

1891 Shopping for Ward and Sons. St Paul's Square [D]

1891 Raising of tower for water tank at Snow Hill for W. P. Rayner & Sons [D]

1891 New premises for Lipscombe and Bayley, Stanhope St after their original premises were destroyed by fire.

1895 Warehouse and workshops, Frederick St/Regent St, Hockley for Adie and Lovekin Ltd, jewellers.

1895 Alterations to industrial premises, Whittal St for Robert Mansell; 1903 alterations

1895 Alterations and additions to premises, Gas St for H. H. Mullinger; 1911 alterations

1895 Addition to shopping for Plant and Green, Warstone Lane

1896 Addition to Tool Works for A. W. Wills and Co., Cuckoo Rd

1896 Manufacturing premises for Mary Bolton, ships' berths manufacturers, 19 Newhall Hill

1896 Shopping for John Mitchell Newhall St/Lionel St

1897 Shopping for Elkington and Co. Ltd, Newhall St

1905 New premises and shopping for Simplex Steel Conduit Company, Maxstoke St

1905 Boiler House for Simplex Steel Conduit Company, Garrison Lane.

1908 Business premises for H. M. Mitchell, Moland St

1908 Additions to 8 Whittal St for W. Hunt and Sons

1908 Alterations to premises in Barford St for City Casting and Metal Company

1911 Alterations to premises owned by J & W Mitchell, Coventry Rd

1914 Shopping, Oxford St for Topham and Snushall

DOMESTIC

1887 House for Alfred Lovekin, Tudor Grange, Blossomfield Solihull; 1900 extensions for Alfred Bird

1890 Coach house and stable for James Adie, rear of 33 Hagley Rd [D]

1895 Bay and two-storey extension for Miss Bolton, 12 Highfield Rd, Edgbaston; 1900 new store with bedroom over. Now used for commercial purposes

1897 Two houses in Park Hill Rd, Harborne for S. J. Green

1895 Alterations to house, 39 Beaufort Rd, Edgbaston for C. H. Lines

1896 House for Rev. G. Litting, Edgbaston Rd

1899 House for Alice Thompson, Hermitage Rd, Edgbaston

1899 Alterations to Hill House, Richmond Hill Rd, Edgbaston for Ernest Kannrenth; 1904 alterations; 1908 additions

1901 House and Stable, Hagley Rd opposite Hagley Rd Station, for Thomas Henry Smith

1901 Alterations and additions to 8, Vicarage Rd for W. F. Hoslam

1903 Alterations to 14 Arthur Rd, Edgbaston for S. Munslow

1906 House for T. H. Smith, Stanmore Rd, Edgbaston

1906 Greenhouse, Portland Rd, Edgbaston for T. H. Bailey

1910 Additions to house, Sir Harry's Rd, Edgbaston for Rev. Canon D. Thompson

1908 Additions to 11, Ampton Rd, Edgbaston for J. Briley

1914 Additions to house in Pritchatt's Rd, Edgbaston for E. Kannreuether

NOTES

[1] A list of their output has been compiled from the Birmingham Building Registers in Birmingham Central Library, Archives and Heritage Services and is given in the List of Works.

[2] *Kelly's Post Office Directories* 1868–1905; RIBA *Directory of British Architects* (London and New York, 2001).

[3] Allan W. Evans, *Tudor Grange — I have a story to tell* (unpublished research paper); private papers of Sir Alfred Bird in the possession of his descendants, including Souvenir Programme of Garden Party held at Tudor Grange, 1913; Solihull Council Offices, Solihull Building Register, app. nos 386, 387, 396, for additions to Tudor Grange including new stable and entrance lodge, 1900–01.

[4] Andy Foster, *Pevsner Architectural Guides: Birmingham* (New Haven and London, 2005) p. 133.

[5] *Ibid* p. 167.

[6] Nikolaus Pevsner and Alexandra Wedgwood, *The Buildings of England: Warwickshire* (Harmondsworth, 1966) p. 12; Foster, *Birmingham*, p. 115.

[7] Census Enumerators' Records, 1891.

[8] *Victoria History of the County of Warwick*, vol 7, *Birmingham*, ed. by R. B. Pugh, (1964) p. 390; Pevsner and Wedgwood, *Warwickshire*, p. 131.

[9] Will of Edward Mansell, 1943.

[10] *The Builder*, 160, 21 March 1941 p. 289.

15 Ewen and J. Alfred Harper

MICHAEL HARPER AND BARBARA SHACKLEY

Ewen Harper (1853–1920) worked as an architect in Birmingham for more than four decades from 1875, when he set up in practice, until his death in 1920. He was a true philanthropist and a staunch Methodist with particularly strong links with the Weslyan Church. Over the years he was responsible for the design of a number of significant buildings in the area, many for the commercial and industrial interests which were fast developing in the city, and produced some notable buildings in terracotta. He was also a prolific designer of non-conformist churches. Non-conformism was a strong force in Birmingham in the second half of this nineteenth-century and Ewen clearly became a prominent member of the community. From 1897, until shortly before his death, Ewen was in partnership with his younger brother, James Alfred Harper (1866–1952) as Ewen Harper and Brother.

Ewen was born on 31 May 1853, the fifth of seven children of James and Amelia Harper of New Street, Darlaston. James was a gunlock filer by occupation and by 1861 had moved to Aston where as a small manu-facturer in the gun trade he employed fifteen people. Ewen was educated at King Edward's School and attended the non-conformist Bloomsbury Institution. He became a national Queen's Medallist at the age of 19 and in 1875, when he was 22, won a South Kensington Art Master's prize, having for some years been a teacher of science and art concurrently with studying architecture. Ewen embarked on his architectural career in 1870 at the age of 16 or 17 when he was articled to David Smith and Son, architects of Cherry Street. Five years later in 1875 he established his own practice at 27 Bennett's Hill. In 1879 he married Amelia Annie Newey

Ewen Harper

Barr and at first lived in Stirling Road, Edgbaston, later moving to Bloemfontein in Shepley Road, Barnt Green, a house he designed for himself. He became a Fellow of the Royal Institute of British Architects in 1907 after more than thirty years in practice. James Alfred Harper also studied at the Birmingham School of Art where he won many prizes and trained in his brother's firm before becoming a partner in 1897. In 1893 he married Mary Purser and lived at Priors Lea, 58 Oxford Road.[1]

Ewen Harper's early commissions were predictably mostly domestic though, judging by the number of jobs entered in his ledger, he seems to have made a good start. In the first five years of practice he was concerned with designing a large number of speculative houses, some shops and small industrial buildings. In 1880 he began his long architectural association with the Wesleyan Church, which was to flourish in later years. His first job for them was to add a classroom to St Martin's Street Chapel's Sunday school followed in 1883 and 1884 with alterations to chapels in St Martin's Street and Stirling Road where he lived. In the latter case, it is recorded, he returned the fee of £100 as a donation, an early indicator of his later philanthropic inclinations.

By 1887 Ewen seems to have been attracting larger scale work. In that year he was commissioned to build a Nurses' House in Bath Row for Queen's Hospital where he was later to add substantial new buildings.[2] In 1890 he was appointed to design alterations to the Assay Office in Newhall Street and in 1889 had his first commission from Joseph Lucas at their premises in Little King Street. In the years to come his relationship with Lucas developed and he was responsible for a number of sizeable projects at their factory in Great King Street/Burberry Street.[3]

By 1894 the practice was flourishing and he was appointed by the Birmingham Electric Supply Company for work at their premises in Dale End. He subsequently carried out several further commissions for this company, designing generating stations.[4] He was also commissioned by the Wesleyan and General Assurance Company to design alterations at their offices in Corporation Street and Old Square. On the commercial front, he continued to work with Lucas and the Birmingham Assay Office throughout the 1890's but also had an interesting appointment from Richard Cadbury, the chocolate manufacturer, to design the Moseley Road Institute in Balsall Heath. This was a centre for an adult school with mission activity and as well as the main hall which seated 2000 people had a lecture hall, gymnasium and numerous classrooms.[5] It was opened shortly after Richard Cadbury's death in 1899. A year before this Ewen Harper had been chosen for another major philanthropic project by Richard Cadbury for the group of 33 Almshouses at Bournville of 1896–97 which Alexandra Wedgwood has described as in

the old tradition: one storey almshouses most attractively set around a spacious grassy quadrangle. Red brick with stone dressings and red tile roofs. The details are all basically Tudor. round-headed entrances to the houses are set in pairs beneath timber framed

Generating Station, Summer Lane, Hockley, designed in 1902. *Courtesy of Michael Harper*

gables. Mullioned windows. The main entrance is of a gatehouse type of two storeys with little turrets to either side and a projecting porch. This centre block has to one side the chapel , a simple rectangular room with pretty roof trusses, and to the other, the matron's rooms. In the middle of the quadrangle is a rest house, similar to the one on The Green, but here it is rectangular with an open arcade supported on wooden columns around the central 'house', and a pyramid roof with gabled dormers in each side, and a lantern.

Harper also designed the nearby group of 38 houses the rents from which pro-vided the endowment for the almshouses, and these too are of brick with Tudor detailing.[6]

In 1897 Ewen Harper took into partnership his younger brother, J. Alfred Harper and the practice became Ewen Harper and Brother. In 1898 the Harpers stepped firmly into the realms of substantial commercial projects. It is at this time that they developed a large commercial building speculatively at the northern end of Corporation Street beyond Old Square. This was the Ruskin Buildings at Nos 179–203 designed in 1898, and from where they subsequently practiced. A similar building was their King Edward Building at Nos 205–13 of 1901 for John Hawkins and Sons, cotton Spinners. Both buildings had shops at street level with

Bournville Almshouses, Maryvale Road, 1896–97

four floors of offices above, a substantial investment at that time by any measure. Ruskin Buildings was finished to a high standard externally, with red brickwork and a vigorous treatment of shallow bays and faience horizontal banding through the first and second floors. The piers between shops are faced in terracotta with sculpted caps. King Edward Building is more simply finished with shaped red brick piers between large timber windows.

Their largest project in Corporation Street was the Central Methodist Hall of 1901–03, with its huge perpendicular windows and towering belfry. This replaced the smaller 1877 Central Hall by Osborn and Reading also in Corporation Street. Alexandra Wedgwood commented on the Harpers' building:

In red brick and terracotta, it is clearly the local men's answer to the Victoria Law Courts opposite to which it does indeed form the perfect complement. It is a large building of three stories, the ground floor with a row of shops, asymmetrical about a tall slender central tower; the seven bays to the other are taken up by the main hall on the first floor. The fenestration also follows this division, with five bays and round-arched traceried windows above convex lower ones to the seven bays. Vigorous details everywhere and good sculpture over the porch. The main hall is rectangular with aisles, rising from the first floor to the full height of the building. Seven bay iron arcade with clerestory above,

Ruskin Buildings, Corporation Street, photographed shortly after completion in 1900.
Courtesy of Michael Harper

King Edward Building, Corporation Street/Steelhouse Lane, 1901

Central Methodist Hall, Corporation Street, 1901–03

Detail of main entrance, Central Methodist Hall

and a gallery on three sides with a good wrought iron balustrade of Art Nouveau flourishes.

The building cost £96,165. It is listed Grade 2* and was a major commission for the practice. The accommodation comprised a central meeting hall, with organ, to seat up to about 2,500, smaller meeting rooms, committee rooms, Sunday School halls, Library, rooms for social occasions and numerous administrative offices, in all over thirty rooms.[7] It covers an area on the ground of about 1.25 acres. Sadly it is now unused and is deteriorating.[8]

Another substantial building of this period with non-conformist overtones was the new YMCA and Temperance Hall in Dale End of 1901 of which Alexandra Wedgwood commented in 1966 'a good example of their red brick and terracotta work. A gabled nine bay symmetrical design, vaguely Jacobean' but which has since been demolished.[9] At the same date they also carried out substantial alterations to an earlier Temperance Hall designed by Yeoville Thomason in Temple Street in 1858, to which they added a new terracotta façade with twin towers. Their work has since been obliterated by further alterations by C. E. Bateman when the Hall was remodelled for the Birmingham Law Society in the 1930s.[10]

Other commercial developments in Birmingham at about the turn of the century were new offices for the Wesleyan and General Assurance in Steelhouse Lane, the Summer Lane Generating Station for Birmingham Electric Supply Co., and Warehouse premises for Bell and Nicolson, who were wholesale drapers, in Cannon Street. The latter was the first fully steel framed building in Birmingham.[11] Later, in 1911, came a new warehouse and offices for Halford Cycle Co. in Moor Street, and in 1916, the Phoenix Building, on a fine site at the corner of Colmore Row and Temple Row for Phoenix Assurance. This is a splendid building of vigorous design, said to be influenced by Selfridges in London, faced in Portland stone with deeply recessed horizontal joints, and ashlar columns in Doric order to the first and second floors.[12] Of these buildings only the Phoenix Assurance Building remains.

Not all their designs for industrial buildings were on a large scale. In Station Street, Bromsgrove, a set of workshops they designed for the Bromsgrove Guild still survive. These date to 1904–08 and are part brick and part corrugated iron.[13]

As already noted, Ewen had close links with the Weslyan Church. He became a director of the Wesleyan and General Assurance Society and, amongst his many commitments to philanthropic institutions, he was twice elected Conference Representative by the Wesleyan District Synod and for eight years was President

Phoenix Assurance Co. Building, Colmore Row, 1916

Bloemfontein, now Rede
House, Shepley Road, Barnt
Green, 1892. *Photo: B. S.*

of the Birmingham City Mission.[14] Throughout his architectural career he worked professionally for the Wesleyan and Baptist Churches and over the ten years from about 1893 to 1903 he designed or altered more than thirty chapels and Sunday schools, included among which were those at King's Norton (1891) Fillongley (1892), Wolverton (1892), Smethwick (1893), King's Heath (1893), Stafford (1893), and Highgate Park Moseley (1893). His chapel at Headless Cross, Redditch of 1897 has an open-work stone spire which was one of his specialitities.[15] He also designed Weslyan chapels in India and one in Durban.

Ewen Harper was successful in a number of competitions and was placed high in the competition held in1890 for Sir Edwin Watkins's Great Tower of London; this he entered in association with John Graham, an engineering colleague. There was a large entry for the competition but the project was never built. In 1903 the practice was also placed third in the competition for Durban Town Hall in Natal.

Although the Harpers included domestic architecture amongst their work much of it was for small villas built as speculative housing. An exception was the large detached house Ewen built for himself in Shepley Road, Barnt Green in 1892. Bloemfontein was of brick with Queen Anne details and had a lodge with a mansard roof. He also built a large house in Barnt Green for Mr J. G. Mood. Two other large detached houses he designed were 21 Ashleigh Road in Solihull for John Petrie of 1896[16] and 26 College Road, Bromsgrove in neo-Georgian style, in 1909.[17] A project of a different nature was the work of the firm in designing several houses in Belcher's Lane and Yardley Green Road for the Ideal Village at Bordesley Green, a scheme of low cost, low density artisans' housing developed by the Ideal Benefit Society just prior to the First War.[18]

In the years 1914 to 1920 which cover the period of the Great War, the practice was kept busy mainly by its clients in the business community, most of whose

House for Mr Mood, Barnt Green, early 20th century photograph. *Courtesy of Jennie McGregor Smith*

names are well known in Birmingham today. They include Marsh & Baxter, Baker & Finnemoor, Taylor & Challon, Allday & Onions, Hortons Estate, Pinsent & Co., Harris & Sheldon, Smith Major & Stevens, The Valor Co., Fysche & Horton, Hoskins & Sewell, and Guardian Assurance.

Ewen died in 1920 after a short illness. His will gives an interesting insight into the man after a career of forty five years in which much had been achieved; he was a real entrepreneur but also, like many of his peers, a true philanthropist. In his will his address is given as Ruskin Buildings, Corporation Street. He made charitable bequests to The National Children's home and Orphanage, The Wesleyan Foreign Missionary School, Birmingham Central Hospital, and the Birmingham Queen's Hospital. In addition to bequests to his immediate family, Ewen left modest amounts to his groom, his gardener, his friends and his curator. There is no mention of his wife so presumably he was a widower. To his son Leonard Ewen, Harper he left all his share and interest in the profession of architect.

After his death the practice continued under the name of Ewen Harper Brother & Co., the name it had assumed in 1919 when Ewen Harper retired, the partners being his younger brother Alfred, and his son Leonard. In due course other

Interior of Mr Mood's house. *Courtesy of Jennie McGregor Smith*

younger members of the family joined the partnership but in 1937, for reasons that are now buried in the past, they decided to split up. Leonard continued to practice from Ruskin Buildings under the name of Ewen Harper & Co. and Alfred set up in partnership with his son, Geoffrey, under the style of J. Alfred Harper & Son, moving into new offices at Union Chambers in Temple Row, a building they had just completed. After World War II a third generation of architects in the family joined their respective practices, Rosslyn (always known as Ross) with his father, Leonard, at Ewen Harper & Co., and Michael with Geoffrey at J. Alfred Harper & Son. Both strands of the family took in other partners and changed the styles under which they were practicing but by 1998, after almost 125 years, both firms had been wound up.

Terracotta griffin on the Ruskin Buildings, Corporation Street

Selected Architectural Works of Ewen and J. Alfred Harper

Ewen Harper (1853–1920) studied at the Birmingham School of Art and served his articles with David Smith and Son of Birmingham. He set up in independent practice in 1875. In 1897 his younger brother J. Alfred Harper (1866–1952) became a partner in the practice which became Ewen Harper and Brother. On Ewen Harper's retirement in 1919 his son, Leonard became a partner and the firm continued as Ewen Harper, Brother and Co. until 1937.

BIRMINGHAM AND ITS ENVIRONS

PUBLIC

1881 Additional classroom for Wesleyan Sunday School, St Martin's St Chapel, Islington

1881 Courthouse, Albert St

1884 School in Carlyle Rd, Edgbaston for Wesleyan Chapel

1885 Highgate Park Baptist Chapel, Moseley Rd; 1894 Sunday School [D]

1888 Nurse's house and extensions for Queen's Hospital [D]

1889 Wesleyan Chapel, Willenhall

1890 Hart Memorial United Methodist Chapel, Gravelly Hill [D]

1890 Lecture room in Stirling Rd

1891 Pershore Rd Wesleyan Chapel, King's Norton

1893 Removed iron chapel from Jenkins St to Blake Lane and built hall and institute for Rev. Odells in Jenkins St and Arthur St

1893 Extensions to St Agnes Church, St Agnes Rd, Moseley

1896 Wesleyan Methodist Chapel, Waterloo Rd, Smethwick

1897 Sunday school, Buck St for the Trustees of the Wesleyan Central Mission

1897 Mission hall for Adults Schools, Farm St, Hockley

1897 Friend's Institute, Moseley Rd, Balsall Heath for Richard Cadbury

1897 Birmingham Town Mission, Tindal St

1900–01 Alterations and additions to Temperance Hall, No. 8 Temple St

1901–03 Methodist Central Hall, Corporation St

1902–04 Y.M.C.A. Building and Temperance Hall, Dale End [D]

1901–02 Wesleyan Methodist Chapel, Pershore Rd South, Cotteridge

1902 Wesleyan Methodist Chapel, Station Rd, Erdington

1905 Grainger's Lane Primitive Methodist Church, Cradley Heath [D]

1906 Park Congregational Hall, Grange Rd, Dudley

1906 Selly Oak Primitive Methodist Chapel, Bristol Rd [D]

1907 New building for Queen's Hospital [D]

1909 Mission Hall, Perrott St

1909 Long Lane Primitive Methodist Chapel, Halesowen

1910 Vicarage Rd Hazelwell Wesleyan Methodist Chapel, King's Heath

COMMERCIAL

1876 3 shops and stabling, Great Lister St for Mr James

1877 8 shops, Church Rd for Mr Oxford

1880 Bakehouse, Bordesley Green

1888 Offices at Rotton Park St, Edgbaston

1890 Extensions to Assay Office, Newhall St; 1897 extensions; 1904–08 alterations and additions; 1914 additional storey

1894 Temporary offices for Wesleyan and General Assurance Co. in Moor St [D]

1895 Alterations to Offices for Wesleyan and General Assurance Co. Corpin St

1897 Work for Wesleyan Central Mission, Buck St

1898 Business premises, Cherry St

1898 Offices, 55, Colmore Row

1899 Ruskin Buildings, Corporation St for Ewen Harper & Bro.

1901 King Edward's Building, Corporation St for John Hawkins and Sons, cotton spinners

1901 Premises for Wesleyan Assurance Co., Steelhouse Lane [D]

1902 Business premises in Newhall St

1906 Warehouse, Cannon St for Bell & Nicolson

1916 Offices for Phoenix Assurance Co., Colmore Row/Temple Row

INDUSTRIAL

1881 Variety Works, Frederick St

1882 Re-fronting of 45 Frederick St

1887 Manufactory, Rupert St for Joseph Stevens

1887 Rolling mill, Montgomery St, Sparkhill for W. & G. Johnson & Co.

1889 Shopping and warehouse, Great King St for Joseph Lucas & Son [D]; 1895 additions

1894 Offices, sheds, engine house and chimney stack, Dale End for The Electric Supply Co.

1895 Factory for a biscuit manufacturer in Moor St

1896 Factory in Great King St/Burbury St for Joseph Lucas & Son [D]; 1899 extensions; 1909 extensions

1896 Offices and warehouses in Newhall St, Water St and Parker St for the Electric Supply Co.

1902 Generating Station, Summer Lane for the Electric Supply Co.

1904 Distillery, Aston Church Rd

1904 Offices at Foundary, Mary Ann St for Taylor Challen; 1914 additions

1904 New premises in Warstone Lane for Joseph Walker [listed Grade II]

1910 Factory, Farm St

1911 Business premises, Moor St for Halford's Cycles

1911 Factory for Baker and Finnemore, Brook St/Newhall St

1912 Premises, Great Charles St

1914 New factory, Eliot St

1914 Factory, Oldknow Rd

1914 Industrial premises, Bagot St for Austin Motors

1914 Industrial premises, New Canal St for Bell and Nicolson

1915 Premises, Camden St for New Hudson Cycle Co.

1915 Premises, Aston Church Rd, Aston for Electricity Supply Co.

1917 Aeroplane Factory, Ryder St for Harris & Sheldon

DOMESTIC

1875 32 houses in Cuckoo Rd, Aston for Mr Birkenhead

1875 12 houses, Edgbaston for Mr Barmeant

1875 32 houses and retail shop Icknield St and Tindale St for Mr Taylor

1876 3 houses in Blenheim St, King's Heath for Mr Edmund Green

1878 House, Pershore Rd for Mr Carling

1878 Villa at Olton for Mr Godfrey

1878 House at Olton for Mr Harvey

1879 3 houses in Acocks Green

1880 Villas in Stirling Rd

1887 22 houses in Coventry Rd

1887 Houses on Dudley Rd, Spring Hill, Hooper St etc. for Mr Colmore

1887 House in Aston Rd for Ernest Booth

1889 3 houses in Cambridge St, Moseley for Henry Lucas

1889 5 houses in Stoney Lane for Joseph Lucas

1890 26 houses in Reservoir Rd, Edgbaston

1891 11 houses in Reservoir Rd

1892 Bloemfontein (now Long Rede) Shepley Rd, Barnt Green for Ewen Harper

1892 36 houses in Brunswick Rd

1893 Houses in Daisy Rd, Leslie Rd and Reservoir Rd

1895 38 houses in Moseley Rd

1895 12 dwellings in Vincent St, Balsall Heath.

1897 Bournville almshouses, Mary Vale Rd for Richard Cadbury

1903 5 houses for J. A. Harper in Railway Terrace.

1906 House 21 Ashleigh Rd, Solihull for John Petrie.

1909 House 26 College Rd, Bromsgrove

1913 Houses in Belchers Lane for Ideal Village for Ideal Benefit Society

1913 Houses in Yardley Rd for Ideal Benefit Society

? date House, Barnt Green for Mr Mood

OUTSIDE BIRMINGHAM

PUBLIC

1892 Chapels in Fillongly, Brackley, Hinton nr Brackley, Wolverton, Stoney Stratford and Bletchley

1893 Chapels in Reading, Sydenham Rd London, Rugby and Port Erin, Isle Of Man

1895 Baptist Church, The Green, Stafford

1897 Headless Cross Wesleyan Methodist Church, Redditch

1903 Wesleyan Methodist Chapel, Llandrindod Wells, Powys

1904 Methodist New Connexion Church, Blackheath, Rowley Regis, Staffs.

Hotels in Cumbria and Aberystwith

Grand Spa Hydro, Clifton

INDUSTRIAL

1904–08 Workshops for the Bromsgrove Guild, Station St, Bromsgrove

OUTSIDE BRITAIN

Two chapels in India

Wesleyan churches in South Africa

NOTES

[1] Biographical and business details of Ewen and J. Arthur Harper are taken from the following sources: Nigel Cameron and Michael Harper's article 'The Harper Family of Architects' (unpublished, 2007); Ledger Books of Ewen Harper and Ewen Harper and Brother in private collection; obituary of Ewen Harper, *Birmingham Post*, 8 February 1920; Birmingham Architectural Association *Green Book* 1953–55, p. 23. The authors are grateful to Nicola Coxon for the use her notes on the Harper Brothers.

[2] Birmingham Central Library, Archives and Heritage Services (hereafter BCL AHS) Birmingham Building Register, app. no. 6086, 1888.

[3] *County Express*, 22 and 29 September and 27 October 1906.

[4] BCL AHS, Birmingham Building Register, app. no. 7043, 1894 Dale End; app. no. 10797, 1895 Newhall St; app. no. 10796, 1895 Parker St; app. no. 11568, 1896 Water St; app. no 16843, 1902 generating station, Summer Lane; app. no. 1843, 1904 sub-station, all for Birmingham Electric Supply Company.

[5] BCL AHS, Birmingham Building Register app. no. 12542, 1897; *Victoria History of the County of Warwick*, vol. 7, *Birmingham*, ed. by W. B. Stephens (1964), p. 457.

[6] Nikolaus Pevsner and Alexandra Wedgwood, *The Buildings of England: Warwickshire* (Harmondsworth, 1966), p. 124; BCL AHS, Northfield Building Register, app. no. 2674, 1897; Iolo A. Williams, *The Firm of Cadbury* (1931), pp. 216–17.

[7] BCL AHS, Birmingham Building Register, app. no. 15221, 1899; *Birmingham Post* 17 September 1903 and 6 February 1920; Pevsner and Wedgwood, *Warwickshire*, p. 113; ' Methodist Central Hall' (unpublished, undated Victorian Society, Birmingham Group File Appendix 1.3); Andy Foster *Pevsner Architectural Guides: Birmingham* (New Haven and London, 2005), pp. 106–07.

[8] Permission for conversion to flats was given in 2006.

[9] BCL AHS, Birmingham Building Register, app. no. 16988, 1902; Pevsner and Wedgwood, *Warwickshire*, p. 125; for an illustration of the YMCA and Temperance Hall see Bryan Little, *Birmingham Buildings: the Architectural Story of a Midland City* (Newton Abbot, 1971), fig. 72.

[10] Foster, *Birmingham*, p. 121.

[11] Dept of Environment, *List of Buildings of Special Architectural Interest: Birmingham*.

[12] Foster, *Birmingham*, p. 96.

[13] Alan Brooks and Nikolaus Pevsner, *The Buildings of England: Worcestershire* (New Haven and London, 2007), p. 202.

[14] Obituary, *Birmingham Post*, 8 February, 1920.

[15] Brooks and Pevsner, *Worcestershire*, p. 561.

[16] Nigel Ian Cameron, *Ashleigh Road, Solihull* (Studley, 2002), p. 52.

[17] Brooks and Pevsner, *Worcestershire*, p. 204.

[18] BCL AHS, Birmingham Building Register, app. nos 20535, 24889, 25686 Houses in Belcher's Lane for Ideal Benefit Society; app. no. 30535, Houses in Yardley Green Road for Ideal Benefit Society 1913; Birmingham City Council Papers relating to Conservation Area no. 27 The Ideal Village, Bordesley Green 1988–96.

16 Frederick William Martin

BARBARA SHACKLEY

For almost one hundred years Frederick William Martin (1859–1917) has been an under-rated and almost unknown architect. Unearthing information about him has been difficult as his architectural ability has been hidden within the work of the partnership. Due to the death of his father's partner, J. H. Chamberlain, Frederick was rapidly promoted to replace him in his father's architectural practice. It was apparent that Frederick was a great designer and had the ability to move with the times. In the last years of the nineteenth century, Frederick's favourite building material was terracotta, which when combined with brick, was popular in Birmingham at this time. When fashions changed he turned to designing in a more restrained style, in rough-cast and brick. Becoming a pioneer of town planning, he designed the whole of the Moor Pool Housing Estate in a very, understated 'Arts & Crafts' style which included all domestic buildings, shops, offices and roads as well as the landscaping. His hospital designs were modern and innovative and his research into the most modern hospital methods created a Children's hospital, which in today's terms would be described as 'state of the art'. He adopted a severe Baroque style for his public buildings and his range of building types included schools, hospitals, libraries as well as domestic, commercial and industrial buildings.

Frederick came to prominence on the early and sudden death of his father's partner, John Henry Chamberlain, in 1883. A young man of twenty four years, with his brother Herbert, he was made a partner in his father's practice at 106, Colmore Row. As Chamberlain had been the inspiration in the partnership there was a void to fill and it was a challenge which Frederick was eventually to meet. The elder son of William Hippisley Martin (1828–1900), Frederick, after a privileged upbringing, living at The Larches, Stratford Road Aston, was educated at Rugby School and at the University of London. He never became a member of the RIBA only becoming a LRIBA in 1911 at the age of fifty-two. He married Mabel Crosskey in 1886, a suffragette and eldest daughter of a prominent Birmingham non-conformist minister who lived at 117, Gough Road, Edgbaston. They set up home at Bournbrook Hall, Stirchley having five children, one of whom served in the First World War.[1] In 1884, he gave a lecture to the Philosophical Society of Birmingham on *The Geological Section along the Railway to King's Norton*.[2] He became part of the liberal, non-conformist community in Birmingham, mixing with many influential people in the Council such as J. S. Nettlefold, William

Kenrick, and W. Beale. He was an active member of the Birmingham Architectural Association, a member of the Committee of the Children's Hospital and a member of the Children's Committee which acquired playing fields at Castle Bromwich for the City.

William Hippisley Martin, was an able businessman and constructional architect and the partner of D. R. Hill, prior to his partnership with Chamberlain. He had never shown great imagination in his designs and Chamberlain, an exponent of Venetian Gothic architecture, seems to have had total control of the drawing board as it was said that not a drawing left the partners' office which was not to his design.[3] In 1883, when Chamberlain died at the age of fifty two, Martin, with the assistance of his sons, Frederick and Herbert, decided to carry on the practice. At first the practice continued to use Chamberlain's designs but as time progressed, the partners developed their own ideas. In the last few years of the century, it is to Frederick Martin that most of the quality of Martin and Chamberlain buildings has been ascribed although it is difficult to ascertain when the father stops and the sons start.[4] After William's death, in 1901 the practice was re-named Martin and Martin.

Most of the commissions the practice received in the years after Chamberlain's death were connected with education and indeed there were thirty Birmingham Board Schools built between 1885 and 1901, as well as many alterations and additions to existing schools. The first of these schools was the Stratford Road Board School of 1885, now listed Grade II.[5] This is an excellent copy of Chamberlain's style, and as there was more money available, many have thought that it was an improvement. The terracotta panels of flowers and plants must have been some of Chamberlain's designs showing his favourite method of blending of naturalism and stylization.

The partnership, at this time, still known as Martin & Chamberlain, became the leading practitioners of the Birmingham's 'terracotta school'. During the next decade, designs changed subtly, the asymmetry advocated by Chamberlain was replaced by more orderly elevations; stained glass disappeared and greater emphasis was given to the position of the tower. Chamberlain had argued like Pugin, that Gothic was the only true vernacular style for Britain. He had however allowed himself freedom to also use the 17th century, country house style. This freedom was carried still further by this new partnership to include the styles, decorative motives, and forms of the sixteenth century and even the Romanesque. Designs became more flamboyant and some have been thought to be brash and even foreign to Gothic architecture. Terracotta was used for facing buildings which allowed a still greater freedom than Chamberlain's use of exterior tiling. Some criticised that terracotta, although being used as an implied structural material, for example for the ribbing or groins, was not actually structural at all. Indeed, terracotta, along with the use of towers became the dominant factors of the new style. However, one has to accept that the designs were truly original.[6]

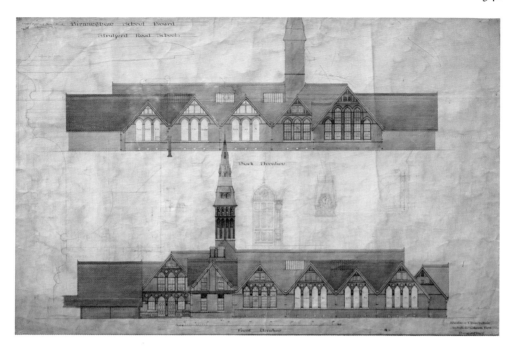

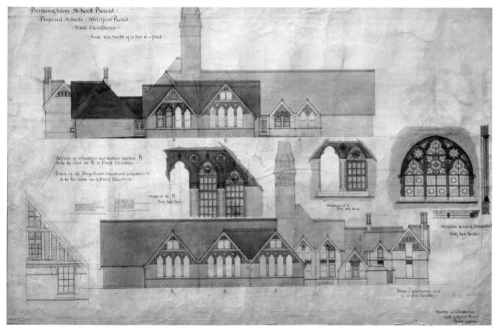

Stratford Road Board School.
TOP Front and back elevations. BELOW Side elevation and window detail, 1884.
Courtesy of Stratford Road Primary School

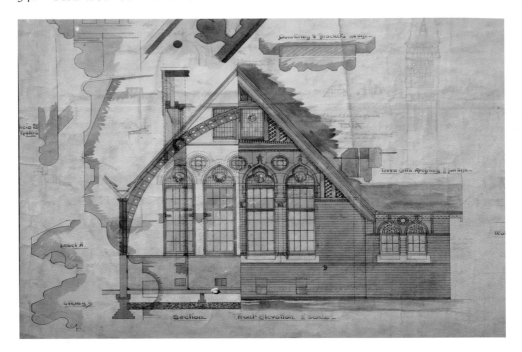

Stratford Road Board School.
TOP Section through main hall and window detail, 1884. BELOW Main hall.
Courtesy of Stratford Road Primary School

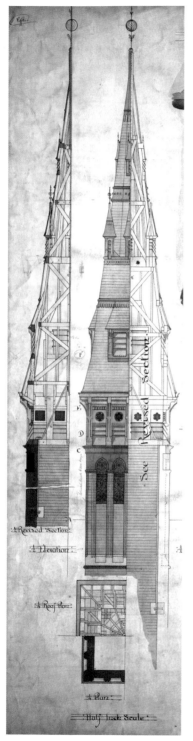

Stratford Road Board School, detail of tower,
1884, and photograph 2003 prior to demolition.
Photo: D. L.

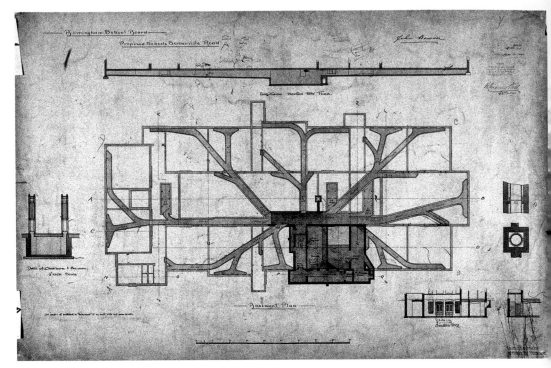

Somerville Board School, heating plan, 1894. *Courtesy of Birmingham Urban Design*

In the *Birmingham Weekly Post* of 1896, it was stated that the newly opened Dennis Road Board School had a ventilation system, in the form of a tower that could keep the temperature 15 degrees below the outside temperature on a hot day, clearing the air in a room as many as four times an hour.[7] The first building completely of terracotta was Barford Road Board School of 1887, the same year that the terracotta Victoria Law Courts was started. The next year, in 1888, another tower (now demolished) was built at Upper Highgate Street Board School, now listed Grade II. The year 1892, saw the building of Waverley Road Higher Grade Board School at Small Heath, with an 82 foot tower and a wealth of detailing. George Dixon, who had realized that intelligent boys were passing at a high standard at the age of twelve years, and would benefit from another two years of schooling, at his own expense in 1884, had opened the Bridge Street Central Board School in the premises of the former Cadbury factory, vacated since the move to Bournville. This had a syllabus which included over eleven hours a week of practical chemistry. Waverley School, funded by the School Board continued these ideas and possibly was the first public forerunner of Technical Colleges, an innovative idea to be taken up nationally. Not everyone was in favour and in 1892, at the opening of the School, John Lowe, a Tory councillor, made the comment that the rate payers should not have to pay for the further education of the artisan classes.[8]

Towards the end of the last decade of the 19th-century, complaints of the virtual monopoly that Martin & Chamberlain enjoyed as Corporation architects obliged the School Board to hold a competition for Yardley Road Board School which they still won. After William Martin's death in 1900, the firm having designed forty one schools, the partners demanded a higher percentage for their designs. This was not agreed upon and they lost their position with the School Board. Those schools that survive are still considered to be the best buildings in their neighbourhood.[9]

The Free Libraries Committee was set up to help to provide free book lending throughout the town. The two libraries of Spring Hill in Icknield Street and Green Lane at Small Heath were opened in 1893, and built of terracotta and brick. Both are now listed Grade II. Green Lane Library and Baths by Herbert Martin was built on a triangular site with a robust tower.[10] This is in contrast to that of Spring

Spring Hill Library, Icknield Street, 1893

Hill by Frederick Martin which is more elegant.[11] Here the short, conical spire rises from a graceful square tower decorated with bunches of pinnacles with a triangular pediment above the clock. The left and rear elevations were completely plain as they were situated next to buildings now demolished. The interior had heavy, red marble columns, Gothic arches, a gallery and an arched ceiling. One can recognise the same designs developed for their schools. The success of the new libraries was striking and immediate, with thousand of books issued each year.[12]

In 1972, the Middle Ring road was planned to pass along the line of Icknield Street and in doing so to cross the site of Spring Hill Library. To alter the line of the Middle Ring Road involved a sharp curve in the line of the road and due to the protests of the Victorian Society in 1974, the Public Works Department considered moving it *en bloc* and it was even thoroughly cleaned in 1978.[13] However Green Lane Library and Baths were closed in 1977, immediately suffering vandalism, tiles being taken off the roof, walls smashed and lead piping ripped out. The religious organization wishing to buy the building began to have misgivings and complained that the council did not allow them to occupy it and by 1979, it seemed that both buildings would be demolished.[14] Fortunately in 1982, new road improvement schemes retained Spring Hill Library, and Green Lane Library was sold to a Moslem religious group.[15]

Martin & Chamberlain had designed Rubery Hill Hospital in 1882 and Frederick Martin during his career also designed several hospitals and many additions to existing hospitals. His first large commission was Hollymoor Hospital. In 1898, it was decided that a new Lunatic Asylum should be built at Hollymoor Farm and six firms of Birmingham architects were asked to send proposed plans. Mr George T. Hine of Westminster, an experienced asylum architect, was appointed as Assessor. An honorarium of 100 guineas was paid to each competing architect and their commission was to be 5% upon the outlay of the building, not including gas fittings or electric lighting. Frederick Martin, using the motif, 'Forward' was chosen for his originality with a building of 4,931,427 cubic feet. The chief feature was the 132 feet high square water tower of brick with classical details, copper roof and lantern.[16] The Asylum accommodated 600 patients, 300 males and 300 females, being made up of pavilions, for women and for men, and including dormitories with wards, for each sex. The principal entrance and official block faced north-west, allowing the patients to enjoy the south side. The Infirmary and an epileptic ward were situated on the ground floor as were offices, stores, kitchens, workshops, laundry, wash houses, a large dining and recreational hall with stage. A detached chapel for 400 people and a residence for the medical superintendent were provided, both with a covered way to the asylum. Suitable apartments for three assistant medical officers, a house keeper, attendants and twelve maids were provided along with accommodation in small houses and cottages for the engineer and gardeners, two of which were to be lodges at the entrance gates for married attendants. Accommodation for thirty two nurses and

Hollymoor Hospital, postcard *c.* 1940

thirty two male attendants with mess rooms and recreational rooms, farmhouses and buildings for twenty four cows, eight horses, eighty pigs, a dairy, a detached infectious hospital and a mortuary for both sexes were provided. No boundary wall was built around the large grounds but the exercising courts were enclosed by walls, palisades, or a sunk fence to allow the best view.[17]

During the First World War, Hollymoor became a War Hospital and was transformed to take wounded soldiers, accommodating as many as 946 men, a total of 21,280 in all. Between the wars it was converted back to a mental hospital but in 1939, patients from the inner city hospitals were evacuated and the hospital was equipped as a General Hospital. By 1940, casualties from Dunkirk arrived and by 1942 it became a military psychiatric hospital. After the war, badly in need of repair it was equipped to cope with Nuclear Attack casualties as well as psychiatric patients. It was demolished in 1995–96 as the new Solihull District General Hospital was opened. The listed chapel and administrative centre were retained and refurbished and opened as an art media centre. The spacious grounds were used for housing and the water tower still stands above them all.[18]

In September 1905, The Birmingham and Midland Hospital for Women, Showell Green Lane, Sparkhill, costing £45,000, and accommodating fifty patients was opened. This was set on a site of 8,500 sq. yards. The administrative buildings and

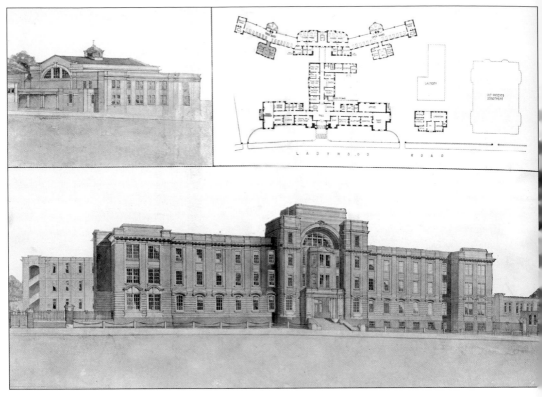

Children's Hospital, Ladywood Road, plan and elevation from *The Builder*, 29 August 1913. *Courtesy of Birmingham Central Library*

nurses' home of two stories faced the road and at the rear, divided by lawns and tennis courts were the wards for patients. These were made up of two storied wings north and south, and contained four wards each with ten beds. The upper wards had balconies on three sides with iron staircases at the ends. All the walls were plastered with non-absorbent material and tinted pale green with white woodwork. Near the centre of the upper corridors were two sets of operating rooms.[19] The hospital closed in the late 1990s and was demolished.

The partnership of Chamberlain and Martin had built the original Children's Hospital, Steelhouse Lane in 1867–68, although in 1870, the in-patients part of the hospital was moved to the Lying-in Hospital in Broad Street. In 1907, the fifty years lease on the building in Broad Street was running out and it was evident that the accommodation was too small. As early as 1905, Frederick Martin had been a member of the Hospital Management Board at Steelhouse Lane and in 1907, the Board of Governors, impressed by the now completed Women's Hospital, appointed him architect at a remuneration of 5% of the cost. It is interesting that the Registered Office of the Management Board was 106, Colmore Row, the address of Frederick's practice. By 1910, the Governors had purchased a three acre site for the new hospital on Ladywood Road, now Ladywood Middleway, at a cost of £17,193 with money raised from public subscription.[20]

It was not until 1913 that building work could start utilising funds raised by a public appeal as a memorial to the late King. The Hospital cost over £30,000, and was named the King Edward VII Memorial Children's Hospital. During the years between 1907 and 1913, Frederick Martin had drawn up the plans for the hospital, taking considerable trouble to research modern hospital layouts, consequently it was at the forefront of modern hospital design. The builder was J. H. Barnsley & Son. The main building which fronted Ladywood Middleway, was of red brick with stone dressings in a Free Renaissance style. The front building, the administrative block and medical residences of four floors, was T-shaped. The main façade was symmetrical with a projecting central doorway with several steps leading up to the main entrance. The windows above the doorway were set in a circular bay. The top floor held the kitchens and food stores and the lower ground floor was for the admission of patients, operating theatres and an X-Ray department. The outpatient department was added in 1925.

The two lines of wards in the rear, made up of two pavilions, three stories high, resembled the spread-out wings of a butterfly. They were built in a gentle curve facing from the north-west to the south-east to provide the optimum amount of sunshine and were inclined at an angle towards each other, to give shelter from the cold winds. Success had attended open air treatment where tried in the Broad Street hospital and the new hospital was planned to provide these facilities. The principle of open wards was carried further than any other hospital, with one side open to the south west. Of the six main wards three were for medical cases and three for surgical. Each ward, contained one large room of fourteen beds, one smaller containing five beds, a single bed room for observation and a small three bedroom high temperature ward for changing dressings – a total of 138 beds. The south fronts of the large wards were filled with collapsible screens which allowed the whole frontage to be thrown open to the sun and air. They were built of Hennebique ferro concrete floors against fire risk and with flat roofs; the later to permit open air treatment. The septic block on the ground floor contained a diphtheria ward for six beds with a tracheotomy room and accommodation for nurses attending diphtheria and other infectious diseases.

Frederick Martin died five months before the building was completed and Herbert, his brother completed the work. The Children's Hospital was taken into the NHS in the late 1940s and the hospital building in Broad Street became part of the Orthopaedic Hospital. It is now a night club and entertainment centre. When the Children's Hospital relocated to what had been the General Hospital (by William Henman), it was returned to its original site.[21]

The firm also undertook some commercial buildings. Selly Oak Electricity Station, designed in 1890, and built in brick and terracotta with stone dressings is a striking building. Which member of the practice designed this building is unknown. From the road this listed Electricity Station appears as a tall version of a two storied French Gothic Royal Chapel, raised on a high rectangular plan. The south east front has a deep flight of steps leading to the portal with a window above. It has steeply hipped tiled roofs, with terracotta floral bracketed eaves, cornice and finials. An apsed transept with stone dressed arcaded light and terracotta eaves projects from the basement. Another commission was for extensions to The Grand Hotel, in Colmore Row. This had been designed in 1876–78 for Horton's Estate by Thomson Plevins. Around 1890 Martin & Chamberlain extended the building at the rear in Barwick Street. In 1893–95 they again extended it, this time designing an eight storey extension in red brick and terracotta with canted bays. This extension included the best interiors of the hotel, the Grosvenor Room, a ball room with an adjoining withdrawing room, both decorated with rich French 18th-century style plasterwork.[22] Again it is unknown which partner was the designer.

Perhaps the New Telephone Exchange, built in 1896, and situated at the corner of Newhall Street and Edmund Street for the National Telephone Company was Frederick's finest commercial building.[23] Built in terracotta and Ruabon brick and listed Grade I, it had four floors. The originality shown by Frederick in his school designs was found again here. Tall arcades ran through the main storeys which were divided by large brick piers topped by clusters of pinnacles, similar to Spring Hill Library. All the windows and the round headed entrance were set within this arcade, and the corner was emphasized by a projecting two storey bay. The blocks of terracotta, made by J. C. Edwards in a purple-red colour created a graduation in decorative effect, from the simple moulded sections on the arches, to a stylised flower-bud pattern and swirling acanthus leaves. Leopard-like animals projected as keystones to the arches or wrapped themselves over the balustrades. A Baroque sense of movement was found in the corner oriel window with more fantastic animals, like gryphons with fish tails, reclining against the balustrade ends. The gables above the entrance and corner bays had roundels with tracery similar to those in the School of Art. The Newhall Street entrance had fine wrought-iron gates.[24]

In the simple interior were offices for the management, offices to-let and, on the top floor, the exchange or switch room. Part of this room could be used by the operators for recreation but when there was a lot of work, it could be extended from 65 to 95 ft long, and as it was 40 ft wide, it could accommodate 200 operators. The girls had their own cloakrooms and a separate entrance. A pamphlet issued by the National Telephone Company described the girl's rest room as 'well warmed and ventilated, the intervals are spent in doing fancy work or in reading, the operators having organized a reading circle for the study of standard authors.' Similar to the designs for school halls, the roof of this room was opened to its full height with pointed trusses. The National Telephone Company was taken over by

The Telephone Exchange, Newhall Street and Edmund Street, 1896

the GPO and in the 1970s this building was threatened as redundant.[25] In 1994, an extra floor was added during alterations and it is now occupied by offices and restaurants.

Of the industrial buildings designed by Martin & Martin, the building for Deakin & Francis, jewellery manufacturers, of 1905–06, situated at 17, Regent Place, was the most interesting. Originally an adapted domestic building of 1824 this underwent partial demolition and was replaced by a new purpose-built workshop and office range. This manufactory was one of a small group in the Jewellery Quarter that incorporated larger houses of the early to mid 19th century, encased within later developments. Described in the *Watchmaker, Jeweller, Silversmith and Optician's Journal* of 1906, the alterations demonstrated advanced characteristics for its type and date. These included the T-plan, giving wide rooms and natural light from the north-lit roof, an internal telephone network, a compressed-air supply and a sophisticated central-heating and cooling system. The cross of the T-form was built in the former front gardens and the façade rose from the pavement to make optimum use of the available land. The design of the façade was influenced by the Birmingham Arts & Crafts Movement. The building was of two storeys with a basement, the rear part having elevations built in a progressive functional style with piers which rose up the full height of the walls and with large uninterrupted steel framed windows forming the panels. The internal structure was built using cast iron columns and cased rolled-steel beams.[26] Today, the Grade

The Telephone Exchange, detail of corner gable

II building remains in use as a jewellery manufactory and the rear workshop range is let out for use by small firms in the jewellery and related trades.

Frederick Martin's domestic work included a pioneering garden suburb development as well as detached middle class housing. The Moor Pool Estate in Harborne was built on the initiative of John Sutton Nettlefold a successful industrialist who had became the first Chairman of Birmingham's Housing Committee in 1901. At first, Nettlefold followed a policy of piecemeal slum clearance, but he realised that this was only a remedy for the housing problem, not a cure. The garden city philosophy advocated that housing was at the root of social problems. Houses should be suitable for ensuring healthy living, for bringing up healthy children; with more air, more gardens, and more open spaces for playgrounds. In 1906, the City Council adopted Nettlefold's report, recommending a Garden Suburb policy. This was three years before the first Housing and Town Planning Act. They agreed to acquire cheap land for houses at a density of ten per acre; to provide open spaces, parks and playgrounds; and to keep road widths flexible; wider for through traffic and narrower for access. Nettlefold was a pioneer, his policies and his sensitivity to the environment, put Birmingham in the forefront

Premises for Deakin & Francis, 17 Regent Place, 1905–06

of British planning. This was expressed in his book, *Town Planning in Practice* of 1914 and its results can be seen in the Moor Pool Estate run by Harborne Tenants Ltd as a co-partnership housing scheme. Tenants were to buy shares in the company and then eventually manage the estate themselves as co-owners. It was one of a dozen similar schemes in England that attempted at reasonable rents, to provide healthy living accommodation, on the outskirts of big towns.

Frederick Martin, employed as architect on the site, also became a pioneer in Town Planning and researching the ideals of the movement, again he created original designs. In 1907, the estate of fifty-four acres was purchased for £15,860 and in 1908 building started. These fifty-four acres were developed at a density of only ten dwellings to the acre instead of the usual 40–50 houses an acre found in the inner city. The houses were built in blocks of two, four, six and eight on either side of the roads, seventy-two feet apart. This was to create a spaciousness which gave more light and air to every house; each window was to look upon greenery. The houses built of brick and roughcast, were designed in a stripped and restrained Arts & Crafts style, with casement windows, gabled roofs with some deep eaves. Because of the cost of their rural setting the interiors of the houses

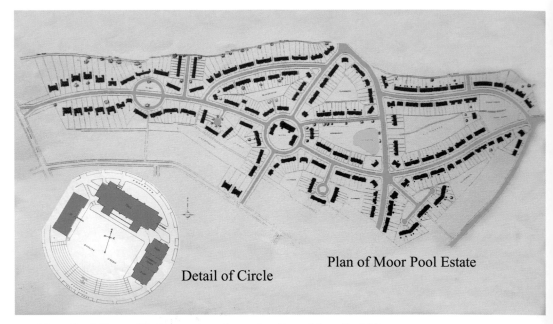

Detail of Circle

Plan of Moor Pool Estate

Moor Pool Estate, Harborne, based on plan from *Moor Pool News*, 1909

were not as roomy as the houses in the city. Some house types had two, three or four bedrooms usually with the w.c. downstairs or in a few types, even outside. Some houses had bathrooms, often downstairs although one style had a bathroom downstairs and one upstairs. The living accommodation was mostly made up of two areas described as scullery and living room with a brick or tiled fireplace, a fuel store and larder. Between the grass and the gardens there was a gravel pathway and between the gardens were beech hedges. The gardens were of moderate size so the tenants would have enough time to tend them. Every road was to have its own character and no house was to darken or offend a neighbour's house.[27]

As the road construction had to be paid for by the tenants, it was decided that the roads should be only sixteen feet wide but with a broad band of trees planted in grass on either side and designed deliberately winding. These roads were less expensive than the normal construction, probably not metalled, but as was pointed out by the society, wide enough for the amount of traffic necessary. Another important item in the cost was the construction of the sewers. This was done by the introduction of a combined drainage system. This modern and cheaper system of road and sewer construction resulted in a saving of between, sixpence and a shilling a week, although the society had to pay for the upkeep of the planted roads. In addition to the principal park, surrounding the Moor Pool, a number of small playgrounds were provided for children. In the Circle in the centre of the estate were shops, a community hall, tennis courts, and a bowling green.

The total rents including rates varied from six shillings to twelve shillings and sixpence a week. Tenants paid a small sum at first and then made weekly contributions until their holding amounted to £200. Of the capital cost to the society a percentage was set aside to build up a sinking fund that would write off the houses in 60 years. Repairs would cost no more than 0.35% as tenants would eventually become their own landlords and thus take care of the properties.

Today, Moor Pool is considered a very good example of a garden suburban development. The whole area is semi-rural with grassed verges, many mature trees and open spaces. The pool is a particularly pleasant feature which attracts many species of wild fowl. The houses reflect the arts and crafts movement in architecture and some are of a particularly enterprising design. For example, the flats in Ravensbourne Road, the two storied terraced dwelling houses where the upper ones are reached by balcony bridges supported on steelwork, listed Grade II are especially interesting.[28] The ideal of co-ownership has never been realized and from the 1970s tenants have been allowed to buy their houses while still retaining shares in the company. Moor Pool was designated as a Conservation Area in 1970.[29] The Circle, an asymmetrical composition, which contains the Public Hall and Club of eight bays and of brick and roughcast with tiled roof, encompasses

Moor Pool Estate houses

Moor Pool Estate, tennis court and rear of shops in the Circle

the shops, offices and bowling green and is listed Grade II as is the Harborne Estates Office.

In 1902, he designed a house in Rotton Park Road for himself along with another twelve houses.[30] Numbers 24 and 26, a pair of brick, three storey, semi-detached houses are among these houses, none very exciting. In 1907, he designed 17, Farquhar Road for himself. This is a listed house in roughcast with a tiled roof in a restrained Arts & Crafts style. A striking house with an unusual double gabled porch, battered buttress and low eaves and partly of two storeys and partly of two with attic; it has four bays with casement windows and leaded lights.[31] A similar house for Mr E. Cheshire must be by him at number 84, Westfield Road. Number 86, Westfield Road was designed by him for G. Martin in 1909 in brick with some timber decoration and a vernacular type of porch.

Frederick died in 1917 at his home in Abbey Cottage, Abbey Road, Harborne from a perforating gastric ulcer, at the early age of fifty seven years, having had peritonitis in 1914. He never entered public life but carried out an excellent practice and was highly esteemed by his profession and by a large circle of private and commercial friends. He was thrust into architectural business life when his

17 Farquhar Road, Edgbaston, 1907

father's talented partner died and he rose to the challenge. He became one of Birmingham's most successful practitioners in the use of terracotta. His Telephone Exchange building is considered by many to be the most successful terracotta building designed by a Birmingham architect. His dedication to the research of what was required enabled him to produce hospitals of the most modern design and the Children's Hospital was one of the most up to date in the country. His enterprising designs on the Moorpool Estate, resulted in pioneer work in town planning and social planning. After the First World War, his son Cyril Martin, entered into partnership with his uncle, Herbert Martin and W. H. Ward. The firm still continues under the name of Martin, Ward and Keeling.

List of Architectural Works of Martin and Chamberlain after 1884, and Martin and Martin, including the Work of Frederick Martin

Frederick Martin (1859–1917) was educated at London University and in 1883 became a partner in the practice of his father, William Martin after the death of J. H. Chamberlain, as did his younger brother, Herbert. In 1901 the practice became Martin and Martin after William Martin's death. After Frederick Martin's death in 1917, his son Cyril Martin joined his Uncle as a partner together with W. H. Ward, the younger.

BUILDINGS IN BIRMINGHAM AND ITS ENVIRONS

PUBLIC

1885 Ada Street Board School, Small Heath for Birmingham School Board (henceforward BSB)

1885 Stratford Road Board School, Sparkbrook for BSB (listed Grade 2*)

1885 Cowper Street Board School, Newtown Row for BSB [D]

1887 Barford Road Board School, Rotton Park for BSB

1888 Upper Highgate Street Board School for BSB [D]

1888 Soho Road Board School, Hockley for BSB (listed Grade II)

1888 Alterations to King Edward's Elementary Girl's School, Gem St for Gem Street (Girls' Free Order) Board School for BSB

1888 St John the Evangelist Church, Sparkhill

1888 Water tower for Victoria Park, Small Heath

1889 Oakley Road Board School, Small Heath for BSB [D except house]

1890 Alterations to factory for Branch School of Art, Vittoria St; 1900 addition of schoolroom

1890 Camden Street Board School, Spring Hill for BSB; 1899 additions [D]

1891–93 Spring Hill Free Library, Icknield St for Birmingham Corporation

1891 Tilton Road Board School, Small Heath for BSB (listed Grade II)

1891 Burbury Street Board School for BSB [D]

1891 Floodgate Street Board School for BSB (listed Grade II)

1892 Waverley Road Higher Grade Board School, Small Heath for BSB (listed Grade II*)

1894 Small Heath Free Library and Public Baths, Green Lane, Small Heath.

1894 Somerville Road Board School, Small Heath for BSB

1895 City Road Board School, Summerfield for BSB

1896 Dennis Road Board School, Balsall Heath for BSB

1896–1905 Hollymoor Mental Hospital for Birmingham Corporation

1898 Yardley Road Board School, Small Heath for BSB

1899 Addition of workshop, Little Green Lane Board School for BSB; 1900 addition of cloakroom and classroom

1899 Alterations and additions to Children's Hospital, Steelhouse Lane

1899 Additions to Nelson Street Board School for BSB

1899 Additions to Icknield Street Board School for BSB

1899 Additions to Lower Windsor Street Board School for BSB

1899 Additions to Broad Street Children's Hospital for Hospital Committee; 1904 additions

1899 Addition of workshop, Summer Lane Board School for BSB

1900 Bordesley Green Board School, Bordesley Green Rd for BSB

1900 Fox Street School for Deaf Children, Gem St for BSB

1900 Station Road Board School, Harborne for BSB

1900 Addition of classroom, Tindale Street Board School, Balsall Heath for BSB

1900 Addition of schoolroom and cloakroom, Oakley Road Board School for BSB

1900 Addition of schoolmaster's room and cloakroom, Summer Lane Board School for BSB

1900 New baths and engineer's house, Green Lane, Bordesley for Birmingham Parks & Baths Dept.

1900 Conway Road Board School, Sparkbrook for BSB

1901 Alum Rock Road Board School for BSB [D]

1901 Additions and Alterations to George Dixon Higher Grade School, Oozells St for BSB

1901 Additions to Dartmouth Street Board School for BSB

1901 Additions to Farm Street Board School for BSB

1901 Addition of latrines, Foundry Road Board School, Winson Green for BSB

1901 Additions to Rea Street South School, Deritend for BSB

1901 Additions to Cowper Street Board School, Newtown Row for BSB

1901 Additions to Lower Windsor Street Board School, Duddeston for BSB

1901 Additions to Highfield Road Board School for Aston School Board

1901 Handsworth New Road Council School for BSB

1902 Station Road Board School, Harborne for BSB

1902 Bordesley Green Board School, for BSB

1903 Additions to Lower Tower Street School, Aston for Rev. J. G. Faulkner

1903 Additions of w.c.s etc. to Domestic Mission, Fazeley St

1903 Alterations to Godon Boys Home, Deritend

1905 Addition to Women's Hospital, Upper Priory for Hospital Committee

1905 Rugby School, Elkington St

1907 Addition of gymnasium and drainage, Edgbaston High School for Girls, 25 Hagley Rd, Edgbaston

1907 Nurses Home, Summer Hill for Birmingham & District Nursing Society

1907 Women's Hospital, Showell Green Lane, Sparkhill; 1913 additions [D]

1913 Hospital for Children, Ladywood Rd; 1914 additions

1913 Alterations to Birmingham and Midland Hospital, Corporation St

1914 Extensions to General Hospital, Steelhouse Lane

COMMERCIAL

1889 Shop, offices and warehouse, Broad St/Gas St

1890–93 Extensions to the rear of the Grand Hotel, Colmore Row.

1896 Offices and exchange for National Telephone Co., 17–19 [56] Newhall St

1899 Fleet Street Stores for National Telephone Co.

1903 Additional storey, 104–106 Colmore Row for Martin & Martin

1905 Re-building of Vales Restaurant, Broad St for E. Cutler

1908 Alterations for W. H. Bowater, Needless Alley

1914 Shop for Harborne Tenants Ltd, The Circle, Moor Pool, Harborne

INDUSTRIAL

1889 Additions to printing works, Needless Alley

1889 Factory and warehouse for Southall Bros. and Barclay, Dalton St; 1902 alterations and additions

1890 Additions to bottling store and additional stable for Mackie and Gladstone, Dale End

1890–92 Longbridge Pumping Station

1890 Selly Oak Electricity Sub Station, Bristol Rd

1890 Addition of Hydraulic Supply Stores, Dalton St for Birmingham Corporation Waterworks

1890 Stabling and mess room for Small Arms Co., Golden Hillock Rd, Small Heath

1899 Shopping for Brampton Bros Oliver Street; 1905 extensions; 1906 extensions; 1909 alterations; 1914 shopping

1900 Additions and alterations for Hadley & Shorthouse, Eyre St

1900 Chimney stack for Rotton Park St Refuse Collection Depot for Health Comm. City Council; 1902 Destructor and stabling etc.

1902 Additions to Mirror Laundry Co., Park Hill Rd

1902 Additions for Southall Bros & Barclay, Alum Rock Rd; 1903 additions

1905 Extension for Deakin and Francis, Regent Place

1905 Shopping, for Brampton Bros, Aston Brook St

1906 Shopping for Birmingham Aluminium Co., Cambridge St

1906 Rebuilding, Digbeth 11 for Tramway Co.

1906 Rebuilding, Digbeth 108 for Tramway Co.

1906 Alterations for Cheshire Brewery Royal Exchange Park Rd, Hockley

1907 Factory for Southall Bros and Co., Alum Park Rd

1907 Shopping for Brampton Bros, Chester St

1908 Factory for E. Cutler, Sheepcote St

1908 Alterations for Speedwell Gearcase Co., Broad St

1910 Alterations and additions Kyott's Lake Rd for Tramway Dept.

1912 Additions Whitmore St for Birmingham Tramways Dept.

1914 Shopping for Brampton Bros, Bloomsbury St

1914 Alterations for Southall Bros & Barclay, Dalton St

1914 Motor garage, for the Mirror Laundries Co., Formans Rd

1914 Alterations for Southall Bros & Barclay, Dale End

DOMESTIC

1886 Addition of conservatory and glasshouses, Whetstone, Somerset Rd for George Kenrick

1886 Additions to 50 Wellington Rd, Edgbaston

1888 Alterations to Kelton, Church Rd, Edgbaston for Thomas Gladstone

1889 22 Artisans dwelling houses, Gem St and Lawrence St for Improvement Committee

1890 Addition of battery room and coach house, Penrhyn, Somerset Rd, Edgbaston for Herbert Chamberlain

1890 Alterations to Hallfield, Priory Rd, Edgbaston for Edward Nettlefold

1901 Alterations and additions, to Harborne Hall, Harborne for Edward Nettlefold

1902 Twelve houses, Rotton Park Rd, Edgbaston

1902 House, Rotton Park Rd, Edgbaston for Frederick Martin

1903 House, Portland Rd, Edgbaston for R. W. Crosskey

1905 House, [?] 84, Westfield Rd, Edgbaston for E. Cheshire

1906 Alterations and additions, 188, Hagley Rd, Edgbaston for F. I. L. Houghton

1906 Alterations to house Mansel Rd, Bordesley Green for Mrs Hastings

1906 Additions to Metchley House, Somerset Rd, Edgbaston for W. B. Kenrick; 1919 additions

1906 House, 86, Westfield Rd, Edgbaston for F. W. Ryland

1907 New Road, Park Hill Rd, Harborne for Harborne Tenants Ltd

1907 House, 17, Farquhar Rd, Edgbaston for F. W. Martin

1908 Alterations to Westmere, Edgbaston Park Rd, Edgbaston for W. Tangye

1909 House Woodbourne Rd, Edgbaston for H. Martin

1909 Housing estate for Harborne Tenants Ltd, Moor Pool, Harborne

1909 Alterations to house, 14, Woodbourne Rd, Edgbaston for E. Beale [D]

1910 Alterations to house, Somerset Rd, Edgbaston for Mr Beale

1912 Alterations to house, Edgbaston Park Rd, Edgbaston for Mr Brampton

1912 Additions to house, Ampton Rd, Edgbaston for A. Wood

1913 Motor house, Wentworth Gate, Harborne for Harborne Tenants

1913 Residence, Blackwell, Barnt Green for Thomas Barclay

NOTES

1 The author is grateful to David Low for the use of his notes on Frederick Martin.

2 Obituary in *Birmingham Post*, 9 July 1917; *The Builder*, 119, 30 September 1920, p. 248; RIBA *Journal*, 27, August 1920, p. 459; *Who's Who in Architecture* (1911).

3 Birmingham Central Library, Archives and Heritage Services (hereafter BCL AHS), *Birmingham Institutions*, Papers from the Philosophical Society of Birmingham.

4 *Catalogue* of Exhibition 'Martin Ward and Keeling Structural Architects' (Birmingham, 1982).

5 Francis W. Greenacre, *Martin & Chamberlain and the Birmingham Board Schools* (unpublished pamphlet, Victorian Society, Birmingham Group 1968), p. 4.

6 BCL AHS, Birmingham Building Register, Planning Applications nos 4227, 12 August 1884; 8139, 13 July 1891; 9694, 31 August 1893; 13929, 9 May 1898 for Stratford Road Board School.

7 Greenacre, *Martin & Chamberlain*, pp. 5–6.

8 *Ibid*, p. 4.

9 *Ibid*, p. 5.

10 Dept. of Environment, *List of Buildings of Special Architectural or Historic Interest: Birmingham*. Grade II listed schools by the partnership in 1880–90 are Cooksey Road and Newlands Centre and Regent Park Annexe; Also Garrison Lane Nursery School Bordesley and Master's House.

11 BCL AHS, Birmingham Building Register, planning application no. 8758. 10 June 1892, for Library and Green Lane Baths.

12 Douglas Hickman, *Warwickshire* (1979), p. 65.

13 BCL AHS, Birmingham City Council Committee, Free Libraries, Minutes, 1893, p. 169.

14 Birmingham City Council Planning Department, *Report to the Conservation Area Advisory Committee*, 1974.

15 *Birmingham Post*, 20 January 1979.

16 Victorian Society Birmingham file, unpublished letter from West Midlands County Council County Planning Department, 25 March 1982.

17 Nikolaus Pevsner and Alexandra Wedgwood, *Buildings of England: Warwickshire* (Harmondsworth, 1966), p. 195.

18 *The Builder*, 73, 16 October 1897, p. 307; 13 November 1897, p. 403; 20 November 1897, p.422; *The Builder*, 74, 15 January 1898, p. 57; 12 March 1898, p. 258; 16 April 1898, p. 370; 7 May 1898, p. 441; BCL, AHS, BCC Sites and Buildings Committee, Lunatic Asylums Visitors Report, May 1898.

19 Fay Crofts, *History of Hollymoor Hospital* (Warwick 1988).

20 *The Builder*, 89, 30 September 1905, p. 348; BCL AHS, Birmingham Building Register., app. no. 24611, 12 August 1913 additions to Women's Hospital.

21 £21,000 was collected by readers of the *Birmingham Mail* as reported in the paper on 4 June 1910.

22 The foregoing sections on the Children's Hospital are based on the following: BCL AHS, BCC Hospital Management Committee Minute Books 1905–1918, 14 Sept 1907, 8 January 1912; BCC Sites and Buildings Committee Minute Books, 1907–1918 *passim*; *The Builder*, 94, 7 March 1908, p. 285; *The Builder*, 99, 8 October 1910, p. 406; *Building News* 105, 29 August 1913, p. 296; *The Builder*, 106, 9 January 1914, p. 53; BCL AHS, Birmingham Building Register, app. no. 25948, 28 July 1914; *Birmingham Daily Post*, 21 December 1917; BCL AHS LF 56.1 Sandra Squires, 'Building History 1, King Edward VII Memorial Children's Hospital' (unpublished, 1994).

23 Andy Foster, *Pevsner Architectural Guides: Birmingham* (New Haven and London, 2005), pp. 98–99.

24 Victorian Society Birmingham file, Minutes of a meeting to discuss threatened buildings, July 1975.

25 Foster, *Birmingham*, pp. 130–31.

26 *Birmingham Post*, 26 November 1979.

27 BCL AHS, Birmingham Building Register, app. no. 18492, 5 April 1905; John Cattell, Sheila Ely and Barry Jones, *The Birmingham Jewellery Quarter* (Swindon, 2002), pp. 172–73.

28 *Birmingham Daily Post*, 28 October 1907.

[29] Pevsner and Wedgwood, *Warwickshire*, p. 186.

[30] *Birmingham Weekly Post*, 2 November 1907 picture of Mrs Nettlefold with spade digging the first sod, *Birmingham Daily Post* 26 April 1908, first house opened; BCL AHS Harborne Tenants' Ltd *Rules* (Birmingham, 1908); BCL AHS *Harborne Tenants' Prospectus* (Birmingham, 1908); BCL AHS Birmingham Building Register, app. no. 20875A, 22 May 1909 and app. no. 24107, 29 March 1913; BCL AHS *Chairman's Address at the Annual General Meeting Harborne Tenants* 23 March 1911; BCL AHS *An address delivered by Mr A. J. Leeson at a meeting of the Birmingham and District Trade and Property Association*, 27 July 1911 and press correspondence 6 January 1912; R. Hudson, P Atkins, T. Demidowicz, *City Villages* (Birmingham City Council Conservation Department, unpublished paper, n.d.).

[31] BCL AHS, Birmingham Building Register, app. no. 16835, 1 May 1902 and app. no. 16964, 15 July 1902.

[32] BCL AHS, Birmingham Building Register, app. no. 19629, 1 March 1907.

Part Four · The Arts and Crafts Movement

17 W. H. Bidlake

TREVOR MITCHELL

William Henry Bidlake (1861–1938) was praised in his lifetime as the 'Man Who Rebuilt Birmingham'.[1] He is regarded as the city's leading Arts and Crafts architect, his work securing national and international recognition.[2] His path into architecture, however, was not straightforward, for although his father and grandfather had both been architects, Bidlake had been intended for a career in the India-rubber trade in Leicester, supplying the Midlands' bicycle industry.[3] It was by his own efforts and skills that he was to forge a distinguished career in Birmingham's architectural, educational and philanthropic communities.

He was born on 12 May 1861 in Wolverhampton, where his father George (1830–92) had built a busy practice designing chapels, town halls, workhouses and schools in Staffordshire and the Welsh Borders. George, the son of an architect, Thomas Bidlake, had been born in London, where he served articles and attended the Royal Academy Schools, winning RIBA Silver Medals for measured drawing and design.[4] He quickly applied his skills to good effect: in the 1850s alone he won at least seven competitions with an early partner, Lovatt.[5] He married Mary Bates, from Leicester, and had four children, of whom William was the eldest, and the only son.[6] In 1865 he published a volume of his chapel designs, which demonstrates a prolific and inventive mind, ability as a draughtsman and an interest in self-publicity.[7] William certainly inherited from his father the latter two attributes, but not so his practice, because in 1872 George retired, passing his business on to Tom Fleeming (1848/9–1935), his last partner, and the family moved to a country house near Leicester.[8]

William remained behind in Wolverhampton, attending Tettenhall College, in

W. H. Bidlake

buildings designed by his father, where he showed an early artistic ability.[9] In 1878 he entered Christ's College, Cambridge, where he read natural sciences, graduating in 1882.[10] In his own account of his studies he stressed their relevance to architecture, claiming to have studied 'physics, chemistry, geology and botany as bearing on the science of building construction and the nature of materials'.[11] He spent part of his university vacations with a Leicester architect, James Tait (1834/5–1915), whose office he entered in January 1882.[12] However, Bidlake's provincial beginnings were brief: as the Cambridge-educated son of a prosperous retired architect, he soon went to London to learn from the work of men with national reputations.

Some time in 1882, Bidlake went to work as an assistant to Colonel Robert W. Edis (1839–1927).[13] Edis was an early and noted exponent of the Queen Anne style, designing houses, flats, shops and hotels from the 1870s. His practice was popular with members of fashionable society, including the royal family.[14] In June 1883 Bidlake gained a place at the Royal Academy Architectural School.[15] The School was run by Richard Phené Spiers (1838–1916), an acknowledged draughtsman and an enthusiastic architectural historian. His work was frequently exhibited in the annual Royal Academy Exhibitions, and he wrote many articles for national periodicals.[16] His achievements may have provided a model for Bidlake, whose career was to be characterised by similar interests in drawing and architectural history. Classes were held on three evenings each week, supervised by three visiting academicians. In the years 1883 to 1886 this role was often taken by Richard Norman Shaw (1831–1912), G. F. Bodley (1827–1907) and Alfred Waterhouse (1830–1905).[17]

At the Academy School Bidlake struck up friendships with fellow students such as E. Guy Dawber (1862–1938) and F. W. Troup (1859–1941). Dawber became a keen explorer of regional vernacular traditions, publishing studies of the farmhouses and cottages of Kent, Sussex and the Cotswolds, where he opened an office in 1890. A member of the Art Workers' Guild, he was successful on both sides of the profession, serving as president of the RIBA and being made a Royal Academician.[18] Troup became an active member of the Art Workers' Guild, designing its premises.[19] In 1884 Bidlake was joined at the School by his cousin, Arnold Bidlake Mitchell (1864–1944), who was also to become a nationally recognised Arts and Crafts architect.[20]

It is not clear how long Bidlake spent at the Academy; he appears not to have progressed to the Upper School.[21] He may have preferred the classes offered by the Architectural Association, which he joined in 1883.[22] He played an active part in this student-organised body, serving on its Sketch Book Committee and Main Committee, alongside such figures as W. A. Pite (1860–1949), brother of A. Beresford Pite (1861–1934) and Leonard Stokes (1858–1925).[23] As president of the Association, Stokes worked to modernise its teaching programme. He later served as president of the RIBA and was a member of the Art Workers' Guild.[24]

In addition to daytime work and evening classes, Bidlake found time to enter several national student competitions. In March 1883 he was placed second in the RIBA's Silver Medal Competition for measured drawings of St Mary's Church, Leicester. A reviewer for *The Builder* thought his work 'truly artistic in touch and feeling', and suggested that it merited first prize.[25] The following year his drawings of St Margaret's Church and the Old Town Hall in Leicester were published in the *Architectural Association Sketch Book*, the first of many inclusions. He was represented in each of the next seven annual volumes, winning prizes in 1887 and 1888.[26]

In 1884 Bidlake won third place in the AA Travelling Studentship Competition, with drawings of the Chapter-House at Southwell Minster which were among the entries 'most commended' by *The Builder*.[27] The next year he won the prestigious Pugin Prize, with drawings of Prior Crauden's Chapel at The Deanery, Ely.[28] The prize, of fifty pounds, was for travelling expenses incurred on a trip to study Gothic architecture. Bidlake envisaged a three-month tour of the cathedrals and churches of the East Midlands and East Anglia, commencing at the end of May 1885. The highlight of his tour was Lincoln, where his response to the vitality of the carved decoration of the Minster echoed the ideas of Ruskin as set out in his *Lamp of Life*.[29] Drawings of Lincoln provided the first of many successful submissions to the Royal Academy Summer Exhibition.[30]

In the event, however, he cut short his trip in order to start work for Bodley and Garner. There Bidlake 'found himself in his real element – becoming immersed in the various phases of Gothic architecture at home and abroad, more particularly in the 14th century English manner'.[31] The office was busy preparing a design for the first Liverpool Cathedral competition and Bidlake played a large part in the preparation of the drawings, working with Leonard Stokes.[32] His time there coincided with work to the cathedrals of York, Ely and Lincoln, the design of St Mary's Church, Clumber and the construction of Hewell Grange, Tardebigge, near Bromsgrove.[33]

Bodley was a follower of Pugin and especially of Ruskin, using their principles as a basis for an architecture characterised by its unity of expression and its restraint. He regarded the architecture of the past as a model for contemporary design because of its harmony with nature and its expression of the life of its makers and users. He believed that new work should follow vernacular traditions 'not only in the use of local material, but in designing in the local manner, and in harmony with surrounding buildings'. Rejecting eclecticism, he argued for a restrained and organised architecture governed by a pursuit of purity and subtlety that he called 'Refinement', ordering all aspects of design: 'the whole building, in its lines and mass, should have the same expression, one rather of reserve and power controlled than of any ostentation or display'.[34] He promoted the applied arts, founding his own firm of decorators, Watts and Co. Bodley passed these ideals on to Bidlake and his generation through his teaching and his buildings, and their influence can be seen in Bidlake's ecclesiastical and domestic work.

The end of Bidlake's year with Bodley and Garner was marked by recognition of his abilities as a designer, when in 1886 his design for a town church won third place and a Medal of Merit in the RIBA's Soane Medallion Competition. His true ability was perhaps not fully expressed in his entry: *The Builder* noted that he had 'produced a design which shows certainly more knowledge and, probably, more power, than any of the others. We should much like to have seen what he could have done with more time and care'.[35] The reviewer for The *British Architect* was 'disappointed with the design', but thought it 'needless to say that the drawings are excellent and show more than ordinary skill'.[36] Bidlake was to have plenty of time to develop his design skills: he was to wait five years for his first commission for a new church. But before beginning his independent career he rounded off his education with a tour through France and Italy.[37]

During his time working in London, Bidlake proved himself to be a very able student. His draughtsmanship was recognised through success in competitions and publication; his knowledge of English Gothic work was demonstrated through the Pugin Studentship and his creativity found favour in the Soane Medallion Competition. In two of London's principal offices he experienced the latest developments in contemporary design. He mixed with many able fellow-students, a gifted generation which pursued wide interests in traditional craft skills and the applied arts as part of an expanded concept of their role. Some went on to have distinguished careers as designers, teachers and leaders of the profession. Thus it was that although Bidlake returned to the Midlands at the end of his training, his personal and professional connections were to give him continued links with national ideas and personalities.

On completion of his studies Bidlake set up in practice in Birmingham. By December 1886, when he applied for membership of the Birmingham Architectural Association, he had opened an office at 24 Waterloo Street, a central location popular with other architects.[38] His business was slow to develop: there is no evidence for any commissions done in his name before October 1888.[39] He presumably found some work assisting others by 'taking in washing'.[40] In the spring of 1887 he spent three months in the Edinburgh office of Dr R. Rowand Anderson (1834–1921), where he worked with Troup on an unsuccessful competition design for the Imperial Institute, London, making the published perspective.[41] He also did work for Stokes, providing perspective views of St Clare's Church, Sefton Park, Liverpool which were shown in the Royal Academy Summer Exhibition in 1889 and 1890.[42] In January 1888 he was elected an Associate of the RIBA, following examination, but this did not result in any immediate improvement to his prospects.[43]

However, Bidlake was not idle, but entered quickly into professional and cultural life. In London he supplemented his success at the Royal Academy with talks to the Architectural Association, that on dry rot being so popular as to merit its publication.[44] In Birmingham he joined several bodies, giving papers to the Archaeological Section of the Birmingham and Midland Institute and becoming an associate of the Birmingham Society of Artists.[45] He thereby established a presence nationally and locally which can only have assisted the favourable reception of his architectural skills.

Within months of joining the BAA he had become a committee member and its librarian. He was to serve on the committee almost continuously until 1918. He gave papers to the General Meeting and took on additional responsibilities such as the organisation of the annual social event, the 'conversazione'. He probably arranged a trip in 1889–90 to see houses by Col. Edis and by Ernest George and Peto, and also one to visit churches by Bodley and Garner. He also joined the annual sketching trips, which in the 1890s focused on the vernacular buildings of the Cotswolds, Shropshire and Oxfordshire. But it was educational work which was to be Bidlake's greatest contribution to the Association and arguably to architecture in Birmingham. In 1888 he was appointed as visiting lecturer to its course in the history of architecture. When architectural education in the city was reorganised in 1892 he became Special Lecturer in Architectural History and Design in Building at the School of Art. He was to teach architecture students in Birmingham until 1925.[46]

It is far from clear how Bidlake supported himself in these early years. That he found things difficult may be judged from remarks in a talk he gave in 1891 to the Architectural Association:

To the architect who has started in practice with few friends and less capital there comes a pinch which tests his fibre. It is just then that he is tempted to work 'for charity' and on approval in the hopes of getting a connexion, and there will never be wanting those who will take advantage of his embarrassment. ... Being hard up is really such a dangerous state for a man to be in, that I do not think the law ought to allow it.[47]

Early financial problems and difficulties encountered in his first commissions may have prompted Bidlake to make a fundamental change in his working arrangements. For by February 1889 he had left his first office for another a few doors away, belonging to John Cotton (1844–1934), an established architect with a moderately-sized business designing churches, schools and houses.[48] Cotton had worked with George Bidlake and James Tait, but had also spent time in London with W. E. Nesfield (1835–88) and Alfred Waterhouse. It would seem that Cotton handed over his practice to Bidlake in 1889 owing to ill health, but stayed on until 1891 to supervise work in hand.[49] In this way Bidlake acquired an established business, and was given the start that he needed.

Two commissions soon came through one of Cotton's clients.[50] St Alphege's Schoolhouse, Solihull (1891), was a rather ordinary piece of work based on Cotton's Gothic Revival school designs. However, it led quickly to a substantial job to

Church of St Oswald, Small Heath, watercolour by Bidlake from *The Architect*, vol. 46, 1891. *Courtesy of Birmingham Central Library*

design St Oswald's Church at Small Heath, Birmingham (1891). The design bor-
rows external features from St Alban's, Bordesley (1879–81), by J. L. Pearson
(1817–97). Inside, the arcades are a development from Cotton's St Chrysostom's,
Winson Green (1887–88). The guiding spirit of Bodley can also be seen in window
tracery and in the handling of decorative detail. The building displays a confident
use of fashionable forms, a concern for the colour and texture of materials and
thoughtful control in the form and location of decorative detail. Bidlake successfully submitted a watercolour of his design to the Royal Academy exhibition of
1891, which was published in *The Architect*.[51]

His next major commission came through his involvement in two philanthropic organisations, the Birmingham Kyrle Society and the Birmingham Guild
of Handicraft. He had become a member of the former by 1890 and was actively
involved in developing its evening craft classes into the new Guild founded in the
same year.[52] In 1892 Bidlake designed the new Kyrle Hall, Sheep Street, Gosta
Green, to house the complementary work of the two groups. Something of the
romantic medievalism of the guild movements of the period was reflected in the
design, with a jettied, half-timbered upper floor bisected by a polygonal brick

Kyrle Hall, Sheep Street, Gosta
Green. Photograph *c.* 1892,
*courtesy of Birmingham Archives
and Heritage Services*

tower. This rather hard-edged composition was softened by carefully-chosen brickwork and leaded glazing, but to judge from contemporary illustrations it did not display the Arts and Crafts sensitivities of later works.[53]

Bidlake was appointed to the Society's Council for 1893–94 and served as vice-president 1894–95.[54] The president was C. E. Mathews, a solicitor whose interest in architecture and craftwork is reflected in his employment in 1893 of W. R. Lethaby (1857–1931), a founder of the Art Workers' Guild and disciple of Philip Webb (1831–1915), to design his home, The Hurst, on the Four Oaks Estate.[55] During the same period Bidlake served as honorary director of the Guild, overseeing its establishment as a limited company.[56] He also served as vice-president of the BAA and taught architectural design and history at the School of Art. Thus by the end of 1895 Bidlake had extensive commitments in the areas of architectural and craft education and a position in the public life of the city.

In a similar burgeoning of his private practice, the following five years found Bidlake at his most productive and creative. Between 1895 and 1901 he won about thirty commissions. Chief among these were ten suburban and rural houses and two churches, which, by virtue of the widespread coverage and favourable criticism that they received, are responsible for Bidlake's reputation as a designer. This key phase began with a family collaboration to build houses at Four Oaks, near Sutton Coldfield.

Sutton Coldfield was a popular destination for Birmingham's city dwellers, with a reputation as a holiday resort and a healthy town, aided by its proximity to a large expanse of public open space, Sutton Park. The Four Oaks Estate, on the edge of the park, had been the home of the Hartopp family until 1879, when the construction of a railway line divided it from the park and it was sold and laid out as a racecourse. In 1881, its first year of operation, the racecourse hosted the Grand National, but the venture failed and in 1891 it was purchased by the Marquis of Clanrickarde and laid out for residential development.

Only fifteen minutes from Birmingham by train, the estate proved popular with the city's professional and business classes.[57] Its large plots, with mature landscape and immediate access to the countryside of Sutton Park, provided ideal sites for the small country houses, 'of moderate size designed for the enjoyment of wealth in retirement', that became the characteristic housing type around the turn of the century and the typical product of the Arts and Crafts architects of the period.[58] The German critic Hermann Muthesius, who made a study of English domestic architecture at this time, identified a set of distinctive features of such houses: they had three reception rooms and a hall, a long, low appearance due to all reception and service rooms being placed on the ground floor and they were often articulated as a principal block with a smaller wing.

Muthesius began his account of this new trend in domestic architecture with reviews of the work of Lethaby and Ernest Newton (1856–1922), former assistants of Norman Shaw and founders of the Art Workers' Guild.[59] Both designed homes for the Four Oaks Estate. It was perhaps through his acquaintance with C. E. Mathews, Lethaby's client, that Bidlake came to know of the Estate and Lethaby's design for it, one of the first houses there. It may therefore have been at Bidlake's instigation that his brother-in-law, a Leicester solicitor, acquired some plots at Four Oaks and employed Bidlake to design houses for them.

Thus Bidlake's first design for Four Oaks, The Dene, Bracebridge Road (1895), was built as a speculation.[60] In its architectural language it does not yet display Bidlake's mature style: the demands of ready saleability may have dictated the use of fashionable tile-hanging and timber-framing, the Old English vocabulary of Norman Shaw. Its use was probably inspired by a recently completed house nearby, The Leasowes, 107 Lichfield Road, by Newton, with which it shares several features.[61] However, in its planning and composition The Dene provided a model for subsequent houses. He employed two blocks – one containing drawing room and study, and the other dining room and kitchen – arranged about a connecting dwelling hall and subsidiary stairwell. This pattern was used with little alteration in houses such as Nuthurst, Hockley Heath (1896) and Withens, Four Oaks (1898). It was also adapted by the addition of a service yard for two larger houses, Garth House, Edgbaston (1900), and Redcroft, Four Oaks (1901).

The Dene also served as a template for the composition of later houses. The plan is articulated as a principal range with horizontal emphasis, contrasting with

The Dene, 2 Bracebridge Road, Four Oaks, 1895, garden front

the verticality of a gabled end bay. This vertical component usually mirrors the side and rear gabled bays of The Dene by presenting near-blind elevations. Tall chimneys are also used to provide vertical accents. Designs usually include lozenge or star-shaped examples in imitation of Elizabethan precedent, but these decorative forms are used in combination with sturdy rectangular stacks, perhaps to suggest a chronological sequence or functional hierarchy.

Bidlake's second design for the Four Oaks Estate, produced in 1896, was Woodgate, a home for his mother and himself, his father having died in 1892.[62] Here he first employed a coherent architectural vocabulary derived from the forms and materials of the sixteenth-century Midlands' vernacular. He combined good quality two-inch brickwork with stone dressings, tall stone-capped gables with kneelers under steeply-pitched roofs, prominent chimneys and mullioned windows. Wilderhope Manor, Shropshire and Beckley Park, Oxfordshire have both been identified as possible historical sources for its detailing.[63] This palette was to be used with the planning and compositional devices found in The Dene to create a successful formula for his future domestic output. He used it again at Ridgewood, Almondbury, Gloucestershire (1900); at Redcroft (1901); The Knoll, Leicester (1905) and The Hurst, Moseley (1908). Judged against the eclecticism of

Woodgate, 37 Hartropp Road, Four Oaks of 1896, Bidlake's own house. Photograph of entrance front, from *The Studio*, vol 3, 1902

The Hurst, 6 Amesbury Road, Moseley, 1908

Newton's Leasowes and even the expressive variety of Lethaby's The Hurst, the external appearance of these houses is restrained and homogenous. This effect is achieved at the risk of a lifeless historicism. If Bidlake's output had been large then this might have been the result. Happily, each house bears the signs of individual and detailed consideration, and is enlivened by hand-crafted decoration and bespoke fittings.

While the vocabulary of Woodgate draws on vernacular sources, Bidlake looked to the work of contemporaries for its composition and planning. Its low embracing roof, ribbon windows, catslide dormer and projecting porch can be seen in the same relationship in the entrance front of Walnut Tree Farm, Castlemorton, Worcestershire, by C. F. A. Voysey (1857–1941), published in 1890.[64] Lethaby's The Hurst, occupying a plot adjacent to Woodgate, provided a model for the paired two-storey bays of the garden front and the subtle symmetry of the hall, while Voysey's room-and-a-corridor plan provided a convincing model for both Woodgate and The Hurst. Another source for the composition of Woodgate may be Inglewood, 32 Ratcliffe Road, Knighton, Leicester (1892), an early design by Ernest Gimson (1864–1920), probably also influenced by Walnut Tree Farm. The design was exhibited at the 1893 Arts and Crafts Exhibition, but Bidlake could also have known it from his connections in Leicester.[65]

Woodgate, photograph of dining room inglenook from *The Studio*, vol. 3, 1902. *Courtesy of Birmingham Central Library*

The intimacy of the low roof and small leaded casements at Woodgate is enhanced inside by use of timber framing, oak beams and inglenooks. The inglenook was a favourite feature, most commonly found in the drawing room, but Bidlake contrived to include three in his own home. The house conveys his notion of Hospitality, through a romantic interpretation of late-medieval features that is not to be found in Voysey's plain interiors, or in Lethaby's free use of eighteenth-century window forms and symmetry.[66] But Bidlake was not immune to the classical elements present in The Hurst. He introduced a degree of symmetry into the hall and the garden front at Woodgate, and played with the use of partial symmetry in subsequent designs, such as Withens, to emphasise the central role of the hall.[67] However, while he praised Georgian house design for its 'restraint and quiet dignity', this appreciation did not lead Bidlake into the Neo-Georgian revival led by figures such as Newton and adopted locally by C. E. Bateman (1863–1947).[68]

In all, Bidlake designed five homes on the Four Oaks Estate. Most of his small country houses received some publicity through publication or exhibition. But it is arguably Garth House, Edgbaston, designed in 1900, that received most attention and has most helped to shape current perceptions of his domestic work. It belongs with the preceding houses because its plan is a development of The

Dene's and its external massing depends on the same mixture of vernacular elements used at Woodgate. But it stands apart from them because its historical references are overlaid with a contemporary aesthetic, reflecting more closely the concerns of those who, unlike Bidlake, were searching for a new style.

Garth House was Bidlake's largest domestic commission to date, built for Ralph Heaton the director of the Birmingham Mint.[69] This is not reflected in additional reception rooms, but rather in their increased size, a greater degree of richness in their decoration and in the addition of a service court. It is perhaps the size of the house more than any other factor which is responsible for the individual qualities of the design. The larger rooms require larger windows and generate a greater external envelope. This gives emphasis to Bidlake's characteristic panels of blind wall, and reduces the frequency with which features punctuate the elevations. This creates an impression of solidity and calm, greatly enhanced by the uncharacteristic introduction of large areas of white-painted pebble-dash render to the first floor and gables.

The idea may have been to introduce a strong horizontal element like the tile-hanging at The Dene or the low eaves of Woodgate. Bidlake had proposed a

Woodgate, garden front, 1896

Garth House, Edgbaston Park Road, Edgbaston, 1900, photograph of entrance front from *The Studio*, vol. 3, 1902. *Courtesy of Birmingham Central Library*

Garth House, garden front

similar upper storey of rough-cast in an unexecuted design for Kyrle Hall in 1891 and had used it for a terrace of houses and shops in 1898.[70] The use of render had been popularised by Voysey, and H. T. Buckland (1869–1951) had built for himself a completely rough-cast house at Edgbaston in 1899.[71] It provides a coherence that brings simplicity to the design and a strong horizontal emphasis. The use of white-painted timber window frames also departs from Bidlake's preferred vocabulary of stone mullions.

The interior of Garth House also sets it apart from other works. The status of the hall reaches its highest level, being equal in size to the reception rooms and having a shallow barrel-vaulted ceiling. Extensive use is made of white-painted woodwork in the manner of Voysey, including raised-and-fielded timber panelling, novel in form but suggesting early eighteenth-century precedent. The drawing room contains a plaster frieze in a vine motif, again finished in white. The absence of oak panelling and expressed timber beams, combined with the larger dimensions of the rooms and the disposition of spaces about the axis of the hall, create a light, ordered environment. Although the medievalising features of hall and inglenook are once more employed, they have been stripped of overt historical references.

Garth House, photograph of the hall from *The Studio*, vol. 3, 1902. *Courtesy of Birmingham Central Library*

This tranquil interior is achieved without the loss of decorative work that illustrates the craft ideal and reflects the taste and wealth of the client. The house is enriched with decorative metalwork, lustre tiles to fireplaces, moulded plaster-work, decorative glazing to the porch and, now lost, figurative stained glass to the staircase window. These represent hand-crafted work by independent, creative minds, and invest the house with a variety of treatment and greater individuality. This was an important objective for Bidlake, who felt that no single architect could reproduce the 'freshness and variety' of a team of craftsmen builders.[72] At the same time, following Bodley, he sought a unified treatment which brought overall 'Harmony'. Seeking a sense of 'Repose' for the occupants, he condemned the 'self-assertive and blatant "special feature" of an architect's misguided originality' as 'an indescribable evil', and felt that 'some of the copper twists and curls that circle round the fireplace ... can be nothing but torture to a sensitive man'.[73]

Arts and Crafts fittings of a similar quality are also found at Woodgate, Withens, Redcroft and in later houses, their extent presumably dictated by the availability of funds. They are found in greatest profusion at The Knoll, Bidlake's largest house: the client's brother-in-law was George Bankart (1866–1929) a specialist in plasterwork and lead casting who worked with Gimson, before mov-ing to Birmingham in about 1900 to work with The Bromsgrove Guild.[74] His work almost certainly appears at The Knoll and he was probably responsible for similar plasterwork in other houses.

Garth House was singled out as an exemplar by Muthesius. It influenced his assessment that Bidlake had 'found a very independent, novel interpretation', especially in his interiors. More generally, he noted Bidlake's use of 'the plainest of brick walls' and 'broad sweeping masses for the roofs'. He praised his houses at Four Oaks as being among the best on the estate:

They are immediately recognisable from their very simple style and the great honesty that they express ... inside as well as outside everything is extremely natural. Yet although his means are of the simplest, he manages to create interiors of great intimacy.[75]

The novelty of Garth House was not to be repeated in later houses. Its breadth of treatment is absent from Redcroft, Four Oaks, designed in the following year, although it is very similar in plan and in the choice and arrangement of eleva-tional features.[76] Redcroft is only slightly smaller, but this is emphasised by smaller, stone-mullioned windows, reduced storey heights and the lowering of the eaves to the entrance front in emulation of Woodgate, its neighbour. A tall corner gable echoes Garth House, but its scale and articulation point to the influence of the Cotswold vernacular, which Bidlake had been sketching in 1899. Inside, oak panelling and beamed ceilings mark a return to tradition that places Garth House on its own. The requirements of a wealthy and informed client may have directed Bidlake towards a fresh, contemporary expression. Once there, he may have

Redcroft, 22 Ladywood Road, Four Oaks, 1901, from Herman Muthesius, *Das Englische Haus*, 1904

considered that the innovation identified by Muthesius was too close to being the mark of an assertive architect, a distraction from the repose and harmony that he sought.

In his approach to domestic design Bidlake reflected his training and interests, demonstrating a consistent rather than a developing view, allied firmly to the vernacular tradition as interpreted by Philip Webb (1831–1915) and followers such as Lethaby. He believed that the adoption of traditional rules of house building generated good design, and argued that in the past 'the house ... was the simple and direct outcome of those rules applied to the wants of the owner and to the limitations of the site and local materials'.[77] But this rational justification was clouded by a romantic vision which acknowledged the 'associations of ideas, and reminiscences' that historical references brought to design.[78] Bidlake sought the comfort and emotional well-being of the occupants and believed that the associational and symbolic value of traditional elements could bring to his designs 'that simple, solid and homely character that we associate with old English life'.[79]

Individual expression could be channelled into the modification of traditional forms to modern requirements, and through the introduction of hand-crafted fixtures and fittings. Art Nouveau demonstrated to his satisfaction that any striving after originality outside accepted traditions was likely to result in the loss of the essential quality of 'reticence'.[80] The house was for Bidlake a place of physical safety and emotional nurture. He sought a familiar expression of home life rather than a new one and wished to re-establish links to an untroubled, hospitable past.

The development of Bidlake's approach to the design of churches followed a similar trajectory to that for his domestic work and ran parallel to it. The completion of Woodgate at the end of 1897 coincided with the start of work on St Patrick's Church, Earlswood, a small, aisleless church replacing a chapel of the 1840s. But there is no hint of the nostalgia which characterises his home. Instead there is a surprisingly modern, direct expression of structure which breaks from the conventionality of St Oswald's, completed four years before. The result placed Bidlake at the forefront of church design and provided the model for his treatment of St Agatha's Church, the building which secured his reputation as one of the leading ecclesiastical architects of his generation.

The plain but carefully considered brick exterior of St Patrick's could be mistaken for the chapel it replaced, but conceals a glorious interior space of great clarity, brought alive by the fluidity of its surfaces and contrasts of lighting and dynamic decoration. The nave is brimming with light: its walls of buff brickwork perhaps follow Cotton's use of this material at nearby St Thomas's, Hockley Heath (1879). They are expressed as alternating triangular piers and windows, with the angled faces of the piers running as splayed reveals into the windows. The front facet of each pier runs up to support the decorated timber ribs of the tunnel-vaulted roof. The ribs sit on deeply carved, gilded stone corbels, which seethe with life as alternating human heads and vegetative forms, the hair of the former imitating the fronds of the latter, both sweeping backwards and upwards.

The chancel is much darker and is set unusually high, being reached by a flight of eight steps which fan out into the nave. The east wall is divided into three planes, the outer two angled. Set beneath the east window is the low, arched opening of the small apsidal sanctuary, a low, vaulted space. Lancets to either side throw a raking light across the altar. The high east window and the dimly-lit recess of the sanctuary below form the visual and liturgical focal points of the building. The angled wall-piers catch raking light and lead the eye eastwards in a rhythm of reflected daylight. This fluidity of movement is reinforced by the absence of stops, capitals or corbels within the height of the walls.

This use of angled planes creates a crisp, sophisticated homogeneity, which conforms well to the contemporary search for a simplified Gothic ordered by system and unity, articulated by contemporary writers such as J. T. Micklethwaite.[81] While St Oswald's shows an interest in surfaces and uses splayed reveals, it does not point to this rapid development of a direct, geometrical expression of structure. Contemporary precedents for the use of angled planes can be found in

Church of St Patrick, Earlswood, 1897, interior. *Photo: D. S.*

Stokes' St Clare's, Sefton Park and his design for a church at Miles Platting.[82] They were also used by C. H. M. Mileham (1837–1917) at St Augustine's, Highgate, London (1882), praised by Bidlake for its spatial qualities.[83] But it is the rich and dynamic schemes of decoration which provide a clue to a new progressive influence on Bidlake's thinking. The beautifully-carved corbels to the nave and chancel, and the painting of the roofs and wallplates, suggest a commitment to the integration of luscious decorative arts found in the work of J. D. Sedding (1838–91) and his successor Henry Wilson (1864–1934). Sedding was the subject of a lecture given to the BAA in February 1897.[84] This connection is strengthened by the design of the west end of St Agatha's, his most renowned church.

   In the Spring of 1898 a competition was held to design a new church at Sparkbrook, to replace the recently-demolished city centre churches of St Peter and Christ Church.[85] The assessor, Sir Arthur Blomfield (1829–99), chose Bidlake's design over entries from national and local figures and work began on St Agatha's

Church in the following year.[86] The site was relatively small and built-up, so the design focuses external incident on the road front, with a soaring tower flanked by porches. Behind is a six-bay nave, with aisles widened to the east to accommodate the projected congregation of one thousand.[87] The chancel of three narrower bays terminates in a sanctuary with canted sides which form reveals to the east window. A square chapel sits between the chancel and the south aisle, with an organ loft above, while an open passage runs along the north side of the chancel, connecting with vestries to the east.

In his previous church commissions Bidlake had been prevented by budget and circumstance from building a tower, but his design for St Agatha's was of such quality and power that its construction was assured. He made free use of the Perpendicular tradition, as refined by Bodley, but also took inspiration from the work of his contemporaries. Its corners are defined by clasping octagonal turrets, cleanly expressed without buttressing. These rise above an open stonework parapet to end in open lanterns. The detailing calls to mind the towers which flank Sedding's Holy Trinity, Sloane Street, London (1888), while elements of the general composition recall the tower which Wilson added to Sedding's St Clement's Church, Bournemouth (1893). There are also similarities with Stokes' designs for Sefton and Miles Platting. The octagonal motif is repeated in piers which frame the porch doorways to either side. The porches give access to the tower, an arrangement suggested by Micklethwaite, so that the body of the church is first viewed through the soaring tower arch.[88]

The principal impressions gained from the interior of St Agatha's are of height, light and fluid space. These are developed from the materials, geometry and decorative schemes employed at St Patrick's. The vertical emphasis of the wall piers at St Patrick's is developed through the novel design of the polygonal arcade piers. The long sides of these meet at an acute angle in front of the wall face, to create a leading edge which rises to the clerestory arches which support the wall plate. The plane of the wall varies against the constant face of these shafts. The nave walls can thus be read as double-height arcades of narrow brickwork piers, with the clerestory bays and the intermediary stone aisle arcades set within. This was a device which he was to use in later commissions. The arcaded and clerestoried chancel is treated as a continuation of the nave, with the same sense of light and volume.

This clarity and uniformity of structure is not obscured by an overlay of decoration, which is confined to two horizontal bands at the two levels of arcading. The uppermost is enlivened by corbels deeply carved with writhing naturalistic foliage that seems to grow from the front edge of the wall shafts. But the lower arcade is more subtly treated, the piers having no capitals. Instead the spandrels are plastered to offer surfaces for decoration, although none is evident. This gives more emphasis to the sinuous, wave-like soffit-moulding of the arches themselves, of Hollington stone, which die into the broad, canted sides of the

Church of St Agatha,
Stratford road, Sparkbrook,
1899–1901

piers. In contrast, the hood-moulds above run horizontally into the leading edges
of the piers, proud of the wall plane, leading the eye from bay to bay.

If St Agatha's presents a development of ideas first employed at St Patrick's, it
also makes clear the debt which both buildings owe to Stokes. A comparison of
the plans and arcade treatments of St Agatha's and St Clare's reveals several similarities, but also highlights the sophistication of Bidlake's design, carefully built up
from a few geometric elements and principles so that the place and purpose of
each can be seen in isolation and as a part of the whole. In Stokes' work this structural clarity appears static and lifeless, while Bidlake has achieved this crispness of
structure without any sacrifice of lively, organic detailing. The rich decoration,
used in restricted, concentrated form, exhibits a directional force which gives life
to the structural grid.

The church was dedicated in July 1901, almost certainly too late to have been
seen in its finished state by Muthesius before the completion of his survey of
English church building of the same year.[89] Yet Bidlake was included there in a list
of 'outstanding English architects' active in modern Anglican church-building in
the Gothic tradition.[90] This international recognition was confirmed at a national

Church of St Agatha, nave arcade

level with the exhibition of a watercolour perspective of the west front at the Royal Academy.[91]

The completion of St Agatha's Church found Bidlake at the top of the local profession. It confirmed his abilities as a church designer, and would be followed before the close of the decade with a further six new places of worship. In the domestic field he had worked steadily in the production of substantial detached houses to a standard which in 1902 was to earn him a monograph in the international arts magazine *The Studio*.[92] His continuing contribution to the artistic and educational life of the city had been marked in 1898 with a commission to build a new Branch School of Art in Balsall Heath, a rare foray into the commercial Baroque language of Shaw.[93]

Among his peers, Bidlake's standing was reflected by his election to the presidency of the BAA in 1899, for three years rather than for the customary two. This was perhaps the busiest point of his career, and yet his dedication to the

OPPOSITE   Bishop Latimer Memorial Church, Handsworth New Road, Winson Green, 1902

Association was such that he missed only one meeting.[94] It is perhaps a measure of his national standing and wide-ranging connections that these years saw a particularly impressive list of speakers who addressed the Association. The subjects covered give an idea of contemporary interests: the study of vernacular buildings and craftwork traditions were the principal topics. Thus Guy Dawber spoke on 'The Cotswold Country', while Arnold Mitchell spoke on 'The Study of English Church Architecture'. George Bankart spoke on 'Old Plasterwork' and Francis Troup gave a talk on 'Ornamental Lead and Lead Casting'.[95] Bidlake's commitment to craftwork found expression, when at his suggestion the BAA became the first professional architectural body to admit craftsmen as associate members.[96]

Bidlake's career was increasingly dominated by church work up to 1914. In the designs that followed St Agatha's, mirroring the pattern of his domestic work, he never again achieved the same freedom from historical precedent or the same combination of structural clarity and expressive, concentrated ornamentation. His next major commission, the Bishop Latimer Memorial Church, Winson Green (1902), is disappointing. It has something of the character of an East Anglian wool church, and conventional detailing masks any expression of structure. Only in the chancel arch do the angled planes of his previous work show themselves. Nevertheless, in 1906 Bidlake's standing as a church designer was reflected in his appointment to the influential committee of honorary consulting architects which advised the Incorporated Church Building Society on the grants it made towards the building and repair of Anglican churches. The committee met monthly and advised on the designs that were submitted for funding. Senior members included Bodley, Shaw and Mileham.[97]

The years 1906–09 were particularly active, and he was helped by an assistant, Alan Brace.[98] He built new parish churches at Wylde Green (1905) and Handsworth (1907), which show a closer relationship to St Agatha's, and added the tower to St Mary's, Wythall (1908). Bidlake also submitted a design for Winnipeg Cathedral.[99] This was not successful, but something of the ambition and quality of his ideas may have found their way into the magnificent lierne-vaulted interior of Handsworth Cemetery Chapel (1908), where structural expression and decoration achieve complete integration, albeit in a historical vocabulary.

By 1910 work had come to an end on most of his church commissions and Bidlake seems to have had relatively few jobs. In 1911 he suffered the death of his mother, who had lived with him at Four Oaks, and for that year and the following there are few recorded commissions.[100] In 1913 he entered a competition for a new church to be dedicated to St Germain, for a site in Edgbaston. Charles Bateman (1863–1947) was the competition assessor and gave the prize to Edwin Reynolds (1875–1949) for a Romanesque design.[101] Reynolds was fourteen years younger than Bidlake, and had been his assistant during the busy years of 1896–1900.[102] A new generation of architects was at work in the city, many taught by Bidlake. But the debt that they owed to their teacher did not prevent them from competing with him for work.

The outbreak of the First World War brought a cessation in construction work, and Bidlake's practice, already reduced, never recovered from the building cost inflation that followed. After the war he designed a small number of memorials, mainly for old clients, but built relatively little otherwise. He put his efforts into assistance for returning servicemen, by reviving the city's architectural course, succeeding J. L. Ball (1852–1933) as Director of the School of Architecture from 1919–22.[103]

Although Bidlake's skills had been widely acknowledged in the years around the turn of the century, he did not apply for fellowship of the RIBA until 1920.[104] He had been elected to the Institute's Council in 1901 and 1904, on both occasions topping the poll, and had served on the Art Standing Committee for 1909–11. He was thus known by those who were active in the Institute, serving alongside contemporaries from his London days, such as Stokes, Dawber and Beresford Pite, as well as older members like Bodley and Spiers.[105] His application was supported by the president of the Institute, J. W. Simpson (1858–1933), and by Dawber, who commented that 'it is quite unnecessary for me to say anything about his qualifications for Fellowship, as his work is well known and admired by all architects'. Dawber knew many of his buildings, and had 'the highest admiration of his professional knowledge and skill', praising his 'artistic powers' and his 'beautiful draughtsmanship'.[106] Bidlake's delay in securing fellowship (Bateman had been granted fellowship in 1898) suggests a reticence concerning his architectural abilities, or a pride in his professional background. Fellowship, unlike Associate membership, could be awarded to those without qualifications. The scarcity of work after the War may have prompted him to obtain this sign of recognition.

Bidlake's retirement from active practice and from teaching was marked by a move away from Birmingham. In 1923 he found a site near Tunbridge Wells where he could 'indulge to the full in his hobby of landscape gardening'.[107] There he built Vespers, complete with inglenooks and timber framing, the house in which he was to spend the rest of his life, not alone, in monastic contemplation, but with a new wife and her three young children, for in March 1924 he married a recently-divorced actress, Gertrude Emma Prendré (1888–1978).[108] Bateman remarked that Bidlake had a 'naturally retiring disposition' caused by deafness, and was 'increasingly elusive'.[109] Perhaps some of the elusiveness may have reflected a desire to avoid comment on his marriage from those who had known him in his bachelor days.

In retirement he continued to find some work in Birmingham and in 1927 he took on a partner, Walter John Knight.[110] His enthusiasm for architecture remained sufficiently keen for him to submit drawings to the competition for Guildford Cathedral in 1930.[111] His last complete ecclesiastical commission came as late as 1932, when he re-used his arcade from St Andrew's Handsworth as a model for Sparkhill Congregational Church.[112] He retained an office in Birmingham until 1930, when on resigning from the BAA he was elected an honorary member. The Association declared itself pleased that by this means it would not 'lose touch entirely with one who, more than anyone else, has been responsible for Architectural Education in Birmingham'.[113]

It is for two buildings, St Agatha's Church and Garth House, rather than for his teaching, that Bidlake is now chiefly remembered. However, his career was far richer and more complex. Architecture was his passion and helping others his delight. Working with little assistance he created many buildings which were selected by others as exemplars for national and international audiences. He maintained a role as lecturer and officer in the country's principal architectural bodies, as well as in Birmingham. He was also an accomplished artist, an active promoter of craftwork and an influential and dedicated teacher. He thus stands alongside the best Arts and Crafts architects of his generation, sharing with them the same broad conception of the range of interests and skills appropriate to their profession. Like most of them also, he explored the possibilities of a new style, but was bound in reverence to the past. Bidlake believed that 'the traditional is no doubt the survival of the fittest' and considered it a mark of good design that 'the traditional has been brought up to date. And what, indeed,' he remarked, 'is all progress but that?'[114]

List of Architectural Works of William Henry Bidlake (1861–1938)

William Henry Bidlake read natural sciences at the University of Cambridge. He entered the office of James Tait of Leicester in 1882 but soon entered the office of Robert Edis of London and also studied at the Royal Academy Architectural School and the Architectural Association. In 1885 he spent a year in the office of Bodley and Garner of London. He set up practice in Birmingham in 1886 and in 1889 took over the practice of John Cotton who continued in the firm until 1891. On retirement in 1923 Bidlake left Birmingham but continued working and in 1927 took on a partner Walter John Knight.

His work up to 1936 has been included in the list.

WORK IN BIRMINGHAM AND ITS ENVIRONS

PUBLIC

1889 Seating plan for Rev. P. E. Wilson, St Crysostom's Church, Park Rd, Hockley, with Cotton

1890 Cottage Hospital for Bromsgrove Hospital Committee, New Rd, Bromsgrove, Worcs., with Cotton

1890 Decoration for Rev. F. H. Weston, St Nicholas's Church, Lower Tower St, with Cotton

1891 School for Canon Charles Evans, St Alphege's Boys' School, Mill Lane, Solihull [D]

1891 Chancel and four bays of nave for Rev. Hubert Sands, St Oswald's Church, St Oswald's Rd, Small Heath; 1899 west front, two nave bays and south-east porch

1891 Renovation for Rev. W. Laporte Payne, All Saints' Church, All Saints' St, Hockley

1892 The Kyrle Hall and Workshops for The Birmingham Kyrle Society, Sheep St, Gosta Green [D]

1894 Repair and redecoration for Rev. J. P. Gardiner, Bishop Ryder Memorial Church, Gem St, Gosta Green [D]

1895 New west front and redecoration for Rev. G. H. Cameron, St Stephen's Church, St Stephen's St, Aston New Town [D]; 1905 mission room for Rev. J. T. Jones; 1906 rebuilding behind west front for Rev. T. S. Dennison

1896 Additions to School for Rev. W. Laporte Payne, All Saints' Schools, All Saints' St, Hockley

1898 Vestry for Rev. W. C. R Bedford, Holy Trinity Church, Trinity Hill, Sutton Coldfield

1898 New Church for Trustees of the Birmingham Churches Fund, St Agatha's Church, Statford Rd, Sparkbrook; 1905 mission room for Rev. G. C. Vecqueray, St Agatha's Church

1898 Branch School of Art for City Museum and School of Art Committee, Moseley Rd, Balsall Heath; 1913 Latrines

1902 New Church for anonymous donor (Pauline Boulton), Bishop Latimer Memorial Church, Handsworth New Rd, Winson Green; 1909 altar table and organ case; 1927 reredos with Knight

1905 West front and four nave bays, Emmanuel Church, Birmingham Rd, Wylde Green, Sutton Coldfield; 1925 eastern nave bay and Chancel

1905 Restoration to Crypt Chapel for Rev. T. B. H Brooks, St Alphege's Church, Solihull and mission room; 1931 Repairs to tower with Knight

1906 Mission Hall for Rev. J. S. Thirtle, for Bishop Latimer Memorial Church, Beeton Rd, Winson Green

1907 New Church for Rev. A. E. Burn and Rev. S. J. Selwyn, Saint Andrew's Church, Oxhill Rd, Handsworth; 1909 reredos with panels by Fred Davis

1908 Cemetery Chapel and Keeper's Lodge for Handsworth Urban District Council, Camp Lane, Handsworth; 1909 Gardener's cottage

1911 Parish Room for Rev. H. Sands, St Oswald's Rd, Small Heath

1912 Redecoration for Rev. D. Card, St Edward's Church, New John Street West, Aston New Town, with Bernard Sleigh

?1914 Porch and vestry, All Saint's Church, Gravelly Hill

1919 War Memorial Cross, The Square, Solihull

1920 Additions to club house, St Stephen's Club House, New Town Row, Aston New Town

1926 Restoration of roof for Rev. Canon E. L. Cochrane, St Edburgha's Church, Yardley

1932 Church and Sunday Schools for Rev. J. Bolton Petts, Sparkhill Congregational Church and Sunday Schools, Stratford Rd, Sparkhill

COMMERCIAL

1895 Alterations for Carter and Carter, accountants, 34 Waterloo St

1895 Additions for Birmingham Coffee Tavern Company, The Coffee House, Winson Green Rd, Winson Green

1900 Extension to premises for Mirror Laundries Ltd, Park Hill Rd, Harborne

1902 Offices and warehouse for Keep Brothers, Great Charles St [D]

INDUSTRIAL

1896 Workshops for Thomas Vann, rear of Arthur Rd, Hay Mills; 1897 extensions

1897 Additions to premises for David Worrall, Garrison Lane, Bordesley

DOMESTIC

1888 Two villas for Edward Cullen, Stratford Rd, Yardley

1894 Cottage for W. J. Day, Park Hill Rd, Harborne

1895 House for Frank Winterton, The Dene, 2 Bracebridge Rd, Four Oaks, Sutton Coldfield

1896 House for W. H. Bidlake, Woodgate, 37 Hartopp Rd, Four Oaks, Sutton Coldfield

1896 Additions for H. F. Keep, The Grange, Highfield Rd, Edgbaston, further additions 1904, 1908, 1918 and 1927.

1896 Additions to house for T. F. Walker, Ashfield, 120 Hagley Rd, Edgbaston

1897 House for F. Winterton, Woodside, 51 Bracebridge Rd, Four Oaks, Sutton Coldfield; 1908 motor house

1897 House for Thomas Vann, Jubilee House, Coventry Rd, Hay Mills [D]

1898 Seven terraced houses, bakery and shop for Little Bromwich Estate Company (Frank Winterton), Green Lane/Fourth Avenue, Little Bromwich [D]

1898 House for John C. Shannon, Withens, 17 Barker Rd, Four Oaks, Sutton Coldfield

1898 House for Rev. Hubert Sands, St Oswald's Vicarage, 18 Dora Rd, Small Heath

1900 House for Canon C. B. Wilcox, St Agatha's Vicarage, 100 Sampson Rd, Sparkbrook

1900 House for Ralph Heaton, Garth House, 47 Edgbaston Park Rd, Edgbaston; 1901 Stables

1901 House for H. J. Yates, Redcroft [St Winnow], 22 Ladywood Rd, Four Oaks, Sutton Coldfield; 1905 motor house and stables

1902 Additions to house for T. S. Stewart-Smith, 38 Westfield Rd, Edgbaston

1903 Alterations to house for Russell Jolly, 1 Ampton Rd, Edgbaston

1904 Additions to house for Rev. J. S. Thirtle, 146 Handsworth New Rd, Winson Green

1906 Seven terraced houses for Rev. J. S. Thirtle, Handsworth New Rd, Winson Green

1906 Additions to house for Dr Arthur Foxwell, Northfield Grange, Bristol Rd South, Northfield [D]

1907 Conversion of three terrace houses to form Vicarage for Canon Frederick McKenzie, St Anne's Vicarage, 84 Cato St, Duddeston [D]

1908 House for A. J. Bowen, The Hurst, 6 Amesbury Rd, Moseley

1910 Extensions to house for Miss G. Smith, 13 Highfield Rd, Edgbaston

1912 House for Rev. David Card, St Edward's Vicarage, New John St West, Aston New Town [D]

1912 Additions to house for Joel Cadbury, Tudor Hill House, Tudor Hill, Sutton Coldfield

1913 House for Dr John Jameson Evans, St Clears, 79 Farquar Rd, Edgbaston; 1919 extension to bedroom

1919 Additions to house for Dr James A. H. White, 186 Monument Rd, Edgbaston

1920 Semi-detached houses for William Wilkinson Ltd, 7 and 7a Endwood Court Rd, Handsworth Wood

1922 House for James A. Lee, Welwyn, Birmingham Rd, Wylde Green, Sutton Coldfield

1936 Two houses for Harry Keep, East House and West House, 85 and 87 Harborne Rd, Edgbaston

WORK OUTSIDE BIRMINGHAM

PUBLIC

1889 Additions including apse for Rev. Hugh Sherrard, St Thomas's Church, Market St, Stourbridge, Staffs, with Cotton; 1891 Memorial Screen for Robert Broomhall

post 1892 Tomb Chest for Bidlake Family, Grave of George Bidlake, St Peter's Churchyard, Broadstairs, Kent

1897 New nave, chancel and vestry for Rev. G. W. Barnard, St Patrick's Church, Salter St, Earlswood

1901 New nave, chancel and north porch for Rev. J. G. Trotter, St Leonard's Church, Dordon, Warks

c. 1902 Triptych, Madresfield Court Chapel, Worcs., with C. M. Gere

1905 Restoration of tower and spire for Rev. T. E. Hamer, St Lawrence's Church, Church St, Darlaston, Staffs; 1907 screens to chapels; 1913 redecoration

1907 Restoration of tower and chancel for Rev. F. T. Bramston, St Peter's Church, Wooton Wawen, Warks.

1908 Tower and vestry for Misses Mynors, St Mary's Church, Chapel Lane, Wythall, Worcs; 1909 Holy table, reredos, chancel screen, clergy desks and choir stalls, reredos by Fred Davis; 1913 organ case, nave furnishings, West Gallery for Florence Mynors

1908 Re-seating and repairs for Rev. A. H. Cheshire, St Matthew's Church, Shuttington, Warks.

1909 Roof repairs for Rev. T. W. Downing, Knowle Parish Church; 1913 organ screen; 1914 alteration of altar table; 1920 furnishings, Soldiers' Chapel; 1921 churchyard cross; 1928 pulpit for Edith M. Richards; 1932 restoration of baptistry

1911 Restoration, The Guildhouse, High St, Knowle

1912 Additions, including Meeting Hall, for Frederick Ernest Muntz, The Institute, Stratford Rd, Hockley Heath,

1918 Repairs, St Paul's Church, Blackheath (ICBS)

1919 War Memorial Tablet for Rev. H. Sands, All Saints' Church, Burbage, Wiltshire

1920 Bellcote and War Memorial Tablet for Rev. T. W. Downing, Mission Chapel, Chapel Lane, Chessett's Wood; 1923 Chancel and Vestry

1920 War Memorial Tablet for Rev. T. W. Downing, The Institute, High St, Knowle

1921 War Memorial, Houghton-on-the-Hill, Leics.

1923 Repairs to tower and chancel, pulpit and lectern for Rev. Dudley Westerman Lee, St Mary's Church, Preston-on-Stour, Warks.

1931 Altar and reredos for Harry T. Grant, St Wilfred's Church, Kibworth Beauchamp, Leics.

1932 Screen for the Buszard family, Lady Chapel, St Mary's Church, Lutterworth, Leics.

COMMERCIAL

1914 Offices and engine house for Knowle and District Gas Co. Ltd (F. E. Muntz)

DOMESTIC

1892 Additions to house for Sir Frederick Peel, The Manor House, High St, Hampton-in-Arden, Warks.

1894 Alterations to house for Frank Winterton, Roundhill, Melton Rd, Thurmaston, Leics.

1896 House for Rev. E. P. Gonner, Saint Thomas's Vicarage [Nuthurst], Nuthurst Lane, Hockley Heath

1896 Estate worker's cottage for Rev. T. H. Mynors, Weatheroak Hall, Brockhill Lane, Wythall, Worcs.

1897 House for Thomas Beaven Clark, Meadow Cottage [Monkshaven], Fountain Lane, Sidcot, Winscombe, Avon

1897 House for Dr Christopher Lewis, Packwood Tower, Windmill Lane, Packwood, Hockley Heath

1899 House for Henry Vaughan Clark, Ridgewood, 19 Old Aust Rd, Almondsbury, Glos.

1899 Additions to house for James Booth, Batt's Hill, Warwick Rd, Knowle

1903 Additions and restoration for J. S. Elliot, The Manor House, Dowles, Bewdley, Worcs.

1905 House for William Henry Winterton, The Knoll, Glebe Rd, Oadby, Leics.

1906 Additions to house for F. E. Muntz, Umberslade Park, Hockley Heath

Pre-1920 [post 1912] Additions to house including library, orangery, and entrance for Hon. Richard Strutt, St Catherine's Court, St Catherine's, Avon

1922 Additions to house and garden for Mary Gertrude Bidlake Winterton, Altamont, Westview Rd, Warlingham, Surrey

1923 House for W. H. Bidlake, Vespers [Lorien], Faircrouch Rd, Best Beech, Wadhurst, East Sussex; 1925 additions

1924 House for Amy Mary Callon, Manor Cottage Bungalow, Ravensdale Lane, Wadhurst, East Sussex

1924 Additions to house for Agnes Mary Connolly, Manor Cottage, Faircrouch Lane, Wadhurst, East Sussex

1926 House for Parsonage Fund Committee, The Curate's House, Manor Rd, Dorridge, with Knight

1931 Alterations and repairs to house for Rev. T. W. Downing, St Anne's Cottage, High St, Knowle

1931 House for Dr Charles Jameson Evans, Alvecote, 35 Church Rd, Fleet, Hants

---

NOTES

[1] *Wolverhampton Express and Star* 13 November 1937.

[2] Alastair Service, *Edwardian Architecture: a Handbook to Building Design in Britain 1890–1914* (1977), p. 80.

[3] *Wolverhampton Express and Star* 13 November 1937.

[4] *Birmingham at the Opening of the Twentieth Century: Contemporary Biographies*, ed. by W. T. Pike (Brighton, n. d.), p. 151; *The Builder*, 62, 1892, p. 364.

[5] R. H. Harper, *Victorian Architectural Competitions: an index to British and Irish Architectural Competitions in The Builder, 1843–1900* (1983), p. 189.

[6] *Ex inform* Ben and Jill Pite, great nephew and great niece of W. H. Bidlake, undated letter and family tree.

[7] George Bidlake, *Sketches of Churches designed for the use of Nonconformists* (Wolverhampton, 1865).

[8] *The Builder*, 62, 1892, p. 364.

[9] *Ibid*; *Wolverhampton Express and Star* 13 November 1937; *Journal of the Royal Institute of British Architects* (hereafter JRIBA), 45, 1938, p. 622.

[10] John Pelie, *Biographical Register of Christ's College 1505–1905, and of the Earlier Foundation, God's House, 1448–1505*, 2 vols (Cambridge, 1910), 2, p. 659.

[11] 'Men who build: No. 38, W. H. Bidlake, M. A. of Birmingham', *The Builder's Journal*, 13, 1896, p. 153.

[12] RIBA, British Architectural Library, RIBA Associate Nomination Papers, vol. 10, p. 9.

[13] *Ibid*.

[14] *Macmillan Encyclopaedia of Architects* ed. by A. K. Placezek, 2 vols. (1982), 2, p. 7.

[15] Royal Academy Library M. S. Collection, C/32/402, Register of Students admitted to the Royal Academy Architecture School, January 1876–January 1906, entry No. 199.

[16] A. Stuart Gray, *Edwardian Architecture: a Biographical Dictionary* (Ware, 1988), p. 335.

[17] Royal Academy *Annual Reports* 1883–1886.

[18] Gray, *Edwardian Architecture*, pp. 160–63.

[19] *Ibid*, p. 357.

[20] *The Builder*, 46, 1883, p. 310.

[21] Royal Academy *Register of Students to R. A. Architecture School*, entry No. 199.

[22] Architectural Association Library Archive, AA Brown Books, 1882–83.

[23] *Ibid*, 1885–86, 1886–87.

[24] John Summerson, *The Architectural Association 1847–1947* (1947), p. 21; Gray, *Edwardian Architecture*, pp. 337–42.

[25] *The Builder*, 44, 1883, p. 310.

[26] *Architectural Association Sketch Book*, new series, 4 (1884), sheets 24, 25; *Architectural Association Sketch Book*, (1884–95).

[27] *The Builder*, 46, 1884, p. 816.

[28] Sutton Webster, 'W. H. Bidlake 1861–1938' *Architecture West Midlands*, 26, 1976, p. 17.

[29] RIBA, British Architectural Library, X(079) P70233.5 (4253), W. H. Bidlake, The Pugin Tour, 1885.

[30] A. Graves, *Royal Academy of Art: a Complete Dictionary of Contributors and their Work from its Foundation in 1769 to 1904* (1905), vol. 1, p. 190.

[31] Sutton Webster, *Notes on some building designs of W. H. Bidlake MA, FRBA 1861–1938* (Birmingham, 1985), p. 4; *JRIBA*, 45, 1938, p. 622.

[32] *Ibid*; *Catalogue of the Drawings Collection of RIBA* ed. by M. Richardson (Farnborough, 1976), vol. 5, p. 115.

[33] *Seven Victorian Architects*, ed. by J. Fawcett (1976), p. 97, p. 154.

[34] G. F. Bodley, 'Some Principles and Characteristics of Ancient Architecture and their Application to the Modern Practice of Art', *JRIBA*, 7, 1899–1900, p. 136, p. 133.

[35] *The Builder*, 50, 1886, p. 387, p. 400.

[36] *British Architect*, 25, 1886, p. 218.

[37] RIBA, British Architectural Library, RIBA Fellowship Nomination Papers, no. 41, Candidate's Separate Statement, 22 March 1920.

[38] RIBA Associateship Nomination Papers, vol. 10, p. 9; RIBA West Midlands Regional Office, Birmingham, Birmingham Architectural Association (hereafter BAA), General Minute Book, (1882–89), minute 840.

[39] Birmingham Central Library, Archives and Heritage Services, (henceforth BCL AHS) Yardley Building Register, app. no. 84a, October 1888.

[40] W. H. Bidlake, 'Pitfalls on Commencing Practice', *The Builder*, 61 (1891), 351–53, 365–68, (p. 352).

[41] S. McKinsty, *Rowan Andersen* (Edinburgh, 1991), p. 117. Drawing published in *The Builder*, 53 (1887), pp. 143–45.

[42] Graves, *Royal Academy of Art*, vol. 4, p. 271.

[43] RIBA Nomination Papers.

[44] W. H. Bidlake, *Dry Rot in Timber* (1889).

[45] Birmingham and Midland Institute (Archaeological Section), *Transactions*, 15, 1889, p. 20; *Ibid*, 17 (1891), p. 150; *Birmingham at the Opening of the Twentieth Century*, p. 151.

[46] BAA Committee Minute Book (1882–96), item 522; Letters Book, letter dated 20 September 1889; Report, session 1889–90, p. 13; Report session 1887–88, p. 13; Committee Minute Book (1882–96), minute 659; Green Books.

[47] Bidlake 'Pitfalls' p. 353.

[48] The preface to 'Dry Rot in Timber' is dated February 1889, and gives Bidlake's address as 37 Waterloo Street.

[49] *Bromsgrove, Droitwich and Redditch Weekly*, 14 April 1934.

[50] *Kent Courier*, 29 October 1937.

[51] *The Architect*, 46, 1891, p. 297

[52] Birmingham Kyrle Society, *Tenth Annual Report* (1890), p. 21.

[53] *The Builder*, 72, 1897, p. 161.

[54] Birmingham Kyrle Society, *Thirteenth Annual Report* (1893), p. 3.

[55] Gray, *Edwardian Architecture*, p. 43; Sutton Coldfield Reference Library, Sutton Coldfield Building Register, vol. 1, (1887–94) app. no. 224 (1893).

[56] BCL AHS, 450350 Birmingham Guild of Handicraft, Committee Minutes, 1890–99, p. 101, p. 137.

[57] D. V. Jones, *The Royal Town of Sutton Coldfield, a Commemorative History* (Sutton Coldfield, 1973), p. 96, pp. 86–89, p. 94; Sutton Coldfield Reference Library, QSH97FOU, newspaper cuttings, Four Oaks Estate, 1890–1984, p. 4.

[58] John Summerson, *The Turn of the Century: Architecture in Britain around 1900* (Glasgow, 1976), p. 5.

[59] *The English House*, ed. by D. Sharp (Oxford, 1979), abridged translation of H. Muthesius, *Das Englische Haus* (2nd ed. pub. Berlin, 1908–11) pp. 127–29; pp. 38–39.

[60] Sutton Coldfield Building Register, vol. 2 (1894–98), app. no. 260 (1895).

[61] *Ibid*, vol.1 (1887–94), app. no. 260. Bidlake's next house design, for Nuthurst, done some six months later, employs a much reduced vocabulary similar to that of J. L. Ball's 17–19 Rotton Park Road, Edgbaston, of the same date.

[62] *Ibid*, vol.2 (1894–98) app. no. 508; *The Builder*, 62, 1892, p. 364.

[63] By Alan Crawford and H. V. Wilde respectively.

[64] *British Architect*, 34, 1890, p. 302.

[65] *Arts and Crafts Exhibition Society Catalogue* (1893), entry no. 450.

[66] A. S. Wainwright, 'Birmingham Architect — W. H. Bidlake', *Studio*, 25, 1902, p. 253.

[67] Sutton Coldfield Building Register, vol. 2 (1894–98), app. no. 742.

[68] *The Modern Home: a Book of British Domestic Architecture for Moderate Incomes*, ed. by W. S. Sparrow (1906), p. 18.

[69] BCL AHS, Birmingham Building Register, app. no. 15978 (1901).

[70] Webster, *Notes*, p. 19.

[71] Buckland's house was 21 Yateley Road. *Architectural Review*, 10 (1901), p. 225.

[72] Sparrow, *The Modern Home*, p. 21.

[73] Wainright, 'Birmingham Architect', p. 246.

[74] M. Greensted, *Gimson and the Barnesleys 'Wonderful furniture of a commonplace kind'* (Stroud, 1991), p. 90; Alan Crawford 'The Birmingham Setting' in *By Hammer and Hand: the Arts and Crafts Movement in Birmingham* ed. by Alan Crawford (Birmingham, 1984), pp. 32–33.

[75] Sharp, *The English House*, p. 55.

[76] Sutton Coldfield Building Register, vol. 3, app. no. 1179 (1902).

[77] Wainright, 'Birmingham Architect', p. 245.

[78] Sharp, *The English House*, p. 24.

[79] *Ibid*, p. 13.

[80] *Ibid*, p. 23.

[81] J. T. Micklethwaite, *Modern Parish Churches* (1874).

[82] *Academy Architecture* (1892), p. 15, exhibit no. 1714.

[83] W. H. Bidlake, 'Imagination in Planning' *JRIBA*, I (1894), p. 242.

[84] BAA, Report of the 23rd Session 1896–97, p. 14.

[85] *The Builder*, 74, 1898, p. 203.

[86] *The Builder*, 74, p. 124. Competitors included Mervyn Macartney (1853–1932), Temple Moore (1856–1920) and John Douglas (1829–1911).

[87] *The Builder*, 84, 1903, p. 40.

[88] Micklethwaite, *Modern Parish Churches*, pp. 18–19.

[89] *Saint Agatha's Magazine — Jubilee Souvenir Number, 1901–1951*, p. 57.

[90] H. Muthesius, *Die neuere Kirkliche Baukunt in England* (Berlin, 1901), p. 48.

[91] Graves, *Royal Academy of Art*, vol. 1, pp. 190–91, exhibit no. 1588.

[92] Wainright, 'Birmingham Architect', pp. 245–53.

[93] Birmingham Building Register, app. no. 14578 (1898).

[94] BAA General Minute Book 1896–1909.

[95] BAA Reports, 1898–1901.

[96] BAA General Minute Book 1896–1909, minutes of 27 October 1899; *JRIBA*, 8 (1900–01), pp. 486–87.

[97] Lambeth Palace Library, Incorporated Church Building Society Annual Reports 1900–26.

[98] BAA, *Green Book, Session 1906–07*, p. 10; *BAA Green Book, Session 1909–10*, p. 12.

[99] RIBA Fellowship Nomination Papers.

[100] Webster, *Notes*, p. 6.

[101] *The Builder*, 106 (1914), p. 70.

[102] RIBA Fellowship Nomination Papers, no. 1820.

[103] University of Central England, School of Art Archive, Reports of Birmingham Municipal School of Art, 1920–25, minutes of meeting of May 1921; minutes of meeting of 28 July 1922.

[104] RIBA Fellowship Nomination Papers, no. 1841.

[105] *JRIBA*, 8, (1901), p. 382; 11 (1904), p. 443; 16 (1909), p. 543; 17 (1910), p. 610.

[106] RIBA Fellowship Nomination Papers, no. 1841.

[107] *Kent Courier*, 29 October 1937.

[108] *Ex inform* Sutton Webster, letter of 23 November 1985.

[109] *JRIBA*, 45 (1938), p. 622.

[110] Webster, *Notes*, p. 6.

[111] *Wolverhampton Express and Star*, 13 November 1937.

[112] Birmingham Building Register, app. no. 57035 (1932).

[113] BAA, *Green Book 1030–31*, p. 33.

[114] Sparrow, *The Modern Home*, p. 24.

18 Joseph Lancaster Ball

REMO GRANELLI

Joseph Lancaster Ball (1852–1933) is perhaps one of the two most accomplished designers to have practised architecture in Birmingham, the other being William Henry Bidlake (1861–1938), and certainly the most rigidly disciplined of them all having no room in his spare designs for 'quaintness' and 'ingle nookery' such as in the work of Joseph Crouch. He enjoyed a long professional career, and a successful one, but not one which was highly productive when compared with certain of his contemporaries such as, for instance, Charles Edward Bateman (1863–1947) who was able to design competently and profusely in any style, neither does Ball show the same inquisitive flair, instead he devoted his life to working assiduously creating his own distinctive style and producing highly detailed drawings of a handful of carefully crafted buildings which were constructed at a period in English architecture when detail-design had become of paramount importance. This is particularly true of his early buildings as an inspection of the Handsworth Wesleyan Theological College admirably demonstrates. Yet over a period of some years he was able to free himself from the influence of the Free Classic Style which had gripped architects so voraciously during the eighties and gradually evolved the style which we associate with his best work for which he, no doubt, would wish to be remembered, that is a design philosophy based on the vernacular of the simple early 17th-century yeoman's house, or prosperous farmhouse.

Ball was a small man, 5'5" high and spare in build, with fair straight hair worn short, a sandy moustache and blue eyes. Normally a quiet and serious man inclined to be thoughtful, he was also capable of a good sense of dry humour. Being a competent and knowledgeable person himself he would not suffer fools gladly, and would become impatient with hesitation, and angry with poor school reports, yet, oddly, he did not see any point in his daughters becoming qualified to do a job of work. Although he could be good company, being an excellent conversationalist, he liked to be quiet for long periods with his pipe and books, particularly the Waverley novels which he enjoyed – not surprising for an architect of his period. He was also a tremendous walker with a particular liking for the Criccieth area where he often stayed, and he was an enthusiastic gardener, an interest which apparently absorbed his home hours when he preferred not be involved with office work.

In the main Ball worked alone and did not easily make friends. Other architects and artists rarely visited his home, and he had little to do with the Birmingham

Group of Artists which is strange when, as Director of the School of Architecture, he surely came into contact with the Group at Margaret Street. Among the few young men who were articled to Ball may be mentioned S. N. Cook who later built up a substantial practice in Birmingham.

Joseph Ball was born in Maltby, Yorkshire in 1852 where his father was serving a three-year term as a Wesleyan Minister. The Ball family were of London origin but Joseph spent much of his early life being taken about the country following his father's ministry and when he was old enough he was sent to London in 1877 to serve his articles with the architect William Wilmot Pocock, the designer of Carpenters' Hall, Throgmorton Avenue in London.[1]

In 1879 when in partnership with the Northumberland architect Algernon R. Goddard, Ball was named winner of the competition for the new Handsworth Wesleyan Theological College and this success provided the incentive for Ball's long and successful association with Birmingham, for on the back of this contract he came to the City the following year and opened an office in Paradise Street. With his sister he took accommodation at Regent House, Greenfield Crescent, Harborne. Being practising Methodists the Balls attended the Wesleyan church at South Street in Harborne which had been built in 1868 to the design of the architect Ewan Harper; and it was there that Ball made the acquaintance of Thomas Barnsley, one of the brothers in John Barnsley and Sons, one of the foremost building firms in Birmingham which then operated from Ryland Street. Also present was Thomas's daughter Edith whose friendship with Ball deepened as he visited the Barnsley's at their home, and they married in 1881.

Soon after their marriage Joseph and Edith moved into a detached red brick quasi-Gothic house of the 1870s at 285 Harborne Road, just above Kingscote Road and almost directly opposite the site upon which Ball later built the Bluecoat School Chapel. While living there he added the flat-roofed bay window on the right of the entrance door and, typically Victorian, he studiously ignored the detailing and character of the existing house.

The Wesleyan Theological College at Handsworth was quite a large job for a young architect of twenty-seven – it is interesting to note how competent Victorian architects were, due no doubt to the hands-on training that they received in their offices. The building of the college, won in the competition in 1879, was begun on site in 1880 and was completed the following year, by then Goddard had disappeared from the scene. The college was initially to accommodate 70 students and its design was based on a colligiate 'E' type plan with library, studies and bedrooms, main entrance and headmaster's house forming the main wing on the west front.

Long cross wings project on north and south, and immediately behind the tower is the chapel, now used as a bar room. The entire design is in a muted red-brown brick with dark red and purple diaper work and buff terracotta dressings, setting a standard for all Ball's future work, not in style, Tudor, but in the rigid

Wesleyan Theological College, Friary Road, Handsworth, 1880–81 and 1904. Postcard

discipline which he exercised over massing and proportioning, and the sensitive, understated detailing of the constructional components of his building. An interesting construction feature not common on earlier buildings is the pre-cast terracotta units used to form lintels over window openings. Because terracotta is constructed to take tensile stress Ball broke down his lintel into small interlocking units, each part taking its share of loading from brickwork above but working together as one continuous unit. The carved pitch pine seating in the library by John and Willis, architectural workers of Birmingham, has now gone and the room is used as a badminton court. In the chapel erected in 1932 there is an egg tempera panel of The Annunciation by Yoxley and Whitford after Fra Angelico's work at St Mark's, Florence, while the east window by the same artists, with two lights has been removed to Trinity Methodist College in Rookery Road.

Before moving on to his second large contract, the Princess Alice Orphanage, he built a composition of shops, warehouses and offices at 10 Cherry Street/ 17 Cannon Street[2] using the Free Classic Style by then in favour among younger men since its introduction by Richard Norman Shaw (1831–1912) in the 1870s. The influence of Shaw's Swan House in Chelsea, 1875 can also be seen. Under Ball's controlled hand a quite different collection of elements have been brought together in a well-balanced and satisfactory composition. The building is basically a rectangular box with a stone coped Dutch gable fronting Cherry Street

expressing many of the elements which gave the style the contemporary designation of 'Queen Anne' such as the small gablets to dormer windows, again repeated in moulded brickwork above string courses, and brick pilasters with moulded terminals at head and foot, probably cast at the brickworks although it was not beyond the skill of a good tradesman to cut the bricks on site and then rub the edges to the required shape with a soft stone. The success of the composition lies in Ball's disciplined use of vertical pilasters and horizontal weathering courses which provide a framework within which his openings sit, he was then able to allow himself the luxury of the three oriel windows with swagged panels.

Ball had well established himself in Birmingham by his ability as an architect, and by his adherence to the non-conformist faith, for this element of local society gave him a great deal of professional support as we see by his appointment as architect for the Princess Alice Orphanage in Chester Road at New Oscott, a large contract built over the years from 1881 to 1923. The scheme was designed as a series of buildings, many of domestic scale, around a 'Village Green', and the buildings in which the children lived were designed to resemble private dwelling houses built as bequests became available to the orphanage, so that although the main buildings which form the frontage were built between 1881–83, the houses were built successively up to 1907, and the hospital which is sited to the east of the Green was built in 1923. Three of the houses, and the Lodge, which fronted the main road, were demolished in the late 1960s.

The main frontage comprising the first building stage of Master's house, teaching and administrative area, chapel and first living quarters, illustrate the most comprehensive range of Classical form and detail from the late sixteenth to early eighteenth centuries to be found anywhere in this area. At the south end of the range there is the Master's house in the Queen Anne style of the early eighteenth century with the coved boxed eaves which Ball used extensively in future domestic work. The Flemish style was used for the central clock tower with a high pepper pot roof and fruity Renaissance ornamentation in red terracotta and moulded brickwork, with the intermediate rough cast areas dovetailed into quoined brickwork. The decorative terracotta work that we see is similar in detail to the ornamental brickwork at Cannon Street but is nearer in spirit to mid-17th than 18th-century work. A charmingly scaled and detailed domestic wing brings this impressive exercise in manners to an end providing living accommodation for children and was designed accordingly in the homely vernacular of the late sixteenth and early seventeenth centuries.

In 1884–85 Ball designed and built a complex of red brickwork on the corner of Corporation Street and Lower Priory for the Birmingham Wesleyans, which included a chapel taking up half the area on the first floor while the remaining half

OPPOSITE   The entrance tower, Wesleyan Theological College

Offices and warehouses on the corner of Cannon Street and Cherry Street, 1881

provided space for Sunday School and staircases. The ground floor provided shops and warehouses, entrances and staircases to the chapel and Sunday school.[3] At this stage of his career Ball showed the eclectic taste of all Victorian architects in being influenced not only by traditional construction methods, which were appropriate, but also by design dictums, and like many other designers he changed the historic style according to the building type that he was designing. In

Princess Alice Orphanage, Oscott, 1881–83 and 1905–22. *Courtesy of Birmingham Archives and Heritage Services (WK/02/26)*

this instance chapel and school would be the main consideration therefore an ecclesiastical expression flavoured with influences from the Continent appeared to be in order for this design which can now only be viewed in illustrations since the building was demolished with many other Victorian buildings in the city centre in the sixties.

In the same year, 1885, Ball built the Asbury Memorial Wesleyan Chapel at Holyhead Road, Handsworth, a small and simple building constructed in brown brickwork with stone dressings to windows. It has a rectangular cell with broad nave and narrow aisles and windows placed high above the aisle roof like extended clerestoreys. The nave projects through in to the main entrance front which in this case faces north, and adjacent to the entrance rises the attached bell tower with saddle-back roof.[4]

During his long career as a practitioner, some fifty-three years, Ball often worked for the Wesleyan Congregation in Birmingham, and on one contract he collaborated with Ernest Barnsley who later gained prominence in the Cotswolds. He was the son of E. W. Barnsley who with his father and brothers managed the prominent firm of Birmingham builders. Ernest and his brother Sidney, both architects, moved to the Cotswolds in 1893 with their friend and collaborator Ernest Gimson, and devoted their working lives to the creation of traditional architecture and furniture with great and pleasing attention to detail and with close adherence to the Arts and Crafts Movement which took hold rapidly in the 1890s. But before moving to the Cotswolds Ernest Barnsley twice collaborated with the architect who had married his cousin, Edith. In the first instance, Ball and Barnsley worked together on extensions to the Wesleyan Chapel on the corner of Sandon and Barnsley Roads which Ewan Harper had built in 1882 when he provided a small chapel and classroom with Gothic facades. The small building still exists but adjoining it is the larger building of 1898 by Ball and Barnsley which is the same plan-type as the Asbury Memorial Chapel having a wide nave, central and side aisles, with the main entrance situated on the north side. The north-west tower shows the banded and chequered stone and brickwork made popular by William Butterfield (1814–1900), but the lead covered fleche above is French influenced while the perforated top storey immediately below is reminiscent of northern Italian architecture. The whole is competent without being thrilling, but the tower is pleasing. In 1901 Ball, working alone, added the transepts and chancel to adjoin Harper's earlier chapel.[5]

A little before, in 1887, he built a detached house for his father-in-law, Thomas Barnsley, in Augustus Road.[6] Unfortunately this house was demolished some years ago and nothing remains to give an idea of its appearance. But two years later he built 'Earlsfield', 20 Westfield Road in Edgbaston, for his brother-in-law John Barnsley who was then twenty-eight and a partner in the Barnsley firm, and destined to become a successful business man, his work culminating with a knighthood. The house is a tight classical design of pre-Queen Anne period and symptomatic of Ball's fastidious attention to detail.[7]

It was in the last decade of the century that Ball began to emerge as a domestic architect of the first rank, and this was still the period of great domestic building in England. As has been discussed Ball mainly concentrated during the first ten years of his practice on large contracts and churches, but during the late eighteen-eighties and through the nineties more one-off houses came his way in addition to the speculative housing which he designed for the Barnsley firm. After the house in Westfield Road that he had designed for John Barnsley he had a spate of one-off houses which helped to establish him as a leading Birmingham architect. 'Briarwood' at 17 Twatling Road, in Barnt Green which he designed and built in 1891 is a modern detached house in large red-brown bricks similar to Birmingham Commons, with hard untextured red brick voussoirs at window heads. The style nudges the classical, or perhaps what might be called 19th-century traditional.[8] He then went on a little later, in 1895, to design for the Barnsley firm two tasteful detached houses, Nos 13 and 15 Rotton Park Road in Edgbaston, as a speculative exercise.[9] But in the same year and on the adjoining site he designed a pair of semi-detatched houses, Nos 17 and 19, for himself.[10] The design of these two houses manifest a complete break with the classical influences which had been apparent in his previous work and display a new interest in the vernacular of the

Wesleyan Chapel, Sandon Road, Edgbaston, 1898. The Chapel by the Harpers is on the left

simple early 17th-century yeoman's house. Ball was now feeling the influence of what has been termed the Arts and Crafts Movement advocated by William Morris and activated in architecture by William R. Lethaby whose influence on Ball's generation is amply illustrated by work produced in this country during the 1890s. Ball accepted this updated vernacular style with relief and in Rotton Park Road features of the seventeenth century can be seen such as the coved plastered eaves with over-sailing roof and the gutter supported by wrought iron bearers fixed to the brickwork The roof is simply pitched, with hand-made brown clay tiles and boarded dormer windows. The brickwork, red-brown and hand-made is in two inch modules. This vernacular expression in domestic architecture was used by Ball on several of his future houses including 'The Cottage', Hagley Road in Edgbaston which he designed in 1902 for Mr Phelps.[11] This was an enlarged and detached version of the cottages in Rotton Park Road but with details from source which influenced 'The Hurst' in Hartopp Road at Four Oaks designed by Lethaby in 1893; for example stone-coped gables, decorative brick weather moulds at mid-gable height, and on the rear elevations Ball had included several softly segmental headed windows. The gable was obviously an important element in the design for apart from the heavily moulded weathering course the square headed windows

17, Rotton Park Road,
Edgbaston, 1895, Ball's
own house

have a lintel deep course of tile creasing, and there is a stone lozenge insert high up in the gable. This design must surely be a run-up for Winterbourne which was started the same year.

Lethaby became an important influence in Ball's professional life at this period and the two came to know each other well, perhaps having first met through the Barnsley brothers who were well acquainted personally with Lethaby and were greatly influenced by him after about 1890. Ball and Lethaby came together in 1899 to build the Eagle Insurance Building in Colmore Row, Birmingham which was initially Lethaby's project, although it would be interesting to know how much designing and detailing Ball did on the project apart from most of the building supervision.[12] How they first came together is unsure, it could have been a shared acquaintance with the Barnsley brothers, but we must remember that Lethaby was well known in Birmingham through his visits to the Art College where he lectured students, and to the Birmingham Architectural Association where he delivered lectures to members. However, it was Ball who supervised the construction of the building, one of the few in Birmingham to be statutorily listed Grade I. A five-bay design was used on a tall slim building with triangular and semi-circular stone hoods over-sailing the windows on the third floor just below the chequerboard pattern of the wall above, similar to the detail that had been used by Ball some ten years earlier on the Sandon Road Methodist Chapel. Below the pre-medieval figuring at roof level the following three storeys depict the classical treatment of the eighteenth century with columns dividing the façade into five equal parts as in ancient temples. But the high ground floor is quite different in expression and sheds past references in its central partition. The building's two entrances with hood moulds and mullioned lights above are classical influenced by the Italian Renaissance. However, the building is considered to be an early introduction to the modern movement in architecture, and is highly thought of by such as Pevsner, but it appears to have made no impression on Birmingham architects of the time who continued to follow the arts and crafts trail. At the completion of this contract Lethaby asked Ball to join him as his partner in London, but knowing that his wife would be unhappy away from her family, Ball felt obliged to refuse.

Those years throughout the nineties and the first decade of the twentieth century were prominent in the English domestic scene by virtue of a new building impetus for the wealthy middle class. Winterbourne in Edgbaston Park Road was one of those that led the way being one of the finest houses of its period in the Birmingham area and comparable with any domestic essay by contemporaries such as Bidlake, Bateman and Buckland.

Ball was probably first approached by John Sutton Nettlefold (1866–1930) after an introduction by Charles Edward Mathews who was a friend of Nettlefold's uncle, the statesman, Joseph Chamberlain, and was previously Lethaby's client on the Eagle Insurance Building, so that he well knew Ball's worth. However Ball and Nettlefold came together their collaboration was a fruitful one in which

Former Eagle Star Insurance Building, Colmore Row, 1899–1900

Nettlefold, having adopted Birmingham as his home, was to acquire through Ball the gently sited, small country house which was exactly appropriate for a middle class gentleman aspiring to the landed values of the aristocracy.

His views had the strong support of his formidable wife, Margaret, née Chamberlain, who was John's second cousin, and a niece of the statesman. They were an interesting couple who shared many civic, in addition to aesthetic, interests, and who enjoyed taking cycling holidays together on the continent. When John suffered his last illness she nursed him with devotion at their home, which was by then at Brampton in Oxfordshire. But despite the apparent closeness between them there had always existed a tension, caused perhaps by a seeking for dominance. Margaret was a Chamberlain, and it has been said that they were always right and had the advantage of knowing it. It has also been said that you never argued with a Nettlefold. In the instance of this relationship it was a case of Greek meets Greek. So how did Ball fare between them? It has been suggested that Margaret would have had a lot to say about the planning of her home, but there is little evidence of her interference in the built design, there are, however, some influences of Lethaby's and no doubt she would have had her say in the planning of the domestic offices. However in the overall planning and expression of the house we see only Ball plus Lethaby's influence. It is understood, however, that the gardens were Margaret's special domain, and it must be added that Arts and Crafts architects when they were allowed to design the garden, usually followed the design dictum, of the mid-seventeenth century, whereas the gardens at Winterbourne are relatively informal.

The house designed by Ball for the Nettlefolds at Winterbourne[13] which he began building in 1902, postulates a break with his work of the past while intimating in its plan form the influence of Lethaby's 'The Hurst' of 1893 which was demolished in the 1960s. In this design the architect moves on from his house designs of 1895 to encompass a larger dwelling with the simple design of a gentleman's house of the late seventeenth century. The building shows external façades of brickwork, there is no stonework to be seen, and windows are simple rectangular casements punched into the brickwork and close to the external face. Gables are high and pointed, and roof lines are, unfortunately, wavy along their ridges to simulate age – this does not sound like the fastidious Ball.[14] Within the building there is a very restrained use of ornamentation taking the form of decorative plasterwork to beams and ceiling by Catterson Smith, and the detailing throughout is puritanic. The long, broad, low ceilinged barrel vaulted gallery had a fireplace opposite the bay window and was an integral part of this space reflecting the use of the gallery in Jacobean times. At the foot of the staircase the full length portrait of Margaret was completed in 1904, when she was thirty-three, by John Byam Shaw – an interesting choice when there were locally available artists of the calibre of the Quaker Joseph Southall and other members of the Birmingham Group, many of them excellent portraitists. The wood panelling remains much as it was

Entrance front of Winterbourne, Edgbaston Park Road, Edgbaston, 1902–04. Ball added a stable block in 1906

but some years ago the bookcase had gone and the gallery was so cluttered with large potted plants and unnecessary furniture that what was left of its once fine grandeur was obscured, panelled doors were unnecessarily flushed with plywood, fortunately this 1960s phase has been played out. All family rooms on the ground floor enjoy a south-east aspect and lovely views across a well designed garden. Those rooms comprise dining and drawing rooms, study, billiards room, and morning room, all of which had access to veranda's on the south-east and south-west of the house. Some of the rooms are of commodious proportions with plaster cast decorations on ceiling beams. On the first floor ceiling just above the oak staircase which has a plastered floorwell decorated with horticultural and wild life subjects is a monogrammed plaque with the initials JSN and the date 1904.

When Winterbourne was completed in 1904 it brought Ball a great deal of publicity being published in the *Architectural Review* and later in *Country Life*.[15] The recognition of his work in addition to his professional relationship with a prominent architect/educator such as Lethaby raised his already sound position in the local architectural hierarchy, and although being late in becoming involved with the office of the Birmingham Architectural Association, he accepted the invitation to act as the BAA's President for a three year term from 1906–09, and his

Presidential address shows his persistent concern with current standards of design when he was at pains to show that architecture was more than a system of arts and crafts strung together.[16]

During the early years of the twentieth century Ball did not complete a great deal of work, BAA demands took time away from practice, and he continued to work mostly alone on one-off houses such as 'The Cottage' in Hagley Road and a little later in 1906 he designed and built another house with similar details at 'Penderell', 24 Somerset Road, Edgbaston, now a nursing home.[17] The alterations and additions to the original building to suit its new function have been considerable but it is still possible to pick out features which name its designer such as the arched stacks, coved plastered eaves, and wide bracketed gutters. Just below the eaves he has introduced a few courses of diaper work to the red-brown facing brickwork. A new design element for Ball at this stage is the introduction of a decorative stone chequer course above the main entrance to the house.

During what appears to be a not very productive period for Ball, and just when he was ending a successful term as President of BAA he was invited to accept the new position to be created of Director of the Birmingham School of Architecture. The school was to be a department of the celebrated Birmingham School of Art in Margaret Street whose deserved reputation had been fostered by its Head, Edward Richard Taylor (1838–1919) who had retired six years before. Ball appears to have been a successful teacher where his scholarly attitude to architecture was exactly what the new school needed, and he was fortunate in his staff which included Bidlake, a very successful architect, and like himself a scholar, and the younger but talented E. F. Reynolds who was appointed as Deputy Director. The Day School which provided full-time education for several days a week to articled assistants and students continued to function until 1916 when Ball retired from the Directorship and the course closed until the end of the war. At its conclusion Bidlake took over the Directorship, and Reynolds remained as his Deputy.

During his time as Director Ball continued his practice and in 1909 he commenced building Furze Hill, now Foxhill Manor, at Willersey, near to Broadway in Gloucestershire, for Mr Hookham.[18] The house is in a lovely situation perched high on a hill above Willersey and the large and attractive village of Broadway commanding wide views of the Cotswold hills and the vale of Evesham. How interesting and perplexing that Ball and Bidlake should move away, partially, from historical styles at the end of the nineteenth century and the beginning of the twentieth century suggesting that they will embrace what we now know to be the beginnings of the modern movement in architecture, only to move back again to historical styles. This is precisely what Ball did, disappointingly, at Furze Hill, where he built for his client a small medieval manor house. But he planned and detail-designed with great care and authority a building which in plan-form was based upon the 'X' or 'butterfly' type plan of Edward Prior (1852–1932) which is seen at The Barn, Exmouth constructed in 1897. This plan-form influenced many

Furze Hill, Willersey, near Broadway, 1900

architects besides Ball, such as Voisey, Lutyens, Baillie Scott and others. But Ball had used only the plan-form which has many advantages from the point of view of aspect, and clothed the exterior of the building with yellow Cotswold stone, coursed and dressed at quoins and in-filled with coursed rubble. All windows are stone framed and transomed, with leaded lights. Gables are steep in the medieval Cotswold tradition and are stone caped. The entrance porch is two storeys high and has a semi-circular hood with arched entrance. It is an impressively detailed essay but has nothing new to offer apart from its plan which is, after all, some ten years old.

While still working as Director at the School of Architecture Ball continued with private practice and in 1911–12 built the church of St Gregory the Great at Oldknow Road, Small Heath, in the Byzantine style with Painswick stone and tile on edge chequer board patterns in window tympana and blind arcading.[19] A year later he added the chapel at St Peters' College, Saltley, in Gothic to match existing buildings using a mottled Hollington stone for the fabric with dressings in white Hollington and red roof tiles to harmonise with the existing college in a pseudo-Romanesque style. The building was erected by John Barnsley & Sons.

A few years later in 1918 Ball, once again in full-time practice, took a commission which was quite different from those he had previously managed, the Carnegie Infant Welfare Institute in Hunter's Road at Handsworth.[20] Working to a tight budget he produced a plain and functional façade which mirrored clearly with its window pattern the disposition of rooms behind. The almost fortress like façade,

St Gregory the Great, Oldknow Road, Small Heath, 1911–12

Exterior of St Gregory the Great

with low pitch tiled hipped roof, is divided into bays by wide brick buttresses, and at the eaves there is decorative moulded brickwork. At the centre of the façade above the brick weather mould is William Bloye's sculptured figure of a Woman and Child.

In 1913 a competition was organised for Birmingham Architects to provide designs for a new Bluecoat School at Harborne on the corner of Harborne Road and Metchley Lane, to replace the original school building which had stood on a site facing onto St Philip's churchyard on Colmore Row since 1724 when the school was founded to provide for both orphans and children of the poor. Twenty-three architects entered for the competition and C. E. Bateman was one of the two assessors who chose three competitors to enter the last phase of the competition. Ball was one of them and was finally chosen as the winner despite accusations from the two unsuccessful architects that his scheme did not answer the conditions of the competition.

The argument appears to have been pointed and lengthy judging from the letters that appeared in subsequent editions of *The Builder* for December 1913 written by the angry two remaining final competitors, Marcus O. Type and Garratt S. Simister. But Ball did not involve himself in this fiasco but instead

Carnegie Infant Welfare Institute, Hunter's Road, Handsworth, 1918

Bluecoat School, Harborne, 1923

proceeded upon the long-term aims involving the erection of the many buildings which now form the school.[21]

The whole school was designed and built in a carefully muted neo-classical style which sits easily in vision but is quite unexciting. In this respect Ball was in step with his Birmingham colleagues in shunning the new Modern Movement in architecture which was beginning to establish itself in some quarters of the country in the 1920s, and he continued to look to dated styles of the past. As Ball came towards the end of his career he worked on succeeding building phases of the Bluecoat School, his last large contract, one which he supervised with great enjoyment probably guessing, if not knowing, that this would be his last big job. On the opening of the school chapel in 1932 he decided at the age of eighty to retire saying to his daughter Phylliss, 'I don't suppose I will take on any more commissions now, so there is no point in keeping on my city office'. He closed his office at 25 Paradise Street and retired to his home at Rotton Park Road where he died the following year on 11 December 1933 aged eighty-one years bringing to an end a long and distinguished career of some fifty-three years. His last years had been saddened by the deaths of several of his near family. Edith had died in 1928, followed the next year by his brilliant surgeon son Lawrence aged forty-five, and his daughter Dorothy who died in 1931, leaving two married daughters, Mrs Hickinbotham and Mrs Davis, and the unmarried Phylliss and Hester.

The architect Edwin Reynolds, himself a sensitive architect and Ball's Deputy at the School of Architecture, wrote in the RIBA Journal for 24 February 1934 an obituary referring to Ball as the doyen of the profession in Birmingham and to the fresh thought and care he gave to each of his buildings – an apt tribute.

List of Architectural Works of J. L. Ball

Joseph Lancaster Ball (1852–1933) was articled to William Wilmot Pocock of London. He was in partnership with Algernon Goddard for a year from 1879. In 1880 he set up in independent practice in Birmingham, continuing until his retirement in 1930.

WORK IN BIRMINGHAM AND ITS ENVIRONS

PUBLIC

1880–81 Wesleyan Theological College, Friary Rd, Handsworth; additions 1904

1881–83 Princess Alice Orphanage, Chester Rd North, Oscott, Sutton Coldfield; 1905–23 additions

1884–85 Wesleyan Chapel and Sunday School, corner of Corporation St and Lower Priory [D]

1885 Asbury Memorial Wesleyan Chapel, Holyhead Rd, Handsworth

1889 Addition of billiards room for The Oratory School, Hagley Rd

1893 Mission Hall, Hatchett St, Newtown Row.

1894 Additions and alterations to Wesleyan Chapel, South St, Harborne

1898 Wesleyan Chapel, corner of Sandon Rd and Barnsley Rd, Harborne (in assoc. with E. Barnsley for first stage)

1899 Additions to Wesleyan Chapel, St Martin's St, Edgbaston

1911–12 Church of St Gregory the Great, Oldknow Rd, Small Heath

1912 Chapel, St Peter's College, Saltley

1918 The Carnegie Infant Welfare Institute, Hunter's Rd, Handsworth

1923, 1929–32 The Bluecoat School, Metchley Lane, Harborne (in assoc. with G. S. Simister for latter phase)

COMMERCIAL

1881 Shops, warehouses and offices at 10 [13–14] Cherry St, Birmingham, for Thomas Smith

1899–1900 Eagle Insurance Building, Colmore Row (in association with W. R. Lethaby)

INDUSTRIAL

1881 Alterations and additions to Manufactory, Buckingham St, off Great Hampton St

1896 Factory for Austin Cycle Co., Monument Rd, Ladywood

1906–10 Factory and offices for C. H. Pugh, Tilton Rd, Bordesley

1907 Shopping and additions for Rudge Whitworth Ltd, Rea St, Digbeth; 1910 additions

1907 Warehouse for B. S. Smith, Price St

1911 Factory for Lanchester Cars, Montgomery St, Small Heath.

DOMESTIC

1886 Additions to Abbey House, corner of St Michael's Rd and Soho Rd, Soho Hill, Handsworth for Dr A. Holdsworth

1887 House, Augustus Rd, Edgbaston for Thomas Barnsley [D]

1889 House, 'Earlsfield', 20 Westfield Rd, Edgbaston for John Barnsley

1895 Five houses for Thomas Wheatley at Wenman St/Vincent Parade, Balsall Heath

1895 Two houses for J. Barnsley and Sons, 13 and 15 Rotton Park Rd, Edgbaston

1895–96 Two houses for J. L. Ball, 17 and 19 Rotten Park Rd, Edgbaston

1896 Eleven houses for Thomas Wheatley, Vincent Parade, Balsall Heath

1896–97 Sixteen houses for J. Barnsley and Sons, east side of Barnsley Rd, Edgbaston

1900 Fourteen semi-detached houses for J. Barnsley and Sons, west side of Barnsley Rd, Edgbaston

1891 House, 'Briarwood', 17 Twatling Rd, Barnt Green, Worcs. for J. A. Christie

1902–03 House, 'The Cottage', Hagley Rd, Edgbaston for Mr Phelps

1902–04 House, Winterbourne, [56] Edgbaston Park Rd, Edgbaston for J. S. Nettlefold; 1906 stables and lodge

1906 'Penderell', 24 Somerset Rd, Edgbaston

1910 'Vernon Court', Vernon Rd, Edgbaston.

WORK OUTSIDE BIRMINGHAM

DOMESTIC

1909–10 House for Mr. Hookham at Furze Hill, Willersey, near Broadway, Gloucs.

NOTES

[1] Family details and the early life of the architect are based on information obtained from his daughters Phylliss and Hester Ball, on a personal visit by the author on 23 May 1978.

[2] Birmingham Central Library, Archives and Heritage Services (hereafter BCL AHS) Birmingham Building Register, app. no. 2911, shops, warehouses and offices, 10 Cherry Street, Birmingham for Thomas Smith.

[3] BCL AHS, Uncatalogued architects' Drawings, Roll 36, drawings by Ball for Weslyan Chapel and Sunday School, Corporation Street/Lower Priory Street. Illustrated in *Building News*, 49 (1885) p. 586.

[4] Victoria and Albert Museum, RIBA Architectural Drawings Collection, drawings by Ball for Asbury Memorial Chapel, 1885.

[5] BCL AHS, Birmingham Building Register, app. no. 14055, additions to Weslyan Chapel, Sandon Road, Edgbaston, 23 June 1898; app. no. 16282, 20 May 1901, addition of transcept and chancel.

[6] BCL AHS, Birmingham Building Register, app. no. 5370, 26 February 1887, house for Thomas Barnesley, Augustus Road, Edgbaston.

[7] BCL, AHS, Birmingham Building Register, app. no. 6469, 22 January 1889, house for John Barnsley, 'Earlsfield' 20 Westfield Road, Edgbaston.

[8] BCL, AHS, Uncatalogued architects' drawings collection, Roll 29 drawings by Ball for 'Briarwood' 17 Twatling Road, Barnt Green; Alan Crawford, *A Tour in North Worcestershire* (Birmingham, 1977), p. 7.

⁹ BCL AHS, Birmingham Building Register, app. no. 10659, 13 December 1894, two houses, 13–15 Rotton Park Road, Edgbaston for J. Barnsley and Sons.

¹⁰ BCL AHS, Birmingham Building Register, app. no. 11160, 3 August 1895, two houses, 17–19 Rotton Park Road, Edgbaston for J. L. Ball.

¹¹ BCL AHS, Uncatalogued architects drawings, Roll 32, drawings by Ball for 'The Cottage'; Birmingham Building Register, app. no. 16742, 24 February 1902, for The Cottage, Hagley Road, Edgbaston for G. Phelps.

¹² BCL AHS, Birmingham Building Register, app. no. 14657, 10 March 1899, for Eagle Insurance Building, Colmore Row, Birmingham.

¹³ BCL AHS, Uncatalogued architects' drawings, Rolls 30 and 31, drawings by Ball for Winterbourne, 1902–4 and 1906; M. E. Macartney, *Recent English Domestic Architecture*, 1, 1908, p. 4 and pp. 42–45 (special supplement to *Architectural Review*); BAA Green Books, 1904, p. 21; Remo Granelli, 'Architecture' in *By Hammer and Hand: the Arts and Crafts Movement in Birmingham*, ed. by Alan Crawford (Birmingham, 1984), pp. 47–50; lecture by Remo Granelli 'Winterbourne, the Nettlefolds and J. L. Ball, 23 June, 1979; *ex inform* Mrs M. Beale, personal details of the Nettlefolds; Phillada Ballard, *A Small Country House in Birmingham: Winterbourne and its Garden 1903–1995*, (Birmingham, 1995).

¹⁴ See J. L. Ball, 'A Study in Roof Building' *Architectural Review*, 18, 1905, pp. 10–13.

¹⁵ *Country Life*, 30, 1 July 1911, Supplement, pp. 7–8.

¹⁶ Birmingham Architectural Association, acc. no. 662093, J. L. Ball's Presidential Addresses for 1906–07, 1907–08, and 1908–09.

¹⁷ BCL AHS, Birmingham Building Register app. no. 18955, 23 January 1906, for house, Pendrell, 24 Somerset Road, Edgbaston; uncatalogued architects' drawings collection, Roll no. 24 Ball's drawings for Pendrell.

¹⁸ *The Builder*, 103, 27 December, 1912, p. 778; Royal Academy Exhibitions 1905–07, p. 79, 1912 'East and West Fronts of Furze Hill, Willersley, Worcs; BAA Green Book 1909–10, p. 26; Lawrence Weaver, *Small Country Houses of Today*, vol. 1, (1922) pp. 50–52.

¹⁹ BCL AHS, Uncatalogued architects' drawings collection, Roll 33, Ball's drawings for church of St Gregory the Great, Oldknow Road, Small Heath Birmingham, 1911–12 and 1928; BAA Green Book 1911–12, description of work in progress, 11 July 1912, p. 28; *The Builder*, 100, 1911, p. 522.

²⁰ BCL AHS, uncatalogued architects' drawings collection, Roll no. 29 Ball's drawings for Carnegie Welfare Centre.

²¹ *Ibid*, Roll no. 25 Ball's drawings for the 1929 scheme; illustrations of the competition scheme and correspondence *The Builder*, 105, p. 513, p. 518, p. 530.

19 Charles Edward Bateman

DAVID DAVIDSON

Charles Edward Bateman (1863–1947) was born in Castle Bromwich on 8 June 1863. He was born into a family of architects – his father, John Jones Bateman, was a prolific architect and first president of the Birmingham Architectural Association. C. E. Bateman's practice was diverse. In housing, he tackled everything from large rural houses for the middle classes to reconfiguring courts of back-to-backs for the Birmingham Corporation Housing Committee.[1] Although rooted in the Arts and Crafts Movement, he was happy to embrace technology, as espoused by Lethaby, to achieve bold designs for industrial buildings. His church work was finely detailed and based on careful study of old work. According to Granelli, he 'never produced anything bad'.[2] Keen observation and study of historical examples inform his work, which was characterised by an unusual sensitivity and honesty.

Charles Bateman received his early education at St Marylebone Grammar School, London and Grange School, Eastbourne. In 1880 he became articled to his father in his practice at 59 Colmore Row, Birmingham. In 1883 the practice became Bateman and Bateman when Charles's older brother, John Joseph Bateman, a surveyor, was taken in, moving to offices at 13 Waterloo Street. He died in an accident in 1885 and in the same year, Charles moved to the offices of Verity and Hunt in Regent Street, London.

Thomas Verity, the son of the theatre architect Frank Verity, had set up in practice with George Hunt on the back of some successful competition entries. The firm had an Evesham office, on the edge of the Cotswolds, which appeared to be run primarily by Hunt, mainly altering

C. E. Bateman

and updating older properties at a period where the value of old houses was being rediscovered. Bateman became involved in enlarging and restoring houses in the area, instilling in him a great love of Cotswolds' building which was to inform his work throughout his life. In his obituary of Bateman, Holland Hobbiss wrote 'it was the work of such men as Sir Guy Dawber, N. Prentice and Charles Bateman who have preserved and carried on the Cotswold tradition'.[3] Bateman's association with the area was to remain and he retired to a pair of cottages he converted in Bourton-on-the Hill in 1924.

Whilst working with Verity and Hunt between 1885 and 1887, Bateman attended classes at the Architectural Association, where his principal tutor was E. J. May. May had been a pupil of Norman Shaw and ran a successful country house practice designing houses that were 'generous and simple, avoiding the Arty and Crafty'.[4] May lived and worked at Bedford Park, building houses in a loose Queen Anne manner.[5] These were clearly an influence on Bateman when he returned to Birmingham, particularly in his work on the Cartland Estate, King's Heath.

In 1887, Bateman returned to become a partner in his father's practice. He quickly got involved with the activities of the Birmingham Architectural Association, an organisation that was to play an important part in his professional life. He had joined in 1883, becoming a committee member in 1884, when he was elected Secretary to the Elementary Class of Design. In 1886 he won the BAA prize for Best Series of Designs while at Verity and Hunt and in 1887 he was appointed Secretary to the Class of Construction and Practice. In the same year he steered through Committee the formal affiliation with the AA in London. With his London connections he was able to call upon the most influential architects of the day to address his Birmingham members including Guy Dawber, Aston Webb, Beresford Pite, E. S. Prior, Charles Holden and Halsey Ricardo.[6]

In 1895 Bateman became an Associate of the RIBA by examination. His papers were signed by George Hunt and William Hale. The same year he became President of the BAA. In his Presidential Address he lists some of his 'heroes'. These include Bodley, Shaw, Mountford, Nesfield and Blomfield but he also expresses admiration for the work of Barry, Inigo Jones, Wren and Pearson.[7]

As well as practicing, Bateman took an interest in teaching architecture. In addition to his frequent lectures to the BAA students on aspects of practical building, he also lectured at the Birmingham School of Art from 1899 until 1905. It was not until 1909 that the Birmingham School of Architecture was founded as a branch of the School of Art and this was achieved with the help of Bateman who felt that the teaching of architecture, based on his own experience and technical knowledge, was an essential part in the training of young architects.

In 1898, Bateman was elected a Fellow of the RIBA. His papers were signed by Frank B. Osborn and William Henman. On the Proposer's Statement, Henman writes, 'My present offices are at 31 Cannon Street, a building of decidedly good character erected from the designs of Mr C. E. Bateman'.[8] That year Bateman and

Bateman moved to new premises at 81A Edmund Street.

Bateman was joined in 1898 by Alfred Hale, son of William Hale, with whom he was to win a number of competitions including High Wycombe Town Hall, 1903,[9] and Northfield Library, Birmingham, 1905. Herbert Tudor Buckland was with the practice for three years from 1890.

Bateman's first work on rejoining his father was at the Priory Estate, King's Heath for John Cartland.[10] King's Heath was already an expanding suburb of the city and Cartland instructed J. J. Bateman to draw up a layout for a new middle class suburb. J. J. Bateman had already carried out work for members of the Cartland Family, extending The Priory in 1855 and enlarging Vectis Lodge, Edgbaston, for John Cartland in the 1880's as well as drawing up plans for the enlargement of Hazelwell Hall, King's Heath, for George Cartland in 1886.[11] In 1889 Major John Howard Cartland inherited The Priory and continued to develop the land.

The development began slowly with two pairs of semi-detached houses at the corners of Melstock Road and Vicarage Road, erected around 1887. Built of brick with tile hung upper storeys and bays with pulvinated friezes, the designs reflect the Queen Anne influence of Bedford Park. Later houses show the younger Bateman's growing confidence, moving from the derivative styles of Shaw and May towards larger gestures and greater simplicity.

The first houses to display his more relaxed Arts and Crafts sensibility are the pairs on the corner of Vicarage Road and Stanley Road, built in 1889. These are asymmetrical compositions with a mix of tile-hung and half-timbered gables, a long ridge line, sturdy chimneys and casement windows. Each house is given a different plan and the pairs and are designed to look like a single unit.

Bateman attempted Midlands' vernacular with nos 4–6 Stanley Road, built in 1892. Two storey and attic with close studding on the upper floor and brick below, the front doors are recessed behind Gothic arches. Each dining room has a bay window tucked under the jettied upper storey, carried on a bressummer supported on stone corbels. When delivering a paper on 'Small Houses' at the Architectural Association in London in 1900, Bateman commented that 'at some time or other, everyone does a half-timber house, and wishes they had not after a later inspection'.[12] He felt that the material required regular maintenance, could be unconvincing when the timber is merely applied and can look harsh. The same paper also refers to the recessed porch, which 'is cheaper, while it gives scale to a small house and will form in the hall a convenient bay window recess'.

Nos 12–14 Stanley Road 1892–93 introduce a more satisfyingly restrained approach to materials. Built in red brick with stone dressings used sparingly to define the openings and decorate the paired central gables, the stone is treated very simply, with no mouldings other then weathering details on the stone coped gables and canted bays. Window mullions, lintels and quoins are flush, reflecting Cotswold traditions. The massive central chimney stack, with blind arch detail,

4–6 Stanley Road, King's Heath, 1892

reflects Bateman's view that 'chimneys should be looked upon a miniature towers, not stalks'.[13]

Bateman used the same materials for the largest pairs of houses on the Priory Estate, built in 1895 to frame the entrance to the newly cut Cartland Road. They are asymmetrical compositions, like Cotswold manor houses in red brick with stone dressings and given a picturesque outline by a combination of coped gables, dormers and substantial chimneys. Bateman wrote, 'There is a particular charm about coped gables, which mark the verticality of the gable in contrast to the horizontal line of the eaves'.[14] Window proportions and gable widths vary to express the spaces within.

The King's Heath houses show Bateman grappling with the question of style and asserting his authority in the practice. They illustrate his practical approach to the design of modest houses for which the practice was known. According to Muthesius, Bateman and Bateman were considered specialists in the design of the smaller house[15] and Bidlake used two pages of Bateman's cottage and house designs in *The Modern Home*.[16] The constraints imposed by the limited budgets available on these buildings did not allow him to demonstrate what he could do

254 Vicarage Road and 1 Cartland Road used by Bateman to frame the road junction, 1895

with a more generous commission. Whilst at work on the Priory Estate, Bateman was commissioned to design 'Firsdene' in Bromsgrove for F. M. Cartland in 1892 on a grand scale and its appearance owes much to Bateman's grounding in the Cotswold vernacular.

The design was illustrated in the *Building News* in December 1892.[17] The perspective shows it to be a large stone house in the style of a 17th-century Cotswold manor. The description explains 'the walls are of Bromsgrove stone in courses, with roofs covered in Colley Weston stone slates in scale with the rest. The chimneys are shown in brickwork. The general effect of the residence, as in old houses, depends on its grouping and main proportions, the details being exceedingly simple'. This may be too kind. The house looks a bit self-consciously styled and lacks the clarity and naturalness of Bateman's mature work.

Also in King's Heath, Bateman designed The Gable House, Cartland Road, in 1896. Built for Walter Fitzmaurice, a builder who was employed by Major Cartland in laying out roads in Priory Estate, it was illustrated in *The Builder* in 1902.[18]

The Gable House, Cartland Road, King's Heath illustrated in *The Builder*, 2 March 1902. *Courtesy of Birmingham Central Library*

The form and planning of the house are unusual. At the centre of the principal elevation, beneath a richly detailed brick and stone banded gable containing a chimney stack and dovecote, is a carriage arch giving access through to the service yard at the rear. The front door is located within this archway. A second smaller gabled bay raises two storeys to create a visual counterpoint, clad in cleft oak boarding. The house is built in thin red bricks with yellow Guiting stone dressings. The windows are leaded timber casements. The roof is covered in old tiles, which Bateman felt 'make a roof warmer than slates, and where sound old ones can be obtained they look all the better for being weathered'.[19]

The front door leads into a small hallway from which all the main rooms are reached. The hall proper, which was a sitting room, is linked to the drawing room by a set of folding doors. Both rooms are panelled, with beamed ceilings, and the folding doors when closed are indistinguishable from the panelling. Bateman wrote that, 'Owning to the smallness of our rooms it is a great advantage to arrange them so that they can be thrown together by using folding doors. If you set the hall in the middle and can throw the room into it on each side, you obtain quite a large and interesting room for special occasions'.[20]

The hall fireplace is set at the corner of the room and is of carved dark red Codsall stone with softly moulded plasterwork on the chimney breast above. An inglenook fireplace in the drawing room is of similar stone, full height with coved cornice inset with rosettes. Short benches are built in to each side.

The year 1896 also saw the construction of 'Birnam' and 'Millbrick', an asymmetrical pair of semi-detached houses in Rectory Road, Castle Bromwich. Built from bricks reclaimed from a nearby mill, the result caused the reviewer in the *Builder's Journal and Architectural Record* to note that 'Messrs Bateman have had them laid with a wide white flat-pointed unstruck joint, and the result must have satisfied their most sanguine conjectures'.[21] Bateman's craftsmanlike approach to surface did not go unnoticed. No 3 has panelling from an 18th-century church at Water Orton.[22]

These houses, with other examples from the Priory Estate and Worcestershire, were illustrated in *The Builder* in March 1900 to accompany a transcript of Bateman's talk to the Architectural Association on 'Small Houses'. The paper he delivered was published in full and provides an insight into the design processes of the architect. He appears as a very practical man, as concerned with the size of the ideal chimney flue as he is with the appearance of the house.

Having moved away from overtly historicist styles and developed a more personal language, the next major house by Bateman is more radical. The Homestead, Woodbourne Road Edgbaston, is an Arts and Crafts house stripped down to its essentials in a way that, for this date, was very progressive in Birmingham and relates to the work of Voysey and Baillie-Scott. A large house for Percival Jones designed in 1896, it sits reticently back from the road at the top of a rising site screened by a high brick wall, in contrast to the Victorian houses adjacent that

The Homestead,
Woodbourne Road,
Edgbaston, 1896

display their showy wares by addressing the street. It is approached by a long winding drive, past terraced gardens, to a court at the side of the house, enclosed by the service wing. An arch leads to the stables, motor house and yard at the rear.

The house is entered through a Gothic stone recessed porch decorated with low relief rosettes and inscribed 'East, West, Home's Best'. An article in *The Builder* explains the plan:

The aspect and view from the site necessitated the dining room being placed at the south east corner, and the kitchens at the opposite diagonal corner to be near the tradesman's entrance and the separated out-offices in the rear, the difficulty of access between the two being got over by placing the pantry under the stairs. This position is found convenient for answering the front door. The hall is in communication with the dining and drawing rooms by wide folding doors, and when these are opened an apartment 56' long is obtained.[23]

The house displays Bateman's flexible internal planning, with the oak floors and panelling unifying the rooms. The interior is fitted out to a high standard. Dining room and hall have oak beamed ceilings; the drawing room, low relief plaster decoration. Fireplaces are stone with Tudoresque details — those in the dining and drawing rooms set in timber inglenooks. To the rear, a billiard room includes an extraordinary light fitting with wrought iron tendrils spreading across the ceiling. Upstairs the main bedroom is fully panelled and provided with built-in furniture, painted white with brass fittings.

Externally the house is stripped of all superfluous detail. 'In the way of ornaments, one need not put in what one can possibly leave out,' wrote Bateman.[24] The materials are roughcast walls with reclaimed brick chimneys; stone details are limited to the entrance and moulded caps to the chimneys. Fenestration is horizontal in emphasis, being leaded timber casements throughout, reflecting Bateman's idea that 'low wide windows perhaps light a room the most agreeably, and prevent the sun's rays from penetrating too far ...'[25] The hall is lit by a taller window set adjacent to the powerful external chimney with battered stack. The house displays an honesty that Muthesius would admiringly describe as 'primitivism'.

The roof is designed simply, punctured by the massive brick chimneys, and covered in stone slates laid in diminishing courses. Bateman wrote, 'the roof in a great measure governs the plan itself ...'[26] The main gable to the front, with stone coping on flush kneelers, breaks the horizontality of the composition. This house is a major break with the earlier work.

In 1900 Bateman built The Grey House in Barnt Green. Occupying a large plot off Mearse Lane, it was illustrated in *The Builder* in 1901.[27] The article states that it was to be finished in roughcast but the house, as built, is brick. It is a more conservative design than the Homestead, being full of the swagger demanded of a wealthy client keen to see where his money was being spent.

The core of the house, the principal rooms, is solidly built of brick with heavy stone mullioned windows and coped gables. However the service wing is more simply expressed, being of plain brickwork with timber casements set flush with the wall. The appearance is of a Tudor manor house extended in a later century. As Davey writes, 'This kind of artificial ageing ... was increasingly loved by clients (particularly those with new money) in the second half of the nineteenth century, and it became an important ingredient in Arts and Crafts thinking ...'[28]

In 1903 Bateman built a modest pair of houses in Anchorage Road, Sutton Coldfield, of vernacular inspiration. These were part of a speculative development begun in 1870 by Richard Sadler who laid out plots suitable for 'Suburban Residence of a Superior Class'.[29] Bateman purchased a small plot and erected his pair of houses designed to appear as one dwelling. The elevations are informal; roughcast on a reclaimed brick ground floor with old tiles on the roof, robust chimneys, flush stone-mullioned windows and canted flat-roofed bays. No. 5, which presents a three storey gabled bay to the road, is entered from the front into a small hallway with staircase rising off it, lit by a tall window above the front door. No. 7 has the main door to the side gable wall which is decorated with two ocular windows. Bateman moved to this house around 1910 and lived in it until his retirement to Bourton-on-the-Hill in 1924. The form of the houses reflects the asymmetrical pairs on the corner of Vicarage Road and Cartland Road, King's Heath but the effect of the reclaimed brick and roughcast is much softer.

The Gable House, The Homestead, the Anchorage Road and the Castle Bromwich houses represent something of a theme in Bateman's mature work to date – the reduction of details (when not overtly historicist), simple rooflines and economical planning. His next houses in Four Oaks are something of a departure, in their different ways.

Between 1902 and 1904 Bateman designed four large houses in Four Oaks which illustrate the development of his mature work. Davey refers to Four Oaks as 'some of England's most beautiful suburbs' and the setting attracted Birmingham's moneyed classes who brought with them the most talented local and national architects.[30] Houses were built by Lethaby (The Hurst) and Ernest Newton (The Leasowes) – with a garden laid out by Bateman as a series of rooms[31] and local men like Reynolds, Bidlake, Hobbiss, Crouch and Butler and Cossins, Peacock and Bewlay.

Bateman's first house in Four Oaks was Redlands, 1903. It was built for Richard Parkes, who demolished a house in Northumberland and brought the bricks with him.[32] The house stands on a large plot off Hartopp Road and, according to Granelli, 'shows Bateman in full command of his technique'.[33] Every element is thoroughly and consistently considered, beginning with the plan, which is twisted on the plot to take advantage of the contours of the site and afternoon sun.[34] In 1900 Bateman had written that 'points which force themselves upon us when laying down a plan are the approach to the land, the aspect, the views obtainable, and the levels, the most important perhaps being the aspect' and this is reflected in the siting of the house.[35] The drawing room has a large bay to catch the late afternoon sun and make the most of views over the garden.

Lawrence Weaver reviewed the house in 1910 and was particularly impressed with Bateman's practical approach to problem solving. He writes, '... successful house-building is based not so much on the gift of large conceptions, as on the observation of ordinary needs and skill in ministering to them. In such work Mr Charles Bateman has built success on large experience, and the arrangement of Redlands is a good example of convenient and economical planning'.[36] The house is entered from a courtyard enclosed by the carriage-house and stable wing with its Bateman trademark arched entrance between. The front door, under a barrel-vaulted canopy on Doric columns, opens directly into the hall, expressed externally by a wide, two-storey gabled bay. The main living rooms lead off this hall, all orientated towards the garden.

In the external treatment of Redlands, Bateman displays a refined simplicity in the detailing, using timber casement windows, long tile roof, richly textured salvaged brickwork. In his description of the house, Weaver writes 'Mr Bateman has eschewed anything like a conscious feature, which is all to the good. He has relied on the dignity which is always secured by a long even roofline. The chimneys, seen from the garden, are bold and their positions, two issuing from the apex and one, that of the kitchen, projecting on the south-east front, reveal

Redlands, 1 Hartopp Road, Four Oaks, 1903

another point of good planning. The sitting room fires are all in inside walls, an arrangement which conserves the heat where it is wanted, whereas the kitchen is the cooler for having its range built into an outside wall. The mass of the kitchen chimney, moreover, joins with the two-storey bay in adding a touch of reasonable variety to the garden front'.[37] Bateman uses the practicalities of the plan as an opportunity to enrich his elevation, and the bold kitchen chimney, breaking through the eaves line, provides a counterpoint to the two storey bay.

After the comparative reticence of Redlands, Bryn Teg, built in 1904, comes as something as a surprise. It is a 'large house in which Bateman's preference for the element of Cotswold building is exploited with relish', according to Granelli.[38] The plan is similar to Redlands, with its entrance forecourt and the main rooms looking over the garden. The treatment, however, is very different. The upper storeys are slate-hung in a mix of Hollington, Grinshill and Penkridge stones. This rests on a base of reclaimed brick with stone dressings. On the entrance front, four gables of differing sizes make up the elevation, with the entrance and hall gables projecting forward. Timber leaded casement windows project slightly, supported on timber brackets and arranged to reflect the rooms behind, the largest lighting the stair. Old clay tiles are used for the roof.

The garden elevation is very different, deriving much of its character from the horizontal emphasis of the fenestration and the broad hipped roof. This horizontality is enhanced by the voids between the window bays and the central balcony suggests a Wealden house. On the left is a deep semi-circular bay supporting the gable. The chimneys are particularly heavy and have distinctive pointed slate chimney pots much used by Bateman.

The interior has modelled plasterwork, mosaic and marble decoration by the St George's Guild of Handicrafts in Birmingham. The front door leads through a narrow passage to a broad corridor which gives access to the principal rooms on the garden side. There is a living hall at the front of the house and both hall and living room can be opened to the corridor by double doors, creating a large entertaining space.

With his next house the influence of the Georgian Revival appears. Hawkesford, in Bracebridge Road, was built for his father, J. J. Bateman, in 1902.[39] It is a large house in full Queen Anne style with heavy cornice, stone voussoir headed sash windows and hipped slate roof. Again, the walls are reclaimed brick. At the centre of the garden front is a two storey canted bay which breaks the repose of the elevation. It is only to this one elevation that Bateman gives a Classical discipline. The other sides of the house are an informal arrangement of sashes and, at the rear, a tall transomed and mullioned window lights the stairs. The effect is of an earlier house refronted in the eighteenth century.

The planning also owes more to Arts and Crafts thinking than to the axial plan of Classical architecture. The entrance is on the side of the house and leads to a hall and corridor which runs the length of the house, giving access to the dining

Bryn Teg, 14 Bracebridge Road, Four Oaks, 1904, front elevation

Bryn Teg, garden elevation

room, study and drawing room which overlook the garden. It was practical and economical. Hawkesford was illustrated in *Recent English Domestic Architecture*.[40]

In 1903 J. J. Bateman died. He had lived only one year in Hawkesford. Charles lived on in the house with his sisters until 1910, when he moved to the house in Anchorage Road. His father's death left him in charge of the firm, assisted by Alfred Hale, son of the architect, William Hale.

Carhampton, a house built in 1902 in Luttrell Road, is similar in style although the two storey bay as been omitted and the front door is wilfully placed on the right of the principle elevation, as Lutyens had done at Crooksbury in 1889.[41] Sash windows vary in width to add movement to an otherwise static façade. The house was built on the site of Four Oaks Hall and is said to have been constructed from materials salvaged from it. The bricks and many of the stone voussiors would seem consistent with this and the stone gate piers at the entrance may be the

Carhampton, Lutterell Road, Four Oaks, 1902

originals. This may explain the choice of the Georgian Revival for both Hawkesford and Carhampton.

It is interesting to note that Bateman was building Hawkesford and Carhampton at the same time as Redlands and Bryn Teg. The radical difference in style was consistent with the English architectural scene at the time. Many architects trained in the Gothic and Arts and Crafts tradition were making a similar switch, discovering the architecture of the Renaissance. This was encouraged by a number of studies, such as Reginald Blomfield's *A Short History of Renaissance Architecture in England 1500–1800* (published in 1897), which spoke to those clients who valued 'taste rather than originality'.[42] Much of Bateman's domestic output after 1902 reflected this shift.

In the early 1890s Bateman carried out the archaeological recording and restoration of St Mary and St Margaret's Church in Castle Bromwich.[43] This seems to have led to the commission to design the new rectory for the church, and led to further such commissions throughout Birmingham as new parishes were formed to serve the expanding city.

The Castle Bromwich rectory was built in 1908; an arresting Queen Anne house, using some of the details already seen at Four Oaks, particularly the sash

The Rectory, Rectory Lane, Castle Bromwich, 1908. *Photo: B. S.*

windows with exposed boxes under stone voussoir heads and tall hipped roof with three stacks arranged symmetrically. The entrance front is rather austere: the main rooms face over the rear garden. Extra height is given by the central projecting bay having a panelled parapet rising above the cornice supported on a giant order of brick pilasters. Windows are artfully arranged; segmental headed casements on the ground floor, sashes above. Three occuli pierce the brick of the central bay. Over the doorcase is a barrel-vaulted hood supported on console brackets. The elevation is much more changeful than those of Hawkesford and Carhampton, and is the most satisfying of Bateman's Classical houses. The interior contains good plasterwork and a delightful oratory with barrel vaulted ceiling and a small stained-glass Crucifixion.

All Bateman's later vicarages are Georgian Revival in spirit, except for the rather eccentric example for St Nicolas, New Town of 1913 and the effortless, sprawling Arts and Crafts design in Maney Hill Road, Sutton Coldfield of 1911.[44] Less lavish in scale than Castle Bromwich is St Peter's vicarage, George Street West, Ladywood, another essay in the Queen Anne. Designed in 1910 for a small site in an inner city parish, the house turns its side to the street, with the main rooms facing south to catch the sun. This front is composed of three two-storey bays,

St Peter's Vicarage, Maney Hill Road, Sutton Coldfield, 1911

with the cornice carried round them. Economy is clearly important and the forms are simple but the effect of the bays is powerful.

The front door leads to a vaulted corridor which runs the length of the house, receptions rooms to one side, service areas and stairs to the other — a similar plan to the Four Oaks houses. Externally hard-fired red-blue brick is used, more befitting an inner city location, with dentilled cornice and rusticated corner pilasters. Pedimented dormers in the hipped roof light the attic, and three tall chimneys decorated with blind arches are again arranged symmetrically.

Bateman's vicarage for St James, Edgbaston, 1911–12, occupies a more generous plot. Bateman located the house below S. S. Teulon's church, with the frontage facing it, allowing the principal rooms views over the substantial gardens. The design is symmetrical with a central pedimented bay. Texture is provided by thin brick quoins and a projecting string course at first floor level, and full use is made of a variety of window sizes to enliven the elevation. This is particularly successful on the garden elevation where the first floor windows are considerably larger than the ground, creating an odd tension in the composition. The recessed bay to the left of the front door contains two blind windows to balance the sashes on the right as the study has been given a bay window to the side garden.

As well as the housing design for which the practice was known, Bateman also undertook commercial work. A particularly influential job came his way from the Cartlands at King's Heath. Birmingham at the beginning of the twentieth century had adopted the principle of 'fewer and better' in the granting of new licences, by which inner-city gin-palaces were closed and licences granted to the breweries to erect new inns of a more respectable type in the expanding suburbs. Bateman was commissioned to build a new public house for Cartland's growing estate.

The Red Lion was designed along the lines of a 17th century Cotswolds coaching inn, with tall bay windows and a richly carved Wildon stone façade.[45] The lofty interior had dark bolection moulded panelling, huge stone fireplaces and was lavishly detailed to reflect its place at the heart of the new community. This commission was to lead to the design of a great number of new pubs and the practice became a specialist in the field, building more pubs in the region than any other firm.[46]

An illustration in the *Builders' Journal and Architectural Record* of February 1900 shows a dramatic design for The Cannon Street Hotel.[47] Positioned on a corner plot, a stone ground floor supports two floors of banded brick and stone. The huge roof accommodates two rows of dormers and is expressed by a massive three storey gabled end. Two heavy stacks are corbelled out over the street elevation. It bears more than a passing resemblance to Shaw's White Star Offices, Liverpool, of 1895.

The design of factories and warehouses for the thriving manufacturing city was another area of work in which Bateman excelled. In 1898, he designed a factory for Westley Richards, a gun manufacturer, in Selly Oak, for whom the firm had

The Red Lion, King's Heath, 1904

already built.[48] The site was a long strip of land bounded by the watercourse of Bourne Brook on one side and the Victorian housing of Selly Oak on the other. Across the river was farm land belonging to the Calthorpe family, on which was soon to be built Aston Webb's University of Birmingham.

The frontage to Grange Road is essentially symmetrical and relies for its impact on simple detailing and the use of vernacular forms. A pair of three storey gables break up the long elevation and announce the entrances to the offices, workshops and the yard at the rear. The materials are red brick and slate, with casement windows throughout. In its details, the factory shares a lot of similarities with A. S. Dixon's Birmingham School of Handicrafts. The use of coped gables, unadorned chimney stacks and particularly the design of the fenestration are all found in Dixon's building. He uses the same arched openings on the ground floor and casement windows under blind arches. The detail of the arched openings is identical – brick on end with cavetto mouldings to give depth to the elevation. It is a fully realised Arts and Crafts factory and the rather romantic illustration for the *Building News* of 2 February 1900 gives it something of the appearance of a large 17th-century farmhouse in a rural setting.

Arts and Crafts architecture, rooted as it was in the revival of vernacular forms found in domestic buildings, could not easily be transplanted to an urban setting. A different approach was required when building in the context of a city street, such as Feeney's printing offices in Cannon Street already referred to by Toni Demidowicz in chapter four. As a contrast to the refined contextualism of this piece of townscape, two unexecuted designs published in *The Builder* in 1902 illustrate an extraordinary boldness in Bateman's work. Both were to be built in reinforced concrete.[49]

The warehouse extension for S. C. Larkins and Son Ltd proposed for a site in Cannon Street appears as a huge gabled six storey tower linked to an earlier building by a second floor bridge. The framing of the structure is clearly expressed, yet lightly dressed in Flemish Renaissance detailing. Two storeys of attics are lit by long rows of dormers. It appears both romantic and rational at the same time.

More spectacular in its robust expression of the machine aesthetic was the printing works for George Jones and Son in Cornwall Street, designed in 1899. Devey describes it thus: 'brick piers support a three-storey gabled roof in which the offices are lighted by dormer windows in the slopes. Between the piers, huge square gridded windows light the machine halls which rise above a base course infilled with glass blocks. It is one of the most daring designs for an industrial building of the period'. Ever practical, Bateman provided iron balconies for window cleaning.

Bateman turned his hand to urban Classicism for the Birmingham and District Bank in Broad Street, Birmingham, in 1898, the same year that he was working on Westley Richards. The bank is in what came to be known as the Wrenaisssance style, but in this case it owes as much to Norman Shaw as to Wren.

Bateman's bank is a well-proportioned block of brick and stone above a rusticated stone base. It is of three storeys and attic, the latter lit by a row of pedimented dormers. On the ground floor, the windows are steel framed with plate glass, but on the first floor, tall sashes in stone architraves with keyed pulvinated friezes and projecting cornices open onto bellied wrought-iron balconettes supported on stone corbels. The tall chimney stacks of banded brick and stone and the blocky stone quoins are borrowed from Shaw.

Bateman undermines the Classical plan by placing his entrance to the side in an unusual triangular porch with a somewhat Jacobean balustrade and much stone-carving; reeded Ionic engaged columns, acanthus decoration to the cornice, cartouches over the doors and foliate decoration to the jambs.

His offices for J. Mountford in Cornwall Street of 1904 display a freedom of expression that displays Arts and Crafts informality with Classicising elements to produce a building of great playfulness.[50]

At first sight this appears to be a symmetrical composition, but on further examination is more complex. The four-storey elevation is divided into five bays. The first is blank; the third carries the entrance to No. 91, with an open scroll pedi-

The Birmingham and District Bank, Broad Street, 1898, photographed in 1973

ment, broken into by a tall window with shell hood. In the fifth bay is the door to No. 89, given a similar but subtly different treatment, its scroll pediment holding a tablet of stone. Bays of sash windows with rusticated heads rise to a gadrooned cornice and display flush stone dressings with diamond patterns at second floor level.

Occular windows with stone surrounds pierce the brickwork between the bays at second floor level. Above this are three sash windows in moulded frames with arched heads and diamonds in the tympana. Diamond shaped frames of stonework fill the spaces between the windows, which are not centred on the bays below. The deep parapet is decorated by wreaths and chequerboard panels of brick and stone. The elevation is built in precise, hard red bricks and carved stone.

Bateman's Birmingham Dental Hospital, also built in 1904 was, if anything, more bizarre, introducing elements of Edwardian Baroque. Sited almost opposite Dixon's Guild of Handicrafts on Great Charles Street, it was essentially a Classical composition, but here Arts and Crafts detailing is more evident. The building was

Offices for J. Mountford 89–91 Cornwall Street, 1904

illustrated in the *Building News* on 5 August 1904. The ground floor is squat, with doors to each side and two large windows to the centre, given stone surrounds and keystones. A cartouche at the centre and two keyed occuli to each side enliven the spaces between the arches. Above the string course are four tall sashes in stone architraves with aprons. Surmounting these architraves are blind brick arches of tile and stone in a chequerboard pattern. On the second floor, the windows are given steep broken pediments supported on pilasters and oversized keystones. Circular and diamond-shaped stone panels fill the spaces between. In his obituary of Bateman, Hobbiss specifically mentions this building as of note.[51]

Church work was another area of interest for Bateman but he was not as successful in this field as some of his contemporaries such as Bidlake, having no grounding in it. Bateman studied churches in England and France on his sketching tours with the Birmingham Architectural Association and wrote articles for the Birmingham and Warwickshire Archaeological Society on historic church buildings.

He designed few churches in his career and none that were fully completed. Bateman entered the competition for the church of St Agatha, Sparkbrook, in 1891, which was won by Bidlake. He acted as assessor for the 1914 competition for St Germain's, Edgbaston, choosing Reynolds' design as the winner.[52]

Two designs for new churches by Bateman were published in the *Architectural Review* in 1906, in a special issue to publicise that year's Royal Academy Exhibition at which the designs were shown (Bateman's Four Oaks houses were also exhibited). The first of these, on Aldridge Road, Four Oaks, was not built but the illustration in *The Builder*, in which the designs were also published, shows a long, low building, without aisles, and with a crenellated tower over the choir, topped by a steeply pitched roof.[53] A sturdy buttressed porch projects from the side of the nave and an external pulpit is inserted at the base of the tower. The interior has a vaulted ceiling. The description in *The Builder* states that the church was designed to seat 300 and was to be built in red sand-stock bricks with stone dressings and stone slate roofs.

Both this and St James' Church, Mere Green Road, were won in competition, the assessor being Bidlake. St James' Church is another long, low design, this time with a squat western tower with heavy clasped buttresses, pyramidal roof and chequerboard parapet.[54] The chancel is differentiated from the nave only by a small bellcote breaking through the ridge of the roof. The aisles are very low and are decorated with the same chequerboard masonry. The organ loft is expressed by a crenellated tower on the side of the chancel, with tall window containing flowing, intricately carved tracery. *The Builder* describes the interior as having a plaster barrel-vaulted ceiling running continuously from east to west.[55] Unfortunately, only the chancel was completed and today sits awkwardly at one end of the early 19th-century church by D. R. Hill that Bateman's was to have replaced.

Another aspect of Bateman's church work included ecclesiastical decoration and church furnishings, often in the manner of Ninian Comper. He designed screens and colour decorations for St. Mary's Lichfield, Wednesbury Parish Church and St James, West Bromwich, as well as church screens and furniture at

Holy Trinity Church, Coleshill Street, Sutton Coldfield, painted roof decoration, 1914 and 1929

King's Heath. Hobbiss wrote that 'the intricate lace-like patterns of his ecclesiastical work were works of art'.[56]

The internal appearance of Holy Trinity, Sutton Coldfield, was totally transformed by Bateman's spectacular decorations in the years between 1914 and 1929.The church dates from the early sixteenth century. Bateman's interventions began in 1914 when he decorated the ceiling of the chancel, which was a plain wooden barrel-vault.[57] His embellishments involved dividing up the ceiling into panels with gilded beading and filling the panels with abstracted foliage and flower patterns reminiscent of a William Morris design. At the junction between the beading and the wall are red and gold shields which depict the instruments of the passion. Above this is a narrow painted banner decorated with inscriptions in Gothic script, and the panels nearest the east window hold angels with further inscribed banners. Gilded low-relief foliate decorations mark the intersection of the beading. The effect is light, despite the strong colour and abundance of gold. In 1929 he completed his scheme with the decoration of the nave roof and the ceiling of the Vesey Chapel.

In 1913, on completing his second term as President of the BAA, Bateman was presented with a portrait by W. J. Wainwright R.W.S., a significant Birmingham artist of his day. The portrait depicts Bateman seated, sketch pad in hand, with a bust of his father on a marble plinth behind him. On the wall at the rear is a portrait of his grandfather, Joseph Bateman, in an oval frame. All three generations of architects captured on one canvas. He donated the portrait to the BAA in 1946.[58]

In 1924, Bateman moved to a house he converted from a pair of cottages in Bourton-on-the-Hill. The change of address did not mean that he was planning retirement (he was sixty-one), and he continued to play an active role in the practice and carry out a great deal of work in his beloved Cotswolds.

He died at Bourton-on-the-Hill on 5 August 1947, aged eighty-five, and was buried at St Mary and St Margaret's Church, Castle Bromwich.

In his obituary in the RIBA *Journal*, Holland Hobbiss wrote 'there has been no Architect in our City of Birmingham who has so much influenced the work of his contemporaries as C. E. Bateman. . . . He has now passed away but his work lives on and will continue to be a source of example and inspiration for succeeding generations'.[59]

Bateman's design philosophy can be summed up in a quote from his paper to the AA in 1900; 'Architecture is nothing but construction, with the addition of a refining and beautifying element, obtained by continued and enthusiastic study, developing a certain natural aptitude'.[60]

List of Architectural Works of C. E. Bateman

C. E. Bateman (1863–1947) was articled to his father, J. J. Bateman in 1880. From 1885 to 1887 he worked for the London architects, Verity and Hunt, and attended classes of the Architectural Association. He became a partner in his father's practice of Bateman and Bateman in 1887. After his father's death he continued the practice assisted by Alfred Hale. He continued working for the firm after moving to the Cotswolds in 1924.

His work up to 1919 has been included in the list.

WORK IN BIRMINGHAM AND ITS ENVIRONS

PUBLIC

1891–93 Restoration and recording of Church of St Mary and St Margaret, Castle Bromwich

1904 Birmingham Dental Hospital, Great Charles St, Birmingham [D]

1905 Free Library, Church Rd, Northfield (with Alfred Hale – won in competition)

1907–09 Addition of chancel, Church of St James, Mere Green Rd, Sutton Coldfield

1908 Alterations and additions to Woodlands Hospital, Bristol Rd for The Crippled children's Union; 1911 Isolation Block [D]

1913 Mission Church of St Paul, Finnemore Rd, Bordesley

1913 Alterations to Church of St John, Warmley

1914 Decoration of Chancel, Holy Trinity Church, Sutton Coldfield; 1929 Decoration of nave and North Chapel

COMMERCIAL

1898 Birmingham and District Bank, Broad St, Birmingham

c. 1899 The Cannon Street Hotel, Birmingham [D]

1903–04 The Red Lion Public House, Vicarage Rd, King's Heath

1904–05 Offices for J. Mountford, Nos 89–91 Cornwall St, Birmingham.

INDUSTRIAL

1894 Offices and printing works for John Feeney, proprietor of the *Birmingham Post* and *Daily Mail*, Cannon St, Birmingham [D]

1898 Westley Richards Gun Factory, Grange Rd, Selly Oak.

1899 Printing works for George Jones & Son, Cornwall St, Birmingham(unexecuted)

1900 Warehouse for S. C. Larkins & Son, Cannon Street, Birmingham (unexecuted)

1901 Factory for Thomas Smith & Sons, Adderley Rd, Saltley

DOMESTIC

Houses on The Cartland Estate, Kings Heath:

1889 Nos 241–43 Vicarage Rd (semi-detached pair of houses)

1892 Nos 247–49 Vicarage Rd (semi–detached pair of houses)

1892 Nos 4–6 Stanley Rd (semi-detached pair of houses)

1892–93 Nos 8 and 10 Stanley Rd (detached houses)

1893 Nos 12–14 Stanley Rd (semi-detached pair of houses)

1894 Nos 258 Vicarage Rd and 2 Cartland Rd (semi-detached pair of houses)

1894 Nos 254 Vicarage Rd and 1 Cartland Rd (semi-detached pair of houses

1894–96 Semi-detached pairs of houses at King's Heath, illustrated in *The Builder*, April 23 1898, p. 395. (It is not known if these houses were built)

1896 The Gable House, 42 Cartland Rd, King's Heath for Walter Fitzmaurice

1903 No. 310 Vicarage Rd

Other Houses

1891 Lodges to Bremesgrove Chase, Mearse Lane and Brookhouse Rd, Barnt Green for Lord Austin

1892 Firsdene, Bromsgrove for F. M. Cartland (? unexecuted)

c. 1895 The Cedars, Calthorpe Rd (*The Builder*, 27 Nov. 1897, p. 440 refers to it as a 'half-timbered house')

1896 Nos 1 and 3 Rectory Lane ('Birnam' and 'Millbrick'), Castle Bromwich. (Semi-detached pair of houses. Bateman and his father lived in one of them)

1897–98 The Homestead, 25 Woodbourne Rd, Edgbaston for Percival Jones

1900 No. 30 Fiery Hill Rd, Barnt Green.

1900 The Grey House, Mearse Lane, Barnt Green

c. 1900 Garden layout for The Leasowes, Lichfield Rd, Four Oaks (house by Ernest Newton)

1901 Conversion and extension, no. 10 Fiery Hill Rd, Barnt Green

1901. House, Barnt Green. Illustrated in *The Builder*, 23 November 1901. (It is not known if this house was built)

1901–02 Carhampton House, no. 11 Luttrell Rd, Four Oaks for J. E. Baines

1901–02 Hawkesford, No. 14 Bracebridge Rd, Four Oaks for J. J. Bateman

1903 No. 3 Anchorage Rd, Sutton Coldfield for Charles Keeling

1903 Nos 5–7 Anchorage Rd, Sutton Coldfield for Charles Keeling. (Bateman lived in no. 5 from 1910 to 1924)

1903 House, Alcester Rd, Moseley, for Richard Smith

1903 Redlands, no. 1 Hartopp Rd, Four Oaks for Frank Parker

1904 Bryn Teg, no. 35 Bracebridge Rd, Four Oaks for H. Scott Jones

1905 Pinfold House, no. 27 Cherry Rd, Barnt Green

1907 House and stabling in Streetly Lane for H. Bevan

1908 Additions to Wootton Green, Balsall Heath for C. E. Clive

1907–08 The Rectory, Rectory Lane, Castle Bromwich

1909 Lovelace Hill, no. 123 Widney Manor Rd, Solihull for Brigadier Ludlow

1910 St Peter's Vicarage, George St West, Ladywood

c. 1910 Extension and conversion of two cottages to a single house, Millmead, Wake Green Rd

1911–12 St James's Vicarage, Edgbaston, Birmingham

1911–12 St Peter's Vicarage, Maney Hill Rd, Sutton Coldfield

1912 and 1920 Twatling Green Farm, no. 19 Twatling Rd, Barnt Green (restoration and additions to timber-framed farmhouse)

1913 St Nicolas' Vicarage, Lower Tower St, New Town, Birmingham

c. 1914 House for Miss Nettlefold, Farquhar Rd, Edgbaston, Birmingham

1914–15 St Wulstan's Vicarage, Bournbrook Rd, Selly Oak

1915 House on corner of Ladywood Road and Bracebridge Rd, Four Oaks for Mrs Burnett

WORK OUTSIDE BIRMINGHAM

PUBLIC

1903–04 Town Hall, High Wycombe, Buckinghamshire (with Alfred Hale – won in competition only partly built)

1913 County Council Schools, Lime Tree Avenue, Broadway

c. 1917 Union of London and Smiths Bank, Nuneaton.

Colour decorations to interior, St Mary's Church, Lichfield, Staffs.

Colour decorations to interior, Parish Church, Wednesbury

Colour decorations to interior, St James's Church, West Bromwich

Cottage Hospital, Moreton-in-the-Marsh, Glos.

COMMERCIAL

1910 Lygon Arms, Broadway for S. B. Russell. Great Hall and kitchen wing; 1911 Rear bedroom wing; 1919 garage wing; 1922 alterations to smoke room and bar

DOMESTIC

1908, Mill Hay, Broadway, alterations and additions to 17th-century house (in association with George Hunt)

c. 1910 Aber Artro, Llanbedr, Gwynedd

1910 West End, Broadway, extensions to 17th-century house

1912–13 Bannuts, Church St, Broadway, addition of rough-cast wing with barrel vaulted hall

c. 1915 Green Close, Snowshill, Glos., alterations and additions to four cottages for Mr H. Peach with terraced gardens at rear

1916 Sands Farm, Broadway, addition of two storey porch for S. B. Russell

1916 Asthall Manor, Asthall, Oxfordshire. Extensions to 17th-century house for Lord Redesdale. Gabled bay added to north *c.* 1918 Honiley Hall, Honiley. Alterations for H. L. Wade. (Dining room illustrated in *The Builder*, 9 July 1919)

c. 1919 Tower Close, Snowshill. Conversion of three 16th-century and 17th-century cottages into one dwelling for S. B. Russell (in association with Gordon Russell)

Manor House, Wroxall, West Midlands. Alterations

Sopworth, Wiltshire. Alterations to house for Colonel the Hon. Algernon Stanley

---

NOTES

[1] J. S. Nettlefold, *Practical Housing* (Letchworth, 1908) p. 32.

[2] Remo Granelli, 'Architecture' in *By Hammer and Hand: The Arts and Crafts Movement in Birmingham*, ed. by Alan Crawford (Birmingham, 1984) p. 50.

[3] Royal Institute of British Architects Journal, September 1947, p. 575.

[4] A. S. Grey, *Edwardian Architecture: A Biographical Dictionary* (1985) p. 259.

[5] T. Affleck Greaves, *Bedford Park: The First Garden Suburb* (1999) p. 8.

[6] Information from Birmingham Architectural Association *Annual Reports*.

[7] BAA *Annual Report*, 1897–98.

[8] Royal Institute of British Architects, Bateman's Fellowship Application.

[9] *The Building News*, 84, 19 June 1903.

[10] See chapter 4.

[11] *Builders' Journal and Architectural Record*, 10, 14 February 1900, p. 19.

[12] C. E. Bateman, 'Small Houses', in *The Builder*, 78, 17 March 1900, pp. 258–62.

[13] *Ibid*, p. 259.

[14] *Ibid*.

[15] Herman Muthesius, *The English House* (first pub. 1904, English translation, 1979) p. 55.

[16] W. H. Bidlake, H. Ricardo, J. Cash, *The Modern Home: A Book of British Domestic Architecture for Moderate Means*, edited by W. S. Sparrow, (1906) pp. 58–59.

[17] *Building News*, 53, 9 December 1892, p. 805.

[18] *The Builder*, 80, 2 March 1901. Birmingham Central Library Archives and Heritage Services (hereafter BCL AHS), Birmingham Building Register, app. no. 2460, 1896.

[19] Bateman, 'Small Houses', p. 259.

[20] *Ibid*, p. 260.

[21] *The Builders' Journal and Architectural Record*, 10, 14 February, 1900, p. 19.

[22] Metropolitan Borough of Solihull and City of Birmingham, Castle Bromwich Conservation Area, April 1980, p. 14.

[23] *The Builder*, 80, 2 March 1901, p. 214.

[24] Bateman, 'Small Houses', p. 260.

[25] *Ibid*.

[26] *Ibid*, p. 258.

[27] *The Builder*, 80, 1 June 1901.

[28] P. Davey, *Arts and Crafts Architecture* (1997) p. 105.

[29] *Scenes from Sutton Coldfield's Past*, edited by R. Lear (Sutton Coldfield, 1989).

[30] *Arts and Crafts Architecture*, p. 105.

[31] Douglas Hickman *et al*, *Conservation in Four Oaks: A Proposal* (unpublished report, Victorian Society, Birmingham Group, 1981).

[32] *Ibid*, p. 3.

[33] Granelli, 'Architecture,' p. 51.

[34] Sutton Coldfield Library (hereafter SCL) Sutton Coldfield Building Register, app. no. 1374, 1903, house, Hartopp Rd for Frank Parker.

[35] Bateman, 'Small Houses'.

[36] Lawrence Weaver, *Small Country Houses of Today* (1910) p. 8.

[37] *Ibid*, p. 10.

[38] Granelli, 'Architecture', p. 51; SCL, Sutton Coldfield Building Register, app. no. 1487, 1904.

[39] SCL, Sutton Coldfield Building Register, app. no. 1214, 1901, house for Bateman and Bateman.

[40] *Recent English Domestic Architecture* edited by M. Macartney (1910).

[41] SCL, Sutton Coldfield Building Register, app. no. 1213, 1901, house for J. E. Baines.

⁴² R. Fellowes, *Edwardian Architecture: Style and Technology* (1995) p. 19.

⁴³ *Transactions of the Birmingham and Warwickshire Archaeological Society*, 1893, pp. 1–7.

⁴⁴ SCL, Sutton Coldfield Building Register, app. no. 2326, 1911, for Vicarage, Maney Hill Road.

⁴⁵ *Building News*, 86, 15 July 1904; BCL AHS, King's Norton and Northfield Building Register, app. no. 1563, 27 July 1903.

⁴⁶ B. Oliver, *The Renaissance of the English Public House* (1947) p. 86.

⁴⁷ *Builders' Journal and Architectural Record*, 10, 14 February 1900, p. 21.

⁴⁸ BCL AHS, King's Norton and Northfield Building Register, app. no. 3433, 15 Sept 1898.

⁴⁹ *The Builder*, 82, 19 July 1902.

⁵⁰ BCL AHS, Birmingham Building Register, app. no. 6162, October 1904.

⁵¹ RIBA *Journal*, September, 1947, p. 576.

⁵² Bryan Little, *Birmingham Buildings* (Newton Abbot, 1971) p. 123.

⁵³ *The Builder*, 90, 26 May 1906, p. 560.

⁵⁴ SCL, Sutton Coldfield Building Register, app. no. 1876, 1907, additions to St James's Church.

⁵⁵ *Ibid.*

⁵⁶ Obituary in BAA *Year Book*, 1947, p. 28.

⁵⁷ Norman Granville Evans and Margaret Gardner, *Holy Trinity, Sutton Coldfield* (1987).

⁵⁸ BAA *Annual Report*, 1946.

⁵⁹ Obituary in RIBA *Journal*, Sept 1947, p. 575.

⁶⁰ Bateman, 'Small Houses', p. 260.

20 Crouch and Butler

RUDI HERBERT AND BARBARA SHACKLEY

The success of Joseph Crouch (1859–1936) was due to his diversity and his energy. He had the ability to respond quickly to the changing building market of the time and to supply what was wanted at attractive prices. His wide interests and connections also provided him with many introductions to Birmingham entrepreneurs. At the beginning these led to the designing of workshops, small industrial premises and commercial buildings but then moved on to working class housing and large domestic dwellings. Thereafter he designed schools, colleges, ten nonconformist churches and several local government buildings. During the thirty years between 1884 and 1914, he designed over sixty industrial and commercial buildings; produced at least thirty working-class housing schemes, which comprised over four hundred and fifty houses and two hostels, and over twenty large prestigious dwelling houses. Out of a total of ten competitions, he won four of them and came second in two. In terms of architectural interest, his public buildings, designed with originality and inspiration, are the most impressive and his greatest successes.

Joseph Crouch was born, educated, and worked throughout his life in the Birmingham area and appears to have followed in the footsteps of his father, William Jeffs Crouch an architect or a builder in a small way.[1] He was educated at King Edward VI Grammar School, Birmingham and at the age of seventeen, articled to David Smith and Sons for four years. From 1880 to 1884, he worked in the offices of Messrs Thomas Naden and F. B. Endells of Birmingham and was a part time student at Birmingham Municipal School of Art. Briefly, whilst working for a Mr Weaver in London, he attended part-time classes in South Kensington.

Joseph Crouch

In 1884, at the age of twenty-five he set up his own practice in 39, Newhall Street, Birmingham, and was joined two years later by his partner Edmund Butler (1862–1936).[2] They moved their office to 67a, New Street in 1923 and in 1934, at the age of seventy-five, Crouch retired, having worked for fifty years.[3] Butler had married Crouch's sister and worked very much in the shadow of his brother-in-law. A third partner, Rupert Savage (1871–1956) joined them in 1902.[4] Joseph Crouch and Edmund Butler were elected fellows of the Royal Institute of British Architects in January 1914.[5] Crouch had two sons, Robert Kenneth, a quantity surveyor, and Alec Leycester, a confectioner, and two daughters, Marjorie and Perry, all of whom survived him.[6]

In 1899, Crouch built Seven Gables for himself in Sutton Coldfield.[7] He moved to Latimer House, Kenilworth in 1911 and then to Quarry House in 1914. He was a man with many outside interests, a Mason, a member of the Birmingham Liberal Association and was closely associated with the non-conformist movement, his brother being a Methodist minister. He was interested in local history and archaeology, organizing major excavations at Kenilworth Abbey.[8] From 1913 to 1922 he served on the Kenilworth Urban District Council, became a member of the Warwick Board of Guardians and was a Justice of the Peace for Warwickshire, from 1917 until his death. In the 1920s he moved to 27a, Dale Street, Leamington Spa where he lived until his death in 1936.

One of the first British architects to study town-planning, Crouch visited Germany for that purpose before the First World War. He designed a number of housing schemes on Tachbrook Road and Leicester Street in Leamington Spa and he was a member of the Town Planning Institute.[9] He wrote four books on architecture and art, the first two written in conjunction with his partner, Edmund Butler. *The Apartments of the House, their Arrangement, Furnishings and Decoration* written in 1900, shows their interest in the architecture, interior design and furnishings of the English House especially during the Elizabethan and Jacobean periods. This book was principally a practical book of advice. In his book *Puritanism in Art: An Enquiry into a Popular Fallacy*, published in 1910, he stated 'that great art was not impossible if theories of Puritanism were to prevail'. Crouch's two books on non-conformist church architecture are instructive in the architecture, decoration and seating arrangement of his churches. The first published in 1901, *Churches, Mission Halls and Schools for Non-Conformists*, explores topics such as sites, planning, acoustics, ventilation, wiring and lighting.[10] Crouch thought that, 'the Gothic type of church without certain modifications was unsuitable for non-conformist purposes, because the sermon plays such an important part in their services'.[11] His fourth book, entitled *Planning and Designing of a Methodist Church*,[12] was a much briefer work, published in 1930 at the end of his career.

Although when Crouch began his practice, England was experiencing an economic depression between 1875 and 1886, it was at this time that many of

Front cover of *The Apartments of the House* by Edmund Crouch and Joseph Butler, published in 1900

Factory for E. L. Gyde,
32 Frederick Street, 1914

Birmingham's factories were built, and Crouch and Butler designed factories, warehouses, storerooms, stables and allied types of industrial and commercial units. Many of these buildings were described as 'shopping' – long, brick buildings, often only one brick thick, with rows of metal windows, often at the rear of industrial premises and used extensively in the Birmingham area. He supplied new factories and small purpose-built workshops for the Jewellery Quarter where employment rose from 14,000 in 1886 to 30,000 in 1914.[13] In Great Hampton Street he designed shopping for George Cadbury in 1887.[14] His work for the jeweller E. L. Gyde included an office showroom and a factory in 1914 at 32, Frederick Street[15] and houses in Four Oaks.[16] The Frederick Street factory, recently refurbished externally and listed Grade II, is designed in the shape of a T. Probably built for multi-occupancy, the cross of the T, formed by a street range of three and a half storeys with a façade of cream coloured terracotta and green-glazed brick, originally contained offices and warehousing. The stem of the T was formed by a three storeyed workshop range built of blue and red brick with a flat asphalt roof.[17] Other industrial buildings include a factory in Lionel Street, an alteration of a warehouse in Great Charles Street and another in Aston, workshops at 50 Bracebridge Street[18] and factories in Chester Street[19] and Oliver Street.[20] In New Town Row he supplied designs for a warehouse and shop[21] and in Saltley, a cycle accessory factory and workshop for Charles Brampton,[22] with a cycle factory for A. W. G. Baxter in Sparkbrook.[23] He designed shops, storerooms[24] and stables[25] in Cheapside, Digbeth and throughout the area he designed the addition of many w.c.s.

Most of the factories and warehouse units were relatively small. One factory on New Town Row, of three storeys had a frontage of 72 feet,[26] whereas the factory in Frederick Street for the jeweller, E. L. Gyde was 135 feet wide[27] and one built for W. J. Baker in Northwood Street, had a frontage of 308 feet.[28] The factories for A. W. G. Baxter in Sparkbrook[29] built in 1896 had ground and first floor windows decorated with keystones and William Pope's factory[30] in Livery Street built in 1895 had Doric pillars at each end of the first floor, whilst the ground floor windows were decorated with brickwork.

The most impressive of Crouch's factory units was for A. R. Dean for whom he had already altered premises in Dalton Street. In 1896, nos 153 and 155, Corporation Street, including a shop/workshop and Pitman's vegetarian restaurant was designed for A. R. Dean who constructed much of the furniture for the houses designed by Crouch. This exuberant design, of four storeys and two attics was built of red brick and buff terracotta and had four sets of different styled windows on each floor and was in two parts vertically with the gable bridging the larger part. The skyline had a small oriel, a tiny octagonal domed top with a huge Flemish gable with a smaller gable to the right. The large gable was decorated with an allegory of Birmingham and Industry by Benjamin Creswick. Uniformity was provided by a frieze, also by Benjamin Creswick, representing carpenters at work and diners at table, with a city coat of arms above the arches and a string course with cable moulding pulled by putti at each end. This is one of the best pieces of terracotta work in Birmingham.[31] In 1896, Birmingham Gaiety Concert Hall in Gem Street was rebuilt for Weldon Watts,[32] followed by Sydenham Hotel on Golden Hillock and Anderton Roads for Thomas Leckie.[33] In 1912, Crouch was responsible for the building of the former Royal Birmingham Society of Artists, on the site of Rickman & Hutchinson's 1820 gallery. It had a top-lit room in a two storey rear block. The original plaque still survives in the new RBSA building in Brook Street.

Demand for factories and warehouses associated with the jewellery trade, dwindled just before the First World War.

Between 1884 and 1914, due to a big rise in population, Bordesley, for instance doubled in size from 38,552 in 1871 to 62,855 in 1911, the building of working class housing increased both in the private and the municipal sector.[34] The Improvement Acts, such as the 1875 Artisans and Labourers' Dwellings Improvement Act, encouraged slum clearance on a large scale and resulted in the construction of Corporation Street in Birmingham. The Birmingham by-laws required thorough

153–155 Corporation Street, 1896

Detail of frieze, 153–155 Corporation Street

ventilation, higher ceilings and improved sanitary services. Crouch carried out at least thirty commissions for working class housing between 1884 and 1914, involving two hostels for women and at least four hundred and fifty houses. Of the houses, two hundred and ninety one were for three principal clients, John Loughton, H. C. Fulford and Frank Sherwood.

In 1888, his first large commission, was for fifty-six houses situated in New-Town Row,[35] followed by ninety seven houses in Kenhelm Road, Smallheath in 1895/6, both for H. C. Fulford.[36] Fulford was a Liberal MP for Birmingham, a councillor for Nechells and chairman of the Markets and Fairs Sub-committee. His firm, Fulfords, family brewers had been taken over by the Holt Brewery Company in 1887.[37] In Saltley, Crouch designed eleven houses in Highfield Road for Alfred Johnson in 1897.[38] For Frank Isherwood he designed forty houses in Farndon Road, Saltley in 1910,[39] followed by houses in three adjoining roads in 1913, comprising eight in Alum Rock Road, one hundred and fourteen in Foxton Road and twelve in Hazelbeach Road.[40] For Mr Clarke, in 1889, he designed ten houses in Lodge Road, Winson Green followed in 1891 by sixteen houses in Villiers

Street opposite Winson Green Prison.[41] In 1887, John Loughton commissioned eight houses in Boulton Road, eight houses off Bacchus Road in 1893,[42] and sixteen houses and a shop at Leonard Street in 1894. These terraced houses, of two bays and two storeys with tunneled access to the rear, were built of red brick. They were set back from a small garden with a small wall. The only decoration was a three or five-sided bay window and buff terracotta lintels above the windows and the doors.

The artisan dwellings which Crouch designed were all of a reasonable standard. The eight houses for John Loughton in Boulton Road, built in 1887, now near the Hockley Flyover have a small entrance hall which is 11 feet 6 inches long and a parlour with a front bay and sitting room, both measuring 14 feet 6 inches by 11 feet 6 inches, considerably larger than those built in Bristol at the same time.[43] The bedrooms and upstairs bathroom were also considerably larger with an upstairs landing. Crouch's designs had two-storey rear annex projections containing three rooms down and three up. However, the ninety houses which Crouch designed for Fulford in Kenelm Road during 1895 and 1896 again with a two-storey rear annex, were considerably smaller and had fewer amenities.[44] The parlour, kitchen and two bedrooms measured 11 feet by 12 feet while the scullery and third bedroom measured only 9 feet by 7 feet. Kenelm Road consisted of long terraces with a tunnel entrance between every two houses. In 1910, Farndon Road, Saltley, the houses were built in rows of six, with a gap separating them from the next row with tunnel access.[45]

John Burnett believes that the lay-out of these houses, influenced by the Birmingham by-laws in 1876 began to breakdown the court system, to improve and control the standards of new houses, invariably built in terraces with access to the rear being through a tunnel or passage at ground level between blocks.[46] The principal drawback of these houses was their lack of sanitation, only nine per cent of them having a wash-house and none a bathroom. By 1914, Birmingham still had about 42,000 back-to-backs, the majority still situated in enclosed courts.[47] J. S. Nettlefold the industrialist and chairman of the Housing Committee opened up the enclosed courts by removing the end houses.[48]

Crouch was probably less concerned with the style of these working class houses and the size of the rooms than meeting the cost requirements of the developer.

The Arts and Crafts houses designed by Crouch and Butler are in complete contrast to those they designed for developers. 'Arts and Crafts' a phrase invented in 1887, stood for craftsmanship brought back to life in an industrial society. It advocated a new sense of the visual arts in which the crafts would have the same dignity as fine art.[49] Writing in his book, *The Apartments of the House, their Arrangement, Furnishing and Decoration*,[50] Crouch attempted to bridge the gap between fine arts and the decorative arts as something precise and challenging when craftsmanship was brought back to life in an industrial city; the crafts should have the same dignity as the fine arts.

This movement in Birmingham flourished most strongly from about 1890 to 1905 and was patronised by the upper middle classes, such as the Kenricks, Nettlefolds and other non-conformist industrialists. It was these people who could afford to purchase expensive hand made products.[51] Architecturally, it searched for a new free style, rooted in vernacular buildings, but the search took individuals down different paths. Of the architects who fostered the movement in Birmingham, Joseph Crouch and Edmund Butler perhaps discounted Philip Webb's low style vernacular revival in favour of the more spectacular, Old English or Elizabethan revival, initiated by George Devey.[52] Both Webb and Devey emphasised the necessity of relating their building to the site and to local traditions of buildings in the area. Crouch and Butler admitted that they were eclectic in their choice of design and felt that style was of little importance compared with design, so long as the result is harmonious.[53] They believed that decorative or applied art was an integral part of the design of a building and it should not be added to later. This would help to raise the status of the decorative arts which the two architects championed.

In Birmingham, 'The Birmingham Group', mostly consisting of former students and teachers of the Birmingham School of Art, became the powerhouse of the decorative craft movement in Birmingham. The Birmingham Guild of Handicraft was founded in 1895 to supply handmade articles superior in beauty of design and soundness of workmanship, to those made by machinery. 'One shall make only what gives pleasure both to the craftsman and to the buyer'.[54] Some of the members of the Guild became closely associated with Crouch and Butler's domestic commissions. Crouch had attended the School of Art and was critical of the mechanical smoothness and perfection of finish of machine-made goods.

Crouch and Butler were foremost in implementing this practice. The interiors of their houses were richly textured with natural materials. They commissioned craftsmen of the Birmingham and Bromsgrove Guilds such as Henry Payne, who undertook the design of stained glass windows, Mary Newill, who was responsible for many of the tapestries and Benjamin Creswick, who created the figured plasterwork. Both Mary Newill, who taught needlework at the School from 1892 to 1920 and Benjamin Creswick, had their work reproduced in the art magazine *The Studio* between 1893 and 1901.[55] Mary embroidered many of the wall hangings for Crouch and Butler's houses, her picture subjects deriving from medieval romance, the first of her Faerie Queene hangings being made to fit between timber framing in Edmund Butler's own house in Sutton Coldfield.[56] Crouch and Butler drew heavily for inspiration from Aston Hall, completed in 1632.

One important feature of the Elizabethan and Jacobean house was the 'Hall' which was re-introduced not only by Crouch and Butler but also by many of their contemporaries. Remo Granelli, in *By Hammer and Hand* said that it tended to

Hall of a house designed by Crouch and Butler illustrated in *The Apartments of the House*

become a central feature, something of a showpiece serving as an antechamber to the various living rooms. The hall's main feature was the inglenook fireplace usually lighted by a small stained glass window above high-backed wooden seats on either side of the fire. Also the frieze played an important part as an in-built decorative feature which was intended to enhance the authentic mood of a Jacobean hall, dining room or drawing room.[57]

The interiors of Crouch and Butler's houses generally followed a basic plan especially on the ground floor with certain variations in size and location of rooms. The Hall often acted both as a sitting area and as an ante-chamber to the various living rooms, as in the case of 59 Salisbury Road, Moseley of 1897, as well as serving as a crossing point to the three main rooms and the kitchen. However in Seven Gables, Sutton Coldfield, the home Joseph Crouch designed for himself, the ground plan shows the hall in a rather isolated position at one end of the ground floor and only leading to the dining room. Douglas Hickman says that, though impressive, it has a dainty domestic scale cunningly achieved by a height of one and a half storeys rather than the medieval two storeys. At the other end a

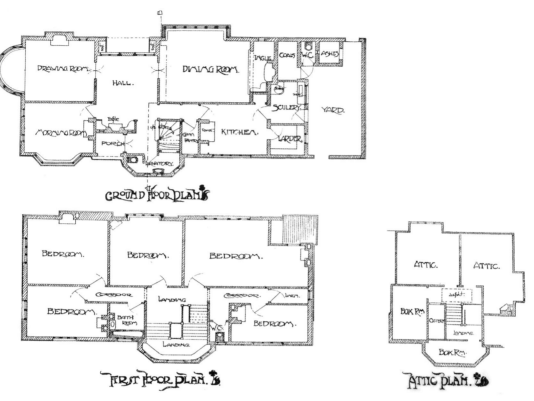

59 Salisbury Road, floor plans, 1897, from *The Apartments of the House*

low inglenook has a copper canopied fire place, flanked by stained glass by Mary Newill representing John Ball and Watt Tyler. A generous bay-window throws light onto a canvas mural made in 1898 by Fred Davis which illustrates Morris's dream of John Ball, leading peasant archers returning from the butts.[58] The ground plan of The Drift, 18, Wentworth Road, Four Oaks built in 1898 for Charles Brampton, cycle accessory manufacturer, shows several inglenooks, a very large one in the hall and another in the drawing room.[59] The houses generally have four good sized bedrooms on the second floor and an attic which provides sleeping quarters for the servants. The galleried hall at The Anchorage in Handsworth, designed in 1898 for A. J. Constantine, shows two frieze paintings by F. W. Davis.[60] These depict a boar hunt and part of 'The Feast of the Peacock'.

Externally the houses often possess a tower which acts as a pivot to the variety of wings and medley of roofs. There are generally two facing materials of equal importance, perhaps thin handmade brick and half-timbering.[61] The elements of stone fragments are incorporated into the brickwork, with stone window frames, battlements, chimneys and sundials. The sundial is a characteristic of these houses and examples of these can be seen at Wyndhurst, 12, The Driffold, Sutton Coldfield[62] and Avoncroft, 21, Four Oaks Road, again for Charles Brampton, and where the sundial has the inscription, 'Count the Sunny Hours'.[63] These decorative features were used by many Arts and Crafts architects but perhaps Crouch employed these features with more emphasis.

Crouch designed at least thirty of these dwellings, six of them on The Driffold and Digby Road, Sutton Coldfield. The earliest house was Newlyn, 5, The Driffold, built in 1892 for Charles Brampton. This set the standard for a number of individually designed houses during the 1890s. Brampton sub-leased part of the land to his younger brother Frederick William who was a Methodist preacher and Mayor of Sutton Coldfield in 1896.[64] On this plot were numbers 7 and 9, distinguished by their Dutch gables and the next plot, 11 and 13, Melbreak, two substantial, semi-detached, Victorian and Venetian-Gothic houses.[65] The later was lived in by Buckler, of Buckler and Webb Ltd, Church Street, printers, and publishers of Crouch and Butler's book *Churches Mission Halls and Schools for Non-conformist* 1901.[66] Opposite stood Top o' the Hill, 14, Driffold which was designed by Edmund Butler for his own occupation.

Eighteen of the houses were built on the Four Oaks estate, which was developed between 1890 and 1908, and was formed from Four Oaks Park which was bought by the Marquess of Clanrikard from a race-course company. Restrictions were imposed on the estate to maintain standards on any development.[67] Cressington, 23, Four Oaks Road, another house designed for Charles Brampton in 1900, shows

Avoncroft, 21
Four Oaks
Road, 1900.
Photo: M. H.
1993

Edmund Butler's own house, Top o'the Hill, 14 The Driffold, Sutton Coldfield, 1899.
Photo: M. H. 1993

Conyar, 16 Luttrell Road, Four Oaks, 1908. Crouch and Butler also designed the adjacent house, no. 18

a fluent handling of features within the whole composition.[68] The layout is L-shaped, the living area in the horizontal of the L, and the domestic area placed on the vertical. One of its most impressive features is the broad chimney stack on the garden elevation which separates the half-timbered part from the brick-faced wing. No. 59 Salisbury Road, Moseley, 1898, is illustrated in their first book.[69] The entrance front with its half-timbered bay is sandwiched between the brick wing and the castellated porch. In 1898, Dale Cross Grange, situated in Barnt Green, was designed for Frank Rabone, a Birmingham industrialist, and a house in Farquhar Road, Edgbaston possibly number 50, were designed in 1904.[70]

How can we assess Crouch and Butler? Alan Crawford has said that, during the period between 1890 and 1905 Crouch and Butler tried to recreate a long lost world and no other Birmingham architects quite indulged themselves so much. One could say that they were pastiche Arts and Crafts architects, borrowing other people's work.[71] Nicholas Cooper is similarly critical – 'Crouch and Butler's houses with their highly contrived attempts to recapture a past that never was, are arty and silly in a peculiarly meretricious way'.[72] Remo Granelli in *By Hammer and Hand*, assesses their work in a similar vein, stating that theirs was a fairly free-and-easy philosophy which enabled them to pirate features and ideas from the rest without conscience.[73] Alan Crawford considers that one of the things the Arts and Crafts could do for a practice is to bring it up in the world. The interiors of

Sketch of 59 Salisbury Road of 1897, from *The Apartments of the House*

Wednesbury
Library and Art
Gallery, 1908.
Photo: M. H. 1993

Crouch and Butler's houses such as the Anchorage, were reproduced in Charles Holmes's *Modern British Domestic Architecture* of 1900 and in *The Studio Special* of 1901. It gave them a higher profile outside Birmingham and brought them into a network of contemporary architects and craftsmen. One might then ask how genuine were Crouch and Butler? Crouch and Butler can claim to be Arts and Crafts architects because of the place they gave to individual craftsmen. For the first three or four years of its life, the bulk of documented work by the Guild was in the houses of Crouch and Butler. The practice was affected by the decline in house building for the upper middle classes during the First World War and the Arts and Crafts movement went out of fashion.[74]

Concurrently with their domestic work, Crouch and Butler undertook many commissions in the Midlands for non-conformist churches, mostly Methodist, together with work for local Education Authorities recently established by the 1902 Education Act. The 1888 Local Government Act stimulated the building of swimming baths, libraries and art galleries. In the first decade of the twentieth century Crouch was successful in four, and second in two, of ten competitions. Seven of these were for buildings outside Birmingham and the West Midlands. Success was due to providing impressive buildings at a reasonable price, the buildings having interesting and varied facades. Crouch obtained the bid for designing the municipal centre at Rawtenstall, Lancashire of which only the domed library at a cost of £5,000 was built.[75] He was awarded a second premium prize in 1904 for Erdington Council House[76] which was never built. He obtained the commission for Wednesbury's Public Library and Art Gallery in 1908 and Pevsner commented that this was the best secular building in Wednesbury.[77] This library has an imposing Renaissance appearance and is faced with red Ruabon brick and

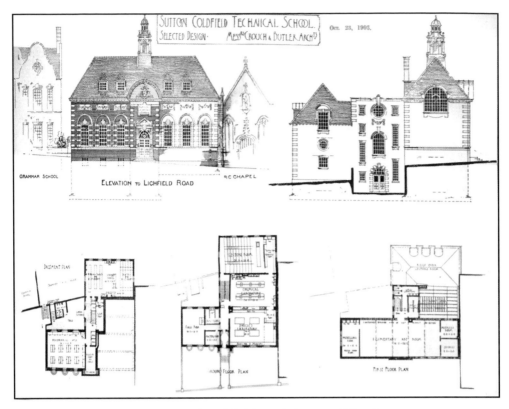

Sutton Coldfield Technical School, Lichfield Road, from *Building News*, 1903

Monk Park stone, the roof covered with green Westmorland tiles. The catalogue celebrating the opening of the Free Library describes the ground floor containing the binding department, with two rows of highly decorated Ionic columns and pilasters, a reminder of a past age. At each end is a newsroom, measuring 50 feet by 30 feet and a lecture room measuring 26 feet by 17 feet which is matched similarly in size on the first floor by the reference library which has an impressive curved plaster ceiling and a magazine room on the far side. It is well lit by windows which serve functional as well as decorative purposes.[78] The most prestigious commission that he won was the first prize for the Manchester Library and Art Gallery in 1911, at a cost of £250,000. His designs consisted of a classical central portico and four Ionic columns on a slightly elevated site. This classical style gave the building a degree of grandeur.[79] Unfortunately because of the First World War this was never built although Crouch received a 500 guineas premium.[80]

After the 1870 Education Act, the creation of School Boards and plans to make elementary education compulsory, commissions for schools and colleges were much more available. The Local Education Authorities were created in 1902 with powers to build secondary grammar schools and teacher training colleges. Crouch took full opportunity of these new architectural challenges. Most of his elementary school designs were in the Birmingham area comprising a variety of types ranging from Wesleyan church schools, built between 1888 and 1908, to the Aston Higher Grade School which was built in 1889. Elementary board schools were built in Yardley in 1892, Sutton Coldfield in 1908 and, in 1911, at King's Heath.

The Technical School in Sutton Coldfield, commissioned in 1903, including fittings, at a cost of £5,000[81] and its extension in 1917, now Sutton Coldfield College of Further Education was an important commission.[82] The school, built on a sloping site provides accommodation on three levels. The basement includes a wood workshop for twenty five pupils and a cooking school; the ground floor has a lecture room for a hundred pupils, chemical and physical laboratories each accommodating twenty five pupils; whilst the first floor contains an art and modelling room for female students. The sloping site effectively obtains the maximum space for teaching facilities. The architectural style is neo-Georgian to complement the adjoining Archbishop Veysey Grammar school, an early eighteenth century brick building.[83]

Dudley Day Training College of 1909, was designed in a neo-Georgian style for 100 day students at a cost of £10,799. It is faced with red Leicester sandstone and Albion stone dressings and the roof is covered with red Hartshill tiles. The design is symmetrical with a two-storied frontage, 120 feet long. It has two sets of four sash windows and three dormers on either side of the central projection topped with an open segmental pediment over the entrance. On each side is a typical Crouch small tower, horizontal banded brickwork and a pierced oval window with stone facings and keystone. The basement is rusticated with smooth ashlar decorated by geometrical grooves. The souvenir brochure of September 1908, commemorating the laying of the foundation stone by the Countess of Dudley, describes the building as consisting of 'an elevated ground floor with a half basement under the front portion and an upper floor over a portion only of the front block'.[84]

Crouch was placed first in the competition for Hull Training College in 1909 by the assessor who spoke very highly of his design because of the balance achieved between the three different buildings which revealed evidence of good planning and design. It was built between 1909 and 1913 and Crouch calculated that the cost of his scheme would be £33,350[85] which was three times as expensive as Dudley College. Crouch's success concerning this building type lay especially in the design of a facade for the larger colleges and features such as striped brick decoration. He provided the maximum of space on the sites to carry out their academic functions. These features were continued by Butler when he designed the new Barnsley and District Grammar School in 1912 for the cost of £15,000.

The design of churches and chapels became the backbone of Crouch's practice. Designs covered two distinct periods: firstly; chapels and mission halls built between 1887 and 1906 mostly for the working class non-conformist and characterised by naves with a capacity to seat large numbers of people; and secondly, churches built post-1906 which had much more decoration and were generally for the middle classes. Between 1887 and 1929, Crouch designed nineteen non-conformist churches which included sixteen Methodist, two Congregational and one Baptist. Of these, seven were in the West Midlands and nine in Birmingham. Crouch's ability to obtain these contracts must have been due to his membership of the Birmingham Liberal Association; coupled with the increased demand for more churches as the population expanded.

Nine chapels were built between 1889 and 1906, for the working classes. Crouch divided the Wesleyan mission hall into two types, firstly the large Hall, seating over 1000, with numerous subsidiary buildings and secondly the central Hall type, with shops to-let, producing an income.[86] One of the problems was the cost of building a large mission hall in a city centre. The first type were very functional and bereft of any decorative features and emphasised the importance of seating provision as seen in the central hall chapel at Inge Street, Long Acre of 1888. Lozells Methodist Church of 1894, was designed as a model for a large hall seating over a thousand. The general form of the plan was based on a Greek cross, and the

Four Oaks Wesleyan Church, Lichfield Road, 1907

Lea Road Congregational
Chapel, Wolverhampton,
1905

whole congregation was accommodated in the main hall at ground level. The interior was of brick with a white painted timber and plaster roof supported on two free-standing columns and had beaten metal gates.[87] Lea Road Congregational Church, Wolverhampton, built in 1905, had a large bare nave with ample seating but little decoration except a small castellated tower, as seen in some of Crouch's houses.

An example of the second type can be seen in the Wesleyan Mission Hall in Newcastle-upon-Tyne, with cupola of 1900, at a cost of £9,000 which was used by Crouch as a trial run for his designs for Westminster Central Hall in 1905.[88]

The design of the post-1906 churches manifested their admiration for English gothic architecture. Their popular 'Greek Cross' foot print allowed a congregation of five to seven hundred to sit no more than 56 feet from the preacher. Permutations concerning the inclusion and exclusion of the nave aisle columns were researched, and consequently the width of a church measuring 64 feet was reduced to 30 feet.[89] Crouch argued that Gothic columns and arches provided an impressive effect and he favoured the introduction of the square western tower containing accommodation for 236 in a gallery. Four Oaks Wesleyan church the first church described in his fourth book was designed in 1907.[90] Although Crouch was only one of many Arts and Crafts architects who had designed houses in the area, it was he who was successful in obtaining this prestigious commission. The church costing £11,000, seating 5,500, has a distinctive design with its church tower placed at the junction of the nave, chancel and transepts similar to some of the great medieval churches like St Peter's, Wolverhampton. The nave with its perpendicular arches and the clerestories gave an impression of spaciousness and antiquity. It is described by Pevsner as ashlar faced with a big crossing tower, perpendicular with tracery and carvings of the Arts and Crafts. The parsonage and caretaker's houses had a Voysey influence.[91] The bay window of the church's parlour was designed in an Arts and Crafts style possibly to act as a bridge between the church and the nearby Four Oaks estate.

Between 1910 and 1920 there were no church commissions, probably because of World War I. In spite of an acute shortage of building materials, between 1920 and 1928, Crouch obtained commissions for four churches in the West Midlands.[92] He wrote his fourth and last book *The Planning and Designing of a Methodist Church* in 1930 at the end of his architectural career.[93]

Examining Crouch's architectural career one can see a progression in terms of size and complexity. His style could be called eclectic. Compared with other Arts and Crafts architects such as Ball, C. E. Bateman and Bidlake, it was Crouch alone who started his career designing factories and working class houses and although he designed many Arts and Crafts houses of charm and interest, his architectural skill, compared to the others has been criticised. However, he did show originality and verve when designing the facades of public and educational buildings such as Wednesbury Free Library and Dudley Training College. These buildings were much more impressive in the way that Crouch used a variety of building material, colour and highlighted window features.

Crouch did not have the same influence as his contemporary Arts and Crafts architects, such as Ball, C. E. Bateman and Bidlake. Ball was Director of the Birmingham School of Architecture and President of the Birmingham Architectural Association. Bateman actively supported the Birmingham Architectural Association of which he was President on two occasions. Bidlake devoted much of his time to the education of architectural students, as a part-time tutor in architectural history, at the School of Architecture. None of these three architects had such an extensive building type portfolio as Crouch but both Bateman and Bidlake earned a national reputation for their work in Birmingham and although Ball's output was limited, what he produced was regarded as of the highest quality. Crouch could never match their national reputation for quality in any of his building types. However, the portfolio of Crouch was much more varied and extensive and it can be concluded that Crouch's strength lay chiefly in his diversity. His success was probably the result of competitive pricing and the ability to develop more sophisticated, economically attractive designs.

List of Architectural Works of Crouch and Butler

Joseph Crouch (1859–1936) was articled to David Smith & Sons of Birmingham and then worked in the office of Thomas Naden of Birmingham. He set up in independent practice in 1884 and took Edmund Butler (1862–1936) into partnership in 1886. In 1902 Rupert Savage (1871–1956) became a partner. Joseph Crouch retired in 1934.
  Crouch and Butler's work up to 1914 has been included in the list.

BIRMINGHAM AND ITS ENVIRONS

PUBLIC

1887 Chapel and additions to school, Great King St

1888 Chapel, Mission Room and Caretaker's House, Inge St, Long Acre

1888 Wesleyan Elementary School, Coventry Rd

1890 Baptist Chapel and School, St Thomas and Charles Henry Streets

1891 Alterations and additions to Liberal Club, 49–50 Gt Hampton St

1892 Red Hill Elementary School, Yardley

1893 Alterations to Birmingham and Midland Providential Dispensary, Farm St, Wednesbury

1894 Lozells Methodist Church, Lozells St

1895 Wesleyan Chapel, Somerset Rd, Handsworth

1896 Birmingham Gaiety Concert Hall at Gem St for Weldon Watts

1892 Red Hill Elementary Board School, Hay Mill; 1894 extension [D]

1898 Aston Higher Grade Elementary School, Whitehead Rd, Aston

1898 Alterations and additions to Homeopathic Hospital, Great Charles St; 1901 additions

1900 Broadway Lower School, Whitehead Rd, Aston (listed Grade II)

1901 Extension to Congregational Chapel, Walsall

1903 Technical School, Lichfield Rd, Sutton Coldfield; 1917 extensions

1903 Chapel at Wesleyan School, Streetley

1906 Holyfield Road Elementary School, Reddicap Heath, Sutton Coldfield

1907 Wesleyan Elementary School, Lichfield Rd, Sutton Coldfield

1907 Four Oaks Methodist Church, church hall, parsonage and caretaker's house, Lichfield Rd, Sutton Coldfield

1908 Public Library, Walsall St, Wednesbury

1909 Wesleyan Church, Tyburn, Birmingham

1909 Wesleyan Church, Stockfield Green, Birmingham

1909 Wesleyan Church, Streetley

1909 Dudley Training College

1910 Hostel for Girls, Corporation St

1911 Brook Lane Elementary School, King's Heath

1912 Women's Hostel, St Mary's Row for Wesleyan Central Committee

COMMERCIAL

1885 Alterations to 36 New St West

1886 Shop front at Binbury St

1885 Shop front, 40 Northhampton St for W. J. Sibley

1889 Storeroom addition, Floodgate St

1891 Offices and shopping, Newhall and Lionel Streets for Dr Parks

1892 Alterations of shops, offices and shopping at 121–22 Gooch St for Davis, Jeweller

1894 Alterations to St Paul's Club, St Paul's Sq/Caroline St

1894 3 shops and houses corner of Drayton & Alcester Rd

1896–9 Business premises and workshops, and restaurant, 153–161, Corporation St for A. R. Dean, furniture retailer and manufacturer

1897 Shop front at Conybere St for Beaumont & Son

1899 Business premises at Lancaster St for Edgar Evans

1900 Sydenham Hotel at Golden Hillock and Anderton Rds, Small Heath for Thomas Leckie

1903 New premises at Barwick St for Barwick Estates

1911 Business premises at Cornwall St for Coud Bros.

1912 New premises for Royal Birmingham Society of Artists, New St

INDUSTRIAL

1884 Store room and workshop, rear of 52, Dale End for Messrs Bagster & Bros.

1884 Shopping, rear of 140–41 Cheapside for Joseph Nochols & Sons

1885 Workshops, Bracebridge St

1887 Alterations of front, 55–57 Vyse St

1887 Shopping, Gt Hampton St for George Cadbury

1888 Workshop, New Town Row

1888 Shopping, Gt Hampton St for Hylton Restall

1888 Shopping and offices, Frederick St for B. J. Round

1889 Alterations and additions, Longmore St for Charles Beaumont

1889 Shopping and alterations, Regent St for Liliselle & Corin

1889 Storeroom addition, Floodgate St for W. H. Fellows

1890 Chimney stack, Norton St for Mr Adams

1890 Shopping and stockroom, Brasshouse Passage

1890 Factory, warehouse and shopping, Oliver St for Brampton & Co.

1890 Manufactory, Hampton St for N. S. Heeley

1891 Two-storey shopping, Gt Hampton St for Green, Caper & Co.

1891 Factory and workshop, St Clement's Rd, Saltley for Brampton and Adcock.

1891 Shopping, 5–7, Hockley Hill for S. Dale

1891 Factory, Price St for Bolt Addis

1892 Warehousing, shopping and alterations, Gt Charles St for Hukin & Heath

1893 Alterations to front and warehousing and shop at New Town Row for Simon T. King

1893 Factory, Northwood St for W. J. Baker

1893 Manufactory, Oliver St for F. Brampton; 1895 alterations and additions

1894 Shopping, 8–9 Northampton St for B. S. Round; 1895 additions to shopping and warehouse; 1901 additions to shopping

1895 Alterations to premises, Dalton St for A. R. Dean

1895 Premises, Livery St for William Pope

1895 Shopping, Schofield St for F. Brampton

1896 Manufactory, Chester St for F. Brampton

1896 Manufactory, Lionel St for Dr Parks

1896 Alterations, 32, Longmore St for W. Worral

1897 Cycle factory at Sampson Rd for A. W. G. Baxter

1897 Shopping at 36 Darwin St for Charles Hodges

1897 Alterations, Gt Hampton St for C. J. Saunders

1900 New kiln, Cliveland St for Morland Bros

1905 New factory, Hockley Hill for S. Wall

1905 Additions, Newhall St for Gorschere & Co.

1905 Alterations and additions, Cambridge St for Butler and Stagg

1906 Alterations, 41 Augusta St for Round and Son

1907 New premises, Dale End for A. R. Baxter

1908 Additions, Frederick St for E. L. Gyde

1908 Alterations and additions, Vittoria St for Heeley & Peart

1908 Alterations, Lombard St for F. Marlborough

1909 Factory, High Park St, Saltley for N. Parkins

1910 Additions, Ludgate Hill for C.W. Heap

1911 Shopping, 47 Adam St for Taylor Law & Co.

1911 Extensions, Hertford St for White & Sons

1912 Stabling, Well St for Wilson & Son

1912 Shopping, Bracebridge St for Benton & Stope Ltd

1913 Alterations, 112, 114, and 116 Bristol St, for Messrs Heath

1914 Shopping, Dartmouth St for Sterend and Sons

1914 Shopping, Fleet St for Myers & Son

1914 Additions, Cornwall St for J. Spicer and Sons

1914 Alterations, Cannon St for Singleton Cole

1914 Factory, offices and showroom, 32 Frederick St for E. L. Gyde Ltd, jewellery manufacturer

DOMESTIC

1879 House, Melbreak, 11–13, The Driffold, Sutton Coldfield for Mr Buckler

1884 Two houses rear of 16–20 Pritchett St

1886 Two houses, Spark St

1886 Two houses, Coventry Rd

1886 Wash houses back of 129–131 Hope St

1887 Six houses, Hunter's Vale

1887 Three houses, Foundry Rd

1887 Three houses, Pounsey Rd

1887 Two houses, Briton Rd

1887 Eight houses, Boulton Rd, Hockley for John Loughton

1887 Four houses, Wright St, Small Heath for Thomas Lakins

1888 Fifty-six houses, three shops, and workshop at New Town Row, St Stephen's St and Ashford St for H. C. Fulford

1889 Two houses, St Oswald's Rd.

1889 Ten houses, Norton St, Winson Green

1889 Five houses, Franklin St for John Hopkins

1889 Ten houses, Woodstock and Anderton Park Rds, Moseley for Richard Rabone

1889 Two houses, Woodstock Rd, Moseley for Richard Rabone

1890 Three houses, Woodstock Rd, Moseley for R. Rabone

1890 Two villas Northfield Rd, King's Norton for Mr Shaw

1890 House, Trevose, 7–9 The Driffold, Sutton Coldfield for F. W. Brampton [D 1967]

1891 Cottage, Lugtrout Lane, Solihull

1891 Sixteen houses, Villiers St, Winson Green

1892 Alterations to 1 Wentworth Rd, Sutton Coldfield

1892 House, Newlyn, 5 The Driffold, Sutton Coldfield for Charles Brampton [D 1967]

1892 Two cottages, Erdington for W. Davis

1893 Eight houses off Bacchus Rd, for John Loughton

1893 Two houses/premises at corner Dudley and Chiswell Rds for A. Tranter

1894 Sixteen houses and shop, Leonard St for John Loughton

1895 Forty-six houses, Kenelm Rd, Small Heath for H. C. Fulford

1896 House, Edgbaston Rd for John Beaumont

1896 Fifty-one houses, Kenhelm Rd, Small Heath for H. C. Fulford

1897 House, [? 48], Farquhar Rd, Edgbaston for R. D. Hayden

1897 House, 59 Salisbury Rd, Moseley for F. Machin

1897 Eleven houses, Highfield Rd for Alfred Johnson

1897 House, Salisbury Rd, Moseley for R. Machin

1898 Five houses, Middleton Hall Rd, King's Norton for A. Tisdall

1898 House, Melbreak, 11 The Driffold, Sutton Coldfield, for Mr Buckler

1898 House, The Anchorage, Hampstead Rd, Handsworth for A. J. Constantine

1898 House, Dale Cross Grange, Mease Lane, Barnt Green for Frank Rabone

1898 House, The Drift, 18 Wentworth Rd, Harborne for Charles Brampton, [D]

1898 House, Seven Gables, 14 Digby Rd, Sutton Coldfield for Joseph Crouch

1899 House, Top o' the Hill, 14 The Driffold, Sutton Coldfield for Edmund Butler

1900 House, Wyndhurst, 12 The Driffold, Sutton Coldfield

1900 House, Avoncroft, 21 Four Oaks Rd, Sutton Coldfield for Charles Brampton (listed Grade II)

1900 House, Cressington, 23 Four Oaks Rd, Sutton Coldfield for Arthur Brampton

1901 House, Luttrell House, 18 Hartopp Rd, Sutton Coldfield for Mr Elvins

1902 House and surgery, 50 Birmingham Rd, Sutton Coldfield for Dr F. A. Brown

1902 House, Anderton Park Rd, Moseley for Joseph White

1903 House, Craithe, Kenilworth Rd, Balsall Common

1903 House, Pritchatt's Rd, Edgbaston for A. Wright

1903 Stabling at Wheeleys Rd for G. Townsend

1903 Four houses, Barmen St for Barwick Estates

1904 House, [?50] Farquhar Rd, Edgbaston for G. Schurhoff

1905 Two houses, 133–135 Handsworth Wood Rd, Handsworth

1906 House, 21 Ladywood Rd, Sutton Coldfield for Charles Brampton

1906 House, 18 Luttrell Rd, Sutton Coldfield for E. L. Gyde

1907 House, Heathercourt, 6 Wentworth Rd, Sutton Coldfield [attrib.]

1907 House, 10 Wentworth Rd, Sutton Coldfield [attrib.]

1908 Two houses, 43 and 45, Four Oaks Rd, Sutton Coldfield for Mr Burley

1908 Wesley Cottage, Sutton Coldfield (listed Grade 11)

1908 House, Conyar, 16 Luttrell Rd, Sutton Coldfield

1910 House Wayside, Sutton Coldfield for H. Lamsdale

1910 Motor house, 17, Carpenter Rd, Edgbaston for Dr L. Green

1910 Forty houses and one milkshop, Farndon Rd, Saltley for Mr Isherwood

1913 House, Wesleyan Manse, 2, Four Oaks Rd, Sutton Coldfield for G. E. Lowe (listed Grade II)

1914 Eight houses, Alum Park Rd, Saltley for F. Isherwood

1914 Motor house, Cotton Lane for C. Vyle

1914 One hundred and fourteen houses, Foxton Rd, Saltley for F. Isherwood

1914 Twelve houses, Hazelbeach Rd, Saltley for F. Isherwood

WORK OUTSIDE BIRMINGHAM

PUBLIC

1900 Wesleyan Mission Hall, Westgate Rd, Newcastle-upon-Tyne

1905 Congregational Chapel, Lea Rd, Penn Fields, Wolverhampton

1906 Wesleyan Church, Briton Ferry, Glamorgan

1906 Rawtenstall Municipal Building and Library, N. Lancs. (Only library built)

1909 Hull Training College

1909 Wesleyan Church, Feltham, Middlesex.

1909 Wesleyan Church, Albany Road, Coventry

1913 Barnsley Grammar School

DOMESTIC

1907 The Quarry, Fieldgate Lane, Kenilworth for Joseph Crouch

?date Housing schemes on Tachbrook Road and Leicester St, Leamington

UNEXECUTED BUILDINGS

1901 South Shields Municipal Buildings (second premium)

1901 Hereford Municipal Buildings

1902 Camberwell Public Baths

1904 Balsall Heath Public Baths

1904 Erdington Council House and Library (second premium)

1905 Methodist Central Hall, Westminster

1909 Berkshire Council House, Reading

1911 Manchester Library and Art Gallery (accepted but cancelled in 1918)

NOTES

[1] Obituary, *The Builder*, 150, 14 April 1936, p. 727; obituary, *Journal of the Royal Institute of British Architects*, 42, 23 May 1936, p. 768.

[2] Correspondence from RIBA British Architectural Library, 13 July 1992; Birmingham Central Library, Archives and Heritage Services (hereafter BCL AHS), Birmingham Building Register, app. no. 6600, 5 April 1889; *Leamington Spa Courier and Warwickshire Standard*, 3 April 1936.

[3] *Leamington Spa Courier* and *Warwickshire Standard*, 3 April 1936.

[4] *Architects' Journal*, 50, 9 July 1919, p. 45.

[5] *Ibid*; RIBA, British Architectural Library, RIBA Fellowship Nomination Papers 16 September 1913.

[6] BCL AHS, Will 25 July 1936, p. 58.

[7] Sutton Coldfield Library (hereafter SCL), Sutton Coldfield Building Register, app. no. 601, 1898.

[8] Victorian Society, Birmingham Branch, File of correspondence from Alan Crawford, 6 October 1991.

9 *Leamington Spa and Warwickshire Standard*, 3 April 1936.

10 Joseph Crouch and Edmund Butler, *Churches, Mission Halls and Schools for Non-Conformists* (Birmingham, 1901).

11 *Ibid*, p. 22.

12 Joseph Crouch, *The Planning and Designing of a Methodist Church* (Birmingham, 1930).

13 Victor Skipp, *A History of Greater Birmingham to 1830* (Birmingham, 1980), pp. 69–71.

14 Birmingham Building Register, app. no. 5697, 12 October 1887.

15 *Ibid*, app. no. 24770, 1 October 1913.

16 SCL, Sutton Coldfield Building Register, app. no. 1711, 18 Luttrell Road, 1906; *Ibid*, app. no. 1819, Conyar, 16 Luttrell Road, 1908.

17 John Cattell, Sheila Elly, and Barry Jones, *The Birmingham Jewellery Quarter* (Swindon, 2002), pp. 222–23.

18 BCL AHS, Birmingham Building Register, app. no. 446, 15 January 1885.

19 *Ibid*, app. no. 12208, 16 September 1896.

20 *Ibid*, app. no. 8759, 10 July 1892.

21 *Ibid*, app. no. 8200, 15 April 1891.

22 *Ibid*, app. no. 8200, 15 April 1891.

23 *Ibid*, app. no. 12138, 20 August 1896.

24 *Ibid*, app. no. 4372, 19 December 1884.

25 *Ibid*, app. no. 425, 5 August 1884.

26 *Ibid*, app. no. 8703, 14 May 1892.

27 *Ibid*, app. no. 24770, 1 October 1913.

28 *Ibid*, app. no. 9679, 19 June 1893.

29 *Ibid*, app. no. 12138, 20 July 1896.

30 *Ibid*, app. no. 11387, 11 November 1895.

31 *Ibid*, app. no. 11497, 13 January 1896; and app. no. 13035, 12 July 1897; Department of the Environment *List of Buildings of Historic and Architectural Interest: Birmingham* (1970), p. 135; Andy Foster, *Pevsner Architectural Guides: Birmingham* (New Haven and London, 2005) p. 105; Nikolaus Pevsner and Alexandra Wedgwood, *The Buildings of England: Warwickshire* (Harmondsworth, 1966), p. 118; *The Architect*, 58, 29 October, 1897, p. 280.

32 BCL AHS, Birmingham Building Register, app. no. 12472, 17 December 1896.

33 *Ibid*, app. no. 15356, 4 January 1900.

34 A. B. Neale and J. D. Wheeler, *City of Birmingham Abstract Statistics* (Birmingham, 1955–57), Table 13.

35 BCL AHS, Birmingham Building Register, app. no. 5836, 15 February 1888.

36 BCL AHS, Birmingham Building Register, app. no. 11191, 20 July 1895; app. no. 12045, 20 July 1896.

37 Alan Crawford and Robert Thorne, *Birmingham Pubs 1890–1939* (Birmingham, 1974), p. 5.

38 BCL AHS, Birmingham Building Register, app. no. 13054, 23 June 1897.

39 *Ibid*, app. no. 21320, 28 February 1910.

40 *Ibid*, app. no. 24218, 28 April 1913.

41 *Ibid*, app. no. 7943, 7 April 1891.

42 *Ibid*, app. no. 9572, 29 July 1893.

43 John Burnett, *A Social History of Housing 1815–1970* (Oxford, 1978), p. 160, figure 9; BCL AHS, Birmingham Building Register, app. no. 5633, 30 August 1887.

44 BCL AHS, Birmingham Building Register, app. no. 11191, 20 August 1895; app. no. 12045, 20 June 1896.

45 *Ibid*, app. no. 21320, 28 February 1910.

46 Burnett, *Housing*, p. 164.

47 *Ibid*, p. 163.

48 C. A. Vince, *History of the Corporation of Birmingham, Volume IV 1900–1914* (Birmingham, 1923) p. 181.

49 Alan Crawford, 'The Arts and Crafts Movement', in *By Hammer and Hand, The Arts and Crafts Movement in Birmingham*, ed. by Alan Crawford (Birmingham, 1984), p. 5.

50 Crouch and Butler, *The Apartments of the House*, Preface VIII.

51 Peter Davey, *Architecture of the Arts and Crafts Movement* (New York, 1980), pp. 86–88.

52 Remo Granelli, 'Architecture' in *By Hammer and Hand*, p. 44.

53 Crouch and Butler, *The Apartments of the House*, p. 67.

54 Alan Crawford, 'The Birmingham Setting' in *By Hammer and Hand*, p. 31.

55 *The Studio, General Index* Vols 1–2 1893–1901 (*The Studio*, London, 1901).

56 Crawford, 'The Birmingham Setting', p. 29.

57 Granelli, 'Architecture', p. 44, p. 46.

58 Douglas Hickman, *Arts and Crafts Houses of Sutton Coldfield* (unpublished Victorian Society Tour Notes, 1975), p. 2.

59 SCL, Sutton Coldfield Building Register, app. no. 825, 18 Wentworth Road, 1898

[60] BCL AHS, King's Norton Building Register, app. no. 2614, The Anchorage, Hamstead Road, Handsworth, 14 September 1898.

[61] Alan Crawford, *Arts and Crafts Architecture in Birmingham* (unpublished, 1990), p. 16.

[62] SCL, Sutton Coldfield Building Register, app. no. 602, Wyndhurst, and 12 Driffold, 1900.

[63] *Vernacular Style Houses in Sutton Coldfield*, ed. by D. K. Cottrell (Birmingham, 1987) p. 10.

[64] Crawford, *Arts and Crafts Architecture in Birmingham*, p. 15.

[65] SCL, Sutton Coldfield Building Register, app. no. 676, 11–13 The Driffold, 1898.

[66] Hickman, *Arts and Crafts Houses of Sutton Coldfield*, p. 3.

[67] *Ibid*, p. 16.

[68] SCL, Sutton Coldfield Building Register, app. no. 826, 23, Four Oaks Road, 1900.

[69] BCL AHS, King's Norton Building Register, app. no. 27191, 59 Salisbury Road, Moseley, 1897.

[70] *Ibid*, Birmingham Building Register, app. no. 18175, house in Farquhar Road, Edgbaston for G. Schurhoff 26 August 1904.

[71] Crawford, *Arts and Crafts Architecture in Birmingham*, p. 16.

[72] Nicholas Cooper, *The Opulent Eye, Late Victorian and Edwardian Taste in Interior Design* (1976), p. 14.

[73] Granelli, 'Architecture', p. 44.

[74] Crawford, 'The Arts and Crafts Movement', p. 17.

[75] Nikolaus Pevsner, *The Buildings of England: North Lancashire* (Harmondsworth, 1969), p. 205.

[76] *British Architect*, 61, 3 June 1904, p. 404.

[77] Nikolaus Pevsner, *The Buildings of England: Staffordshire* (Harmondsworth, 1974), p. 299.

[78] *Souvenir Catalogue Opening of the New Free Library, Walsall Street, Wednesbury* (Wednesbury, 1908).

[79] *The Builder*, 101, 15 December 1911, p. 706.

[80] Correspondence with the Librarian, Manchester Reference Library, 18 February 1991. The authors are grateful for a copy of the minutes of the Council Meeting of 2 October 1918.

[81] *Building News*, 85, 1903, p. 548.

[82] *The Builder*, 113, 30 November 1917, p. 316.

[83] Pevsner and Wedgewood, *Warwickshire*, p. 427.

[84] *Souvenir Brochure The Laying of the Foundation Stone Dudley Training College* (Dudley, 1908).

[85] *The Builder*, 97, 20 November 1909, p. 557.

[86] Crouch and Butler, *Churches, Mission Halls and Schools*, pp. 38–39.

[87] Douglas Hickman, *Birmingham* (1970), p. 45.

[88] Crouch and Butler, *Churches. Mission Halls and Schools*, p. 38, p. 42.

[89] *Ibid*, pp. 25–39.

[90] *Architects' Journal*, 50, 1919, p. 48.

[91] *Building News*, 99, 1910, p. 654.

[92] These were Hall Green in 1924, Beckminster in 1926, Stourbridge in 1928 and Warley Wood in 1928.

[93] Joseph Crouch, *The Planning and Designing of a Methodist Church* (Birmingham, 1930).

21 Newton and Cheatle

NIKY RATHBONE AND JOHN BASSINDALE

The partnership of Thomas Newton (1862–1903) and A. E. Cheatle (1871–1941) dates from 1892, with their most important work concentrated into a short but very intensive period from around 1897 to 1903 when Newton died suddenly, aged only forty.[1] Before 1897 Newton and Cheatle designed a number of domestic houses, some as family speculations, and worked regularly for local business men, particularly the estate agent Frank Taylor, and did routine alterations to houses and factories. Their most important work during this period was probably the Perambulator Works for James Lloyd & Co. on Hurst Street, now demolished. In 1897 Newton succeeded in interesting local businessmen in a major project to develop arcades between Union Street, High Street and New Street. Simultaneously, Newton was designing residential chambers and small office buildings intended for doctors and other professional men around the Colmore Estate, in Newhall, Edmund, Church and Cornwall Streets. The firm was also responsible for major developments on John Bright Street and Station Street for Frank Taylor and Chambers Ltd. In the suburb of Moseley they built The Fighting Cocks for the Holt Brewery Company.

Throughout his career Newton also designed a number of attractive Arts and Crafts houses mainly in the suburbs of Moseley and Northfield, where he and members of his family lived, and in Barnt Green and Walsall. The firm built Arts and Crafts houses in Four Oaks, Sutton Coldfield, where Cheatle and his wife's relatives lived. After Newton's sudden death in 1903 the work of the firm continued, though less intensively. Charles Stansbury Madeley had joined by 1927, and the firm was listed as at 67A New Street in the 1941 Kelly's *Directory of Birmingham*. Cheatle died on 29 November 1941.

Thomas Walter Francis Newton was born in 1862 at Wiveliscombe, Somerset.[2] He was educated at Taunton Independent College. In 1881 he was living in Taunton with his mother and grandmother, his father having died. Newton was articled to Osborn and Reading, 13 Bennett's Hill, Birmingham and *Kelly's Directory* then lists Walter Newton living at 12 Trafalgar Road, Moseley by 1883. His future brother-in-law and close friend, Charles Huffer Wakeman lived at number 1. From 1886 the Newton family were living at Mardon's Croft, 19, Strensham Road, Moseley, later no. 19 Strensham Hill, now demolished, and probably named for Newton's mother, Mary Elizabeth Mardon Newton. Newton designed this house, with no. 17, which was owned by Henry Lockwood, and it is probably an early example of Newton's speculative building.[3] Newton married Fanny Jane Wakeman in 1890. She was the daughter of John Wakeman, Works Manager of Guest Keen and Nettlefold,[4] living at Ashleigh, 45 Park Road, Moseley; in 1886 Newton had designed a bathroom for John Wakeman, and in 1895 worked on alterations to no. 47 which Wakeman also owned. Newton and Cheatle later designed Westholme, 186 West Heath Road and The Croft, 101 West Heath Road for Fanny's brother Charles, building no. 97, The Dell, for himself and his wife and 99, Red House which he rented.[5] Newton and his family then moved to Quarry Farm, Quarry Lane, Northfield, which he altered and renovated. This property has, unfortunately, since been very much altered.

Kelly's *Directory of Birmingham* for 1884 lists T. W. F. Newton's architectural practice at 7 Waterloo Street, the same address as the architectural practice of Joseph Crouch, and the earliest directory entry for both. The two firms were to remain closely linked. By 1888 Newton had moved to 121 Colmore Row. From 1899 *Kelly's Directory* lists Newton and Cheatle's address as 39 Newhall Street, Crouch and Butler are listed there in 1900. This premises, and the firm's records, was destroyed during the War. The two firms did not actually work together, though they shared a secretary, and continued to occupy the same building, 67A New Street, after the War.[6]

Alfred Edward Robie Farmer Cheatle was baptised in 1871 at Dosthill, Kingsbury, Warwickshire, the son of a gentleman farmer, and educated at Christ's Hospital school, Hertford.[7] The work of the partners is first registered in the Plan Books in 1892, previous to this date only Newton's name is listed in the register. Cheatle certainly brought important business to the firm through his connections. He married Rhoda Beatrice Barker, sister of Herbert and Frank Barker of Barker Brothers, later Barker, Ellis & Co., a major firm of Birmingham silversmiths.[8] Newton and Cheatle designed Barker's manufactory on Constitution Hill. They also submitted plans for Barker Road and Beaconsfield Road, Four Oaks, on behalf of the Trustees of William Barker and worked on private houses for members of the Barker family.[9] Cheatle and his wife lived at Four Oaks House, 28 Walsall Road, Four Oaks until about 1920, then at The Oaklands, Penns Lane, Walmley until around 1926, then moving to Chalford, 65, Belwell Lane, Four Oaks, where they were living when Cheatle died in 1941.[10]

T. W. F. Newton presented a paper on 'The Small Country House' to the Birmingham Architectural Association, which was printed in the *Building News* in 1895. Newton's theories were very much expressions of the Arts and Crafts movement of the time, and he goes into considerable detail. Houses should be built for comfort and practicality. No long passages, preferably a single roof. He recommends avoidance of multiple valleys, gutters and hips, in his article. Newton liked decorative gutter brackets. He recommended high chimneys, set on inside walls, with small chimney pots, a practical detail intended to maximise warmth and avoid smoke. Newton preferred small green Westmorland or Colleyweston

26 Barker Road, Four Oaks, 1901

slates, hard brick with wide mortar joints, and relatively small areas of roughcast. He favoured breadth of effect rather than prettiness and ornament in the decoration. He advocates high, light, airy principal rooms, with light, wide, well-lit principal stairs. The dining room should have good kitchen access, and be east and, if possible, south facing, with a beamed ceiling and window seat. The drawing room should face south west, preferably square, with bay window, inglenook and ribbed plaster ceiling.

He goes on to describe the utilities in detail, a good size kitchen, facing north or east for coolness, a scullery, larder, pantry, tradesmen's entrance and yard, shelter for coals, ash and wood, all well away from the front door, with an enclosed back porch, w.c. and tool house. There should be a large bathroom, and he goes into considerable practical detail about hygiene. Some of the bedrooms would be built with attractive sloping ceilings.

Newton also describes in considerable detail the ideal fittings and decoration. Simple brass door furniture, oak board or oak block floor to the hallway, leaded light windows with iron casements, or wide glazing bars, always with small panes of glass, and decorative window fastenings. He advocates feature staircases, preferably dog-legged, and possibly with the balusters placed at an angle, as they often are in the work of Harvey and Voysey. He is fond of simple wallpapers, unlike Morris, and stained woodwork, either dark oak, walnut or green. Newton would use stone fireplaces in the principal rooms, and simple wooden surrounds in

The Pines, 3
Plymouth Road,
Barnt Green

bedrooms. The Pines, 3, Plymouth Road Barnt Green, one of six houses described in Newton's article which he had designed, still survives and is a fine example of his style at this time. It is a half timbered red brick four bedroomed house on a simple rectangular plot, with a long sloping roof and strikingly tall chimneys. The typically Arts and Crafts hall has a large fireplace with an ingle-nook. There is an imposing timbered porch, plain leaded lights and some elaborate ironwork, including the original bell-pull. The outbuildings have been demolished, but otherwise the house is very little altered. He also designed 6 and 8 Plymouth Road. It is possible that other houses in the vicinity may also have been designed by Newton; the cottage in Barnt Green mentioned in his article has not yet been traced.[11]

Remo Granelli in *By Hammer and Hand* comments on the similarity between the domestic work of Newton and that of Crouch and Butler, particularly in the Jacobean-influenced use of half-timbering and important porches.[12] Newton's work also has similarities to the work of Norman Shaw, who is probably the nationally known architect who most influenced him. Newton's comfortable detached and semi-detached villas are typically, asymmetric in appearance, with the various elements well balanced. He makes skilful use of decorative timbering and sometimes combines this with tile hanging or roughcast. His houses typically have substantial porches, often set into a corner of an L-shaped or irregular ground plan. It is probably fair to say that Newton's houses never fit into a simple square or rectangle, he uses jutting bays, single storey or double, or sets part of a house back. His larger houses contrive to suggest buildings that have been attractively added to over many years. He frequently used Art Nouveau leaded and stained glass, particularly in his porches. Decorative dormer windows are also a frequent feature. Chimneys are often imposing. Newton used decorative brick or terracotta, but not as extensively as many other architects of the period, and to a far less extent than in his commercial buildings. Some fine examples of Newton's earlier houses are to be seen in Park Hill Road, Moseley.[13] These show all the characteristics of Newton's houses; asymmetric design, a mixture of brick and white rough-cast, hung tiling or half timbering, small-paned windows, usually with wooden glazing bars, Art Nouveau stained glass, particularly on porch windows, occasional use of stone mullions. Frequently these houses have dormer windows to the roofs.

Probably Newton's largest house was 'Crossways', Highgate Road, Walsall, designed for the JP, W. E. Blyth, and described in the *Building News* in August 1899.[14] The principal rooms were at the back, overlooking the grounds. There was once what must have been a spectacular entrance hall described as 'habitable as a room if desired', with an upper gallery over the main staircase. The drawing room was divided in two by an archway so that the smaller section could be converted

Plans and Elevations of Crossways, Highgate, Walsall from *The Building News*, 18 August 1899

to a boudoir. The dining room had a large ingle-nook with cupboards over, decorated with leaded lights, very typical of Arts and Crafts architecture. This house is now a nursing home, but has not been extensively altered.

Some of the best of Newton's later work is to be found in Barker and Beaconsfield Roads on the Four Oaks Estate at Sutton Coldfield.[15] These houses are larger than the Park Hill examples, detached, but using essentially the same vocabulary with great assurance and charm. Number 26 Barker Road is particularly attractive, with Art Nouveau leaded windows and tapering decorative stonework like decorative buttresses to the ground floor. Number 5 Beaconsfield Road has an Art Nouveau curved parapet, and no. 26 Barker Road has a decorative swirling carved stone set into the brickwork just under the eaves which can be compared with decorative detail on the firm's smaller chambers and offices around the Colmore Estate in central Birmingham.

The firm's domestic and commercial work, however, is very dissimilar. Although the work of Norman Shaw clearly had a strong influence on Newton, particularly in his early work, probably he was most influenced by the work of other Birmingham Arts and Crafts architects with whom he met and shared ideas, particularly Owen Parsons, Crouch and Butler, William Harvey, W. H. Bidlake, J. L. Ball, Arthur Dixon, and Charles Bateman.

The Fighting Cocks, Moseley, is the only complete public house known to have been built by the partnership, though they were certainly responsible for alterations and additions to several others.[16] The distinctive corner tower dominates the High Street. The building includes typical Newton detail such as the shallow jutting bays to the upper floor function rooms, the corner porch, the decorative leaded lights, though these are more Art Deco in character than on most Newton buildings. Most typical, however, are the four curving gables. These are reminiscent of many Continental buildings in Belgium or Germany. The panelling of the porch and tiled interior of the public bar are still intact, though most of the interior fittings have been altered or removed. Many of the public houses in and around Birmingham suburbs are in the domestic Arts and Crafts style, whereas the Fighting Cocks is much closer in style to Newton and Cheatle's commercial chambers and offices than it is to their domestic work. The actual builder of The Fighting Cocks was Edward John Charles, who also built 26 Barker Road and 6 Beaconsfield Road in Sutton Coldfield with Newton and Cheatle.

In Birmingham City Centre, the best-known work of the partnership is probably what remains of the City and Midland Arcades, with its two very striking domes either side of the central gable. The Arcades were built between 1898 and 1901 and originally ran from Union Street through to New Street and High Street. The City Arcades were owned by the City Arcades, Birmingham, Ltd and the Midland Arcade by the Midland Arcade, Birmingham Ltd. Both private companies

OPPOSITE   The Fighting Cocks, Moseley, 1898

Entrance to the City Arcades, Union Street, 1901

involved a number of prominent local businessmen. They were not the first or last arcades to be built in Birmingham, but were among the most popular and success-ful. The Arcades were largely destroyed in the 1941 air raids, but their original line can still be traced through the modern covered walkways replacing them. One entrance on New Street was to the City Arcades, the other to the Midland Arcade. The frontages were five storeys high, the top storey within the roof, in buff terra-cotta, similar to the remaining frontages on Union Street. The frontages show similarity to the work of Essex, Nicol and Goodman at Newton Chambers, New Street and Cannon Street. The interiors of the arcades were two storeys high, also similar to the remaining section on Union Street. The windows of the remaining section are reminiscent of Jacobean mansions, the street front is banded with a decorative terracotta frieze of sea creatures, like those found on William de

Detail of interior of Arcades

Morgan tiles. Plain brickwork contrasts with pale terracotta. The building would not be out of place in Brussels or Amsterdam. Internally, an arched steel and glass roof protects shopping and premises on two levels. There is a very unusual balcony running the length of the first floor constructed from green majolica tiles, decorated with sea creatures, interwoven tiled strapwork, small Chinese style cupolas, and further green tile-work between the shop fronts, all supplied by Doulton & Co. of Lambeth.[17] According to the Prospectus, the 'glazed Terra-Cotta of various colours, will add considerably to the effect when the buildings are illuminated at night, and will render the decoration of a permanent character and materially reduce the cost of maintenance and re-decoration.'[18] The interior of the arcade has decorative arched windows to the first floor. Subways gave goods and services access to the shops.

For Frank Taylor and Chambers Ltd, they designed an extensive development of shops and business premises centred on John Bright Street. The earliest plans are dated 1899. This area has subsequently been re-developed.

The firm also designed several interesting buildings around Church Street, Edmund Street, Suffolk Street and Cornwall Street, including the premises they shared with Crouch and Butler at 39 Newhall Street, now demolished.[19] However, the residential chambers and offices they built for King-Patten, Palk & Co., chartered accountants, 56–60 Newhall Street, does survive. This building is built of red brick and buff stone, typical of Newton's commercial buildings, which manage to evoke the spirit of Jacobean brick-built mansions or Northern European town houses in Amsterdam or Brussels. It has twin gables, decorated with chequers of red brick and buff stone, with a central dormer window between, a feature of several Newton buildings. Exuberant art nouveau figures guard the entrance, where the decoration seems to become almost rococo. The roof line is remarkable for a spectacular cluster of massed chimney pots.[20]

Another building in the same area is no. 134 Edmund Street built for the coal and coke company of G. J. Eveson. This has the ethos of a town house rather than a commercial building. This small four storey red brick and buff terracotta building has two full height bays, highly decorative small-paned windows divided by stone mullions, and fantastic rococo friezes separating the floors.[21] Entirely different is no. 95 Cornwall Street, dwelling house and consulting rooms built in 1901 for Priestley Smith, opthalmic surgeon, also a four-storey town house in red brick and buff stone, but quite austere. Here sash windows are separated by verticals of red brick, decorated with squares of buff stone. Again there are dormer windows, but here a wide buff stone parapet with an Art Nouveau curve upswept at each end.[22] No. 93 Cornwall Street built for Sir James Sawyer, physician, in 1901 is also a four-storey town house, in red brick and buff stone, but here the dormer windows have triangular pediments and the curve of the buff stone parapet almost reverses that of the neighbouring house. Both buildings have simple town house porches set to the right, art nouveau rain water heads, and are separated from the street and basement area by decorative Art Nouveau railings.[23]

Some of Newton and Cheatle's business chambers now appear overwhelmed by later developments, like the charming evocation of town houses at nos 37–39 and nos 41–43 Church Street of 1901 and 1899 respectively. These are again four storeys high, but in strongly contrasting styles. The first is in red brick and buff stone, with curved porches, the second pair, also in red brick, has two distinctive shallow bays, with triangular leaded roofs, originally slate, further leading between the windows to each floor, and sinuously curved rainwater pipes.[24] The factory designed for Buckler and Webb, printers, by Newton and Cheatle in 1898, which once stood next to these, has disappeared under a towering modern block.[25]

OPPOSITE   Offices at 134 Edmund Street for the coal company, G. J. Eveson, 1897

The firm designed a number of manufactories, of which the most important still remaining is the magnificent temple to commerce, built for the Birmingham silversmiths Herbert and Frank Barker, brothers of Cheatle's wife Rhoda, between 1901 and 1914. The completed manufactory covered most of the block bounded by Constitution Hill, Henrietta Street and Water Street and was one of the largest in the Jewellery Quarter with its own gas and electricity supplies. The Constitution Hill frontage of Barker Brothers' manufactory, all of dark red terracotta, is divided into six sections, probably to manage the sloping site. The wide central section is topped by a massive arch, which is topped by a triangular cornice and a pediment. Within the main arch is an arched doorway, the surround decorated with stained glass. This gives onto an Art Nouveau hallway and staircase. There were originally retail shops in the smaller arches along the Constitution hill frontage of the building, no doubt including jewellers. The upper floors of the building on either side of the centre block are defined by undecorated rounded pillars dividing the windows at first floor level, square pillars divide the windows of the upper floors. The central section of the building is topped on the Constitution Hill frontage by a long pediment, with a mansard roof above, and, set into this, are dormer windows, with those distinctive curving central glazing bars which Newton and Cheatle often used on commercial buildings. The two further side sections of the main frontage are distinguished at first floor level by square pillars with curved decorative cornices above this, topped by a further triangular cornice, echoing that over the central section. The left hand side of the building has a further block to the corner with Water Street, six storeys high, each with five square pillars dividing tall, narrow windows. This design is carried round into Water Street, and relates to the similar, much smaller building which it adjoins. The Water Street facade is five storeys high, each floor defined by further squared pillars, with tall windows inset between.[26]

Newton and Cheatle were also responsible for alterations to manufactories and some other smaller buildings around the area of Constitution Hill which do not appear to have survived. For James Lloyd and Co. they designed a perambulator works on Hurst Street, between Thorp and Inge Street, in 1893, the site adjacent to the Hippodrome. This must have been an imposing building and an important development, extended in 1896 with a further storey and shopping.[27]

A group of houses on West Heath Road, built from 1893–1902 have been demolished, while the houses they built on Sandon Road are now in a sorry state.[28] The firm's most enduring memorials are the remaining sections of the City Arcades, the chambers and offices around the Colmore Estate, the Fighting Cocks, Moseley, and their Arts and Crafts houses in Park Hill, Moseley, Four Oaks, Sutton Coldfield, Walsall and Barnt Green.

OPPOSITE   Town House, 93 Cornwall Street, 1901

RIGHT Business
Chambers at 41–43 Church
Street, 1899

BELOW The former
Barker Bros. Manufactory,
Constitution Hill,
1900–1914

List of the Principal Architectural Works of Newton and Cheatle

Thomas Newton (1862–1903) was articled to Osborn and Reading of Birmingham. He set up in practice in 1884 and was joined by A. E. Cheatle (1871–1941) as a partner in 1892. After Newton's death in 1903 Cheatle continued the firm, being joined by C. S. Madeley in 1927.

Newton and Cheatle's work up to 1912 has been included in the List

WORK IN BIRMINGHAM AND ITS ENVIRONS

PUBLIC

1885 Competition for Moseley Rd Wesleyan Chapel Sunday School (unsuccessful)

COMMERCIAL

1888 Extension to shop, Spiceal St [D]

1892 Alterations to shop fronts, 53–54 Great Lister St for F. Taylor

1894 Four shop fronts and alterations to 12 houses at back, 37–40 Hurst St for F. Taylor [D]

1894 Two shop fronts, wash houses, w.c.s and alterations to 12 bay windows, 29–30 Hurst St for F. Taylor [D]

1895 Alterations to two shops and workshop, 280, 282 Coventry Rd for R. W. Tullett, linen draper

1895 Alterations and additions to 3 shops, bakehouse and oven, 62–65 Hurst St for F. Taylor

1895 Alterations to offices, 15 Newhall St for Mayo, Powell and Thompson, chartered accountants [D]

1895 Warehouse, 46–47 Price St for B. Shirley Smith (conversion of two 18th century houses)

1895 Alterations to premises, 22 Newhall St for Dr J. W. Taylor

1896 Alterations to offices, 20–21 Cato St North for City Brewery Co.

1896 Alterations to Britannia Inn, Nechells Place for City Brewery Co.

1897 Business premises, 134 Edmund St for G. J. Eveson, Coke and Coal Ltd

1897 Alterations to premises, 83 High St for Innes, Smith and Co wine and spirit merchants

1897 Business premises, 31–39 Newhall St for Frank Marsh, surgeon and F. Taylor, Birmingham Offices Co. [destroyed in air raid 1941]

1898 Public House, The Fighting Cocks, Alcester Rd, Moseley for Holt Brewery

1898 Business premises, 121–123 Edmund St for G. H. Willetts

1898 Business premises, 125–131 Edmund St for Frank Taylor

1898 Shopping arcade, High St for City Arcades, Birmingham Ltd; 1899 shopping arcade New St; 1901 shopping arcades New St and Union Passage [partly D]

1899 Business premises, 41–43 Church St for R. W. Palk

1899 Business premises and 7 shops, 25, 27, 29 John Bright St, 99, 101, 103, 105 Station St, 13, 14 Suffolk St for F. Taylor and Chambers Ltd; 1899 2 shops and business premises 59, 61, 63 John Bright St [D]

1899 Bridge and tunnel under, Union Passage [D]

1899 Alterations and additions, 19–20 Temple St for Ludlow and Briscoe, surveyors and auctioneers

1901 Offices and Warehouse, 37–39 Church St, for H. B. Perry and Co., export hardware merchants

1902 Business premises, 14 New St for New St Ltd

1902 Stabling, King's Norton Station for T. and M. Dixon, coal merchants

1903 Alterations, 36 Paradise St for John R. Lee, paper hangings dealers [D]

1911 Alterations, 3 Waterloo St for Charles Arnold, solicitor [D]

1912 The Horse and Jockey, Inkford Brook, Alcester Rd

INDUSTRIAL

1887 Warehouse, St Paul's Works, 7 Legge Lane for G. W. Hughes, steel pen maker

1893 Factory, 35–45 Hurst St for James Lloyd and Co. perambulator manufacturers; 1896 additional storey to shopping; 1897 additional stories to shopping and new stable [bombed and demolished *c.* 1941]

1895 Alterations to factory, Lower Priory for Southall Bros. and Barclay, manufacturing pharmaceutical chemists

1897 Factory, Smithfield Passage for J. Truman [D]

1897 Factory 62–63 Hampton St for John Sarsons Walford, cock maker (possibly Paragon Cock Foundry) [D]

1897 Eagle Works, 31 Green St/Alcester St, Deritend for Sarsons and Butt, brassfounders

1898 Printing Works, 45–47 Church St for Buckler and Webb, printers and bookbinders [D]

1898 Shopping, Manor House, 147, Spring Hill for Richard Brown and Sons, sauce manufacturers; 1899 shopping, warehouses, stabling

1900–1901 Manufactory, Water St and Constitution Hill for Barker Bros, silversmiths; 1902 additions; 1903 additions; 1910 additions; 1911 casting shop and shopping; 1914 new stack, coal store and shopping [now Bishmillah Building converted to flats 1992–93]

1901 Additions to Royal Works, Brearley St for R. and H. Phillips

1902 New Premises and depository, 130–131 Suffolk St for Chamberlain, King and Jones, cabinet makers; 1905 additions

1903 Alterations, [40?]Great Charles St for Handley and Shanks, electrical engineers

1904 Alterations, 110–114 Bristol St for Bennet Bros. Ltd, cabinet makers

1910 Warehouse, Cheapside, for Barker Bros. Trustees

DOMESTIC

1885 Lynton Villa, 54 Trafalgar Rd, Moseley for H. J. Gristwood

1885 Woodhurst, 65 Trafalgar Rd, Moseley for H. J. Gristwood

1885 Mornington, 17 Strensham Rd [Strensham Hill], Moseley for H. J. Gristwood

1885 Mardons Croft, 19 Strensham Rd [Strensham Hill], Moseley for T. W. F. Newton

1886 Westfield, 46 [106] Park Road, Moseley for James Bowker

1886 Bathroom for 45 Park Hill, Moseley for John Wakeman

1887 Greengate, 42 [98] Park Hill, Moseley for T. W. F. Newton

1887 Arden Bank, 44 [102] Park Hill, Moseley for T. W. F. Newton

1887 36, 38, 40, Park Hill, Moseley for T. W. F. Newton (unexecuted)

1888 Glaisdale, 38, 40 [96a, 96] Park Hill, Moseley for W. E. Adlard; 1896 stable and billiard room to no. 40 [96] for Adlard

1889 The Dell, [33] Park Hill, Moseley for Rose Fuller

1890 Alterations to Woodville, Elmdon Rd [St Mary's Hospice, 176 Raddlebarn Rd] for J. S. Downing

1890 Heatherdene, 26 Moor Green Lane, Moseley for J. L. Tustin

1892 Alterations and additions, 199 and 200 Aston Rd for Frank Powell

1892 Seven wash houses, 136–143 Cattell Rd for F. Taylor [D]

1892 Five wash houses and w.c.s, Tennant St for F. Taylor

1892 The Oaks, 6 Plymouth Road, Barnt Green

1892 Tanglewood, 8 Plymouth Road, Barnt Green

1892 The Dell, 97 West Heath Rd, Northfield for T. W. F. Newton; 1898 alterations and additions and re-drainage for Prof. P. Frankland [D]

1892 Red House, 99 West Heath Rd, Northfield for T. W. F. Newton; 1897 alterations for Dr John Taylor [D]

1892 The Croft, 101 West Heath Rd, Northfield for C. H. Wakeman [D]

1893 The Gables, 16 Forest Rd, Moseley for A. J. Ball [D]

1894 Two houses and alterations, Bromsgrove St and Essex St for F. Taylor [D]

1894 Meadow House, 1211 Bristol Rd South, Longbridge for H. G. Tanner [D]

1894 Alterations to Granton, 180 Middleton Hall Rd, King's Norton for Dr B. Fourneaux Jordan

1894 8–10 Ashfield Avenue, King's Heath for David Edwards [also probably nos 5, 7, 9, 11, 12, 14]

pre 1895 The Pines, Barnt Green [3 Plymouth Rd]

pre 1895 The Cottage, Barnt Green

1895 Alterations to five houses, Eyre St for Smith, Derry and Taylor

1895 Alterations to fronts and wash houses, alterations at back and w.c.s, 104–107 Bromsgrove St for F. Taylor

1895 Alterations to Albany Villa, 47 Park Rd, Moseley for John Wakeman

1895 Alterations to 88 Hagley Rd, Edgbaston for B. S. Smith

1895 Rangeworthy, 82, 84 [647,649] Bristol Rd South, Northfield for Joseph Hull [D]

1895 Gardener's Lodge to Lyne Orchard, Lyndon End, Olton for G. T. Smith

1896 Broomhill, 103 West Heath Rd, Northfield for C. J. Thursfield [D]

1896 Addition of veranda, coach house and stable to Yew Tree Cottage [Heath House], 164 West Heath Rd, Northfield for Franklin Davies; 1902 additional wing

1896 Gardener's Cottage to Tessall House, 1163 Bristol Road South, Longbridge for Frederick Harding

1897 Westholme, 186 West Heath Rd, Northfield for C. H. Wakeman [D]

1898 Additions and alterations to Quarry Farm [British Legion Club], Quarry Lane, Northfield for T. W. F. Newton

1898 Additions to Sandown, 124 Middleton Hall Rd, Northfield for James Pool

1898 The Glen, 36 [88] Park Hill, Moseley for J. Husband

1898 Addition of billiard room and bathroom to Ruskin Lodge, 19 Tudor Hill Sutton Coldfield for Edward Barker

1898 Four new streets in Four Oaks for Trustees of William Barker (not executed)

1898 Two new streets, Barker Rd and Beaconsfield Rd, Sutton Coldfield for Trustees of William Barker

1898 Two houses, Hampton Lane, Solihull for Alfred Hull

1899 Two houses, Bishops Rd, Sutton Coldfield for E. J. Charles

1899 Alterations to Copsewood, 17 Tudor Hill, Sutton Coldfield for F. E. Barker

1899 Welbeck, [38] Sandon Rd, Edgbaston for William Sheldon

1899 Glynliffen [36] Sandon Road, Edgbaston for Charles Sheldon; 1900 addition of stables and coach house

1899 Crossways, Highgate Rd, Walsall for W. E. Blyth, JP

1900 House, consulting rooms and offices, 95 Cornwall St for Dr Smith Priestley

1900 Residential chambers and offices, 56–60 Newhall St for R. W. Palk, chartered accountant and Birmingham City Offices Ltd.

1900 Two houses, Bishops Rd, Sutton Coldfield for E. J. Charles (not approved)

1900 Alterations to house, Birmingham Rd, Sutton Coldfield for Trustees of George Barker

1900 Beaconsfield, 26 Barker Rd, Four Oaks for Edwin Moore

1900 6 Beaconhurst Rd, Four Oaks for Trustees of George Barker

1900 House, Henrietta St, for Barker Bros. (? not executed)

1901 House and consulting room, 93 Cornwall St for Sir James Sawyer

1901–03 Highcliffe, 105 West Heath Rd, King's Norton [D]

1902 Lodge to Four Oaks House, 28 Walsall Rd for A. E. Cheatle [D]

1902 1 and 2 Kingsbury Villas, [10 and 12], Jordan Rd, Four Oaks for Ann Barker

1902 Alterations to The Island, West Heath Road, Northfield [D]

1903 House, consulting rooms and offices, 61 Newhall St/39 Great Charles St for
   Dr Alfred Carter

1904 The Bungalow, 7 Clarence Rd and The Cottage, 72 Greenhill Rd, Moseley for
   G. W. Taylor

1911 House, Marshall Lake Rd, for E. Bettridge

1912 Alterations to Witton Lodge Farm, Perry Common Rd, Erdington for W. Bellamy

---

NOTES

[1] In the Building Plan registers the listing of T. W. F. Newton changes to Newton and Cheatle by July 1892.

[2] Biographical information is based on the following sources: 1881 Census records; Kelly's *Directories of Birmingham, Worcestershire* and *Warwickshire*; King's Norton Poor Rate Records; Obituaries in the *Building News*, 74, 23 January 1903, p. 119, *The Builder*, 84, 31 January 1903, p. 120, *Birmingham Daily Gazette*, 19 January 1903 and *Birmingham Evening Dispatch*, 20 January 1903.

[3] Birmingham Central Library, Archives and Heritage Services, King's Norton Building Register, plan no. 789 for two houses, [17 & 19] Stensham Hill, Moseley, for H. J. Lockwood and T. Newton, 1885. Newton designed two other house for Lockwood in 1885, nos. 54 and 56 Trafalgar Road, Moseley.

[4] RIBA, British Architectural Library, Biography file, letter from Mrs Macnamara, 1986 giving personal details of the Newton family. She was a friend of Newton's widow.

[5] The houses on West Heath Road designed by Newton, and their occupants, have been identified using the entries in the King's Norton Building Register, OS maps and Kelly's *Directories*. They are The Dell [no. 97], Red House [no. 99], The Croft [no. 101], Broomhill [no. 103], all of 1892 and possibly Highcliffe [no. 105] of 1901–03. He was also responsible for alterations to Brookside [no. 164] and Westholme [no. 186] owned by his brother-in-law.

[6] *Ex inform* G. S. Madeley, son of C. S. Madeley, partner in Newton and Cheatle, telephone conversation, 2003.

[7] 1881 Census; Register of Births, Marriages and Deaths.

[8] For details of Barker, Ellis and Co. Silversmiths see *The Silversmiths of Birmingham and their Marks 1750–1980*, ed. by K. C. Jones (1981), pp. 306–07.

[9] Sutton Coldfield Library, Sutton Coldfield Building Register plan no. 723 for Barker and Beaconsfield Roads, 1898.

[10] Sutton Coldfield Telephone Directories; Electoral Rolls.

[11] T. W. F. Newton, 'The Small Country House', *Building News*, 68, 1895, pp. 366–69. The six houses described in the article were The Dell and The Red House in West Heath Road owned by Newton; Meadow House, 1211 Bristol Road South described as 'house at Longbridge'; and The Gables, 16 Forest Road, Moseley built for Arthur Jesse Ball, an estate agent. These four houses have been demolished. The Pines, 3 Plymouth Road, Barnt Green survives. 'Cottage, Barnt Green' has not been identified. Worcester Record Office has no Barnt Green building plans for the relevant dates.

[12] Remo Granelli, 'Architecture' in *By Hammer and Hand: the Arts and Crafts Movement in Birmingham*, ed. by Alan Crawford (Birmingham, 1984), pp. 41–42.

[13] For details see the list of domestic buildings by Newton and Cheatle at the end of the chapter. The house numbers on Park Hill have changed since the houses were built. The entries in the King's Norton Building Registers are not complete. It is possible that some other houses on the road may be by Newton and Cheatle.

[14] *Building News*, 77, 18 August 1899, p. 193 and illustration 'House at Walsall for Mr W. E. Blyth.'

[15] Sutton Coldfield Building Register plans for work connected with the Barker family on the Four Oaks Estate are as follows: Four new streets, plan no. 688, 1898 (unexecuted); two new streets, plan no. 725, 1898; alterations to 17 Tudor Hill Road for F. E. Barker plan no. 808, 1899; alterations to house in Birmingham Road for trustees of late George Barker, plan no. 990, 1900; house for trustees of George Barker, 6 Beaconsfield Road, plan no. 1005, 1900; two houses for Ann Mary Barker, widow of William Barker, Nos 1 & 2 [10 &12] Jordan Road, plan no. 1317, 1902.

[16] Public House, The Fighting Cocks, Alcester Road, Moseley, for Holt Brewery, King's Norton Building Register plan no. 110, 1898. Between 1896–97 Newton and Cheatle had carried out minor alterations to four pubs for City Brewery in the centre of Birmingham.

[17] John Bassindale, 'The British Shopping Arcade' 1896–1939 (unpublished thesis, Gloucester College of Art and Design and RIBA, 1982), part 2, pp. 58–95 and Appendix pp. 68–101.

[18] BCL, AHS, 243102, The City Arcades, Birmingham Ltd *Prospectus*, 1897; Birmingham Building Register plans, nos 14268, 15320, 15138, 15447, 16366.

[19] Birmingham Building Register, plan no. 13504, 1897, for business premises at 31–39 Newhall Street for Frank Marsh, surgeon and F. Taylor.

[20] Birmingham Building Register, plans nos 15370 and 15519, 1900, for residential chambers for R. W. Palk, chartered accountant of King-Patten, Palk and Co.

[21] Birmingham Building Register, plan no. 12836, 1897, business premises for G. J. Eveson Coal and Coke company.

[22] Birmingham Building Register, plan no. 16560, 1901, house, consulting rooms and offices for J. Priestley Smith, physician. This is building no. 80 in Douglas Hickman's *Birmingham* and is incorrectly described as 'house for Smith Priestley.'

[23] Birmingham Building Register, plan no. 16560, 1901, house and consulting rooms for Sir James Sawyer, physician.

[24] Birmingham Building Register, plan no. 14882, 1899, for business premises for R. W. Palk at 41–43 Church Street and plan no. 16553, 1901, for offices and warehouses for H. B. Perry and Co. Ltd, at 37–39 Church Street.

[25] Birmingham Building Register, plan no. 13933, 1898, for business premises for Buckler and Webb, printers. Illustrated as building no. 73 in Douglas Hickman's *Birmingham*.

[26] Birmingham Building Register, plan nos 15386, 1900 and 16029, 1901, manufactory for Barker Bros., silversmiths, Water Street and Constitution Hill. Additions were made in 1902 (plan no. 17012); 1903 (plan no. 17264); 1910 (plan nos 21362, 21783); 1911 (plan nos 22188, 22318, 22240); and 1914 (plan nos 25221, 25364, 25879). The factory has been converted to flats.

[27] Birmingham Building Register Plan no. 9222, 1893, perambulator works for James Lloyd and Co., 35–45 Hurst Street; additions plan nos 12160, 1896 and 12643, 13130, 1897.

[28] Birmingham Building Register Plan no. 15231, 1899 for house, Glynliften [36] Sandon Road for Charles Sheldon; plan no. 15817, 1900 for stables and Coach house; plan no. 15232 for house, Welbeck [38] Sandon Rd for William Sheldon.

22 Buckland and Farmer

MARY WORSFOLD

The firm of Buckland and Farmer may not be the most well known of firms of Birmingham architects, but in any analysis of the Arts and Crafts movement in Birmingham their contribution, particularly that of Herbert Buckland, is widely acknowledged to be of considerable importance. 'Among the first generation of Arts and Crafts architects the most significant in terms of skill, influence and productivity may be named Joseph Lancaster Ball, Joseph Crouch, A. S. Dixon, W. H. Bidlake, Charles Bateman and Herbert Tudor Buckland'.[1] This contribution was also noted at the time – 'The Birmingham School has become a recognised term in architectural circles, and it is almost needless to add that this distinction is based upon the excellent work that Birmingham architects have produced in recent years. It is also curious to note how many names of well known members in the Birmingham school begin with the second letter of the alphabet, Bidlake, Bateman and Bateman, Ball, Butler of Crouch and Butler, and Buckland'.[2] The firm continued to design buildings, with Buckland as the senior partner, into the 1950s, although by then it was known as Buckland and Haywood.[3] Buckland had commenced in practice on his own account in 1897.

Although they were predominantly a Birmingham practice they are known to have designed buildings as far away as Surrey and Suffolk in the south and Barnsley and Glasgow to the north, not to mention their work in the Elan Valley in Wales, where there was an obvious Birmingham connection.

Herbert Tudor Buckland was born in 1869, in Barmouth, Monmouth-shire, but was living in Birmingham with his mother and sister by 1871. He was educated at King Edward's Grammar School, Birmingham. He initially planned on becoming a mechanical engineer, but a few months of working on trial at Boulton and Watt resulted in

Herbert Tudor Buckland

disillusionment, and he drifted into architecture.[4] He entered into articles with Henry Clere, a quantity surveyor, in 1886, while studying at the Municipal School of Art. He joined the Birmingham Architectural Association (BAA) and became acquainted with Charles Bateman, who had recently gone into practice with his father. The Batemans' office was in the same building as Henry Clere, and the latter frequently prepared bills of quantities for the Bateman Firm.[5]

Buckland, having a good deal of spare time at his disposal assisted the Batemans with some of their drawings. This experience and attendance at BAA classes gradually imbued him with an interest in architecture, and on completing his articles he went into the office of Messrs Bateman in 1891. He stayed until 1895, becoming a good friend of Charles Bateman and entering several national competitions with him.[6]

C. E. Bateman was one of only a few Birmingham architects at this time to be attributed with national importance, others being Bidlake, Ball and Butler. The practice of Bateman and Bateman were responsible for a large number of houses in the West Midlands, in Sutton Coldfield in particular, many in a Cotswolds style, notably Redlands, no. 1 Hartopp Road. The practice was not however just a residential one and they were responsible for a large number of commercial premises constructed in the early part of the 20th Century.

In 1895 Buckland left Bateman and Bateman and entered into partnership with Henry Clere, the firm undertaking architectural as well as quantity surveying work,[7] one of their first commissions being alterations to the Navigation Inn, Bromford. Other work during this period included alterations and additions for Ind Coope, the owners of the Navigation Inn. He also extended the Bournbrook Hotel (now The Old Varsity Tavern), designing the Grange Road elevation. In 1897 Herbert Tudor Buckland dissolved the partnership and commenced practice alone. He would appear to have continued doing alteration work for Ind Coope, as well as some minor shops and housing schemes.

Buckland was joined by Edward Haywood-Farmer as an assistant in 1898, taking him into partnership in 1899. Edward Haywood-Farmer was born near Tamworth in 1871, and was educated at Oundle School, Northamptonshire. After leaving school he was articled to a Mr Josiah Mander, architect of Northampton, before moving to Birmingham in 1898. From the research carried out it has been almost impossible to attribute individual buildings to either Buckland or Farmer. The strong design style that is seen in the Bournbrook Hotel and in Buckland's own house, figures in many of the buildings by the partnership suggesting that Buckland was perhaps the driving force in the design side of the partnership. However planning applications were made in the name of the firm and their work was extensively published, but was always attributed to the partnership. Enticingly some articles, notably those by Lawrence Weaver do attribute work, Moorcroft and Blythe Court to Buckland, and the school applications are generally in Buckland's name although in the journals they are attributed to the partnership.

Edward Haywood-Farmer, from the *Builders'*
Journal, 6 January 1910

Only Haywood-Farmer's house in Sutton Coldfield is attributed solely to him,[8]
although the planning application is from the partnership. In discussing the work
of the partnership in *By Hammer and Hand*, Remo Granelli also refers only to
Buckland.[9]

The two major areas of work for the firm were houses and schools. The
majority of their domestic work was constructed between 1899 and 1911 during
which time they designed over fifteen houses, at least ten of them in Birmingham,
with others as far away as Surrey and Bridlington. The houses were generally
modest sized detached houses, exceptions being Moorcroft and Great Roke which
probably fall into the 'lesser country house' size category, to use Lawrence
Weaver's description. Their clients were a mixture of businessmen such as Henry
Hope, the window manufacturer (Moorcroft) and Hubert Adie, Adie Brothers,
silversmiths (17 Yateley Road), but also professional men, Harry Barling, a surgeon
(Blythe Court). It has not been possible to identify the owners of all the houses
located outside Birmingham, nor to establish how the firm may have been
instructed, Great Roke being an exception. It was constructed for Charles Dixon,
son of George Dixon MP, and a member of the Birmingham firm of H. H. Ward
and Co., machine tool makers. Before building Great Roke he had lived in Westbourne Road, Edgbaston.

Number 15 Yateley Road appears to have been built speculatively by Buckland
and Farmer, but was purchased and extended, to plans by the partnership, for
John Henry Barker in 1908. He was the managing Director of Birmingham Metal

21 Yateley Road, Edgbaston, front elevation, 1899

and Munitions. Buckland and Farmer were responsible for designing their new factory and various extensions between 1912 and 1917.

Remo Granelli describes Buckland's no. 21 Yateley Road house as 'simple and unremarkable, it is an advanced vernacular mode of building based on 17th century work'.[10] This is an accurate description of his earlier houses such as the Yateley Road houses, Moorcroft and Great Roke. Overall their houses do exhibit an air of simplicity, but with carefully thought out simple detailing; features such as semi circular headed recessed reveals above windows, a dentil course at the eaves, sprocketed roofs and the Birmingham eyebrow above the door, figure again and again. They are seen from the smallest house, for example the caretaker's/ master's house at Handsworth Road School up to Great Roke, Surrey, a huge house that still has a simple air, with exquisite detailing that emphasises the simplicity.

In 1899 Buckland designed two modest houses, one in Sandon Road and no. 21 Yateley Road, his own house. Although 21 Yateley Road was one of Buckland's earliest works, it is widely considered one of his best, and is one of only twenty-two buildings in Birmingham listed at Grade I. Roderick Gradidge when writing about the house in *Country Life* in 1990, stated that it is the only 'Birmingham Arts and Crafts house that it is really well preserved'.[11] It was also illustrated in

Rear elevation of 21 Yateley Road, from the *Architectural Review*, December 1901

contemporary journals and books, including the *Architectural Review*[12] and *Das Land Haus und Garten* by Hermann Muthesius.[13] It was lived in by Buckland until his death in 1951 and has had only two owners since who have obviously appreciated its unique quality. The house is cottage-like with a high, steeply pitched, and generously sprocketed, hipped roof. The roof stops just above the first floor windows to the front elevation, but to the rear, it goes down to the ground floor windows. To the front and rear are gables, each with windows to the second floor. The front door has a semi circular head, surmounted by a deep hood, decorated with abstract symbols. Roderick Gradidge suggests they are based on signs of the zodiac. This might suggest the influence of W. R. Lethaby. It is well known that Lethaby was very interested in symbolism. His ideas were explained in his book, *Architecture, Mysticism and Myth*, published in 1891. Gradidge states that 'Buckland's work is characterised by a simplicity and good taste which shows the influence of Webb and Lethaby',[14] and this house does exhibit a plainness and effortlessness reminiscent of The Hurst, Lethaby's house for Charles Mathews in Sutton Coldfield and Red House, Philip Webb's house for William Morris in Kent.

Lethaby's influence on Buckland can be seen in a number of his works. Lethaby designed two buildings in Birmingham, The Hurst, mentioned above and The

Eagle Insurance Building in Colmore Row. Both were, and still are, considered to be highly important not just in terms of architecture but in the aesthetic they represented, and would have influenced many of the architects working in Birmingham, at the turn of the century. Lethaby's influence was noted by Lawrence Weaver, in 1911 writing in *Country Life* about Buckland's house, Moorcroft, discussed below. In praising the Birmingham School he asserts that part of their success is due to the influence of Lethaby:

nor is it in anything but a spirit of praise (of Birmingham Architects) that one sets down the belief that no little of this unity is due to the example set some years ago by the work done in the neighbourhood by that distinguished artist and critic, Professor Lethaby, though himself not a Midland man. The prevailing excellence of the work being done today can in some sort be traced to the example he set by building The Hurst, Four Oaks'.[15]

It is interesting that despite Lethaby's architectural output being so small two of his most prominent buildings were in the City.

Lethaby's influence was not just confined to architecture in terms of the buildings he designed. He also had strong connections with the School of Art in Birmingham. Buckland lectured in Elementary and Advanced design at the school from around 1895 until 1909. During this time Lethaby set up the Central School of Art in London, and drew heavily on the experience of the Birmingham School of Art, which was considered to be 'one of the more successful state schools'.[16] Edward R. Taylor, the Head of the School of Art from 1885 to 1903 advised Lethaby. His successor as Head of the school was Robert Catteson-Smith. Catteson-Smith came from the heart of the Arts and Craft Movement.[17] He had taught at the Central School of Art,[18] and had worked under Lethaby as an Inspector of Schools of Art and Art Classes for the L.C.C.'s Technical Education Board.[19] Catteson-Smith worked on several of Buckland's houses, designing the plasterwork. A number of lecturers who trained at the Central School of Art, later went on to run classes at the Birmingham School of Art. Interestingly Lethaby lectured twice at the School in 1901 on Morris as a Work Master[20] and the Study and Practice of Artistic Crafts.[21] It was almost inevitable that the Lethaby philosophy would permeate the culture of the School of Art and influence the work of the architects strongly connected to the school, such as Buckland and Ball.

Number 21 Yateley Road was followed in 1901 by nos 15 and 19 Yateley Road, the latter was built for the first Lord Mayor of Birmingham, James Smith, both are listed Grade II. Number 15 Yateley Road, now much altered, was built in brick, and left unrendered with a projecting gable to the right hand side. It does however have similar casement windows and a steeply pitched, sprocketed roof, to number 21. Number 19, again altered, does not have a strong resemblance to 21, except to have a steeply pitched roof, but it does have two projecting bays, a feature that is seen in Buckland's later houses.

60 Russell Road, Moseley, 1906

In 1906 Buckland designed Greystoke, 60 Russell Road, Moseley. It was illustrated in *The Architectural Review* in 1908[22] and also in the *Architects' and Builders'*
Journal of 1911, where it was described as 'a quiet example of English domestic
work free from affectation or eccentricity'.[23] It is of rendered brick construction
beneath a steeply pitched tiled roof with a prominent three-storey asymmetrical
gable to the front elevation. The windows are sashes, made up of small panes of
glass, with shallow recessed arched panels above, reminiscent of Philip Webb, at
Red House, and a feature common to a number of Buckland's buildings at this
time, not just houses but schools as well which will be considered later. Very similar to Greystoke is Number 17 Yateley Road, which was designed for Hubert Adie
in 1907. It featured in the *Builders' Journal* and *Architectural Engineer* in 1909.[24] It
is two storey with attics, of brick construction, rendered in cement rough-cast
with brick detailing, beneath a steeply pitched red sand faced tiled roof. It is
asymmetrical in design, with an off centre three storey gable, a common feature
to a number of their houses built around this time. The first floor windows again
have shallow recessed arched panels, and there are casement windows of various
sizes. Five steps lead up to the main entrance, positioned in the gabled block,

which has a segmental hood above in the typical 'eyebrow' style, a feature used by a number of Birmingham Arts and Crafts Architects. The following year saw the design of no. 15 Farquhar Road, a large detached house in Edgbaston, listed Grade II. It is not as distinctively a product of Buckland and Farmer as the houses considered so far, but does pick up smaller details seen in their earlier houses, steeply pitched roofs, projecting gables, mullioned and transomed windows.[25]

Possibly Buckland's most interesting house in Birmingham was Moorcroft, built for Henry Hope, the window manufacturer, designed in 1904, and now, sadly, demolished. Pevsner describes it as 'one of the best Arts and Crafts houses in Birmingham'.[26] A 'small country house' in terms of size, it was located to the rear of Nos 62 and 64 Russell Road, and would have had commanding views over Cannon Hill Park, towards Edgbaston and the city centre. Although there is now a very lively skyline, the view from this aspect would have been somewhat different in 1904. The rear of the house would have faced north-west towards the centre of Birmingham and the view would have been largely green and rural. Moorcroft was constructed in red brick beneath pitched tiled roofs. The house comprised a two storey gabled building, with second floor attics. There were projecting twin gables to the front and rear. Lawrence Weaver describes them as follows: 'a neat point in the design of the main gables is however, hardly visible in the pictures; they are not straight sided, but built to a slight curve, which gives a pleasant and legitimate touch of interest to their outline'.[27] It had a number of other well detailed but simple features; the dominant chimney that grew straight up out of the ground on the left hand side at the front, the projecting porch with stone copings, and the main entrance surmounted by the 'eyebrow' created out of curved/recessed bricks; the decorative brick patterning seen above the door, above the door on the wall behind, and on the rear gables. Lawrence Weaver comments that 'the general merits of the house bear witness to his (Buckland's) devotion to the weightier matter of the law, which is art in building'.[28]

Buckland's work was not restricted to Birmingham. He designed a house which was almost identical to no. 21 Yateley Road, in Bridlington.[29] The floor plan is a mirror image of the Yateley Road house to make the best of the site and position. Another house, not too dissimilar to no. 60 Russell Road and no. 17 Yateley Road, was constructed in Wigginton, Staffordshire. In Rugeley he designed a house, Etching Hill, that bears a marked similarity to Moorcroft, but slightly smaller.[30] The house also has distinctive plasterwork by Catteson-Smith. It has not been possible to date these houses precisely, but they were all written up in architectural journals between 1905 and 1909, indicating they were all probably designed around the time of the Birmingham houses, and, like the Birmingham houses, well publicised.[31]

The largest house Buckland designed was Great Roke, Witley, Surrey and it was described by Remo Granelli as 'the biggest, most ambitious house by the partners and arguably the finest house produced by the movement in Birmingham ...

Great Roke, Witley, Surrey, 1909.
Photo: D. S.

surely one of the last of the important essays in the Arts and Crafts manner'.[32] The house overlooks the village of Witley, and has three wings, in an 'S' plan. It is at present unlisted. It was built externally in random rubble with a cavity and a brick lining, and following the sympathies of the Arts and Crafts Movement the external face is finished in the local Bargate stone, the dressings are of Doulting stone and it is roofed in clay tiles. It is a huge house in comparison to Buckland's other houses, considerably larger than Moorcroft. However it exhibits many of the features of the Birmingham houses, the steeply pitched roofs which sweep down very low as at the Yateley Road houses, the pronounced projecting gables as at Moorcroft, also like Moorcroft a chimney that grows out of the ground. Not seen elsewhere are the two tiered hipped gabled roofs, a local detail, the top tier terminating in a gablet. There are high chimneys, gabled dormers and plain dormer windows, all together producing the ultimate lively roofline. The rear elevation (and to a lesser extent the front elevation), step forward and back due to the projecting gables, increasing the liveliness of the whole composition. The windows are predominately stone mullioned and transomed, with opening metal opening casements, by the Birmingham firm of Messrs Henry Hope & Sons Ltd. The two most exciting features are the two storey music room, complete with a full height, imposing stone bay window, overlooking the entrance to the house and the internal decorative plasterwork which was executed by Robert Catteson-Smith. The plasterwork is highly ornate, detailed and extensive. The beams in the entrance hall and reception rooms are all highly ornamented. Pictures and plans of the house were extensively published in all the technical journals at the time, and the plasterwork including close ups of a number of the finer details were as publicised as the exterior views of the house.

There are also 'Birmingham' details, the eyebrow curve to the front doorway with a small diamond detail above, very similar to the detail above the entrance at

Blythe Court, Norfolk Road, Edgbaston, 1911

Moorcroft. There is also the influence of Lethaby with the chequerboard pattern above the entrance to the music room.

Finally in respect of houses there is Blythe Court, Edgbaston, probably Buckland's last major house in Birmingham, designed in 1911. Of all his houses this one appears to have had the most coverage in the architectural press in the few years after it was constructed.[33] Perhaps more than the others it exhibits the simplicity of The Hurst and the influence of Lethaby. It is a plain building of brick construction under a hipped clay tiled roof with a decorative dentil detail under wide eaves, with two projecting hipped gables to the rear and one to the front elevation. The windows are simple leaded casements. Although asymmetrical in plan due to the layout of the rooms taking precedence in the design, it still has an air of simplicity due to the broad expanses of plain brick, and simple roof design. A small Lethaby decorative detail is the wavy line in the tiling below the first floor windows, a detail also seen at the Women's Hostel, Birmingham University.

Surprisingly Buckland and Farmer carried out very little work in Four Oaks and Sutton Coldfield during these years. The other Birmingham Arts and Crafts architects, Bateman, Crouch and Butler, and Bidlake designed a large number of

12 Bracebridge Road, Sutton Coldfield, designed by Haywood-Farmer for his own occupation, entrance front, 1906

houses in these areas. Farmer's own house, and the only building that seems to be attributed to him, is no. 12 Bracebridge Road of 1906. Two other houses are stylistically attributed to the practice, nos 22 and 24 Anchorage Road, however there is no documentary evidence available.[34] They are listed Grade II.

Buckland is particularly well known in Birmingham as the architect to the Council's Education Department, a post he held from 1903 until the 1930s. He had initially been employed as the salaried architect to the School Board from 1901 following the termination of the Martin and Martin contract, until the 1902 Education Act abolished School Boards and transferred their duties to the municipalities. The majority of Buckland's work appeared to comprise extensions to preexisting schools within Birmingham during the period 1901 to 1918. He designed nine new schools during this period. These were mainly elementary schools, with an infant wing, although the George Dixon Schools in City Road and Cherryhill Road had secondary wings. Children could, at this period, remain at an elementary school until the age of fifteen.[35] Buckland continued to pursue the central hall type of school, as did many urban authorities, despite the ongoing debate concerning the health benefits of pavilion style schools. Accommodation in elementary schools comprised classrooms and an assembly hall, however in the larger schools there was usually more than one hall, for example at City Road there were four, one each for senior girls and boys, one for the elementary school and one for the infant school. Secondary schools also required science and domestic science rooms to be accommodated. The separation of the sexes also resulted in a tendency to build symmetrically, leading to large facades, which perhaps encouraged the use of neo-classical architecture, particularly for secondary schools. In a period during which Seaborn and Lowe state that there was a 'dearth of style in elementary school design', Buckland produced several innovatively designed schools.[36] The majority of Buckland's schools are located in what are now the inner city areas of Birmingham, although these were the areas that were being rapidly developed in the early part of the 20th century. His first schools, Handsworth New Road Council School of 1901, now listed Grade II, Oldknow Road Council School of 1903, listed Grade II, George Dixon County School and George Dixon Council Secondary Schools, City Road of 1904 and Leigh Road Council School of 1908, are all of very different styles.

Often Buckland used the neo-Georgian Style, typical of the period for school buildings[37] particularly with his later schools and the number of alterations and additions he carried out to existing school buildings in Birmingham. Within the scope of this essay it is not possible to look at all his schools but some have been selected which show the most originality in terms of style, including those noted above, and others that were given a significant degree of exposure in the technical publications at the time. It is worth highlighting that Buckland gave a number of presentations on school planning, and these were reported in the professional press. It would appear that he was something of an expert, perhaps hardly surprising as he was the Birmingham Education Authority Architect. During a period of prolific school building and extending, he worked on excess of ninety schools between 1901 and 1918.

Handsworth New Road Council School, won in competition, comprises a largely symmetrical composition with five projecting gables, each with a highly unusual parabolic arched window, and two further bays each with a cubic bay to the front, with a pyramidal roof, surmounted by a finial. There is a further gabled wing, again with a parabolic window, but also hipped gable dormer windows. The neighbouring caretaker's house, no. 17 Handsworth New Road, separately listed Grade II, although different in style to the school, is reminiscent of Buckland houses constructed around this time, although obviously considerably smaller. It exhibits a small hipped gabled, sprocketed roof, a steep pitch to the rear and panelled casement windows, all features common to Buckland's work. For a small house it is finely detailed, especially the iron work brackets supporting the porch roof.

In 1903 Buckland designed Oldknow Road Council School, positioned in what was to become the rear of the site.[38] Seaborn and Lowe state 'in Birmingham it was

Oldknow Road School, Small Heath, 1903

thirty years before elementary schools were built in any style other than Gothic, the first full blown departure being at Oldknow Road (1903), where a Byzantine style was adopted with domed two storey porches and barrel vaulted classrooms'. Could this have been the influence of Westminster Cathedral, under construction at this time? The elevations are a clear expression of the internal plan, and the unusual form of the building is achieved due to the construction of the roofs, concrete covered with asphalt, and the attempt to provide the central halls with light from the side rather than from the rooflights. Contemporary accounts state that the reason for the roofs was to reduce the cost of maintenance. Using side lights rather than rooflights improved the internal appearance of the halls, and the possibility of a more architectural treatment. The use of relatively simple detailing has produced rich and ornate elevations. The barrel vaulted classroom elevations are surmounted by dentil brick courses underneath curved sandstone coping stones, simple in design, but rich in appearance. Beneath the roofs of the halls, and beneath the parapets to the two storey entrances are raised diamond patterns in the brickwork, with a course of zigzag raised bricks above. The positioning of downpipes and the design of the detailing to the original hoppers (now unfortunately replaced) also adds to the interest of the façade. The windows to the halls are very much typical of Buckland, particularly in his later schools, high, rectangular, with semi circular headed recessed reveals above.

The school is listed Grade II, as is the Master's house which is located on the Oldknow Road frontage. Like the school, it is flat roofed with sash windows to the first floor with segmental heads, set back from the wall face, which between the outer bays is carried down between the windows and stopped on corbels. There is the same decorative dentil brick course beneath the sandstone coping stones on the parapet, as the school. Outside the master's house and the adjacent school building, are the only original railings and brick piers that have survived, although similar railings and piers are seen in contemporary photographs on the side of the site. They are separately listed Grade II, and are described in the list description as of 'quiet Arts and Crafts originality'.[39] They are typical of the railings that were found outside all Buckland's schools and it is an obviously typical Arts and Crafts feature to make use of other decorative arts in the architectural composition of a building. It is this attention to detail which makes Buckland's buildings so exciting to look at, and is very much an identifiable feature.

Oldknow Road was followed in 1904 by the George Dixon Schools in City Road,[40] a huge project with two secondary schools, and an elementary and infants school, and as a consequence four central halls, boys', girls', elementary and infants.' This building could not be architecturally more different to Oldknow Road, being Jacobean in style and obviously influenced by the early seventeenth century Aston Hall, in Birmingham. It bears little obvious resemblance to his other schools, but there is an attention to detail which is typical of his work, and the Arts and Crafts Movement. The detailed stone carving above and around the doors, can also be seen on the tower. The tower has an extraordinary ogee lead roof topped with a finial. To the coping stones on the main range are carved letters and numbers, a lesson in stone. However there are neo-classical elements that became a common feature of his later schools, the columns to the boys' entrance and either side of the central ground floor windows on the projecting bays, as well as the wreath of olive leaves above the girls' entrance. Overall the building comprises a fine Jacobean style composition with sandstone mullioned windows, diaper work, and a fine Dutch gable to the left hand side. The caretaker's house is a miniature version with projecting gables, stone mullioned casement window, a single storey stone bay and decorative brickwork. To the front of the school and the City Road are Buckland's distinctive railings and brick piers surmounted by sandstone caps.

Buckland's next major school, although there were also numerous extensions, was Leigh Road Council School designed in 1908, another brick and sandstone building, but more of a mixture of styles. At first glance it appears to be almost vernacular, like his houses, rather than Jacobean, but it also clearly has Arts and Crafts influences as well as Edwardian neo-classicism. It is extremely finely detailed. The front elevation is a mixture of projecting gables with large stone

George Dixon Schools, City Road, 1904

mullioned windows, and almost full height oriel windows, again constructed in stone. The gables have an interesting pilaster detail on either end becoming a buttress on the return. The guttering is of stone with cast iron downpipes with decorative hoppers. The Arts and Crafts detailing includes chequerboard patterning in brick and sandstone above the doorways and the air vents to the gables. There are the usual high quality railings and brick stone piers seen at other schools, the railings having almost neo-classical columns, with a Voysey like detail either side. There is also some very neo-classical detailing to the foundation stone with a pediment, rope carving detailing to the foundation stone and above the doorways. The tower has classical openings at the top to each side with broken headed rounded pediments with ornate neo-classical ironwork in the openings. It is a splendid composition, but the detail is typical of Buckland, and many of the finer points are seen in his later schools and other buildings.

1911 saw the construction of St Benedict's and Cherrywood Road schools.[41] St Benedict's Road Council School comprises a two block, two storey junior school to the rear of the site fronting Heather Road, and a single storey infants' school to the front. Overall it is in an Edwardian neo-classical style. The rear elevation to the Junior School, the most visible, is a two storey building, with a repetitive arrangement of windows separated by full height pilasters which run up into a parapet. The top floor windows have a dentil brick decorative arch above. Between the tops of the pilasters at parapet level are decorative infill panels of concrete rather than stone, a sign of economy perhaps, as the piers to the railings also appear to be concrete blocks. Between the ground and first floor windows are panels of diagonal chequerboard patterned bricks. Similar detailing can be seen to the Infants' School to the front of the site where only the assembly hall has the parapet detail. The single storey building has concrete coping stones and some decorative brickwork below. Like Oldknow Road, the elevations are an outward expression of the internal layout. On the east elevation there are two floors of classrooms, with the ends set back, subservient, containing cloakrooms and stair-cases. There is only one assembly hall, two storeys in height, the large, elaborate arched windows indicating the status of the interior.

Cherrywood Road Council School is another interesting composition, however it is necessary to look at contemporary photographs to ascertain the most impor-tant details. The school has been significantly altered in recent years, leaving it a relatively nondescript building. In plan it is a simple building, rectangular, with mixed senior accommodation on the first floor and mixed junior accommodation on the ground floor. Again the elevations reflect the internal planning the middle five bays, slightly forward of the rest of the building contain the assembly hall, with entrances, cloakrooms located at either end of the main building, where the elevations are somewhat plainer. The interesting thing about this building is the simple but very effective decorative treatment to the main elevation, slightly more simple on the rear but still of interest. There is a definite Byzantine feel with the domed arches on the five central bays and the striped brickwork. There is also a noticeable Lethaby influence with a mixture of rounded arches and pointed arches to windows, reflecting the Eagle Insurance building of 1900 and also the chequerboard detail in the recessed round arches. These rounded arches with the same chequerboard infill appear to two bays at either end of the rear elevation again with striped brickwork. These bays step forward slightly.

Buckland's early schools described above exhibit much of the attention to detail of the Arts and Crafts architecture that is seen in his houses. In terms of planning, to a certain degree the schools illustrate the gradual changes in school design that occurred from the late 19th century through to the First World War. Oldknow Road is of a central hall design, which was typical of the end of the 19th century. This design became less popular for elementary schools at the beginning of the 20th century due to concerns about hygiene and ventilation. Buckland, or maybe the Education Committee in Birmingham, did not pursue the pavilion style school popular in Staffordshire at the time, but St Benedict's and Cherrywood Road are clearly moving away from the pure central hall layout. George Dixon, slightly earlier, is still following the central hall design however this school was for infants, elementary and secondary children, and central halls remained a popular design for secondary schools. The need to accommodate so many children on a fairly narrow site on a main road, may have determined the layout as much as anything.

As mentioned before, Buckland's school work was not restricted to Birmingham. He entered a number of competitions, and achieved a degree of success and designed schools as far away as Barnsley, where he designed the High School, now listed Grade II, but converted to flats. The building was well documented in the professional journals of the day. It was designed in 1907, constructed in 1909 and therefore at the same time as Leigh Road. The two buildings could not be more different, illustrating Buckland's versatility as an architect. Barnsley High School is a Free Classical Style, two storey symmetrical composition. Overall the building presents itself as a composed piece of architecture, with central stone stairs up to the piano nobile level. It is constructed in brick with ashlar dressings beneath a pitched Westmorland slate roof. It has typical Buckland chequerboard detailing, and the ventilation shaft is a decorative tower. However there was some criticism levelled at the design in the professional press, not for its appearance but for its poorly thought out design, with a sick room next to a cookery room, for example. In terms of arrangement, the classrooms organised around a central hall with art room, laboratories etc. on the first floor, the school is fairly typical of secondary schools of the period as well as neo-classical in style.

Although outside the scope of this essay it is worth pointing out that Buckland with his later partner, William Haywood, designed The Royal Hospital School, Holbrook, near Ipswich (1925–33). 'A very large strictly axial composition of buildings in the neo-Wren to neo-Georgian style, culminating in a tall stone spire on the tower … .' Pevsner also describes 'a big chapel with Byzantinesque domes', in concrete. This is a huge school building, although Pevsner finishes his description of the building by saying 'the whole is certainly neither imaginative nor inventive, but it is in its scale and uniformity undeniably impressive'.[42] It is listed Grade II.

Buckland's designs and layouts generally follow established principles, but it is in the outward design, finish and attention to detail, that distinguish Buckland's schools, especially his early work.

Apart from schools the firm also designed other educational buildings, notably the Women's Hostel at Birmingham University, constructed in 1908, and extended in 1913. It is an imposing Queen Anne style building, two storeys in height with attics. The east elevation, overlooks the gardens, and down hill to the Bristol Road. The west elevation exhibits slightly more Arts and Crafts touches being less symmetrical, with interesting almost Byzantine carving above the door and also the 'wavy line' tile detail seen later at Blythe Court, reminiscent of Lethaby. 'University Hall is of special interest within the context of the development of the women's movement in the late Victorian and Edwardian periods … and as a distinguished and characteristically Edwardian interpretation of the Queen Anne style'. This was the first women's university halls, as opposed to the self contained colleges of the Oxford, Cambridge and London Universities. Although its architectural style is

Women's Hostel,
Birmingham
University, 1908

influenced by the Queen Anne movement, a common architectural style at the time for school buildings although not a style used by Buckland, it was a style used by the 'colleges which spearheaded the entry of women into higher education from the late 19th century', such as Newnham College Cambridge, by Basil Champneys 1874–1910, Somerville, Oxford, 1882, by T. J. Jackson and Lady Margaret Hall, Oxford, 1881–83, by Champneys. The Women's Hostel is not pure Queen Anne, but the plan was 'clearly based on these colleges, each room having its own fireplace and facing away from any northern aspects'.[43] Interestingly Buckland went on to design St Hugh's College, Oxford, a women's college, in 1914–16, but in a symmetrical neo-Georgian style, and, much later in 1940, an extension to Newnham College, Cambridge.

Probably due to Buckland's position with the Education Department, the practice designed the estate village in the Elan Valley, Wales in 1906–09 for the maintenance workers for the Elan Dam and reservoirs, the water supply for the City of Birmingham. Birmingham purchased seventy one square miles of the Elan Valley and over twelve years the City constructed, at a cost of six million pounds, a series of dams, aqueducts and reservoirs to hold and transport water. A village of wooden structures was initially constructed to house the workers who built the Elan Valley Dams. This was replaced by the estate village for the maintenance workers by Buckland and Farmer.[44] The village is a small and well preserved garden village positioned below the lowest dam at Caban Coch on the south bank of the River Elan. The village comprises eleven detached and semi-detached houses, a school, Co-op store, superintendent's house and office, with iron railings and gate, shelter and fountain and a small stone bridge. The buildings are of an obviously Arts and Crafts style, rather than a vernacular style, although they are constructed in local materials, a rough random stone, with Bath stone dressings, beneath pitched slate roofs. The buildings with their high pitched roofs, including the occasional sprocketed roof, mansarded gables and mullioned windows, are all very reminiscent of Buckland's houses. His attention to detail in respect of the shelter and small footbridge, both exhibiting the eyebrow detail and also seen as dormer window feature in a pair of cottages at one end of the village, is typical of the quality of Buckland's work.

Professionally Buckland not only practiced as an architect but also taught design to architecture students at the School of Art, before the creation of the School of Architecture. He was also involved with the Birmingham Architecture Association holding a number of positions including honorary secretary as early as 1894/95, and vice-president from 1898/99 to 1901. He would appear to have served as a council member on and off until the 1920s. In 1920 he became President of the Birmingham Architectural Association, a post he held for two years. He became a fellow of RIBA in 1914, and was vice-president of the RIBA from 1923 to 1925.

The firm of Buckland and Farmer, and in particular Herbert Buckland, may not have achieved the status of Bidlake or Bateman, but they were undoubtedly one of the most important practices in Birmingham in the early part of the 20th century, they were at their most prolific during the period 1900 to 1914. Their success was widely acknowledged during this time, evidenced by the large number of their projects that were reported in the professional journals, including extensive articles in *Country Life* by Lawrence Weaver in respect of two of their houses, Moorcroft and Blythe Court, as well as in *Land Haus und Garten* by Hermann Muthesius.

School in Elan Valley Estate Village, 1906–09. *Photo: M. W.*

Cottages, Elan Valley Estate Village. *Photo: M. W.*

Their success was not limited to their domestic work for Birmingham industrialists but is notable in terms of their breadth of building types, range of clients and locations. Although many of their buildings are in Birmingham, they designed buildings as far away as Glasgow, Essex and Surrey. Being the architect to Birmingham's Education Department Buckland designed several schools in Birmingham and extended many more, as well as entering numerous competitions to construct schools further afield. He became an 'expert' in the field, addressing the RIBA on the subject in 1909.[45] In addition to schools, his work in the education field included the Women's Hostel at Birmingham University, and work at women's colleges in Oxford and Cambridge. The practice also designed several industrial buildings in Birmingham. Their largest project was probably the garden village in the Elan Valley, built for the maintenance workers, in an Arts and Crafts style, using local materials.

Buckland and Farmer's work is characterised by a simplicity and attention to detail which draws upon 17th century vernacular domestic buildings, but also shows the influence of Philip Webb and William Lethaby. The latter, through his connection with the School of Art and his two major works in the city, had a major impact on a number of Birmingham architects of the period, and Buckland's work shows how this influence inspired a rich and varied practice of great quality.

List of Architectural Works of Buckland and Farmer

Herbert Tudor Buckland (1869–1951) was articled to a Birmingham quantity sur-
veyor, Henry Clere in 1885 and from 1891–95 worked in the office of Bateman and
Bateman. He set up in practice in partnership with Henry Clere in 1895, but went
into independent practice in 1897. In 1899 he entered a partnership with Edward
Haywood-Farmer (1871–1917). Farmer had been articled to Josiah Mander of Wolver-
hampton. In 1914 William Haywood (1879–1957) became a partner and the firm
became Buckland and Haywood-Farmer. After Farmer's death the practice became
Buckland and Haywood (in 1919).

The work of the practice up to 1919 has been included in the list.

WORK IN BIRMINGHAM AND ITS ENVIRONS

PUBLIC

1900 Handsworth New Rd Council School, Handsworth

1902 Cloakroom and teachers' room for Corksley Rd School

1902 Alterations to Lawley St and Little Barr St Board School, Bordesley

1902 Alterations to Dixon Rd Board School, Small Heath

1902 Additions to Lower Windsor St Board School, Duddeston

1903 Alterations and additions to Arden Rd Board School, Saltley

1903 Alterations to Chandos Rd Board School, Highgate

1903 Additions to Elkington St Board School, New Town Row

1903 Alterations to Elliot St Board School; 1910 urinals

1903 Alterations to Farm St Board School, Summer Hill

1903 Alterations to Foundry Rd Board School, Winson Green; 1904 alterations; 1908 additions

1903 Alterations to Floodgate St Board School; 1904 additions

1903 Additions to Little Green Lane Board School, Small Heath

1903 Oldknow Rd Council School, Small Heath; 1904 addition of science centre

1903 Alterations to Rea St South Board School, Deritend

1904 Latrines for Ada St Board School, Small Heath

1904 Additions to Clifton Rd Board School, Deritend

1904 Addition of Manual Training Centre to Camden St Board School, Spring Hill

1904 George Dixon Council Secondary Schools, City Rd and George Dixon Council School, City Rd

1904 Additions to Dudley Rd Board School, Winson Green; 1911 addition of handicraft centre

1904 Additions to Dennis Rd Board School, Balshall Heath; 1911 addition of laundry centre

1904 Latrines for Fox St Board School

1904 Additions to Jenkins St Board School, Small Heath

1904 Latrines for Norton St Board School, Hockley

1904 New cloakrooms and w.c.s for the Botanical Gardens, Westbourne Rd, Edgbaston

1904 Additions to Warley Road School

1905 Additions of laboratories to Dartmouth St Board School, Ashted; 1906 latrines; 1910 additions

1905 Additions to school for the Education Committee, Garrison Lane Board School, Bordesly; 1910 lavatories

1905 Additions to George Dixon Higher Grade Council School, Oozells St

1905 Addition of woodworking shop to Sherbourne Rd Board School, Balsall Heath

1905 Addition of laundry and cookery rooms to Station Rd Board School, Harborne; 1911 new infant school and additions

1905 Additions to Tilton Rd Board School, Small Heath; 1911 addition of new infants' school

1905 Additions to Tindal St Board School, Balsall Heath

1905 Addition of laundry to Upper Highgate St Board School; 1911 addition of cookery centre

1905 Additions to Yardley Rd Board School, Small Heath; 1910 new latrines

1906 Manual training centre for Chequers Walk Board School

1906 George St West Special School, Brookfields

1906 Alterations to Gem St School; 1910 additions; 1911 alterations

1906 Cloakrooms for Stratford Rd Board School, Sparkbrook

1906 Latrines for Severn St Board School

1907 Women's Hostel, Edgbaston Park Rd for University of Birmingham; 1913 additions

1907 Lavatories for Moseley Rd Board School

1907 Lavatories for Mary St Board School, Balsall Heath

1908 Curator's House for the Edgbaston Assembly Rooms, Hagley Rd, Edgbaston

1908 Leigh Road Council School, Washwood Heath; 1909 caretaker's house

1908 Special school at Little Green Lane Board School, Small Heath

1909 W.c.s etc. for Clifton Road Board School, Balsall Heath; 1911 additions

1909 Additions to Moseley Rd Deaf and Dumb School, Balsall Heath

1909 Additions to Steward Road Board School, Spring Hill

1910 Charles Arthur St Council School, Nechells; 1912 additions [D]

1910 Additions to Floodgate St Board School, Digbeth

1910 Additions to Goodrick St School, Nechells

1910 Additions to school for the Education Committee, Nelson Street Board School

1910 Additional classroom for Osler St Board School, Rotton Park

1910 Sladefied Rd Council School and caretaker's house, Ward End

1910 Latrines for Steward St Board School, Spring Hill

1910 New classrooms for the managers, Trinity Terrace School, Camp Hill

1910 Additions to school for the managers of the Moseley National School, School Rd, Moseley [D]

1911 Addition of Manual Instruction Centre to Burbury St Board School, Lozells

1911 Cherrywood Rd Council School, Bordesley Green

1911 Addition of laundry centre to Oakley Rd Board School, Small Heath

1911 Alterations to St Peter's C of E School, Old Church Rd, Harborne

1911 Alterations to Pitsford St School

1911 St Benedict's Rd Council School, Small Heath

1911 Alterations to Lower Windsor St Board School

1912 Additions to Montgomery St Board School, Sparkbrook

1912 Lavatories for Pershore Rd School, King's Norton

1913 Lavatories for Ada St Board School, Small Heath

COMMERCIAL

1896 Shop and four dwelling houses and a shop for J. White, Elkington St and Bracebridge St

1896 Alterations to Station Hotel, Bordesley Green Rd, for Ind Coope and Co.

1897 Alterations to Fox and Goose Public House, Castle Bromwich Rd, for Ind Coope and Co.

1897 Alterations to a public house, Great Colmore St, for Ind Coope and Co.

1897 Additions to The Bournbrook Hotel, Grange Rd for Ind Coope and Co.

1898 The Navigation Inn at Bromford, Erdington for Ind Coope and Co. [D]

1898 Alterations and additions to a public house, Sun St West, for Ind Coope

1898 Two shops and four houses for I. Larkin Smith, Cherrywood Rd, Bordesley Green

1898 Alterations to shops to form post office for The Fathers of the Oratory, Hagley Rd, Birmingham

1908 Alterations to Lee Longlands, Broad St

1911 New club for Indoor Sports Ltd, Suffolk St

1909 Club house for Harborne Golf Club, Harborne Lane

1914 Pavilion for Harborne Golf Club, Harborne Lane

INDUSTRIAL

1902 Shopping for Thomas Smith and Sons, Lawley St and Little Barr St

1903 Shed for Smith Corn Stores, Watery Lane

1903 Alterations for J. E. Charles, Wheeleys Lane [? D]

1904 Shopping for J. Brough, Loveday St

1905 New tower for J. & M. G. Wolsey, Bordesley Green Rd

1906 Shopping for Wolsey Tool and Motor Company, Bordesley Green Rd

1906 Additional shopping for Hopkiss and Co., Goodman St; 1907 alterations

1907 Additions for Edmonds & Sons, Warstone Lane

1909 Additions for Electric and Ordnance, Cheston Rd

1910 Additions for Hipkiss and Co., Anderton St

1910 Alterations for C. J. Thursfield & Co., Clement St

1910 Shopping for Electric and Ordnance Co., Cheston Rd

1910 Alterations and additions for Jewellers Association, Frederick St

1911 Alterations for Birmingham Corporation, Digbeth

1911 Factory for J. Walker and Sons, Oxford St; 1913 shopping

1911 Alterations for Stewart Smith Ltd, Westfield Rd

1912 Shopping for Smith and Sons, Adderley Rd

1912 Additional storey for Birmingham Metal Co., Adderley Rd

1912 Factory for unknown company, Cerx? St

1912 Shopping for Lyons Dennis, Canal St

1912 Factory for Brampton Bros., Cambridge St

1913 Shopping for The Cinema Co. Ltd, Broad St

1913 Alterations for Thursfield and Co., Clement St

1913 Shopping for the Electric Ordnance and Co., Cheston Rd

1914 Extension of works for Birmingham Metal & Munitions Co., Landor St; 1915 munitions factory, sub-station, castings shops, latrines, warehouse, rolling mill, additions to offices, boiler house; 1916 store

1915 Shopping and chimney for J. Booth and Co., Argyle St; 1916 blacksmiths' shop, motor sheds, warehouse and drainage plan; 1917 tube rolling mill and casting shop, engine house, petrol store, offices and w.c.s, messroom and women's w.c.s; 1918 canteen and laboratory

1915 Alterations and additions to factory for Birmingham Metals & Munitions Co., Drew's Lane

1915 New premises for Mild Steel Castings, King's Rd

1915 Dining hall, garage, stables, cycle house and drainage plan for Kynoch Ltd, Wellhead Lane; 1916 entrance lodge, gate house, garage and alterations to office [D]

1916 New premises for H. Taylor, Argyle St, Acock's Green

1917 Staff w.c.s for Birmingham Metal & Munitions Ltd, Adderley Rd

1917 W.c.s and office block for Birmingham Metal & Munitions Ltd, Landor St

1918 Alterations to gas producer for Tanks Ltd, Moseley St

DOMESTIC

1899 House, Sandon Rd, Edgbaston for Mr Goodman

1899 House, 21 Yateley Rd, Edgbaston for H. T. Buckland

1901 House, 13 [15] Yateley Rd, Edgbaston for Buckland and Farmer; 1908 additions for J. H. Barker; 1910 additions

1901 House, 19 Yateley Rd, Edgbaston for Sir James Smith

1901 Houses for Rev. A. W. Charles at Lickey Square, Barnt Green

1902 House for E. Farmer, 12 Bracebridge Rd, Four Oaks, Sutton Coldfield

1903 Eight Houses for A. Woodward, Mansell Rd

1903 Alterations to house for P. H. Carter, 7 Yateley Rd, Edgbaston

1903 Houses, 22 and 24 Anchorage Rd, Sutton Coldfield (attrib. by D. Hickman)

1906 House for Donald Hope, Moorcroft, Russell Rd, Moseley [D 1970s]

1906 House for John Chamberlain, Greystoke, 60 Russell Rd, Moseley

1907 Alterations for S. Taunton, Westfield Rd, Edgbaston

1907 House for C. C. Harding, 15 Farquhar Rd, Edgbaston

1907 House for H. W. Adie, 17 Yateley Rd, Edgbaston

1907 Additions for Buckland and Farmer 15 Yateley Rd, Edgbaston

1909 Additions for W. Bromett, Woodbourne Rd, Edgbaston

1910 Alterations for E. Morcom, Woodbourne Rd, Edgbaston

1910 Additions for Mole Roland, Westfield Rd, Edgbaston

1911 House for Dr G. Barling, Blythe Court, Norfolk Rd, Edgbaston

1911 Additions to Woodbourne, Augustus Rd, Edgbaston for H. D. Bingley

1912 New bedrooms for I. Osler, Harborne Rd, Edgbaston

1912 Motor house for F. Willmott, Vicarage Rd, Edgbaston

WORK OUTSIDE BIRMINGHAM

PUBLIC

1907 Mission rooms for Rev. R. W. Stephenson, St Hilda's, Warley

1906–09 Village for maintenance workers including new school, for Birmingham Corporation, Elan Valley, Wales

1909 Barnsley High School, Huddersfield Rd, Barnsley

1909 Prince Henry's High School, Victoria Avenue, Evesham

1911 New municipal offices for the City of Coventry, Earl St, Coventry

1913 Alterations and additions for the Board of Education, Shuttington School, Warks.

1914–16 St Hugh's College, St Margaret's Rd, Oxford

DOMESTIC

1902 House for T. O'Callaghan, near Coleshill

1905 House for J. H. Dewes Esq. at Wigginton Staffs., near Tamworth

1906 House at Bridlington

1906 Additions for Major Leslie Renton MP, Naseby Hall, Leics.

1905 House at Lyndon End

1909 House for Mr Charles Dixon, Great Roke, Surrey

1911 Houses at Gidea Park, Romford Garden Suburb

1911 House at Etching Hill, Rugely, Staffs.

NOTES

[1] Remo Granelli, 'Architecture' in *By Hammer and Hand: the Arts and Crafts Movement in Birmingham*, ed. by Alan Crawford (Birmingham, 1984) p. 41.

[2] 'Architects of the Day, Messrs Buckland and Haywood-Farmer of Birmingham', the *Architects' and Builders' Journal*, 31, 6 April 1910, pp. 260–69.

[3] William Haywood (1876–1957) was articled to Johnson & Clark, Architects and Surveyors, in Birmingham from 1892–95. He then attended the Birmingham School of Art from 1895–98, winning the Pugin Scholarship in 1897. He was an assistant to W. H. Bidlake in 1899, before commencing independent practice from 1899 to 1914. It was then that he went into partnership with Buckland and Farmer, the practice being known as Buckland and Haywood-Farmer until 1919 when it became Buckland and Haywood.

[4] 'Architects of the Day, Messrs Buckland and Haywood-Farmer'.

[5] *Ibid.*

[6] *Ibid.*

[7] *Ibid.*

[8] M. MacCartney, 'Recent English Domestic Architecture', the *Architectural Review*, 66, 1908, pp. 7–8.

[9] Remo Granelli, 'Architecture', p. 41, p. 43, pp. 55–56.

[10] *Ibid* p. 55.

[11] I. R. Gradidge, 'A traditional craft', *Country Life*, 184, No. 28, 12 July, 1990, p. 109.

[12] *Architectural Review*, 61, December 1901, 225.

[13] Hermann Muthesius, *Das Land Haus und Garten* (Munich, 1907).

[14] Gradidge, ' A traditional craft', 109.

[15] Lawrence Weaver 'The Lesser Country Houses of Today, Moorcroft, Moor Green, Birmingham', Architectural Supplement, *Country Life*, 30, 1 July 1911, pp. 7–11.

[16] Godfrey Rubens, *William Richard Lethaby: His Life and Work 1857–1931* (1986) p. 178.

[17] Granelli, 'Architecture', p. 38.

[18] Rubens, *Lethaby*, p. 178.

[19] Granelli, 'Architecture', p. 38.

[20] W. R. Lethaby, *Morris as a Work Master*, (1901).

[21] W. R. Lethaby, *The Study and Practice of artistic crafts: an address to the Birmingham Municipal School of Art*, (1901).

[22] Mervyn E. Macartney, 'Recent English Domestic Architecture', *Architectural Review*, 66, 1908, p. 78, p. 65.

[23] 'House at Moor Green, Birmingham', *Architects' and Builders' Journal*, 33, 25 January 1911, pp. 94–95.

[24] *The Builders' Journal and Architectural Record*, 30, 20 October 1909, pp. 298–99.

[25] *Architectural Review*, 67, 1909, p. 35, pp. 38–39.

[26] Nikolaus Pevsner and Alexandra Wedgwood, *The Buildings of England: Warwickshire* (Harmondsworth, 1966) p. 187.

[27] Lawrence Weaver 'The Lesser Country Houses of Today, Moorcroft, Moor Green, Birmingham' Architectural Supplement, *Country Life*, 30, 1911, pp. 7–11.

[28] *Ibid.*

[29] J. H. Elder, *Country Cottages and Weekend Homes*, (1906) pp. 102, 134–36; *Builders' Journal and Architectural Record*, 21, 4 July 1906, p. 3. Elder also cites a house at Lyndon End, Olton, built by Buckland and Farmer (p. 101, p. 128).

[30] *The Architectural Review*, 67, 1909, pp. 35–37.

[31] Other domestic work includes houses at Gidea Park, Romford Garden Suburb, *The Hundred Best Houses, The Book of the House and Cottage Exhibition 1911*, pp. 76–77, pp. 121–22; *Garden City House and Domestic, Interior*

Details (4th ed. 1942) p. 39 and additions to Naseby Hall, Leicestershire, *Builders' Journal and Architectural Record*, 21, 29 August, 1906, p. 101.

[32] Granelli 'Architecture', p. 38.

[33] Lawrence Weaver *Small Country Houses of Today*, second series, (1919), pp. 145–50.

[34] Douglas Hickman, *The Arts and Crafts House of Sutton Coldfield* (typescript of tour for Victorian Society, Birmingham Group, 1975).

[35] Herbert Buckland 'Extracts of a Paper to the Architectural Association on 5th February 1909' *Architect and Contract Reporter*, 81, 12 February 1909, pp. 113–15 and 19 February 1909 pp. 129–32; Also reported in *Builders' Journal and Architectural Record*, 29, 10 February 1909, pp. 113–14 and 17 February 1909, pp. 139–40 and *The Builder*, 96, 20 February 1909, pp. 210–13.

[36] M. Seaborn and R. Lowe, *The English School and its Architecture and Organisation*, 2 vols (1977) II, p. 67.

[37] *Ibid.*

[38] *Builders' Journal and Architectural Record*, 25, 27 December 1905, p. 366, and *Ibid*, 27, 2 October 1907, p. 170.

[39] Department of the Environment *List of Buildings of Special Architectural or Historic Interest: City of Birmingham* (1982).

[40] *Builders' Journal and Architectural Record*, 27, 25 December 1907, pp. 209–10 and *Architectural Review*, 21, 1907, pp. 114–20.

[41] *The Builder*, 106, 31 October 1913, pp. 456–57.

[42] Nikolaus Pevsner, *The Buildings of England: Suffolk* (1974), p. 61, p. 275.

[43] Department of the Environment, *List of Buildings of Special Architectural or Historic Interest: City of Birmingham* (1982).

[44] Supplement to *Builders' Journal and Architectural Record*, 30, 27 October, p. 322; *Academy Architecture*, 36, 1909, pp. 24–26; Richard Haslam, *The Buildings of Wales: Powys* (Cardiff, 1979), p. 318; www.cpat.org.uk/projects/longer/histland/élan/evintr.htm.

[45] Granelli, 'Architecture' p. 38, p. 55.

23 William Alexander Harvey

MICHAEL HARRISON

William Alexander Harvey (1874–1951) was in practice as an architect in Birmingham for over fifty years. Although he received the Bronze Medal of the Royal Institute of British Architects in 1934 for his designs for the Municipal Offices at Dudley, Harvey is best remembered for his early work at Bournville. He was recruited as a very young man by George Cadbury to design cottages for the new Bournville Estate in 1895. 'The appointment,' one commentator rightly noted, 'while giving him the first big opportunity for the exercise of his gifts, proved to be of incalculable value to this pioneering housing experiment.'[1]

The Cadbury Brothers had built their new factory in the countryside in 1879 and named it Bournville. They did not commence their model village until nearly twenty years later. The stated object of the Bournville Estate was 'to make it easy for working men to own houses with large gardens secure from the danger of being spoilt either by the building of factories or by interference of the enjoyment of sun, light and air'.[2] The intention was to construct a replicable low-density 'model village' with attractive and convenient 'cottage homes' for a socially mixed population, which was not restricted to their employees.[3] It was a more practical exemplar than the heavily subsidised and elaborate contemporary scheme developed by W. H. Lever for his workforce at Port Sunlight.

Members of the Cadbury family commissioned many of the early dwellings. Others sought cottage designs from W. A. Harvey for their own use. The earliest houses were sold on 999-year leases. After 1900, the running of the Estate was taken over by the Bournville Village Trust. Their initial policy was to build houses

W. A Harvey on right, at laying of foundation stone for Bournville Infant School in 1910

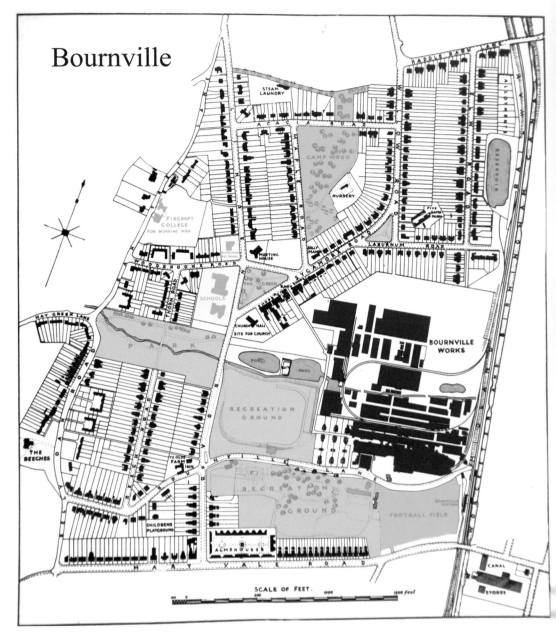

Plan of Bournville based on a plan of 1914. *Courtesy of Bournville Village Trust*

for rent and only allow the sale of properties on 99-year leases. The shift was partly the result of finding out that some early leaseholders had made a big profit on the sale of their houses.

William Alexander Harvey came from an artistic Birmingham family. His father and his brother Ernest were artists in stained glass. The latter was a partner in the firm of Harvey and Ashby, based in John Bright Street.[4] W. A. Harvey was educated privately.[5] It was originally intended that he should take up engraving as a profession but Harvey chose architecture instead. Between 1890 and 1894 Harvey was articled to David Smith and Son of Birmingham whose most significant work was the Classical Wesleyan Chapel at Small Heath of 1876.[6] Harvey also attended classes at the Birmingham Municipal School of Art, where he was taught architectural history and design by W. H. Bidlake, the prominent local Arts and Crafts architect.[7] He also came across Benjamin Creswick, an ardent follower of John Ruskin and Modelling Master at the School.[8] Harvey won prizes at the School of Art for his sketches of local medieval and vernacular architecture.[9] He also frequently travelled abroad, and his visits to the cities of Italy, France, Spain, Germany and America were said to have been 'a rich source of inspiration to him'.[10]

Almost from the very start of his career W. A. Harvey was involved with a range of professional organisations. He became an associate of the Birmingham Architectural Association in 1896, was elected to its council in 1902 and served as president of the Association between 1917 and 1919.[11] Harvey was a founder member of the Town Planning Institute in 1914.[12] He became a fellow of the RIBA in 1918 and received the RIBA Distinction in Town Planning in 1936.[13] In addition, Harvey was a member of many local artistic, musical and horticultural societies. He was also chairman of the Edgbaston Golf Club.[14] This dedicated committee man also had charm and integrity. It was said that 'his quiet, unassuming personality endeared him to all'.[15]

It is not clear how W. A. Harvey came to be employed as architect for the Bournville Estate. He was not a Quaker like George Cadbury, or the surveyor, A. P. Walker, who produced the original street plan for the Estate in April 1895. He was barely twenty-one years old and an architectural novice when he first started work at the Bournville Estate Office. Harvey must have been seen as a promising and committed young designer who could bring together 'the two movements of housing reform and the revival in domestic architecture' and realise Cadbury's dream for 'the model village'[16] It must be remembered that at that time architects were rarely involved in the design of working class or lower middle class housing. Harvey clearly learned from others as he worked towards 'a new conception of design applied to small and medium-sized suburban houses' and sought to explore their relationship to their surroundings. 'Harvey,' one of his successors remarked, 'was one of those pioneers of Garden City architecture who struggled to lift the design of "cottages", as the "romantics" of that period liked to call them, above the level of Victorian speculative builders' terraces'.[17]

Harvey first appears in the Bournville records as a witness to the designs by A. P. Walker for the first houses on the Estate in 1895.[18] The earliest Bournville plan by Harvey was produced in December 1895, but his design for four three-storeyed houses with timber-framing and dormers was never executed.[19] By March 1896 Harvey had clearly become the chief architect of Bournville Village.[20] Harvey's first houses are to be found on Row Heath Road (later called Selly Oak Road), the southern end of Linden Road, Bournville Lane, Mary Vale Road and Raddlebarn Road. These were soon followed by dwellings on Beech and Elm Roads. Harvey did not immediately break away from the typical Birmingham tunnel-back house plan with long back projections. The Bournville plots were, however, more generous than suburban developments elsewhere in the city, and Harvey's façades were treated with greater freedom and simplicity. At first, there was less difference between Harvey's cottages than later. Identical pairs of semi-detached houses are to be found along Bournville Lane and most of the dwellings on Mary Vale Road display only minor variations.[21] Harvey soon began to try to self-consciously produce more varied streetscapes in the Village. A series of panoramic sketches of Beech Road by Harvey exemplify this quest for variety. At this stage nearly all the cottages were semi-detached. A small number of more elaborate and larger dwellings and public buildings were constructed in the late 1890s. This enabled Harvey to achieve a more varied disposition of buildings and a more bucolic atmosphere in the Estate. 'We must study variety and artistic effect,' Harvey told members of the Oxford University Fabian Society in 1902. Harvey later argued that it was 'in the interesting disposition of houses of varying sizes [lay] one of the secrets of beautiful village building'.[22] He believed many old villages proved this hypothesis and sought in his work to emulate such settlements.

As a very young and inexperienced designer embarking upon a scheme that required 'satisfactory accommodation and artistic appearances' Harvey drew not only on the regional vernacular for inspiration but also some of the leading Arts and Crafts architects of the day.[23] Some of the larger houses on Bournville Lane look back to Bedford Park.[24] The pebble-dashed pair of cottages and the shops on Mary Vale Road, with their horizontal emphasis and prominent buttresses, were clearly influenced by the work of C. F. A. Voysey.[25] A number of early half-timbered dwellings and public buildings, like the Bath-house in Laurel Grove and the elaborate shops at the corner of Linden Road and Mary Vale Road, are reminiscent of Shaw's 'old English' work and that of Baillie-Scott.[26] The three blocks of houses in Holly Grove, constructed in 1900, display a wealth of Arts and Crafts details.[27] The picturesque end block makes use of hand-made bricks, half-timbering and pebble-dash and incorporates elaborate Elizabethan-style chimney stacks, elegant dormers of the kind used in the late 17th century and the angled buttresses favoured by Voysey. This group of four houses was deliberately

Pair of houses on Linden Road of 1898. Harvey lived here. Illustrated in *The Model Village and its Cottages: Bournville* (1906)

designed in a way that it made it look as if it had evolved over a period of time. This was a method used by Crouch and Butler for some of their larger suburban houses in Birmingham.[28]

Most of Harvey's early house designs for the Bournville Estate were more simply treated than those described above. The cottages were largely constructed of brick with hand-made tile or Welsh slate roofs. Pantiles were occasionally used to good effect on unbroken and hipped roofs. Some of his most satisfying early designs have long sweeping roofs, which give the designs a comforting grounded feel. Periodically, Harvey gave special treatment to dormers and chimney stacks. His cottages frequently had overhanging eaves, and on a number of dwellings Harvey introduced eaves that curved like eyebrows. Although some of the houses at Bournville designed by Harvey had leaded lights, he used casement windows for the majority of his houses. In the early 1900s, Venetian windows were introduced into some of his designs on Sycamore Road and Woodbrooke Road. On the whole ornament was restricted, but half-timbering, decorative brickwork, pargetting, colouring, metalwork and wood-carving (usually by Creswick) were to be found on some of the Estate's buildings. 'An extensive elevation,' Harvey suggested, 'may also be made interesting by the treatment of a porch here, the addition of a bay window there, and the use of rough cast somewhere else.'[29] Monotony could be avoided 'by variety in combination and disposition' of the

Block of four houses in Holly Grove built in 1900 illustrated in W. A. Harvey *The Model Village and its Cottages: Bournville* (1906)

Another block of four houses in Holly Grove built in 1900 illustrated in *The Studio*, 24, 1902

different designs and the use of irregular building lines. Even where the same plan was used, as in the group of three pairs of semi-detached cottages on Sycamore Road, variety was achieved by the different treatment of the façades. Lawrence Weaver noted that the curved eaves and stepped chimney of the first pair gave them 'just that touch of character which marks them as architecture when compared with sheer utilitarianism'.[30] The streetscape of the largely rectilinear Estate plan was also improved by giving greater attention to the houses situated at road junctions, as can be seen in the designs for the pair of cottages at the junction of Willow Road and Laburnum Road, and the detached house at the junction of Beech Road and Bournville Lane and the block of three cottages on the corner of Linden Road and Acacia Road.

Most contemporary accounts of the Estate stressed its picturesqueness. *The Studio* noted in 1902 that Harvey had 'introduced a large variety into his designs, which are very quaint and picturesque and revive the best traditions of country architecture'.[31] Housing experts and journalists praised the scheme and commented on the picturesque and artistic appearance of the garden suburb.[32] It should also be noted that much of the appeal was generated by the mature trees, flourishing gardens and open spaces of the Estate. Harvey's own published account of his work at Bournville also tends to highlight the more ornate and

A road junction house at the corner of Laburnum Road and Elm Road

variegated houses designed around 1900.[33] One reviewer suggested that its pictures made it 'a delight for the lover of domestic architecture'.[34]

By the time Harvey began to lecture and write about his work between 1904 and 1906 he believed that the designer of cottage homes should meet 'the demands both of satisfactory accommodation and artistic appearance'.[35] Harvey and the Bournville Village Trust had come under some pressure in 1901–02 to design cheaper cottages. Harvey began to recognise that one of his key tasks was to 'satisfy the demands of both art and economy'.[36] 'I strongly urge that the only legitimate way of diminishing cost,' Harvey told a group of London architects in 1902, 'is by the avoidance of unnecessary ornament and by the advancing of a pleasing simplicity.'[37]

One largely successful way of reconciling these potentially conflicting demands was to use long, sloping roofs to produce pleasing proportions for the frontages and at the same time reduce the cost of the brickwork for the walls. The move towards simplified, compact and regular plans was a means of achieving economies. Further savings could also be made by adapting the dimensions of dwellings to the stock sizes of building materials. Although Harvey usually paid particular attention to the quality of materials and made a point of avoiding mechanically-made bricks, he believed that worthy stock articles could be used to advantage. He advocated the use of simple and inexpensive internal fittings in cottages to be let at low rents. Harvey continued to stress the importance of building homes that would last, for he recognised that the 'true cost of economy is that which takes into account the cost of repairs at the end of ten years'.[38]

Harvey's earliest response to the demand for cheaper cottages can be seen in his design for a block of four dwellings on Bournville Lane. 'Economy of construction has been the main object in design,' Harvey explained.[39] This austere block was completed in 1902 (much to the consternation of nearby long leaseholders who had complained to the Trust that such properties would lower the value of their homes).[40] Despite the quest for economy, Harvey believed that the essentials of a cottage home – privacy, homeliness of appearance and a pleasant environment – had been achieved. In retrospect, such simple and cheap blocks were to become the prototype for the council houses of the inter-war period.[41]

These were the first two-bedroomed dwellings in the Village, and tenants were quickly found for them. Most of the cottages in the Model Village had three bedrooms and three rooms downstairs. Harvey, like Parker and Unwin, complained about 'the useless front room in small cottages'.[42] He therefore began to design houses with one large living room, which had the advantage of allowing light and air in from two directions. J. H. Whitehouse described this move to abolish the parlour as 'an attempt ... to get rid of an absurd convention'.[43] Although there seems to have been no difficulty in letting these through houses, the demand for more traditionally-planned parlour houses at Bournville was acknowledged and accepted.[44]

Cottage interior
from W. A. Harvey
*The Model Village
and its Cottages:
Bournville* (1906)

Generally, the street pattern of the Bournville Estate did not allow Harvey as
much freedom in terms of orientation as he would have liked. Where the prospect
was favourable, he did design a number of larger houses (including his own) with
the principal rooms at the back. The large and broad plots of almost all the houses
at Bournville allowed Harvey to take advantage of their generosity by placing the
scullery or kitchen overlooking the garden, so as to afford the housewife a glimpse
of nature.[45]

Besides having adequate accommodation and a pleasing exterior, it was felt that
every home at Bournville should also have a bath (an unusual feature in working-
class homes at the time).[46] The provision of a separate bathroom for the larger
houses was straightforward, but in the smaller cottages various expedients had to
be tried. The placing of the bath in the kitchen was considered the most suitable
arrangement as hot water was usually to hand from the boiler or range. Several
devices were tried by Harvey. These included the sunken bath, a bath covered with
a work surface and the Patent Adjustable Cabinet Bath, which was stored in a
built-in cupboard. The latter was regarded as being the most successful of the
three alternatives.

By the early 1900s the Village and its architect were achieving some recognition.
The Trust's secretary was reporting that 'it is evident that the Village has come to
be regarded as the place that ought to be seen by all who are interested in housing
and kindred questions'.[47] It was hardly surprising that Harvey's salary was raised

from £156 to £306 in July 1901.[48] By the beginning of 1902 Harvey was reporting that he had received 'numerous applications for plans' and so arrangements were put in place relating to Harvey's outside work. Among the private work that Harvey carried out at about this time were larger dwellings for J. H. Barlow, the Trust's Secretary and George Cadbury Junior at Griffin's Hill and houses on Bunbury Road, Northfield and St Agnes Road, Moseley.[49] In May 1902, Harvey was invited to prepare plans for a Ruskin Memorial building to be erected at Bournville.[50]

Harvey continued his domestic work for the Trust, designing houses on Sycamore Road, Acacia Road, Maple Road and Thorn Road between 1901 and 1904. He also did some infill work in Bournville Lane and Beech Road.[51] The desire to produce more economical dwellings at Bournville led to the appointment of Leonard P. Appleton as Building Manager. 'Some such arrangement as this,' the Trustees noted late in 1902, 'has been found necessary owing to the excessive cost of recent building work on the Estate.'[52] In the summer of 1903, concerns about Harvey's designs were raised by the Village Council. The Council members expressed a preference for sash, rather than casement, windows, stairs from the parlour rather than the kitchen, table baths rather than sunken baths and wooden floors (except in rooms containing a copper). One immediate consequence of this was that Harvey was instructed to amend his designs for some cottages in Thorn Road to include sash windows. This was not the end of the matter. In December 1903, George Cadbury Junior presented a critical memorandum to the Trustees complaining about the 'unnecessary cost' of the new houses designed by Harvey in Thorn Road and Acacia Road. Cadbury raised points about the 'unsatisfactory or expensive planning', the use of semi-circular windows, the hand-made bricks and the tiling over doors and windows. The Trustees came to the conclusion that 'in future new plans should be dispensed with as far as possible'. It was also suggested 'that the time had come when W. A. Harvey should cease to give his whole time to the work of the Trust'.[53] He was, however, retained as a Consulting Architect and continued work on the Junior School and the Quaker Meeting House.

On hearing of the discussions, Harvey expressed his desire to leave the Trust immediately and set up his own practice in Bennett's Hill without delay.[54] He was joined by two Trust employees, H. G. Wicks and F. H. Bromhead. It is difficult to know whether Harvey was wounded by this apparent criticism of his work. He continued to have the support of George Cadbury for major projects in the Village and he was aware of the opportunity he had been given at Bournville. 'I should like to add,' Harvey wrote to the Trustees 'that I shall always look back with pleasure upon the period of my service in connection with the Estate'.[55]

Harvey was not without work. His plans for the Friends' Meeting House at Bournville and the Junior School had been submitted to the local authority in August 1904.[56] A lecture to the Architectural Association in London in 1904 was fully reported in *The Builder*.[57] Harvey's own book, *The Model Village and its Cot-*

tages: Bournville, was published, with the Trust's blessing, in 1906. Both undoubtedly helped to bolster his career. Harvey's site plan for the twenty-acre co-partnership scheme being developed on an outlying part of the Bournville Village Trust's estate off Northfield Road was accepted in December 1906. Harvey was to go on and design the majority of the houses on this estate. Harvey also won the First Prize in the competition for the laying out of the Sheffield Corporation estate at Wincobank in conjunction with the Model Cottage Exhibition organised by the National Housing Reform Council in 1907.[58]

The period immediately after the setting up of his own firm in 1904 was taken up with the completion of the first three of Harvey's major public buildings on The Green at Bournville. The Friends' Meeting House, on the North side of The Green, was commissioned and paid for by George and Elizabeth Cadbury. It has a strikingly simple and effective Y-shaped plan. In plan, though not in materials, it is similar to the First Church of Christ Scientist in Manchester. Its architect, Edgar Wood was well-known in Birmingham and his design had been published in *The Builder* in 1904. The front of the Meeting house has a prominent gable, simple mullioned and transomed window and octagonal stair turret. The side arms and Norman style entrance draw the worshipper into the building. The side elevations have sloping buttresses and dormer windows. The interior is simple but striking.

The Friends' Meeting House, The Green, 1905

Its main architectural feature is its timber-framed roof, which has trusses that rise from wall plates in the manner of a cruck-framed roof.[59]

As early as November 1901 the tenants of Bournville had called upon the Trustees to 'secure satisfactory accommodation for the children of the Village'.[60] Having little confidence in the local School Board, the Trustees resolved to build the school themselves. They were anxious that 'the school buildings should be the best possible and so serve as an object lesson to the country'.[61] In early February 1902 Harvey was told to complete the plans of the school and ascertain the approximate costs of the project. Two months later, realising the large expenditure that would have been required, the Trustees willingly accepted George Cadbury's offer to pay for the school himself.[62] The Trustees did, however, provide the site for the school.

Harvey's plans were submitted to E. R. Robson, an authority on school architecture and designer of many London Board Schools, before being sent for approval to the Board of Education in London. They sanctioned the scheme in September 1903 and the final plans were passed by the local authority in August 1904.[63] J. Bowen and Sons of Balsall Heath began work on the school in the Autumn and the school was formally opened in April 1906. The estimated cost of the school was £20,000.[64] It was clearly the intention to provide the best possible teaching environment, according to the standards of the time.

Harvey's plan was based on a large central hall of 84 feet by 32 feet with twelve classrooms grouped around it. The classrooms could take 540 pupils in rooms which were meant to accommodate either 40 or 50 children each. This was quite generous at a time when classes of 60 were the norm. The slope of the site allowed for specially constructed rooms in the basement for craft work and technical instruction for boys and cookery and laundry work for girls. There were separate rooms for the male and female teachers, and a spacious library and a laboratory were provided in the tower.[65] As contemporary photographs show, the main hall was used, among other things, for physical instruction. The large playgound, the school gardens and the nearby park also afforded opportunities for outdoor activities of the kind encouraged elsewhere by George Cadbury.

The large hall has a roof with curved timber braces rather similar to that in the Friends' Meeting Hall. It is lit by dormers and a traceried window to the north. The gabled classrooms have large tri-partite windows to provide a healthy and well-lit teaching environment. An early engraving shows that Harvey originally intended to have stone-mullioned Venetian windows for these classrooms. Their replacement was held by one contemporary critic to be a mistake.[66]

The school is largely constructed of brick, with stone mouldings and it is roofed in graded Welsh slate. On its south-east corner it has a prominent square entrance tower. It has a large Gothic entrance, an ornate oriel window with a steep roof and a half-octagonal staircase turret. The carved panels and mouldings were the work of Benjamin Creswick. 'Everything is being done in the carving of details,' Harvey

Bournville Estate Schools, the Infants' School of 1910 and the Junior School of 1905

explained, 'to make the building itself a permanent means of educating the children.'[67] Besides Creswick's carving, there was decorative plasterwork in the corridors and library and a set of fine iron gates by the Birmingham Guild. A little later, between 1913 and 1915, Mary Sargent Florence and Mary Creighton McDowell produced a series of frescoes illustrating the life of Christ on the walls of the school hall.[68]

Ruskin Hall was the brainchild of J. H. Whitehouse, Secretary of the Birmingham Ruskin Society, Bournville resident and, for a short time, editor of the *Bournville Works Magazine*. Early in 1902 he proposed a national monument to John Ruskin which should 'take the form of a Village Library, Art Gallery and Museum' to be situated in Bournville.[69] The Trustees welcomed the scheme and made a gift of the freehold of the site so long as 'it should be used for the purpose for which it was given'. Harvey was invited to prepare initial plans for the Ruskin Memorial 'to embrace the Library and Lecture Room'.[70] That building was to be seen as the nucleus to which subsequent additions could be made when additional funds became available. Harvey felt that it would be necessary to limit the decorative work in order to work within the prescribed limit of £2500.[71]

Fund-raising did not go smoothly. George Cadbury gave the Ruskin Memorial Committee a loan in the summer of 1903, but Ruskin Hall (as it was to become known) was transferred to the Bournville Village Trust in December of that year.[72] The following spring it was decided that the building be used as an infant school for the young children of Bournville. Ruskin Hall soon developed as an important social, recreational and artistic centre for the Village.

Ruskin Hall sits to the west of the Friends' Meeting House and to the north of the Junior School. The three buildings, although different in stylistic detail, form an impressive but not over-sized group at the north corner of The Green. Ruskin Hall is an L-shaped building made of brick with stone dressings. It has prominent gables and mullioned windows. It has a modestly decorated stone porch and a large, angled bay window. The style is essentially Tudor, but Pevsner noted 'several wilful Art Nouveau details'.[73] The well-lit interior is simply treated, but some decorative plasterwork and metalwork can be found.

The Trustees clearly had no doubts about Harvey's capacity to design the public buildings on the Estate. In the summer of 1908 they decided that 'no buildings should be erected in the centre of the Village without the plans being first submitted to W. A. Harvey.'[74] In his role as Consultant Architect, Harvey had already commented unfavourably on the design of the shops on the Green by his successor, H. Bedford Tylor. Harvey objected to the half-timbering on the grounds that it was 'not in favour with the leading architects, expensive in construction and also in maintenance'.[75] Interestingly, Harvey's Elizabethan-style Infant School, which was planned in 1909 and completed by August 1910, not only had decorative chimney stacks but also half-timbered bays. The removal work that was being considered on The Rookery (or Selly Manor as it was later called) might have influenced Harvey at this point. It is also significant that Harvey only used proper half-timbering for whole units of his buildings.[76]

Despite its obvious historicist features the school had a reinforced concrete floor and a hall with segmental vaults and window openings. Harvey's slightly eclectic but sensitive approach can also be noted in the windows of the school. Many of the windows have leaded lights, but they are also set at a low height so that the children would get the advantage of the light and the views.

Compared to its predecessor, the Infant School was built without incident. It was designed by W. A. Harvey in 1909 and constructed by William Bishop by August 1910. It was paid for by George and Elizabeth Cadbury. The Infant School has an H-shaped plan, with the central hall occupying the cross-piece. Besides the hall, the school had four classrooms, a 'babies' room, teachers' rooms, a museum, cloak rooms and toilets. Harvey's plan included provision of an open-air classroom over the cloak rooms, which was reached from the first floor landing. This area was sheltered from winds from the north and east and provided a fine view of the Park. The Infant School was intended to accommodate 250 pupils.[77] Whilst working on the Infant School at Bournville, Harvey was also engaged by King's Norton and Northfield Urban District Council to design further accommodation for the schools at Charlotte Road, Stirchley.[78]

The most noticeable feature on The Green at Bournville is the centrally placed Rest House. Constructed just before the First World War, this octagonal structure was built to commemorate George and Elizabeth Cadbury's Silver Wedding. It was paid for by contributions from Cadbury workers from around the world and designed by Harvey and Wicks.[79] It was not a typical attempt to give new life to vernacular forms, but a close copy of the 16th century Market Hall at Dunster in Somerset. Unlike the stone original, the Bournville Rest House is constructed of brick with stone dressings and has a steeply-pitched tiled roof topped with a lantern. The eaves of the building, which are supported on large brackets, overhang significantly and provide shelter and shade for the villagers. Above them are projecting gables containing windows with two lights.[80]

Whilst it is evident from some of his work that Harvey was interested in the vernacular, so were some of his Cadbury patrons. George Cadbury bought Selly Manor, 'a mere derelict in the midst of modern work of the poorest architectural character', in 1907. After several years of investigation it was dismantled and a site for it was sought in Bournville.[81] Harvey considered re-erecting it on The Green. The Trustees decided to consult Raymond Unwin who dismissed the idea;

From the point of view of the village I feel that a building in the centre of the Green will tend to prevent you securing eventually a sense of a group of buildings surrounding a Green, and also think perhaps that very prominent and central position for a building which, after all, has no special connection with Bournville, is hardly justified.[82]

Whilst Selly Manor may not have seemed to be a suitable centrepiece for the Village, clearly the Trustees later felt that a Rest House dedicated to George and Elizabeth Cadbury was.

Selly Manor's 'new and fitting site' was just off The Green. It was envisaged that its reconstruction would help 'in the retention of both its artistic and its educative value'. As much of the original structure was salvaged as was possible, and further appropriate material was collected elsewhere in the West Midlands. It was clear that the Manor house, which seems to have been constructed between 14th and 17th centuries, had a complex building history. Whilst Harvey could justifiably claim that 'no piece of timber that could possibly be used was discarded', it is clear that he was less interested in preservation than 'interpretative restoration'.[83] He introduced a staircase which had not survived, but for which there was some evidence in a drawing by David Cox. Some of the timbering, especially at the rear, and some of the windows were significantly changed. The end result was a slightly speculative but picturesque reconstruction which seems to give an air of authenticity to the Model Village.

Harvey and Wicks went on to rescue the remnants of a 14th century cruck-framed hall house from Minworth Greaves. Here the fragments of original material were fewer and the prospects for historical accuracy were more unlikely. As early as 1914 George Cadbury had had his eye on the house. After the purchase of Minworth Greaves, the timbers were surveyed, numbered, dismantled and stored behind Selly Manor for several years. Laurence Cadbury became interested in the project and proposed an approach to Harvey:

Concentrate on the main item of old construction and aim merely at producing one room which would be more or less in the nature of a hall, not bothering about the rest of the building.[84]

Harvey accepted Laurence Cadbury's proposal about the hall, but suggested that the reconstructed building be extended from two to three bays and that a 'minstrel's gallery' be included. After discussions within the Cadbury family Harvey was given the go-ahead for this more drastic and romantic reconstruction of Minworth Greaves in 1929. In both projects, Harvey and Wicks were helped by Charles Mitchell. Whilst Laurence Cadbury stressed the educational value of these structures, it has only been in more recent years that they have developed as museums and galleries.

The last of Harvey and Wicks contributions to the buildings on The Green at Bournville was the Church and Church Hall of St Francis of Assisi. Favourable consideration had been given to the Vicar of Selly Oak when he had made a request for a site for an Anglican Church at Bournville in 1905.[85] The first site offered was on the corner of The Green at the bottom of Maple Road. By the time that sufficient money had been raised to start the project, another site on the opposite corner of The Green had been allocated to the Church of England.[86]

W. A. Harvey and Rev. E. A. Hartland presented the plans for the first part of the scheme, the Church Hall, to the Trustees in October 1912. The plans were accepted, but it was made clear that 'they are not what the Trustees would have chosen'. They also emphasised the need for good materials and high quality workmanship.[87] Their response was conditioned by a concern about matters of style and money rather than a worry about Harvey's interest in high quality craftsmanship.

The style adopted by Harvey for this (and later religious buildings) has been characterised as Early Christian and Romanesque.[88] It was a style that was currently being adopted by Anglicans, but it was certainly different from the Tudor and vernacular elements favoured by Harvey for the buildings he had previously designed on the Bournville Estate. Contemporaries noted that the style struck 'a new note' and Pevsner later suggested that the completed scheme looked 'rather stand-offish and foreign'.[89] Its Italianate, or Lombardic, presence does mark it out in this corner of 'Merrie England', but there can be no doubting the quality of materials and the detailing.

The Parish Hall which was completed in 1913 was a simple structure with small semi-circular headed windows and blind arcading in the gables. The materials used were Wellington bricks and Italian tiles. The hall, which could accommodate 300 people, was used for services until the Church of St Francis of Assisi was com-

Sketch design for the Church and Parish Hall, Bournville from *Bournville Works Magazine* April 1913. *Courtesy of Bournville Village Trust*

pleted in 1925. The designs for the whole complex, which was intended to include the Parish Hall, the Church, a campanile (which was never constructed) and an arcade, were published in 1913.[90]

The Church itself was not constructed until 1925, while the linking arcade was not completed until the 1930s. Nevertheless, this was a design that had been completed before the outbreak of the First World War. One commentator suggested that the Church was built 'from designs which were some twenty years old' and claimed, with some justification, that it was 'a very early example of the revival of interest in the Early Christian and Lombardic styles'.[91] In layout and style it can be compared with similar churches in the Birmingham area.[92] The Church of St Francis of Assisi at Bournville has a basilican plan with an apsidal chancel to the east, a shallow apse for the baptistery to the west and passage The walls of the nave are supported on granite columns with Portland stone capitals (the first four

Church of St Francis, Bournville, 1925

of which were carved in a neo-Byzantine style by William Bloye).[93] The walls have clerestory lights above the semi-circular arches of the arcade. The walls were pre-pared for frescoes, which have never appeared. The roof is carried by a series of king-post trusses. The interior is well-proportioned and has a calm, integrated feel.

Externally, the church, like the Parish Hall, is constructed of brick and Italian tiles. It is a well-crafted church designed in a simple, but effective Italian Roman-esque round-arched style. It was 'the first example of the new phase in Mr Harvey's development'.[94] It marked the beginning of a run of religious building by Harvey and Wicks in this Early Christian basilican style. These included the Church of Immanuel at Highter's Heath, St Francis of Assisi, Friar Park, Wednes-bury (1940) and the Robin Hood, Solihull Cemetery Chapel (1932).

Harvey was also the architect of choice for some of the religiously-based colleges erected on the land of the Bournville Village Trust at Selly Oak. He designed Kingsmead, a Quaker college for training foreign missionaries, in 1905. Westhill College, a non-denominational centre for the training of youth leaders and welfare workers, followed two years later. Carey Hall, completed in 1912, was a joint venture serving the Baptists, the Presbyterians and the London Missionary Society. Westhill is the most architecturally ambitious of the colleges, while Kingsmead has a more domestic feel to it. Another venture aimed at educating working men, Fircroft, eventually found a home in the brick, stone and timber-framed house that Harvey had designed for George Cadbury at Griffin's Hill in 1901.[95]

At the same time as Harvey was working on public buildings on The Green, he produced the site plan and the majority of the house designs for the Bournville Tenants estate, a co-partnership venture on land leased by the Bournville Village Trust started in 1906.[96] Like Bournville Village it contained a triangular green and recreation grounds and it was developed at low density. In this case the number of dwellings per acre was restricted to eleven. Whilst a significant number of semi-detached houses were erected on Northfield Road and Woodlands Park Road, on Kingsley Road Harvey achieved a different effect by grouping blocks of houses in a simple but effective manner. Certain dwellings, especially those on Hawthorne Road, were treated in a more decorative manner. Although brick and clay tiles were the dominant building materials, half-timbering, roughcast, pargetting, dormers and more elaborate chimney stacks were again used by Harvey. The more richly treated groups provide an artistic counterpoint to the simpler blocks. Harvey also continued to give emphasis to corner blocks, as can be seen at the junctions of Northfield Road and Hawthorne Road and Kingsley Road and Woodlands Park Road.

The dwellings on the Bournville Tenants' estate ranged from two-bedroomed cottages with just a living room and kitchen through to quite large semi-detached houses with a hall, drawing room, dining room, kitchen, scullery, three bedrooms and an attic. The majority of the houses designed by Harvey (and Wicks), whether as semi-detached dwellings or as terraced houses, had three bedrooms cottages and either two or three rooms downstairs.[97]

These 'cottages with gardens' in 'The Beauty Spot of the Midlands' were admired locally, though this scheme was not as widely publicised as 'The Model Village'.[98]

By the time of the First World War Harvey was regarded as 'one of our experts on the cheap cottage problem'.[99] Harvey and Wicks won first prize in the 1914 *Country Life* competition to design a pair of cottages for £250. A slightly later design for a pair of cottages drawing on the Kent vernacular was also commended by the same journal.[100] Harvey continued to advise the Bournville Village Trust after the First World War. Early designs for housing types for the Bournville Works Housing Society were drawn up in consultation with Harvey and Wicks.[101] The partners were involved in a number of municipal housing schemes as 'the Homes for Heroes' campaign got under way.[102] As one of Harvey's obituarists noted, 'He . . . left the impress of his personality, taste and skill, not only on Bournville, but on domestic architecture throughout the Midlands, indeed throughout the country.'[103]

The reconstruction work continued. The partners restored the old Tudor Grimshaw Hall at Knowle and the early 18th century Edgbaston Hall. In these cases the partners were not dealing with derelict structures and their work was altogether more tactful and respectful.[104]

After the First World War, Harvey got an increasing number of commissions for public buildings. Their most widely admired work in this period were the Town Hall and Municipal Offices at Dudley, for which Harvey and Wicks were awarded the Bronze Medal of the RIBA in 1934. Later award-winning designs for Oldbury Civic Centre and Municipal Offices and Bedford Town Hall were never executed.[105]

'The church architecture, schools and other public buildings by Mr Harvey,' it was noted, 'illustrate the variety of his architectural styles in which he expressed his genius, though not as a copyist, for his aims were consciously to give new individuality of spirit to old forms.'[106] Harvey's larger buildings were soundly constructed and well-designed and most have a freshness that still appeals. 'As the years went by, he came to a mastery of the use of building materials as a means of achieving colour and texture. This skill together with his love of delicate detail, placed his work on a very high level.'[107] This can be seen in the domestic work, the public buildings and the two churches dedicated to St Francis. The range and quality of Harvey's work warranted the claim made on his death that he was 'one of the most distinguished architects in the Midlands.' Indeed, his early work at Bournville had a much wider impact.[108]

List of Architectural Works of William Alexander Harvey (1874–1951)

W. A. Harvey (1874–1951) was articled to David Smith of Birmingham from 1890 to 1894 and also studied with W. H. Bidlake at the Municipal School of Art. In 1895 he joined the Bournville Estate Office and by 1896 was the chief architect. He left there in 1904 and set up in independent practice, taking H. Graham Wicks into partnership in 1912.

The list below is of Harvey's work up to 1914.

WORK IN BIRMINGHAM AND ENVIRONS

PUBLIC

1900 Meeting Hall, Classrooms and Caretaker's House, Watford Rd, Cotteridge for George Cadbury

1902 Public Hall, Linden Rd for The Ruskin Society

1904 Friends' Meeting House, Linden Rd for George Cadbury

1904 Boy's and Girl's Elementary School Linden Rd, for G. Cadbury and others

1909 Infant's School, Linden Rd for George and Elizabeth Cadbury

1909 Infants' School, Charlotte Rd, Stirchley for Kings Norton and Northfield UDC

1911 Men's Hostel and Warden's House, Griffins Hill for Friends' Foreign Missionary Society

1912 Church Hall, The Green, Linden Rd for Rev. Hartland

1913 Rest House, The Green, Linden Rd for Cadbury Bros.

COMMERCIAL

1896 Washing Baths and Lodge, Bournville Lane for George Cadbury

1896 Extensions to Estate Office, Bournville Lane for George Cadbury

1897 Four Shops and Houses, Maryvale Rd and Linden Rd for George Cadbury

1899 Shops and Houses, Maryvale Rd for George Cadbury

1900 Conversion of shops and houses, Raddlebarn Lane, Selly Oak for George Cadbury

1900 Additions to Frogett's Farm for Refreshment Room for George Cadbury

1901 Gardener's Office, off Sycamore Rd for BVT

1903 Extensions to Estate Office, Bournville Lane for Cadbury Bros.

INDUSTRIAL

1913 Factory, Bishopgate St for Edmonds and Co.

DOMESTIC

1895 Three House, Stirchley Rd and two houses, Ivy Rd, Stirchley for A. Mason

1896 Two Houses, Linden Rd, Bournville for W. B. Bird

1896 Two houses, Maryvale Rd, for Messrs Holbeche and Leach

1896 Two Houses, Maryvale Rd, for H. G. Pugh and Barrow Cadbury

1896 Eight Houses, Row Heath Rd [now Selly Oak Rd] for George Cadbury

1896 Pair of houses for Edwin Short

1896 Two Houses, Maryvale Rd, for Messrs Sandbrook and Watson

1896 Two Houses, Bournville Lane for Messrs Greatrex and Head

1896 Two Houses, Mary Vale Rd for W. Pasant and Amos Hunt

1896 Two Houses Bournville Lane for Messrs Smith and Ellerker

1896 Cottages, Bournville Lane, Maryvale Rd , Linden Rd and King's Norton Rd for George Cadbury

1896 Two houses, Bournville Lane, two houses Maryvale Rd for George Cadbury

1896 Two Houses, Bournville Lane, two houses Maryvale Rd for George Cadbury

1896 Two houses, Maryvale Rd for George Cadbury

1896 Two houses, Bournville Lane, corner of Beech Lane for George Cadbury

1896 Two houses, Bournville Lane for George Cadbury

1896 Four cottages, King's Norton Rd for George Cadbury

1897 Two houses, Maryvale Rd for George Cadbury

1897 Additions to The Beeches for George Cadbury

1897 Two houses, Bournville Lane for Mr Knowles

1897 Two houses, Laburnum Rd for George Cadbury

1897 Four houses, Laburnum Rd for George Cadbury

1897 House, Bournville Lane for G. Gulliver

1897 Forty five houses, Beech Lane for George Cadbury

1897 One house, Mary Vale Rd for George Cadbury

1897 One house, Elm Rd, one house, Laburnum Rd for George Cadbury

1898 Thirty eight houses, Elm Rd, fifty houses, Linden Rd for George Cadbury

1898 Sixteen houses, Linden Rd for George Cadbury

1898 Twenty nine house, Linden Rd, ten houses, Raddlebarn Rd, four houses Acacia Rd, four houses, Sycamore Rd for George Cadbury

1898 Twenty houses, Raddlebarn Lane for George Cadbury

1898 Six houses, Laburnum Rd, two houses, Bournville Lane for George Cadbury

1898 House, Woodland Rd, Northfield (with A. G. Dunn) for A. Chambers

1899 Ten Houses, off Laburnum Rd [Holly Grove] for George Cadbury

1899 Two houses, Sycamore Rd for Messrs Walker and Restall

1899 Five houses, Elm Rd for George Cadbury

1899 Two Houses, Maple Rd for H. Lane

1900 Four houses, Beech Rd and Bournville Lane for George Cadbury

1901 House [Primrose Hill], Griffin's Hill for George Cadbury Junior

1901 House, Griffin's Hill for J. H. Barlow

1901 Six cottages, Bournville Lane for George Cadbury

1901 House, Beech Rd/Bournville Lane for BVT

1901 Two houses, Willow Rd/Laburnum Rd for BVT

1901 Six pairs of houses, Sycamore Rd for George Cadbury

1902 Two cottages, Sycamore Rd for George Cadbury

1902 House, Church Hill, King's Norton for Thomas Locker

1902 Ten dwelling houses, Acacia Rd and Willow Rd for Edward Cadbury

1902 Dwelling house on Manor House grounds, Bristol Rd for George Cadbury

1902 House, Bunbury Rd for Herbert Johnson

1902 Pair of houses, Bournville Lane for Samuel Jones

1902 Two houses, Acacia Rd for Barrow Cadbury

1902 Two houses, Linden Rd for Margaret Cadbury

1902 Four cottages, Bournville Lane for BVT

1902 Pair of cottages, Beech Rd for BVT

1902 Seven cottages, Row Heath Lane for BVT

1903 Three houses, Maple Rd for Elsie Cadbury

1903 Pair of dwellings, Maple Rd for BVT

1903 Six cottages, Thorn Rd for BVT

1903 Pair of semi-detached houses, Griffin's Hill for George Cadbury

1903 Seventeen cottages, Thorn Rd for George Cadbury

1903 Two pairs of semi-detached houses, Maple Rd for W. A. Cadbury

1903 One pair of semi-detached houses, Maple Rd for W. A. Cadbury

1903 Two blocks of four and one pair of cottages, Acacia Rd for BVT

1903 Three dwellings, Linden Rd/Acacia Rd for BVT

1904 Seven Dwelling houses, Linden Rd for BVT

1904 Nine Houses, Linden Rd for BVT

1904 Thirteen houses, Linden Rd for BVT

1904 House and outbuildings, Moor Green Lane for Miss Helen Cadbury

1906 Four houses, Wychall Lane for A. Rowse and W. A. Harvey

1906 House, Oak Tree Lane for W. Littleboy

1906 Six houses, Northfield Rd for Bournville Tenants

1906 Eight houses, Woodlands Park Rd for Bournville Tenants

1906 Four houses, Woodlands Park Rd for Bournville Tenants

1907 Extensions to The Croft, West Heath Rd for Dr R. Green

1907 On pair of houses, Woodlands Park Rd for Bournville Tenants

1907 Two pair of houses, Woodlands Park Rd for Bournville Tenants

1907 Two cottages, Woodlands Park Rd for Bournville Tenants

1907 House, Bournville Lane for George Archibald

1907 Eight houses in new road off Woodland Park Rd [Kingsley Rd], for Bournville Tenants

1907 Four cottages, Kingsley Rd for Bournville Tenants

1907 Four cottages, Northfield Rd for Bournville Tenants

1907 One pair of houses, Northfield Rd for Bournville Tenants

1907 Eleven cottages, Kinsley Rd for Bournville Tenants

1907 Four cottages, Northfield Rd for Bournville Tenants

1907 Four Cottages, Woodlands Park Rd/Kingsley Rd for Bournville Tenants

1907 Pair of semi-detached houses, Woodlands Park Rd for Bournville Tenants

1908 Eight cottages, Kingsley Rd, for Bournville Tenants

1908 Eight cottages, Kingsley Rd for Bournville Tenants

1908 Two cottages, Northfield Rd for Bournville Tenants

1908 Four cottages, Kingsley Rd for Bournville Tenants

1908 Twelve cottages, Kingsley Rd for Bournville Tenants

1908 Four cottages, Kingsley Rd for Bournville Tenants

1908 Pair of cottages, Kingsley Rd for Bournville Tenants

1908 Three cottages, Northfield Rd for Bournville Tenants

1909 Pair of houses, Northfield Rd for Bournville Tenants

1909 Three cottages, corner of Northfield Rd for Bournville Tenants

1909 Two cottages, Hawthorn Rd for Bournville Tenants

1909 Additions for Primrose Hill, Bristol Rd for George Cadbury Junior

1909 House, Northfield Rd for J. Cartwright

1909 Six cottages, Hawthorn Rd for Bournville Tenants

1909 Two cottages, Hawthorn Rd for Bournville Tenants

1909 Two pairs of cottages, Hawthorn Rd for Bournville Tenants

1909 Eight cottages, Hawthorn Rd for Bournville Tenants

1909 Small house, Beaks Hill Rd, King's Norton for R. H. Roberts, Birmingham Guild

1909 Eight cottages, Kingsley Rd for Bournville Tenants

1910 Six cottages, Kingsley Rd for Bournville Tenants

1910 Alterations to Leasowes Farm, Weatheroak, for Miss E. M. Mynors

1910 Additions and alterations to Weatheroak Hall for Miss E. M. Mynors

1910 Pair of dwellings, Northfield Rd for Bournville Tenants

1911 Pair of cottages (Block 50) Northfield Rd for Bournville Tenants

1911 Development of portions of Kingswood Estate

1911 Additions to Primrose Hill, Bristol Rd for George Cadbury Junior

1913 House Selly Wick Rd, Selly Park for Mrs Higgs

1914 Six houses, Sycamore Rd for Cadbury Bros.

1914 Four houses, Laburnum Rd for Cadbury Bros.

NOTES

[1] *Journal of the Royal Institute of British Architects*, April 1951, p. 247.

[2] Birmingham Central Library, Archives and Heritage Services (hereafter BCL AHS), MS 1536 Archives of the Bournville Village Trust, Prospectus for the Bournville Building Estate.

[3] W. A. Harvey, *The Model Village and its Cottages: Bournville* (1906), p. 2; MS 1536 BVT Archives 1536 Manuscript Box 49/B. J. H. Barlow 'The Village of Bournville', May 1904.

[4] *JRIBA* April 1951, p. 247; Kelly's *Directory of Birmingham* 1913.

[5] Obituary in *Birmingham Mail*, 7 February 1951.

[6] *VCH Warwick Vol. VII The City of Birmingham*, ed. by W. B. Stevens (1964) p. 464. The Small Heath Chapel has been demolished; Application for Admission as a Fellow of RIBA, 16 October 1918.

[7] Birmingham Municipal School of Art, *Programme for the Session 1892–93*.

[8] Alan Crawford 'The Birmingham Setting' in *By Hammer and Hand: The Arts and Crafts Movement in Birmingham*, ed. by Alan Crawford (Birmingham, 1984) p. 27.

[9] Birmingham Municipal School of Art, *Prize Lists 1892, 1894, 1895*.

[10] *JRIBA*, April 1951, p. 247.

[11] Birmingham Architectural Association, *Report of the 23rd Session, 1899–1897 and the Syllabus for the 24th Session 1897–98* (1896); MS 1536 BVT Archives, Minutes of Committee, 580, 9 July 1902. Harvey was congratulated and his appointment was sanctioned; *JRIBA*, April 1915, p. 247.

[12] Obituary in *Journal of the Royal Town Planning Institute*, 37, no. 4, February 1951.

[13] *Ibid*.

[14] *JRIBA*, April 1951, p. 247.

[15] *JRTPI*, 37, no. 4, February 1951.

[16] Harvey, *Model Village*, p. 6. See also Michael Harrison, *Bournville: Model Village to Garden Suburb* (Chichester, 1999) chapter 4.

[17] Obituary in *Bournville Works Magazine* (hereafter *BWM*) March 1951, p. 84.

[18] MS 1536 BVT Archives, Plans 14/03.

[19] *Ibid*, Plans 03/2

[20] *Ibid*, Plans 14/02, 14/05, 14/08 houses and Plan 14/10 Shops Mary Vale Road.

[21] J. L. Hoffman, 'Imaging the Industrial Village: Architecture, Art and Visual Culture in the Garden Community of Bournville England', (unpublished Ph.D thesis, University of Yale, 1993) p. 277.

[22] Harvey, *Model Village*, p. 3.

[23] [W. A. Harvey] 'Cottage Homes', *The Builder*, 86, 13 February 1904, p. 159.

[24] W. Creese, *The Search for Environment* (New Haven, 1992 ed.), p. 99, Fig. 37.

[25] *British Architect*, 42, 1894, p. 5. See also J. Brandon-Jones *et al*, *C. F. A. Voysey: architect and designer 1857–1941*, (1978) and H. Hitchmough, *C. F. A. Voysey*, (New Haven, 1995).

[26] See A. Saint, *Richard Norman Shaw*, (New Haven, 1976) p. 24 *passim*.

[27] BCL AHS, King's Norton and Northfield Building Register, app. nos 314–15, 10 houses off Laburnum Road (Holly Grove) for George Cadbury, 28 April 1899.

[28] Remo Granelli 'Architecture' in *By Hammer and Hand*, p. 47.

[29] Harvey, 'Cottage Homes' p. 159.

[30] Lawrence Weaver, *The 'Country Life' Book of Cottage Homes*, (1919 ed.) p. 68.

[31] J. H. Whitehouse, 'Bournville: A Study in Housing Reform', *The Studio*, 24, 1902, p. 168.

[32] W. Thompson, *The Housing Handbook*, (1903) pp. 196–98; *Birmingham Daily Mail* 21 September 1901; *Birmingham Daily Gazette* 21 September 1901; *Church Times* 8 August 1902; *Brotherhood* December 1901; Ebenezer Howard 'A garden village has been built; a Garden City is but a step beyond', cited in R. Fishman, *Urban Utopias in the 20th Century* (1977), p. 61

[33] Harvey, *Model Village*.

[34] J. A. Dale 'Bournville', *Economic Review* January 1907, p. 26.

[35] Harvey, 'Cottage Homes' p. 59.

[36] Harvey, *Model Village* p. 6.

[37] Harvey, 'Cottage Homes' p. 159.

[38] Harvey, *Model Village* p. 21.

[39] *Ibid*, p. 17.

[40] MS 1536 BVT Archives, Minutes 'Secretary's Report' May 1901.

[41] See Carl Chinn, *Homes for People* (Birmingham, 1991).

[42] Harvey, *Model Village* p. 31; M. Miller, 'Raymond Unwin 1863–1940' in *Pioneers in British Planning*, ed. by Gordon Cherry (1981).

[43] Whitehouse, *Bournville; a study in Housing Reform* p. 168.

[44] Bournville Village Trust, *Typical Plans* (Birmingham, 1911).

[45] Harvey, *Model Village* p. 5.

[46] *Ibid* pp. 5–6.

[47] MS 1536 BVT Archives, Minutes 'Secretary's Report', August 1902.

[48] *Ibid* Minutes 3 July 1901.

[49] King's Norton and Bournville Building Register app. no. 921 house for George Cadbury, junior, at Griffens Hill, 1901; app. no. 922 house for J. H. Barlow at Griffens Hill, 1901; app. no. 1233 house for Herbert E. Johnson, Bunbury Road, 17 April 1901.

[50] King's Norton and Northfield Building Register, app. no. 1353 Public Hall in Linden Road for Ruskin Society, 18 September 1902.

[51] King's Norton and Northfield Building Register, app. no. 979 six cottages, Bournville Lane, for George Cadbury, 25 April 1901.

[52] MS 1536 BVT Archives, Minutes 9 October 1902.

[53] *Ibid*, Minutes 16 December 1903.

[54] *Ibid*, Minutes 6 January 1904

[55] *Ibid*, Minutes 13 January 1904.

[56] King's Norton and Northfield Building Register, app. no. 1779 Friends' Meeting House, Bournville for George Cadbury and app. no. 1780 Boys' and Girls' Elementary School, Bournville 27 August 1904.

[57] MS 1536 BVT Archives, Minutes 'Secretary's Report' 31 December 1906.

[58] W. Thompson, *Housing up-to-date* (1907) p. 161; S. M. Gaskell, 'Sheffield City Council and the development of suburban areas prior to World War 1', in *Essays in the Economic and Social History of South Yorkshire* ed. by S. Pollard and C. Holmes (Sheffield, 1976) pp. 192–95.

[59] Nikolaus Pevsner and Alexandra Wedgwood, *The Buildings of England: Warwickshire* (Harmondsworth, 1964) p. 158; Granelli 'Architecture' p. 57.

[60] MS 1536 BVT Archives, Minutes 14 November 1901; 21 November 1901.

[61] *Ibid*, Minutes 30 January 1903.

[62] *Ibid*, Minutes 23 April 1903

[63] *Ibid*, Minutes 17 September 1903; King's Norton and Northfield Building Register app. no. 1780, Boys' and Girls' Elementary School, Bournville for G. Cadbury and others, August 27 1904.

[64] *BWM*, 3, no. 1, November 1904, p. 4.

[65] *Ibid*; Harvey *Model Village* p.14.

[66] Dale 'Bournville' p. 26.

[67] Harvey *Model Village* p. 14.

[68] Pevsner and Wedgwood *Warwickshire* p. 156.

[69] MS 1536 BVT Archives, Minutes, 30 January 1902; 5 February 1902.

[70] *Ibid*, Minutes 1 May 1902; 25 June 1902; 4 July 1902.

[71] *Ibid*, 19 September 1902.

[72] *Ibid*, 16 July 1903.

[73] Pevsner and Wedgwood, *Warwickshire* p. 159.

[74] MS 1536 BVT Archives, Minutes 2 July 1908.

[75] *Ibid*, 13 March 1905.

[76] See P. Atkins, 'The Architecture of Bournville 1879–1914 in *Made in Birmingham: Design and Industry 1889–1989* ed. by B. Tilson (Studley, 1989) p. 45.

[77] Pevsner and Wedgwood *Warwickshire* p. 158.

[78] King's Norton and Northfield Building Register, app. no. 2980, Infant's School, Charlotte Road, Stirchley for KN & NUDC, 8 September 1909.

[79] MS 1536 BVT Archives, Plans Working Drawing of Rest House, August 1903. Harvey seems to have taken his nephew, H. Graham Wicks into partnership in 1912. See designs for Kingsley Road July 1912, plans 09/15 and 09/16.

[80] *BWM* , July 1913, pp. 195–99.

[81] See Photographic Albums in Selly Manor Museum.

[82] Copies of the correspondence and printed material relating to Selly Manor and Minworth Greaves are held at Selly Manor Museum.

[83] Hofman 'Imaging the Industrial Village' p. 645. See the images displayed at Selly Manor Museum.

[84] Selly Manor Collection.

[85] MS 1536 BVT Archives, Minutes 8 March 1905.

[86] *BWM*, January 1913.

[87] MS 1356 BVT Archives, Minutes 16 October 1912.

[88] Pevsner and Wedgwood, *Warwickshire* p. 157; *BWM* April 1913 and September 1924.

[89] *BWM*, April 1913 p. 126; Pevsner and Wedgwood *Warwickshire* p. 157.

[90] *BWM*, April 1913.

[91] *BWM*, December 1929, p. 364.

[92] *Ibid*. See also Pevsner and Wedgwood *Warwickshire*. Local examples are St Basil's, Deritend (A. S. Dixon, 1910); St Andrew's, Barnt Green (A. S. Dixon, 1909–14) and St Germain, City Road (E. F. Reynolds, 1915–17).

[93] *BWM*, December 1929; Pevsner and Wedgwood, *Warwickshire* p. 157; G. T. Noszlopy, *Public Sculpture of Birmingham* (Liverpool, 1998) pp. 81–81.

[94] *JRIBA*, April 1951, p. 248.

[95] See Harrison, *Bournville* p. 71.

[96] For co-partnership schemes see K. Skilleter, 'The role of public utility societies in early British town planning and housing reform, *Planning Perspectives*, 8, 1993, pp. 125–65.

[97] See the Bournville Tenants' plans, mostly by Harvey and Wicks in MS 1356 BVT Archives.

[98] *Birmingham Post* 10 July 1910.

[99] Weaver, *Book of Cottages* pp.19–23.

[100] *Ibid*, pp. 79–81.

[101] See two sets of plans dated 1920 in MS 1536 BVT Archives.

[102] See M. Swenarton, *Homes Fit for Heroes* (1981).

103 *BWM*, March 1951 pp. 83–84; *JRIBA*, April 1951, p. 248.

104 *JRIBA*, April 1951, p. 248.

105 *Ibid*; *The Builder*, 13 December 1935, p. 1050 and 20 December 1935, p. 1110; *Architects' Journal* 26 December 1940, p. 153.

106 *JRIBA*, April 1951, p. 247.

107 *BWM*, March 1951, p. 84.

108 Harrison, *Bournville* p. 86 *passim*.

24 Owen Parsons

NIKY RATHBONE AND JOHN BASSINDALE

Owen Parsons (1876–1944) was involved in building attractive Arts and Crafts dwelling houses around Moseley and King's Heath. He also built some interesting houses in Selly Park and some in Barnt Green and on the Four Oaks Estate, Sutton Coldfield. His more important early commissions appear to be influenced by Norman Shaw, but his later work is far more similar to that of Gilbert Scott or Voysey. His work has similarities to that of local Arts and Crafts architects de Lacy Aherne, J. L. Ball and C. E. Bateman. It is possible that Parsons is relatively little known because he confined himself almost entirely to domestic architecture, rather than church architecture or city centre commercial buildings.[1]

Parsons was born in 1876 in Balsall Heath, Birmingham. His father was Councillor Thomas Parsons, the manager of a local brewery, his mother was Elizabeth Cox, through whom he was related to the Birmingham artist David Cox.[2] Owen Parsons was articled to Sam Owen, architect and surveyor, of 14 Temple Street. He was then articled to John George Bland for two years and went into independent practice in 1895, at Victoria Chambers, Martineau Street. In 1898 he succeeded J. G. Bland in that practice. He became a LRIBA in 1911.[3] From 1897–1930 the firm had offices at 14 Temple Street, and from 1913 to 1919 there was a further practice at 40 High Street Erdington. From 1931 to 1943 the firm was located at Newton Chambers, 43 Cannon Street, premises destroyed in an air raid. Following the War Parsons was appointed to the War Damage Commission as an assessor. From probably, 1944 to 1945 the firm was again at Newton Chambers, 43 Cannon Street. It has not been possible

Owen Parsons

to identify the family name of his wife, Winifred, but they had one son, Flight Lieutenant Antony Parsons, and one daughter and lived from 1916 to 1944 at Holmwood, Greenhill Road, Wylde Green, a house he designed. Parsons died unexpectedly at his office in 1944. In addition to his architectural practice, Parsons was a talented water-colour artist and regularly exhibited with the Royal Birmingham Society of Artists.[4]

Parsons began his career in the early 1890s doing jobbing work; alterations and additions to small industrial and commercial premises around what is now the Birmingham inner city area. This included the addition of shopping to industrial premises in Lower Hurst Street and conversion of some houses to shops in Moseley Road.[5] In 1894 he was responsible for building 'Houses, Bk between 91, 92' on Lower Edwards Street, which appears to describe insanitary back houses.[6]

No public buildings by Parsons have been identified, though he was responsible for alterations to the Moseley and Balsall Heath Institute, Alcester Road, in 1904.[7] Parsons principally worked, however, on domestic houses in a variety of styles. Like de Lacy Aherne, he was involved in designing both speculative housing for rent, of varying quality, and private commissions. For example one of his earliest commissions was in 1892, for sixteen undistinguished terraced dwelling houses for G. East, on Clifton and Ladypool Roads at Balsall Heath.[8] A similar commission for C. Pegram followed in 1898. This time it was for eighteen houses on Chatham and Maas Roads at Northfield.[9] This work apparently led to two further rather cheap speculations for Mr Pegram in Barnt Green. Numbers 35 and 37 Fiery Hill Road built in 1924, are typical Edwardian villas. The other commission, 49–61 Fiery Hill Road, built in 1924, is slightly more interesting. The plans specify four semi-detached houses, and these can easily be identified, from the plans. The buildings again appear cheaply built, but have unusual Dutch gables. They have decorative half-timbering to the upper storeys, but the timbers are too thin.[10] Probably Mr Pegram was concerned to build his properties for rent as cheaply as possible.

The contrast with Owen Parsons's quite distinguished designs for speculative housing around Selly Park could not be greater. Numbers 47–65 Selly Park Road were built for Carr & Layton in 1906 and 1907 and employ, on a small scale, Parsons' typical Arts and Crafts vocabulary. They are L-shaped semi-detached houses, and Parsons combines three storey end gables with long, low roofs. Details include tile hanging and half-timbering or smooth plain white plaster with decorative central motifs to the gable ends, Arts and Crafts porches, sometimes in the angle of the L, simple small-paned windows and tall chimney stacks.[11] Possibly other similar houses on Selly Park Road are by Parsons.[12]

Parsons was responsible for two semi-detached villas on Salisbury Road, Moseley for J. Dean and F. Harrison, built in 1901, which can be identified as numbers 19–21.[13] These appear to be further speculative building as number 19 was listed in the Rate Books as owned by 'Dean' but occupied by Charles Smith. In

55–57 Selly Park Road, Selly Park, 1906–07

19–21 Salisbury Road, Moseley, 1901

1906 Parsons was the architect for 'two cottages' on Bristol Road, Northfield, also for John Dean. In 1909 he was the architect of Wylands, 20 Amesbury Road Moseley for the 'Trustees of the late J. H. Dean' and in 1910 he designed six villas on Bristol Road, Northfield, also for Trustees of the late J. H. Dean.[14]

While Parsons worked on these speculations, he was also engaged as architect for some much larger private houses. There are plans listed for a house, Hazelhurst, 34 Russell Road, Moseley, built in 1898 for George Yorke Iliffe, for whom he had also designed additions to his industrial premises in the form of shopping. The house has been demolished, and the plans are missing.[15] In 1902 Parsons designed a further large house on Russell Road, since demolished, for Thomas Cond. This appears to have been Parsons's first major commission. The three storey house, with coach house and outbuildings, was in the Arts and Crafts style, with attractive contrasts between the horizontal line of the windows and eaves and the verticals of the chimneys and stepped gable. The porch surround echoed the stepped gable end and the curved top of the front door echoed the curved doors of the coach house and the curved roof of one of the dormers. The windows had Parsons's usual decorative leaded lights.[16]

Number 4 Amesbury Road, listed Grade I, is probably Owen Parsons's most important surviving commission.[17] Built in 1909 for John Nicolson, Kilmuir is distinguished by its excellent brickwork, worked into diaper patterns of blue on red. There are long, sweeping roofs, deep eaves, tall chimneys, some diagonally set. To the right at the front is a shallow double height bay with decoratively patterned leading between the upper and lower windows. These windows are used to give horizontal lines in the design, in contrast to the vertical lines of the tall chimneys. The house has an elaborate, rather church-like gabled black timber porch with white interior plaster-work and above this a gallery-effect suggested by medieval-looking leaded windows divided by studded black timbers. The door furniture, window catches, decorative lead rain-water heads and gutter supports are all in typical late Arts and Crafts style. The interior, which apparently survives, is described as a 'restrained mixture of Arts and Crafts and classical mouldings.'[18] Wylands, 20 Amesbury Road, is probably Springholm, designed by Parsons in 1909 for J. H. Dean. This relatively small detached house has a long, sweeping roof which comes down over the porch and looks similar to no. 36 Amesbury Road built by Owen Parsons in 1910 for A. B. Wood. Here the roof sweeps down, long and low over the porch to the garage. The porch itself has elaborately carved black timbers. There is an attractive small bay window to the ground floor, and both the upper and lower windows have decorative plain glass leaded lights.[19]

Probably the most important of Parsons's other surviving houses in the Moseley area is Kingsthorpe, 40 Wake Green Road, listed Grade II, and built in 1910–11. This substantial house on the corner of Wake Green Road and Cotton Lane has three double height bays, the outer ones asymmetrical, the centre a tall Dutch gable which recalls the much cheaper houses on Fiery Road at Barnt Green.

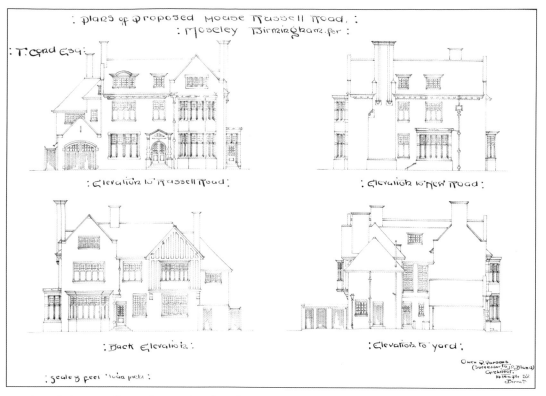

Overdale, Russell Road, Moseley for Thomas Cond, elevation drawings, 1901. *Courtesy of Birmingham Archives and Heritage Services*

In this gable is a band of decorative blue brick diaper-work, similar to that on no. 40 Amesbury Road. The entrance porch is recessed behind slightly tapered Tuscan pillars and has a small balcony above. As at 40 Amesbury Road the brickwork is of very fine quality, there are similar long, sweeping tiled roofs, tall chimneys, contrasting horizontal and vertical lines in the overall design, mullioned windows and leaded-lights.[20]

Similar fine brickwork distinguishes Brereton, 12 Forest Road Moseley, built in 1902 for F. Dingley. This three storey house has a full-height gable with a narrow arrow-slit window to the second floor and a bay to the ground floor. There is a half-timbered upper storey to the right of this gable end, which projects over an arched porch and ground-floor window with leaded lights.[21] A second house on Forest Road, no. 31, for which he made additions, does not survive

From 1907 Parsons was also designing houses around Sutton Coldfield. He moved to Holmswood, 14 Greenhill Road, which he had built for the developers Brooks and Mason in 1912.[22] He was responsible for several other very attractive houses here and in the adjoining Beech Hill Road, which looked onto Walmley

Kilmuir, 4 Amesbury Road, Moseley, 1909, front elevation

Kilmuir, front porch

Golf Club for which he designed the club house, now demolished. These houses all employ his distinctive vocabulary of tall chimneys, sweeping roof-line, small-paned windows, occasionally set to the corner of the building, tile-hanging and half-timbering, studded Arts and Crafts doors and elaborate porches, and exceptionally fine brick-work,[23] with the single exception of Rose Mullion, Greenhill Road, where he used reclaimed brick.[24]

On the prestigious Four Oaks Estate Parsons built at least three fine houses. The earliest of these is 16 Bracebridge Road, completed in 1900, for H. B. Barker, an attractive half-timbered house with stone mullioned windows. This was followed by Hindecliffe, 25 Bracebridge Road, of 1905, a very attractive L-shaped three-storey house with smooth white render, and a studded Arts and Crafts garage door typical of his work. He also designed Culross House, 5 Luttrell Road, for T. Combe, in 1928, another half-timbered L-shaped three-storey house in very dark red brick, half-timbered, with stone mullion windows to the lower floor with low, sweeping roofs.[25]

In 1920 Parsons designed an early group of council houses for Sutton Cold-field Housing Committee. These have been identified as Hollyfield Crescent on Hollyfield Road, an attractive group of eighteen houses with Arts and Crafts

36 Amesbury Road, Moseley, 1910

12 Forest Road, Moseley, 1902

Holmwood, 14 Greenhill Road, Sutton Coldfield, 1912, Parsons's own house

decorative detail, similar to William Harvey's very simple group of cottages on Bournville Lane, Birmingham, for the Bournville Village Trust.[26]

Parsons continued to design and build houses around Birmingham and Sutton Coldfield until his death in 1944. Further research would probably reveal him as the architect of additional houses around Greenhill Road, on the Four Oaks Estate and, possibly, on Amesbury Road in Moseley.

Selected List of Architectural Works of Owen Parsons (1876–1944)

Owen Parsons was articled to Samuel Owen of Birmingham and subsequently to J. G. Bland, also of Birmingham. Parsons set up in independent practice in 1895 and in 1898 took over the practice of J. G. Bland. He continued working until his death in 1944.

His domestic work has been listed up to 1929, and other work up to 1914

WORK IN BIRMINGHAM AND ITS ENVIRONS

PUBLIC

1904 Alterations to Moseley and Balshall Heath Institute, Alcester Rd

COMMERCIAL

1896 Alterations and additions to Stork Inn, Newtown Row for E. Wright

1897 Alterations to two shops, Herbert Rd for W. Bradbury

1897 Conversion of houses to shops, 386, 388, 390, 392, Moseley Rd for James and Type

1898 Victoria Bar Public House, Spring Hill for W. Pickering

1900 Busines premises, shop, living room, bakehouse, shopping, stabling, Washwood Heath Rd for E. Harley

INDUSTRIAL

1893 Shopping, Lower Essex St for G. Y. Iliffe

1894 Shopping, Balshall Heath for Cannon, Wright and Co.

1895 Chimney shaft for Victoria Laundry, Grafton St

1896 Alterations to manufactory, Spencer St, Hockley Hill for R. Wheatley and Son

1897 Shopping, Skinner Lane for G. Y. Iliffe

1914 Premises at Hay Mills for Hoskins and Sewell; 1914 w.c.s

DOMESTIC

1892 16 dwelling houses, Clifton Rd and Ladypool Rd, Birmingham for G. East

1893 3 houses Longbridge Rd for E. Carter

1894 Houses, Bk between nos 91 and 92 Lower Edwards St, Birmingham for W. Bradbury

1896 Scullery and closets to back houses Clifton Rd, Balsall Heath for Mr Arnott, Russell Rd, Moseley

1896 Alterations to 549, Moseley Rd, Birmingham for W. Bradbury

1898 House, Hazelhurst, 34 Russell Rd, Moseley for George York Iliffe [D]

1898 2 houses, Cambridge Rd, Moseley for G. Webster

1898 18 houses Chatham and Moss Rds, Northfield for C. Pegram

1898 2 houses and one shop, Mill Lane, Northfield for C. Pegram

1899 House, The Lawns, 16 Bracebridge Rd, Four Oaks for H. B. Barker

1899 House, Bristol Rd, Northfield for Harry Iliffe

1901 2 houses, 19 and 21 Salisbury Rd, Moseley for J. Dean and F. Harrison

1901 House, Overdale, Russell Rd, Moseley for Thomas Cond; 1903 motor house [D]

1902 House, Brereton, 12 Forest Rd, Moseley, for Francis Dingley

1905 10 houses, 47–65 Selly Park Rd, Selly Park for Carr and Layton

1905 House, Hindecliffe, 23 [25] Bracebridge Rd, Four Oaks for A. Washbourne

1905 2 houses nr The White Lion, Alcester Rd, Beoley for Harry Iliffe

1906 2 cottages, Bristol Rd, Northfield for J. Dean

1906 2 villas, Selly Park Rd, Selly Park for Carr and Layton

1907 6 villas, Selly Park Rd, Selly Park for Carr and Layton

1907 Additions of reception room and bedroom to 31 Forest Rd, Moseley for F. Rogers

1909 House, Kilmuir, 4 Amesbury Drive for John Nicolson

1909 House, Wylands [Springholm] 20 Amesbury Rd, Moseley for J. Dean

1910 House, 36 Amesbury Rd, Moseley for A. B. Wood

1910 6 villas Bristol Rd, Northfield for trustees of J. Dean

1910 Kingsthorpe, 40 Wake Green Rd, Moseley for Frank Banks

1911 House, Sutton Rd, Erdington for J. Drinkels

1911 House[?no. 16] Greenhill Rd, Sutton Coldfield for Brooks and Mason

1912 2 villas, Mossfield Rd, King's Heath for J. Arnold

1912 House, Holmwood, 14 Greenhill Rd, Sutton Coldfield for Brooks and Mason (Parson's own house); 1922 motor house

1913 2 houses [one built] Greenhill Rd, Sutton Coldfield for Frank Matthews

1913 Alterations to stable for house, Green Lane, Sutton Coldfield for Brooks and Mason

1913 House in Greenhill Rd, Sutton Coldfield for Frank Matthews

1914 4 houses, Station Rd, King's Heath for C. Marston

1915 House, Greenhill Rd, Sutton Coldfield for E. Lawley

1916 Additions and garage for Holly Bank, Birmingham Rd, Sutton Coldfield for J. B. Simmons

1918 Additions to The Norlands, Bracebridge Rd, Four Oaks for S. G. Lawley; 1919 motor house

1919 Club House, Greenhill Rd for Walmley Golf Club [D]

1919 Motor house to house in Penns Lane, Sutton Coldfield for L. Laskins

1919 House, Tintagel, Greenhill Rd, Sutton Coldfield for F. Davies

1919 House, 12 Greenhill Rd Sutton Coldfield for W. Vining

1920 Covered yard and motor house, Hollyhust, Birmingham Rd, Sutton Coldfield for Mr Sobey

1920 18 houses Hollyfield Rd, Sutton Coldfield for Sutton Coldfield Housing Committee

1920 Stables for house in Greenhill Rd, Sutton Coldfield for Frank Matthews

1920 House, Donegal, 3 Beech Hill Rd, Sutton Coldfield for W. Nook

1921 Motor house, Wychelm, Lichfield Rd, Sutton Coldfield for E. Withington

1923 House, Talgarth, 2 Greenhill Rd, Sutton Coldfield for Mr Farmer

1923 Bungalow [? no.] Birmingham Rd, Sutton Coldfield for H. Thompson

1923 House [? no. 5] Beech Hill Rd, Sutton Coldfield for W. T. Wiggins Davis

1924 House, Greenhill Cottage, 10 Greenhill Rd, Sutton Coldfield for W. T. Wiggins Davis

1924 House, Four Oaks Rd, Sutton Coldfield for Norman Steeley

1924 Four villas, 49–61 Fiery Hill Rd, Barnt Green for Mr Pegram

1926 Two villas, 35–37 Fiery Hill Rd, Barnt Green for Mr Pegram

1928 House, Culross House, 5 Luttrell Rd, Sutton Coldfield for T. Combe

1929 House, Red Mullion, 8 Bracebridge Rd, Four Oaks for A. W. Small

---

NOTES

[1] The authors are grateful to Alan Crawford who first drew their attention to this important and, hitherto, neglected Arts and Crafts architect.

[2] Obituary in *The Builder*, 166, 3 March 1944, p. 172.

[3] Obituaries in *Birmingham Post*, 16 February 1944 and *Birmingham Mail*, 16 February 1944.

[4] The card index to RBSA in Birmingham Central Library, Archives and Heritage Services (hereafter BCL AHS), includes 'A Perspective View of a bungalow proposed to be created in Austria' by Owen Parsons, Spring 1894.

[5] BCL AHS, Birmingham Building Register plan no. 12370 (1896) shopping in Lower Hurst Street for G. Yorke and app. no. 13383 (1897) alterations to convert houses to shops, nos 386, 388, 390, 392 Moseley Road for James and Type.

[6] Birmingham Building Register app. no. 10547 (1896) for 'houses Bk between 91 and 92' Lower Edwards Street for W. Bradbury.

[7] Birmingham Building Register app. no. 17979 (1904) for alterations to Moseley and Balshall Heath Institute, Moseley Road 1904.

[8] Birmingham Building Register app. no. 9706 (1892) for 16 dwelling houses, Clifton and Ladypool Roads for G. East.

[9] BCL AHS King's Norton Building Register app. nos 85–88 (1898) for 18 houses, Chatham and Maas Roads for C. Pegram.

[10] Worcestershire Record Office, 6461 Boxes 12–13, miscellaneous plans of early houses for the Barnt Green Estate, near Bromsgrove. Fiery Hill Road was originally Station Road and Cherry Hill Road was originally Fiery Hill Road. Houses nos 48–61 are on the corner. Information courtesy of Alan Brooke.

[11] King's Norton Building Register plan no. 1924 (1905) for 10 semi-detached houses [nos 47–65] Selly Park Road, Selly Park for Carr and Layton.

[12] Carr and Layton commissioned plans for a further eight villas from Parsons in Selly Park Road between 1906 and 1907. There is also an attractive small detached house next to nos 47 to 65. According to the owner this was originally built 'by an architect for his mistress'. Diligent searching of the plan books and rate books has however failed to substantiate this.

[13] King's Norton Building Register app. no. 934 (1901) for two houses [nos 19–21] Salisbury Road, Moseley, for J. Dean and F. Harrison.

[14] These plans in the King's Norton Building Register are app. no. 2147 (1906); app. no. 2991 (1909) and plan no. 3173 (1910).

[15] King's Norton Building Register app. no. 31 (1898) for house, Russell Road Moseley, for George Yorke Iliffe.

[16] King's Norton Building Register app. no. 1143 (1901) for house, Russell Road, Moseley, for Thomas Cond.

[17] King's Norton Building Register app. no.2486 (1909) for house, Russell Road, Moseley, for John Nicolson.

[18] Department of the Environment, *List of Buildings of Special Architectural or Historic Interest: City of Birmingham* (1982) p. 9.

[19] King's Norton Building Register app. no. 3141 (1910) for house, [36] Amesbury Road, Moseley for A. B. Wood.

[20] King's Norton Building Register app. no. 3392 (1910) for house [40] Wake Green Road, Moseley for Frank Banks.

[21] King's Norton Building Register app. no. 1174 (1902) for house [12] Forrest Road, Moseley for Francis Dingley.

[22] Sutton Coldfield Reference Library, Sutton Coldfield Building Register app. no. 2437 (1912) for house [14] Greenhill Road, Sutton Coldfield for Brooks and Mason.

[23] His houses in Beech Hill Road are no. 5 Donegal (Sutton Coldfield Building Register app. no. 3053) and Tudor House (Sutton Coldfield Building Register app. no. 3554). It is stylistically likely that Parsons was responsible for other houses on this attractive road. In Greenhill road he designed eleven houses between 1912 and 1924. A study of their plans in the Sutton Coldfield Building Register indicates that some of the houses were modified in construction. Brooks and Mason apparently owned a large property, Highfield House, a private road off Greenhill Road, now redeveloped, and developed about half the road using various architects.

[24] Rose Mullion is no. 1 Greenhill Road which has been identified from the drawings and personal visit.

[25] The Four Oaks Estate houses have the following application numbers in the Sutton Coldfield Building Register: app. no. 903 (The Lawns, Bracebridge Road), app. no. 1648 (Hindecliffe, Bracebridge Road) and app. no. 4767 (Culross House, Luttrell Road). In 1929 he designed a further house Red Mullion, 8 Bracebridge Road (app. no. 5082) for A. W. Small. This house appears to have been demolished.

[26] Sutton Coldfield Building Register app. no. 3024. The plans were not available but have been identified by personal visit as the group of eighteen council houses.

25 William de Lacy Aherne

CHRISTINE WOOD

William de Lacy Aherne (1867/8–1945) was not a major architect but at the turn of the twentieth century, he was significant in Birmingham. His significance lies mainly in his dominance in the first decade of the twentieth century throughout the area that was then Moseley. In Oxford Road, for instance, he designed eighteen of the houses built between 1904 and 1907 while in Amesbury Road, now part of the Moseley Conservation area, ten of the eighteen houses built between 1906 and 1911 were his. His commissioned designs were attractive and imaginative. Some show the influence of other architects; some, such as his Grade II listed houses in the St Agnes Conservation area in Moseley, decidedly belong to the Arts and Crafts Movement, which was flourishing and highly regarded in Birmingham at that time.

It was in building houses for the professional middle classes that de Lacy Aherne was prolific. He was an architect in the right place at the right time. Landowners in Moseley, whose families had established sizeable estates in the eighteenth century, were releasing this land for building. New roads were being developed, providing, in an increasingly popular suburb, a ready market for substantial detached and semi-detached homes. He built outside Moseley too but nowhere else achieved the same unusual level of dominance. These Moseley houses have generally remained in single family occupancy. Of generous but manageable proportions, they are as desirable for the professional middle classes at the beginning of this century as they were at the beginning of the last. Appreciating the pleasing design, many owners, in making alterations and installing essentials of modern life, have sought to preserve the exterior appearance and original features.

De Lacy Aherne's earlier work shows considerable diversity of style and a desire to ensure that his houses were in keeping with buildings in the vicinity. Most of the larger houses still standing, particularly in King's Norton, then a rural area, have been

William de Lacy Aherne

subject to considerable alteration. After 1903, de Lacy Aherne moved strongly into the speculative market, often in conjunction with local builders. To sustain a relatively expensive lifestyle without private means, he needed more money than he could make from an architect's fees for private residences.

Whatever claims de Lacy Aherne may have to recognition as an architect, he was easily surpassed in achievement of fame and fortune by his son Brian Aherne, the actor and Hollywood star. Brian's autobiography has supplied many biographical details for his father.[1] His account, invaluable though it is, inevitably contains inaccuracies, some detected when they do not match information from contemporary sources. For the early years Brian depended on accounts related to him. Of de Lacy Aherne's three children he spent least time at home and almost all his adult life abroad. Naturally his narrative is coloured by his own perception of events. Since his principal objectives were to tell a good story and sell a book, the accuracy of historical detail was not his main concern.

Brian's explanation of the correct form of his father's name makes an interesting anecdote but is not supported by such evidence as exists. Since references and contemporary newspaper reports show variations in spelling and first name, some explanation is, however, needed. William de Lacy Aherne was born in Cheam, Surrey in 1867 or 1868. The 1881 census records his age as thirteen and his forenames as William Dlay.[2] This implies that 'de Lacy' was a name Aherne was given, unlike Willoughby, which later replaced the more mundane William in Kelly's *Directories* and newspaper reports. In official listings, such as the 1901 Census[3] and the BAA journals, the entry is always under Aherne. His practice operated under the name 'de Lacy Aherne' and thus he signed his name. Willoughby never appeared on official documents; in his will, made the year before he died, he is again William de Lacy Aherne.[4]

The eldest of three sons in a family of ten children, de Lacy Aherne's childhood was somewhat unusual. His paternal grandfather was a Dublin academic and his father was Secretary of the Investment Trust Corporation. Both parents were devout Plymouth Brethren. William Aherne senior invested skilfully for the Trust but spurned, as immoral gains, money he could have made from personal investment. He lived modestly without servants, unusual in a family of the Ahernes' income and social status. Large donations to missionaries meant that there was no money to pay for the children's schooling. Thus, according to Brian, only de Lacy Aherne's youngest sister received any formal education. However, the indications are that de Lacy Aherne was both literate and cultured. Brian says that he taught himself to play the violin and to paint in oils. Not surprisingly he ceased to share his parents' religious convictions. His will states firmly that he desired 'no flowers mourning or religious ceremony'.

His father apparently made no effort to help him train and establish himself in a suitable profession. At the age of nineteen (1886 or 1887), presumably acting on his own initiative, he took a job as an architect's apprentice in Birmingham at a salary of £1 a week. He travelled from Surrey to start his career armed only with his father's gift of £5, his good looks and a talent for drawing. The latter two were to stand him in good stead.

There is evidence that he served his apprenticeship with the King's Norton and Northfield Sanitary Authority under Mr Godfrey, the surveyor.[5] This Authority completed the design and erection of the Fever Hospital and Pavilion at West Heath in 1888, a project in which he was involved. On the earliest of the Building plans he submitted, de Lacy Aherne gave his professional address as 23 Valentine Road, the address of the King's Norton Sanitary Authority offices. He never acquired formal qualifications although, by 1890, he is listed as an 'Architect and Surveyor' with an office at 8 Corporation Street, Birmingham. 'Surveyor' is not mentioned again but his status as an architect is confirmed by his election to the BAA in 1896.[6] He became a Licentiate of RIBA in 1926 and a Fellow of RIBA in 1931.[7]

The first recorded Building Plan submission under his own name was in 1889 for a house and Post Office in King's Norton.[8] This building is now Lloyd's Bank, 100, The Green. The pattern of windows in the upper floors and the decorative timber framing in the gable accord with the Building Plan; the ground floor has undergone considerable alteration. In 1897 he designed two more houses, later converted to shops, on The Green, now within the King's Norton Conservation area.[9]

His earliest commissions were predominantly in the King's Norton area and included some substantial properties for people of importance locally. One such was Hurst Green on the Pershore Road, designed for Aaron Jones in 1893, now part of The Cotteridge Village Inn.[10] The original design, still discernible, is, for de Lacy Aherne, unique in being Georgian influenced. An earlier design in 1890, now a Funeral Directors at 277–279 Pershore Road, has a front elevation with an oriel window below a hipped gable.[11]

In 1894 de Lacy Aherne moved into the same premises as the Auctioneers and Estate Agents, Whittindale and Dyer, at 55 Colmore Row. The association with the Whittindale family, doubtless valuable for him when he began extensive speculative building, was a long one. He shared premises with them again at 5 Waterloo Street and finally took over their premises at 55 Newhall Street in 1931. In 1895 he designed a house in Kenilworth for Mrs Whittindale, in a splendid location overlooking both the castle and the Abbey grounds. Built as 'The Bungalow', it is known today as 'Ford House'.[12]

Early and current alterations to The Bungalow follow, where possible, the style and features of de Lacy Aherne's original design. It was built with solid brick walls and heavy timber framing, the outside walls being rendered. On the back elevation, one side has a gable over two storeys; on the other side the bedroom windows are topped by small gables set into a roof carrying down to the first floor. This roof has overhanging eaves forming a verandah, bordered by a wooden

The Bungalow [Ford House] Kenilworth. *Photograph from sale particulars of 1904, courtesy of Mr and Mrs Convey*

railing which once continued round the house. The railing was originally replicated on the upper floor enclosing a balcony leading from a bedroom. The ground floor is raised well above the surrounding ground level. It is unlike any house de Lacy Aherne designed in Birmingham and supports the theory that he preferred to design to suit the surroundings and client rather than adhere to a particular style.

In the summer of 1898 de Lacy Aherne married Annie Louise Thomas, known as Lulu.[13] She was the daughter of William Thomas, a lawyer and Councillor living in Moseley. Reputed to be pretty, lively and popular, she had a passion and talent for the theatre which she indulged on the amateur stage. A personal friend of Barry Jackson, she later became a founder member of the Birmingham Repertory Company. Thomas must have had serious doubts that de Lacy Aherne, in spite of his good looks and increasing popularity as an architect, could maintain his daughter in an appropriate style. However, he agreed to the match and, although there is no record of the row of suburban houses for which Brian says he put up money, he did commission two houses to be built in 1896–97. The Spinney, no. 63 Salisbury Road, Moseley, he occupied himself.[14] The other was in Chantry Road (no. 25), Moseley.[15] In 1897 de Lacy Aherne submitted a Building Plan for Mere End (no. 60) in Salisbury Road for Percy Hudson[16] and the next year he built No. 112 speculatively.[17] Mere End is a substantial double-fronted, black and white house with two storeys and an attic. It is almost symmetrical, unusual for de Lacy Aherne. Large twin gables at the front have vertical beams carrying down to the base of the windows on the ground floor. Horizontal beams follow the lines of the top and base of the windows. Large canted bays with latticed windows are set forward from the gables with flat roofs on the second floor.

It is likely that William Thomas financed some speculative building and had friends and connections helpful to the rising young architect. Sadly for the family, Thomas died in 1901. His widow moved from The Spinney to a house de Lacy Aherne designed for her in 1902 on the opposite side of Salisbury Road, Goodrest no. 76.[18] Two of the adjacent three houses which he designed, he built as a speculation for himself.

De Lacy Aherne apparently had a good friend in F. C. Box, editor of *The Moseley and King's Heath Journal*. Between January 1896 and January 1898, contrary to the *Journal's* usual practice in an age in which architects did not advertise, glowing reports of his work explicitly named him as architect and gave his office address. Two pages with photographs are devoted to 'The Bungalow', despite Kenilworth being somewhat out of the area ordinarily covered. An article on the early development of Salisbury Road, Moseley, describes him as building a pretty house there, probably Mere End.[19] Even the newly appointed City of Birmingham surveyor moving into 25 Chantry Road provided an opportunity to remind readers that its architect was the fashionable de Lacy Aherne.[20]

Also reported, with accompanying congratulations, is de Lacy Aherne's winning entry for the competition to design the new Moseley Presbyterian Church of England to be built at the junction of Alcester Road and Chantry Road.[21] The architect's drawing of the projected new church is included. The competition took place in 1897, all entries being submitted anonymously. De Lacy Aherne and Arthur G. McKewan, in equal partnership, were first. Crouch and Butler were awarded the £10 second prize. Unfortunately, although the site had been leased and the architects' costings were within the budget set, the church was unable to

Mere End, 60
Salisbury Road,
Moseley, 1897.
Photo: A.W.

raise a sum of money approaching that required. The project was shelved, never to come to fruition. The winning architects were instead invited to design a Lecture Hall. This was built and served as the church until its demolition in 1939.[22] It was disappointing for de Lacy Aherne that a church of so grand a design in such a prominent position was never built. Similar commissions might have followed and his career could have taken a somewhat different path.

Shortly after their marriage the de Lacy Ahernes moved into The Pleasaunce. In 1901 they had two live-in domestic servants and a nurse to care for their son, Patrick, born that year. Brian was born in 1902 and their daughter, Elana, in 1903. With horses and gardens also maintained in an attractive rural setting, the family's lifestyle must have been extremely pleasant, if rather expensive.

The Pleasaunce featured in a series on architects' own homes in *The Birmingham Magazine of Arts and Industries, 1901 to 1903*.[23] Today, renamed Barbara Hart House, it belongs to the NHS. Alterations and the disappearance of the gardens and surrounding countryside render it far less attractive than it appears in contemporary photographs taken for the magazine article. The article includes de Lacy Aherne's own sketch of the house, as envisaged upon completion. It is splendid indeed. Built in the style of an Elizabethan manor house, it again belongs to the Arts and Crafts Movement, while differing considerably from de Lacy Aherne's other Arts and Crafts houses. Timbered gables use reclaimed oak beams, there are Georgian rain-water spout heads of beaten lead and a Queen Anne wrought-iron weather-vane on the roof, which is tiled in reclaimed hand-made sand tiles. The interior has reclaimed oak beams and panelling. It also has a magnificent Jacobean oak staircase, acquired by de Lacy Aherne from nearby Monyhull Hall.

As well as commissions for relatively large new houses, de Lacy Aherne's early work included alterations and some designs for blocks of smaller houses built to let. Commercial work included shops, alterations and numerous renewals of drains. From about 1903 domestic work increased while commercial work decreased, and speculative building began to dominate. In 1903 de Lacy Aherne submitted plans in his own name for six houses in Cartland Road, King's Heath,[24] and two in Salisbury Road, Moseley.[25] In 1905 and 1906 there followed plans in Moseley for six in Russell Road in his own name[26] and a share in ten houses in Oxford Road with the builders Urwin & Fisher.[27] In 1907 and 1908, there were plans for three in Amesbury Road for himself and a share in twenty-five houses in Reddings Road with Fred Charley, another local builder.[28]

Starting in 1907, twenty-five houses were built on the North side of Reddings Road over three years. After a first detached house, the initial development consisted of semi-detached houses, with entrances side-by-side in the middle. All have front gables set well forward of the main entrances with flat-roofed two-storied bays and verandah porches formed by lean-to roofs. The result is a striking line of gables running down the road. The main roofs are tiled, except for one slate pair, and hipped in line with the side faces of the gables. There are two tall chim-

The Pleasaunce, Monyhull Road, King's Norton, 1898 designed by de Lacy Aherne for his own occupation, now Barbara Hart House. Photograph from *The Birmingham Magazine of Arts and Industries*, 1901–3, *courtesy of Birmingham Archives and Heritage Services*

neys on the outsides and two, the front one decorated, on the party line. The shapes of the bays vary considerably as does the decoration at the gable apex. Following this initial successful development, two identical pairs of semis were built in St Agnes Road, Moseley in 1909[29] and two more in Four Oaks Road, Sutton Coldfield. Plans for larger detached houses on the remaining ten plots were submitted during 1908, four for named owners and six on speculation. The design is similar, but the main entrances are set further forward and the ridges of the main roof go right across the width thus providing space for attics. Eight of the houses have additional smaller gables in the roof above the main entrance.

The Grade II listed houses by de Lacy Aherne in the St Agnes Conservation area are Whitecroft, no. 9 St Agnes Road, and a pair of houses, Silverbeech and Bleak House, nos 110 and 112 Oxford Road.[30] This attractive and unusual pair of Arts and Crafts houses was designed for the builders, James Urwin and Frank Fisher with whose firm, Urwin and Fisher, de Lacy Aherne worked frequently in Moseley. Originally these houses were detached. The garage block with a shared billiard room above was added later, then divided when Fisher left in 1916, so making the houses semi-detached.[31] Both are two-storey houses of patterned brick with decorative tile work and brick diapering. The roofs are Westmorland slates with

The North side of Reddings Road, Moseley about 1910, postcard

62 St Agnes Road, Moseley, 1909. This successful design was used for a large number of houses in Reddings Road and elsewhere

overhanging eaves. They are fronted by broad gables with cross roofs behind. There are corniced pent slate roofs over canted bay windows on the ground floor at the front. In no. 110 the apex of this roof is symetrically below the four-light casement window on the first floor and the apex of the main gable. In no. 112 it is well to the side whereas the main gable is symmetrical, stopping between floors at similar heights on both sides. In no. 110 it is higher on one side then sweeps right down over the verandah porch on the other. Thus the symmetric and asymmetric are juxtaposed in a pleasing albeit different way in each of the two houses. The overall impression is of a pair and an integrated design, an impression enhanced by the wrought iron overthrows, carrying plaques with street numbers, and the matching front walls and gate piers which are also Grade II listed.

Frank Davis was another of several local builders with whom de Lacy Aherne worked frequently. Brian felt that his father was stiff and formal and found social relationships difficult but his working relationships suggest otherwise.

In 1905 when plans were submitted for Whitecroft, a substantial and attractive house, de Lacy Aherne also submitted plans for six speculatively built houses in Russell Road, Moseley.[32] These, again rendered, have, in some cases, decorative features similar to those at Whitecroft, for example a chequered tile lunette and buttressed porch. The chequered tile lunette and buttressing is used again in a group of three later houses in Wake Green Road of 1911, of similar basic design to the Russell Road houses. These Arts and Crafts houses incorporate a variety of other features. No. 44 Wake Green Road has a decorated hexagonal tower above

Silverbeach and Bleak House, 110 and 112 Oxford Road, Moseley, built 1906–7, *courtesy of Roy Thomas*

Roanoke, 22 Russell Rd, Moseley, 1906. *Photo: A.W.*

the porch on the right and No. 46 has a small decorative lean-to roof supported on brackets above the first floor window on the right. The chequered lunette occurs again on two houses in Vesey Road, Wylde Green.

The speculatively built houses are similar to many built contemporaneously. Nonetheless there are features which typify de Lacy Aherne's houses. Canted bays, of one or two stories, tend to be flat-roofed and in only one of the houses identified does a gable come out right over a canted bay. Windows are usually leaded, rectangular or, less frequently, diamond latticed. Almost all his houses have gables and many are half-timbered, with considerable variation in the patterning. Long roof lines are typical. At the backs of the houses there are frequently gables and features to enhance the appearance. Some of the three-storey houses have third floor windows only at the sides and verandah porches are not uncommon, particularly in the earlier designs.

Birmingham Building Registers show plans for four sets of industrial premises, the earliest in 1899 and the last in 1912. These suggest a desire to make

44 Wake Green Road, Moseley, 1911

such buildings attractive rather than depressingly utilitarian. The first three have been demolished. Only Siviter House in Ludgate Hill (probably no. 17), built as a glass display and warehouse for A. Kohn, remains.[33] Now called Ludgate Lofts, it has been converted to apartments.

Prosperity for de Lacy Aherne lasted perhaps until 1911. He then faced a financial crisis. Demand for middle class housing had slowed, leaving him with unsold properties, cash flow problems and no further investment potential. He was forced to sell The Pleasaunce, his horses and much of his antique furniture. By then the nearby Monyhull Hall had been sold and converted into a lunatic asylum, depressing the sale price of The Pleasaunce. The family moved into a succession of unsold properties in Russell Road, Moseley (nos 191, 189 and 187) then, in 1917, to 32 Oakfield Road for a couple of years, and finally to Norbrook (no. 43) Park Hill.

After the end of the First World War the work began to come in again. In 1920 de Lacy Aherne submitted twelve sets of plans in Birmingham including twenty-two new houses, six of which were individual commissions for detached houses. Brian Aherne says that he designed a house in Malvern for Sir Barry Jackson and indeed Blackhill, built in 1917, in its beautiful situation on the Malvern hills, could well have been designed by de Lacy Aherne. The de Lacy Ahernes' friendship with Sir Barry also makes it very probable he was the architect but the Building Registers have not survived and to date it has not been possible to find conclusive contemporary evidence.

De Lacy Aherne never regained his former prosperity and country-gentleman life-style, but must have been comfortable enough. Brian Aherne records his parents taking holidays in Europe. Reginald Edmunds, a retired architect, recalls waiting for the tram in his student days with de Lacy Aherne and the latter's friends. De Lacy Aherne, who always liked to look imposing, wore a dark suit and stylish hat with a white gardenia in his lapel.[34] The style was Edwardian and therefore somewhat eccentric in the late 1920s. Visiting Brian in sunny California more than ten years later, even on the beach, de Lacy Aherne still wore a double-breasted suit.

Brian tried to persuade his parents, holidaying with him in the USA, to stay on when war seemed inevitable. He could not understand why his father preferred to return to Norbrook, his suburban home in smoky, industrial Birmingham. The war forced de Lacy Aherne and Lulu to take lodgings in Stratford-upon-Avon. Brian saw his father once more, after Lulu's death, on a brief visit there in 1944. De Lacy Aherne died on 4 December 1945 of acute bronchitis. His age is given as 76.[35] This is irreconcilable with the ages on the 1881 and 1901 censuses, the latter given by de Lacy Aherne himself. It is therefore likely that his elder son Patrick, who registered the death, was mistaken and he was at least 77.

List of Architectural Works of William De Lacy Aherne

William de Lacy Aherne (1868/7–1945) was born in Cheam and trained in Birmingham under Mr Godfrey the surveyor to the King's Norton Sanitary Authority. He commenced working as an independent architect in Birmingham in 1889. He was still working up to 1941. His work has been listed up to 1915.

WORK IN BIRMINGHAM AND ITS ENVIRONS

PUBLIC

1897 Lecture Hall for The Committee Moseley Presbyterian Church of England, Chantry Rd Moseley[D 1939]

1902 Meeting room for J. Genders Secretary to the Christadelphian Synod, Institute Rd, King's Heath (No recognisable features left)

COMMERCIAL

(A number of shops, and conversions to shops, no longer identifiable)

INDUSTRIAL

1899 Manufactory for Samuel Cassel & Sons, 94, 96 and 98 Lombard St, Highgate [D]

1904 New premises for Messrs Ellis & Co, 3 and 4 Hall St, Birmingham [D]

1909 Business premises for Messrs Goodwin Bros., 110 Sandpits, Birmingham [D]

1912 New premises for A Kohn, Siviter House, no. 17 Ludgate Hill, Birmingham [Converted to flats]

DOMESTIC

1889 House and post office for Josiah Hands, no. 100 The Green, King's Norton (now Lloyds Bank)

1890 One house for R. W. Foster, nos 277–279 Pershore Rd South, King's Norton

1891 Four houses for W. Coton, possibly nos 1536, 1538, 1540 and 1542 Pershore Rd, Stirchley

1891 Two cottages for Thomas Seward, nos 30 and 32 Bell Lane, Walker's Heath

1893 One house for Aaron Jones, Hurst Green, Pershore Rd, King's Norton [part of The Cotteridge Village Inn Pershore Rd South]

1895 Three cottages for Mrs Hodgetts, Rose Cottages, nos 1, 2 and 3 The Fordrough, West Heath

1895 House for Theodore Pritchett, Wood Norton, no. 64 Redditch Rd, King's Norton [D]

1896 House for W. Thomas, no. 25 Chantry Rd, Moseley

1897 Residence for Wm. Thomas, The Spinney, no. 63 Salisbury Rd, Moseley

1897 One House for Percy Hudson, Mere End, no. 60 Salisbury Rd, Moseley

1897 Two houses for Mr Foster, nos 2 and 2A The Green, King's Norton

1897 One house for J. Dobson, Meldon, no. 17 Grove Avenue, Moseley

1898 Seven houses for W. Kentish Jnr, nos 1, 3, 5, 7, 9, 11, 13 St Albans Rd, Moseley (Started November 1900)

1898 Fourteen (two built) houses for W. Kentish Jnr, nos 67 and 69 Pershore Rd South, King's Norton

1898 House for W. de Lacy Aherne, no. 112 Salisbury Rd, Moseley

1898 Four houses for J. Horne, nos 71, 73, 75 and 77 Cotton Lane, Moseley

1898 Cottage residence for W. de Lacy Aherne, The Pleasaunce (now Barbara Hart House) Monyhull Hall Rd, King's Norton; 1904 extensions

1898 Two houses for G. Wright Jnr, nos 44 and 46 Bell Lane, King's Norton

1899 Pair of villas for F. Charley Esq., nos 207 and 209 Alcester Rd, Moseley

1899 Fourty-four houses for J. Hough, probably includes nos 3 to 25 Baldwin Rd, nos 4 to 24 Baldwin Rd and nos 4 to 24 Parson's Hill, King's Norton

1899 Residence for F. W. Blake, no. 67 Cotton Lane, Moseley

1899 Two villa residences for Supt. J. Wasley, 183 and 185 Alcester Rd, Moseley

1900 House for W. de Lacy Aherne, Eastcote, no. 13 St Agnes Rd, Moseley

1900 House for E. E. Lamb, Somerville Rd Sutton Coldfield [D]

1900 Dwelling house for J. Tarry, Studholme, no. 45 Greenhill Rd, Moseley [D]

1900 House for Hubert Gibbs, no. 41 Dyott Rd, Moseley

1900 House for Mr Charles Arnold, Hartopp Rd, Sutton Coldfield [D]

1901 House for Mr A. W. Price, Dunster, no. 19 Four Oaks Rd, Four Oaks

1901 Two houses for A. E .Starkey, nos 75 and 77 Stanmore Road, Edgbaston

1901 Conversion of a bake house and coach house to a cottage for J. C. Gilbert, Barston Lane, Solihull

1902 House for W. H. Starkey, no. 417 Hagley Rd, Edgbaston

1902 House for T. F. Ash, no. 39 Dyott Rd, Moseley

1902 Two pairs of houses for Frank Davis, Fernlea, Clavendon, Rathen and Tresco, nos 59, 61, 63 and 65 Cotton Lane, Moseley

1902 Dwelling house for Mrs W. Thomas, Goodrest, no. 76 Salisbury Rd, Moseley

1902 Two residences for Mrs Hookham, no. 18 and Wake Green Lodge Hotel, Wake Green Rd, Moseley

1903 Two houses for W. de Lacy Aherne, Station Rd, Hazelwell, nos 3 and 5, Cartland Rd, King's Heath

1903 Three houses for Ernest Goode (one house) and W. De Lacy Aherne (two houses), nos 70, 72 and 74 Salisbury Rd, Moseley

1903 Two houses for Messrs Sandford & Evans, nos 128 and 130 College Rd, Moseley

1903 Pair of villas for Messrs Edwards & Davis, 132 and 134 College Rd, Moseley

1903 Six houses and stabling for Chas Morrell, nos 20, 22, 24, 26, 28 and 30 Willow Avenue, Bearwood

1903 Six houses for W. de Lacy Aherne, nos 7, 9, 11, 13, 15 and 17 Cartland Road, Kings's Heath

1903 Two houses for E. Allday, nos 127 and 129 Sandon Rd, Bearwood

1903 Three houses for E. Allday, nos 17, 19 and 21 Willow Avenue, Bearwood

1903 House for Mrs H. Preece, Cranmore Drive, Shirley [D]

1904 Two houses for Urwin & Fisher, nos 105 and 107 Oxford Rd, Moseley

1904 Five houses for G. F. Assinder, nos 56, 58, 60, 62 and 64 Wake Green Rd, Moseley

1904 House for Mrs A. Stokes, 20 Ashleigh Rd, Solihull

1904 One House for J. Spillsbury, The Nook, Wake Green Rd, Moseley [D]

1905 Two houses for F. Davis, nos 109 and 111 Wake Green Rd, Moseley

1905 Six houses for Urwin & Fisher and W. de Lacy Aherne, nos 90, 92, 94, 96, 98 and 100 Oxford Road, Moseley

1905 Four houses for W. de Lacy Aherne and Urwin & Fisher, nos 102, 104, 106 and 108 Oxford Road, Moseley

1905 House for W. B. Incledon, Whitecroft, no. 9 St Agnes Road, Moseley

1906 Six (three built) houses for W. de Lacy Aherne, nos 22, 24 and 26 Russell Rd, Moseley

1906 Two houses for W. Scammells, nos 19 and 21 Woodlands Rd, Sparkhill

1906 Two houses for Riley & Richards, nos 41 and 43 Poplar Avenue, Bearwood

1906 Four houses for J. Brooke (sic) of Bromsgrove, nos 7, 9, 11 and 15 Vesey Rd, Wylde Green

1906 Two houses for Urwin & Fisher, nos 110 and 112 Oxford Rd, Moseley

1906 Two houses for A. Davies, nos 79 and 81 West Hill Rd, King's Norton

1906 Three houses for W. de Lacy Aherne, nos 16, 18 and 20 Russell Rd, Moseley (Revision of earlier plan of 1906, completed 1909)

1907 Four houses for Urwin & Fisher, nos 113, 115, 117 and 119 Oxford Rd, Moseley

1907 Seven houses for F. Charley and W. de Lacy Aherne, nos 1, 2, 3, 4, 5, 6 and 7 [nos 2, 4, 6, 8, 10, 12 and 14] Reddings Rd, Moseley

1907 House for J. B. Brookes (sic) of Bromsgrove, no. 17 Vesey Rd, Wylde Green

1907 Two houses for Streather & Hill, Haytor, no. 386 and Heswall, no. 378 Lichfield Rd, Four Oaks

1907 Three houses for J. D. Brooks (sic) of Bromsgrove, Shelsley, no. 1, nos 3 and 5 Vesey Rd, Wylde Green

1907 Six (two pairs built) houses for Messrs G. F. Assinder and H. W. Horton, nos 62, 64, 66 and 68 St Agnes Rd, Moseley

1907 Two houses for F. Charley and W. de Lacy Aherne, nos 8, 9, [nos 16 and 18] Reddings Rd, Moseley

1907 Three pairs of houses for F. Charley and W. de Lacy Aherne, nos 10, 11, 12, 13, 14 and 15 [nos 20, 22, 24, 26, 28 and 30] Reddings Rd, Moseley

1907 House for T. Morton Esq., Lichfield Rd Hill, Four Oaks [D]

1907 Three houses for W. de Lacy Aherne, St Columb, Woodview and Walton House, nos 8, 10 and 12 Amesbury Rd, Moseley (First shown occupied in 1910)

1908 House for Rev. Geo. Avery, no. 16 [no. 32] Reddings Rd, Moseley

1908 One house for C. H. Whittaker, no. 26 or 52 Reddings Rd, [no. 41 Amesbury Rd] Moseley

1908 Detached house for A. W. Currall, no. 18 [no. 36] Reddings Rd, Moseley

1908 Detached house for Bernard Moore, no. 19 [no. 38] Reddings Rd, Moseley

1908 One house for F. Charley and W. de Lacy Aherne, no. 17 [no. 34] Reddings Rd, Moseley

1908 Two houses for S. A. Richards & Co., nos 37 and 39 Poplar Avenue, Bearwood

1908 Detached house for Ernest D. Clark, no. 20 [no. 40] Reddings Rd, Moseley

1908 Private residence for L. C. T. Hadley, Alvechurch Rd [Hampstead House, Condover Rd] West Heath

1908 Six (four built) houses for John Chas Turner, The Grey House, no. 28, and nos 30, 32 and 34 Amesbury Rd, Moseley (Occupied 1911/12)

1908 Five Detached houses for F. Charley and W. de Lacy Aherne, nos 21, 22, 23, 24 and 25; [nos 42, 44, 46, 48 and 50] Reddings Rd, Moseley

1910 Detached residence for Theodore Pritchett, Burford, no. 277 Redditch Rd, King's Norton [D]

1910 House for Josiah Bendall, no. 40 Somerville Rd, Sutton Coldfield

1911 Three houses for W. de Lacy Aherne, nos 189, 191 and 193 Russell Rd, Moseley

1911 Three houses for W. de Lacy Aherne, nos 42, 44 and 46 Wake Green Rd, Moseley

1911 Three houses for W. de Lacy Aherne, Richmond, no. 50, Inverblair, no. 52 and no. 54 Sommerville Rd, Sutton Coldfield

1914 Five houses for J. Richards, nos 78, 80, 82, 84 and 86 Eastern Rd, Wylde Green

1914 House for W. de Lacy Aherne, no. 187 Russell Rd, Moseley

1915 House for W. de Lacy Aherne, no. 179, Russell Rd, Moseley

1915 House for Miss Blick, no. 55 Russell Rd, Moseley

WORK OUTSIDE BIRMINGHAM

DOMESTIC

1896 House for Mrs Whittindale, The Bungalow [Ford House] Castle Rd, Kenilworth

1901 Alterations for S. Jevons, Eastcote Hall, Meriden

1903 Addition of living accommodation to the Post Office, High St, Knowle

---

NOTES

[1] Brian Aherne, *A Proper Job* (Boston, Mass., 1969). Most of the biographical information on the architect is taken from this book. Contemporary sources confirm some of it; some inaccuracies have been detected but it is possible some remain, particularly in the anecdotes.

[2] National Archive, 1881 Census, RG 11, piece 0759 folio 97 p. 13.

[3] Birmingham Central Library, Archives and Heritage Services (hereafter BCL AHS), 1901 Census, RG 13/2804/55.

[4] BCL, AHS, Birmingham District Probate Registry, Will dated 13 July 1945.

[5] *Moseley and King's Heath Journal*, January 1896, p. 352.

[6] Birmingham Architectural Association *Journals* and Kelly's *Directories of Birmingham*.

[7] BAA *Journals* and RIBA.

[8] BCL, AHS, King's Norton Building Register (1889), app. no. 1070, house and Post Office, 100 The Green, King's Norton for Joseph Hands. The following Building Registers have been consulted for the period from 1880–1916: BCL, AHS, King's Norton RDC, King's Norton and Northfield RDC, Birmingham, and Yardley; Sutton Coldfield Library, Sutton Coldfield RDC. In addition some plans for Solihull RDC were consulted, but consultation to identify relevant plans is only allowed by Building Control by their own staff on a fee basis.

[9] King's Norton Building Register, (1887), app. no. 2967, 2 houses for Mr Foster, 2 and 2A, The Green, King's Norton.

[10] King's Norton Building Register, app. no. 1644 (1893), house for Aaron Jones, Hurst Green, Pershore Road South.

[11] King's Norton Building Register, app. no. 1280 (1890), house for Mr Foster, 277–279, Pershore Road South.

[12] *Moseley and King's Heath Journal*, January 1896, p. 352; sales particulars, dated 1904, in the possession of Mr and Mrs Convey, the current owners of The Bungalow [Ford House].

[13] Register of Marriages, King's Norton District, vol. 6c p. 765.

[14] King's Norton Building Register, app. no. 2758 (1897), residence for William Thomas, The Spinney, Salisbury Road, Moseley.

[15] King's Norton Building Register, app. no. 2340 (1896), house for William Thomas, 25 Chantry Road, Moseley.

[16] King's Norton Building Register, app. no. 2927 (1897), house for Percy Hudson, Mere End, Salisbury Road, Moseley.

[17] King's Norton Building Register, app. no. 3347 (1898), house for W. de Lacy Aherne, 112, Salisbury Road, Moseley.

[18] King's Norton Building Register, app. no. 1265 (1902), Dwelling house for Mrs W. Thomas, Goodrest, Salisbury Road, Moseley.

[19] *Moseley and King's Heath Journal*, January 1898, p. 348.

[20] *Ibid*, October 1896, pp. 186–87.

[21] *Ibid*, April 1897, pp. 479–80.

[22] Fred Price, *Moseley Presbyterian Church: A Candid History* (Birmingham, 1991); archive material at BCL, AHS, and at the church. The church was originally called Moseley Presbyterian Church of England. It is now called St Columba United Reform Church.

[23] *Birmingham Magazine of Arts and Industries*, vol. 3, 1901–1903, pp. 138–39; King's Norton Building Register app. no. 3423 (1898) cottage residence for W. de Lacy Aherne, The Pleasaunce, Monyhull Hall Road, King's Norton.

[24] King's Norton and Northfield Building Register, app. no.1480 (1903), six house for W. de Lacy Aherne, nos 7, 9, 11, 13, 17, and 17, Cartland Road, King's Heath.

[25] King's Norton and Northfield Building Register app. no. 1457 (1903), three houses, (one for Ernest Goode and two for W. de lacy Aherne) nos 70, 72 and 74 Salisbury Road, Moseley; Ibid.

[26] King's Norton and Northfield Building Register app. no. 2107 (1906), six houses (3 built) for W. de Lacy Aherne, nos 22, 24 and 26.

[27] King's Norton and Northfield Building Register app. no. 1880 (1905), six house for Unwin and Fisher and W. de Lacy Aherne, nos 92, 94, 96, 98 and 100 Oxford Road, Moseley.

[28] King's Norton and Northfield Building Register app. no. 2479 (1907), three house for W. de Lacy Aherne, St Columb, Woodview and Walton House, Amesbury Road; the applications in Reddings Road are app. no. 2406 (1907), app. no. 2442 (1907), app. no. 2676 (1908), and app. no. 2815 (1908).

[29] Yardley Building Register app. no. 1874 (1907), six house (4 built) for G. F. Assinder and H. W. Horton, nos 62, 64, 66, and 68 St Agnes Road, Moseley.

[30] Chris Pancheri, *St Agnes Moseley Conservation Area, a guided walk* (unpublished leaflet for Birmingham Development Department, 1987). The Moseley Society has produced an updated leaflet for a guided walk.

[31] *The Listed Buildings of Moseley* (Moseley Local History Society, 1995).

[32] King's Norton and Northfield Building Register app. no. 2107 (1906), six houses (three built) for W. de Lacy Aherne, nos 22, 24 and 26 Russell Road, Moseley.

[33] Birmingham Building Register app. no. 22759 (1912)

[34] *Ex inform* Reginald Edmunds, formerly working as an architect in Birmingham.

[35] Death Certificate reference HC 751484, Metropolitan Borough of Stoke Newington.

26 Arthur Stansfeld Dixon

ANDY FOSTER

In April 1908, Janet Ashbee, the wife of C. R. Ashbee – craftsman, architect, socialist, and founder of the Guild of Handicraft, then at Chipping Campden – visited her friends in Birmingham, Arthur Dixon and his wife Gertrude. She saw Dixon, at fifty-two, as 'an elderly man, a disappointed & baffled artist. "I can't get any architecture to do ..." he said to me with the ghost of his former merry twinkle "so I have taken to governing the town – Education Committee, Church defence committee, Licensing Bill opposition committees, etc etc – one must do something for the city one belongs to." His ritualistic fanaticism has increased – & the number of things he finds it necessary to believe took my breath away'.[1] Every aspect of Dixon, his political and business background, his 'singularly devout and zealous'[2] Anglo-Catholic faith, his left views, his love of craftsmanship, his personal charm, and his unusual role as a part time architect, is present or implied in this description. His many roles are all worth study, and it is necessary to be selective. This essay concentrates on his architectural work, especially on his churches, and in conformity with the scope of the book, those built before the Great War.

Arthur Stansfeld Dixon was born in 1856 into one of the handful of leading upper middle class families of a rapidly growing Birmingham. His father George Dixon was a manufacturer and merchant, a liberal Anglican in religion, and an active and prominent Liberal in politics. He was a town councillor from 1863, and Mayor in 1866–67, when his decisive actions helped stop the 'Murphy riots', the violent protests of the city's Irish Roman Catholic community against the lectures of the ex-Catholic, protestant agitator William Murphy.[3] He was elected MP for Birmingham in 1867. George Dixon was a liberal Anglican who 'detested religious bigotry of all kinds'. With the young

Arthur Stansfeld Dixon, drawing by Charles M. Gere, 1929, in a private collection

Joseph Chamberlain he founded the National Education League to campaign for secular elementary education, and in 1869 became its first President. He attended his local Church of England parish churches, St John, Ladywood, and later St Augustine, Edgbaston. The young Arthur and his sister Katie were not impressed by this religion. Arthur compared the vicar at Ladywood, Rev. Morse, to a bad pear he had eaten, and Katie described services at St Augustine's as 'musical, large choir and all that, the way rich people make up for want of ritual; they must have something I suppose ...'[4]

The League made George Dixon into a figure in national politics, and the young Arthur must have met Liberal politicians of the first rank. He may also have met one Oxford don, the idealist philosopher Thomas Hill Green, who had local educational connections as a governor of King Edward's School. He was sent to 'a weekly boarding school, Miss Shirt's somewhere near Perry Barr, he came home on Sunday',[5] then to Rugby school. He entered University College, Oxford, in October 1875, and took his BA in 1879.[6] He returned to his family with the latest social fashions – Katie remembered him introducing them to cocktails before dinner – and it is likely that it was at Oxford that he became a High Churchman, an Anglo-Catholic: a believer in the sacred nature of the Church, the authority of its dogmas, and their expression through religious ritual. Marion Rathbone, Dixon's niece, wrote of her uncle 'He'd been to Oxford, coming under the influence of the Oxford Movement'.[7]

Growing up in Edgbaston, Dixon would have become aware of the Oxford Movement at an early age: Newman was living in the Oratory, not half a mile from his home. In the 1870s Oxford was still the home of Newman's Anglican friend and former collaborator in the Movement, E. B. Pusey, and the centre of High Anglicanism under Pusey's follower, H. P. Liddon and a young Trinity College don coming to prominence, Charles Gore. He was already gathering round him the group of friends, all then young dons, known as the 'Holy Party' or later the 'Longworth group': significant figures in the Anglican church in the late nineteenth and early twentieth century, including the writer and theologian Henry Scott Holland, the first warden of Keble College and later bishop, Edward Talbot, and another bishop to be, Francis Paget.[8] In an intellectual atmosphere conditioned by the idealist philosophy of T. H. Green – Scott Holland was regarded as Green's most important disciple – they were a particularly fashionable and attractive intellectual group. They were more progressive socially than earlier High Churchmen. Gore had been influenced by the left Anglo-Catholic Father Arthur Stanton, and later became a founder member and Vice-President of the Christian Social Union.[9] They were also progressive theologically, as was to be shown in the famous and controversial symposium 'Lux Mundi' of 1890. And they were cultured, Gore had a lifelong love of the Mediterranean and its art. In 1886 he 'roamed about Italy, seeing the sights'; his invitations to the contributors to 'Lux

Mundi' were sent from Italy; and later, when a Bishop, he was in North Africa in 1903, Rome in 1904, followed by Sicily, and the Balearic Isles in 1906.[10]

These attitudes would have attracted a young Liberal, dissatisfied with his father's liberal religion. 'Undergraduates flocked to Gore' slightly later, when he became Principal of Pusey House in 1884.[11] There is no direct evidence, but it likely that Dixon came to know Gore and his friends when he was a student. It is very tempting to see a connection through T. H. Green and Scott Holland. By 1884, when he married Gertrude Bevan, 'Artie was now a churchman (that is, a High Churchman) really a very unbending one in many ways .... They went to live in a new house near the reservoir, really a very nice house, in Montague Road. This was more or less Morris all through by the time they had done with it, and they got some lovely old furniture'.[12] Their daughter Mary was born in 1887. Their elder son Humphrey followed in 1891, by when they had moved to 3 Augustus Road where they remained for over thirty years. Their younger son Evelyn was born in 1895.[13]

'When Artie grew up,' his sister recalled, 'he went to Oxford and took his degree, on the understanding he would come into the business afterwards'.[14] Rabone Bros. were merchants, 'trading mostly with the West Indies, Cuba we always used to hear of',[15] and the business involved a lot of foreign travel. Arthur Dixon, along with his father and brothers, went to Spain 'to study Spain and Spanish ways'. When Katie came home from Newnham College, Cambridge, 'Artie who had just come home from Australia was there too ...'. He stated in 1907 that he had visited and drawn buildings in 'Seville, Cordova, Burgos, Florence & Pisa. Sienna Modena, Amiens Beauvais Rouen Bruges Ghent Ypres etc. Nuremburg, Rothenburg etc'.[16] His sister remembered being with him in Ravenna, with its Early Christian churches, and said 'He was a beautiful draughtsman, and his notebooks were full of delightful drawings'.[17]

In 1890 he helped to found the Birmingham Guild of Handicraft, an offshoot of the Kyrle Society, a philanthropic cultural organisation aimed at working people. The Guild was part of what is now called the Arts and Crafts Movement, and one of a number of radical experiments in craft workshops at about this time, following the example of the Guild of Handicraft in London, founded by C. R. Ashbee in the East End in 1888, and based at Chipping Campden from 1902.[18] The Birmingham Guild, always small, ran classes in craft skills and slowly built up a self-supporting co-operative workshop, which became a separate limited company in 1895. As well as running the workshop, the Guild published a quarterly magazine, The Quest, from 1895.[19] The leading lights apart from Dixon were Montague Fordham, a solicitor, Claude Napier-Clavering, who was a student at the School of Art but married into the wealthy Kenrick family, and the architect W. H. Bidlake. William Kenrick, Napier-Clavering's father-in-law, invested in the Guild, and in about 1898 became Chairman. Dixon acted for a while as the Guild's director, and wrote an account of it in The Quest in 1896. He probably designed much of the metalwork produced by the Guild, items in which Glennys Wild and Alan Crawford find his 'austere hand', and tendency to exaggerate constructional details for aesthetic effect, 'an intellectual aspiring to be earthy'.[20]

It may have been his involvement with the Guild which gave Dixon links to national Arts and Crafts figures. C. R. Ashbee spoke at the inauguration of the Birmingham Guild on 26 September 1890.[21] An incident that day is commemorated by a silver spoon with an ivory handle, made by the London Guild and for Gertrude Dixon, inscribed 'In Mindfulness of a Rebuke. Sep. 26. 90'.[22] Dixon was elected to the committee of the London Guild in 1892 at Ashbee's suggestion, and Ashbee lectured at the Birmingham Guild in the same year.[23] The Birmingham Guild exhibited at the Arts and Crafts Exhibition Society from 1893. By then Dixon knew Norman Shaw, not an Arts and Crafts figure, but close to many in the Movement. One possible link is Shaw's former chief assistant, W. R. Lethaby, the most important thinker of the Movement. In 1892 Lethaby had designed a house in Four Oaks, The Hurst. It introduced his simple and functional style to local architects. Dixon greatly admired Lethaby's work. In 1903 he said of the Eagle Insurance building, 'It honestly expresses in its design the purpose for which it was intended; it can be labeled with the name of no dead style ... (it) is so thoroughly thought out and adapted to its purposes and surroundings, every line and every proportion is so unerringly set out, and every material is treated with such sympathetic understanding as to give the building unfailing interest and dignity'.[24]

In 1898 the Ashbees stayed with the Dixons in March, and again in the autumn.[25] In 1902 the Dixons stayed with the Ashbees at Drayton St Leonard. 'On Sunday we took Arthur Dixon to mass at Dorchester Abbey, & he said it was the most beautiful service he knew. Ritual means a great deal to him; & from the opposite pole of free thought he seems steadily coming towards the Extreme High Churchman's point of view ... Dixon came out in Raptures – "Well" he said "that is a thing to be thankful for!" He is thankful for so many things, & a most responsive & gracious little guest. The sunshine, the frost, the icebound river & the bronzing willow rods – the cosy room – the singing, the Nyon pottery, the lacquer spoons, the mutton, the eggs, the lemonade, the toast, all aroused his enthusiasm'.[26] In November 1904 Janet came to Birmingham. '... Mrs. Dixon had planned one of her delightful dinner parties for me last night, & as Friday was the only day the Lodges could come, Arthur Dixon had to forgo all the excellent meats provided – in fact it was against his ritualistic conscience to have even the social conviviality that day: but he stretched a point for me ... (His) green eyes twinkled sadly at me from behind a mound of conscientious salad'.[27] By 1908, when she found him elderly and baffled, Janet was more critical: 'His ritualistic fanaticism has increased – & the number of things he finds it necessary to believe took my breath away ... it is impossible to carry on any discussion with Arthur because of his crystalised 'parti pris' on any subject connected with Religion, politics, or

Guild of Handicraft, Great Charles Street and New Market Street, 1897–98

property – at a given moment click goes a little door – & he even says "Oh if that's what you think, I can't discuss it any further" & changes the subject'.[28]

The Ashbees were at the radical end of the Movement, but Dixon's account of the Birmingham Guild is careful and temperate, perhaps not wanting to put off potential supporters.[29] He starts with Ruskinian praise of the craftsman compared to machine production, contrasting 'Commercial development, the invention of mechanical methods, division of labour' which has 'divided the craftsman into lifeless pieces', with a Japanese house, which has 'few, if any, purely decorative objects' but 'perfect decoration ... everything is made for a definite purpose, and in addition it is made as comely as the workman knows how to make it'. But his Ruskinism is moderate: 'the use of machinery and the division of labour will continue to be developed', but 'we are beginning to understand that the machine cannot do everything, and that its department must be limited ... The Birmingham Guild of Handicraft, like its prototype in the Mile End Road, has a modest ambition to provide workshops in which the craftsman may work as far as possible apart from the difficulties above referred to'. This account of a craftsmen's guild contains one slightly unusual element, a significant interest in architecture, the Japanese house at the start, and a discussion of 'What shall we say ... of the circular saw and the brickmaking machine? Houses built of machine made bricks, roofs made of timbers sawn square and planed will always look wrong; they lack the human look which the hand gave to the old bricks and the adze to the timber'.

The invocation of Japan, recalling the Aesthetic Movement of Whistler and Beardsley, does sound like an intellectual looking at craftsmen, but the fundamental argument from Ruskin would come naturally to someone in Birmingham. Geoffrey Tyack has referred to the 'rediscovery of Ruskin by younger architects in the 1880s',[30] but in Birmingham, even slightly later, Ruskin was still present. J. H. Shorthouse, the close friend of his later years, lived in the city (and moved to Bournville in 1897), and the national memorial to Ruskin was built in Bournville in 1902. Dixon may have met Ruskin when he visited Birmingham in 1877; when young, he would certainly have known both the architect J. H. Chamberlain and the Liberal politician George Baker, who knew Ruskin personally.

Dixon's role, as a young member of the city's business and political elite becoming involved in artistic ventures, was not surprising. In 1891 he followed his father into politics as a city councillor for St Mary's ward.[31] But then his career took an unconventional turning. He 'had always wanted to be an architect ... (and) after some years his old wishes became too strong, and he did actually become an architect. He had a big unused room opposite to the other door of my father's office, and he set up there'.[32] He started training in 1893, and retired from the Council the following year. His training was unconventional. By his own account it consisted of private reading, six months 'principally in the life class' at the Birmingham School of Art, making 'measured drawings of Southwold Church Suffolk & of several houses in Gloucestershire,' and making 'copies of a set of drawings lent me by Mr. Norman Shaw & of a set by Mr. W.H. Bidlake and attended the carrying out of the latter on the job and at the builder's shop'.[33] He seems never to have become an Associate of the RIBA, but was elected a Fellow in 1907, his proposers being J. L. Ball, C. E. Bateman, and Thomas Cooper, William Henman's partner and former assistant to Alfred Waterhouse. His sister's account condenses the facts, because his office was at first at 32 Waterloo Street, the offices of the Guild of Handicraft, but at about the time of his father's death in 1898, when the Guild had moved to Great Charles Street, he moved his architectural practice into Rabone's office at 297 Broad Street. He remained all his life a part time architect, combining it with his work, and travelling, for Rabones. He mentions in his 1911 lecture as President of the Birmingham Architectural Association that he wrote it 'on a steamship in the Baltic'.

Dixon's architectural work falls into two phases. The first is mostly domestic. His first known building is an extension of 1895–96 to a house in Yateley Road, Edgbaston.[34] The house had been built in 1891 and designed by William Henman. It is modest in size for nineteenth century Edgbaston, one of a row of four in the Old English style, with brick and half-timbering, deriving from the early work of Norman Shaw and Eden Nesfield. Dixon's wing makes this quite simple house look ornate. It is an absolutely undecorated brick block with a full height rectangular bay, which has a lead roof. There are casement windows set flush with the wall, the preferred method of the leading local Arts and Crafts architects, and found, for example, on Bidlake's Garth House of 1901.

His first complete house, The Gables, in Hartopp Road on the Four Oaks Estate in Sutton Coldfield, was begun in May 1896 and completed at the end of 1897.[35] It was built for Montague Fordham of the Guild of Handicraft. The house, which was demolished in the 1960s, was small by the standards of the Estate, and is called 'Cottage' on the drawings. It used the simple language of the Yateley Road extension, which is here more clearly revealed as deriving from Cotswold cottages, despite the use of local brick. On the front, the upper windows nestled right under the eaves, and there was a big central gable flush with the wall, filled by a big mullion-and-transom window lighting the landing. The entrance was in a wide recessed porch. To the right of gable and porch, the roof stepped down, and the lower part to the right was broken up by a projecting chimney. The other chimneys were picturesquely disposed, on the left gable end and on the rear to the left of the gable. The garden front had its entrance to the left, below the step in the roof. Above the step, to the right, were two tall tight gabled bays with big mullion-and-transom windows on both floors. The planning was not so sophisticated, with bathroom and storeroom upstairs pushed into corners to manage direct access to each bedroom.

Dixon used an experienced Birmingham builder, James Smith and Sons of Great Tindal Street, but his inexperience led to many troubles with C. F. Marston, the Sutton Coldfield Borough Council's surveyor. Before work started he had to alter the design to use steel floor joists, to add a siphon to the cesspool, and to use a proprietary bitumen damp course. He also seems to have extended all the cross walls inside up to the gable, and redesigned the small service wing, which was originally placed at a 45 degree angle to the garden front. Fordham had moved in by October 1897 but an inspection on the 29th meant more work. On 16 November Dixon told Marston he had given the order to the builder and it would be done in a few days.

By this time Dixon was already at work on the Guild of Handicraft's building on the corner of Great Charles Street and New Market Street on the edge of Birmingham city centre. This was begun in May 1897.[36] The builders were James Smith and Sons again. It is also domestic in appearance: unusual at first sight for an office and workshops, but the Guild was established to revive traditional craft skills, often carried out in the past in small workshops attached to houses, so a domestic design symbolises something central to its purpose. The bricks are rough-faced, probably hand-made, and wire-cut, laid with wide mortar joints. Again there are casement windows throughout. The simplicity of the design is artful, deceptive; the composition is remarkably sophisticated for so inexperienced an architect. The Birmingham Architectural Association visited it on 16 April 1898, when it must have been substantially complete.[37] The *Architectural Review*, commenting on the perspective drawing shown at the Arts and Crafts Exhibition

Society in 1899, called it 'ably planned, and the exterior view is decidedly picturesque'.[38] On New Market Street, two three storey gabled blocks are separated by a
two storey range with a deep swept roof and big dormers. The gabled blocks are
quietly different: the left one has its windows linked by sunk panels, the right one
has that hallmark of the artistic Arts and Crafts house, a slightly tapering chimney
rising flush from one side of the gable. The Great Charles Street front is a com-
pressed version of the same composition, stepped uphill. This makes the corner
block into a kind of cross-gabled tower, an effective focus just at the most prominent point of the design, and a more subtle version of the corner turrets then so
popular with commercial architects. All the arches are round-headed or, particularly the relieving arches, three-centred. Dixon never used a pointed arch unless it
was unavoidable. Remo Granelli has reasonably suggested that the design is influenced by the Manor Farm at Withington, Gloucestershire, where Dixon lived for
a while; but the corner tower must surely be inspired by the High Building at
Daneway House, Gloucestershire, which Ernest Barnsley, whom Dixon would
have known through Birmingham and Cotswold connections, repaired in 1896.

The domestic work and the Guild building, along with contemporary work by
J. L. Ball, are early examples of an exceptionally simple kind of Arts and Crafts
architecture. Remo Granelli has said of their work of this period, 'This gift for
understatement is something which Dixon and Ball share, their success as
designers lay in what they left off their buildings'.[39] W. H. Bidlake's greatest
achievements of this kind come slightly later (Woodgate, 1897; Garth House, 1901)
and so do C. E. Bateman's (Redlands, 1903). At this point, in the closing years of
the century, Dixon seems to lead where they follow; the combination of sheer
gable and sweeping roof on the New Market Street front of the Guild building
comes from mediaeval Midlands' manor houses, as does Bidlake's dramatic use of
the same combination at 22 Ladywood Road, Four Oaks (1901); but one wonders
if Bidlake's version would have happened in quite the same way without Dixon's.
The immediate source of this manner is Lethaby and his house, The Hurst. Ball
knew Lethaby well, and acted as his executant architect on the Eagle Insurance
Building. Dixon probably knew him and, as we have seen, admired his work
greatly. The Gables was on the neighbouring plot in Four Oaks to The Hurst,
symbolic of the major influence on Dixon and Ball's early houses.

Dixon's approach at this period is illustrated by his 'Notes upon Some of the
Differences Between Ancient and Modern Building'.[40] He wants 'No ornament at
all, unless you can get a man of real imagination to do it, and that means, in most
cases, no ornament at all'. He discusses mouldings and the problem of the lack of
a living tradition: 'each man has to pick his moulding out of a dead heap,' the
styles of the past, 'or else invent one himself . . . the moment you leave the simplest
forms the difficulty begins'. He does not think new invention is possible, so 'the
conclusion seems to be, for the present no ornament, or as little as possible'. Since
Pevsner wrote *Pioneers of Modern Design*, the radical Arts and Crafts architecture

of around 1900, with its lack of decoration, has been seen as a forerunner of the Modern Movement. For Dixon, at least, it was largely the result of concern about contemporary standards of craftsmanship. The austere and reticent manner of Dixon's work parallels that of C. R. Ashbee's cottages at Campden and his small houses, such as the Shoehorn at Orpington of 1900, where 'one is aware, not just of neatness and sturdiness, but of a tense, negative feeling, of the many obvious elaborations which have been refused'.[41]

There are a scatter of minor works at this period: small extensions to houses for himself and his sister, and rather larger extensions, side wings, at Harborne House, now Bishop's Croft, Old Church Road, for Arthur Kenrick, where Dixon's simple manner allows the Georgian house to retain its primacy.[42] There is also a small but interesting piece of church work, a baptistery of 1904 at Christ Church, Wellington, Shropshire.[43] It fits into the south-west corner of a broad Commissioners' church nave. There is simple square framed panelling on the wall, though with posts that rise above the panels, in a manner reminiscent of Voysey, and a massive, very slightly tapering purple-grey stone bowl on heavy pillars. The floor is of green and white marble, laid in radiating lines which curve in S-shapes. It is clearly designed by someone who is aware of the Early Christian or Byzantine Revival manner then being used by progressive church architects, a manner also associated with Lethaby, and to which Dixon will return.

In 1903 Dixon designed a clergy house for St Aidan's church, Small Heath, a church by Frederick T. Proud which he admired as 'lofty and well-proportioned'.[44] It is linked to the church, and Dixon's low proportions and simple style ensure that the house does not compete with the church, or detract from its soaring clerestory.[45] It was built quickly and completed in August 1903, and in December he began a second private house, Tennal Grange, Harborne, which was not completed until January 1905.[46] Again the client came from the circle round the Guild: Claude Napier-Clavering was a member of its management committee.

Tennal Grange is a larger house than The Gables. The entrance front again derives from Cotswold patterns: the E-plan type, with three projecting full height gables, the middle one slightly shorter than the end ones. The material is red and blue brick laid in Sussex bond, with an occasional extra stretcher slipped in between the headers, four rather than three. The roofs are steep, and the gabled wings thin for their height, giving the whole composition a slightly stark, almost gawky quality, with none of the smoothness and elegance of Bidlake's and Bateman's work. This feeling is intensified by the left hand wing, nearest as you approach from the road, having no front window on the ground floor. This may derive from the first floor treatment of the tower on Bidlake's 22 Ladywood Road of 1901, but Dixon's treatment is markedly tougher, with a big central chimney rising right up to the gable, though mitigated by a generous shallow bow window on the side elevation. The chimney is a feature more typical of High Victorian Ruskinian Gothic, the work of J. H. Chamberlain, than other local Arts and Crafts

Tennal Grange, Tennal Lane, Harborne, 1903–05, entrance front

Tennal Grange, garden front

architects. Dixon is closer to Ruskin than Bidlake and Bateman, as we might expect.

This unusual arrangement, which lights the library, sets the tone for the unconventional planning of the rest. We look for the entrance in the front of the central projection, but it isn't there. Instead it is pushed leftwards, into a single storey block linking left and centre wings, perhaps deriving from the added entrance block to The Gables. Where the door would conventionally be are two small windows lighting lavatories. Behind the entrance is a hall again running across the house to a recessed loggia on the garden front; the recessed porch has moved from front to back, where it sits between two wings which do not match those on the front. To the left of the hall, behind the library, is the drawing room: to the right, the dining room. The staircase rises up in the central projection. This works well as planning, putting the dining room next to a generous servants' wing. All three floors of the right hand front wing house servants' rooms: effective planning, but also a symbolic gesture that the servants are part of the central core of the house, rather than being banished to a separate, low servants' wing. In practical and symbolic terms Tennal is more democratic than most large Edwardian houses, perhaps reflecting Dixon's, and presumably Napier-Clavering's, socialist views. The interior has been altered but the hall retains its fireplace with hand-moulded plaster overmantel. It is now the West Midlands Territorial Army Headquarters.

Tennal Grange was, in 1903, just starting to become old-fashioned; the simple style of the years of around 1900 was giving way to the revival of classicism. The move is symbolised by the change in the *Architectural Review*. Founded in 1897 and first edited by the metalworker and architect Henry Wilson, it was sympathetic to Arts and Crafts radicalism. By 1899 Wilson had been replaced by Mervyn Macartney, who despite an Arts and Crafts background, started to move the magazine towards classical houses. Lutyens, perhaps the greatest architect of the time, moved from the simple domestic revival of Tigbourne Court (1899) to the complex classicism of Heathcote (1906), a manner he came to call 'the High Game'. After Tennal, Dixon's practice comes almost to a halt. Between January 1905 and November 1908 there are only some repairs at Swainswick church, near Bath, where 'my chief aim was to conceal the fact that an architect had been there',[47] a pulpit for St Alban, Bordesley, and an unexecuted scheme for a church at Sumburgh, Orkney, shown at the Arts and Crafts Exhibition Society in 1906. He was puzzled and discomfited by the change in fashion, 'the strange thing is that after a lull of nearly fifty years pediments and Ionic columns are back again,' he said in 1911.

This was the time when Janet Ashbee found him looking old and disappointed, talking about going into local politics, more dogmatic in his views, and difficult to argue with. He had been churchwarden at St Alban's Bordesley from 1899 to 1907.[48] Now he became a JP in 1909,[49] and served as treasurer of the Diocese's Ordination Candidates' Fund.[50] He found time to write a long and detailed article for the *Journal* of the RIBA on 'Early Roman Churches'.[51] For two years, 1909–11, he was President of the Birmingham Architectural Association, and gave the annual lecture to its members. Dixon's article and his two contrasting lectures give us an account of how his thinking has developed since his early houses, and how he reacted to the re-appearance of history, and pediments. They also give us a remarkable picture of his detailed design practice.

The article on Roman churches is mostly historical and descriptive, and shows us some of the reasons for Dixon's love of Early Christian and Romanesque buildings, rather than Gothic. As an Anglo-Catholic, he relates the buildings to the growth of the early church, describing basilican planning and its evolution from pagan halls of justice, and detailing early ritual layouts, particularly at S. Clemente (which scholars then thought a building of the fifth century). He describes at length

The Roman basilicas built of red brick ... inside they were plastered when marble plates or mosaic was not used. The roofs were of low pitch, covered with red tiles; the tiles are half round channels set alternately convex and concavewise interlocking each other. On some of the tie beams, purlins, and rafters, are to be seen remains of coloured decoration in small geometrical patterns .... The clerestory wall, pierced with small square or round-headed windows, was carried in the earliest buildings on colonnades of marble pillars often taken from pagan temples ... later, arcades of small round arches took the place of the horizontal entablature over the columns. The floors were covered with marble mosaic work composed of pieces of red, green, and white marble three or four inches square set in a great variety of geometrical patterns; and the apse, the arch over it ... were decorated with pictures in glass mosaic.

There is a long description of these early church mosaics, focusing on central figures of Christ, the symbols of the Good Shepherd and the fish, and references to the book of Revelations.

The first lecture is theoretical: 'A number of observations of a rather general kind'.[52] There is a sad tone to much of it, a disparity between the problems he defines and the solutions he offers, which mirrors what Janet Ashbee saw. It is still Ruskinian, but he no longer hopes for radical changes in the processes of building. He rehearses Ruskin's ideas on the nature of Gothic and contemporary architecture, and the relationship of architect and craftsman. We long ago lost 'the life of Gothic art'; 'the styles of the past have been based on a definite set of aims and objectives', but now 'we are groping in the dark'. There has been 'an enormous improvement in jewellery ... largely ... due to Birmingham men', and a similar improvement in other practical arts such as plasterwork, because 'the divorce between the craftsman and designer has been dissolved'. The effect of the modern system on craftsmen is 'deadly', 'the man has no scope for individual thought' and he 'inevitably tends to lose ideas of right and wrong altogether'. But 'I am not of course for a moment suggesting that the same sort of thing can be done in building'. (One can almost hear the sigh of relief from part of the audience here.) He has in fact only two suggestions, modest by the standards of the Arts and Crafts radicalism of ten years earlier. First, if 'we could have the same architect working for years together with the same company of men, the effect on the architect and on the men would be enormous', and second, that architects should have 'some opportunity of getting in touch with materials and tools just so much as will enable him to think in terms of tools and materials instead of in terms of paper and ink', perhaps 'a few weeks only' of bricklaying and carpentry. This sounds almost desperate: please let the young men have just a little time in a builder's yard as well as their classes in formal design and their training in building regulations. And what follows is 'dangerously stretched', in Alan Crawford's words,[53] describing the tenuous link between craftsmanship and industrial processes, because he talks of the 'splendid opportunity' of ferro-concrete for 'the development of fine form and beautiful composition of line'.

He ends by trying to relate historic styles and ideas. He remarks on how in the late mediaeval period the rise of the artisan class caused 'prosperous and beautiful commercial cities came into existence in Italy, Flanders, Germany, France and England', an argument he would have heard often in earlier years, when the Birmingham Liberals, including his father, saw cities such as Florence as the prototypes for what they were creating in Birmingham. And there is, again, a heartfelt passage on 'The great style which we variously call Early Christian or Early Romanesque … the basilicas built in Rome and other parts of Italy between the 3rd and 10th centuries suggest in their mosaic pictures that men's minds … were full of the vision of the heavenly kingdom'.

Dixon's interest in this style and period, shown in this lecture and his RIBA article, place him among a network of architects and clergy with strong links to the Arts and Crafts Movement in one direction, and with strong Roman and Anglo-Catholic links in another. An important link to his domestic architectural is Lethaby, who in 1894 co-authored a book on the Sancta Sophia in Constantinople.[54] The most important work is J. F. Bentley's Westminster Cathedral of 1896–1902: Bentley, prevented from visiting Constantinople, read Lethaby's account of the Sancta Sophia instead, and 'San Vitale at Ravenna and Lethaby's book told me all I wanted'.[55] Lethaby in return called the Cathedral 'nobly planned, soundly balanced, and carefully constructed'.[56] Arts and Crafts architects and designers worked on its decoration, especially Robert Weir Schultz in St Andrew's Chapel.[57] In Anglo-Catholic churches the most famous work is Henry Wilson's fittings at St Bartholomew's, Brighton.[58] From the opposite direction, Robert Weir Schultz and Sidney Barnsley, brought up in Birmingham, and the cousin by marriage of Dixon's friend, J. L. Ball, published a magnificently illustrated account of *The Monastery of Saint Luke of Stiris in Phocis* in 1901. For many of these people, Early Christian or Byzantine influences were a way out of a Gothic Revival which they saw as tired and associated with evangelical or liberal churchmanship. Dixon, as we have seen, was not impressed by the services at St Augustine's. For Arts and Crafts architects, the style epitomised sound functional construction and good materials; for Catholic clergy, it served to recall the united Church of the early Fathers, important to both Roman and Anglo-Catholics.

The interest spread well beyond architects and clergy, and was popularized by the great Italian exhibition of 1904. It can be seen in the writings of E. M. Forster, who found the 'Venice by Night' scene at the exhibition 'absurdly moving'.[59] His first novel set in Italy, *Where Angels Fear to Tread*, appeared in 1905, and *A Room with a View* in 1908. Forster, a member of the SPAB, brings architecture into his short story, 'The Eternal Moment', written in 1904, and set in Cortina d'Ampezzo, where the modern Grand Hotel des Alpes, 'an enormous distended chalet ... from which ... asphalt paths trickled over the adjacent country', and which is advertised by electric light, is contrasted with the old-fashioned Albergo Biscione where 'the antique spirit had not yet departed .... The great manner, only to be obtained without effort, ruled throughout. In each bedroom were three or four beautiful things — a little piece of silk tapestry, a fragment of rococo carving, some blue tiles, framed and hung upon the whitewashed wall'.[60] Here we are very close to Dixon's Japanese house, and Italian traditions stand for honest and simple building.

At the start of the second lecture Dixon explains that H. W. Simister, the Secretary of the Association, had suggested 'Tell us how you do your work', and 'I will try and do as I am told and talk about details of practice and treatment of materials'.[61] The suggestion points to what local architects would find interesting in Dixon's work. He might have little experience of drains and Borough Surveyors, but his experience as a craftsman had given him a skill in the visual judgment of materials as good as, but different from, full time professionals. Dixon's response is an example of his Arts and Crafts approach. A more conventional architect might have talked about design, proportioning, composition; Dixon talks about how he treats materials. It is a lecture rare, if not unique, in Birmingham architectural history, giving away trade secrets, as it were, but Dixon, with a secure background and income, had no reservations. It is also much more interesting, full of life, than the theoretical one. However disillusioned Dixon was politically, he could lose himself in architectural practice.

The first and longest section is on bricks. He prefers 'Black Country' blue, brindled, and red bricks for facings, because they don't decay, and softer red Warwickshires inside the wall, because they aren't as porous. These are 'machine made — I mean wire cut' bricks, but not the hard machine pressed bricks which would have been used for facings in the nineteenth century — when Dixon's brindled bricks would have been classed as seconds and used inside the wall. When he can afford it he will use hand made bricks and have them thinner than the ugly modern standard size. But otherwise 'if we make a flush joint and spread the mortar a little over the edges of the bricks we can still further improve the proportions.'

Joints are 'a great help also in the matter of colour . . . . Black Country bricks laid all together are nothing better than a dingy smudge, but divide them with clean light coloured joints and a really wonderful series of colours come out, and these combine together in quite delightful harmony'.

Dixon continues by discussing brick bonding. English Bond is 'very ugly' and Flemish 'too mechanically regular'. He wants 'to rebel against this tyranny of bonds' and use 'one header to three of four stretchers in each course or one course of alternate headers and stretchers, or even of one header and two stretchers, with two or three courses of stretchers'. The first of these is exactly the Sussex Bond Dixon used at Tennal Grange, which is occasionally found elsewhere in Birmingham, and the second, Flemish Stretcher Bond, often used on Victorian terraced houses. He recommends courses of tiles for binding together stone walls (an echo of SPAB practice). He discusses jointing, starting with a long quotation from Ruskin, and significantly from the intense visual sensitivity and emphasis on colour of *The Stones of Venice*, the passage in Book 1 on 'The Wall Veil' which condemns joints in masonry which draw attention to themselves, and conversely any attempt 'studiously to conceal' them. He likes the traditions of patterning with bricks: mixing them with terracotta in Italy, and especially the mixture of 'little red and grey bricks ... white stone, and grey flint, with white mortar joints' in the 'half-magic skill' of bricklayers in Normandy.

Dixon's account of brickwork places him in a tradition beginning with Ruskin and going through the most important theorist of architecture in the Arts and Crafts Movement, W. R. Lethaby. He would have known the celebration of brickwork in the chapter on 'Gothic Palaces' in Book 2 of *The Stones of Venice*: 'just as many of the finest works of the Italian sculptors were executed in porcelain, many of the best thoughts of their architects are expressed in brick, or in the softer material of terracotta',[62] and also the description and illustrations of complex brickwork in the Duomo of Murano: 'a string course composed of two layers of red bricks, of which the uppermost projects as a cornice, and is sustained by an intermediate course of irregular brackets, obtained by setting the thick yellow bricks edgeways, in the manner common to this day'.[63] This is the practice known as cogging, as common in the Victorian terraces of Birmingham and other cities as it was in tenth and twelfth century Venice. He would also have known well the principles of surface decoration which Ruskin lays down in his account of St Mark's: light and delicate plinths and string courses, and solid shafts.[64]

Lethaby, in the monograph on the Sancta Sophia, Constantinople, which he wrote with Harold Swainson, remarks that 'Byzantine architecture was developed by the use of brick in its fullest and frankest manner',[65] and explicitly recommends Byzantine practice as an example for contemporary architects, 'a conviction of the necessity of finding the root of architecture once again in sound common-sense building and pleasurable craftsmanship remains as the final result of our study of S. Sophia, that marvellous work . . .'.[66] This interest informed the practice of many

Arts and Crafts architects: the patterning of brick and stone in the parapet of Lethaby's Eagle Insurance building, and the corbelled-out door hoods on Randall Wells' cottages of 1908 at Fallings Park, Wolverhampton, to cite two local examples.

In talking of brick – and he mentions that he has 'very little experience of any other masonry than brickwork', seeing bricks and stone as part of the same thing – Dixon is also following the Arts and Crafts tradition of looking to local materials for his work. Birmingham has no workable local stone. The city is built on friable sand and pebble beds. But this material is excellent for brick-making. Nineteenth century maps of the area show innumerable small brick pits, and large extraction continued near Minworth until the nineteen sixties.

Dixon continues by discussing roofs, where he wants slates 'quarried thick and rough'. He 'used to think roofs should be steep, over 45 degrees in pitch', but for cost reasons and to get good ventilation has been trying shallower pitches. He will use ridged tiles, single and double Roman, but 'large flat tiles turned up at either edge and the joints covered with tapered ridges' are better, as are 'tapered channel tiles set alternately concave and convex'. He talks conventionally of internal treatments, of plaster and mediaeval painting on it, and stained glass, and Gothic vaulting, but also mentions Italian screens where 'the timber is only partly covered in colour, and the colour of the timber itself forms a very effective background' and discusses the pigments needed for this work, and the problem of the timber changing colour with age. He prefers plastering interiors to leaving the bricks bare, but explains its difficulties, particularly its combination with stone, where he likes 'the light fillet or moulding which often divides the one from the other ... the dividing line must, I think, be acknowledged .... Nothing is uglier than the unpremeditated line between the plaster and the quoin stones of window and door recesses.' He discusses decoration, again quoting *The Stones of Venice* at length, on its need for vividness, but in the right place. Finally he criticises, as has been mentioned, the return of classicism.

Dixon's second lecture has the air of someone wrestling with real problems of design and materials: the smell of the drawing board and the building site. By the time he delivered it, he had indeed started producing significant work again: the four churches of 1908 to 1913. This revival of his career had its origin in changes to the Church of England in Birmingham. Charles Gore, who probably influenced him at Oxford, became Bishop of Worcester in 1902, and when the Diocese of Birmingham was carved out of Worcester in 1905, he moved to become its first Bishop. His appointment as a bishop was a bold move, and caused protests, for Anglo-Catholicism was still not respectable and there was much campaigning by Protestants against ritual in the years around 1900. When Gore was at Worcester he let the suffragan Bishop Knox of Coventry, an evangelical, run Birmingham affairs, but in 1905 he took charge. He instantly displayed a concern for the poor among his flock, visiting a working-class parish in Small Heath and to local astonishment staying overnight in a terraced house in the area.

Gore tended to work through small groups and liked having friends around him. Two members of his inner circle of friends, the 'Longworth group', moved to the area. Bishop Louis Mylne of Calcutta returned to England to be Rector of Alvechurch, and Winfrid Burrows, a close ally of Gore's in Oxford, became vicar of St Augustine, Edgbaston, and Archdeacon of Birmingham.[67] Gore's presence also attracted young clergy who admired and followed him to the area, including a rich young curate, John Ludlow Lopes. When Gore moved, rather reluctantly, to be Bishop of Oxford in 1911, his replacement was Henry Russell Wakefield, a High Churchman if not an Anglo-Catholic, and a Liberal in politics as well. For Dixon, Anglo-Catholic and socialist, this was a blessed change. From being a member of a dubious minority in the Church, he was suddenly among friends. If he and Gore were not friends before, they became so now. Many years later, in 1924, Gore, now retired, returned to Birmingham to address the students of the School of Art, with Dixon in the chair, and his words show both old friendship and a wry appreciation of Dixon's persuasive skills: 'I dare say you know something of your chairman and that when he persists he gets his way'.[68]

Dixon's churches were built in this new atmosphere. They are all mission buildings, and three of them are linked to church work in working-class areas. As we might expect from his essay and lectures, they mark a sharp change in Birmingham church architecture, a change which reflects a national movement but which happens here with great suddenness. The years around 1900 saw the flowering of a powerful but scholarly late Gothic Revival in the work of W. H. Bidlake: St Agatha, Sparkbrook, Bishop Latimer, Handsworth and St Andrew, Handsworth, inspired by late mediaeval work, but transfigured by the care for quality of materials and handling typical of the Arts and Crafts Movement. The part rebuilding of St James at Hill, Sutton Coldfield, by Bidlake's friend, C. E. Bateman, is similar. Then this beautiful architecture disappears almost overnight. Bidlake started no new Anglican church after 1909, and Bateman only one more. No church is ever again designed in the city in a recognizable Gothic Revival manner. The late Gothic Revival, found elsewhere in Britain in, for example, the work of Sir Charles Nicholson, is absent from Birmingham.

Dixon's first church was an extremely modest mission hall, St John the Evangelist, in Foundry Lane, Smethwick. His plans were approved on 5 November 1908, but the building was not completed until October 1910.[69] The hall, closed in 1967 and demolished, was built in the parish of St Stephen, Smethwick, a church with an Anglo-Catholic tradition. It had a five bay nave with a hipped roof and big casement windows, almost like a bungalow, and a narrower extension at the rear as a chancel, though with a kitchen and vestry behind the altar wall. The sides of the chancel each had a pair of windows with simple round arched heads almost certainly turned with tiles: the only detail in the whole building which signified its religious purpose. There were no historic motifs or decoration, and the historic

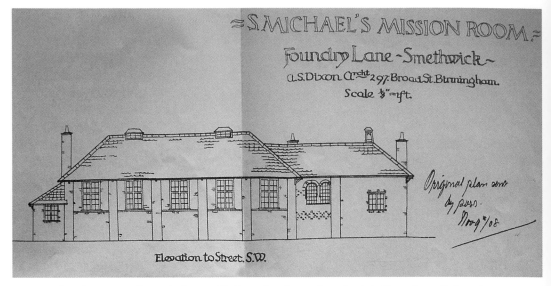

St John the Evangelist Mission Hall, Foundry Lane, Smethwick. Drawing of elevations, 1908. The mission was initially intended to be dedicated to St Michael. *Courtesy of Sandwell Metropolitan Borough Council, Planning Department*

allusion of the windows grew simply out of their method of construction. Materials and constructional detail were more important than style, though what style there was recalled 'the basilicas built in Rome and other parts of Italy between the 3rd and 10th centuries'. Theology, architectural theory and history have all been bound together. The result is a manner both subtle and flexible; two pairs of windows on their own can change significantly the nature of a building, signifying 'church' where everything else is domestic.

Before St John's was finished, Dixon had started work on another mission church. The foundation stone of St Andrew, Barnt Green, was laid on 27 November 1909. The apse, chancel and a bay of the nave were built and dedicated on 28 May 1910; two more bays, with flanking aisles, followed in 1913.[70] Dixon's design included a fourth bay, with the entrance, and a short, stubby, north-west tower with a pyramid roof, which remained unexecuted. It was built in the parish of Alvechurch, where the rector was Gore's friend, and member of the 'Longworth group,' Louis Mylne.

It is a massive and squat little building, a miniature apsed basilica. There is a blunt and windowless buttressed apse. The aisles are articulated by massive straight buttresses which pierce the eaves of the roofs to support the trusses inside, and exactly the same process repeats at clerestory level. A small quadrant link from chancel to south aisle — for processions — bluntly echoes the apse. Paired windows are articulated by absolutely plain square stone piers and blunt capitals which have a single outward quarter curve. String courses are shallow or

Original design drawing for St Andrew, Barnt Green, *courtesy of the Vicar and P. C. C.*

St Andrew, Barnt Green, 1909–10, exterior. *Photo: A.F.*

St Andrew, Barnt Green, 1909–13, interior. *Photo: A.F.*

non-existent. However undecorated, both capitals and strings conform to Ruskin's laws in his description of St Mark's, laws which underlie the massiveness of Dixon's manner. A triplet on the south side of the chancel projects under a gable. Something about this deliberately heavy, three-dimensional, articulation is only just not frightening, as if the building were a huge insect with the projecting buttresses its pairs of legs, and might move.

There is a fascinating surface texture. The Black Country facing bricks in the apse shades in individual bricks from red to deep blue. In the aisles there is more maroon. The walls rise from a chamfered plinth which is delineated by blue bricks. The mortar joints are wide and the mortar tends to spread over the brick. The bond is a kind of modified Flemish with extra headers in the apse, probably for strength on the curve, but Sussex bond with occasional extra stretchers, four rather than three, in the aisles. The apse has diagonal patterning of blue bricks against red, and a band of tilework. The roof has a shallow pitch and the tiles are mostly single Romans, but with some single curved tiles set downwards and linked by smaller pieces across their top edges. Bricks, mortar, bonding, and tiling all follow the principles laid down in Dixon's 1911 lecture. Again, they derive from Ruskin, this time his description of Murano. The windows are round-headed pairs and triplets, turned with tiles. Conscious and obvious applied 'style' in the sense which a slightly earlier architect or critic might have used the word, in, say, calling a Gothic Revival 'Second Pointed', is absent. The windows are the only specific historical allusion, and one growing out of construction more than deliberately applied. The tower, if built, would have looked more obviously Italian, but its shape is as much about simplicity and economy. Noble planning is obviously not possible, but everything is soundly balanced and carefully constructed.

The interior is entirely plastered. The absolutely unmoulded round arches of the arcades spring from equally plain piers. No conscious style here either. But the Early Christian architecture of Italy is evoked by the clerestory windows, made by Richard Stubington of the School of Art, with their leadings including round lights, filled with turned 'bottle' ends, where fifth century churches had stone transennae. The roof shows early Christian inspiration and modest budgets coming together: plain king-post trusses with diagonal trusses. The screen, added in 1915, has a heavy beam supported by slightly tapering square posts. This is exactly the type of Italian screen with painted decoration described in Dixon's 1911 lecture, and, at the same time, by Frederick Bligh Bond and others.[71]

With St Andrew's partly built, Dixon started work on St Basil, Deritend, in early 1910. The plans were approved by the Council on 15 February.[72] The foundation stone is dated 1 October, but foundations and lower walls must have been constructed by then. The church was completed and consecrated on 18 November 1911.[73] This is the church which gave Dixon an enduring, if small, reputation in church and architectural circles. The interior perspective was exhibited at the Royal Birmingham Society of Artists and reproduced in the society's history. A threat of redundancy in the 1930s was fought off by Dixon's friends led by John Willmott, the company secretary of Rabones. There is a small entry in that classic meeting place of architectural history and Anglo-Catholic piety, John Betjeman's *Collins Guide to English Parish Churches*.[74]

It is a larger church than St Andrew's, and it was completed. There is slightly more stylistic reference, but there is also greater complexity and sophistication in the use of materials. The street front displays the same bricks, in colour and bonding, the same chamfered plinth, and the same two light windows with tile heads and blunt mullions. Between the entrances is a west apse, and this together with the windows gives the whole front a Romanesque flavour. Dixon's original scheme had a turret with a pyramid roof, a miniature version of the tower proposed for St Andrew's, but in execution this was changed to a transverse bell turret. There is the same massive treatment, with the entrances set in relieving arches, and another relieving arch running up into the bell turret. What is different is the complexity of texture. The apse has two tile bands set above brick rows with blue headers, and above them a diagonal pattern of tiles and brick headers. The relieving arches are even more complex, with two areas of diagonal patterning separated by tile bands and chequered rows of brick; the gable is articulated by a tile band at the impost level of the windows; there are more tile bands on the bell

St Basil, Heath Mill Lane, Deritend, 1910–11. *Photo: A.F.*

turret. The texture starts to approach that of the complex brick, stone and tile patterns and cloisonné work described by historians of middle and late Byzantine architecture and found, among other places at Hosios Lukas (St Luke of Stiris).[75]

Inside, we are again in a basilica, with a nave of five bays and narrow passage aisles. Again we have Dixon's lectures put into practice, though here the account of Roman churches is more prominent. 'The clerestory wall, pierced with small square or round-headed windows, was carried … on … arcades of small round arches.' Here the arcades are tapering granite monoliths, with cushion capitals, decorated with scenes from the life of St Basil painted by Humphrey Dixon, the architect's son.[76] The roof has simple king post trusses, with a pair of trusses marking the division between nave and chancel. It is the east end which is the glory of St Basil's. First there is another, slightly richer, early type of screen, with solid dado, tapering square posts with slight chamfering, and heavy beam. It is painted with stylized flowers and patterns, and supports rood figures said to have been brought back from Italy by Dixon. Beyond, there is a chancel and apse, with a mosaic of Christ with St John the Baptist and St Basil, and marble panelling, the verticals with a V-pattern. A piscina has a stepped in arch of Westminster

OPPOSITE   St Basil, the apse

Cathedral type. The floor is 'covered with marble mosaic work composed of pieces of red, green, and white marble three or four inches square' though not here in geometrical patterns. The altar and lectern are of immensely heavy design. The exterior of St Basil's seems to grow out of the brick factories and warehouses, some of which still surround it, and make their way of building beautiful; the interior is an unexpected, holy cave.

The official client for St Basil's was the Rev. C. J. Tompkins, the vicar. Much of the money, however, seems to have come from his rich young Anglo-Catholic curate, Rev. John Ludlow Lopes, whose obituary records that St Basil's 'owes much to his generosity'.[77] Lopes began as curate to Fr. James Adderley, a famous Anglo-Catholic socialist, at Saltley. Again there is a link to Gore. It was Lopes's 'interest in social matters, stemming from Dr. Gore's Christian socialism', that brought him to St Basil's and the slums of Deritend in 1909. Lopes was another Anglo-Catholic who liked Early Christian and Byzantine architecture, probably as a symbol of the early undivided Catholic church, because he went on in 1912–15 to build the St Edmund's Boys' Home in High Street, Deritend, designed by Edward Mansell.[78] Its buildings survive in secular uses, including the chapel with its campanile closely based on S. Giorgio al Velabro which is still such a landmark on the main road.[79]

The last of this group of Dixon churches returned to the simplicity of the first mission hall. The College of Grey Ladies in Coventry was not as otherworldly as it sounds. It was 'a Society of Women living together as friends for the purpose of helping in the work of the Church of England'.[80] Many were parish workers in the area, and the college had accommodation and a chapel for retreats and conferences: something both progressive, in enhancing the role of women in the church, and in the Catholic tradition. Dixon designed for it a small building which was a chapel but also had bedrooms above. It was begun in late 1912[81] and opened in June 1913.[82] Here the flexibility of his manner was evident again. The front had two storeys, a hipped roof, domestic looking chimneys, and little oriel bay windows upstairs — a house. But the ground floor elevation had a projecting gable, with a doorway set below four round-headed windows — unmistakably ecclesiastical. Yet because the detail was subsidiary to massing and materials, these references are easily integrated. The interior of the chapel had a remarkable beamed ceiling supported on long steep struts with curved braces.

Designing this group of churches while working for Rabones must have kept Dixon very busy. As we have seen, he wrote his 1911 lecture on board ship, almost certainly on business. Gore paid tribute to his organizing ability and persuasiveness, and at this time he seems to have acted as a link between clients needing new buildings and Arts and Crafts architects, almost like an impresario, when he did not have time for the work. The house, Great Roke at Witley, Surrey, of 1909 by Buckland and Haywood-Farmer, was built for his brother Charles.[83] The same architects designed the factory at 58 Oxford Street of 1911 for Thomas Walker and

WEST ELEVATION

Chapel of the Grey Ladies, Coventry, elevation drawing 1912. *Courtesy of City of Coventry (Plan 6840 approved 19 Nov. 1912)*

Son — the Walker family were Dixon's relatives. Dixon must have played a similar role in the style of a church which needs to be considered here, as it is so close in design and approach to his work at Barnt Green and Deritend. St Gregory the Great, Small Heath started as the Mission of the Good Shepherd, in the Anglo-Catholic parish of All Saints, Small Heath. The permanent church was begun in 1910, though only the apse and two bays of the nave were then built. Fr. Lopes is known to have given the hanging rood, and probably paid for much more. The architect was Dixon's friend, J. L. Ball.[84] Ball was a lifelong Methodist with no connection to the Catholic tradition of the Church of England except for his friendship with Dixon, who was a patronage trustee of All Saints.[85] His design uses the same Early Christian style as St Basil's, re-creating a Roman basilica of the fifth century. There is the same richly textured brick and tile exterior, but St Gregory's is on a much bigger scale than Dixon's churches and its magnificent apse, with bands of deliberately uneven tile and stone decoration, is the grandest work of its kind in the city. As with their houses of the 1890s, Dixon and Ball seem to work closely in step with each other.

In 1913 there was a competition for a new church in Edgbaston, now St Germain's, built in St Augustine's parish and promoted by the vicar, Gore's friend, Winfrid Burrows. Dixon entered, along with Ball and Bidlake, but the winner came from a younger generation: Edwin Reynolds, assistant director to Ball at the School of Architecture. The church, built in 1915–17, is amply and confidently planned in a way Dixon never attempted, but its crusty brick style and signature bonding — Flemish Stretcher bond with a single row of stretchers between each Flemish row — owe much to Dixon's example. All other church work was stopped by the Great War. Dixon carried on with public duties, becoming chairman of the Diocesan Board of Finance in 1915. In the atmosphere of 1914 people must have noticed his German second name, from his mother's family. His wife's first name sounded German. During the war, she stopped calling herself Gertrude and used her second name, Emily.[86] Their younger son, Evelyn, was killed in 1916.

After the War Dixon still did some church work. In 1922 Bishop Wakefield moved to the present Bishop's Croft, the former Harborne House, which Dixon had worked on for Arthur Kenrick. Dixon designed him a chapel, separate from the house but linked to it.[87] It is in brick with stone blocks in the quoins, and the stylistic references are Jacobean — buttresses with consoles set upright on the tops, the same motif used on an open bellcote, and a simplified Dutch gable arrangement on the ends, with central pediments. It seems very classical for Dixon, but the style has references to a famous period for Anglo-Catholics, the reign of Charles I and the time of George Herbert, and Nicholas Ferrar at Little Gidding. The interior is wainscoted in rectangular panels to door head height, and painted white above, an arrangement which suggests that Dixon knew Philip Webb's Rochester Diocesan Deaconess Institution Chapel of 1896 (itself a parallel to the College of Grey Ladies).[88] The plain groined vault above is a feature Lethaby used frequently, e.g. in the side lobby of the Eagle Insurance building in Colmore Row. Fine woodwork includes a lobby screen and stalls arranged like a college chapel. It was completed in 1923.

Also in 1922 he started the rebuilding of St Giles, Rowley Regis, and the church was consecrated on 29 September 1923.[89] The drawings are signed by Dixon and the younger Arts and Crafts architect Holland W. Hobbiss.[90] It looks as if the design is Dixon's, with Hobbiss acting as executant architect. The previous church of 1904, a Gothic Revival design by Lewis Sheppard and Son of Worcester, was mostly destroyed by fire in 1913. The east end partly survived, and was incorporated into the new building. So the arcades and windows are pointed, to conform with the older work, Dixon's only use of these Gothic motifs. In other ways the building uses the language of the his earlier churches: plain brick walls with simple lancet windows, plain rendered arcades inside, and a powerful west

The Bishop's Chapel, Old Church Road, Harborne, 1922

The Bishop's Chapel, interior. *Photo: A.F.*

tower, sharply cut off at the top by a blunt parapet: a landmark, on its hill, for miles around.

After Rowley his work in Birmingham stops. Bishop Wakefield retired in 1924. His successor, Bishop Barnes, was a liberal evangelical, almost a Modernist, and was opposed by Dixon's friends, the Anglo-Catholic clergy, from the moment of his appointment. They were soon in a long public dispute, the so-called 'rebellion', which lasted nearly thirty years.

In 1922 his daughter Mary died after an operation. In that year he and his wife left Edgbaston and moved to Deddington in Oxfordshire. Emily Dixon wanted to move. 'We have sold 3 Augustus Rd,' she wrote with obvious relief to Janet Ashbee.[91] The move must explain Hobbiss' role at Rowley. Janet Ashbee visited Deddington in 1926 and described it as 'a sad little yellow-grey stone village, with a huge bare derelict-looking market square'.[92] When he moved, Dixon gave up his chairmanship of the Diocesan Board of Finance, but remained as Chairman of the School of Art and a member of the Diocesan Advisory Committee, and visited the city regularly.[93] He kept a friendly interest in St Andrew, Barnt Green, designing a timber organ gallery in 1926, presenting an Austrian processional cross, a Florentine alms dish, and small copies of Old Masters to hang on the aisle walls.[94] We are almost back at Forster's Albergo Biscione, where 'in each bedroom were three or four beautiful things'.

St Giles, Rowley Regis, 1922–23. (The transept end on the right is of 1904.) *Photo: A. F.*

He was still working at one major project, the Anglican Cathedral in Seoul, Korea. The Anglican church in Korea was Catholic in tradition, and Bishop Trollope, appointed in 1911, had been vicar of St Alban, Bordesley.[95] Dixon's first design, of 1922, was cruciform, with an aisled nave, central tower and smaller towers in the re-entrant angles of the transepts.[96] The transepts were large and contained separate churches for English and Japanese services. The chancel had an external arcade, for processions, and there was a large undercroft. The design is consciously Italian Romanesque; the arcades have cushion capitals similar to those at St Basil's. His sister said 'his cathedral has a great look of San Vitale.'[97] Construction was underway by 1925, but the large transepts were cut down in execution. Dixon appears to have visited Seoul at least twice. There is a sketch plan marked 'Seoul June 1927' for mission buildings around the Cathedral. He almost certainly attended the consecration on 2 May 1928, when chancel, transepts and a stub of the nave had been completed.

He died suddenly in January 1929, and was buried at Witley, Surrey, near the home of his brother Charles.[98]

Selected List of Works by Arthur Stansfeld Dixon (1856–1929)

A. S. Dixon was a partner in the Birmingham mercantile house of Rabone Brothers, but also worked as a part-time architect. He started training in 1893 through private study and classes at the Birmingham School of Art and his first work dates from 1895. He was still working as an architect when he died in 1929.

WORK IN BIRMINGHAM AND ENVIRONS

PUBLIC

1907 Addition of pulpit to St Alban's Church, Bordesley [D]; *c.* 1919 addition of panelling in north transept

1908–10 St John the Evangelist Mission Room, Foundry Lane, Smethwick [D]

1908 Addition of altar to St Philip's Cathedral, Birmingham; 1920 memorial tablet to soldiers of the Royal Warwickshire Regiment

1909–10 Chancel and one bay of nave of St Andrew's Church, Barnt Green, Worcs., for Bishop Louis Mylne, Rector of Alvechurch; 1913–14 remainder of nave and aisles; 1915 Screen; 1926 Organ gallery [2001 organ gallery removed for large new semi-circular porch by Liz Jeavons Fellows]

1910 Club Rooms, St Basil's Church, Heath Mill Lane, Deritend for Rev. C. J. Tomkins [D]

1910–11 St Basil's Church, Heath Mill Lane, Deritend for Rev. C. J. Tomkins [converted to offices after 1982. Chancel retained intact]; 1911–12 Mortuary Chapel and remodelling of schoolrooms [now St Basil's Centre]

1922–23 Addition of Bishop's Chapel to Bishop's Croft (formerly Harborne House), Old Church Rd, Harborne for Rt Revd Russell Wakefield, Bishop of Birmingham

1922–23 Rebuilding of Chuch of St Giles, Rowley Regis, Staffs., designed jointly with Holland W. Hobbiss

COMMERCIAL

1897–98 Birmingham Guild of Handicraft offices and works, Great Charles St and New Market St, Birmingham [rear workshops D; interior gutted on conversion to offices 1988–89]

DOMESTIC

1895–96 Additions to 'Llantrisant', Yateley Rd, Edgbaston, for Philip A. Carter

1896 Additions to 3 Augustus Rd, Edgbaston, for A. S. Dixon [D]

1897 The Gables, Four Oaks, Sutton Coldfield for Montague Fordham [D]

1897–98 Additions to House in Fellows Lane, Harborne, for Claude Napier-Clavering

1898–99 Additions to House in Westbourne Rd, Edgbaston for C. W. Dixon [D]

c. 1898 Addition of Stables to Ladywood Court, Hartopp Rd, Four Oaks, for Frederick and Katie Rathbone [D]

1899 Additions to 36 Harborne Rd, Edgbaston, for Miss H. M. Dixon; 1914 alterations

1902–03 Additional wings to Harborne House, [Bishop's Croft] Old Church Rd, Harborne for Arthur Kenrick; 1910 alterations for J. Archibald Kenrick

1903 St Aidan's Clergy House, Herbert Rd, Small Heath, for Canon C. N. Long [Converted to meeting and community rooms for St Aidan's, now All Saints Church, c. 2000]

1903–05 Tennal Grange, Tennal Rd, Harborne, for Claude Napier-Clavering

1909 Addition to Fairoaks, Farquhar Rd, Edgbaston for Allen Tangye; 1910 additions

1914 Alterations to 36 Harborne Rd [Birmingham Medical Institute], Edgbaston

WORK OUTSIDE BIRMINGHAM

PUBLIC

1902 Altar, reredos and repairs to Sibson Church, Leics; 1910 screen

1904 Addition of Baptistery and font to Christ Church, Wellington, Salop.

1905 Repairs to St Mary's Church, Swainswick, Somerset

1912–13 Chapel of the College of Grey Ladies, Coventry [D]

1922–28 St Mary and St Nicholas Cathedral, Seoul, Korea

DOMESTIC

1898 Cottages and farm buildings, Borden Wood, Hants.

NOTES

[1] King's College, Cambridge, Ashbee Journals, letter of 28 April 1908.
[2] Obituary of A. S. Dixon, *Birmingham Mail*, 10 January 1929.
[3] *D. N. B.* George Dixon; also the source for his involvement in the National Education League.

[4] Katie Rathbone, *The Dales: Growing up in a Victorian Family*, ed. by S. T. ('Bob') and Harlan Walker (Ledbury, 1989), pp. 4–5. The book also includes reminiscences by Katie Rathbone's daughter, Marion.

[5] *Ibid*, p. 21.

[6] Joseph Foster, *Alumni Oxonienses 1715–1886* (Oxford, 1886), p. 373.

[7] Rathbone, *The Dales*, p. 130.

[8] G. L. Prestige, *The Life of Charles Gore* (1935), ch. 2 *passim*.

[9] Prestige, *Gore*, p. 11, p. 91.

[10] *Ibid*, p. 88, p. 98, p. 247.

[11] *Ibid*, p. 70.

[12] Rathbone, *The Dales*, p. 89.

[13] Family tree in *ibid*; *The Birmingham Red Book*, 1891.

[14] Rathbone, *The Dales*, p. 5.

[15] *Ibid*, p. 99.

[16] RIBA, British Architectural Library, Application for fellowship of the RIBA, 1907.

[17] Rathbone, *The Dales*, pp. 5–6.

[18] Alan Crawford, *C. R. Ashbee, Architect, Designer & Romantic Socialist* (New Haven and London, 1985), *passim*.

[19] Alan Crawford, 'The Birmingham Setting: A Curious Mixture of Bourgeoisie and Romance' in *By Hammer and Hand: The Arts and Crafts Movement in Birmingham*, ed. by Alan Crawford (Birmingham, 1984), pp. 31–32.

[20] Glennys Wild and Alan Crawford, 'Metalwork: By Hammer and Hand' in *By Hammer and Hand*, pp. 98–99.

[21] *Birmingham Daily Post*, 27 September 1890. I owe this and the following references to Alan Crawford.

[22] Illustrated in *The Art Journal*, 1894, p. 183. Source: Victoria and Albert Museum, *Catalogue of an exhibition of Victorian & Edwardian Decorative Arts*, 1952, item no. P5.

[23] V&A, National Art Library, Minutes of the School of Handicraft; *British Architect*, 38, 9 July 1892; Birmingham Central Library, Archives and Heritage Services (henceforth BCL, AHS), Minutes of the Committee Meetings of the Birmingham Guild of Handicraft 1890–1899.

[24] A. S. Dixon, 'Some Notes on Civil and other Buildings in Birmingham', in The General Association of Church School Managers and Teachers, Birmingham Congress, *Official Guide 1903* (Birmingham, 1903), p. 60.

[25] Letters in the possession of Felicity Ashbee, information from Alan Crawford.

[26] King's College, Cambridge, Ashbee Journals, letter of 18 February 1902.

[27] Ashbee Journals, letter of 5 November 1904.

[28] Ashbee Journals, letter of 28 April 1908.

[29] A. S. Dixon, 'Manufacture and Handicraft, with some account of the Guild of Handicraft in Birmingham', *The Quest*, no. 2, March 1895, pp. 21–27.

[30] Geoffrey Tyack, 'Ruskin and the English House', in *Ruskin and Architecture*, ed. by Rebecca Daniels and Geoff Brandwood (Reading, 2003), p. 113.

[31] *The Birmingham Red Book*, 1891 et. seq.

[32] Rathbone, *The Dales*, p. 99.

[33] Application for fellowship of the RIBA, 1907.

[34] BCL AHS, Birmingham Building Register, app. no. 11408, 21 November 1895; *Builders' Journal*, 17, 5 March 1902, p. 40.

[35] Sutton Coldfield Library, Sutton Coldfield Building Register, app. no. 431. The dates of the building are from the notices filed with the plan. The correspondence between Dixon and the Borough Surveyor is in the plan docket. See also *Builders' Journal and Architectural Record*, 5, 5 March 1902, pp. 39–40 and supplement.

[36] Birmingham Building Register, app. no. 12964, 15 May 1897. No drawings survive but Dixon's name is in the plan register; *Architectural Review*, 6, 1899, p. 274; *Building News*, 77, 1899, p. 577

[37] *BAA Green Book* 1897–98, p. 23, report of visit to buildings in progress.

[38] *Architectural Review*, 6, 1899, p. 271.

[39] Remo Granelli, 'Architecture: All the World and Time Enough' in *By Hammer and Hand*, pp. 54–55.

[40] *The Quest*, no. 5, March 1896, pp. 54–66.

[41] Alan Crawford, *C. R. Ashbee*, p. 269.

[42] Birmingham Building Register, app. no. 16990, 30 July 1902; also app. no. 21648, 9 August 1910; Application for fellowship of the RIBA, 1907.

[43] Application for fellowship of the RIBA, 1907.

[44] A. S. Dixon, 'Some Notes on Ecclesiastical Buildings', p. 58.

[45] Birmingham Building Register, app. no. 17445, 8 May 1903. The building was completed 20 August 1903.

[46] Birmingham Building Register, app. no. 17769, approved 1 December 1903.

[47] See fn 61 below.

[48] [Rachel Waterhouse], *Guide Book to S. Alban & S. Patrick Birmingham 12* (n.d. *c.* 1984).

[49] *Cornish's Guide to Birmingham*, 1927, entry on Arthur Stansfeld Dixon.

[50] *Birmingham Diocesan Directory*, 1910.

51 RIBA *Journal*, 15, 1908–09, pp. 664–78.

52 BCL AHS, Birmingham Architectural Association, Presidential Address, Session 1909–10, by A. S. Dixon.

53 Alan Crawford, 'Conclusion: A Famous City of White Stone' in *By Hammer and Hand*, p. 129.

54 W. R. Lethaby and Harold Swainson, *The Church of Sancta Sophia Constantinople: A Study of Byzantine Building* (London and New York, 1894).

55 Winefride de l'Hôpital, *Westminster Cathedral and its Architect* (1919), vol. 1, p. 35.

56 W. R. Lethaby, introduction, in *Westminster Cathedral*, vol. 1, p. vii.

57 Gavin Stamp, *Robert Weir Schultz – Architect – and his work for the Marquesses of Bute – an essay*, (Mount Stuart, 1891), p. 60 *passim*.

58 Nicholas Taylor, 'Byzantium in Brighton', in *Edwardian Architecture and its Origin*, ed. by Alistair Service (1975), p. 280 etc.

59 P. N. Furbank, *E. M. Forster:* vol. 1 *The Growth of a Novelist* (1977), p. 116.

60 E. M. Forster, *The Eternal Moment* (1947 edition), pp. 214–15, pp. 221–22.

61 Birmingham Architectural Association, Presidential Address, Session 1910–11, by A. S. Dixon; private collection; *The Builder*, 98, 29 October 1910, pp. 527–30.

62 John Ruskin, *The Stones of Venice*, 3 vols, book 2, ch. VII, para. XXXVIII (1851–53).

63 *Ibid*, book 2, ch. III, para. XXVI.

64 *Ibid*, book 2, ch. IV, paras. XXX et. seq.

65 Lethaby and Swainson, *Sancta Sophia*, p. 199.

66 *Ibid*, preface.

67 For Burrows, see Prestige, *Gore*, p. 114, p. 241. He was Registrar of Pusey House, where Gore was Head, in 1889 and helped Gore in the controversy over 'Lux Mundi'. Burrows and Mylne appear in a group photograph taken at Longworth in 1902, opposite p. 376. Gore's papers, which were left to the Community of the Resurrection at Mirfield, were destroyed, probably in the 1950s.

68 'Address of Right Rev. Dr. Charles Gore, February 1924' in *Fourteen Addresses delivered to students of the Birmingham Municipal School of Art now the College of Arts and Crafts Margaret Street*, ed. by Leonard Jay (n.d., Birmingham).

69 Sandwell MBC Planning Dept., Borough of Smethwick Building Register, app. no. 64 (2782), 5 Nov 1908; *Victoria County History of Staffordshire*, vol XVII (1976) p. 127; *Smethwick Telephone*, 8 October 1910.

70 Foundation stone on church; Architect's signed perspective drawing, copy hanging in church; Alan Brooks and Nikolaus Pevsner, *The Buildings of England. Worcestershire* (revised ed., 2007), p. 122; *Birmingham Diocesan Calendar* 1911 p. 203, 1914 p. 195. *History of St Andrew, Barnt Green*, complied by E. Victor Goodrich (1968); Appeal letter for extension of the church, January 1913, including copy of the architect's signed plan; Typescript history of the church, n.d. The last three all in the possession of the parish, 1993, and copied for the author by Sheila Parker.

71 F. Bligh Bond and Dom Bede Camm, *Roodscreens and Roodlofts* (1909), ch. 1 *passim*. Bligh Bond was responsible for the rood beam of 1911 in St Aidan, Small Heath.

72 Birmingham Building Register, app. no. 21291.

73 Copy of the order of service in the author's possession.

74 *Collins Guide to English Parish Churches*, ed. by John Betjeman (1958, revised ed. 1959) p. 377. See also Douglas Hickman, *Birmingham* (1970), p. 56; Joseph Hill and William Midgley, *The History of the Royal Birmingham Society of Artists* (c. 1930, Birmingham) pl. 100; *Birmingham Diocesan Calendar*, 1912 p. 202 and 1913 pp. 196–98; Nikolaus Pevsner and Alexandra Wedgwood, *The Buildings of England: Warwickshire* (Harmondsworth, 1966), pp. 130–31; Andy Foster, *Pevsner Architectural Guides: Birmingham* (New Haven and London), p. 185.

75 See for example Richard Krautheimer, *Early Christian and Byzantine Architecture* (Harmondsworth, 4th. ed. 1986), parts six & seven, p. 331 *passim*.

76 This attribution was given by S. T. Walker (Dixon's nephew) to George Price and noted in the copy of Douglas Hickman's *Birmingham* in the Conservation Group, Department of Planning and Regeneration.

77 *Birmingham Post*, 21 September 1961.

78 Birmingham Building Register, app. no. 23601.

79 Fr. Adderley had similar tastes in architecture to his curate, building two mission churches in Saltley made of 'frazzi', artificial stone blocks which he thought particularly Italian. They were designed by P. Morley Horder of London.

80 Coventry City Archives DR637/1, constitution of the College of Grey Ladies.

81 Coventry City Archives, Coventry Building Register, app. no. 6840 approved 19 November 1912.

82 Coventry City Archives DR637/2, minute book of the College of Grey Ladies 1912–17.

83 Remo Granelli, 'Architecture', p. 56; Rathbone, *The Dales*, p. 132 (Marion Rathbone).

84 Birmingham Building Register, app. no. 21540, approved 13 June 1910; church Year Book 1950 in the author's possession.

85 BCL AHS, Birmingham Diocesan Records, BDR/D1/116/3.

[86] Rathbone, *The Dales*, p. 131 (Marion Rathbone).

[87] Birmingham Building Register, app. no. 33465, 27 January 1922.

[88] Sheila Kirk, *Philip Webb: Pioneer of Arts and Crafts Architecture* (Chichester, 2005), pp. 258–61. The chapel was never published but Kirk points out that Webb's admirers would have known it. J. L. Ball uses cross beams in aisles at Sandon Road Methodist Church, Edgbaston (1889) and St Gregory the Great, Small Heath, which probably derive from the south aisle of Webb's St Martin, Brampton, Cumbria (1874 etc.).

[89] M. C. Warby, *St Giles Rowley Regis. 75th Anniversary of the Fourth Church 1932–1998: A History of the Church's Early Days* (Sandwell, 1998).

[90] Birmingham Diocesan Records, BDR/C6/1/445, application 23 October 1922, faculty of 7 June 1923. It seems that the work began before the formal granting of the faculty. The superb font of 1926 with carvings of Evangelical symbols by William Bloye was designed by Hobbiss alone.

[91] Ashbee Journals, letter from E. G. Dixon, 1 July 1922.

[92] *Ibid*, letter of April 1926.

[93] Birmingham Diocesan Directories, *passim.*

[94] Birmingham Diocesan Records, BDR/C6/1 and BRD/C6/1/531; *History of St Andrew Barnt Green* complied by E. Victor Goodrich, 1968.

[95] Basil Clarke, *Anglican Cathedrals Outside the British Isles* (1958), p. 120.

[96] Many drawings for Seoul Cathedral survive in a private collection.

[97] Rathbone, *The Dales*, pp. 5–6.

[98] Obituary, *Birmingham Mail*, 10 January 1929.

Index

References to figures are given in italic type.

Birmingham's Victorian and Edwardian Architects

EDITED BY PHILLADA BALLARD

PUBLISHED BY OBLONG FOR THE BIRMINGHAM
AND WEST MIDLANDS GROUP OF THE
VICTORIAN SOCIETY · 2009

Frst published by Oblong Creative Ltd for the
Birmingham and West Midlands Group
of the Victorian Society 2009

ISBN 978 0 9556576 2 7

Designed and produced in the UK
by Oblong Creative Ltd,
416B Thorp Arch Estate,
Wetherby LS23 7FG

Contents